Third Workshop on Speech and Language Technologies for Dravidian Languages (DravidianLangTech 2023)

Varna, Bulgaria
7 September 2023

ISBN: 978-1-7138-9043-0

Printed from e-media with permission by:

Curran Associates, Inc.
57 Morehouse Lane
Red Hook, NY 12571

Some format issues inherent in the e-media version may also appear in this print version.

Association for Computational Linguistics
209 N. Eighth Street
Stroudsburg, Pennsylvania 18360

Phone: 1-570-476-8006
Fax: 1-570-476-0860

acl@aclweb.org

Additional copies of this publication are available from:

Curran Associates, Inc.
57 Morehouse Lane
Red Hook, NY 12571 USA
Phone: 845-758-0400
Fax: 845-758-2633
Email: curran@proceedings.com
Web: www.proceedings.com

DravidianLangTech 2023

Third Workshop on Speech and Language Technologies for Dravidian Languages

associated with

The 14th International Conference on Recent Advances in Natural Language Processing RANLP'2023

PROCEEDINGS

September 7, 2023

THIRD WORKSHOP ON SPEECH AND LANGUAGE TECHNOLOGIES FOR DRAVIDIAN LANGUAGES
ASSOCIATED WITH THE INTERNATIONAL CONFERENCE
RECENT ADVANCES IN NATURAL LANGUAGE PROCESSING'2023

PROCEEDINGS

September 7, 2023

Designed by INCOMA Ltd.
Shoumen, BULGARIA

Message from the General Chair

The development of technology increases our internet use, and most of the global languages have adapted themselves to the digital era. However, many regional, under-resourced languages face challenges as they still lack developments in language technology. One such language family is the Dravidian (Tamil) family of languages. Dravidian is the name for the Tamil languages or Tamil people in Sanskrit, and all the current Dravidian languages were called a branch of Tamil in old Jain, Bhraminic, and Buddhist literature (Caldwell, 1875). Tamil languages are primarily spoken in south India, Sri Lanka, and Singapore. Pockets of speakers are found in Nepal, Pakistan, Malaysia, other parts of India, and elsewhere globally. The Tamil languages, which are 4,500 years old and spoken by millions of speakers, are underresourced in speech and natural language processing. The Dravidian languages were first documented in Tamili script on pottery and cave walls in the Keezhadi (Keeladi), Madurai and Tirunelveli regions of Tamil Nadu, India, from the 6th century BCE. The Tamil languages are divided into four groups: South, South-Central, Central, and North groups. Tamil morphology is agglutinating and exclusively suffixal. Syntactically, Tamil languages are head- final and left-branching. They are free-constituent order languages. To improve access to and production of information for monolingual speakers of Dravidian (Tamil) languages, it is necessary to have speech and languages technologies. These workshops aim to save the Dravidian languages from extinction in technology.

Organizing Committee

- Bharathi Raja Chakravarthi, School of Computer Science, University of Galway, Ireland
- Ruba Priyadharshini, Gandhigram Rural Institute-Deemed to be University, India
- Anand Kumar M, Department of Information Technology, National Institute of Technology Karnataka Surathkal, India.
- Sajeetha Thavareesan, Senior Lecturer in Computer Science, Dept. of Computing, Eastern University, Sri Lanka.
- Elizabeth Sherly, Indian Institute of Information Technology and Management-Kerala, India

Programme Committee

- Judith Jeyafreeda Andrew, University of Manchester
- Bharathi B, SSN College of Engineering, India
- Premjith B, Amrita School of Artificial Intelligence, Coimbatore, Amrita Vishwa Vidyapeetham, India
- Abhinaba Bala, International Institute of Information Technology-Hyderabad, India
- Fazlourrahman Balouchzahi, Instituto Politecnico Nacional (IPN), Centro de Investigacion en Computacion (CIC)
- Shubhankar Barman, BITSPilani, India
- Sean Benhur, PSG College of Arts and Science, India
- Shankar Biradar, Indian Institute of Information Technology Dharwad, India
- Mukund Choudhary, International Institute of Information Technology Hyderabad, India
- Sharal Coelho, Mangalore University, India
- Thenmozhi D, SSN College of Engineering, India
- Priyanka Dasari, International Institute of Information Technology Hyderabad, India
- Nikhil E, International Institute of Information Technology Hyderabad, India
- Toqeer Ehsan, University of Gujrat, India
- Kavya G, Mangalore University, India
- Jyothish Lal G, Amrita School of Engineering, India
- Asha Hegde, Mangalore University, India
- Nitesh Jindal, University of Galway, Ireland
- Rachana K, Mangalore University, India

- Selam Kanta, Instituto Politecnico Nacional Centro de Investigacion en Computacion centro
- Sai Prashanth Karnati, Amrita School of Engineering, India
- Parameswari Krishnamurthy, International Institute of Information Technology Hyderabad, India
- Prasanna Kumar Kumaresan, University of Galway, Ireland
- Kirti Kumari, Indian Institute of Information Technology Ranchi, India
- Yves Lepage, Waseda University
- Sainik Mahata, Jadavpur University
- Manish Nadella, Amrita Vishwa Vidyapeetham
- Bhavish Pahwa, Bits Pilani University
- Nikhil Chowdary Paleti, Amrita School of Artificial Intelligence
- Shantanu Patankar, Pune Institute of Computer Technology
- Shiva Kumar Pentyala, Salesforce AI
- Rahul Ponnusamy, University of Galway
- Hariharan R L, National Institute of Technology Karnataka
- Amrish Raaj P, College of Engineering, Guindy, Anna University, India
- Eduri Raja, National Institute of Technology Silchar
- Surangika Ranathunga, University of Moratuwa
- Manikandan Ravikiran, Georgia Institute of Technology, Hitachi India Pvt Ltd
- Ankitha Reddy, SSN College of Engineering, India
- Malliga S, Kongu Engineering College, India
- Angel Deborah S, SSN College of Engineering, India
- Ramaneswaran S, VIT University, India
- Kogilavani S V, Kongu Engineering College, India
- Richard Saldanha, National Institute of Technology Karnataka, India
- Hosahalli Lakshmaiah Shashirekha, Mangalore University, India
- Poorvi Shetty, JSS Science and Technology University
- Rajalakshmi Sivanaiah, SSN College of Engineering, India
- Musica Supriya, Manipal Institute of Technology, Manipal Academy of Higher Education
- Anil Kumar Vuppala, International Institute of Information Technology Hyderabad, India
- Mesay Gemeda Yigezu, Computer Research Center, National Polytechnic Institute

Table of Contents

This page intentionally left blank.

Conference Program

Thursday, September 07, 2023

14:30–16:00 **Paper Presentation**
Chairs: Bharathi Raja Chakravarthi, Prasanna Kumar Kumaresan

14:30–14:37 *On the Errors in Code-Mixed Tamil-English Offensive Span Identification*
Manikandan Ravikiran and Bharathi Raja Chakravarthi

14:37–14:44 *Hate and Offensive Keyword Extraction from CodeMix Malayalam Social Media Text Using Contextual Embedding*
Mariya Raphel, Premjith B, Sreelakshmi K and Bharathi Raja Chakravarthi

14:44–14:51 *Acoustic Analysis of the Fifth Liquid in Malayalam*
Punnoose A K

14:51–14:58 *Transformer-based Context Aware Morphological Analyzer for Telugu*
Priyanka Dasari, Abhijith Chelpuri, Nagaraju Vuppala, Mounika Marreddy, Parameshwari Krishnamurthy and Radhika Mamidi

14:58–15:05 *Improving Reinfocement Learning Agent Training using Text based Guidance: A study using Commands in Dravidian Languages*
Nikhil Chowdary Paleti, Sai Aravind Vadlapudi, Sai Aashish Menta, Sai Akshay Menta, Vishnu Vardhan Gorantla V N S L, Janakiram Chandu, Soman K P and Sachin Kumar S

15:05–15:12 *Social Media Data Analysis for Malayalam YouTube Comments: Sentiment Analysis and Emotion Detection using ML and DL Models*
Abeera V P, Dr. Sachin Kumar and Dr. Soman K P

15:12–15:19 *Findings of the Second Shared Task on Offensive Span Identification from Code-Mixed Tamil-English Comments*
Manikandan Ravikiran, Ananth Ganesh, Anand Kumar M, R Rajalakshmi and Bharathi Raja Chakravarthi

15:19–15:26 *Overview of the shared task on Fake News Detection from Social Media Text*
Malliga S, Bharathi Raja Chakravarthi, Kogilavani S V, Santhiya Pandiyan, Prasanna Kumar Kumaresan, Balasubramanian Palani and Muskaan Singh

15:26–15:33 *Findings of the Shared Task on Sentiment Analysis in Tamil and Tulu Code-Mixed Text*
Asha Hegde, Bharathi Raja Chakravarthi, Hosahalli Lakshmaiah Shashirekha, Rahul Ponnusamy, SUBALALITHA CN, Lavanya S K, Thenmozhi D., Martha Karunakar, Shreya Shreeram and Sarah Aymen

15:33–15:40 *Findings of the Shared Task on Multimodal Abusive Language Detection and Sentiment Analysis in Tamil and Malayalam*
Premjith B, Jyothish Lal G, Sowmya V, Bharathi Raja Chakravarthi, Rajeswari Natarajan, Nandhini K, Abirami Murugappan, Bharathi B, Kaushik M, Prasanth SN, Aswin Raj R and Vijai Simmon S

Thursday, September 07, 2023 (continued)

15:40–15:46 *Overview of Shared-task on Abusive Comment Detection in Tamil and Telugu*
Ruba Priyadharshini, Bharathi Raja Chakravarthi, Malliga S, SUBALALITHA CN, Kogilavani S V, Premjith B, Abirami Murugappan and Prasanna Kumar Kumaresan

15:47–15:50 *CoPara: The First Dravidian Paragraph-level n-way Aligned Corpus*
Nikhil E, Mukund Choudhary and Radhika Mamidi

15:50–15:53 *ChatGPT_Powered_Tourist_Aid_Applications__Proficient_in_Hindi__Yet_To_Master_Telugu_and_Kannada*
Sanjana Kolar and Rohit Kumar

15:53–15:56 *Enhancing Telugu News Understanding: Comparative Study of ML Algorithms for Category Prediction*
Manish Rama Gopal Nadella, Venkata Krishna Rayalu Garapati, Eswar Sudhan S.K., Gouthami Jangala, Soman K.P. and Sachin Kumar

15:56–16:00 *Revisiting Automatic Speech Recognition for Tamil and Hindi Connected Number Recognition*
Rahul Mishra, Senthil Raja Gunaseela Boopathy, Manikandan Ravikiran, Shreyas Kulkarni, Mayurakshi Mukherjee, Ananth Ganesh and Kingshuk Banerjee

16:30–17:30 Poster Presentation
Chairs: Anand Kumar M, Rahul Ponnusamy

16:30–17:30 *Poorvi@DravidianLangTech: Sentiment Analysis on Code-Mixed Tulu and Tamil Corpus*
Poorvi Shetty

16:30–17:30 *NLP_SSN_CSE@DravidianLangTech: Fake News Detection in Dravidian Languages using Transformer Models*
Varsha Balaji, Shahul Hameed T and Bharathi B

16:30–17:30 *AbhiPaw@DravidianLangTech: Multimodal Abusive Language Detection and Sentiment Analysis*
Abhinaba Bala and Parameswari Krishnamurthy

16:30–17:30 *Athena@DravidianLangTech: Abusive Comment Detection in Code-Mixed Languages using Machine Learning Techniques*
Hema M, Anza Prem, Rajalakshmi Sivanaiah and Angel Deborah S

16:30–17:30 *AlphaBrains@DravidianLangTech: Sentiment Analysis of Code-Mixed Tamil and Tulu by Training Contextualized ELMo Word Representations*
Toqeer Ehsan, Amina Tehseen, Kengatharaiyer Sarveswaran and Amjad Ali

16:30–17:30 *HARMONY@DravidianLangTech: Transformer-based Ensemble Learning for Abusive Comment Detection*
Amrish Raaj P, Abirami Murugappan, Lysa Packiam R S and Deivamani M

Thursday, September 07, 2023 (continued)

16:30–17:30 *Avalanche@DravidianLangTech: Abusive Comment Detection in Code Mixed Data Using Machine Learning Techniques with Under Sampling*
Rajalakshmi Sivanaiah, Rajasekar S, Srilakshmisai K, Angel Deborah S and Mirnalinee ThankaNadar

16:30–17:30 *DeepBlueAI@DravidianLangTech-RANLP 2023*
Zhipeng Luo and Jiahui Wang

16:30–17:30 *Team_AJNS@DravidianLangTech: Offensive Language Identification on Multilingual Code-Mixing Text*
Atharva Joshi, Narayan Subramanian and Ratnavel Rajalakshmi

16:30–17:30 *Selam@DravidianLangTech:Sentiment Analysis of Code-Mixed Dravidian Texts using SVM Classification*
Selam Kanta and Grigori Sidorov

16:30–17:30 *LIDOMA@DravidianLangTech: Convolutional Neural Networks for Studying Correlation Between Lexical Features and Sentiment Polarity in Tamil and Tulu Languages*
Moein Tash, Jesus Armenta-Segura, zahra ahani, olga kolesnikova, Grigori Sidorov and Alexander Gelbukh

16:30–17:30 *nlpt malayalm@DravidianLangTech : Fake News Detection in Malayalam using Optimized XLM-RoBERTa Model*
Eduri Raja, Badal Soni and Sami Kumar Borgohain

16:30–17:30 *ML&AI_IIITRanchi@DravidianLangTech: Fine-Tuning IndicBERT for Exploring Language-specific Features for Sentiment Classification in Code-Mixed Dravidian Languages*
Kirti Kumari, Shirish Shekhar Jha, Zarikunte Kunal Dayanand and Praneesh Sharma

16:30–17:30 *ML&AI_IIITRanchi@DravidianLangTech:Leveraging Transfer Learning for the discernment of Fake News within the Linguistic Domain of Dravidian Language*
Kirti Kumari, Shirish Shekhar Jha, Zarikunte Kunal Dayanand and Praneesh Sharma

16:30–17:30 *NITK-IT-NLP@DravidianLangTech: Impact of Focal Loss on Malayalam Fake News Detection using Transformers*
Hariharan R L and Anand Kumar M

16:30–17:30 *VEL@DravidianLangTech: Sentiment Analysis of Tamil and Tulu*
Kishore Kumar Ponnusamy, Charmathi Rajkumar, Prasanna Kumar Kumaresan, Elizabeth Sherly and Ruba Priyadharshini

16:30–17:30 *hate-alert@DravidianLangTech: Multimodal Abusive Language Detection and Sentiment Analysis in Dravidian Languages*
Shubhankar Barman and Mithun Das

16:30–17:30 *Supernova@DravidianLangTech 2023@Abusive Comment Detection in Tamil and Telugu - (Tamil, Tamil-English, Telugu-English)*
Ankitha Reddy, Pranav Moorthi and Ann Maria Thomas

16:30–17:30 *AbhiPaw@ DravidianLangTech: Abusive Comment Detection in Tamil and Telugu using Logistic Regression*
Abhinaba Bala and Parameswari Krishnamurthy

16:30–17:30 *AbhiPaw@ DravidianLangTech: Fake News Detection in Dravidian Languages using Multilingual BERT*
Abhinaba Bala and Parameswari Krishnamurthy

16:30–17:30 *Habesha@DravidianLangTech: Utilizing Deep and Transfer Learning Approaches for Sentiment Analysis.*
Mesay Gemeda Yigezu, Tadesse Kebede, Olga Kolesnikova, Grigori Sidorov and Alexander Gelbukh

16:30–17:30 *Habesha@DravidianLangTech: Abusive Comment Detection using Deep Learning Approach*
Mesay Gemeda Yigezu, Selam Kanta, Olga Kolesnikova, Grigori Sidorov and Alexander Gelbukh

16:30–17:30 *SADTech@DravidianLangTech: Multimodal Sentiment Analysis of Tamil and Malayalam*
Abhinav Patil, Sam Briggs, Tara Wueger and Daniel D. O'Connell

16:30–17:30 *MUCS@DravidianLangTech2023: Sentiment Analysis in Code-mixed Tamil and Tulu Texts using fastText*
Rachana K, Prajnashree M, Asha Hegde and H. L Shashirekha

16:30–17:30 *MUCS@DravidianLangTech2023: Leveraging Learning Models to Identify Abusive Comments in Code-mixed Dravidian Languages*
Asha Hegde, Kavya G, Sharal Coelho and Hosahalli Lakshmaiah Shashirekha

16:30–17:30 *MUNLP@DravidianLangTech2023: Learning Approaches for Sentiment Analysis in Code-mixed Tamil and Tulu Text*
Asha Hegde, Kavya G, Sharal Coelho, Pooja Lamani and Hosahalli Lakshmaiah Shashirekha

16:30–17:30 *MUCSD@DravidianLangTech2023: Predicting Sentiment in Social Media Text using Machine Learning Techniques*
Sharal Coelho, Asha Hegde, Pooja Lamani, Kavya G and Hosahalli Lakshmaiah Shashirekha

16:30–17:30 *MUCS@DravidianLangTech2023: Malayalam Fake News Detection Using Machine Learning Approach*
Sharal Coelho, Asha Hegde, Kavya G and Hosahalli Lakshmaiah Shashirekha

16:30–17:30 *KEC_AI_NLP@DravidianLangTech: Abusive Comment Detection in Tamil Language*
Kogilavani Shanmugavadivel, Malliga Subramanian, Shri Durga R, SRIGHA S, Sree Harene J S and Yasvanth Bala P

16:30–17:30 *KEC_AI_NLP@DravidianLangTech: Sentiment Analysis in Code Mixture Language*
Kogilavani Shanmugavadivel, Malliga Subaramanian, VetriVendhan S, Pramoth Kumar M, Karthickeyan S and Kavin Vishnu N

Thursday, September 07, 2023 (continued)

16:30–17:30 *CSSCUTN@DravidianLangTech:Abusive comments Detection in Tamil and Telugu*
Kathiravan Pannerselvam, Saranya Rajiakodi, Rahul Ponnusamy and Sajeetha Thavareesan

On the Errors in Code-Mixed Tamil-English Offensive Span Identification

Manikandan Ravikiran[†*], Bharathi Raja Chakravarthi[‡]
[†]Georgia Institute of Technology, Atlanta, Georgia
[‡]School of Computer Science, University of Galway, Ireland
mravikiran3@gatech.edu, bharathi.raja@insight-centre.org

Abstract

In recent times, offensive span identification in code-mixed Tamil-English language has seen traction with the release of datasets, shared tasks, and the development of multiple methods. However, the details of various errors shown by these methods are currently unclear. This paper presents a detailed analysis of various errors in state-of-the-art Tamil-English offensive span identification methods. Our study reveals the strengths and weaknesses of the widely used sequence labeling and zero-shot models for offensive span identification. In the due process, we identify data-related errors, improve data annotation and release additional diagnostic data to evaluate models' quality and stability. *Disclaimer: This paper contains examples that may be considered profane, vulgar, or offensive. The examples do not represent the views of the authors or their employers/graduate schools towards any person(s), group(s), practice(s), or entity/entities. Instead, they emphasize the complexity of various errors and linguistic research challenges.*

1 Introduction

Offensive span identification from code-mixed Tamil-English social media comments (Ravikiran and Annamalai, 2021) focuses on extracting character offsets corresponding to tokens contributing to offensiveness. Identifying such offensive spans is helpful in multiple facets ranging from assisting content moderators for quicker moderation to the development of semi-automated tools which can provide thorough attribution related to the intervened offensive content. Recently there are numerous methods (Ravikiran et al., 2022; Hariharan RamakrishnaIyer LekshmiAmmal, 2022) that are capable of identifying these offensive spans with accuracy as high as 60% on very hard-to-understand short sentences with limited contextual information.

However many of these methods rely on large code-mixed datasets (Chakravarthi, 2022, 2023; Chakravarthi et al., 2022a,b; Kumaresan et al., 2022) and pre-trained language models (Ravikiran and Annamalai, 2021). Nevertheless, these methods are still far away from solving offensive span identification despite such large success. To advance further with this, we need to understand better the sources of errors in the offensive span identification. Such an analysis will, in turn, help introduce inductive biases to extract the spans effectively. Thus, we analyze errors on the Tamil-English code-mixed offensive span identification dataset (DOSA-v2) which consists of 4816 (train) and 876 (test) offensive comments obtained from YouTube movie trailers with span annotations (Ravikiran et al., 2022).

Specifically, this work focuses on models' prediction errors and data-related errors. For the former case, we comprehensively investigate the predictions of 8 different models that currently exist for offensive span identification. Accordingly, we find that all the existing models suffer from issues ranging lack of identification of words or phrases that are commonly used to making mistakes due to context ambiguity. Based on this, we create eight different error categories suitable to measure the quality of models' predictions.

In the latter case, we find very few works to focus on error analysis of offensive span identification, with a predominant concentration on the English Language (Ding and Jurgens, 2021). Additionally, some works focus on error analysis of sequence labeling method (Stanislawek et al., 2019; Niklaus et al., 2018; Nguyen et al., 2019), but not from the point of offensive spans. In this work, in line with Ding and Jurgens (2021) we use human intervention for error analysis. More specifically, we create multiple error analysis teams consisting

* Corresponding Author: Work done during graduate school

Third Workshop on Speech and Language Technologies for Dravidian Languages, pages 1–9, Varna, Bulgaria, Sep 7, 2023.
https://doi.org/10.26615/978-954-452-085-4_001

Methods	Model	F1
Token Labeling (Ravikiran and Annamalai, 2021)	Multilingual-BERT (M1)	0.5688
	RoBERTA (M2)	0.5721
	XLM-RoBERTA (M3)	0.5793
Zero-shot Rationale Extraction (Ravikiran and Chakravarthi, 2022)	RoBERTA+LIME (M4)	0.4886
	XLM-RoBERTA+LIME (M5)	0.4845
	XLM-RoBERTA+IG (M6)	0.4923
	XLM-RoBERTA + IG + Augmentation (M7)	0.5023
	RoBERTA + LIME + Multilabel training (M8)	0.4723

Table 1: Results reported in authors publications about offensive span identification models on the DOSA_v2 test set. There is no script available to test models from Ravikiran and Annamalai (2021), rather models are reproduced based on description of models in original paper. Zero shot model results are reproduced based on code from `https://github.com/manikandan-ravikiran/zero-shot-offensive-span`. **IG**: Integrated Gradients, **LIME**: Local Interpretable Model Agnostic Explanations.

of data scientists and NLP researchers to review the errors to see if there are any data-related errors. In the due process, we find around 9% of the test data show errors due to missing or incorrect annotation. Overall the contributions of this paper are as follows.

- We reproduce results of existing models for offensive span identification in code-mixed Tamil-English Language.
- We extend six different error categories from earlier works of Named Entity Recognition (Stanislawek et al., 2019) and Toxic Span Identification (Ding and Jurgens, 2021), to context of code-mixed Tamil-English offensive span identification. Additionally, we introduce two new categories specifically focusing on Tamil-English code mixed comments. In the due process, we systematically inspect and categorize various identified errors from the existing offensive span identification models.
- We identify various data-related errors and re-annotate the dataset to improve overall data quality.
- Finally, we release additional diagnostic datasets to help researchers understand various strengths and weaknesses of the offensive span identification models[1].

The rest of the paper is organized as follows. In section 2, we present the offensive span identification models, error categories, re-annotation, and diagnostic data creation process. Meanwhile in section 3, we discuss each results with discussion of key findings in section 4 and conclude in section 5.

2 Methods

In this work, we start our analysis by reproducing selected models for the DOSA-v2 dataset. Following this, the models' errors and errors in the test dataset itself are analyzed multiple times across each sentence. After reviewing the various errors, we define different error categories that help identify and diagnose common and important errors (Section 2.2). Finally, we re-annotate the dataset based on identified dataset errors to find a few improvements in overall results (Section 2.4).

2.1 Offensive Span Identification Models

Various models developed for offensive span identification to date in literature are shown in Table 1. Most of them are widely used across other NLP tasks beginning with transformer-based sequence labeling, which are bi-directional language models with an encoder architecture made of BERT (Devlin et al., 2019), RoBERTa (Liu et al., 2019), or XLM-RoBERTA (Conneau et al., 2020) with an output layer fine-tuned for labeling individual tokens. Also, there are zero-shot models that couple transformer-based sentence classifiers with rationale extraction methods of Local Interpretable Model Agnostic Explanations (LIME) (Ribeiro et al., 2016) and Integrated Gradients (IG) (Sundararajan et al., 2017). Occasionally, these models use additional bells, and whistles involving masked data augmentation and multilabel training to identify the offensive spans better (Ravikiran and Chakravarthi, 2022). We selected the highlighted models from Table 1 in this work due to their high results.

[1] `https://drive.google.com/drive/folders/1VGJcGEdcx4rUIUNT3WReRBGMWX1WKUAA?usp=sharing`

2.2 Error Categories

Shortform	Error Category
DE-	Dataset Error
DE-M	Missing Annotation Error
DE-I	Incorrect Annotation Error
PE-	Prediction Errors
PE-M	Prediction Missing Offensive Word
PE-AMB	Prediction Error due to Sentence Ambiguity
PE-UN	Error due to Unrelated Prediction
PE-LC	Prediction Error with Larger Context
PE-SL	Prediction Error with Smaller Context
PE-UKN	Uncategorized Prediction Errors

Table 2: Error categories used in this work

Since much of the offensive content is spread across social media, from a human moderation perspective, the task of identifying of offensive span relies upon multiple factors, namely (a) context around the offensive utterance, (b) situation when the offensive content was posted, (c) awareness of commonly used offensive words in the particular domain, (d) inconsistency in usage of words that are viewed by some as offensive and (e) general knowledge about the world.

Specifically, inline with Ding and Jurgens (2021), we created **DE-M**, **DE-I** and **PE-UN** error categories. Meanwhile to identify errors where the model identifies part of the ground truth or identifies words/phrases that are not present in ground truth we created **PE-LC** and **PE-SC** error categories. These errors are similar to token level errors in NER systems but previously unexplored in offensive span or toxic span identification problem.

Additionally Dravidian languages including Tamil often exhibit phenomenon of place sensitive word choices i.e depending on place where it is spoken certain words are more common than the others. For example, the phrase `vaaya moodu (shut your mouth)` is widely used. Meanwhile the phrase `Poda berika mandaiya (go you peach head)` is not common, rather find heavy localization within northern regions of Tamil Nadu. As such to accommodate these and cases where the word is explicitly offensive irrespective of context, we create **PE-M** error category.

Finally, for the sentences where the understanding of offensiveness is not directly possible only through the words in the sentence; instead requires additional world knowledge. we created **PE-UKN** error category. All the developed error categories shown in Table 2. Each of these error categories is described briefly in the following sections with examples.

- **DE-M**: **Missing Annotation Errors** are errors that are part of the gold standard annotation. As a result, the models' performance may be over or underestimated. For example, in the sentence `Amma Silluku da Silluku da (Your mother is a w**e)`, the gold standard annotation has only one instance of `Silluku da` identified, leading to a second prediction by the model identified as an error. In this case, both of the instances should be annotated.
- **DE-I**: **Incorrect Annotation Errors** are annotations that include part of the sentence that is in the context of an offensive word but do not directly contribute to offensiveness. For example, in the sentence `Anda parambarai p****a parambarai nu vadhuduraga da`, the offensive part is only `p****a parambarai.` Instead, the annotation has `Anda parambarai p****a parambarai`, resulting in an incorrect estimation of the models' accuracy.
- **PE-M**: **Prediction Missing Offensive Word** is the error where the model misses the word that are often used in offensive conversation and sometime are localized to a given region. For example, phrase `Poda berika mandaiya (go you peach head)` the offensive part is `berika mandaiya.`
- **PE-AMB**: **Prediction Error due to Sentence Ambiguity** is the most challenging case where the inferring offensive span is complex, as these sentences are often sarcastic and indirect. For example, in the sentence `Mr. X! Mr. Y kitta pesuriya Manda battharam`, the sentence is offensive to Mr. X because of the word `Manda battharam`, which means "take care of your head." The sentence implies that when talking to Mr. Y, Mr. X should be careful of their head which is a sarcastic offensive statement towards Mr. Y.
- **PE-UN**: **Error due to Unrelated Prediction** by the model are errors where the model predicts offensive spans that are entirely different from the ground truth annotation. These

are the errors that reduce the model's accuracy significantly.

- **PE-LC**: **Prediction errors with larger context** are the offensive span errors, where the model, in addition to identifying the offensive part, also accounts for a few more words before or after it. For example, in the sentence `Enna da innum trending aagala thuu (What man, it is not trending yet, shit)`, the ground truth annotation for the offensive part is `thuu`. However, the model extracts `trending aagala thuu`.
- **PE-SC**: **Prediction Errors with smaller context** are the offensive span errors, where the model identifies only part of the ground truth annotation but not wholly. For example, in sentence `Hindi villanunga tholla thaanga mudilapa saami (Unable to bear the nuisance by Hindi villains)`, the ground truth annotation for the offensive part is `tholla thaanga mudilapa`. However, the model extracts only `tholla`.
- **PE-UKN**: **Errors that are uncategorized**: These are the sentences where the offensive span identification is not possible without the world knowledge. For example, in the sentence `Mr X sir trending neenga late sir` one can argue that this is not offensive solely based on context words without any world knowledge. However, the sentence is offensive trolling towards Mr. X, saying he is not trending due to the late release of his movie. So the part of the sentence making the sentence offensive is the phrase `late sir`.

2.3 Data Review and Re-Annotation Method

Two teams analyzed the sentences identified as part of the offensive span. Each team consisted of an NLP researcher and a data scientist with former being linguist with deep knowledge of Tamil literature and later is from computer science background, often developing models for on actual application. As such, this combination of people is useful for considering linguistic properties (if any) and need of actual application. Each team reviewed the predicted offensive spans of all the models and categorized and re-annotated the sentences as shown in the following steps.

- A set of error categories were established. See section 2.2.
- The results obtained were distributed across two teams equally along with ground truth annotation, where first, each team would review their share of results and assign one or more error categories. To this end, the teams assign each sentence to one of the error categories.
- After this, the two teams created annotations for DE-M and DE-I errors, respectively.
- Finally, the two teams checked each others' re-annotated sentences for consistency and quality. Conflict, if any, was resolved via debate on the reasoning behind such annotation. In this work, we often saw conflicts where the annotations of one team failed to account for one or more phrases considered in annotation of the other team.

Error Category	Agreement (%)	Kappa
DE-M	94.12	0.4767
DE-I	84.80	0.4119
PE-AMB	84.97	0.4052
PE-UKN	93.89	0.3801

Table 3: Inter-annotator statistics (agreement and Kappa) during error review process, before discussing each controversial example and the re-annotation stage.

Irrespective of ease of annotation, only for a few categories, the two teams annotated all the sentences in the test data of DOSA-v2. The inter-annotator agreement statistics and Kappa measures are shown in Table 3 for DE-M, DE-I, PE-AMB, and PE-UKN. For some sentences, especially involving PE-AMB, the data scientists across both teams argued that these sentences are difficult to identify spans, as it took them a fair amount of time to categorize such errors and proposed removing them. The NLP researchers reviewed such examples independently and agreed that they are needed for improving the overall systems. For categories PE-U and PE-M, the teams employed a semi-automatic approach to increase review speed. Specifically, the steps used are as follows.

- For PE-UN the teams directly checked if spans had any overlap between the ground truth and prediction. If not, they were categorized as PE-UN.
- For PE-M, we use the offensive dictionary from Ravikiran and Chakravarthi (2022). In

each of the sentences, offensive words were noted and checked to see if the model missed any of them.

PE-UKN is the hardest among all, which often lead to disagreements. To this end, we found that team that argued against categorizing sentences as PE-UKN often knew the context behind such sentences. Such discrepancy, in turn, emphasized the need for world knowledge to solve errors under such categories.

2.4 Diagnostic Data Creation Procedure

Once the errors were identified, analyzed, and categorized, the next step was to create diagnostic datasets. The purpose was to develop more examples that account for some of the minimal and commonly encountered examples in the real world that are to be must identified by the developed methods. Specifically, these diagnostic examples correspond to (i) sentences having words that are commonly used under offensive context, which will help to check if models' are failing in most straightforward cases (ii) sentences with ambiguity due to sarcasm, where the model can identify sarcastic offensiveness and (iii) large sentences where the context is extensive, which the model need to essentially capture to identify offensive spans but at the same time avoid PE-LC errors.

To this end, we select the semi-supervised data released as part of the DOSA-v2. The data consists of the 526 code-mixed sentences from the domain different from DOSA-v2 used in error analysis and have no associated span annotation. From this, we form the first diagnostic dataset (DSET-A) to account for each of the three categories mentioned earlier.

For (i), the DSET-A introduces more offensive words previously unseen in DOSA-v2 train and test datasets. These words are offensive irrespective of their context and often have varying pronunciations. For (ii), the diagnostic dataset consists of spans that highlight sarcastic offensiveness. These are often the most challenging cases for the models to identify, and if specified, one can agree that the models can understand the context effectively and may work across domains. For (iii), the uses sentences with more than 50 characters and accounts for the previous two characteristics. All of these three were created as follows.

- We created noisy annotations using the best performing supervised model M4 for each sentence.
- Divide the identified noisy annotations across the two teams which originally did the error analysis.
- Each team reviewed and corrected annotation errors if any. They also ignored sentences that are not part of this previously mentioned category.
- Finally, the annotations were merged and assigned to each category.

Additionally, we form two more diagnostic datasets, which are pretty straightforward. The second dataset (DSET-B) was generated from random words that are not offensive. Its purpose is to check if a model over-fits on offensive parts of a particular data set. A well-developed model should not return any entities on these random sentences. We generated two thousand of these sentences. The third diagnostic dataset (DSET-C) consisted of one thousand sentences with only offensive words or phrases, which tests if the model identifies all the offensive spans if there are any. DSET-C was again created using the offensive word dictionary from Ravikiran and Chakravarthi (2022).

3 Results

3.1 Overall Errors

In the DOSA-v2 test set, we selected sentences where at least one of the select models made mistakes in recognizing correct offensive spans. Table 4, shows representation of different types of errors across these models for DOSA-v2 test set along with their character level F1 score respectively. Specifically, we categorize each of the 876 test sentence to belong to one of the error categories from section 2.2.

From the table we can see multiple interesting characterstics.

- Supervised models tend to be more accurate (higher F1), while the zero-shot model accounts for more words with lower probability, which often leads to a drop in results.
- Both supervised and zero-shot models encompass more DE-I errors than DE-M errors.

	Models							
Error Type	**M1**	**M2**	**M3**	**M4**	**M5**	**M6**	**M7**	**M8**
DE-M	8	6	6	11	7	5	5	8
DE-I	34	33	32	29	29	17	17	23
PE-M	57	56	63	31	62	192	192	120
PE-AMB	146	136	132	64	31	0	0	35
PE-UN	62	70	67	80	78	80	80	79
PE-LC	234	241	245	593	601	577	577	553
PE-SC	330	329	336	63	63	0	0	53
PE-UKN	5	5	5	5	5	5	5	5
F1	0.5688	0.5721	0.5793	0.4886	0.4845	0.50231	0.5023	0.472
F1@30	0.6979	0.7066	0.708	0.58667	0.5965	0.5947	0.5947	0.587
F1@50	0.6835	0.686	0.6999	0.576	0.5835	0.5701	0.5701	0.572
F1@>50	0.5335	0.5244	0.5644	0.451	0.442	0.4709	0.4709	0.431

Table 4: Errors for a each model across various categories of errors.

- Meanwhile, for PE-M, we can see zero-shot XLMRoBERTA-based models (M6, M7, M8) show a relatively higher error (>100) than the rest.
- Zero-shot models tend to predict more unrelated PE-UN errors than the supervised approaches. But, at the same time, they show fewer errors in the PE-AMB category.
- Across both zero-shot and supervised models, most errors are concentrated in PE-LC and PE-SC categories, with PE-LC dominating zero-shot approaches and PE-SC dominating supervised models. We believe this is because of the high precision nature of sequence labeling compared to threshold-based scoring used in zero-shot models.
- Moreover, we can see that the errors are in similar ranges for PE-LC and PE-SC categories across different methods within the same category.
- PE-UKN is very less and is the same across all the methods.
- Finally, we can see XLM-RoBERTA encoder dominate across both supervised and zero-shot approaches with high results.

3.2 Effect of Re-Annotation

Table 5, shows results after re-annotation. Firstly comparing Table 4 with 5, we can see that across all the models' errors due to incorrect annotation and missing annotation are zero. Meanwhile, The overall F1 reduced with re-annotation, indicating an overestimating of existing models' performance. We can see that the models' performance dropped by 0.5%. To understand this drop further, we investigated sentences of different lengths, i.e., (i) sentences with less than 30 characters (F1@30), (ii) sentences with 30-50 characters (F1@50), (iii) sentences with more than 50 characters (F1@>50) in line with Ravikiran et al. (2022).

Table 5, shows each of these results. From the table 5 we can see that for F1@30, the results have an average improvement of 1.7% with re-annotation indicating re-annotation improved the data quality. From the results, we can note two additional points. Firstly, for large sentences beyond 50 characters, the drop of result is high, indicating the complicated structure of sentences, often where the true offensive span is hard to obtain. In fact, during re-annotation, we noticed that during the categorization of PE-LC within each team, there was a significant discussion on why particular spans an error considering they are capture sentence structure. Second for sentences with less than 30 characters, often we see that most of the sentences are part of the offensive span. In that sense correcting data-related errors is expected to improve overall results.

3.3 Results on Diagnostic datasets

Looking at the models' results for our three diagnostic datasets (Table 6), the critical observation is that we achieved significantly lower results than initially on the DOSA-v2 dataset from Table 4. Such a result is because we selected samples for DSET-A from different domains, such as homophobia and transphobia, while the original train and test set are from the domain of movie reviews. In particular, we selected 491 sentences, with 256 of them having new offensive words previously unseen in train or test. Meanwhile, 60 are ambiguous, and the rest are all sentences with more than 50 characters that are either ambiguous or have new offensive words or both. Moreover, few of these sentences have entirely different sentence structures than train and test sets.

As far as the results of the DSET-A were concerned, we observed much better results for su-

	Models							
Error Type	**M1**	**M2**	**M3**	**M4**	**M5**	**M6**	**M7**	**M8**
DE-M	0	0	0	0	0	0	0	0
DE-I	0	0	0	0	0	0	0	0
PE-M	56	57	53	64	61	192	192	118
PE-AMB	151	138	134	32	34	0	0	40
PE-UN	60	69	64	80	78	80	80	79
PE-LC	243	248	254	595	597	578	578	554
PE-SC	342	339	347	63	64	0	0	55
PE-UKN	5	5	5	5	5	5	5	5
F1	0.5636	0.5683	0.5747	0.483	0.4789	0.4943	0.4943	0.466
F1@30	0.7067	0.7195	0.7214	0.604	0.614	0.6099	0.6099	0.604
F1@50	0.6335	0.656	0.6789	0.5689	0.5756	0.5616	0.5616	0.559
F1@>50	0.5135	0.5181	0.5635	0.444	0.4366	0.4633	0.4633	0.425

Table 5: Errors for a each model across each categories of errors after re-annotation.

Models	**M1**	**M3**	**M4**	**M5**	**M6**	**M8**	**M9**	**M10**
DSET-A	0.4022	0.3884	0.3839	0.3499	0.3779	0.4429	0.383	0.3549
DSET-B	0.4349	0.4426	0.4568	0.5128	0.4578	0.5108	0.58	0.5238
DSET-C	0.87185	0.7579	0.9022	0.9092	0.8972	0.8302	0.757	0.7392

Table 6: Results (character level F1) of selected models across diagnostic datasets

pervised models than for zero-shot approaches. Specifically, we see all the models show results around 40% in F1. Further, we could see the models fail in identifying new offensive words 86% of the time.

Meanwhile, we see surprising results when tested with all the models on DSET-B and DSET-C. Firstly for DSET-B, where all the words in a sentence are offensive, the models fail by a large margin. This suggests that the existing benchmark dataset set alone is insufficient to estimate the models' ability to know the offensive words.

Meanwhile, for DSET-C, we can see almost all the models show results lower than 100% indicating many of them are indeed predicting non-offensive words as offensive. This is not good considering, upon practical application may lead to over censoring of contents. However, we believe models which show high scores on this DSET-B are helpful for actual application due to reduced false positives.

4 Discussion

Since the field of offensive span identification from code-mixed Tamil English language is in the nascent stage, based on previous results, we draw the following minimal takeaways that could be adopted in upcoming publications of offensive span identification models.

- Firstly, any assessment of new methods and models should be broadened to understand their common mistakes, specifically via the usage of DSET-B and DSET-C, respectively. This, in turn, will help identify why these models perform well or poorly in test set examples.
- Complex linguistic syntax and sentences structures with completely new words are common in social media. In that sense benchmarking using DSET-A is useful
- While deriving error categories, we realized many errors could be further expanded into sub-categories. For example, PE-M errors with different language origins where the offensive words are from Tamil or English. In that sense, detailed error analysis with automatic identification of different categories is warranted.
- Though data annotation is complex and time-consuming, it is important to check precise results rather than only accuracy numbers. Especially with many of them being released as part of shared tasks, one could employ the need for error analysis. This will, in turn, ensure models stability and improve the quality of data before much of the research community starts moving the field further.
- The identified errors shows that PE-M to form significant portion of errors, right after PE-LC and PE-SC hinting on need to identify the same.
- Meanwhile, data annotation for offensive span identification is ambiguous, with different annotators arguing for different parts of sentences to be considered for spans. This means that metrics such as F1 are not sufficient. Instead, metrics that account for neces-

sary and sufficient parts of spans must be introduced for a fair comparison of developed models.

- While benchmarking is vital, we could see the failure of models when extending to different domains. This suggests the need to accommodate other data domains in code-mixed low resource languages.
- Also, none of the models solved the PE-UKN category indicating the need for world knowledge beyond sentences to identify such offensive sentences. To this end, we find this type of errors are difficult to identify both manually and automatically. This is because often the world knowledge is subjective to individual person.
- Finally, the DOSA-v2 test set is too small to test a model's generalization and stability. Faced with this issue, we must find new techniques to prevent the over-fitting of the model and test exhaustively on diagnostic sets to ensure model quality.

5 Conclusion

Overall in this work, we studied errors in offensive span identification models. To this end, we considered both zero-shot and supervised sequence labeling approaches. We started with analyzing predictions of 8 different models and creating various error categories. Based on the analysis, we re-annotated the DOSA-v2 test set and re-benchmarked the results to find the re-annotation was fruitful in improving the outcomes of sentences with less than 30 characters simultaneously highlighted the failure of methods across large sentences. We additionally developed diagnostic datasets to assist in identifying critical errors. Finally, we discussed some of our key findings, which could be adapted in future works, including developing metrics that effectively capture models' performance development of cross-domain data and knowledge sources for context understanding.

Ethics Statement

In this paper, we report on the errors of existing state-of-the-art Tamil-English offensive span identification models, by drawing perspectives from problems such as Named Entity Recognition and Toxic span identification. To this end, we reproduce existing models, create new error categories and study data related errors, by creating a new diagnostic dataset for offensive span identification. The data collection process did not involve any human participants. So, no ethics board approval was necessary. All the datasets used in this work are available under permissive licenses that allow sharing and redistributing. We believe that the NLP systems developed using current released dataset may lead to better understanding of errors, in turn contributing to systems for identification of offensive language across multiple platforms, with broader societal implications. If used as intended the models and dataset could improve the quality of social media conversation. An important point to note is potential skew in error analysis and datasets used themselves. Any analysis may often skew in a certain direction. For example, in this work the datasets used are small and error analysis may be biased towards one of more groups of people. However, to mitigate this to certain extent, we have considered offensive contents targeted towards underrepresented transgender, LGBTQ communities to avoid potential bias and negative impacts.

Acknowledgements

We thank our anonymous reviewers for their valuable feedback. Any opinions, findings, and conclusion or recommendations expressed in this material are those of the authors only and does not reflect the view of their employing organization or graduate schools. The analysis was result of series projects done during CS7646-ML4T (Fall 2020), CS6460-Edtech Foundations (Spring 2020) and CS7643-Deep learning (Spring 2022) at Georgia Institute of Technology (OMSCS Program) in collaboration with researchers at NUI Galway. Bharathi Raja Chakravarthi were supported in part by a research grant from Science Foundation Ireland (SFI) under Grant Number SFI/12/RC/2289_P2 (Insight_2).

References

Bharathi Raja Chakravarthi. 2022. Multilingual hope speech detection in English and Dravidian languages. *International Journal of Data Science and Analytics*, 14(4):389–406.

Bharathi Raja Chakravarthi. 2023. Detection of homophobia and transphobia in Youtube comments. *International Journal of Data Science and Analytics*, pages 1–20.

Bharathi Raja Chakravarthi, Adeep Hande, Rahul Ponnusamy, Prasanna Kumar Kumaresan, and Ruba Priyadharshini. 2022a. How can we detect homophobia and transphobia? experiments in a multilingual code-mixed setting for social media governance. *International Journal of Information Management Data Insights*, 2(2):100119.

Bharathi Raja Chakravarthi, Ruba Priyadharshini, Thenmozhi Durairaj, John McCrae, Paul Buitelaar, Prasanna Kumaresan, and Rahul Ponnusamy. 2022b. Overview of the shared task on homophobia and transphobia detection in social media comments. In *Proceedings of the Second Workshop on Language Technology for Equality, Diversity and Inclusion*, pages 369–377, Dublin, Ireland. Association for Computational Linguistics.

Alexis Conneau, Kartikay Khandelwal, Naman Goyal, Vishrav Chaudhary, Guillaume Wenzek, Francisco Guzmán, Edouard Grave, Myle Ott, Luke Zettlemoyer, and Veselin Stoyanov. 2020. Unsupervised cross-lingual representation learning at scale. In *Proceedings of the 58th Annual Meeting of the Association for Computational Linguistics, ACL 2020, Online, July 5-10, 2020*, pages 8440–8451. Association for Computational Linguistics.

Jacob Devlin, Ming-Wei Chang, Kenton Lee, and Kristina Toutanova. 2019. BERT: pre-training of deep bidirectional transformers for language understanding. In *Proceedings of the 2019 Conference of the North American Chapter of the Association for Computational Linguistics: Human Language Technologies, NAACL-HLT 2019, Minneapolis, MN, USA, June 2-7, 2019, Volume 1 (Long and Short Papers)*, pages 4171–4186. Association for Computational Linguistics.

Huiyang Ding and David Jurgens. 2021. HamiltonDinggg at SemEval-2021 task 5: Investigating toxic span detection using RoBERTa pre-training. In *Proceedings of the 15th International Workshop on Semantic Evaluation (SemEval-2021)*, pages 263–269, Online. Association for Computational Linguistics.

Manikandan Ravikiran Hariharan RamakrishnaIyer LekshmiAmmal, Anand Kumar Madasamy. 2022. Nitk-it_nlp@tamilnlp-acl2022: Transformer based model for toxic span identification in tamil. In *Proceedings of the Second Workshop on Speech and Language Technologies for Dravidian Languages*. Association for Computational Linguistics.

Prasanna Kumar Kumaresan, Rahul Ponnusamy, Elizabeth Sherly, Sangeetha Sivanesan, and Bharathi Raja Chakravarthi. 2022. Transformer based hope speech comment classification in code-mixed text. In *International Conference on Speech and Language Technologies for Low-resource Languages*, pages 120–137. Springer.

Yinhan Liu, Myle Ott, Naman Goyal, Jingfei Du, Mandar Joshi, Danqi Chen, Omer Levy, Mike Lewis, Luke Zettlemoyer, and Veselin Stoyanov. 2019. Roberta: A robustly optimized BERT pretraining approach. *CoRR*, abs/1907.11692.

Binh An Nguyen, Kiet Van Nguyen, and Ngan Luu-Thuy Nguyen. 2019. Error analysis for vietnamese named entity recognition on deep neural network models. *CoRR*, abs/1911.07228.

Christina Niklaus, Matthias Cetto, André Freitas, and Siegfried Handschuh. 2018. A survey on open information extraction. In *Proceedings of the 27th International Conference on Computational Linguistics*, pages 3866–3878, Santa Fe, New Mexico, USA. Association for Computational Linguistics.

Manikandan Ravikiran and Subbiah Annamalai. 2021. DOSA: Dravidian code-mixed offensive span identification dataset. In *Proceedings of the First Workshop on Speech and Language Technologies for Dravidian Languages*, pages 10–17, Kyiv. Association for Computational Linguistics.

Manikandan Ravikiran and Bharathi Raja Chakravarthi. 2022. Zero-shot code-mixed offensive span identification through rationale extraction. *Proceedings of the Second Workshop on Speech and Language Technologies for Dravidian Languages. Association for Computational Linguistics, 2022.*

Manikandan Ravikiran, Bharathi Raja Chakravarthi, Anand Kumar Madasamy, Sangeetha Sivanesan, Ratnavel Rajalakshmi, Sajeetha Thavareesan, Rahul Ponnusamy, and Shankar Mahadevan. 2022. Findings of the shared task on Offensive Span Identification in code-mixed Tamil-English comments. In *Proceedings of the Second Workshop on Speech and Language Technologies for Dravidian Languages*. Association for Computational Linguistics.

Marco Túlio Ribeiro, Sameer Singh, and Carlos Guestrin. 2016. "why should I trust you?": Explaining the predictions of any classifier. In *Proceedings of the Demonstrations Session, NAACL HLT 2016, The 2016 Conference of the North American Chapter of the Association for Computational Linguistics: Human Language Technologies, San Diego California, USA, June 12-17, 2016*, pages 97–101. The Association for Computational Linguistics.

Tomasz Stanislawek, Anna Wróblewska, Alicja Wójcicka, Daniel Ziembicki, and Przemyslaw Biecek. 2019. Named entity recognition - is there a glass ceiling? In *Proceedings of the 23rd Conference on Computational Natural Language Learning (CoNLL)*, pages 624–633, Hong Kong, China. Association for Computational Linguistics.

Mukund Sundararajan, Ankur Taly, and Qiqi Yan. 2017. Axiomatic attribution for deep networks. In *Proceedings of the 34th International Conference on Machine Learning, ICML 2017, Sydney, NSW, Australia, 6-11 August 2017*, volume 70 of *Proceedings of Machine Learning Research*, pages 3319–3328. PMLR.

Hate and Offensive Keyword Extraction from CodeMix Malayalam Social Media Text Using Contextual Embedding

Mariya Raphel, Premjith B, Sreelakshmi K
Amrita School of Artificial Intelligence,
Coimbatore,
Amrita Vishwa Vidyapeetham, India
b_premjith@cb.amrita.edu

Bharathi Raja Chakravarthi
School of Computer Science,
University Of Galway,
Galway, Ireland

Abstract

This paper focuses on identifying hate and offensive keywords from codemix Malayalam social media text. As part of this work, a dataset for hate and offensive keyword extraction for codemix Malayalam language was created. Two different methods were experimented to extract Hate and Offensive language (HOL) keywords from social media text. In the first method, intrinsic evaluation was performed on the dataset to identify the hate and offensive keywords. Three different approaches namely – unigram approach, bigram approach and trigram approach were performed to extract the HOL keywords, sequence of HOL words and the sequence that contribute HOL meaning even in the absence of a HOL word. Five different transformer models were used in each of the approaches for extracting the embeddings for the ngrams. Later, HOL keywords were extracted based on the similarity score obtained using the cosine similarity. Out of the five transformer models, the best results were obtained with multilingual BERT. In the second method, multilingual BERT transformer model was fine tuned with the dataset to develop a HOL keyword tagger model. This work is a new beginning for HOL keyword identification in Dravidian language – Malayalam.

1 Introduction

Social networking sites are the platforms where users can create their own profiles and communicate with other users regardless of any kind of limitations. The freedom to share any content on social media led to the rise of hate and offensive posts on online social media (OSN) (Bharathi and Agnusimmaculate Silvia, 2021; Bharathi and Varsha, 2022; Swaminathan et al., 2022). Hate and offensive posts pose a severe risk to victims' physical and mental health and lead to serious consequences (Chakravarthi, 2022a,b; Kumaresan et al., 2022). This emphasis the importance of automatically detecting hate and offensive content from social media (Sreelakshmi et al., 2021), (Chakravarthi et al., 2023).

The identification of words which make the text hate or offensive is even more critical because it helps to restrict users from posting as well as reading comments containing such words. Therefore, the automatic extraction of the keywords from a social media post has the equal significance of detecting hate content from a social media post. HOL keyword extraction models are available in some languages. However, such models are not yet implemented in Dravidian languages like Malayalam, Tamil, Kannada etc. This task is challenging in Dravidian languages because Dravidian languages are abundant in morphology and can generate numerous word forms by joining a sequence of morphemes to the root word (Chakravarthi et al., 2022a,b; Chakravarthi, 2023). Besides, the social media posts are codemixed and low-resource for Dravidian languages, which poses other challenges in developing an automatic keyword extraction model. Despite of the challenges, developing a HOL keyword extraction model for Dravidian languages is necessary due to its increased use in social media.

Developing a model on codemix data is really challenging. The unavailability of an annotated dataset for HOL keyword extraction on codemix data was the other main challenge. Therefore, we developed an annotated dataset where all the HOL words are labelled in each social media text. Further, we prepared a dictionary of hate and offensive words. Thus, through this work, we addressed the main challenge which hindered any research in HOL keyword extraction in Malayalam by developing the HOL keyword extraction dataset. Later, we performed an intrinsic evaluation on the dataset using five different multilingual sentence transform-

Third Workshop on Speech and Language Technologies for Dravidian Languages, pages 10–18, Varna, Bulgaria, Sep 7, 2023.
https://doi.org/10.26615/978-954-452-085-4_002

ers.

This paper investigates the efficacy of different multilingual transformer-based embedding models for automatically extracting the keywords from Malayalam codemixed social media posts. We experimented three approaches namely, unigram approach, bigram approach and trigram approach for this. Unigram approach was meant for extracting HOL keywords. In addition, we used the transformer-based models to identify the multiword expressions that make a sentence which does not have a hate or offensive word, hate or offensive text. Here, we define the multiword expression as a sequence of two words (bi-gram) or three words (tri-gram). We considered the intrinsic evaluation scheme in all these approaches for detecting the keywords and multiword expressions from a social media comment. Likewise we developed a transformer based model (Vaswani et al., 2017) and performed various analysis to evaluate the efficacy of our model.

The major contributions of this paper are:

- A model for extracting keyword/multiword expression from social media posts in Malayalam codemix text.
- An annotated dataset for detecting hate and offensive keywords from social media posts in Malayalam codemix text.
- A comparison between the performance of different multilingual transformer models on identifying HOL keyword/multiword expression.
- A transformer-based model for HOL keyword identification

2 Related Works

Hate and offensive content is a pervasive and developing social trend because of the surge of social media technology usage. There are many works related to hate and offensive language identification.

In (Hande et al., 2021), the work was on identifying the offensive language in the low-resourced code-mixed Dravidian languages - Tamil, Kannada, and Malayalam. They constructed a dataset by transliterating all the code-mixed texts into the respective Dravidian language and then pseudo labels were generated for it. They used different pretrained language for extracting the embeddings and then it was given to recurrent neural networks. The best results were obtained when they used the ULM fit model. Their model gave an F1 score of 0.79 for Tamil-English, 0.96 for Malayalam-English and 0.73 for Kannada-English.

In (Sreelakshmi et al., 2021), the authors developed three deep neural architectures for offensive language identification in Dravidian languages. The first architecture was a hybrid model including a convolutional layer, a Bi-LSTM layer and a hidden layer. The second architecture contains a Bi-LSTM and the third architecture contains a Bi-RNN. They mainly focused on the code-mixed Tamil-English, Malayalam-English and Kannada-English for their work. On evaluation, the hybrid model gave them the best results with an F1 score of 0.64 for Tamil- English, 0.90 for Malayalam-English and 0.65 for Kannada-English.

Various approaches were used by different works for identifying hate and offensive language identification. However, we couldn't find any works on hate or offensive keyword extraction from Dravidian languages. Lack of HOL keyword annotated dataset is one of the main reason behind it. On the contrary, works on hate and offensive keyword extraction exists for languages except Dravidian.

In (Sarracén and Rosso, 2023), the work was on extracting Offensive keyword from English comments. OffensEval 2019 and OffensEval 2020 were the datasets used for this work. The offensive keyword extraction was done based on the attention mechanism of BERT and the eigenvector centrality using a graph representation. On testing, they obtained an F1 score of 0.5687 on Off20-OFF19 and 0.5798 on Off19-OFF20.

In (Pamungkas et al., 2022), the authors investigated the role of swear words in detecting the abusive language. They proposed the guidelines for tagging the HOL keywords. They developed a swear word abusive dataset for English language using twitter comments. They also performed certain intrinsic evaluations such as sequence labelling on their dataset. They obtained an f1 score of 0.75 for non-abusive swear word, 0.42 for abusive swear word and 0.99 for not a swear word.

In (Martinc et al., 2022), the authors proposed Transformer-based Neural Tagger for Keyword Identification (TNT-KID) to extract one or multiword phrase which represents the key aspects of a document. For this task, they collected a dataset of scientific abstracts and extracted keywords. According to their work, keyword tagging task was modeled as a binary classification task and predict if a word in the sequence is a keyword or not. The model was trained and tested accordingly and they obtained an F1-score of 0.63.

Though the HOL keyword extraction was put forward by few works, it is not yet implemented in Dravidian languages. This was the major research gap that motivated us for our work. It is necessary to develop a HOL keyword extraction model for Dravidian languages, because, it is widely spoken in south India and commonly used in social media for posting comments. Hence our work focuses on implementing HOL keyword extraction in Dravidian language. As mentioned earlier, lack of dataset was the main challenge for this. Therefore, we created a HOL keyword dataset for code-mixed Malayalam language. Thus we tackled the prime cause for the research gap. Our work is a new beginning for HOL keyword extracton in Dravidian language.

3 DATASET

Since dataset for HOL keyword extraction were not existing for Malayalam language, creation of the dataset was our prime motive. Tweets and YouTube comments were the sources of data. We extended the existing 'HASCO' dataset (Chakravarthi et al., 2020) to create our new HOL keyword dataset. The HASOC dataset comprises of code-mixed malayalam comments labelled as 'Hate' or 'Not Hate'. We focused on the negative comments (labelled as 'Hate') for finding the HOL keywords. The dataset consisted of 8943 comments. Out of that 3092 comments were of HOL nature and remaining 5851comments were normal. On analysing the negative comments in perspective of HOL keywords, we could notice two types of negative comments. We categorised the comments into two. The first category consisted of negative comments with a HOL word(s). The second category contained negative comments which did not have a HOL word in it.

Keyword annotations process then was narrowed down to first category. The dataset creation (annotation) steps are illustrated in Fig. ??.

The first step was to search for HOL keywords from the comments belonging to category one. For the ease of identifying negative words, we created a custom list of HOL keywords from swear word website.The HOL words in each comment was then identified by referring to this custom list. In order to label the identified HOL keywords, we followed the guidelines proposed by (Pamungkas et al., 2022). According to this, each offensive/hate keyword was tagged using <b> and </b> . If any comments contain multiple negative words, that comments can be replicated to mark those words. We tagged the keywords accordingly to create the final annotated dataset. The final list of HOL list contained 1082 words in it. The test set used in this work comprised of 756 comments.

4 Methodology

We followed two methodologies for extracting hate and offensive keyword from codemix Malayalam social media text. The first method involves an intrinsic evaluation whereas the second method follows a transformer based approach.

4.1 Data Preprocessing

Preprocessing was performed on the annotated dataset. This step focuses on conversion of letters into lower case, punctuation removal, emoji removal and username removal. Python's built-in package "`re`" was used for the removal of punctuations and username.

4.2 Method - 1:

Our first methodology involves the following steps as illustrated below in Fig. 1. The overall model has four main stages, namely, dataset creation, preprocessing, extracting embedding and HOL identification.

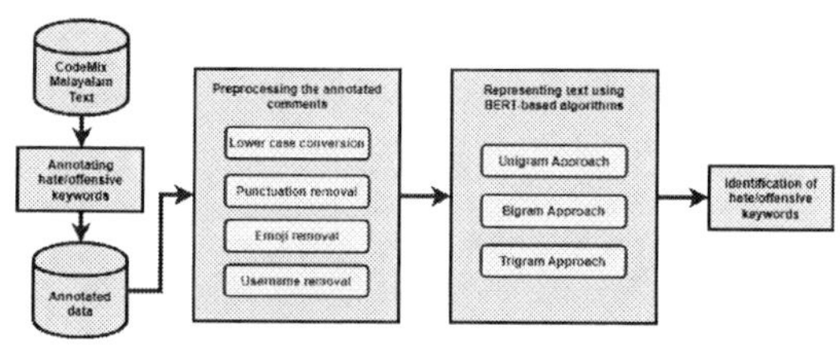

Figure 1: Proposed Architecture - 1

4.2.1 Generate Embeddings

Embedding helps to represent a word and its semantic information in a vector format. Words that are close in vector space are likely to have similar meanings. Therefore, in this work, we have generated embeddings for the n-grams to represent them in the vector space. The model will be able to segregate the HOL words and other normal words as the HOL words will be closer in the vector space. Various BERT based multilingual algorithms were used for representing the text and generating the embeddings. Five different sentence transformers (Devlin et al., 2018) (Sanh et al., 2019) (Das et al., 2022) (Kakwani et al., 2020) were used for the same.

At this stage, three approaches were followed for generating the embeddings - Unigram, bigram and trigram

4.2.2 Unigram Approach

In this approach, we considered words or unigrams obtained by tokenizing the input text. Later, the word embeddings were generated using the embedding models mentioned above. This embedding can be matched against the embeddings of the hate and offensive dictionary words.

4.2.3 Bigram Approach

In this approach, a two-word sequence or bigrams were considered. Bigrams were obtained by using an overlapping window approach over the comments. The window size was two and the overlapping size was one. Embedding of the bigrams were then generated using the chosen embedding models. These embeddings were used to compare with the embeddings of the hate and offensive dictionary words in the later stages. Thus, during the final identification phase in this approach, a sequence of two words will be predicted.

4.2.4 Trigram Approach

In this approach, a three-word sequence or trigrams were considered. We used the the overlapping window approach to obtain trigram with minor modifications in window size. In order to generate trigrams, the window size was set to three and the overlapping size was one. Later, the word embeddings were generated using the embedding models. These embeddings were used to match against the embeddings of the hate and offensive dictionary words. According to this approach, a sequence of three words will be predicted during the identification phase.

The bigram and trigram approaches were done to extract the sequence of HOL words from the comments. Similarly, there may be comments which does not contain a hate word. However the whole sentence might contribute a HOL context. In order to tackle these two possibilities, bigram approach and trigram approach were introduced.

4.3 Identify Hate and Offensive Keywords

The hate and offensive keywords were identified using similarity score. Cosine similarity was used for this purpose. After generating the embeddings for both the list of hate words and the tokenised comments (ngrams), cosine similarity between each of the ngrams and the hate word was calculated. Based on this similarity score, top five words (ngrams) were extracted as the hate words. Let W denotes the word vector and H denotes the hate word vector, then the cosine similarity can be given as:

$$CosineSimilarity(W, H) = \frac{W.H}{||W||||H||} \quad (1)$$

4.4 Method - 2:

Our second methodology follows a transformer based approach. Fig. 2 illustrates the steps involved in this method.

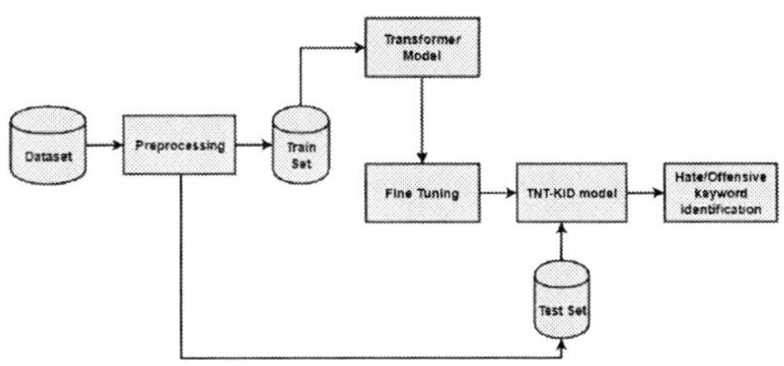

Figure 2: Proposed Architecture - 2

We started with our annotated HOL keyword dataset. The preprocessing step was same as in the method - 1. The dataset was then split into train set and test set. Train set was used developing and fine tuning our transformer model.

4.4.1 Model Development and Fine Tuning:

Pre-trained 'bert-base-multilingual-cased' transformer model was used as the base model in this method. The task of identifying HOL keywords was modelled as a binary class token classification problem. Therefore, our model have a task-specific output layer on top of the transformer model. Since it is a token classification task, the value at each index position in the output vector denotes whether the token at that index position in the comment vector is a hateword/offensive or normal.

We prepared two lists based on the train set. The first list contained all the comments of the train set. The second list contained the HOL words if any present in the corresponding sentence. The lists were named as 'sentences' and 'hatewords' respectively. Later both the lists were tokenised and the embeddings were generated. Comments in the 'sentences' list were padded to form a vector of length 256. Subsequently, label vectors of length

256 were prepared. The values in the label vectors were 1s and 0s. 1 represents HOL token and 0 represents a normal token.

'FULL_FINETUNING' was set to true in our model. Therefore, all the parameters of the pre-trained model were fine-tuned except the parameters like gama, bias etc. The weight_decay_rate was set to 0.01 for the non-normalization parameters and to 0.0 for the normalization parameters. Normalization parameters (e.g., gamma and beta) are typically used to scale and shift the outputs of a layer during training to improve performance. These parameters are not typically fine-tuned because they are usually set to some reasonable initial values and then fixed during training to prevent overfitting. This is because these parameters control the normalization of the activations across training examples, and overfitting on this normalization can lead to poor generalization performance on new data. By fixing these parameters during training, the model can learn better representations that are less dependent on the normalization parameters and thus more likely to generalize to new data.

5 Experiments and Results

In each approach of method-1, the comments were tokenized to form ngrams. Five different sentence transformers were used to generate the embedding of the ngram. Finally, cosine similarity was employed for finding the HOL keyword.

The models were trained with 3425 HOL comments and 6174 normal comments. Later, they were tested with 84 HOL comments. As this is a task where HOL words are detected, the no.of comments in the test set might not create any bias. The 84 test cases were prepared meticulously. The test cases included only those comments which contained HOL words that weren't listed on the custom list. This was done to know how efficiently the model could recognize unseen HOL words.

The performance of five different sentence transformers in extracting HOL words are compared in this section.

5.1 Unigram Approach

The results obtained on testing unigrams using different transformers are as follows:

5.1.1 BERT-base-multilingual-cased

Some sample results of this model for comments typed in English alone, Malayalam alone and including both are given in Fig. 3. For multilingual BERT it can be see that, the expected words are present in the predicted for first and second comments. But missed one word in last case. But still, since the expected words can be found in the predicted, this can be considered as a good performance.

Comment	Expected Words	Predicted Words
അയ്യേ നട്ടെല്ലില്ലാത്ത അവതാരക... അഭിമാനം എന്നൊന്നില്ലാത്ത അവതാരക...	അയ്യേ, നട്ടെല്ലില്ലാത്ത, അഭിമാനം എന്നൊന്നില്ലാത്ത	'നട്ടെല്ലില്ലാത്ത', 'എന്നൊന്നില്ലാത്ത', 'അയ്യേ', 'അവതാരക', 'അഭിമാനം'
ഇൻസൾട്ട് ചെയ്താൽ അടുത്ത ഗോൾഡൻ ബമ്പർ കിട്ടും .. സേച്ചി ഒന്നും തോന്നരുത് podii പിത്തക്കാടി	podii, പിത്തക്കാടി	'podii', 'പിത്തക്കാടി!', 'തോന്നരുത്', 'ബമ്പർ', 'ഇൻസൾട്ട്'
poi chavadi ena. Oro durandangal. Online cla ss kanum vegam vitto	poi chavadi, Oro durandangal	'chavadi', 'durandangal', 'kanum', 'vegam', 'ena'

Figure 3: Unigram - bert-base-multilingual-cased

5.1.2 distilbert-base-multilingual-cased

For multilingual distilbert, some of the expected words were present in the predicted list. On analysing the similarity scores it was seen that, the non hate words got a higher score than the hate words in the comments which include both English and Malayalam. However, this can also be regarded as a fair performance as the expected words were predicted.

5.1.3 Hate-speech-CNERG/indic-abusive-allInOne-MuRIL

This model follows a similar pattern as that of multilingual disitil bert. Some of the expected words were found in the predicted lists But for the comments typed in Malayalam alone, the non hate word has got a higher score than hate words.

5.1.4 ai4bharat/indic-bert

On inspecting the words predicted by this model, it was noted that few of the expected keywords were missed in the comments typed in English. Similarly non hate words got a higher score than the hate words in the comments typed in Malayalam.

5.1.5 Hate-speech-CNERG/malayalam-codemixed-abusive-MuRIL

In case of codemixed-abusive-MuRIL, a satisfactory result was not obtained for any of the comments.The model is not predicting well for English based comments. Therefore, for the comments typed in English alone and comments typed in English-malyalam, the predictions were not as desired. Even for the comments typed in Malayalam alone, non hate words had higher scores. In fact the scores are very similar or very high for the all words . This can be one of the causes for not distinguishing hate and non hate words properly and for the incorrect predictions.

The prediction accuracy of each model on testing with unigram approach is given in Table 1

5.2 Bigram Approach

In this approach, sequences of two words were predicted. Performance of the sentence transformers in the bigram approach has a similar pattern as that of the unigrams approach. The comments that do not contain a hate word, but a negative context are presented below. The results obtained on testing bigrams using different transformers are as follows:

5.2.1 BERT-base-multilingual-cased

The predictions obtained by this model is given in Fig. 4. On inspecting the predictions, it can be found that the sequences predicted by multilingual BERT contributes a negative meaning for all the three comments.

Comment	Expected Words	Predicted Words
ഈ മുഖഭാവം കണ്ട് ആരും അത്ഭുധപെടേണ്ട. സന്തോഷ് പണ്ഡിറ്റ് നേക്കാളും കിടുവ	സന്തോഷ് പണ്ഡിറ്റ് നേക്കാളും കിടുവ	'നേക്കാളും കിടുവ', 'അത്ഭുധപെടേണ്ട സന്തോഷ്', 'പണ്ഡിറ്റ് നേക്കാളും', 'ആരും അത്ഭുധപെടേണ്ട', 'മുഖഭാവം കണ്ട്'
No violence only peace. ഗോപാലൻ പണ്ടേ പീസിന്റെ ആളാണല്ലോ	പീസിന്റെ ആളാണല്ലോ	'പണ്ടേ പീസിന്റെ', 'പീസിന്റെ ആളാണല്ലോ', 'ഗോപാലൻ പണ്ടേ', 'peace ഗോപാലൻ', 'only peace'
Ikka fansinte 25 k dislike undallo... dislike adi chittu karanjolu	adichittu karanjolu	'adichittu karanjolu', 'dislike undallo', 'undallo dislike', 'dislike adichittu', 'ikka fansinte'

Figure 4: Bigram - BERT-base-multilingual-cased

5.2.2 distilbert-base-multilingual-cased

Multilingual distilbert model was able to extract negative sequences from the comments typed in English alone and Malayalam alone. Whereas, for the comment typed in English-Malayalam s.a discrepancy was seen in the predicted sequences.

5.2.3 Hate-speech-CNERG/indic-abusive-allInOne-MuRIL

The performance of this model using bigram approach was not satisfactory. The similarity scores of the bigrams were higher and closer. Hence, the predictions obtained were not accurate.

5.2.4 ai4bharat/indic-bert

The performance of this model was similar to that of the previous model. Even in this model, the predictions were not satisfactory because the model predicted incorrect bigram sequences as HOL for the comments.

5.2.5 Hate-speech-CNERG/malayalam-codemixed-abusive-MuRIL

Wrong predictions were obtained for the comments typed in Malayalam alone and English alone. Comparatively, better predictions were obtained for the comment typed in English and Malayalam.

The prediction accuracy of each model on testing with bigram approach is given in Table 2 On analysing the performance of different sentence transformer models in the bigram approach, it can be concluded that the multilingual bert outperforms the other models.

5.3 Trigram Approach

In trigram approach, sequences of three words were predicted. Performance of the sentence transformers in trigram approach follows a similar pattern as that of the bigram approach. The results obtained on testing trigrams using different transformers are as follows:

5.3.1 BERT-base-multilingual-cased

The predictions obtained by this model is given in Fig. 5. On inspecting the predictions, it can be found that the correct sequences were predicted by multilingual bert and they contributed a negative meaning for all the three comments.

Comment	Expected Words	Predicted Words
ഈ മുഖഭാവം കണ്ട് ആരും അത്ഭുധപെടേണ്ട. സന്തോഷ് പണ്ഡിറ്റ് നേക്കാളും കിടുവ	സന്തോഷ് പണ്ഡിറ്റ് നേക്കാളും കിടുവ	'ആരും അത്ഭുധപെടേണ്ട സന്തോഷ്', 'പണ്ഡിറ്റ് നേക്കാളും കിടുവ', 'കണ്ട് ആരും അത്ഭുധപെടേണ്ട', 'അത്ഭുധപെടേണ്ട സന്തോഷ് പണ്ഡിറ്റ്', 'സന്തോഷ് പണ്ഡിറ്റ് നേക്കാളും'
No violence only peace. ഗോപാലൻ പണ്ടേ പീസിന്റെ ആളാണല്ലോ	പണ്ടേ പീസിന്റെ ആളാണല്ലോ	'പണ്ടേ പീസിന്റെ ആളാണല്ലോ', 'ഗോപാലൻ പണ്ടേ പീസിന്റെ', 'peace ഗോപാലൻ പണ്ടേ', 'only peace ഗോപാലൻ', 'violence only peace'
Ikka fansinte 25 k dislike undallo... dislike adichittu karanjolu	dislike adichittu karanjolu	'dislike adichittu karanjolu', 'undallo dislike adichittu', 'k dislike undallo', 'dislike undallo dislike', 'ikka fansinte 25'

Figure 5: Trigram - BERT-base-multilingual-cased

5.3.2 distilbert-base-multilingual-cased

Multilingual distilbert gave a good result in trigram approach when compared with the bigram approach. It predicted the negative sequences from all the three types of comments.

5.3.3 Hate-speech-CNERG/indic-abusive-allInOne-MuRIL

The performance of this model in trigram approach follows the same pattern as that of its bigram approach. The results obtained with this model in the trigram approach is not satisfactory as the predictions obtained were inaccurate due to the higher similarity scores of all the trigrams.

Model	# of predicted hate words	Prediction accuracy
BERT-base-multilingual-cased	85	76.58%
distilbert-base-multilingual-cased	89	80.18%
ai4bharat/indic-bert	76	68.47%
Hate-speech-CNERG/indic-abusive-allInOne-MuRIL	73	65.76%
Hate-speech-CNERG/malayalam-codemixed-abusive-MuRIL	60	54.05%

Table 1: Results of Unigram-based approach

Model	# of predicted hate words	Prediction accuracy
BERT-base-multilingual-cased	100	86.20%
distilbert-base-multilingual-cased	97	83.62%
ai4bharat/indic-bert	88	75.86%
Hate-speech-CNERG/indic-abusive-allInOne-MuRIL	87	75%
Hate-speech-CNERG/malayalam-codemixed-abusive-MuRIL	71	61.20%

Table 2: Results of Bigram-based approach

5.3.4 ai4bharat/indic-bert

On inspecting the predictions obtained with this model, it was seen that the predictions obtained for the comments typed using English script and Malayalam script were better than the predictions generated for the comments typed using English-Malayalam.

5.3.5 Hate-speech-CNERG/malayalam-codemixed-abusive-MuRIL

The similarity scores of trigrams obtained with this model were too close and higher. The model couldn't discern the hate/offensive sequences. Hence, incorrect predictions were obtained in most of the cases.

The prediction accuracy of each model on testing with trigram approach is given in Table 3 On comparing the performance of different sentence transformer models in the trigram approach, it is evident that the multilingual bert model performs better than the other models.

6 Performance of Method-2

This section presents the results of method-2. The train set was divided for training and validation in the ratio 8:2. The model was trained and validated for 30 epochs using Adam and RMSprop optimizers with learning rate 3e-5. Later the model was tested on the test set comprising of 84 comments. The performance of the model on the comments typed in English, comments typed in malayalam and comments including both Malayalam and English were evaluated. Table 4 and Table 5 denote the results obtained for Adam and RMSprop optimizers respectively. A validation accuracy of 88.80% was obtained for the former model and 89.65% was attained for the latter. The best results were obtained with Adam optimizer.

7 Discussion

On analysing the dataset and results obtained in method-1, it was seen that in most of the cases the hate words had a similarity score >=0.7. On analysing the performance of transformer models, we could see that the best results were obtained with multilingual bert.

Multilingual bert is trained on a large corpus and it has a huge number.of parameters when compared with the other models. This can be one of the reasons behind the excellent performance of the model in all the three categories of comments (typed in English alone, malayalam alone and including both).

Multilingual bert is followed by Multilingual distilbert whose performance is a bit lower in the category of comments including both English and Malayalam. Multilingual distilbert is a distilled version of multilingual bert with lower number of parameters. This can be the cause for lower performance of multilingual distilbert when compared with the multilingual bert.

The indic-abusive-allInOne-MuRIL model has a lower performance in the category of comments typed in Malayalam alone when compared with the other two categories. But we can see that indic-abusive-allInOne-MuRIL and multilingual distilbert showed a similar pattern of fair performance and it is better than indic bert.

The indic-bert gave a medium performace in all the three categories of comments, but lower than

Model	# of predicted hate words	Prediction accuracy
BERT-base-multilingual-cased	88	84.62%
distilbert-base-multilingual-cased	87	83.65%
ai4bharat/indic-bert	86	82.69%
Hate-speech-CNERG/indic-abusive-allInOne-MuRIL	85	81.73%
Hate-speech-CNERG/malayalam-codemixed-abusive-MuRIL	71	68.27%

Table 3: Results of Trigram-based approach

Comment Type	# of predicted hate words	Prediction accuracy
English	24	70.58%
Malayalam	23	45.09%
Eng-Mal	10	52.63%

Table 4: Results of Model with Adam Optimizer

Comment Type	# of predicted hate words	Prediction accuracy
English	20	58.82%
Malayalam	23	45.09%
Eng-Mal	8	42.11%

Table 5: Results of Model with RMSprop Optimizer

the above 3 models. It can be due to the fewer number of parameters in this model. And finally, the malayalam-codemixed-abusive-MuRIL, gave a lower-than expected result. Even though this model is trained on Malayalam codemix abusive language, the performance was not as expected.

On comparing bigram and trigram approaches, bigram approach yields a better result than the latter.

Based on the results obtained in method-2, we could see that (the best performance of the model was evident on English based comments. Comparatively good performance was seen on Malayalam comments and English-Malayalam comments.) Though we evaluated the performance of the model with various optimizers, Adam optimizer was performing best on our dataset.

8 Conclusion and future work

In order to fulfil the gap of lack of annotated data for HOL keywords in Malayalam, a dataset was created for the same as part of this paper. Later, the hate and offensive keywords in the dataset were identified based on cosine similarity using unigram approach. Apart from this, hate and offensive sequences were extracted from the sentences even in the absence of a hate word using bigram and trigram approach. On comparing the performance of various sentence transformer models, "`bert-base-multilingual-cased`" turned out to be the best model for extracting hate keywords from code-mix Malayalam social media text.

Being the best model, the "`bert-base-multilingual-cased`" was utilized for developing the transformer model in the second method. Based on the results obtained in method-2, the best performance of the model was evident on English based comments. Comparatively good performance can be seen on Malayalam comments and English-Malayalam comments.

As a future work, the explainability concept(Peyrard et al., 2021)can be employed to improve the performance of the current model. Also, the performance of indic-abusive-allInOne-MuRIL and malayalam-codemixed-abusive-MuRIL models can be further investigated. Likewise, the effect of different dialects can be analysed to know its role in identifying HOL keywords.

Acknowledgments

The author Bharathi Raja Chakravarthi was supported in part by a research grant from Science Foundation Ireland (SFI) under Grant Number SFI/12/RC/2289_P2(Insight_2).

References

B Bharathi and A Agnusimmaculate Silvia. 2021. SSNCSE_NLP@DravidianLangTech-EACL2021: Offensive language identification on multilingual code mixing text. In *Proceedings of the First Workshop on Speech and Language Technologies for Dravidian Languages*, pages 313–318, Kyiv. Association for Computational Linguistics.

B Bharathi and Josephine Varsha. 2022. SSNCSE NLP@TamilNLP-ACL2022: Transformer based approach for detection of abusive comment for Tamil language. In *Proceedings of the Second Workshop on Speech and Language Technologies for Dravidian Languages*, pages 158–164, Dublin, Ireland. Association for Computational Linguistics.

Bharathi Raja Chakravarthi. 2022a. Hope speech detection in Youtube comments. *Social Network Analysis and Mining*, 12(1):75.

Bharathi Raja Chakravarthi. 2022b. Multilingual hope speech detection in English and Dravidian languages. *International Journal of Data Science and Analytics*, 14(4):389–406.

Bharathi Raja Chakravarthi. 2023. Detection of homophobia and transphobia in Youtube comments. *International Journal of Data Science and Analytics*, pages 1–20.

Bharathi Raja Chakravarthi, Adeep Hande, Rahul Ponnusamy, Prasanna Kumar Kumaresan, and Ruba Priyadharshini. 2022a. How can we detect homophobia and transphobia? experiments in a multilingual code-mixed setting for social media governance. *International Journal of Information Management Data Insights*, 2(2):100119.

Bharathi Raja Chakravarthi, Manoj Balaji Jagadeeshan, Vasanth Palanikumar, and Ruba Priyadharshini. 2023. Offensive language identification in dravidian languages using mpnet and cnn. *International Journal of Information Management Data Insights*, 3(1):100151.

Bharathi Raja Chakravarthi, Anand Kumar M, John P McCrae, B Premjith, KP Soman, and Thomas Mandl. 2020. Overview of the track on hasoc-offensive language identification-dravidiancodemix. In *FIRE (Working notes)*, pages 112–120.

Bharathi Raja Chakravarthi, Ruba Priyadharshini, Thenmozhi Durairaj, John McCrae, Paul Buitelaar, Prasanna Kumaresan, and Rahul Ponnusamy. 2022b. Overview of the shared task on homophobia and transphobia detection in social media comments. In *Proceedings of the Second Workshop on Language Technology for Equality, Diversity and Inclusion*, pages 369–377, Dublin, Ireland. Association for Computational Linguistics.

Mithun Das, Somnath Banerjee, and Animesh Mukherjee. 2022. Data bootstrapping approaches to improve low resource abusive language detection for indic languages. In *Proceedings of the 33rd ACM Conference on Hypertext and Social Media*, pages 32–42.

Jacob Devlin, Ming-Wei Chang, Kenton Lee, and Kristina Toutanova. 2018. Bert: Pre-training of deep bidirectional transformers for language understanding. *arXiv preprint arXiv:1810.04805*.

Adeep Hande, Karthik Puranik, Konthala Yasaswini, Ruba Priyadharshini, Sajeetha Thavareesan, Anbukkarasi Sampath, Kogilavani Shanmugavadivel, Durairaj Thenmozhi, and Bharathi Raja Chakravarthi. 2021. Offensive language identification in low-resourced code-mixed dravidian languages using pseudo-labeling. *arXiv preprint arXiv:2108.12177*.

Divyanshu Kakwani, Anoop Kunchukuttan, Satish Golla, Gokul N.C., Avik Bhattacharyya, Mitesh M. Khapra, and Pratyush Kumar. 2020. IndicNLPSuite: Monolingual Corpora, Evaluation Benchmarks and Pre-trained Multilingual Language Models for Indian Languages. In *Findings of EMNLP*.

Prasanna Kumar Kumaresan, Rahul Ponnusamy, Elizabeth Sherly, Sangeetha Sivanesan, and Bharathi Raja Chakravarthi. 2022. Transformer based hope speech comment classification in code-mixed text. In *International Conference on Speech and Language Technologies for Low-resource Languages*, pages 120–137. Springer.

Matej Martinc, Blaž Škrlj, and Senja Pollak. 2022. Tnt-kid: Transformer-based neural tagger for keyword identification. *Natural Language Engineering*, 28(4):409–448.

Endang Wahyu Pamungkas, Valerio Basile, and Viviana Patti. 2022. Investigating the role of swear words in abusive language detection tasks. *Language Resources and Evaluation*, pages 1–34.

Maxime Peyrard, Beatriz Borges, Kristina Gligorić, and Robert West. 2021. Laughing heads: Can transformers detect what makes a sentence funny? *arXiv preprint arXiv:2105.09142*.

Victor Sanh, Lysandre Debut, Julien Chaumond, and Thomas Wolf. 2019. Distilbert, a distilled version of bert: smaller, faster, cheaper and lighter. *arXiv preprint arXiv:1910.01108*.

Gretel Liz De la Peña Sarracén and Paolo Rosso. 2023. Offensive keyword extraction based on the attention mechanism of bert and the eigenvector centrality using a graph representation. *Personal and Ubiquitous Computing*, 27(1):45–57.

K Sreelakshmi, B Premjith, and Soman Kp. 2021. Amrita_cen_nlp@ dravidianlangtech-eacl2021: deep learning-based offensive language identification in malayalam, tamil and kannada. In *Proceedings of the First Workshop on Speech and Language Technologies for Dravidian Languages*, pages 249–254.

Krithika Swaminathan, Bharathi B, Gayathri G L, and Hrishik Sampath. 2022. SSNCSE_NLP@LT-EDI-ACL2022: Homophobia/transphobia detection in multiple languages using SVM classifiers and BERT-based transformers. In *Proceedings of the Second Workshop on Language Technology for Equality, Diversity and Inclusion*, pages 239–244, Dublin, Ireland. Association for Computational Linguistics.

Ashish Vaswani, Noam Shazeer, Niki Parmar, Jakob Uszkoreit, Llion Jones, Aidan N Gomez, Łukasz Kaiser, and Illia Polosukhin. 2017. Attention is all you need. *Advances in neural information processing systems*, 30.

Acoustic Analysis of the Fifth Liquid in Malayalam

Punnoose A K
Flare Speech Systems
punnoose@flarespeech.com

Abstract

This paper investigates the claim of rhoticity of the fifth liquid in Malayalam using various acoustic characteristics. The Malayalam liquid phonemes are analyzed in terms of the smoothness of the pitch window, formants, formant bandwidth, F3 rhoticity, the effect on surrounding vowels, duration, and classification patterns by an unrelated classifier. We report, for the fifth liquid, a noticeable difference in terms of pitch smoothness with the rhotics. In terms of the formants and formant bandwidth, the difference between the fifth liquid and the other liquids is significant, irrespective of gender. As for F3 rhoticity, there is no evidence for the rhotics F3 being lower compared to laterals F3, especially for females. The effect of the fifth liquid on the surrounding vowels is inconclusive. The phoneme duration of the fifth liquid is significantly different from all the other liquids. Classification of the fifth liquid section implies higher order signal level similarity with both laterals and rhotics.

1 Introduction

Malayalam along with Tamil has five liquid phonemes. Alveolar lateral /l/, retroflex lateral /ɭ/, alveolar tap /r/, alveolar trill /r/ and a fifth liquid /z̢/. There have been attempts to classify the fifth liquid /z̢/ in Malayalam either to laterals or to rhotics. The fifth liquid in Tamil /z̢/ is reported to be acoustically more similar to lateral /ɭ/ (Narayanan et al., 1999). Based on the phonetic and phonological characteristics, there were suggestions on the rhoticity of the fifth liquid in Malayalam (Punnoose et al., 2013; Kochetov et al., 2020). Phonological characteristics like non-gemination or occurrence at only the inter-vocalic positions point toward the fifth liquid's supposed rhoticity. To analyze the Malayalam liquids, other than just using voice signals, other modalities like static MRI and ultrasound are used, especially in uncovering the articulatory configurations (Kochetov et al., 2020; M. et al., 2013). In (Kochetov et al., 2020), although the authors support the rhoticity of the fifth liquid overall, they report that the position and configuration of articulators vary widely among the rhotics, for the same word for different speakers.

In this paper, we seek acoustic-phonetic data patterns for any similarities between the fifth liquid and rhotics/laterals. The rest of the paper is organized as follows. First, the details of the Malayalam liquid dataset used for analysis are discussed. Next, a pitch smoothness function is introduced and the pitch smoothness of Malayalam liquids is measured and compared. Then, the formants of the fifth liquid are compared with the laterals and the rhotics genderwise. After that, the claim of low F3 for rhotics compared to that of laterals is assessed. Then, the formant bandwidth of liquids is analyzed genderwise. Next, the effect of the liquids on the surrounding vowel formants is discussed. After that, liquids are analyzed in terms of their duration. Finally, an unrelated English frame-based phoneme classifier is used to understand the classification patterns of the fifth liquid section in Malayalam.

1.1 Dataset Used

Due to the unavailability of a public Malayalam liquid dataset, we record the data from a modest 10 speakers. All the speakers are middle-aged and from central Kerala. Speakers are asked to read unrelated words put in the form of 2 sentences 5 times. The words transcribe to

1. /maz̢u/, /maz̢a/, /miz̢i/, /kuz̢i/, /paz̢am/, /puz̢a/, /piz̢avu/, /vaz̢ii/, /viz̢upp/
(axe, rain, eyes, hole, fruit, river, mistake, way, baggage)

2. /malayaɭam/, /puravastu/, /purappad/
(Malayalam, antique object, leaving)

The liquid segments are manually time labelled for all the words using Audacity.

Third Workshop on Speech and Language Technologies for Dravidian Languages, pages 19–24, Varna, Bulgaria, Sep 7, 2023.
https://doi.org/10.26615/978-954-452-085-4_003

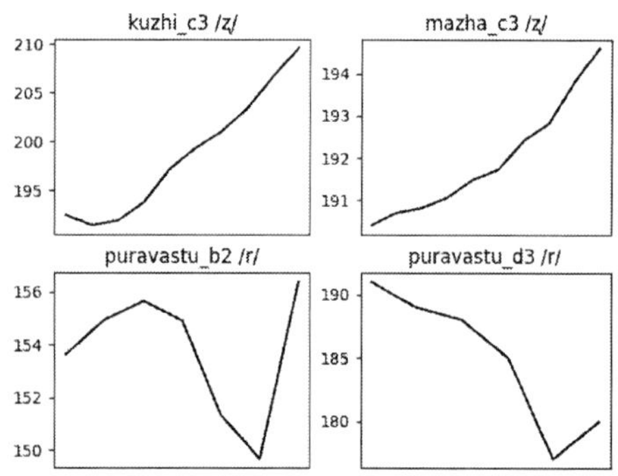

Figure 1: pitch smoothness of the fifth liquid vs rhotics

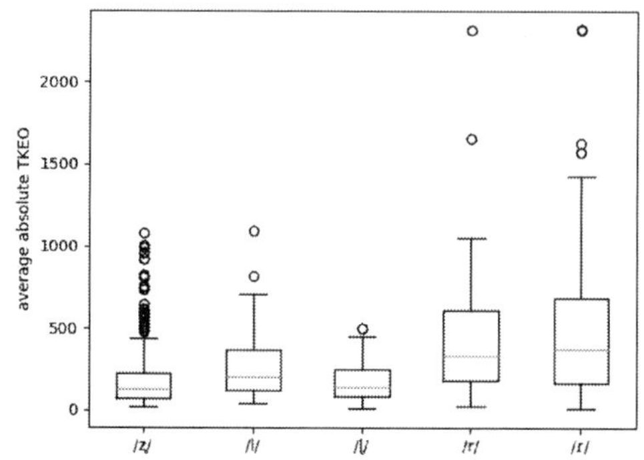

Figure 2: Average absolute TKEO value of pitch window of Malayalam liquid phonemes

2 Analysis

Every similarity analysis (except for the pitch smoothness and the classifier-based analysis) is formulated as a statistical hypothesis test that compares the relevant acoustic feature from 2 broad phonemic classes. The null hypothesis is that there is no difference between the acoustic feature in consideration between 2 phonemic classes.

2.1 Pitch Smoothness Analysis

Our first observation is that rhotics /r/ and /ɾ/ seems to have an abrupt change in the pitch contour. Figure 1 shows the pitch smoothness of /ʐ/ and /r/. To measure this abrupt change in pitch, given a pitch window of N values, we compute the average absolute Teager-Kaiser Energy Operator (TKEO) in its discrete form, denoted by δ,

$$\delta = \frac{1}{N-2} \sum_{k=1}^{N-1} \left| x[k]^2 - x[k-1]x[k+1] \right| \quad (1)$$

The absolute value ensures that any abrupt change in either direction is accounted for. Figure 2 plots the average absolute TKEO value of the pitch window of Malayalam liquid phonemes. The pitch value is programmatically extracted using Parcelmouth library (Jadoul et al., 2018), which is a Python port of the popular Praat (Boersma and Weenink, 2021). The relevant instances from all the words are pooled for /ʐ/. The pitch window duration is 40ms with a shift of 10ms. Every frame where the pitch is not detected is discarded. From the plot, it is clear that the pitch transition abruptness is the lowest for /ʐ/ and highest for /ɾ/. On the other hand, /ɭ/ is similar to /ʐ/.

Table 1: percentage of recordings with atleast one undetected pitch frame in the liquid segment

phoneme	percentage
/ʐ/	0.007
/l/	0
/ɭ/	0
/r/	0.04
/ɾ/	0.14

It is instructive to note that for certain liquid phonemes, pitch is not detected for certain frames. Table 1 shows the percentage of recordings where atleast one pitch frame in the liquid segment is undetected. /ɾ/ seems to have a disproportionate number of undetected pitch frames. This could be attributed to the insufficiency of Praat's pitch detection algorithm or the absence of a voiced region in the liquid segment.

2.2 Formant Analysis

The formant value varies between male and female speech (Huber et al., 1999; Diehl et al., 1996). We first validate this with the null hypothesis that, for Malayalam liquids, the male and female formant values are similar. Midpoint formants of all the liquids are extracted using Praat. Note that for rhotics, formants tend to be discontinuous or tend to abruptly change. In the case of a missing formant value due to discontinuity, the nearest formant value in the same liquid segment is taken. Table 2 shows the results of a 2 tailed t-test for 2 means of formants between males and females of all liquid phonemes. Significance level $\alpha = 0.05$ is used for all statistical tests throughout this paper.

From Table 2, it is clear that there is no de-

Table 2: p-value of 2 tailed t-test for 2 means for formants between male and female

ph	p-val F1	p-val F2	p-val F3
/z̨/	0.8808	< 0.0001	< 0.0001
/l/	0.7868	0.5857	0.1669
/l̨/	0.963	< 0.001	0.1132
/r/	0.2010	0.7738	0.0824
/ɾ/	0.2135	0.3527	0.6783

tectable difference between male and female formant values for rhotics and /l/. For /l̨/, F2 seems to be different between males and females. For /z̨/, F2 and F3 seem to be different between males and females. This warrants the analysis of formants, gender-wise.

Table 3: mean and standard deviation of the formants of male speakers

ph	$F1_\mu$	$F1_\sigma$	$F2_\mu$	$F2_\sigma$	$F3_\mu$	$F2_\sigma$
/z̨/	407	242	1867	271	2556	345
/r/	565	453	1893	312	2780	376
/ɾ/	577	100	1436	284	2628	625
/l/	378	84	1896	332	3209	598
/l̨/	492	39	1153	569	2649	400

Table 4: p-value of 2 tailed t-test for 2 means for liquid phoneme formants of males

ph1	ph2	p-val F1	p-val F2	p-val F3
/z̨/	/r/	0.0158	0.6987	0.0078
/z̨/	/ɾ/	0.0037	< 0.0001	0.4480
/z̨/	/l/	0.6013	0.6627	< 0.0001
/z̨/	/l̨/	0.1188	< 0.0001	0.2682

Table 3 shows the formants computed at the midpoint of all the liquid phoneme segments for males. Table 4 shows the p-value of 2 tailed t-test for 2 means between the fifth liquid and the other 4 liquids, for males. For any 2 liquid phonemes in consideration, the null hypothesis is that the formants characterize a broader phonemic class that comprises those 2 phonemes. The difference between /z̨/ and /l/ in terms of F3 is significant. In terms of F2 values, /z̨/ is different from /ɾ/ and /l̨/. In terms of F1 values, the fifth liquid is different from both the rhotic phonemes.

Table 5 shows the formants computed at the midpoint of all the liquid phoneme segments for females. Table 6 shows the p-value of 2 tailed t-test for 2 means between the fifth liquid and the other 4 liquids, for females. /z̨/ is different from /r/ and /l/ in terms of F3. /z̨/ is statistically different from all the other liquids in terms of F2. /z̨/ is different from /ɾ/ in terms of F1.

Table 5: mean and standard deviation of the formants of female speakers

ph	$F1_\mu$	$F1_\sigma$	$F2_\mu$	$F2_\sigma$	$F3_\mu$	$F2_\sigma$
/z̨/	403	246	2124	301	2776	377
/r/	436	251	1914	218	2939	258
/ɾ/	609	75	1497	167	2675	370
/l/	373	56	1945	293	3004	258
/l̨/	492	57	1490	180	2792	222

Table 6: p-value of 2 tailed t-test for 2 means for liquid phoneme formants of females

ph1	ph2	p-val F1	p-val F2	p-val F3
/z̨/	/r/	0.5940	0.0003	0.0227
/z̨/	/ɾ/	< 0.0001	< 0.0001	0.1700
/z̨/	/l/	0.4402	0.0024	0.0015
/z̨/	/l̨/	0.0811	< 0.0001	0.8237

2.3 F3 Rhoticity in Malayalam

In (Delattre and Freeman, 1968), authors suggest that rhotics in English are characterized by low F3 compared to that of laterals. We pooled the rhotics and laterals F3 data and test whether the hypothesis holds in Malayalam. Table 7 shows the result of the test, gender-wise.

Table 7: Comparison of F3 of rhotics vs laterals, genderwise

H_1 condition	formant	gender	p-val
(/r/, /ɾ/) < (/l/, /l̨/)	F3	m	0.03874
(/r/, /ɾ/) < (/l/, /l̨/)	F3	f	0.05358
(/r/, /ɾ/) < /z̨/	F3	m	0.9853
(/r/, /ɾ/) < /z̨/	F3	f	0.7191
/z̨/ < (/l/, /l̨/)	F3	m	< 0.0001
/z̨/ < (/l/, /l̨/)	F3	f	0.009

(/r/, /ɾ/) denotes the combined rhotic data. For males, there seems to have sufficient evidence to accept the alternate hypothesis that rhotics F3 is lower compared to laterals F3. The fifth liquid F3 is lower than the lateral F3 for both males and females.

2.4 Formant Bandwidth

Formant bandwidth does not have much impact on vowel intelligibility (Rosner and Pickering, 1994)

but affects the identification of competing vowels (de Cheveigné, 1999). The formant bandwidth of the liquids is programmatically extracted and checked for any similarity between the fifth liquid and the other liquids.

Table 8: p-value of 2 tailed t-test for 2 means for liquid phoneme formant bandwidth of males

ph1	ph2	p-val F1	p-val F2	p-val F3
/ʐ/	/r/	0.0170	< 0.0001	0.2805
/ʐ/	/ɾ/	< 0.0001	< 0.0001	0.264
/ʐ/	/l/	0.3269	0.0002	0.9601
/ʐ/	/ɭ/	0.7120	< 0.0001	0.2219

Table 9: p-value of 2 tailed t-test for 2 means for liquid phoneme formant bandwidth of females

ph1	ph2	p-val F1	p-val F2	p-val F3
/ʐ/	/r/	< 0.0001	< 0.0001	0.1722
/ʐ/	/ɾ/	< 0.0001	0.1023	0.0339
/ʐ/	/l/	0.5560	< 0.0001	0.0358
/ʐ/	/ɭ/	0.4253	0.8113	0.0272

Tables 8 and 9 show the result of the p-value of 2 tailed t-test for 2 means for formant bandwidth of male and female voices respectively. The null hypothesis is that the formant bandwidth values are similar for the 2 phonetic classes. For males, in terms of F1 bandwidth /ʐ/ is different from rhotics. In terms of F2 bandwidth, /ʐ/ is different from every other liquid. For females, in terms of F1 bandwidth, /ʐ/ is different from rhotics. In terms of F2 bandwidth, /ʐ/ is different from /r/ and /l/. In terms of F3 bandwidth, /ʐ/ is different from all the other liquids except /r/. Though the results don't conclusively place the /ʐ/ to either lateral or rhotic camp, overall the formant bandwidth seems to be more similar to laterals compared to that of rhotics.

2.5 Formants of the Vowels Surrounding the Fifth Liquid

In (Punnoose et al., 2013), authors hypothesize that the F1 of the vowels surrounding the /ʐ/ tends to be lower than those surrounding /r/ and /ɭ/. Further, F2 of the vowels surrounding the /ʐ/ is greater than those surrounding /r/ and /ɭ/. We test these hypotheses with the words puʐha, malayaɭam, and puravastu. All the vowels surrounding /ʐ/, /r/, /ɭ/ is manually labelled and F1 and F2 at the midpoint is programmatically extracted. For consistency, we test the F1 of the vowel /uh/ preceding /ʐ/ in puʐha with F1 of /uh/ preceding /r/ in puravastu. Likewise, F1 of /aa/ following /ʐ/ in puʐha is compared with F1 of /aa/ following /ɭ/ in malayaɭam.

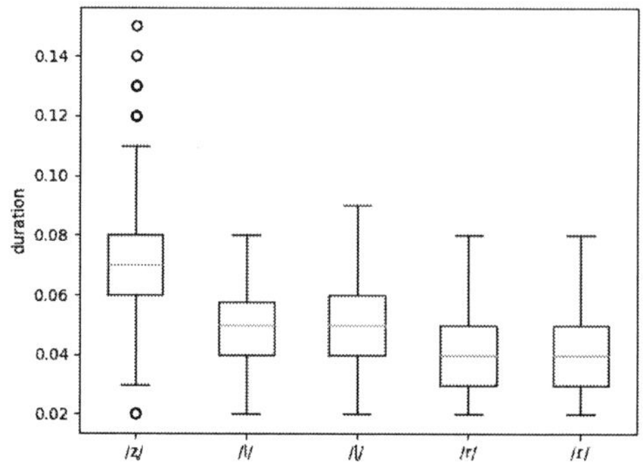

Figure 3: Duration of the Malayalam liquids

Table 10: formants of the vowels surrounding the fifth liquid

H_1 condition	formant	p-value
/uh ʐ/ < /uh r/	F1	0.0008707
/ ʐ aa/ < / ɭ aa/	F1	1
/ uh ʐ/ > /uh r/	F2	0.9997
/ ʐ aa/ > / ɭ aa/	F2	0.02349

Table 10 shows the result of the comparison of various conditions on F1 and F2 between /ʐ/, /r/, /ɭ/. The F1 of the vowel /uh/ before /ʐ/ is lower than the F1 of the vowel /uh/ before /r/. Likewise, F2 of /aa/ following /ʐ/ is greater than the F2 of /aa/ following /ɭ/. The rest 2 conditions do not hold.

2.6 Duration Analysis

Figure 3 plots the duration of all the liquids. It is clear that the 2 laterals /l/ and /ɭ/ are very close in terms of duration statistics. The two rhotics /r/ and /ɾ/ are also similar in duration. Table 11 shows the result of 2 tailed t-test for 2 means for comparing the duration of all pairs of liquid phonemes. The null hypothesis is that any two liquid phonemes have the same duration. The difference in duration between the fifth liquid /ʐ/ and any other liquids is significant.

The difference in phoneme duration between any Malayalam laterals and rhotics is statistically significant. This strongly suggests that duration is a distinctive feature of a broad phonemic class.

Table 11: p-value of 2 tailed t-test for 2 means for the duration of the fifth liquid vs other liquids

ph1	ph2	p-value
/ʐ/	/r/	< 0.0001
/ʐ/	/ɾ/	< 0.0001
/ʐ/	/l/	< 0.0001
/ʐ/	/ɭ/	< 0.0001
/l/	/ɭ/	0.8625
/r/	/ɾ/	0.4882
/l/	/r/	0.0033
/l/	/ɾ/	0.0002
/ɭ/	/r/	0.0031
/ɭ/	/ɾ/	0.0002

2.7 Classifier Based Analysis

Apart from formants, spectral level higher-order features might capture not-so-interpretable acoustic features, especially with a phoneme discriminative objective. We trained a frame-based phoneme classifier with perceptual linear coefficients (PLP) features as input to classify a frame with sufficient left and right context. A frame corresponding to 25 ms is appended with left and right 4 frames each with a 10 ms shift is considered as the input segment. 13 PLP features along with delta and double delta coefficients form an input vector of size 351. With ICSI Quicknet (Johnson., 2004) a multi-layer perceptron of the architecture 351x1000x1000x1000x40 is trained. The 40 units at the output correspond to standard 40 English phonemes. The softmax layer is used at the output and the network is trained with cross-entropy loss.

Approximately 35 hours of publically available Voxforge dataset (Voxforge.org) is used for training the classifier. Voxforge is an uncurated read-out English speech dataset. The labels for training the classifier are obtained by forced alignment of the same dataset using Kaldi speech recognition toolkit (Povey et al., 2011). For a given 9 frame input, the classifier outputs a probability vector, where each component corresponds to a phoneme. The phoneme with the highest probability is the classified phoneme for that input. Note that the frame classifier is trained with one lateral /l/ and 2 rhotics /r/ and /er/.

All the Malayalam words with fifth liquid /ʐ/ is run through the frame classifier. Out of the frames detected as /l/, only 27% are at the actual fifth liquid position. Whereas out of the frame detected as /r/, 91% is at the actual fifth liquid position, and out of the frame detected as /er/, 65% is at the actual fifth liquid position. The rest of the fifth liquid position is filled by vowel phonemes, /g/, etc. This shows that irrespective of the language, at the higher order signal feature level, the fifth liquid share some similarities with laterals and rhotics. Despite the low precision of lateral /l/, the fifth liquid /ʐ/ is a category of its own and cannot be categorized conclusively into laterals or rhotics.

3 Conclusion and Future work

The claim of rhoticity of the fifth liquid in Malayalam is analyzed using various acoustic-phonetic characteristics. First, the details of a small Malayalam liquids dataset are described. The average absolute Teager-Kaiser energy operator is used to measure the smoothness of the pitch window of various Malayalam liquids. For the fifth liquid, there is a noticeable difference in terms of pitch smoothness with the rhotics. Next, the formants are used to measure the similarity between the fifth liquid and the other liquids, gender-wise. The difference between the formants of the fifth liquid and the other liquids is significant, irrespective of gender. Next, the hypothesis that the F3 of rhotics is lower than that of the laterals is tested. For females, there is no evidence for the rhotics F3 being lower compared to laterals F3.

Then, we analyze the formant bandwidth gender-wise. Formant bandwidth does not seem to offer any definite evidence to classify the fifth liquid as either laterals or rhotics. After that, the assumption of the fifth liquid affecting the F1 and F2 of the surrounding vowels in specific ways, compared to that of laterals and rhotics is analyzed. No definite evidence could be obtained that supports this assumption. Then, the duration of the fifth liquid is analyzed and contrasted with the remaining liquids to find any similarities. No statistically significant similarity is observed for the duration between the fifth liquid and any other liquids. Finally, an unrelated classifier is used to classify the fifth liquid section to see the generic frame-level recognition pattern. Classification of the fifth liquid section implies higher order signal level similarity with both laterals and rhotics.

Articulatory configurations, not provably reflecting in signal level data, cannot be the mere deciding factor for broad phoneme classification. More data-driven spectral level features from context dependant realization of the fifth liquid may provide more insights into how similar the fifth liquid is to laterals/rhotics. The recent advances in multilingual acoustic representation learning could provide further insights into the real nature of the fifth liquids (Babu et al., 2021; Baevski et al., 2020). The various acoustic pieces of evidence considered, in the context of this paper, are not sufficient enough to conclusively classify the fifth liquid in Malayalam as rhotic.

4 Limitations

This paper describes a purely data-driven approach to determine whether the fifth liquid in Malayalam is similar to rhotics or laterals. In the context of this paper, we don't associate acoustic measurements with any assumptions about the articulatory configurations or phonotactic constraints of the fifth liquid. This results in pure acoustic-phonetic conclusions about the rhoticity of the fifth liquid.

References

Arun Babu, Changhan Wang, Andros Tjandra, Kushal Lakhotia, Qiantong Xu, Naman Goyal, Kritika Singh, Patrick von Platen, Yatharth Saraf, Juan Pino, Alexei Baevski, Alexis Conneau, and Michael Auli. 2021. XLS-R: self-supervised cross-lingual speech representation learning at scale. *CoRR*, abs/2111.09296.

Alexei Baevski, Yuhao Zhou, Abdelrahman Mohamed, and Michael Auli. 2020. wav2vec 2.0: A framework for self-supervised learning of speech representations. In *Advances in Neural Information Processing Systems*, volume 33, pages 12449–12460. Curran Associates, Inc.

Paul Boersma and David Weenink. 2021. Praat: doing phonetics by computer [Computer program]. Version 6.1.38, retrieved 2 January 2021 http://www.praat.org/.

Alain de Cheveigné. 1999. Formant bandwidth affects the identification of competing vowels.

Pierre Delattre and Donald C. Freeman. 1968. A dialect study of american r's by x-ray motion picture.

Randy L. Diehl, Björn Lindblom, Kathryn A. Hoemeke, and Richard P. Fahey. 1996. On explaining certain male-female differences in the phonetic realization of vowel categories. *Journal of Phonetics*, 24(2):187–208.

Jessica Huber, Elaine Stathopoulos, Gina Curione, Theresa Ash, and Kenneth Johnson. 1999. Formants of children, women, and men: The effects of vocal intensity variation. *The Journal of the Acoustical Society of America*, 106:1532–42.

Yannick Jadoul, Bill Thompson, and Bart de Boer. 2018. Introducing Parselmouth: A Python interface to Praat. *Journal of Phonetics*, 71:1–15.

D. Johnson. 2004. Icsi quicknet software package. http://www.icsi.berkeley.edu/Speech/qn.html. Accessed 06/25/2014.

Alexei Kochetov, Christophe Savariaux, Laurent Lamalle, Camille Noûs, and Pierre Badin. 2020. Malayalam three-way rhotics contrast: Articulatory modelling based on mri data.

James Scobbie M., Reenu Punnoose, and Ghada Khattab. 2013. Articulating five liquids: A single speaker ultrasound study of malayalam.

Shrikanth Narayanan, Dani Byrd, and Abigail Kaun. 1999. Geometry, kinematics, and acoustics of tamil liquid consonants. *The Journal of the Acoustical Society of America*, 106:1993–2007.

Daniel Povey, Arnab Ghoshal, Gilles Boulianne, Lukas Burget, Ondrej Glembek, Nagendra Goel, Mirko Hannemann, Petr Motlicek, Yanmin Qian, Petr Schwarz, Jan Silovsky, Georg Stemmer, and Karel Vesely. 2011. The kaldi speech recognition toolkit. In *IEEE 2011 Workshop on Automatic Speech Recognition and Understanding*. IEEE Signal Processing Society. IEEE Catalog No.: CFP11SRW-USB.

Reenu Punnoose, Ghada Khattab, and Jalal Al-Tamimi. 2013. The contested fifth liquid in malayalam: A window into the lateral-rhotic relationship in dravidian languages. *Phonetica*, 70:274–97.

B. S. Rosner and J. B. Pickering. 1994. *Vowel Perception and Production*. Oxford University Press.

Voxforge.org. Free speech... recognition (linux, windows and mac) - voxforge.org. http://www.voxforge.org/. Accessed 06/25/2014.

Transformer-based Context Aware Morphological Analyzer for Telugu

Priyanka Dasari [1*], Abhijith Chelpuri [1*], Nagaraju Vuppala,
Mounika Marreddy, Parameswari Krishnamurthy, Radhika Mamidi
International Institute of Information Technology, Hyderabad, India
(priyanka.dasari, abhijith.chelpuri)@research.iiit.ac.in

Abstract

This paper addresses the challenges faced by Indian languages in leveraging deep learning for natural language processing (NLP) due to limited resources, annotated datasets, and Transformer-based architectures. We specifically focus on Telugu and aim to construct a Telugu morph analyzer dataset comprising 10,000 sentences. Furthermore, we assess the performance of established multi-lingual Transformer models (m-Bert, XLM-R, IndicBERT) and mono-lingual Transformer model BERT-Te (trained from scratch on an extensive Telugu corpus comprising 80,15,588 sentences). Our findings demonstrate the efficacy of Transformer-based representations pre-trained on Telugu data improved the performance of the Telugu morph analyzer, surpassing existing multi-lingual approaches. This highlights the necessity of developing dedicated corpora, annotated datasets, and machine learning models in a mono-lingual setting. Using our dataset, we present benchmark results for the Telugu morph analyzer achieved through simple fine-tuning on BERT-Te. The morph analyzer dataset [1] and codes are open-sourced and available here.

1 Introduction

A Morphological Analyzer is a valuable tool in natural language processing (NLP) that analyzes words by breaking them down into constituent morphemes. It provides crucial grammatical information, including gender, number, person, case markers (GNP), tense-aspect-modal information, and other linguistic features, which are indispensable features for understanding the morphology of a given language(Rao and Kulkarni, 2006). Many agglutinative languages have these grammatical features as part of their words. Hence, building a morph analyzer that parses and provides this information is important. This expansion would greatly benefit various NLP tasks and applications tailored to Indian languages.

This work aims to develop a Transformer based context-aware morphological analyzer for Telugu. Telugu is known for its agglutinative nature, and various affixes were attached to the root word to convey different grammatical meanings. Nouns and pronouns in Telugu are inflected for gender, number, person and case markers, followed by clitics. Verbs exhibit extensive inflections based on tense, aspect, mood and agreement features such as gender, number, and person (GNP). Additionally, Telugu also uses productive derivational suffixes, where nouns are converted into an adjective by the addition of the suffix *-ayna* and an adverb by the addition of the suffix *-gā* and by the addition of the suffix *-aḍaM* allows verb roots to function as gerunds, thereby allowing for noun inflections (Krishnamurti and Gwynn, 1985).

The complexity of Telugu morphology necessitates a robust morphological analyzer, which plays a crucial role in various NLP applications such as speech synthesis, information extraction, information retrieval, and machine translation (Rao et al., 2011). A morphological analyzer takes a single word in isolation and provides all possible analysis. Although a word may have multiple valid analysis, when considering the context in which the word is used, often only one analysis is appropriate or meaningful. This is because the context helps determine the word's intended meaning, which can help narrow down the possible analysis. Traditionally, morphological analyzers for Indian languages have been rule-based. Still, there is a recent shift towards utilizing machine learning techniques to build computational models with the development of Transformer based models from scratch in Telugu (Marreddy et al., 2022a)

[1] https://github.com/parameshkrishnaa/Telugu-Morph-Dataset/

[1*] The first two authors contributed equally to the work.

Third Workshop on Speech and Language Technologies for Dravidian Languages, pages 25–32, Varna, Bulgaria, Sep 7, 2023.
https://doi.org/10.26615/978-954-452-085-4_004

on 80,15,588 sentences. This shift leverages advancements in downstream NLP tasks in Telugu like named entity recognition (Duggenpudi et al., 2022), sentiment analysis, emotion identification, sarcasm detection (Marreddy et al., 2022b), clickbait detection (Marreddy et al., 2021), and summarization (Vakada et al., 2023). Also, we see it is important to explore and compare existing multi-lingual Transformer based language models like mBERT (Pires et al., 2019), IndicBERT (Kakwani et al., 2020) and XLM (Conneau et al., 2019) with Telugu Transfer models (monolingual setting) like BERT-Te for the low-resource language, Telugu.

The main contributions of this paper are as follows:

- Creation of annotated Telugu Morphological analyzer dataset of 10,000 sentences.
- We created the benchmark results for Telugu morphological analyzer.
- Extensive experimentation with available Telugu Transformers models and existing multi-lingual Transformer models.
- On our dataset, BERT-Te outperforms the existing multi-lingual Transformer models.

The rest of the paper is organized as follows: Section 2 discusses the review and comparison of existing approaches. Section 3 describes the preparation of the dataset. Section 4 provides an overview of the experiment and evaluation of approaches followed using the dataset to train different models on the Telugu morphological features. Sections 5 and 6 discuss the ethical statement, conclusion, and future work.

2 Related Work

This section discusses the related work on building a corpus for morphological analysis focusing on Indian languages, existing Telugu BERT models, and Multi-lingual models. We also review the various common approaches used to build morphological analyzers. In the case of many Indian languages, morphological analysis has traditionally used a rule-based approach. It can be helpful in linguistic research because they provide a framework for formal analysis and understanding of language structures and patterns.

A Telugu Morphological Analyzer (Rao et al., 2011) is an example of organizing a linguistic database and employing computing resources effectively. The accuracy and coverage of this morph analyzer is 95-97%. This work is based on the word and paradigm approach (Hockett, 1954). A set of morpho-phonemically different forms in their inflection and derivation processes are identified. The failure of the presence of a root word in the morphological dictionary decreases the accuracy of the morph analyzer because it cannot analyze the root word. So, it shows issues with the OOV (Out-of-Vocabulary) and is not a context-based-morphological analyzer.

(Sunitha and Kalyani, 2009) have discussed an unsupervised stemmer that provides information about various decomposition of the word inflected by many morphemes. Firstly, the given Telugu words are processed by the (TMA) Telugu rule-based morph analyzer (Rao et al., 2011). The unsupervised stemmer further processes unrecognized words by the TMA to identify the components of the stem.

(Sneha and Bharadwaja, 2013) discussed a simple framework for designing and building a Morph Analyzer for Telugu noun forms applying the Telugu orthographic rules set with Finite State Machine (FSM). (Srinivasu and Manivannan, 2018) created a computational morphological analyzer and generator for Telugu using Item and Process linguistic model and FSM as a computational algorithm. (Kanuparthi et al., 2012) developed Hindi derivational morphological analyzer with 22 derivational suffixes (Goyal and Lehal, 2008) to analyse the derivation patterns in Hindi. For Tamil, (Parameshwari, 2011) implemented the APERTIUM Morphological Analyzer and Generator by defining and specifying the relevant linguistic database required for their development. The paper additionally discusses the module's efficacy, coverage, and speed compared to large corpora. (Veerappan et al., 2011), implements the morphological analyzer and generator for Kannada based on a rule-based finite state transducer that includes suitable morphological feature information and well-written morphophonemic rules. Morphological Analyzer for Gujarati (Baxi et al., 2015) introduces a hybrid approach combining statistical, knowledge-based, and paradigm-based approaches is used to develop the Morph analyzer.

Using the paradigm-based inflectional system and finite state systems to represent the language modelling, (Bapat et al., 2010) developed a highly accurate morphological analyzer for Marathi. (Baxi and Bhatt, 2022) based on the unimorph schema or the Universal Dependency Framework with the dataset contains 16527 distinct Gujarati inflected words with their morphological segmentation and grammatical feature tagging information is annotated and evaluated using the baseline format. Deep neural network-based models have recently been widely employed for building morphological analyzers. (Premjith et al., 2018) study discusses the Malayalam morphological analysis as a character-level sequence labeling problem that has been achieved with deep learning architectures such as Recurrent Neural Networks (RNN), Long Short-Term Memory (LSTM) and Gated Recurrent Units (GRU). The model was trained using a 128-embedding size. According to their results, GRU has the highest accuracy score. (Gupta et al., 2020) studied the performance of different composite neural models for Sanskrit morphological tagging. Using neural architecture. (Chakrabarty et al., 2016) built a lemmatizer for Bengali and studied how it performed on the problem of word sense disambiguation.

Transformer-based language models like BERT-Te are available in Telugu (Marreddy et al., 2022a) trained on 80,15,588 sentences. These representations resulted in downstream NLP tasks in Telugu like named entity recognition (Duggenpudi et al., 2022), sentiment analysis, emotion identification, sarcasm detection (Marreddy et al., 2022b), and clickbait detection (Marreddy et al., 2021), and summarization (Vakada et al., 2023).

3 Dataset Description

This section elaborates on the dataset that is used to build our Transformer-based morph analyzer. We used a collection of generic Telugu corpus of 10,000 sentences as the basis for our work. Detailed statistics of lexical categories of this dataset can be found in Table 1. In order to ensure the quality of the data, we performed various cleaning and normalization procedures on the raw text. This included tasks such as correcting spelling inconsistencies and errors. By carrying out these measures, we aimed to enhance the reliability and consistency of the dataset. To facilitate further processing, we used a tokenizer[2] for dividing the text into individual tokens and to identify sentence boundaries. The tokenizer takes raw text as an input and produces the output in Shakti Standard Format (SSF) format (Bharati et al., 2007).

Lexical Categories	**Types**	**Tokens**
Nouns	4817	24904
Verbs	1636	15648
Pronouns	163	5025
Adjectives	174	2000
Adverbs	70	1018
Number words	195	716
Nouns of space & time	27	52
avyayas (indeclinables)	405	5731
Total	7,487	55,094

Table 1: Statistics of lexical categories from the dataset.

We used the LT toolbox[3] version of Telugu Morph Analyzer, which is developed by (Rao et al., 2011). To identify the POS tags within sentences, we use an existing ILMT POS tagger (Bharati and Sangal, 2007). The POS tagger assists in determining the role of each word in the sentence. Telugu morphological analyzer generates multiple possible analysis for a given word. To select the most appropriate contextual morph analysis, we used the same technique as mentioned in (Krishnamurthy, 2019) wherein we used the POS tagger that selects the relevant POS tag based on the POS category of the word. POS tagger provides the POS tag for the word in context, and then we prune out the multiple analysis in the morph based on the POS tagger's output, if any. For example, if a word has multiple morph analysis with different lexical categories, such as a noun or a verb, the POS tagger selects the noun or verb analysis according to the pruning output. If the pruning module fails, we resort to the pick-one morph strategy that selects the first analysis as the output for the word. However, it should be noted that errors in POS tagging can lead to mistakes in selecting the correct morph, thereby affecting the contextual awareness of the words in a sentence. Manual validation is necessary to identify the errors in selecting context-aware morphological analysis. We have discussed

[2]https://github.com/nagaraju291990/sentence-tokenizer

[3]https://github.com/parameshkrishnaa/Telugu-Morph-lttoolbox

specific errors pertaining to wrong GNP marking, incorrect case-marking, *sandhi* split errors and the like.

The following examples explicate the errors:

1. Wrong POS tag leads to selecting the wrong lexical category.

(1) vāṭi-ni **pagalu** aMtā mēp-āli
They-ACC day all graze-HORT
'They should be grazed all day.'

In example (1), *pagalu* is wrongly tagged as VM (verb main) *pagalu* 'to break ', instead of a noun (NN) *pagalu* 'day'. This lead to errors in further stages of processing.

2. Ambiguous words which show no difference in number, person, or direct/oblique differences.

(2) madhya-lō baḍi mānēs-ina vāḷḷu
middle-LOC school stop-REL they
kūḍā **cēr-ā-ru**.
also join-PST-3.PL
'Those who left school in the middle also joined.'

In example (2), the subject agreement of *cēr-ā-ru* 'to join' can be analysed both as 2nd person (exclusive or honorofic pronoun (*mīru* 'you') and 3rd person. However, in the example (2), the subject *vāḷḷu* 'they' is the third person pronoun that resolves the ambiguity. It is noted that the morph analyser fails to provide the correct analysis in such cases.

(3) ilā **amma pani** kūḍā nā netti-na
this-way mother-OBL work also I-GEN
paḍ-iM-di.
head-LOC fall-PST-3.PL.FN
'This way, mother's work also fell on me.'

In Telugu, not all nouns overtly show differences in direct and oblique case marking. One such example, as in (3), is noted in the corpus. The noun *amma* 'mother' here, when associated with another noun *pani* leading to a chunk *amma pani* 'mother's work', does not show any change in form. This leads to an error in the marking of the case for *amma* 'mother'. It is observed that the noun is marked with a direct case instead of an oblique case.

3. *sandhi* split errors

Other common errors include the *sandhi* splitting errors. Telugu being rich in *sandhi*, requires a *sandhi* splitting module before morph analysis for appropriate marking of features. In some cases, *sandhi* splitter fails to split certain words as in (4), where *āḍavāḷlaMdarikī* 'all women' is not split. It should be split into *āḍavāḷlu* & *aMdarikī* 'women' & 'all; only then morph analyser provides an accurate analysis. *sandhi* splitting is also done manually. Consider the example:

(4) **āḍavāḷḷaMdari-kī** ī śakti rāv-āli
women+all-DAT this power get-HORT
'All women should get this power.'

To ensure the reliability of our dataset, we conducted extensive manual validation. Our analysis found that some words needed to be listed in the dictionary, resulting in the tool's inability to analyze those words automatically. To solve this, we manually assigned paradigms to these Out-Of-Vocabulary (OOV) words, ensuring they could be processed effectively and provides the analysis. We made 34% of changes in the dataset due to pre-processing errors. This validation process played a crucial role in enhancing the accuracy and quality of the dataset, providing reliable results for our analysis. Continuous refining of the dataset through manual validation makes the development of transformer-based context-aware morphological analysis more accurate.

4 Methodology

We first obtain the sentences with morphological tags for each word in the sentences, and then we feed those sentences to our language model to refine it using this dataset. We segregate the words' properties, such as lexical category, gender, and person, after acquiring the morphological tags for each word in the sentence before feeding them separately to the classifiers. In this section, we develop a comprehensive exploration of the different language models analyzed for the morph tag prediction study, elucidating their configuration

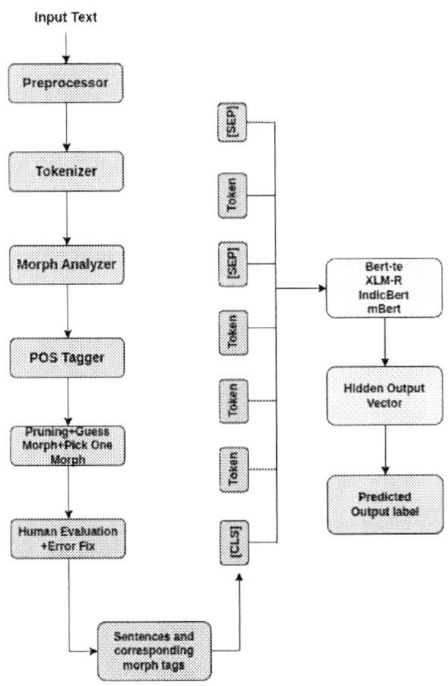

Figure 1: Flowchart of the work

in greater detail. In a later section of this article, we present results from language models that were examined in relation to several types of morphological tags. Figure 1 depicts the overall process flowchart.

4.1 Approaches

This section provides a description of the language models utilized, followed by an evaluation of their performances in the later section.

Bert-Te: Similar to the pre-trained BERT model introduced by (Devlin et al., 2019) in 2019, which is trained on the BooksCorpus and English Wikipedia, we opted for a model based on the Transformer architecture called BERT-basecased for Telugu. This Telugu variant of BERT is trained on a large corpus comprising 8 million sentences. The BERT-basecased model has 110 million parameters in total, 12 transformer blocks, 768 hidden layers, and 12 self-attention blocks.(Marreddy et al., 2022a) For the purposes of our investigation, we adjusted a BERT-Te model separately. We identified the following hyperparameters for fine-tuning the BERT-Te model to obtain optimal performance: (i) 64 batch size (ii) 3e-5 learning rate (iii) Number of training epochs: 30. To address the overfitting issue, we monitored the validation loss and stopped training if it did not decrease for five consecutive epochs.

IndicBERT: AI4Bharat, an AI research organization, has created a multilingual " IndicBERT " model that focuses on Indian languages and utilizes the BERT architecture(Kakwani et al., 2020). IndicBERT has undergone training on a large corpus of text originating from various Indian languages, including Hindi, Bengali, Tamil, and Telugu. This training enables the model to incorporate and understand these languages' unique linguistic characteristics and complexities. As a result, IndicBERT can comprehend and generate text within the context of multilingual Indian languages.

Multilingual BERT: Multilingual BERT (Bidirectional Encoder Representations from Transformers) is a variant of the BERT model that has been specifically trained on multilingual text data(Pires et al., 2019). This training enables the model to comprehend and generate text in multiple languages, making it a valuable tool for various multilingual natural language processing (NLP) tasks. Multilingual BERT has gained significant popularity within the NLP community.

The architecture of multilingual BERT closely resembles that of the original BERT model. It consists of a transformer-based neural network that utilizes self-attention mechanisms to capture contextual information from both the left and right contexts of each word in a given sentence. This mechanism allows the model to grasp the subtleties of language and the relationships between words.

During the training process of multilingual BERT, the model undergoes pretraining on an extensive corpus of text encompassing multiple languages. Throughout this pretraining phase, the model learns to predict missing words in sentences, which helps it develop a profound understanding of language structures and semantics. By training on a diverse range of languages, multilingual BERT can effectively capture cross-lingual information and transfer knowledge between different languages.

XLM-R: XLM-R (Cross-lingual Language Model - RoBERTa) is an advanced multilingual language model developed by Facebook AI. It is an extension of RoBERTa, which is itself a variant of the BERT model(Conneau et al., 2020). XLM-R has been specifically designed to excel in multilingual natural language processing (NLP) tasks and supports a wide array of languages.

The architecture of XLM-R is based on the transformer neural network, similar to

Model/Category	Bert-te			Indicbert			mBert			XLM-R		
	P	R	F1	P	R	F1	P	R	F1	P	R	F1
Lexical category	0.642	0.821	0.602	0.951	0.706	0.702	0.623	0.822	0.581	0.720	0.688	0.576
number	0.906	0.77	0.738	0.821	0.703	0.607	0.819	0.781	0.680	0.726	0.74	0.590
person	0.820	0.771	0.704	0.665	0.554	0.475	0.796	0.78	0.690	0.672	0.770	0.570
gender	0.875	0.833	0.778	0.854	0.535	0.527	0.805	0.843	0.729	0.757	0.809	0.624
TAM/CM	0.588	0.78	0.515	0.549	0.503	0.409	0.575	0.696	0.564	0.720	0.530	0.527

Table 2: Precision,Recall and F1 scores for models tested

BERT. It comprises multiple layers of self-attention mechanisms that effectively capture contextual information from the input text. This enables the model to comprehend the intricate relationships between words and sentences, and learn representations that accurately capture the semantics of the text.

One notable feature of XLM-R is its capability to align representations across various languages. By learning a shared representation space, XLM-R can proficiently transfer knowledge from high-resource languages to low-resource languages, even in scenarios where training data is limited. This makes XLM-R particularly valuable for multilingual transfer learning tasks, as it can utilize the knowledge acquired from one language to enhance performance in another.

4.2 Dataset Splitting

The dataset we used consists of 10,000 sentences, which we divided into two parts. The testing set accounts for 20 percent of the data, while the training set accounts for the remaining 80 percent. We evaluated the performance of the models mentioned earlier using the test data, and the precision, recall, and f1 scores obtained are presented in the following section.

4.3 Results

Precision, recall, and F1 score are common evaluation measures to gauge the performance of classification models. These metrics are derived by comparing a model's predictions with the actual labels assigned to the data. By providing valuable insights into the effectiveness of a classification model, these evaluation metrics assist practitioners in assessing and optimizing its utility. Below, we showcase the precision, recall, and F1 scores of the different models examined in this section.

In our study, for each category, we developed separate classifiers, and the performance of each classifier using various models is shown in Figure 2. We can see from the results (Table- 2) that Bert-te outperforms all other models in terms of F1 scores for the person (0.70), gender (0.77), and number (0.73) categories. Bert-te surpasses all other models in their respective categories with recall scores of 0.82 for lexical category, 0.77 for number, 0.83 for gender, and 0.77 for person. Bert-te has the greatest precision score in the person category (0.90), which completely outperforms all other models in that category. We discovered that our model, Bert-te, which is trained purely on Telugu language data, performs better than other multilingual models trained on various languages.

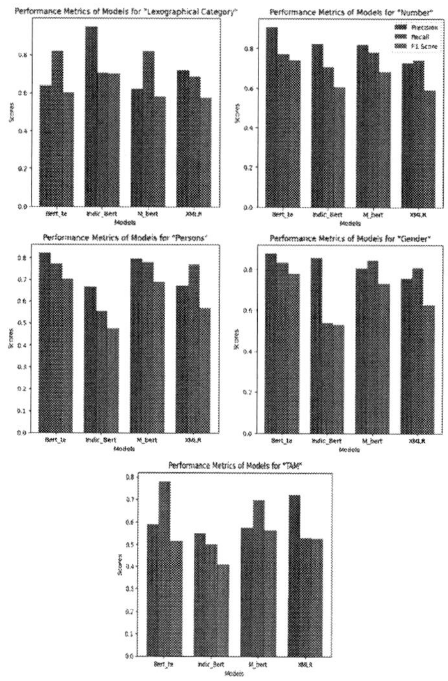

Figure 2: Comparision between all the different Models run for different tags.

The Bert-te model is specifically able to understand the complexities and nuances peculiar to Telugu owing to the concentrated Telugu language instruction. As a result, when compared to the more broad multilingual models, it exhibits improved performance in Telugu language-related tasks.

This result emphasizes the value of domain-specific training and shows that optimizing models for a particular language can improve performance in tasks requiring that language. The Bert-te model's ability to outperform other multilingual models demonstrates the value of specialized language instruction in generating superior outcomes.

5 Ethical Statement

We created a dataset for the Telugu Morph Analyzer and open source the dataset [4]. The codes can be downloaded from here. We reused publicly available Telugu Transformer models (BERT-Te) to compare with existing multi-lingual Transformers models (IndicBERT, XLM-R, mBERT).

6 Conclusion and Future Work

Understanding the structure of individual words is made easier by morphological analysis. In terms of morph information, we have produced a trustworthy dataset. Various NLP tasks can now use this dataset. With the aid of the Morph Analyser, language models can effectively learn and utilize the additional details provided, enabling them to make more accurate predictions, generate more coherent and contextually appropriate responses, and better comprehend the subtleties of human language. By leveraging the insights from the Morph Analyser, language models become more efficient at processing and utilizing the available information, leading to improved language processing capabilities and more refined language generation.

References

Mugdha Bapat, Harshada Gune, and Pushpak Bhattacharyya. 2010. A paradigm-based finite state morphological analyzer for marathi. In *Proceedings of the 1st Workshop on South and Southeast Asian Natural Language Processing*, pages 26–34.

Jatayu Baxi and Brijesh Bhatt. 2022. Gujmorph-a dataset for creating gujarati morphological analyzer. In *Proceedings of the Thirteenth Language Resources and Evaluation Conference*, pages 7088–7095.

Jatayu Baxi, Pooja Patel, and Brijesh Bhatt. 2015. Morphological analyzer for gujarati using paradigm based approach with knowledge based and statistical methods. In *Proceedings of the 12th International Conference on Natural Language Processing*, pages 178–182.

Akshar Bharati and Rajeev Sangal. 2007. Computational paninian grammar framework. *Supertagging: Using Complex Lexical Descriptions in Natural Language Processing*, 355.

Akshar Bharati, Rajeev Sangal, and Dipti M Sharma. 2007. Ssf: Shakti standard format guide. *Language Technologies Research Centre, International Institute of Information Technology, Hyderabad, India*, pages 1–25.

Abhisek Chakrabarty, Akshay Chaturvedi, and Utpal Garain. 2016. A neural lemmatizer for bengali. In *Proceedings of the Tenth International Conference on Language Resources and Evaluation (LREC'16)*, pages 2558–2561.

Alexis Conneau, Kartikay Khandelwal, Naman Goyal, Vishrav Chaudhary, Guillaume Wenzek, Francisco Guzmán, Edouard Grave, Myle Ott, Luke Zettlemoyer, and Veselin Stoyanov. 2019. Unsupervised cross-lingual representation learning at scale. *arXiv preprint arXiv:1911.02116*.

Alexis Conneau, Kartikay Khandelwal, Naman Goyal, Vishrav Chaudhary, Guillaume Wenzek, Francisco Guzmán, Edouard Grave, Myle Ott, Luke Zettlemoyer, and Veselin Stoyanov. 2020. Unsupervised cross-lingual representation learning at scale. In *Proceedings of the 58th Annual Meeting of the Association for Computational Linguistics*, pages 8440–8451. Association for Computational Linguistics.

Jacob Devlin, Ming-Wei Chang, Kenton Lee, and Kristina Toutanova. 2019. Bert: Pre-training of deep bidirectional transformers for language understanding. *arXiv preprint arXiv:1810.04805*.

Suma Reddy Duggenpudi, Subba Reddy Oota, Mounika Marreddy, and Radhika Mamidi. 2022. Teluguner: Leveraging multi-domain named entity recognition with deep transformers. In *Proceedings of the 60th Annual Meeting of the Association for Computational Linguistics: Student Research Workshop*, pages 262–272.

Vishal Goyal and Gurpreet Singh Lehal. 2008. Hindi morphological analyzer and generator. In *2008 First International Conference on Emerging Trends in Engineering and Technology*, pages 1156–1159. IEEE.

Ashim Gupta, Amrith Krishna, Pawan Goyal, and Oliver Hellwig. 2020. Evaluating neural morphological taggers for sanskrit. *arXiv preprint arXiv:2005.10893*.

[4]https://github.com/parameshkrishnaa/Telugu-Morph-Dataset/

Charles F Hockett. 1954. Two models of grammatical description. *Word*, 10(2-3):210–234.

Divyanshu Kakwani, Anoop Kunchukuttan, Satish Golla, NC Gokul, Avik Bhattacharyya, Mitesh M Khapra, and Pratyush Kumar. 2020. inlpsuite: Monolingual corpora, evaluation benchmarks and pre-trained multilingual language models for indian languages. In *Proceedings of the 2020 Conference on Empirical Methods in Natural Language Processing: Findings*, pages 4948–4961.

Nikhil Kanuparthi, Abhilash Inumella, and Dipti Misra Sharma. 2012. Hindi derivational morphological analyzer. In *Proceedings of the Twelfth Meeting of the Special Interest Group on Computational Morphology and Phonology*, pages 10–16.

Parameswari Krishnamurthy. 2019. Development of telugu-tamil transfer-based machine translation system: An improvization using divergence index. *Journal of Intelligent Systems*, 28(3):493–504.

Bhadriraju Krishnamurti and John Peter Lucius Gwynn. 1985. *A grammar of modern Telugu*. Oxford University Press, USA.

Mounika Marreddy, Subba Reddy Oota, Lakshmi Sireesha Vakada, Venkata Charan Chinni, and Radhika Mamidi. 2021. Clickbait detection in telugu: Overcoming nlp challenges in resource-poor languages using benchmarked techniques. In *2021 International Joint Conference on Neural Networks (IJCNN)*, pages 1–8. IEEE.

Mounika Marreddy, Subba Reddy Oota, Lakshmi Sireesha Vakada, Venkata Charan Chinni, and Radhika Mamidi. 2022a. Am i a resource-poor language? data sets, embeddings, models and analysis for four different nlp tasks in telugu language. *ACM Transactions on Asian and Low-Resource Language Information Processing*, 22(1):1–34.

Mounika Marreddy, Subba Reddy Oota, Lakshmi Sireesha Vakada, Venkata Charan Chinni, and Radhika Mamidi. 2022b. Multi-task text classification using graph convolutional networks for large-scale low resource language. In *2022 International Joint Conference on Neural Networks (IJCNN)*, pages 1–8. IEEE.

K Parameshwari. 2011. An implementation of apertium morphological analyzer and generator for tamil. *Parsing in Indian Languages*, 41.

Telmo Pires, Eva Schlinger, and Dan Garrette. 2019. How multilingual is multilingual bert? *arXiv preprint arXiv:1906.01502*.

B Premjith, KP Soman, and M Anand Kumar. 2018. A deep learning approach for malayalam morphological analysis at character level. *Procedia computer science*, 132:47–54.

G. Uma Maheshwar Rao and Amba P. Kulkarni. 2006. Computer applications in indian languages.

G. Uma Maheshwar Rao, Amba P. Kulkarni, and Christopher M. 2011. A telugu morphological analyzer. *International Telugu Internet Conference Proceedings*.

DL Sneha and K Bharadwaja. 2013. A novel approach for morphing telugu noun forms using finite state transducers. *IJERT*, 2(7):550.

B Srinivasu and R Manivannan. 2018. Computational morphology for telugu. *Journal of Computational and Theoretical Nanoscience*, 15(6-7):2373–2378.

KVN Sunitha and N Kalyani. 2009. A novel approach to improve rule based telugu morphological analyzer. In *2009 World Congress on Nature & Biologically Inspired Computing (NaBIC)*, pages 1649–1652. IEEE.

Lakshmi Sireesha Vakada, Anudeep Ch, Mounika Marreddy, Subba Reddy Oota, and Radhika Mamidi. 2023. Gae-isumm: Unsupervised graph-based summarization for indian languages. In *2023 International Joint Conference on Neural Networks (IJCNN)*, pages 1–8. IEEE.

Ramasamy Veerappan, PJ Antony, S Saravanan, and KP Soman. 2011. A rule based kannada morphological analyzer and generator using finite state transducer. *International Journal of Computer Applications*, 27(10):45–52.

Improving Reinforcement Learning Agent Training using Text-based Guidance: A Study using Commands in Dravidian Languages

Nikhil Chowdary Paleti, Sai Aravind Vadlapudi, Sai Aashish Menta, Sai Akshay Menta, Vishnu Vardhan Gorantla V N S L, Janakiram Chandu, Soman K P, and **Sachin Kumar S**
Amrita School of Artificial Intelligence, Coimbatore,
Amrita Vishwa Vidyapeetham, India.
s_sachinkumar@cb.amrita.edu, nikhil.paleti@outlook.com

Abstract

Reinforcement learning (RL) agents have achieved remarkable success in various domains, such as game-playing and protein structure prediction. However, most RL agents rely on exploration to find optimal solutions without explicit guidance. This paper proposes a methodology for training RL agents using text-based instructions in Dravidian Languages, including Telugu, Tamil, and Malayalam along with using the English language. The agents are trained in a modified Lunar Lander environment, where they must follow specific paths to successfully land the lander. The methodology involves collecting a dataset of human demonstrations and textual instructions, encoding the instructions into numerical representations using text-based embeddings, and training RL agents using state-of-the-art algorithms. The results demonstrate that the trained Soft Actor-Critic (SAC) agent can effectively understand and generalize instructions in different languages, outperforming other RL algorithms such as Proximal Policy Optimization (PPO) and Deep Deterministic Policy Gradient (DDPG).

1 Introduction

Reinforcement learning (RL) has developed by leaps and bounds in the past few years, there have been agents capable of beating world champions in games like go Silver et al. (2016), there have been agents capable of predicting protein structures Senior et al. (2020) and more recently there has also been an RL agent capable of optimizing computer code Mankowitz et al. (2023). However, most of the RL agents optimally find the best solution by themselves through exploration of the environment and there lacks a technique through which these agents can be guided so that we can control the path or trajectory that the agent takes while reaching the optimal solution.

There has been little work done to guide or help the RL agents get to the goal state through text-based instructions, especially in the Dravidian languages. The current literature Kaplan et al. (2017) and (Li et al., 2022) provide a basis for this approach where they have constructed a Bimodal embedding network to guide the RL agent on text-based instructions. However, existing literature doesn't compare various Reinforcement learning algorithms and they also don't consider the possibility of training the agents to understand the text instructions in multiple languages.

This paper aims to address this literature gap by proposing a methodology for training reinforcement learning agents in the lunar lander game using text-based embeddings in four languages: English, Telugu, Tamil, and Malayalam (K et al., 2021). By encoding instructions into meaningful numerical representations (Nagasai et al., 2021), the agents can effectively understand and respond to natural language instructions, leading to more immersive and intuitive user-agent interactions.

The proposed methodology for training RL agents with natural language guidance in the lunar lander game involves: 1) collecting a dataset of human demonstrations and textual instructions in multiple languages, 2) encoding the instructions into numerical representations using text-based embeddings, 3) employing RL algorithms with the embeddings as input to train the RL agent, optimizing for successful landings, 4) evaluating the effectiveness of the methodology for unseen paths. we show that

Third Workshop on Speech and Language Technologies for Dravidian Languages, pages 33–42, Varna, Bulgaria, Sep 7, 2023.
https://doi.org/10.26615/978-954-452-085-4_005

the trained Soft Actor-Critic agent is capable of generalizing well to act according to the instruction given in any language.

The organization of the remainder of the paper is as follows: Section 2 details the related works. Section 3 provides a detailed description of the environment used for training the RL agents. Section 4 presents the proposed methodology and the results are discussed in section 5. Finally, we conclude in Section 6 while providing future directions for research.

2 Related Work

Existing work that combines reinforcement learning and natural language can be categorized into two tasks. In the first task, RL agents are trained in environments where the environment is rendered using only text descriptions, unlike the standard 2D or 3D environments that we traditionally see Jansen (2022). The second task focuses on helping or guiding Reinforcement learning agents through natural language, which the present work focuses on.

In Kaplan et al. (2017), a methodology was presented to use natural language to train a reinforcement learning agent to beat "MONTEZUMAS REVENGE", a game that standard RL agents like A3C fail to solve. To prepare a dataset, games were played manually by humans, and snapshots of the game state were taken. The snapshots along with text instructions were used to train CNN and RNN networks using cosine similarity loss to produce text and image embeddings of the game state. These embeddings were given to the RL agent as observations and a new reward function was designed which incorporated a similarity measure reward based on the text and image embeddings. The agent trained obtained a score of 3500 which outperformed the best model at that time by a score of 1000.

The authors in Li et al. (2022) used a similar methodology to (Kaplan et al., 2017) but they replaced the RNN-based network for text embedding with a pre-trained Bert model. This model supports giving instructions using synonyms of original instructions and the model would still be able to understand the instructions. Through their experiments, the authors say that the agent is able to get to the goal state 24 times out of 100 test tasks with a bert-distance model and 17 times with a bert-cosine model.

In recent times, work has focused on using Large Language Models (LLMs) as RL agents. In Wang et al. (2023), the authors have presented Voyager which uses LLM as an RL agent. The LLM harnesses the world language learned to generate consistent action plans or executable policies. The methodology presented in Voyager relies on using a Black-Box LLM (GPT-4) and skips any need to train or finetune the model. The methodology is comprised of three components: An automatic curriculum which is based on the goal of "discovering as many diverse things as possible". A skill library to store and retrieve code generated by the LLM based on embeddings of the generated function descriptions. An iterative prompting mechanism that generates code for various tasks. Finally, there is also a self-evaluation component where the LLM acts as a critic to evaluate the generated function. Though the voyager agent performs well when compared with other similar agents, it, however, has its own downsides like significant cost incurred through GPT-4 API, Hallucinations, and inaccuracies in generating a new skill. Most of the drawbacks can be improved by employing a multimodal LLM that can benefit from both text and visual data or finetuning an LLM with knowledge about various aspects of the environment to reduce inaccuracies and hallucinations. We still require advancements in research in the domain to tackle other problems like the high inference time of LLMs and computational costs of finetuning.

Existing literature did not explore the possibility of using multiple languages to guide Reinforcement learning agents, and there has not been a comparative study on various reinforcement learning algorithms for natural language-guided learning. The present work aims to tackle these research gaps by presenting a methodology to train Reinforcement learning agents through text guidance in various languages including Dravidian languages and also perform a comparative study on the employability of various state-of-the-art Reinforcement learning algorithms for text guidance.

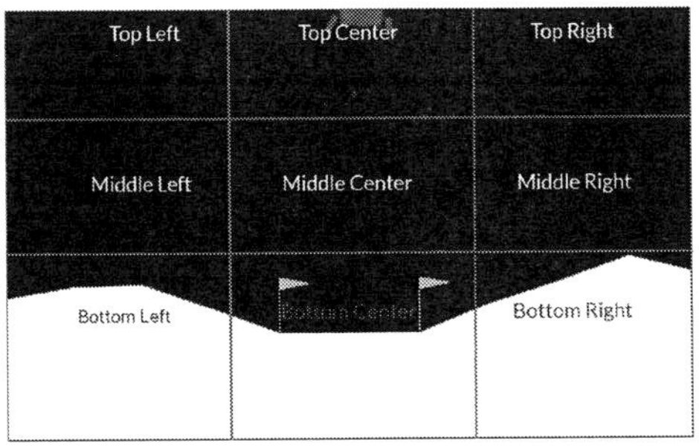

Figure 1: Modified Lunar Lander Environment

3 Environment

The environment used in this study is a modified version of the Lunar Lander environment which is a part of the Box2D environments from the open-source Python library "Gymnasium". The environment is a typical rocket trajectory optimization problem and the goal of the environment is to land the lander on the landing pad. The environment supports both continuous state configuration and discrete state configuration. The continuous state version of the original environment is considered in this study which contains eight observations: the coordinates of the lander in x & y, its linear velocities in x & y, its angle, its angular velocity, two booleans that represent whether each leg is in contact with the ground or not and the action space consists of two continuous actions: The first coordinate of an action determines the throttle of the main engine, while the second coordinate specifies the throttle of the lateral boosters.

The original environment is partitioned into 9 regions as shown in Figure 1 to construct the modified environment. The new goal of the environment is to trace the lander along the path that is given (An example path can be: Top center, Top right, Middle Right, and Bottom center) and finally land on the landing pad. A random path from the preconfigured list of paths is automatically assigned by the environment every time the environment is reset. The path given to the environment can contain locations of the environment in the following languages: English, Telugu, Tamil, and Malayalam. Refer to Appendix A for a detailed list of the paths that can be generated.

A newly shaped reward function is defined through which the lander receives a reward of

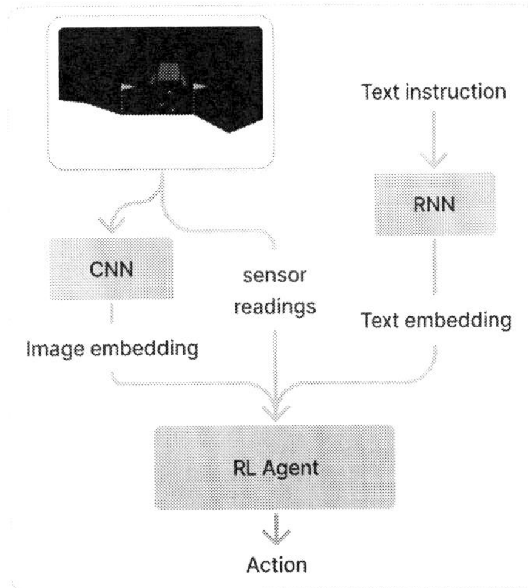

Figure 2: High-level overview of methodology

0 if it moves closer to the target location along the path, -1 if it moves away or deviates from the path, a negative reward based on the angle tilted if its more than 45 degrees, 100 for each leg in contact with the landing pad, and -20 if it tries to land without going along the path. This will effectively punish the agent if it is not following the trajectory given and will reward the agent if it follows along the trajectory and successfully lands. With the mentioned changes, the modified environment still has 8 observations and 2 actions but there is an added feature to generate to path and a new shaped reward function that we employ.

4 Methodology

A high-level overview of the methodology is presented in Figure 2. The 8 sensor observations from the lander along with image embedding of the current state and text embedding of the current target location will go in as input to the Reinforcement learning Agent which gives an action to be taken. The text instruction to the RNN can be in the following languages: English, Telugu, Tamil, and Malayalam. The training of these networks can be split into two stages, in the first stage the embedding networks CNN and RNN are trained together (Kumar et al., 2015) using a cosine similarity loss, and then in the second stage, the RL agent is trained.

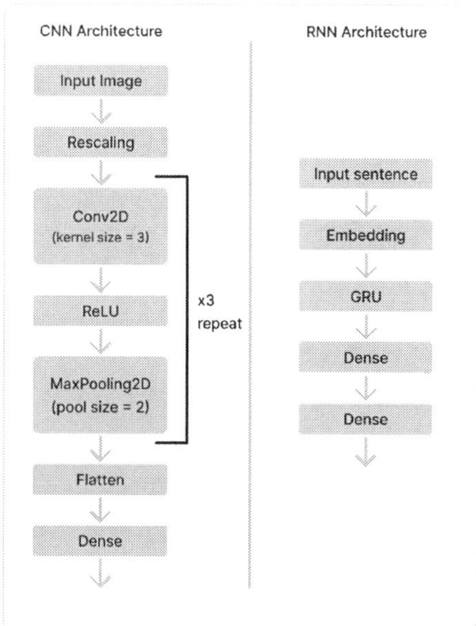

Figure 3: Left: Architecture of CNN network
Right: Architecture of RNN network

4.1 Bimodal Embedding networks

To capture the current state of the environment a CNN-based network is used and to capture the text instruction an RNN-based network is used. Both of these networks are trained together based on cosine embedding loss. Each of the networks outputs an embedding of length 10. The architecture of the two networks is presented in Figure 3.

4.1.1 Dataset

The dataset used to train the embedding network consists of image and text pairs.

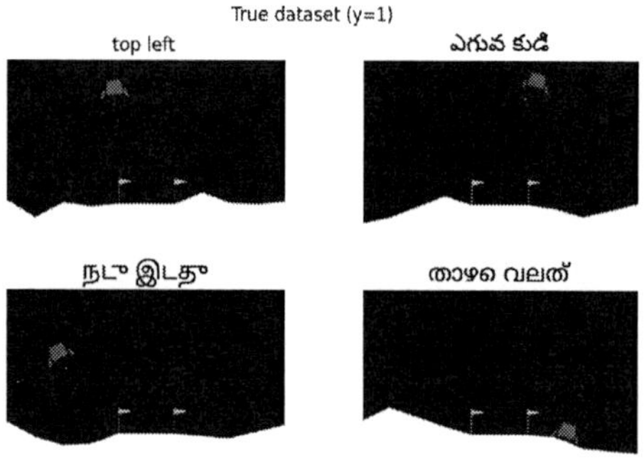

Figure 4: True class of embeddings dataset

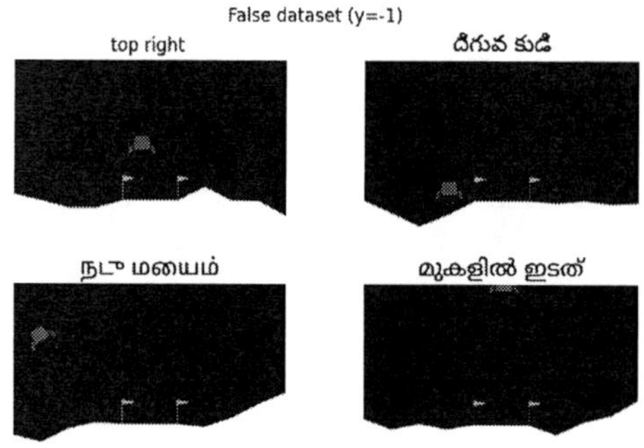

Figure 5: False class of embeddings dataset

The game was played manually and at each timestep, a snapshot of the game state was saved. The snapshots were then manually assigned a text description based on the 9 regions in the modified environment. The dataset consists of two classes: The true class (y = 1) is shown in Figure 4 and represents image, text pairs where text is an accurate description of the image. The false class (y = -1) shown in Figure 5 represents the image, text pairs where text is a false description of the image.

There are 876 image and text pairs for a language and in total, across four languages there are a total of 3,504 pairs. The images are 200px in height, 300px in width and have RGB channels. The text description consists of two words representing the position of the rover in the image according to the regions presented in Figure 1.

4.2 Reinforcement Learning

The Reinforcement Learning (RL) agent is responsible for determining the best action possible given the current environment state. For Guided reinforcement learning, along with the sensor information, the two embedding vectors are also taken in by the algorithm as input. There is a wide spectrum of algorithms (Sreedevi and Rao, 2019) that have the capacity to learn in continuous observation space, among them Deep Deterministic Policy Gradients (DDPG), Proximal Policy Optimization (PPO) and Soft Actor-Critic (SAC) have been considered in this study. The implementations of the algorithms are taken from the open source python library "StableBaselines3" presented by Raffin et al. (2021).

4.2.1 PPO

The authors in Schulman et al. (2017), have presented a new family of policy gradient methods that optimize a "surrogate" by performing a stochastic gradient ascent. In contrast to the standard policy gradient when an update happens per data sample, a novel objective function is proposed that can perform minibatch updates. It has its roots in TRPO but is much simpler to implement. The authors show that this new algorithm strikes a balance between sample complexity, simplicity, and wall time.

4.2.2 DDPG

The authors, Lillicrap et al. (2019), have adapted the technique based on Deep Q-Learning technique for the continuous action space domain. DDPG is a model-free algorithm that can solve more than 20 simulated physics tasks using the same neural network architecture and hyperparameters. To solve the exploration problem in continuous action spaces, the authors have used noise generated using the Ornstein-Uhlenbeck process. The same was adapted for our environment.

4.2.3 SAC

Standard model-free RL algorithms suffer from high sample complexity and brittle convergence properties which requires careful hyperparameter tuning. In Haarnoja et al. (2018), the authors propose an off-policy actor-critic algorithm that maximizes the expected reward while also maximizing entropy. It tries to achieve the goal while also being as random as possible. This feature of the SAC algorithm enables the agent to find out optimal solutions even when the environment is changing or even when there is an obstacle in the standard optimal path, the agent will learn to maneuver around it.

4.3 Training

The embedding networks were trained on a standard Google Colab instance with a T4 GPU. The networks were trained using a batch size of 64 for 600 epochs using Adam optimizer with a learning rate 1e-4. The training loss is presented in Figure 6.

The Reinforcement learning agents were put to training on a lambda labs instance equipped with an Nvidia A10 GPU, which has a compute capability of 8.6, 30vCPUs, 200GiB RAM, and 1.4 TiB SSD. Default Stable baselines 3 parameters were used to train the models as they have been already tuned to work with diverse sets of environments.

Two experiments were run using RL algorithms, In the first experiment the agent received instructions only in the Telugu language, and in the second experiment, the agent received instructions in all 4 languages (English, Telugu, Tamil, and Malayalam). Table 1 describes various training step lengths that were used to train.

The training results of the Multi-Language SAC agent which was trained for 50 Million steps are presented in Figure 7. The agent is able to achieve a score close to 200 with an episode length close to 500 after training.

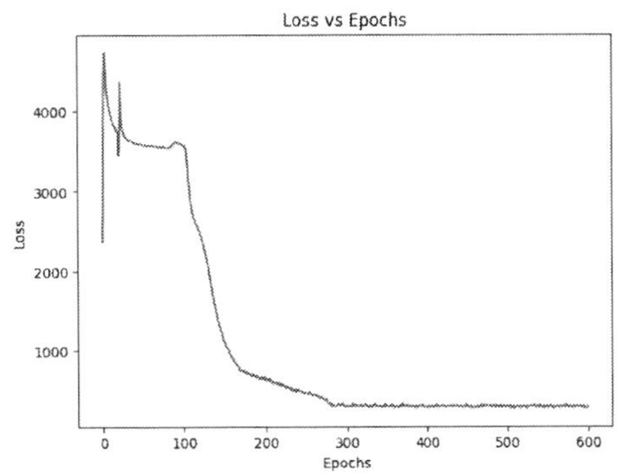

Figure 6: Embeddings networks loss

Algorithm	Telugu Language	Multi Language
DDPG	30 Million	30 Million
PPO	40 Million	40 Million
SAC	30 Million	50 Million

Table 1: Training steps for RL algorithms

5 Results and discussion

Figure 8 shows a visualization of the input text embeddings plotted using UMAP McInnes et al. (2020). The plot depicts similar instructions being plotted together in the low dimensional space indicating that our embedding network has learned to build connections among the vocabulary used for training it. Table 2 shows the top 5 cosine similarity values computed between the embedding of ఎగువ

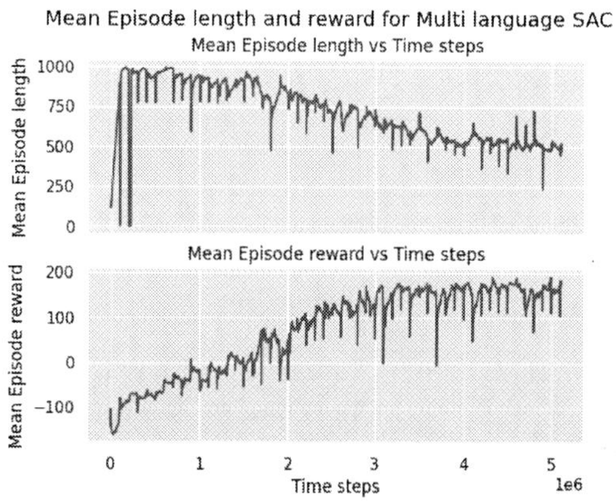

Figure 7: Episode length and reward for Multi Language SAC

Figure 8: UMAP visualization of input instructions

Instruction	Cosine Similarity to ఎగువ ఎడమ (top left)
మధ్య ఎడమ (middle left)	0.98
ఎగువ కుడి (top right)	0.06
దిగువ ఎడమ (bottom left)	0.05
ఎగువ కేంద్రం (top center)	0.02
మధ్య కుడి (middle right)	-0.08

Table 2: Cosine similarity of text embeddings

ఎడమ which means "top left" to other Telugu text instructions. The similarity values further strengthen the claim about the model understanding the underlying patterns in the input text.

As discussed before, 9 unique paths were used for training and a total of 36 paths are made from the 9 paths by translating them to various Dravidian languages. Appendix A provides an overview of the paths used in training. For the first experiment, only 9 paths in the Telugu language were considered and 3 RL agents were trained. The SAC agent obtained an average reward of 192.94, the PPO agent obtained an average reward of -184.53 and the DDPG agent obtained an average reward of -344.46.

In order to test the ability of RL agents to generalize to unseen paths, a few experiments are conducted as presented in Table 3. The paths included transitions that the agent never got to see during training. The unseen paths included transitions like going from middle center to middle right which tests the agent on its capability to fly the lander in the opposite direction and also transitions like going from middle left to top left which tests the agent's capability to fly up in the opposite direction. It should be noted that the agent was never instructed to fly in the opposite direction during training.

The results in Table 3 demonstrate the capability of SAC to generalize well to unseen instructions. Across all the experiments it has maintained a positive reward while the PPO and DDPG agents struggled to perform well.

S.No	Path	SAC Average Reward	PPO Average Reward	DDPG Average Reward
1	ఎగువ కేంద్రం, మధ్య కుడి, ఎగువ కుడి, మధ్య కేంద్రం, దిగువ కేంద్రం (top center, middle right, top right middle center, bottom center)	181	-418.5	-180.5
2	ఎగువ కేంద్రం, మధ్య కుడి, మధ్య కేంద్రం, దిగువ కేంద్రం (top center, middle right, middle center, bottom center)	187	-95.4	-453.7
3	ఎగువ కేంద్రం, ఎగువ కుడి, ఎగువ కేంద్రం, ఎగువ ఎడమ, మధ్య కేంద్రం, దిగువ కేంద్రం (top center, top right, top center, top left, middle center, bottom center)	182	-299.7	-668.2
4	ఎగువ కేంద్రం, ఎగువ ఎడమ, ఎగువ కేంద్రం, ఎగువ కుడి, మధ్య కుడి, మధ్య కేంద్రం, దిగువ కేంద్రం (top center, top left, top center, top right, middle right, middle center, bottom center)	185	-265.7	-441.9
5	ఎగువ కేంద్రం, మధ్య కుడి, మధ్య కేంద్రం, మధ్య ఎడమ, దిగువ కేంద్రం (top center, middle right, middle center, middle left, bottom center)	181	-87.9	-558.2

Table 3: Rewards of the unseen paths tested on RL agents trained on Telugu language instructions.

The second set of experiments consisted of training the RL agents using instructions from all 4 languages: English, Telugu, Tamil, and Malayalam. The total number of instructions considered is 36 (9 from each language). The trained SAC agent obtained an average reward of 187.19, the PPO agent obtained -262.8, and the DDPG agent obtained a -419.37 reward. We can observe that the performance of the Agent trained on multi-language instructions is lower compared with the agent trained on a single language. Though the SAC agent received 20M additional training steps for multiple languages, it obtained less average reward than a single language agent. PPO and DDPG showed similar performance to single language agents, failing to converge.

For the agents trained on instructions from multiple languages first a test was performed to evaluate the agents on using combinations of languages. Presented in Table 4, for multi-language combination paths, the SAC agent obtained an average score of 186.9 while PPO and DDPG obtained -312 and -326.8 respectively. These results indicate that the SAC agent is not confusing among languages and is able to reach the goal state successfully even if the input consisted of instructions from multiple languages.

The final set of tests as presented in Table 5 consisted of evaluating the RL agent train on multi-language instructions on unseen paths. These paths again consisted of transitions that were never seen during training and this time the paths included instructions from multiple languages. The results again show that SAC is able to generalize well to the unseen paths compared to PPO and DDPG. These tests can be viewed by accessing `https://www.youtube.com/watch?v=oxADf4oV74w`

6 Conclusion and Future Works

We have successfully demonstrated a methodology to guide the reinforcement learning agents through text instructions in multiple Dravidian languages. PPO, DDPG, and SAC algorithms were put to use for the task and results showed that SAC generalized well even for unseen paths. When unseen instructions from a mix of Dravidian Languages were given

S.No	Path	SAC Average Reward	PPO Average Reward	DDPG Average Reward
1	top center, మధ్య కేంద్రం, கீழ் மையம் (top center, middle center, bottom center)	190.6	-185.6	-453.1
2	മുകളിൽ മധ്യം, நடு மையம், దిగువ కేంద్రం (top center, middle center, bottom center)	195.1	-263.5	-159.1
3	மேல் மையம், മുകളിൽ വലത് middle right, దిగువ కేంద్రం (top center, top right, middle right, bottom center)	181.5	-423.6	-218.8
4	ఎగువ కేంద్రం, top left நடு இடது, താഴെ മധ്യം (top center, top left, middle left, bottom center)	180.7	-375.4	-476.4

Table 4: Evaluating Agents on paths constructed from multiple languages

S.No	Path	SAC Average Reward	PPO Average Reward	DDPG Average Reward
1	top center, మధ్య ఎడమ, மேல் இடது, മുകളിൽ മധ്യം, top right, നടുക്ക് മധ്യം, താഴെ മധ്യം (top center, middle left, top left, top center, top right, middle center, bottom center)	180	-710.4	-230.2
2	മുകളിൽ മധ്യം, நடு இடது, ఎగువ ఎడమ top center, நடு மையம், దిగువ కేంద్రం (top center, middle left, top left, top center, middle center, bottom center)	165	-617.4	-252.9
3	ఎగువ కేంద్రం, middle left, மேல் இடது, മുകളിൽ മധ്യം, நடு மையம், దిగువ కేంద్రం (top center, middle left, top left, top center, middle center, bottom center)	148	-564.5	-198.1
4	மேல் மையம், ఎగువ ఎడమ, മുകളിൽ മധ്യം, top right, നടുക്ക് വലത് మధ్య కేంద్రం, bottom center (top center, top left, top center, top right, middle right, middle center, bottom center)	-69	-366.7	-382.3
5	ఎగువ కేంద్రం, നടുക്ക് വലത്, நடு மையம், நடு இடது, bottom center (top center, middle right, middle center, middle left, bottom center)	175.3	-188.6	-278.3

Table 5: Rewards of the unseen paths tested on RL agents trained on Multi-language instructions.

to the SAC agent, it obtained an average reward of 119.8 while an SAC agent trained on Telugu language instructions alone obtained an average reward of 183.2 for unseen Telugu instructions. The correctness of the embeddings was also verified through the UMAP plot and cosine similarity.

The work presented in this paper can be extended by using various architectures for embedding networks and making them more efficient. Another direction that can be explored is the use of MultiModal Multilanguage Large Language Models which are capable of understanding images and text in multiple languages, providing access to good computational infrastructure one can try training these LLMs to understand Dravidian languages and also act as Reinforcement Learning agents.

References

Tuomas Haarnoja, Aurick Zhou, Pieter Abbeel, and Sergey Levine. 2018. Soft actor-critic: Off-policy maximum entropy deep reinforcement learning with a stochastic actor.

Peter Jansen. 2022. A systematic survey of text worlds as embodied natural language environments. In *Proceedings of the 3rd Wordplay: When Language Meets Games Workshop (Wordplay 2022)*, pages 1–15, Seattle, United States. Association for Computational Linguistics.

Sreelakshmi K, Premjith B, and Soman Kp. 2021. Amrita_CEN_NLP@DravidianLangTech-EACL2021: Deep learning-based offensive language identification in Malayalam, Tamil and Kannada. In *Proceedings of the First Workshop on Speech and Language Technologies for Dravidian Languages*, pages 249–254, Kyiv. Association for Computational Linguistics.

Russell Kaplan, Christopher Sauer, and Alexander Sosa. 2017. Beating atari with natural language guided reinforcement learning.

S. Sachin Kumar, B. Premjith, M. Anand Kumar, and K. P. Soman. 2015. Amrita_cen-nlp@sail2015: Sentiment analysis in indian language using regularized least square approach with randomized feature learning. In *Mining Intelligence and Knowledge Exploration*, pages 671–683, Cham. Springer International Publishing.

Xin Li, Yu Zhang, Junren Luo, and Yifeng Liu. 2022. Pre-trained bert for natural language guided reinforcement learning in atari game. In *2022 34th Chinese Control and Decision Conference (CCDC)*, pages 5119–5124.

Timothy P. Lillicrap, Jonathan J. Hunt, Alexander Pritzel, Nicolas Heess, Tom Erez, Yuval Tassa, David Silver, and Daan Wierstra. 2019. Continuous control with deep reinforcement learning.

Daniel J Mankowitz, Andrea Michi, Anton Zhernov, Marco Gelmi, Marco Selvi, Cosmin Paduraru, Edouard Leurent, Shariq Iqbal, Jean-Baptiste Lespiau, Alex Ahern, et al. 2023. Faster sorting algorithms discovered using deep reinforcement learning. *Nature*, 618(7964):257–263.

Leland McInnes, John Healy, and James Melville. 2020. Umap: Uniform manifold approximation and projection for dimension reduction.

L. S. Nagasai, V. J. Sriprasath, V. V. SajithVariyar, V. Sowmya, K. Aniketh, T. V. Sarath, and K. P. Soman. 2021. Electric vehicle steering design and automated control using cnn and reinforcement learning. In *Soft Computing and Signal Processing*, pages 513–523, Singapore. Springer Singapore.

Antonin Raffin, Ashley Hill, Adam Gleave, Anssi Kanervisto, Maximilian Ernestus, and Noah Dormann. 2021. Stable-baselines3: Reliable reinforcement learning implementations. *Journal of Machine Learning Research*, 22(268):1–8.

John Schulman, Filip Wolski, Prafulla Dhariwal, Alec Radford, and Oleg Klimov. 2017. Proximal policy optimization algorithms.

Andrew W Senior, Richard Evans, John Jumper, James Kirkpatrick, Laurent Sifre, Tim Green, Chongli Qin, Augustin Žídek, Alexander WR Nelson, Alex Bridgland, et al. 2020. Improved protein structure prediction using potentials from deep learning. *Nature*, 577(7792):706–710.

David Silver, Aja Huang, Chris J Maddison, Arthur Guez, Laurent Sifre, George Van Den Driessche, Julian Schrittwieser, Ioannis Antonoglou, Veda Panneershelvam, Marc Lanctot, et al. 2016. Mastering the game of go with deep neural networks and tree search. *nature*, 529(7587):484–489.

A. G. Sreedevi and Thipparaju Rama Rao. 2019. Reinforcement learning algorithm for 5g indoor devicetodevice communications. *Transactions on Emerging Telecommunications Technologies*, 30.

Guanzhi Wang, Yuqi Xie, Yunfan Jiang, Ajay Mandlekar, Chaowei Xiao, Yuke Zhu, Linxi Fan, and Anima Anandkumar. 2023. Voyager: An open-ended embodied agent with large language models.

Appendix

A Preconfigured Paths

The modified environment has a set of 36 preconfigured paths from which one is randomly assigned every time the environment is reset. There are a total of 9 unique paths to go from the start location to the landing pad which is listed in Table 6.

S.no	English Instruction
1	top center, middle center, bottom center
2	top center, top right, middle right, middle center, bottom center
3	top center, top right, middle center, bottom center
4	top center, top left, middle left, middle center, bottom center
5	top center, middle left, bottom center
6	top center, middle right, bottom center
7	top center, top left, middle left, bottom center
8	top center, top left, middle center bottom center
9	top center, top right, middle right bottom center

Table 6: Instructions used for training

All the other paths are translations of these 9 paths in Dravidian languages: Telugu, Tamil, and Malayalam. The help of google translate has been taken to get the translations in various Dravidian languages. Table 7 lists out the translations of locations in the languages considered.

S.no	English	Translation
1	top center	Telugu: ఎగువ కేంద్రం Tamil: மேல் மையம் Malayalam: മുകളിൽ മധ്യം
2	top left	Telugu: ఎగువ ఎడమ Tamil: மேல் இடது Malayalam: മുകളിൽ ഇടത്
3	top right	Telugu: ఎగువ కుడి Tamil: மேல் வலது Malayalam: മുകളിൽ വലത്
4	middle center	Telugu: మధ్య కేంద్రం Tamil: நடு மையம் Malayalam: നടുക്ക് മധ്യം
5	middle left	Telugu: మధ్య ఎడమ Tamil: நடு இடது Malayalam: നടുക്ക് ഇടത്
6	middle right	Telugu: మధ్య కుడి Tamil: நடு வலது Malayalam: നടുക്ക് വലത്
7	bottom center	Telugu: దిగువ కేంద్రం Tamil: கீழ் மையம் Malayalam: താഴെ മധ്യം
8	bottom left	Telugu: దిగువ ఎడమ Tamil: கீழ் இடது Malayalam: താഴെ ഇടത്
9	bottom right	Telugu: దిగువ కుడి Tamil: கீழ் வலது Malayalam: താഴെ വലത്

Table 7: Translation of locations

Social Media Data Analysis for Malayalam YouTube Comments: Sentiment Analysis and Emotion Detection using ML and DL Models

Abeera V P , Sachin Kumar , Soman K P
Amrita School of Artificial Intelligence,Coimbatore,
Amrita Vishwa Vidyapeetham,India
vp_abeera@cb.students.amrita.edu
s_sachinkumar@cb.amrita.edu
kp_soman@amrita.edu

Abstract

In this paper, we present a study on social media data analysis of Malayalam YouTube comments, specifically focusing on sentiment analysis and emotion detection. Our research aims to investigate the effectiveness of various machine learning (ML) and deep learning (DL) models in addressing these two tasks. For sentiment analysis, we collected a dataset consisting of 3064 comments, while for two-class emotion detection, we used a dataset of 817 comments.In the sentiment analysis phase, we explored multiple ML and DL models, including traditional algorithms such as Support Vector Machines (SVM), Naive Bayes, K-Nearest Neighbors (KNN), MLP Classifier, Decision Tree, and Random Forests. Additionally, we utilized DL models such as Recurrent Neural Networks (RNN),Long Short-Term Memory (LSTM) and Gated Recurrent Unit(GRU). To enhance the performance of these models, we preprocessed the Malayalam YouTube comments by tokenizing and removing stop words. Experimental results revealed that DL models achieved higher accuracy compared to ML models, indicating their ability to capture the complex patterns and nuances in the Malayalam language.Furthermore, we extended our analysis to emotion detection, which involved dealing with limited annotated data. This task is closely related to social media data analysis. For emotion detection, we employed the same ML models used in the sentiment analysis phase. Our dataset of 817 comments was annotated with two emotions: Happy and Sad. We trained the models to classify the comments into these emotion classes and analyzed the accuracy of the different models.

1 Introduction

Social media platforms have revolutionized the way people communicate and express their opinions. With the exponential growth of user-generated content, analyzing social media data has become essential for understanding public sentiment and emotional responses. In this context, YouTube, one of the most popular video-sharing platforms, provides a wealth of data in the form of user comments. Analyzing these comments can offer valuable insights into the sentiments and emotions of viewers, which can be utilized for various applications, such as content recommendation, user engagement, and market research.

This work focuses on social media data analysis for Malayalam YouTube comments, specifically targeting sentiment analysis and emotion detection. Malayalam, a Dravidian language predominantly spoken in the Indian state of Kerala, presents unique challenges due to its complex grammar and distinct linguistic features. Analyzing sentiments and emotions in Malayalam comments requires a deep understanding of the language's nuances and cultural context.The main challenge of the Malayalam language is the lack of an available annotated dataset(Soumya and Pramod, 2020).Therefore, we have begun our work by creating our own dataset.

The primary objective of this research is to explore the effectiveness of different machine learning (ML) and deep learning (DL) models in tackling sentiment analysis and emotion detection tasks for Malayalam YouTube comments. Sentiment analysis aims to classify comments as positive, negative, or neutral, providing an overall sentiment polarity associated with the content. On the other hand, emotion detection focuses on categorizing comments into predefined emotion classes, such as happiness, anger, sadness, or surprise,etc.

To conduct this study, we collected a sizable dataset of 3,064 comments for sentiment analysis and an additional 817 comments for two-class emotion detection. We employed various ML and DL models, including traditional algorithms such as Support Vector Machines (SVM), Naive Bayes, K-Nearest Neighbors (KNN), MLP Classifier, Decision Tree, and Random Forests. Additionally, we utilized DL models such as Recurrent Neural

Third Workshop on Speech and Language Technologies for Dravidian Languages, pages 43–51, Varna, Bulgaria, Sep 7, 2023.
https://doi.org/10.26615/978-954-452-085-4_006

Networks (RNN), LSTM, and GRU. The dataset was preprocessed by tokenizing the comments and removing stopwords to enhance the models' performance.

The main focus of our investigation is to compare the accuracy of the ML and DL models in sentiment analysis and emotion detection tasks. We hypothesize that DL models will outperform ML models due to their ability to capture complex patterns and linguistic nuances present in the Malayalam language. The findings of this study will contribute to the growing field of social media analytics, providing valuable insights into the sentiment and emotional responses of YouTube users in the Malayalam language.

Overall, this work aims to shed light on the effectiveness of ML and DL models for social media data analysis of Malayalam YouTube comments, emphasizing the importance of accurately understanding sentiments and emotions expressed in regional languages. The outcomes of this study can benefit content creators, marketers, and researchers seeking to leverage social media data for decision-making and understanding user preferences in the context of Malayalam YouTube content.

2 Literature

Social media platforms have become prominent sources of user-generated content, providing vast amounts of data for analysis. With the increasing popularity of regional languages, there is a growing need to develop effective techniques for analyzing text data in languages other than English. In the context of Malayalam, a Dravidian language predominantly spoken in Kerala, India, social media data analysis using machine learning (ML) and deep learning (DL) models has gained attention. This literature review examines relevant studies focusing on social media data analysis of Malayalam text data, specifically employing ML and DL models.Most of the Malayalam Social Media Data analysis work is carried out in sentiment analysis problem.The table 1 below provides a literature review focusing on sentiment analysis in social media data analysis problems.

We conducted a survey on several social media data analysis problems, including offensive language identification, part-of-speech tagging, emotion detection, sarcasm detection, humor detection, and more, in various languages. The table 2 show some works related to these topics.

In summary, the literature review demonstrates a growing interest in social media data analysis of Malayalam text data using ML and DL models. Existing studies have explored sentiment analysis and emotion detection, highlighting the effectiveness of both traditional ML algorithms and advanced DL models in capturing sentiments and emotions expressed in Malayalam text. However, the focus has been on specific domains or platforms, such as news headlines, tweets, or movie reviews, leaving a gap in the analysis of Malayalam YouTube comments. This work aims to fill this gap by implementing sentiment analysis and emotion detection specifically for Malayalam YouTube comments using ML and DL models.

3 Objectives

The goals of this work is to explore the application of machine learning (ML) and deep learning (DL) models for social media data analysis of Malayalam text data, with a specific focus on sentiment analysis and emotion detection in Malayalam YouTube comments. The key objectives of this study are as follows:

- Implement sentiment analysis: Develop ML and DL models to classify Malayalam YouTube comments into sentiment categories, such as positive, negative, or neutral. Compare the performance of ML and DL models in terms of accuracy, precision, recall, and F1-score.

- Perform emotion detection: Train ML models to detect emotions expressed in Malayalam YouTube comments, such as happiness and sadness. Evaluate the performance of MLmodels in accurately identifying emotions.

- Compare ML and DL models: Compare the performance of ML models (such as KNN,SVM, Naive Bayes,MLP classifier,Decision Trees and Randm Forset) with DL models (such as RNN,LSTM and GRU) in sentiment analysis and emotion detection tasks. Assess the superiority of DL models in capturing the nuances of Malayalam language and achieving higher accuracy compared to ML models.

- Analyze the challenges and limitations: Identify the challenges and limitations specific to

Reference of the work.	Dataset	Algorithms Used	Metrics
(Soumya and Pramod, 2020)	3184 Malayalam tweets	NB,SVM,and RF	RF classifier with Unigram with Sentiwordnet including negation words, got the highest accuracy,95.6%
(Rahul et al., 2018)	1286 Malayalam sentences	CRF and SVM	Accuracy:52.75%
(Kumar et al., 2017)	12922 malayalam tweets	CNN,LSTM	LSTM with SELU achieved best results:F1-score:0.9823, Recall:0.9824,Precision:0.9823, Accuracy: 0.9824
(Pavan Kumar et al., 2021)	Youtube comments(codemix text),facebook posts etc	CNN,LSTM,Bi-LSTM	Bi-LSTM got highest accuracy
(Soumya and Pramod, 2022)	Malayalam Tweets	Hybrid Models-CNN with variants of RNN(LSTM,Bi-LSTM,GRU)	Hybrid models improve the performance of Sentiment Classification compared to baseline models LSTM, Bi-LSTM and GRU.
(Hande et al., 2021)	Code-mixed YouTube comments for Tamil, Malayalam, and Kannada languages.	Pretrained transformer-based models that have been used for both STL and MTL	Multi-task learning model can achieve high results compared with single-task learning while reducing the time and space constraints required to train the models on individual tasks.
(Thara and Poornachandran, 2022)	Malayalam – English code-mixed data set	DL models-uni-/bi-directional, hybrid,and transformer models	F1-Score- 0.76

Table 1: Literature on sentiment Analysis.

Reference of the work	Topic and Dataset	Algorithms Used	Metrics
(Sasidhar et al., 2020)	Emotion Detection,12000 Hindi-English code-mixed texts	1D-CNN,Bi-LSTM,CNN-LSTM,CNN-BiLSTM	CNN-BiLSTM gave better performance with 83.21% classification accuracy
(Kumar et al., 2019)	POS Tagger,9915 Malyalam Tweets	RNN,GRU,LSTM, and bidirectional LSTM	GRU model at word level gave the highest f1-measure of 0.9254;at character-level,the BiLSTM model gave the highest f1-measure of 0.8739
(Sreelakshmi et al., 2021)	Offensive Language Identification, code-mixed sentences	Hybrid network models with Bi-LSTM and Bi-RNN	Hybrid network exhibited better training performance.
(Al-Ghadhban et al., 2017)	Sarcasm Detection,Arabic tweets	Weka classifier model	Precision-0.659,Recall- 0.710,F-score-0.676
(Mao and Liu, 2019)	Humor Detection,24000 English tweets	BERT-based approach	Accuracy-0.822
(Dhanya and Balakrishnan, 2022)	Offensive speech Detection, Malayalam-English Code Mixed Data	SVM,logistic regression,K-NN,random forest and XGBoost	XGBoost achieved good results with 80% accuracy and with high precision, recall and F1-score.

Table 2: Literature on different social media data anlaysis

sentiment analysis and emotion detection in Malayalam YouTube comments.

By achieving these objectives, this work aims to contribute to the field of social media data analysis by providing insights into the effectiveness of ML and DL models for sentiment analysis and emotion detection in the context of Malayalam YouTube comments. The findings can inform decision-making processes, content recommendation systems, and user engagement strategies for regional language-based social media platforms.

4 Theoretical Background

4.1 Social Media Data Analysis

Social media platforms have become a treasure trove of user-generated content, offering valuable insights into user opinions, sentiments, and emotions. Social media data analysis involves extracting, processing, and analyzing this vast amount of data to gain valuable insights(Rahul et al., 2018). It enables researchers and organizations to understand user behavior, preferences, and trends, and make data-driven decisions.

4.2 Sentiment Analysis

Sentiment analysis, also known as opinion mining, is a natural language processing (NLP) technique that aims to identify and extract subjective information from text data. It involves determining the sentiment or polarity associated with a particular piece of text, such as positive, negative, or neutral. Sentiment analysis has gained significant attention in recent years due to the widespread use of social media platforms and the need to understand public opinion and sentiment towards various entities, including products, services, and events. Various approaches can be employed for sentiment analysis, including rule-based methods, lexicon-based methods, and machine learning-based methods(Nandwani and Verma, 2021). Rule-based methods utilize predefined linguistic rules and patterns to determine sentiment. Lexicon-based methods rely on sentiment lexicons or dictionaries containing words with associated sentiment scores. Machine learning-based methods involve training models on labeled datasets to learn patterns and classify text based on sentiment.

4.3 Emotion Detection

Emotion detection is a subfield of affective computing that focuses on recognizing and classifying emotions expressed in text, speech, or other forms of data. Emotions are complex psychological states that play a crucial role in human communication and decision-making. Emotion detection aims to automatically identify and categorize emotions such as happiness, anger, sadness, fear, surprise, and disgust from textual data(Sasidhar et al., 2020). Similar to sentiment analysis, emotion detection can be approached using different techniques. These include lexicon-based methods, machine learning-based methods, and deep learning-based methods. Lexicon-based methods utilize emotion lexicons containing words and their associated emotional labels. Machine learning-based methods involve training classifiers on labeled datasets, where features are extracted from the text data to predict emotions. Deep learning-based methods, such as recurrent neural networks (RNNs) and convolutional neural networks (CNNs), can capture the contextual and sequential dependencies in the data, leading to improved emotion detection performance.

4.4 Machine Learning (ML) Models

Machine learning models are computational algorithms that can learn from data and make predictions or decisions without being explicitly programmed. ML models have been widely used in various NLP tasks, including sentiment analysis and emotion detection. Traditional ML algorithms, such as Support Vector Machines (SVM),KNN,MLP Classifier,Decision Tree, Naive Bayes, and Random Forests, have been applied successfully to sentiment analysis and emotion detection tasks. These models require feature engineering, where relevant features are extracted from the text data using TF-IDF feature extraction method(Soumya and Pramod, 2020) and used as input to the ML algorithms.

4.5 Deep Learning (DL) Models

Deep learning models are a subset of ML models that utilize artificial neural networks with multiple layers to automatically learn hierarchical representations from data. DL models have demonstrated remarkable performance in various NLP tasks, surpassing traditional ML algorithms(Pavan Kumar et al., 2021). In sentiment analysis created DL models, such as Recurrent Neural Networks (RNNs),LSTM, and GRU.

4.6 Malayalam Text Data

Malayalam is a Dravidian language predominantly spoken in the Indian state of Kerala. Analyzing sentiment and emotions in Malayalam text data presents unique challenges due to the language's specific linguistic features, grammar, and cultural nuances.The main challenge in Malayalam is the scarcity of annotated data(Soumya and Pramod, 2020). Therefore, we created our own dataset and tackled two problems using a small dataset. We are continuously working to expand our dataset size.

4.7 Evaluation Metrics

In sentiment analysis and emotion detection tasks, evaluation metrics are used to assess the performance of the models. Common metrics include accuracy, precision, recall, F1-score, and confusion matrices. Accuracy measures the overall correctness of predictions, while precision and recall provide insights into the models' ability to correctly identify specific sentiment or emotion categories. F1-score balances precision and recall, offering a single metric to evaluate model performance.

5 Methodology

5.1 Dataset Collection and labelling

The first step in the methodology involves gathering a Malayalam YouTube comment dataset for sentiment analysis and emotion detection. For this purpose, we developed a web scraping program to retrieve YouTube comments. A total of 7,500 YouTube comments were extracted from a variety of videos using automated web scraping techniques. From this collection, 3,064 comments were manually annotated to capture distinct sentiments for sentiment analysis, while 817 comments were assigned different emotions for emotion detection. The annotation process is being conducted by a team of three individuals to ensure accuracy; the final labels will be established after completion by all three team members. Due to the meticulous nature of this process, it is time-consuming, and thus, the annotation is ongoing. Currently, 3,064 comments have been labeled for sentiment analysis and 817 comments for emotion detection. Consequently, we have employed these labeled datasets for our study.

5.1.1 Data Labelling for sentiment analysis

The dataset was labeled or annotated for sentiment analysis. It was annotated with different sentiments, including positive, negative, and neutral. A total of 3,064 comments were labeled by three different individuals, and the majority vote was taken as the final label. To facilitate dataset labeling, we created a user interface using recat for easy annotation. The Fig. 1 shows a screenshot of the user interface. Table 3 shows the count of comments labeled with different sentiments.With this 3064 sentiments annotated dataset,we have created different ML and DL models.

Sentiments	number of comments
Positive	1548
Negative	575
Neutral	941
Total	3064

Table 3: count of different sentiments

m

Figure 1: UI for Labelling Sentiment Analysis

5.1.2 Data Labelling for Emotion Detection

The dataset was labeled or annotated for Emotion Detection. Out of 7500 comments, 1000 comments were labeled with 10 different emotions, including Happy, Sad, Anger, Fear, Surprise, Affection/Love, Abusive, Sarcasm, Humor, and Excitement(Sasidhar et al., 2020). Each comment was labeled by three individuals, and the target label was determined based on majority votes. Data labeling was conducted through online and offline modes. Online modes included WhatsApp polls, Google Forms, and Google Sheets, while offline mode involved using hard copies of the form.

The Fig. 2 shows a screenshot of the WhatsApp poll used for annotation.Table 4 shows the count of comments labeled with different sentiments.The Fig. 3 shows a screenshot of the diferent emotions labelled comments.Due to the limited number of annotated samples per emotion, we have currently worked with two classes: happy and sad. We have implemented a two-class emotion detection using ML algorithms.

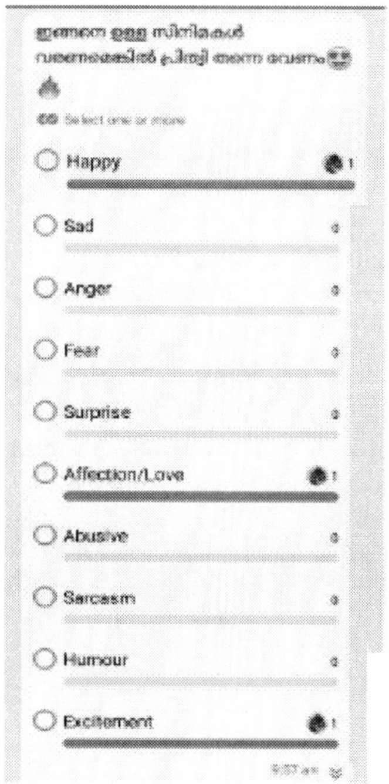

Figure 2: WhatsApp poll for Labelling

Emotions	number of comments
Happy	417
Sad	400
Anger	50
Fear	10
Surprise	20
Affection/love	100
Abusive	15
Sarcasm	10
Humour	25
Excitement	30
Total	1000

Table 4: count of different emotions

Emotions labelled comments

Sl No.	Comments	(1) Happy	(2) Sad	(3) Anger	(4) Fear	(5) Surprise	(6) Affection/	(7) Abusive	(8) Sarcasm	(9) Humour	(10) Exciteme
1	ദൈവത്തെ ഓർത്തു ഇനി സം.. വിധാനം ചെയ്യരുത് 🙏🙏🙏 മോഹൻലാലിനോട് ഇഷ്ടം ഉള്ളത് കൊണ്ടാണ് ഇറങ്ങി പോകാത്തത് 🙏🙏	0	1	1	0	0	1	0	0	0	0
2	തിയേറ്ററിൽ ആളുകൾ ഉറങ്ങിയാണല്ലോ ആറാട്ട് നെ സ്വീകരിച്ചത്	0	0	0	0	0	0	0	1	1	0
3	അപ്പൊ തുടങ്ങിയല്ലേ നെയ്യാറ്റിൻകര ഗോപന്റെ ആറാട്ട്	1	0	0	0	0	1	0	0	0	1
4	ആർക്കോ വേണ്ടി കോമാളിത്തരം കാണിക്കുന്ന സൂപ്പർ സ്റ്റാറുകളെക്കാൾ എത്രയോ മുകളിൽ ആണ് പ്രിത്വിരാജ്..	1	0	0	0	0	1	0	0	0	0
5	Adipoli movie 5/5. Unexpected climax	1	0	0	0	0	1	0	0	0	1

Figure 3: Emotions labelled comments

5.2 Data Preprocessing

Once the dataset is collected, it needs to be preprocessed to enhance the performance of the sentiment analysis and emotion detection models. Preprocessing steps may include tokenization, removing stop words, stemming or lemmatization, and handling special characters or emoticons specific to the Malayalam language(Rahul et al., 2018). This ensures that the text data is in a suitable format for further analysis.

5.3 Feature Extraction

In sentiment analysis and emotion detection, relevant features need to be extracted from the preprocessed text data. For sentiment analysis, the TF-IDF feature extraction method(Soumya and Pramod, 2020) is used in the creation of various ML models, while the Text-to-Sequence and Word2Vec methods are employed for creating DL models.The TF-IDF feature extraction method is also utilized in emotion detection with ML models.

5.4 Machine Learning Models

For sentiment analysis and emotion detection, ML models can be employed.The dataset was split into 80% training and 20% testing data, and various ML models were created, including NB, KNN, SVM, MLP classifiers, Decision Tree, and Random Forest.

5.5 Deep Learning Models

Sentiment analysis was implemented using different Deep Learning algorithms on the same dataset. The dataset was split into 80% training and 20% testing data, and various DL models, including DNN, RNN, LSTM, and GRU, were created(Kumar et al., 2017).These models can automatically learn representations and patterns from the text data.Pretrained word embeddings such as Word2Vec and feature extraction methods like text-to-sequence were utilized for implementing DL models.

5.6 Model Training and Evaluation

The ML and DL models are trained on the labeled dataset, with sentiment labels for sentiment analysis and emotion labels for emotion detection. The dataset can be divided into training, validation, and test sets to assess the models' performance. Accuracy, precision, recall, F1-score, and confusion matrices are common evaluation metrics. The models can be fine-tuned and retrained as necessary to achieve the best performance.

5.7 Performance Comparison

The performance of the ML and DL models is compared in terms of accuracy, precision, recall, and F1-score. The focus is on evaluating the performance of DL models against traditional ML models, particularly in terms of their ability to handle the nuances and complexities of the Malayalam language.

6 Experimental results and discussion

Sentiment analysis and emotion detection in our work are carried out using machine learning (ML) and deep learning (DL) techniques, implemented using the Python programming language.

6.1 Sentiment Analysis Results

For sentiment analysis of Malayalam YouTube comments, we implemented both machine learning (ML) and deep learning (DL) models. The ML models included NB, KNN, SVM, MLP classifiers, Decision Tree, and Random Forest, while the DL models comprised RNN,LSTM,and GRU.

6.1.1 Experimental results of sentiment analysis using ML Models

20% of the dataset, which consisted of 613 comments, was used for evaluating different ML models. The figures below show the confusion matrix of the different models using the same test data.The Fig. 4, 5,shows confusion matrix of different ML Models.

The table 5 displays the performance metrics of various ML models, including accuracy, precision, recall, and F1 score. it is clear that the MLP classifier and KNN with 15 neighbors achieved the highest accuracy.

Models	Accuracy	Precision	Recall	F1-Score
NB	43.72	0.4198	0.4184	0.410
KNN	54.32	0.4831	0.4451	0.4448
SVM	50.57	0.1711	0.3312	0.2256
MLP Classifier	54.32	0.4831	0.4451	0.4448
Decision Tree	49.27	0.4227	0.4037	0.4012
Random Forest	51.71	0.4249	0.3668	0.3177

Table 5: Performance Metrics of SA using ML Models

6.1.2 Experimental results of sentiment analysis using DL Models

20% of the dataset, which consisted of 613 comments, was used for evaluating different DL models.The table 6 displays the performance metrics of various DL models with text-to-sequence feature extraction methods,including accuracy, precision, recall, and F1 score.From the performance metrics table, it is clear that the GRU model achieved an accuracy of 54.21%, which is higher than that of the simple RNN and LSTM models.

Models	Accuracy	Precision	Recall	F1-Score
Simple RNN	52.23	0.4595	0.4470	0.4478
LSTM	52.89	0.4618	0.4471	0.4484
GRU	54.21	0.4717	0.4275	0.4189

Table 6: Performance Metrics of SA using DL Models

The table 7 displays the performance metrics of various DL models with Word2Vec,including accuracy, precision, recall, and F1 score.From the performance metrics table, it is clear that the LSTM model achieved an accuracy of 52.40%, which is higher than that of the simple RNN and GRU models.

Models	Accuracy	Precision	Recall	F1-Score
Simple RNN	49.26	0.4173	0.4072	0.4047
LSTM	52.40	0.4705	0.4400	0.4435
GRU	51.40	0.4501	0.4264	0.4273

Table 7: Performance Metrics of SA using DL

6.2 Emotion Detection Results

From the 1000 comments labelled with different emotions, 817 comments were selected for two-class emotion classification (happy and sad). We implemented various ML models for this task, including NB, KNN, SVM, MLP classifier, Decision Tree, and Random Forest. TF-IDF feature extraction was used to extract features.20% of the data, specifically 164 comments, were reserved for testing the different ML models.The table 8 displays the performance measures of various ML models, including accuracy, precision, recall, and F1 score. it is clear that the MLP classifier achieved an highest accuracy of 81.71%.

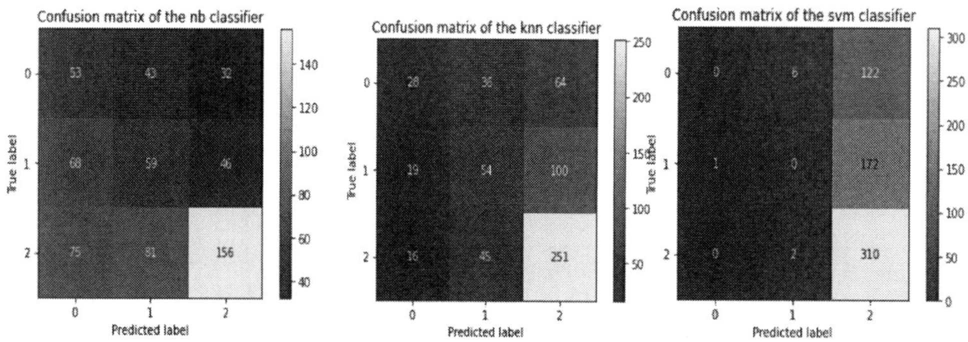

Figure 4: Confusion Matrix of NB,KNN and SVM

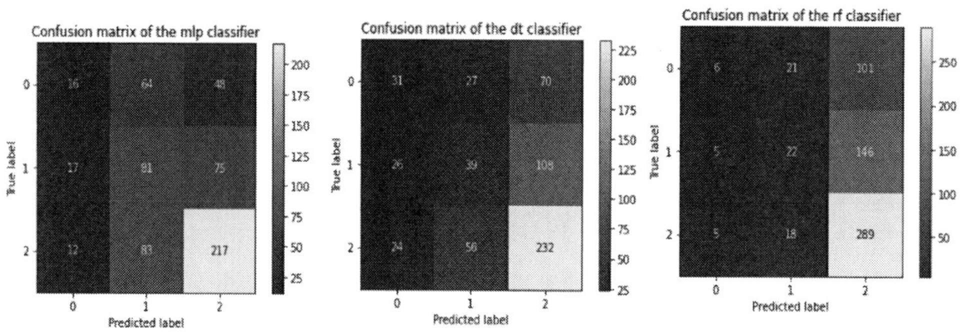

Figure 5: Confusion Matrix of MLP Classifier,Decision Tree and RF

Models	Accuracy	Precision	Recall	F1-Score
NB	76.22	0.5221	0.5157	0.5180
KNN	73.78	0.4913	0.5005	0.4958
SVM	78.05	0.0.5556	0.5229	0.5178
MLP Classifier	81.71	0.5516	0.5520	0.5485
Decision Tree	68.90	0.4757	0.4626	0.4603
Random Forest	74.39	0.5360	0.4970	0.4895

Table 8: Perormance Metrics of Emotion Detection

7 Conclusion

In this paper addresses the challenges posed by the unavailability of annotated datasets for the Malayalam language in the field of natural language processing (NLP). To overcome this challenge, we created our own dataset with manual annotation and focused on two social media problems: sentiment analysis and emotion detection.For sentiment analysis, we utilized a dataset of 3064 annotated comments and implemented various machine learning (ML) and deep learning (DL) models. Among the ML models, MLP classifier and KNN with 15 neighbors demonstrated the highest accuracy. On the other hand, among the DL models, GRU and LSTM exhibited the highest accuracy. ML models were trained using TF-IDF feature vectorization, while DL models utilized Word2Vec embeddings.Additionally, we implemented two-class emotion detection using ML models, with MLP classifier achieving the highest accuracy.As part of our future work, we aim to increase the size of our dataset and implement more transformer models to further enhance the accuracy of our models.Overall, this research highlights the importance of creating annotated datasets for under-resourced languages like Malayalam and demonstrates the effectiveness of ML and DL models in addressing sentiment analysis and emotion detection tasks. The findings provide valuable insights for future studies in NLP for the Malayalam language and contribute to the growing body of research in this field.

References

Dana Al-Ghadhban, Eman Alnkhilan, Lamma Tatwany, and Muna Alrazgan. 2017. Arabic sarcasm detection in twitter. In *2017 International Conference on Engineering & MIS (ICEMIS)*, pages 1–7. IEEE.

LK Dhanya and Kannan Balakrishnan. 2022. Comparative performance of machine learning algorithms in detecting offensive speech in malayalam-english code-mixed data. In *Advances in Distributed Computing and Machine Learning: Proceedings of ICADCML 2022*, pages 687–696. Springer.

Adeep Hande, Siddhanth U Hegde, Ruba Priyadharshini, Rahul Ponnusamy, Prasanna Kumar Kumaresan, Sajeetha Thavareesan, and Bharathi Raja Chakravarthi. 2021. Benchmarking multi-task learning for sentiment analysis and offensive language identification in under-resourced dravidian languages. *arXiv preprint arXiv:2108.03867*.

S Kumar, M Anand Kumar, and KP Soman. 2019. Deep learning based part-of-speech tagging for malayalam twitter data (special issue: deep learning techniques for natural language processing). *Journal of Intelligent Systems*, 28(3):423–435.

S Sachin Kumar, M Anand Kumar, and KP Soman. 2017. Sentiment analysis of tweets in malayalam using long short-term memory units and convolutional neural nets. In *Mining Intelligence and Knowledge Exploration: 5th International Conference, MIKE 2017, Hyderabad, India, December 13–15, 2017, Proceedings 5*, pages 320–334. Springer.

Jihang Mao and Wanli Liu. 2019. A bert-based approach for automatic humor detection and scoring. In *IberLEF@ SEPLN*, pages 197–202.

Pansy Nandwani and Rupali Verma. 2021. A review on sentiment analysis and emotion detection from text. *Social Network Analysis and Mining*, 11(1):81.

PHV Pavan Kumar, B Premjith, JP Sanjanasri, and KP Soman. 2021. Deep learning based sentiment analysis for malayalam, tamil and kannada languages.

M Rahul, RR Rajeev, and S Shine. 2018. Social media sentiment analysis for malayalam. *Int. J. Comput. Sci. Eng*, 6(06):48–53.

T Tulasi Sasidhar, B Premjith, and KP Soman. 2020. Emotion detection in hinglish (hindi+ english) code-mixed social media text. *Procedia Computer Science*, 171:1346–1352.

S Soumya and KV Pramod. 2020. Sentiment analysis of malayalam tweets using machine learning techniques. *ICT Express*, 6(4):300–305.

S Soumya and KV Pramod. 2022. Hybrid deep learning approach for sentiment classification of malayalam tweets. *International Journal of Advanced Computer Science and Applications*, 13(4).

K Sreelakshmi, B Premjith, and Soman Kp. 2021. Amrita_cen_nlp@ dravidianlangtech-eacl2021: deep learning-based offensive language identification in malayalam, tamil and kannada. In *Proceedings of the First Workshop on Speech and Language Technologies for Dravidian Languages*, pages 249–254.

S Thara and Prabaharan Poornachandran. 2022. Social media text analytics of malayalam–english code-mixed using deep learning. *Journal of big Data*, 9(1):45.

Findings of the Second Shared Task on Offensive Span Identification from Code-Mixed Tamil-English Comments

Manikandan Ravikiran[†*], **Ananth Ganesh, Anand Kumar Madasamy**[⋆]
Ratnavel Rajalakshmi [⊕], **Bharathi Raja Chakravarthi**[‡]
[†]Georgia Institute of Technology, Atlanta, Georgia
[⋆]National Institute of Technology Karnataka Surathkal, India
[⊕]Vellore Institute of Technology, Chennai, India
[‡]School of Computer Science, Univeristy of Galway, Ireland
mravikiran3@gatech.edu, bharathi.raja@insight-centre.org

Abstract

Maintaining effective control over offensive content is essential on social media platforms to foster constructive online discussions. Yet, when it comes to code-mixed Dravidian languages, the current prevalence of offensive content moderation is restricted to categorizing entire comments, failing to identify specific portions that contribute to the offensiveness. Such limitation is primarily due to the lack of annotated data and open source systems for offensive spans. To alleviate this issue, in this shared task, we offer a collection of Tamil-English code-mixed social comments that include offensive comments. This paper provides an overview of the released dataset, the algorithms employed, and the outcomes achieved by the systems submitted for this task.

1 Introduction

Combating offensive content is crucial for different entities involved in content moderation, which includes social media companies as well as individuals (Subramanian et al., 2022; Chinnaudayar Navaneethakrishnan et al., 2023). To this end, moderation is often restrictive with either usage of human content moderators, who are expected to read through the content and flag the offensive mentions (Arsht and Etcovitch, 2018). Alternatively, there are semi-automated and automated tools that employ trivial algorithms and block lists (Jhaver et al., 2018). Though content moderation looks like a one-way street, where either it should be allowed or removed, such decision-making is fairly hard (Bharathi and Agnusimmaculate Silvia, 2021; Bharathi and Varsha, 2022; Swaminathan et al., 2022). This is more significant, especially on social media platforms, where the sheer volume of content is overwhelming for human moderators especially (Kumaresan et al., 2022; Chakravarthi, 2022b,a). With ever increasing offensive social media contents focusing on offensive comments and statements semi-automated and fully automated content moderation is favored (Ravikiran et al., 2022; Chakravarthi, 2023; Chakravarthi et al., 2023a).

Tamil is an classical ancient language (Subalalitha, 2019a; Anita and Subalalitha, 2019a; Thavareesan and Mahesan, 2019, 2020a,b) with a history dating back to 580 BCE (Sivanantham and Seran, 2019). It is primarily spoken in Tamil Nadu, India, and also in Sri Lanka, Malaysia, and Singapore. Tamil holds official language status in Tamil Nadu, Sri Lanka, Singapore, and the Union Territory of Puducherry (Subalalitha, 2019b; Sakuntharaj and Mahesan, 2016, 2017, 2021). Additionally, there are significant Tamil-speaking communities in Kerala, Karnataka, Andhra Pradesh, Telangana, and the Andaman and Nicobar Islands. The Tamil diaspora is spread across countries across the world and is recognized as a scheduled language in the Indian Constitution. It has a rich literary tradition dating back to the 6th century BCE (Anita and Subalalitha, 2019b), with rock edicts and "hero stones" serving as some of the earliest known written records. De-

* Corresponding Author, Work done during graduate school

Third Workshop on Speech and Language Technologies for Dravidian Languages, pages 52–58, Varna, Bulgaria, Sep 7, 2023.
https://doi.org/10.26615/978-954-452-085-4_007

spite its own script, with the advent of social media, code-switching has permeated into the Tamil language across informal contexts like forums and messaging outlets (Ravikiran et al., 2022). As a result, code-switched content is part and parcel of offensive conversations in social media.

Despite many recent NLP advancements, handling code-mixed offensive content is still a challenge in Dravidian Languages (Sitaram et al., 2019) including Tamil owing to limitations in data and tools. However, recently the research of offensive code-mixed texts in Dravidian languages has seen traction (Priyadharshini et al., 2020; Chakravarthi, 2020; Chakravarthi et al., 2023a,b). Yet, very few of these focus on identifying the spans that make a comment offensive (Ravikiran and Annamalai, 2021; Ravikiran et al., 2022). However, highlighting these specific spans segments can greatly assist content moderators and semi-automated tools that prioritize identifying and attributing offensive content. In line with this objective, we presented second iteration of code-mixed social media text in Tamil, including offensive spans, and invited participants to develop and submit systems under two distinct settings for this shared task. Our CodaLab website[1] will remain open to foster further research in this area.

2 Related Work

2.1 Offensive Span Identification

Existing literature on identifying offensive spans primarily finds its origins in SemEval Offensive Span Identification shared task, which predominantly centers around the English language (Pavlopoulos et al., 2021). More than 36 different systems have been developed using various approaches. For Dravidian Languages there are quite few works namely Ravikiran and Annamalai (2021); LekshmiAmmal et al. (2022); Rajalakshmi et al. (2022).

3 Task Description

Our task of offensive span identification required participants to identify offensive spans i.e, character offsets that were responsible for the offensive of the comments, when identifying such spans was possible. To this end, we created two subtasks each of which are as described.

[1]https://codalab.lisn.upsaclay.fr/competitions/11174

3.1 Subtask 1: Supervised Offensive Span Identification

Given comments and annotated offensive spans for training, here the systems were asked to identify the offensive spans in each of the comments in test data. This task could be approached as supervised sequence labeling, training on the provided posts with gold offensive spans. It could also be treated as rationale extraction using classifiers trained on other datasets of posts manually annotated for offensiveness classification, without any span annotations.

3.2 Subtask 2: Less data Offensive Span Identification

All the participants of subtask 1 are encouraged to also submit a *Less Data approach*, where the participants are expected to submit a model while using only parts (not fully) of training data of subtask 1. Participants were asked to develop systems to achieve competitive performance with limited data. To this end, participants were empowered to use creative ways to do this including data subset selection, coreset theory etc.

4 Dataset

For this shared task, we build upon dataset from earlier work of Ravikiran et al. (2022), which originally released 4786 code-mixed Tamil-English comments with 6202 offensive spans. We released this dataset to the participants during training phase for model development. Additionally, the test set from the same work with 1006 samples were released for development/validation purposes. Meanwhile for testing we extended this dataset with new additional annotated comments. To this end, we use dataset of Priyadharshini et al. (2022) that consist of abusive comments. From this we selected 366 comments for testing purpose.

Split	Train	Test
Number of Sentences	4786	361
Number of unique tokens	22096	2947
Number of annotated spans	6202	677
Average size of spans (# of characters)	21	21
Min size of spans (# of characters)	4	4
Max size of spans (# of characters)	82	58

Table 1: Dataset Statistics used in this shared task

Following previous research (Ravikiran et al., 2022), we created span-level annotations for 361 newly selected test comments. We followed the same process and guidelines for annotation, anonymity maintenance etc. Profanity in data was explained apriori with an option to withdraw from the annotation process if necessary. To ensure quality each annotation was verified by one or more annotation verifier, prior to merging and creating gold standard test set. The overall dataset statistics is given in the Table 1. Overall for the 361 comments we obtained Cohen's Kappa inter-annotator agreement of 0.64 inline with Ravikiran et al. (2022).

5 Competition Phases

5.1 Training Phase

In the training phase, the train split with 4786 comments, and their annotated spans were released for model development. Participants were given training data and offensive spans. Along with this development/validation set was also released. Participants were also emphasized on cross-validation by creating their splits for preliminary evaluations or hyperparameter tuning. In total, 48 participants registered for the task and downloaded the dataset.

5.2 Testing Phase

Test set comments without any span annotation were released in the testing phase. Each participating team was asked to submit their generated span predictions for evaluation. Predictions are submitted via Google form, which was used to evaluate the systems. Though CodaLab supports evaluation inherently, we used google form due to its simplicity. Finally, we assessed the submitted spans of the test set and were scored using character-based F1 (See section 7.2).

6 System Descriptions

Overall we received only a total of 3 submissions from three teams out of 48 registered participants. All these were only for subtask 1. No submissions were made for subtask 2. Each of their respective systems are as described.

6.1 The AJNS Submission

The best performing system from AJNS experimented with rationale extraction (Atharva et al., 2023) by training offensive language classifiers and employing model-agnostic rationale extraction mechanisms to produce toxic spans as explanations of the decisions of the classifier. Specifically to achieve accurate classification, it employed the Bidirectional and Autoregressive Transformers model (Lewis et al., 2020), which is based on zero-shot learning and effectively captures the semantic meaning and context of the input text. BART's ability to generalize from limited labeled data allows for higher accuracy despite using less data compared to traditional models. This initial classification step helps us narrow down the focus to offensive spans within the text. Once the offensive spans are identified, we further process them using the Bidirectional Encoder Representations from Transformers (Devlin et al., 2019) in conjunction with the Local Interpretable Model-Agnostic Explanations (Ribeiro et al., 2016). The BERT+LIME model extracts specific span words and their positions within the parent sentence. They obtain F1 score of 0.2858

6.2 The DLRG-R1 and DLRG-R2 submission

The DLRG team formulated the problem as a combination of token labeling and span extraction. Specifically, the team created word-level BIO tags i.e., words were labelled as B (beginning word of a offensive span), I (inside word of a offensive span), or O (outside of any offensive span). Following which character level embeddings is created and an LSTM model (DLRG-R1) is trained. This system produces F1 of 0.2254. The DLRG-R2 employed similar strategy like DLRG-R2 team except they used GRU instead of LSTM. This system produces F1 of 0.2134.

6.3 The DLRG-R2 submission

7 Evaluation

This section focuses on the evaluation framework of the task. First, the official measure that was used to evaluate the participating systems is described. Then, we discuss baseline models that were selected as benchmarks for comparison reasons. Finally, the results are presented.

7.1 Evaluation Measure

In line with work of Pavlopoulos et al. (2021) each system was evaluated F1 score computed on character offset. For each system, we computed the F1 score per comments, between the predicted and the ground truth character offsets. Following this we calculated macro-average score over all the 876 test comments. If in case both ground truth and predicted character offsets were empty we assigned a F1 of 1 other wise 0 and vice versa.

7.2 Benchmark

To establish fair comparison we first created following baseline benchmark system which are as described.

- BENCHMARK is a random baseline model which randomly labels 50% of characters in comments to belong to be offensive. To this end, we run this benchmark 10 times and average results are presented in Table 2.

Table 2: Official rank and F1 score (%) of the 3 participating teams that submitted systems. The baselines benchmarks are also shown.

RANK	TEAM	F1 (%)
BASELINE	BENCHMARK	37.24
1	AJNS	28.58
2	DLRG-R1	22.54
2	DLRG-R2	21.34

8 Analysis, Discussion and Remarks

In general, we were pleased to witness the level of engagement in this shared task, with numerous participants signing up, expressing interest in obtaining datasets, and seeking potential baseline codes for the project. Although only three teams ultimately submitted their systems, the variety of approaches taken to tackle the problem is quite promising. Nevertheless, we have included some of our observations below, which stem from our evaluation and the insights gained from the results.

Table 2 shows the scores and ranks of two teams that made their submission. NITK-IT_NLP (Section 6.1) was ranked first, followed by DLRG (Section 6.3) that scored 27% lower was ranked second. The median score was 31.08%, which is far below the top ranked team and the benchmark baseline models.

BENCHMARK 1 achieves a considerably high score and, hence, is very highly ranked with character F1 of 37.24%. Combination of BART with LIME interpretability by model AJNS is behind BENCHMARK 1 by 9%, indicating the language models ability to not so effectively rationalize and identify the spans. Meanwhile DLRG-R1 and DLRG-R2 has large gap compared to random baselines, indicating the proposed approaches by these teams are not suitable for practical use. To this end, these methods employ direct token labeling which is more surprising.

Table 3: Results of submitted systems across comments of different lengths.

	F1@30 (%)	F1@50 (%)	F1@>50 (%)
AJNS	41.01	41.61	22.48
DLRG-R1	38.03	34.39	17.03
DLRG-R2	31.03	30.33	16.06

8.1 General remarks on the approaches

Though neither of teams that made final submissions created any simple baselines, we could see that all the submissions use well established approaches in recent NLP focusing on pretrained language models. Meanwhile DLRG used well-grounded Non-Transformer based approach. Yet neither of teams used any ensembles, data augmentation strategies or modifications to loss functions that are seen for the task of span identification in the past across shared tasks.

8.2 Error Analysis

Table 2 shows maximum result of 37.24% for baseline model with AJNS showing highest result of 28.58% with DLRG failing significantly compared to random baseline. To this end, we wonder if potentially these approaches have any weaknesses or strengths. To understand this, first we study the character F1 results across sentences of different lengths. Specifically we analysis results of (a) comments with less than 30 characters (F1@30) (b) comments with 30-50 characters (F1@50) (c) comments with more than 50 characters (F1@>50). The results so obtained are as shown in Table 3.

Firstly from Table 3 we can see though AJNS shows high results overall for cases of comments with larger lengths the model fails significantly by 19%. Meanwhile for DLRG-R1 and DLRG-R2 the results are more mixed, especially we can see that for comments with less than 30 characters the model shows improvement in F1 by around 10%. Meanwhile for shorter comments, the results high indicating the methods are indeed useful. However these short sentences often contained only cuss words or clearly abusive words that are easily identifiable and often present in the train set, indicating the deficiency of the submitted systems.

9 Conclusion

In this work, we set up a second shared task that was centred on locating offensive language spans in code-mixed Tamil-English text. Compared to our earlier iteration, we had 6,153 social media comments that were tagged to identify abusive spans. Only three teams submitted their systems out of 48 registered participants. We described their strategies in this study and talked about the results they got. It's interesting that a strategy for reason extraction that combines BART and LIME was effective but was not able to beat random baseline. The LSTM/GRU model, on the other hand, performed noticeably worse than the random baseline and showed sensitivity to shorter sentences. We have made the baseline models and information available to the public in order to aid future research. Moving forward, we intend to redo the offensive span identification task under multitask setup with identification of different types of offensiveness alongside the offensive spans.

Acknowledgements

We thank our anonymous reviewers for their valuable feedback. Any opinions, findings, and conclusion or recommendations expressed in this material are those of the authors only and does not reflect the view of their employing organization or graduate schools. The shared task was result of series projects done during CS7646-ML4T (Fall 2020), CS6460-Edtech Foundations (Spring 2020) and CS7643-Deep learning (Spring 2022) at Georgia Institute of Technology (OMSCS Program). Bharathi Raja Chakravarthi were supported in part by a research grant from Science Foundation Ireland (SFI) under Grant Number SFI/12/RC/2289_P2 (Insight_2).

References

R Anita and CN Subalalitha. 2019a. An approach to cluster tamil literatures using discourse connectives. In *2019 IEEE 1st International Conference on Energy, Systems and Information Processing (ICESIP)*, pages 1–4. IEEE.

R Anita and CN Subalalitha. 2019b. Building discourse parser for Thirukkural. In *Proceedings of the 16th International Conference on Natural Language Processing*, pages 18–25.

Andrew Arsht and Daniel Etcovitch. 2018. The human cost of online content moderation. *Harvard Journal of Law & Technology*.

Joshi Atharva, Subramanian Narayanan, and Rajalakshmi Ratnavel. 2023. Team_ajns@dravidianlangtech: Offensive langauge identification on multilingual code mixed text. In *Proceedings of the Third Workshop on Speech and Language Technologies for Dravidian Languages*, Varna, Bulgaria. Recent Advances in Natural Language Processing.

B Bharathi and A Agnusimmaculate Silvia. 2021. SSNCSE_NLP@DravidianLangTech-EACL2021: Offensive language identification on multilingual code mixing text. In *Proceedings of the First Workshop on Speech and Language Technologies for Dravidian Languages*, pages 313–318, Kyiv. Association for Computational Linguistics.

B Bharathi and Josephine Varsha. 2022. SSNCSE NLP@TamilNLP-ACL2022: Transformer based approach for detection of abusive comment for Tamil language. In *Proceedings of the Second Workshop on Speech and Language Technologies for Dravidian Languages*, pages 158–164, Dublin, Ireland. Association for Computational Linguistics.

Bharathi Raja Chakravarthi. 2020. HopeEDI: A multilingual hope speech detection dataset for equality, diversity, and inclusion. In *Proceedings of the Third Workshop on Computational Modeling of People's Opinions, Personality, and Emotion's in Social Media*, pages 41–53, Barcelona, Spain (Online). Association for Computational Linguistics.

Bharathi Raja Chakravarthi. 2022a. Hope speech detection in youtube comments. *Social Network Analysis and Mining*, 12(1):75.

Bharathi Raja Chakravarthi. 2022b. Multilingual hope speech detection in english and dravidian languages. *International Journal of Data Science and Analytics*, 14(4):389–406.

Bharathi Raja Chakravarthi. 2023. Detection of homophobia and transphobia in youtube comments. *International Journal of Data Science and Analytics*, pages 1–20.

Bharathi Raja Chakravarthi, Manoj Balaji Jagadeeshan, Vasanth Palanikumar, and Ruba Priyadharshini. 2023a. Offensive language identification in dravidian languages using mpnet and cnn. *International Journal of Information Management Data Insights*, 3(1):100151.

Bharathi Raja Chakravarthi, Ruba Priyadharshini, Shubanker Banerjee, Manoj Balaji Jagadeeshan, Prasanna Kumar Kumaresan, Rahul Ponnusamy, Sean Benhur, and John Philip McCrae. 2023b. Detecting abusive comments at a fine-grained level in a low-resource language. *Natural Language Processing Journal*, 3:100006.

Subalalitha Chinnaudayar Navaneethakrishnan, Bharathi Raja Chakravarthi, Kogilavani Shanmugavadivel, Malliga Subramanian, Prasanna Kumar Kumaresan, Bharathi, Lavanya Sambath Kumar, and Rahul Ponnusamy. 2023. Findings of shared task on sentiment analysis and homophobia detection of youtube comments in code-mixed dravidian languages. In *Proceedings of the 14th Annual Meeting of the Forum for Information Retrieval*

Evaluation, FIRE '22, page 18–21, New York, NY, USA. Association for Computing Machinery.

Jacob Devlin, Ming-Wei Chang, Kenton Lee, and Kristina Toutanova. 2019. BERT: pre-training of deep bidirectional transformers for language understanding. In *Proceedings of the 2019 Conference of the North American Chapter of the Association for Computational Linguistics: Human Language Technologies, NAACL-HLT 2019, Minneapolis, MN, USA, June 2-7, 2019, Volume 1 (Long and Short Papers)*, pages 4171–4186. Association for Computational Linguistics.

Shagun Jhaver, Sucheta Ghoshal, Amy S. Bruckman, and Eric Gilbert. 2018. Online harassment and content moderation: The case of blocklists. *ACM Trans. Comput. Hum. Interact.*, 25(2):12:1–12:33.

Prasanna Kumar Kumaresan, Rahul Ponnusamy, Elizabeth Sherly, Sangeetha Sivanesan, and Bharathi Raja Chakravarthi. 2022. Transformer based hope speech comment classification in code-mixed text. In *International Conference on Speech and Language Technologies for Low-resource Languages*, pages 120–137. Springer.

Hariharan LekshmiAmmal, Manikandan Ravikiran, and Anand Kumar Madasamy. 2022. NITK-IT_NLP@TamilNLP-ACL2022: Transformer based model for toxic span identification in Tamil. In *Proceedings of the Second Workshop on Speech and Language Technologies for Dravidian Languages*, pages 75–78, Dublin, Ireland. Association for Computational Linguistics.

Mike Lewis, Yinhan Liu, Naman Goyal, Marjan Ghazvininejad, Abdelrahman Mohamed, Omer Levy, Veselin Stoyanov, and Luke Zettlemoyer. 2020. BART: Denoising sequence-to-sequence pre-training for natural language generation, translation, and comprehension. In *Proceedings of the 58th Annual Meeting of the Association for Computational Linguistics*, pages 7871–7880, Online. Association for Computational Linguistics.

John Pavlopoulos, Léo Laugier, Jeffrey Sorensen, and Ion Androutsopoulos. 2021. Semeval-2021 task 5: Toxic spans detection (to appear). In *Proceedings of the 15th International Workshop on Semantic Evaluation*.

Ruba Priyadharshini, Bharathi Raja Chakravarthi, Subalalitha Cn, Thenmozhi Durairaj, Malliga Subramanian, Kogilavani Shanmugavadivel, Siddhanth U Hegde, and Prasanna Kumaresan. 2022. Overview of abusive comment detection in Tamil-ACL 2022. In *Proceedings of the Second Workshop on Speech and Language Technologies for Dravidian Languages*, pages 292–298, Dublin, Ireland. Association for Computational Linguistics.

Ruba Priyadharshini, Bharathi Raja Chakravarthi, Mani Vegupatti, and John P McCrae. 2020. Named entity recognition for code-mixed Indian corpus using meta embedding. In *2020 6th international conference on advanced computing and communication systems (ICACCS)*, pages 68–72. IEEE.

Ratnavel Rajalakshmi, Mohit More, Bhamatipati Shrikriti, Gitansh Saharan, Hanchate Samyuktha, and Sayantan Nandy. 2022. DLRG@TamilNLP-ACL2022: Offensive span identification in Tamil usingBiLSTM-CRF approach. In *Proceedings of the Second Workshop on Speech and Language Technologies for Dravidian Languages*, pages 248–253, Dublin, Ireland. Association for Computational Linguistics.

Manikandan Ravikiran and Subbiah Annamalai. 2021. DOSA: Dravidian code-mixed offensive span identification dataset. In *Proceedings of the First Workshop on Speech and Language Technologies for Dravidian Languages*, pages 10–17, Kyiv. Association for Computational Linguistics.

Manikandan Ravikiran, Bharathi Raja Chakravarthi, Anand Kumar Madasamy, Sangeetha S, Ratnavel Rajalakshmi, Sajeetha Thavareesan, Rahul Ponnusamy, and Shankar Mahadevan. 2022. Findings of the shared task on offensive span identification fromCode-mixed Tamil-English comments. In *Proceedings of the Second Workshop on Speech and Language Technologies for Dravidian Languages*, pages 261–270, Dublin, Ireland. Association for Computational Linguistics.

Marco Túlio Ribeiro, Sameer Singh, and Carlos Guestrin. 2016. "why should I trust you?": Explaining the predictions of any classifier. In *Proceedings of the Demonstrations Session, NAACL HLT 2016, The 2016 Conference of the North American Chapter of the Association for Computational Linguistics: Human Language Technologies, San Diego California, USA, June 12-17, 2016*, pages 97–101. The Association for Computational Linguistics.

Ratnasingam Sakuntharaj and Sinnathamby Mahesan. 2016. A novel hybrid approach to detect and correct spelling in tamil text. In *2016 IEEE international conference on information and automation for sustainability (ICIAfS)*, pages 1–6. IEEE.

Ratnasingam Sakuntharaj and Sinnathamby Mahesan. 2017. Use of a novel hash-table for speeding-up suggestions for misspelt tamil words. In *2017 IEEE international conference on industrial and information systems (ICIIS)*, pages 1–5. IEEE.

Ratnasingam Sakuntharaj and Sinnathamby Mahesan. 2021. Missing word detection and correction based on context of tamil sentences using n-grams. In *2021 10th International Conference on Information and Automation for Sustainability (ICIAfS)*, pages 42–47. IEEE.

Sunayana Sitaram, Khyathi Raghavi Chandu, Sai Krishna Rallabandi, and A. Black. 2019. A survey of code-switched speech and language processing. *ArXiv*, abs/1904.00784.

R Sivanantham and M Seran. 2019. Keeladi: An urban settlement of sangam age on the banks of river vaigai. *India: Department of Archaeology, Government of Tamil Nadu, Chennai*.

C. N. Subalalitha. 2019a. Information extraction framework for Kurunthogai. *Sādhanā*, 44(7):156.

CN Subalalitha. 2019b. Information extraction framework for kurunthogai. *Sādhanā*, 44(7):156.

Malliga Subramanian, Rahul Ponnusamy, Sean Benhur, Kogilavani Shanmugavadivel, Adhithiya Ganesan, Deepti Ravi, Gowtham Krishnan Shanmugasundaram, Ruba Priyadharshini, and Bharathi Raja Chakravarthi. 2022. Offensive language detection in tamil youtube comments by adapters and cross-domain knowledge transfer. *Computer Speech & Language*, 76:101404.

Krithika Swaminathan, Bharathi B, Gayathri G L, and Hrishik Sampath. 2022. SSNCSE_NLP@LT-EDI-ACL2022: Homophobia/transphobia detection in multiple languages using SVM classifiers and BERT-based transformers. In *Proceedings of the Second Workshop on Language Technology for Equality, Diversity and Inclusion*, pages 239–244, Dublin, Ireland. Association for Computational Linguistics.

Sajeetha Thavareesan and Sinnathamby Mahesan. 2019. Sentiment analysis in tamil texts: A study on machine learning techniques and feature representation. In *2019 14th Conference on industrial and information systems (ICIIS)*, pages 320–325. IEEE.

Sajeetha Thavareesan and Sinnathamby Mahesan. 2020a. Sentiment lexicon expansion using word2vec and fasttext for sentiment prediction in tamil texts. In *2020 Moratuwa engineering research conference (MERCon)*, pages 272–276. IEEE.

Sajeetha Thavareesan and Sinnathamby Mahesan. 2020b. Word embedding-based part of speech tagging in tamil texts. In *2020 IEEE 15th International conference on industrial and information systems (ICIIS)*, pages 478–482. IEEE.

Overview of the shared task on Fake News Detection from Social Media Text

Malliga Subramanian[1], **Bharathi Raja Chakravarthi**[2],
Kogilavani Shanmugavadivel[1], **Santhiya Pandiyan**[1],
Prasanna Kumar Kumaresan[2], **Balasubramanian Palani**[3], **Muskaan Singh**[4],
Sandhiya Raja[1], **Vanaja**[1], **Mithunajha S**[1]
[1]Kongu Engineering College, Tamil Nadu, India
[2]Insight SFI Research Centre for Data Analytics, School of Computer Science, University of Galway, Ireland
[3]Indian Institute of Information Technology, Kottayam, India
[4]Ulster University, UK
mallinishanth72@gmail.com

Abstract

The rapid proliferation of fake news has emerged as a significant challenge to the credibility of online information, largely due to the swift dissemination of content on social media platforms. This article provides a concise summary of the findings of the shared task on "Fake News Detection in Dravidian Languages[1] - DravidianLangTech@RANLP 2023". The aim of this shared task is to categorize social media posts as either fake or original, specifically focusing on content in Malayalam. The shared task garnered participation from 8 teams who presented their systems. These systems encompassed a spectrum of methodologies including machine learning techniques and transformer-based models like MuRIL, XLMRoBERTa, and Indic BERT. Notably, the XLMRoBERTa-based model demonstrated exceptional performance, achieving a macro F1-score of 0.90.

1 Introduction

Online social network (OSN) platforms such as Twitter, Facebook, WhatsApp, and Instagram are extensively used by millions of users in this modern internet era to publish and spread the news about emergent events to many people more quickly and without any validation or verification. According to the (Pennycook, 2020) the core ideas in cascading news and sensitive information are ingrained in truth notions and communication accuracy theories. According to a recent statistics report given in statistica 2023[2], Facebook has 2.96 billion monthly active users, while the count for Twitter has reached 556 million monthly active users, whereas WhatsApp, as well as Instagram, have more than 2 billion active users 1. A vast amount of news is shared and propagated among socially connected network users without knowing the authenticity of the news during the election campaign, trending events, and pandemic emergencies. Misinformation creators are intentionally flooding falsified and unverified information for various political and commercial purposes. Hence, a significant amount of misinformation and false news has proliferated over OSNs, negatively influencing readers, and causing numerous negative consequences on the economy, politics, and social security. Therefore, fake news detection (FND) is demanding in the current scenario. In (Pennycook et al., 2020) the authors identified primary methods currently available to spot false news and how these methods might be used in various contexts by conducting a systematic literature review. A pertinent example, the difficulties, and the ideal setting in which to use a certain technique are all provided for some approaches.

In general, FND methods can be categorized into two types: social context-based and content-based methods as shown in Figure 1. The former is more concerned with the user engagement data such as comments, reposts, and ratings, while the latter is associated with the article's news content like title, text, image, and video (Shu et al., 2017). The social context-based methods can be further divided into two categories: propagation structure-based and post-based methods. The propagation structure-based methods concentrate on propagation patterns or trends of fake news on social networks, while post-based methods examine the opinions or emotions expressed by the users in their posts. Due to the unstructured nature of the data, these two types of social-context techniques face

[1]https://codalab.lisn.upsaclay.fr/competitions/11176
[2]https://shorturl.at/dloDF

Third Workshop on Speech and Language Technologies for Dravidian Languages, pages 59–63, Varna, Bulgaria, Sep 7, 2023.
https://doi.org/10.26615/978-954-452-085-4_008

the following challenges: data collection and analysis, noisy data, and missing data. Hence, the focus of this shared task is on content-based strategy. The Content-based methods are more straightforward and convenient to detect fake news, particularly at an early stage.

Transfer learning-based FND system is introduced in (Palani and Elango, 2023a) According to their perspective, BERT is a bidirectional language model since it considers the context of both a word's left and right sides. In contrast, GPT and ELMo are only trained in the right-to-left context and the left-to-right context, respectively. The local contextual features over space and the global semantic relation features over time are then extracted in the feature representation layer using multichannel CNN and stacked BiLSTM. The model may learn many characteristics from several viewpoints using a multichannel CNN. The model's various channels each extract features from the same input in their own unique ways, producing a more reliable representation(Shanmugavadivel et al., 2022).

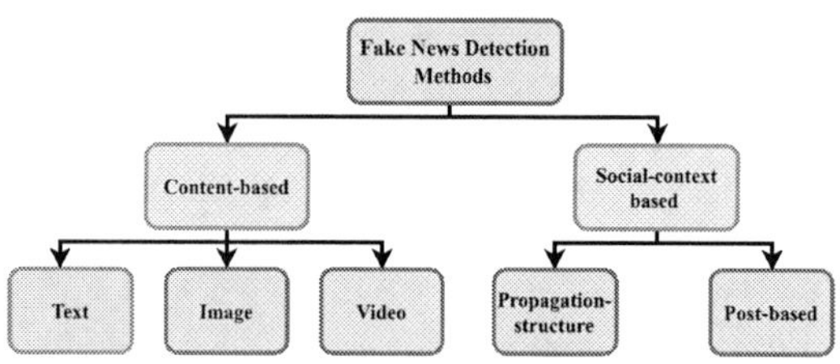

Figure 1: Categorization of FND methods

In (Ahmad et al., 2020), the authors applied machine learning-based ensemble methods with the help of textual properties to distinguish fake news from the original one.

2 Related Work

The researchers used pre-trained language models such as BERT, and RoBERTa for contextual word embedding and then used DL-based models to detect fake news. In (Palani and Elango, 2023b), authors present the DL-based FND framework in which RoBERTa and FFN are used to extract contextual dependent features and to detect fake news respectively. Similar to FND there are numerous works published such as Hope speech detection (Chakravarthi et al., 2022a) and Homophobia, Transphobia Detection (Chakravarthi et al., 2022b) in social media posts. The author in (Chakravarthi, 2022) employs a DL-based hope speech detection model in which T5-sentence and Indic-BERT are used for word embedding to capture the contextual relationship among words. Then the contextual features are sent as input to CNN to detect the hope speech comments(Subramanian et al., 2022). The proposed model's performance is evaluated on a multilingual dataset named HopeEDI which is introduced in the shared task 2021 (Chakravarthi, 2020).

Dhivya (Chinnappa, 2021) proposed a two-stage hope detection process in which the language detector identifies the language of the model, and the hope detector classifies the text into hope speech, non-hope speech, or not lang. The various pre-trained language models and DL-based models are proposed, and their performance is evaluated on three hope speech datasets in English, Tamil, and Malayalam.

3 Task Description

The task aims to identify fake news from the posts or comments in Dravidian Languages such as Malayalam which is collected from the YouTube OSN. Each comment/post is annotated at the comment/post level and assigned the class labels fake or real.

4 Dataset Description

The dataset is balanced since the number of samples in fake and real classes is almost nearer. The dataset contains a total of 5,091 comments of which 2,512 are fake news and 2,579 are real news. The dataset is split into training, validation, and testing. The detail of the dataset is shown in Table 1.

Table 1: Summary of the dataset

Dataset	Fake News	Real News	Total
Training	1,599	1,658	3,257
Validation	406	409	815
Testing	507	512	1,019
Total	2,512	2,579	5,091

5 Methodology

In this shared task, there are eight teams actively participated and implemented their models. They evaluated their model's performance on our fake news dataset.

DeepBlueAI (Luo and Wang, 2023): Team DeepBlueAI used a pre-trained language model such as XLM-RoBERTa to identify fake news. The authors employed the XLM-RoBERTa model to extract the context-aware features from the textual news. Then the contextual feature vector is sent as input to the fully connected layer with softmax to classify fake or real news. Their model achieves an F1-score of 0.90 in this task.

AbhiPaw (Bala and Krishnamurthy, 2023): Team AbhiPaw_ ABHi presented a Multilingual Representations for Indian Languages (MuRIL) for FND. The F1-score of 0.87 is achieved with their proposed model.

NITK-IT-NLP (R L and Kumar M, 2023): Team NITK-IT-NLP used a multilingual version of the transformer-based MuRIL model for developing the FND system. They also introduced focal loss as the loss function while training the model. The model achieves the F1-score of 0.87 for FND.

NLPT (Raja et al., 2023): Team NLPT_Malayalam employed a pre-trained language model called XLM-RoBERTa for FND. The proposed model achieves an F1-score of 0.87 which is better than the ML-based models. The reasons for the improvement are a self-attention mechanism of transformers, a byte-level BPE, and a dynamic masking pattern during training.

MUCS (Sharal Coelho and Shashirekha, 2023): Team MUCS proposed TF-IDF to convert words into vectors based on the occurrence of the words. The extracted features of TF-IDF are passed as input to the different ML-based classifiers to predict the given news as fake or real. The model achieves the F1-score of 0.83 for FND.

ML_AI_IIITRanchi (Kumari et al., 2023): Team ML_AI_IIITRanchi proposed an ensemble ML-based FND system which uses Bag-of-words and Indic BERT for the textual features extraction. Then, ensemble ML-based classifiers such as Random Forest (RF) and AdaBoost are employed to detect the fake news. The F1-score of 0.78 is achieved with their proposed model for FND. DLRG_RR: Team DLRG_RR presents the ML-based FND system in which TF-IDF is used to transform the words into vectors and Passive Aggressive Classifier (PAC) is adopted for FND. Their model achieves the F1-score of 0.73.

NLP_SSN_CSE (Balaji et al., 2023): Team NLP_SSN_CSE employed various pre-trained transformer-based language models, such as BERT, ALBERT, and XLNET for FND. These models are effective in extracting the contextual relationships within the text which lead to improved accuracy in FND tasks for the Malayalam language. Self-attention mechanism captures the most relevant features from the text to detect fake news. The precision, recall, and F1 measure are around 0.75, indicating a balanced performance in identifying both real and fake news. The accuracy of 0.75 suggests the model's ability to make correct predictions overall.

6 Results and Discussions

The performance assessment of the proposed models by the participating teams was conducted using the macro F1 score metric, which is a widely used measure for evaluating classification models. The results of this evaluation are presented in Table 2 below, showcasing the ranking of the teams that took part in the collaborative task. In total, eight teams submitted their respective solutions for evaluation.

Securing the top position, the team "DeepBlueAI" which achieved the first rank demonstrated an impressive macro F1 score of 0.90. Their accomplishment was attributed to the adept utilization of the XLM-RoBERTa model. This pre-trained transformer model was fine-tuned by the team's authors to effectively discern fake comments. This achievement underscores the efficacy of leveraging powerful transformer-based architectures for addressing the task.

Moving on, teams ranked 2nd, 3rd, and 4th garnered identical macro F1 scores of 0.87, highlighting their consistent performance. Among these, the team "AbhiPaw," positioned at the 2nd rank, strategically employed the Multilingual Representations for Indian Languages (MuRIL) model. While MuRIL was primarily designed as a multilingual language model for Indian languages, the team harnessed its potential for the classification task. This innovative approach signifies the adaptability of pre-trained models across diverse downstream applications.

In the lower rankings, the last two teams, securing the 7th and 8th positions, achieved a macro F1 score of 0.73. Their methodology involved the implementation of the Passive Aggressive Classifier (PAC) coupled with the feature weighting technique known as Term Frequency-Inverse Document Frequency (TF-IDF). The teams meticulously experimented with various configurations of the maximum document frequency parameter in the

Table 2: Rank list for Malayalam task

S.No.	Team Name	Macro F1	Rank
1	DeepBlueAI(Luo and Wang, 2023)	0.90	1
2	AbhiPaw(Bala and Krishnamurthy, 2023)	0.87	2
3	NITK-iIT-NLP(R L and Kumar M, 2023)	0.87	2
4	NLPT(Raja et al., 2023)	0.87	2
5	MUCS(Sharal Coelho and Shashirekha, 2023)	0.83	3
6	ML_AI_IIITRanch(Kumari et al., 2023)	0.78	4
7	DLRG_RR	0.73	5
8	NLP_SSN_CSE(Balaji et al., 2023)	0.73	5

Tfidfvectorizer, leading to their placement at the 7th rank. Similarly, the team "NLP_SSN_CSE," positioned at rank 8, employed a similar approach, utilizing an array of pre-trained transformer models like BERT, ALBERT, XLNet, and mBERT. Despite their diverse model ensemble, their performance closely aligned with the team ranked 7th.

Overall, the ranking table provides a comprehensive overview of the distinct strategies and models adopted by each participating team. This evaluation sheds light on the varying degrees of success achieved by exploiting transformer-based models, language-specific architectures, and traditional classification techniques, all contributing to the advancement of fake news detection.

7 Conclusion

This paper presents an overview of the fake news detection shared task conducted at DravidianLangTech-RANLP 2023, specifically focusing on the Malayalam language. The task garnered participation from eight teams, each submitting predictions for evaluation. The methods employed by these teams varied, spanning from traditional TF-IDF vectorizers with machine learning to contemporary pre-trained transformer models for data representation. An analysis of the methodologies revealed a consistent trend: transformer-based methods outperformed other techniques, as indicated by evaluation metrics such as classification accuracy and confusion matrices. This suggests the potency of transformer models in effectively capturing fake news detection performance. In summary, the paper summarizes the DravidianLangTech 2023 fake news detection shared task for Malayalam, highlighting diverse strategies, and underscoring the prevalence of transformer-based methods for improved performance.

Acknowledgments

The author Bharathi Raja Chakravarthi was supported in part by a research grant from Science Foundation Ireland (SFI) under Grant Number SFI/12/RC/2289_P2(Insight_2).

References

Iftikhar Ahmad, Muhammad Yousaf, Suhail Yousaf, and Muhammad Ovais Ahmad. 2020. Fake news detection using machine learning ensemble methods. *Complexity*, 2020:1–11.

Abhinaba Bala and Parameswari Krishnamurthy. 2023. Abhipaw @ fake news detection in dravidian languages-dravidianlangtech@ranlp 2023. In *Proceedings of the Third Workshop on Speech and Language Technologies for Dravidian Languages*, Varna, Bulgaria. Recent Advances in Natural Language Processing.

Varsha Balaji, Shahul Hameed T, and Bharathi B. 2023. Nlp_ssn_cse@dravidianlangtech-ranlp 2023: Fake news detection in dravidian languages using transformer models. In *Proceedings of the Third Workshop on Speech and Language Technologies for Dravidian Languages*, Varna, Bulgaria. Recent Advances in Natural Language Processing.

Bharathi Raja Chakravarthi. 2020. Hopeedi: A multilingual hope speech detection dataset for equality, diversity, and inclusion. In *Proceedings of the Third Workshop on Computational Modeling of People's Opinions, Personality, and Emotion's in Social Media*, pages 41–53.

Bharathi Raja Chakravarthi. 2022. Hope speech detection in youtube comments. *Social Network Analysis and Mining*, 12(1):75.

Bharathi Raja Chakravarthi, Vigneshwaran Muralidaran, Ruba Priyadharshini, Subalalitha Cn, John Philip McCrae, Miguel Ángel García, Salud María Jiménez-Zafra, Rafael Valencia-García, Prasanna Kumaresan, Rahul Ponnusamy, et al. 2022a. Overview of the shared task on hope speech detection for equality, diversity, and inclusion. In *Proceedings of the second workshop on language technology for equality, diversity and inclusion*, pages 378–388.

Bharathi Raja Chakravarthi, Ruba Priyadharshini, Thenmozhi Durairaj, John Philip McCrae, Paul Buitelaar, Prasanna Kumaresan, and Rahul Ponnusamy. 2022b. Overview of the shared task on homophobia and transphobia detection in social media comments. In *Proceedings of the Second Workshop on Language Technology for Equality, Diversity and Inclusion*, pages 369–377.

Dhivya Chinnappa. 2021. dhivya-hope-detection@ lt-edi-eacl2021: multilingual hope speech detection for code-mixed and transliterated texts. In *Proceedings of the First Workshop on Language Technology for Equality, Diversity and Inclusion*, pages 73–78.

Kirti Kumari, Shirish Shekhar Jha, Zarikunte Kunal Dayanand, and Praneesh Sharma. 2023. Ml&ai_iiitranchi@dravidianlangtech-ranlp 2023:leveraging transfer learning for the discernment of fake news within the linguistic domain of dravidian language. In *Proceedings of the Third Workshop on Speech and Language Technologies for Dravidian Languages*, Varna, Bulgaria. Recent Advances in Natural Language Processing.

Zhipeng Luo and Jiahui Wang. 2023. Deepblueai@dravidianlangtech-ranlp 2023. In *Proceedings of the Third Workshop on Speech and Language Technologies for Dravidian Languages*, Varna, Bulgaria. Recent Advances in Natural Language Processing.

Balasubramanian Palani and Sivasankar Elango. 2023a. Bbc-fnd: An ensemble of deep learning framework for textual fake news detection. *Computers and Electrical Engineering*, 110:108866.

Balasubramanian Palani and Sivasankar Elango. 2023b. Ctrl-fnd: content-based transfer learning approach for fake news detection on social media. *International Journal of System Assurance Engineering and Management*, 14(3):903–918.

Gordon Pennycook, Jonathon McPhetres, Yunhao Zhang, Jackson G Lu, and David G Rand. 2020. Fighting covid-19 misinformation on social media: Experimental evidence for a scalable accuracy-nudge intervention. *Psychological science*, 31(7):770–780.

McPhetres J. Zhang Y. Lu J. G. Rand D. G. Pennycook, G. 2020. Fighting covid-19 misinformation on social media: Experimental evidence for a scalable accuracy-nudge intervention. *Psychological Science*, 31(7):770–780.

Hariharan R L and Anand Kumar M. 2023. Nitk-it-nlp@dravidianlangtech-ranlp 2023: Impact of focal loss on malayalam fake news detection using transformers. In *Proceedings of the Third Workshop on Speech and Language Technologies for Dravidian Languages*, Varna, Bulgaria. Recent Advances in Natural Language Processing.

Eduri Raja, Badal Soni, and Sami Kumar Borgohain. 2023. nlpt malayalm@dravidianlangtech : Fake news detection in malayalam using optimized xlm-roberta model. In *Proceedings of the Third Workshop on Speech and Language Technologies for Dravidian Languages*, Varna, Bulgaria. Recent Advances in Natural Language Processing.

Kogilavani Shanmugavadivel, Sai Haritha Sampath, Pramod Nandhakumar, Prasath Mahalingam, Malliga Subramanian, Prasanna Kumar Kumaresan, and Ruba Priyadharshini. 2022. An analysis of machine learning models for sentiment analysis of tamil code-mixed data. *Computer Speech & Language*, 76:101407.

Kavya G Sharal Coelho, Asha Hegde and Hosahalli Lakshmaiah Shashirekha. 2023. Mucs@dravidianlangtech2023: Malayalam fake news detection using machine learning approach. In *Proceedings of the Third Workshop on Speech and Language Technologies for Dravidian Languages*, Varna, Bulgaria. Recent Advances in Natural Language Processing.

Kai Shu, Amy Sliva, Suhang Wang, Jiliang Tang, and Huan Liu. 2017. Fake news detection on social media: A data mining perspective. *ACM SIGKDD explorations newsletter*, 19(1):22–36.

Malliga Subramanian, Ramya Chinnasamy, Prasanna Kumar Kumaresan, Vasanth Palanikumar, Madhoora Mohan, and Kogilavani Shanmugavadivel. 2022. Development of multi-lingual models for detecting hope speech texts from social media comments. In *International Conference on Speech and Language Technologies for Low-resource Languages*, pages 209–219. Springer.

Findings of the Shared Task on Sentiment Analysis in Tamil and Tulu Code-Mixed Text

Asha Hegde[1], Bharathi Raja Chakravarthi[2], Hosahalli Lakshmaiah Shashirekha[1], Rahul Ponnusamy[2], Subalalitha Chinnaudayar Navaneethakrishnan[3], Lavanya Sambath Kumar[4], Durairaj Thenmozhi[5], Martha Karunakar[5], Shreya Sriram[5], Sarah Aymen[5]

[1]Department of Computer Science, Mangalore University, Mangalore, India
[2]National University of Ireland Galway, Ireland
[3]SRM Institute of Science And Technology, Tamil Nadu
[4]Madras Institute of Technology, Tamil Nadu, [5]SSN College of Engineering, Tamil Nadu
bharathiraja.akr@gmail.com

Abstract

In recent years, there has been a growing focus on Sentiment Analysis (SA) of code-mixed Dravidian languages. Despite this, there is currently lack of research on SA specifically tailored for code-mixed Dravidian languages, highlighting the need for further exploration and development in this domain. In this view, "Sentiment Analysis in Tamil and Tulu - DravidianLangTech" shared task at Recent Advances in Natural Language Processing (RANLP) - 2023 is organized. This shared task consists two language tracks: code-mixed Tamil and Tulu texts. Tulu text is first ever explored in public domain for SA in this shared task. Fifty seven research teams registered for the shared task and we received 27 systems each for code-mixed Tamil and Tulu texts. The performance of the systems (developed by participants) has been evaluated in terms of macro average F1 score. The top system for code-mixed Tamil and Tulu texts scored macro average F1 scores of 0.32, and 0.542 respectively. The high quality and substantial quantity of submissions demonstrate a significant interest and attention in the analysis of code-mixed Dravidian languages like Tamil and Tulu.

1 Introduction

Sentiment Analysis (SA) is a task to understand how people perceive and react to a particular topic, and it has gained significant attention in both academic and industrial settings over the past two decades. On social media, SA provides insights into the opinions and emotions expressed by individuals towards a brand or product online, or a video, movie, or an incident (Chakravarthi et al., 2022). The field of SA has evolved to encompass the collection and analysis of data from social media posts, allowing organizations to gain a comprehensive understanding of public sentiment towards their brand. By utilizing SA techniques, companies can gauge the overall perception of their brand, identify positive or negative sentiments, and make informed decisions about marketing strategies or customer relationship management. Unlike a simple examination of mentions or comments, SA delves deeper into the sentiments and evaluations conveyed in terms of posts shared by people on various social media platforms (Chakravarthi et al., 2020c).

One specific challenge in SA on social media is dealing with code-mixed texts. Code-mixing is a common occurrence in multilingual communities, where individuals blend words, morphemes, and phrases from two or more languages in their speech or writing (Kachru, 1978; Bali et al., 2014). This phenomenon poses a challenge for SA systems, particularly when they are written in non-native scripts, such as using roman characters to represent languages that traditionally use different scripts (Hegde and Shashirekha, 2022). The complexity arises from the presence of code-switching at various linguistic levels, including phonological, lexical, and syntactic aspects of the text. These intricate language patterns make it difficult for SA models trained on monolingual data to accurately interpret the sentiments expressed in code-mixed texts.

The demand for SA on social media texts, particularly those that are code-mixed, has been on the rise. Companies recognize the importance of understanding the sentiments and opinions expressed in diverse linguistic contexts, as it enables them to cater to a broader range of customers and tailor their marketing strategies accordingly. Researchers and practitioners continue to develop and refine SA techniques to effectively handle code-mixed texts and provide accurate SA results in multilingual settings Balouchzahi and Shashirekha (2020). To effectively analyze sentiment in code-mixed texts, specialized techniques and models need to be de-

Third Workshop on Speech and Language Technologies for Dravidian Languages, pages 64–71, Varna, Bulgaria, Sep 7, 2023.
https://doi.org/10.26615/978-954-452-085-4_009

veloped. These approaches should consider the unique linguistic characteristics of code-mixing, including the mixing of different languages, the potential shifts in sentiment across languages, and the context-dependent nature of sentiment interpretation Chakravarthi et al. (2020a). Researchers and practitioners are actively working on improving SA systems to handle code-mixed data, as the prevalence of code-mixing on social media and other online platforms continues to grow Chakravarthi et al. (2021).

This shared task introduces two gold standard corpora for SA of code-mixed text in Dravidian languages, namely Tamil-English and Tulu-Kannada-English. The corpora serve as a valuable resource for researchers and practitioners working on SA in multilingual contexts, allowing them to develop and evaluate models that can effectively handle code-mixed data in these specific language pairs. The objective of this task is to determine the sentiment polarity of code-mixed comments/posts in Tamil-English and Tulu-Kannada-English, sourced from social media. This dataset includes annotations of sentiment polarity at the comment/post level, aiming to identify whether the sentiment expressed is 'Positive', 'Negative', 'Neutral', or 'Mixed Feeling'. The training and development sets contain 33,989 and 3,786 sentences for Tamil, and 6,458 and 781 sentences for Tulu, respectively. Further details regarding the dataset annotation can be found in references Chakravarthi et al. (2020b) and Hegde et al. (2022a).

Tamil - is the first language considered as one of the longest surviving classical languages in India Subalalitha (2019); Srinivasan and Subalalitha (2019). It is a scheduled language under the Indian constitution and official language of the Indian states of Tamil Nadu and Puducherry. In addition, it is considered as one of the national languages of Singapore and SriLanka. Tamil is spoken by sizable minority in four more south Indian states, in addition to Kerala, Karnataka, Andhra Pradesh, Telangana, and the Union Territory of Andaman and Nicobar Islands. The Tamil Nadu State Department of Archaeology and Archaeological Survey of India has recorded first Tamil script in 580 BCE on pottery from Keezhadi, Sivagangai, and Madurai districts of Tamil Nadu, India Sivanantham and Seran (2019). Tamil script is known as Tamili or Tamil-Brahmi and it consists of 18 consonants, 12 vowels, and 216 compound letters followed by a special character Hewavitharana and Fernando (2002); Hegde et al. (2022b).

Tulu - is a prominent Dravidian language spoken by approximately 2.5 million individuals primarily in the Dakshina Kannada and Udupi districts of Karnataka, as well as some parts of Kasaragod in Kerala. It holds great significance as the mother tongue for its speakers, who have made significant contributions to Karnataka's cultural history and, in turn, to Indian culture as a whole. Tulu retains several features of ancient Dravidian languages while also introducing innovations not found in other Dravidian languages Padmanabha Kekunnaya. It utilizes its own script called Tigalari, derived from the Grantha script, which is no longer in use. The Tulu script consists of 52 letters, including 16 vowels and 36 consonants Antony et al. (2012); Hegde et al. (2022c).

2 Task Description

Sentiment analysis in Tamil and Tulu aims to determine the sentiment polarity of social media comments and posts that are written in both Tamil-English and Tulu-English. The following schema was used to annotate the data for sentiments.

- Positive state: The text contains an explicit or implicit signal that the speaker is in a positive state, such as content, appreciative, at ease, and forgiving.
- Negative state: The language contains a clue that indicates the speaker is in a negative state, such as sad, angry, nervous, or violent.
- Mixed Feeling: The sentence contains a clue, either explicitly or implicitly, indicating the speaker is having both good and bad feelings.
- Neutral/unknown state: The text does not contain any explicit or implicit clue of the speaker's feelings.

To aid in improved understanding, the text was translated into Tamil and Tulu and sent to the annotators. A minimum of three annotators contributed to each sentence's annotation.

Sentiment analysis in Tamil and Tulu task involves polarity categorization at the message level. Systems must categorize a YouTube comment into one of the four classes: positive, negative, neutral, or mixed emotions for Tamil-English dataset and positive, negative, unknown, or mixed emotions for Tulu-English dataset. Our datasets include code-switching at three different levels: tag, intra-sentential, and inter-sentential. The comments for the Tamil-English dataset were typed in Roman characters using either Tamil vocabulary and English grammar, or vice versa. Similar to this, comments from the Tulu-English dataset were typed in Roman characters using either Tulu or English grammar and lexicon. The following Tamil-English dataset samples show how this scripting pattern is used.

- Hotel vechu govrama vaalra thirunangaigalum irukaanga.ithu pondra theru porukki kalum irukaanga.-*There are trans women who live with respect by owning hotel. There are street vendors like this.* Tag switching with English words.
- 5rs kudutha pogamatamga 10 or 20 kuduka sollu thittuvaanga ! Idhukku Peru dha vazhipari. - *If we give 5 rupees they won't leave they will scold to give 10 or 20 rupees. This is what named as robbery.* Tamil words written in Roman script with no English switch.
- Hello eallarum apadi illa. nanum tirunagai than. nalaiku si exam elutha poren. tnpsc grp 2 eluthiruken. theriyama ellarum ore mathiri nu ninaikathinga - *Everybody is not like this.I am also a trans woman. Tomorrow going to write SI exam. Written TNPSC group 2 exam. Without knowing do not think like this.*. Inter-sentential switch
- True i didn't give single Paisa to this people. - *True I didn't give single paise to these people.* Intra-sentential switch between clauses.

The following Tulu-English dataset samples show how this scripting pattern is used.

- ayyo encha la onji love letter unda- *Oh is there a love letter like this.* -Tag switching with English words.
- Aye dayeg mandde kanatha patherunu - *Why he is talking like a mad-* Tulu words written in Roman script with no English switch.
- Super Arpit Anna picture tuvodunde ejji devere Mande haal and Kali review tude - *Super Arpith brother, no need to see the picture. Oh God by seeing the review itself mind got ruined.* Intra-sentential switch
- masth edde ithand. super brother. - *It was very nice. Super brother.* Inter-sentential switch between clauses.

3 Related work

A 3-parallel Long Short Term Memory (LSTM) architecture which takes random, Word2Vec and random character embeddings to categorize sentiment of Dravidian code-mixed YouTube comments was implemented by Mishra et al. (2021). They obtained 15th, 12th, and 12th positions respectively for Tamil, Malayalam, and Kannada datasets. SR et al. (2022) experimented with Kernel based Extreme Learning Machines (ELM) for sentiment analysis. They concluded that Polynomial kernels works best in the ELM architecture for Code-Switched Dravidian Languages.
A deep learning-based framework using Bidirectional-LSTM (Bi-LSTM) was proposed by Roy and Kumar (2021) to extract the features from input sentences and classify the sentiment in code-mixed languages. Shanmugavadivel et al. (2022) proposed sentiment analysis and offensive language identification on multilingual code-mixed data. They worked on extraction of semantically meaningful information from code-mixed data using word embedding for sentiment classification. Yadav and Chakraborty (2021) proposed an unsupervised method for Sentiment Analysis of Code-mixed Data. They employed multilingual and cross-lingual embeddings of monolingual text to find the sentiment in code-mixed text. Clustering of Tamil text with and with-out considering class-wise information for sentiment analysis was proposed by Thavareesan and Mahesan (2021). They tested by varying number of centroids in k-means clustering and k-nearest neighbour classifier. They achieved better results using FastText embeddings when compared to Bag Of Words (BOW) embeddings.

4 Methodology

We received a total of 27 submissions for both Tamil and Tulu. The systems were evaluated based on macro average F1 scores and a rank list was prepared. Table 1 and Table 2 show the rank lists of code-mixed Tamil and Tulu texts respectively. We briefly describe below the methodologies used by the top five teams.

- DeepBlueAI (Luo and Wang, 2023): The authors fine-tuned XLM-RoBERTa, a pre-trained multilingual language model, as the base model and they also combined various language datasets in different proportions.

Team name	Macro F1 score	Rank
DeepBlueAI (Luo and Wang, 2023)	0.32	1
MUNLP (G et al., 2023)	0.269	2
Poorvi (Shetty, 2023)	0.268	3
AK-NLP	0.242	4
AlphaBrains (Ehsan et al., 2023)	0.215	5
Habesha (Yigezu et al., 2023)	0.208	6
lidoma (Tash et al., 2023)	0.199	7
MUCSD (Coelho et al., 2023)	0.19	8
TU-PM	0.18	9
selam (Kanta, 2023)	0.147	10
AbhiPaw	0.143	11
Team-Tamil (Ponnusamy et al., 2023)	0.142	12
MUCS (Kulal et al., 2023)	0.141	13
ML&AI_IIITRanchi (Kumari et al., 2023)	0.124	14
Muhammad	0.12	15

Table 1: Rank list based on macro average F1 score for code-mixed Tamil text

Team name	Macro F1 score	Rank
DeepBlueAI (Luo and Wang, 2023)	0.542	1
MUNLP (G et al., 2023)	0.533	2
TU-PM	0.529	3
AK-NLP	0.523	4
AlphaBrains (Ehsan et al., 2023)	0.522	5
selam (Kanta, 2023)	0.518	6
lidoma (Tash et al., 2023)	0.516	7
Muhammad	0.514	8
MUCSD (Coelho et al., 2023)	0.508	9
L&AI_IIITRanc (Kumari et al., 2023)	0.471	10
AbhiPaw	0.442	11
Team-Tamil (Ponnusamy et al., 2023)	0.442	12
Habeesha (Yigezu et al., 2023)	0.352	13
Poorvi (Shetty, 2023)	0.268	14
MUCS (Kulal et al., 2023)	0.204	15

Table 2: Rank list based on macro average F1 score for code-mixed Tulu text

They also used cross-validation to assess the performance and generalization of the fine-tuned model across multiple languages. They achieved the best macro F1 scores for both Tamil and Tulu code-mixed text securing the 1st place in the shared task.

- MUNLP (G et al., 2023): This team used two distinct approaches for Tamil and Tulu code-mixed texts. They fine-tuned Tamil sentiment BERT with the oversampled train data for Tamil. Whereas, for Tulu, they combined FastText pre-trained word embeddings with Tulu byte pair embeddings to train LinearSVC model. Their system achieved Rank 2 for both Tamil and Tulu.

- Poorvi (Shetty, 2023): Authors trained ensemble of ML (LinearSVC, Random Forest, MultinomialNB, and Logistic Regression) classifiers considering TF-IDF of n-grams in the range n = (1, 2). Their model secured 3rd and 14th ranks for Tamil and Tulu respectively.

- AK-NLP: This team trained LSTM model fed with TF-IDF features for both code-mixed Tamil and Tulu texts. They achieved Rank 4 for both Tamil and Tulu.

- TU-PM: Authors fine-tuned XLM-RoBERTa-base for both code-mixed Tamil and Tulu. Their proposed models achieved 3rd and 9th ranks for Tulu and Tamil code-mixed texts.

- AlphaBrains (Ehsan et al., 2023): Using trainsliteration, this team augmented the existing Tamil and Tulu text before training their proposed models. They used TL by training character based contextualized ELMO representations for both Tamil and Tulu. Their proposed models secured 5th rank for both Tamil and Tulu code-mixed texts.

5 Evaluation

The distribution of the sentiment classes are imbalanced in both the datasets. In the Tamil code-mixed dataset, we have a class imbalance with the majority of comments belonging to Positive (20,070) class. Similarly, the Tulu code-mixed dataset has class imbalance with Positive (3,118) and Neutral (1,719) being the majority classes.

To address class imbalance, we utilized the macro average F1 score for ranking the systems. Macro F1 scores are often used in evaluating models trained on imbalanced data because they provide a balanced assessment of model performance across all classes, regardless of class distribution. In imbalanced datasets, accuracy alone can be misleading, as a model may achieve high accuracy by simply predicting the majority class. By using the macro average F1 score, equal importance is given to each class, making it a suitable metric to evaluate model performance in scenarios where class imbalances exist. This score is computed by averaging the F1 scores of each class in the multi-class classification problem. To facilitate this calculation, we leveraged the classification report tool from Scikit-learn[1], which provided comprehensive metrics and insights for evaluating the performance of the systems.

$$Precision = \frac{TP}{TP + FP} \quad (1)$$

$$Recall = \frac{TP}{TP + FN} \quad (2)$$

$$F1score = 2 * \frac{Precision * Recall}{Precision + Recall} \quad (3)$$

6 Results and Discussion

The sentiment analysis shared task focused on two languages: code-mixed Tamil and Tulu. A total of 57 participants registered for the shared task, out of which 27 teams submitted their systems for both Tamil and Tulu language tracks. Table 1 and Table 2 present the rank lists for Tamil and Tulu languages respectively, showcasing the performance of the submitted systems. It is worth noting that the majority of submissions were designed to handle SA for both languages, as indicated earlier. In this section, we present the top-ranked results for both the languages based on the macro average F1 scores. The rankings reflect the performance of the systems on the dataset, with the top positions indicating the highest macro average F1 scores across all classes.

Teams have commonly employed transformer-based models like XLM-RoBERTa, Tamil sentiment BERT, DeBERTa-Large, MuRIL, and IndicBERT, even though these models were not originally pre-trained on code-mixed text. In addition, some teams have also experimented with pre-trained word embeddings like FastText and BPEmb.

[1]Macro F1 score

Using these linguistic representations, a range of machine learning (ML) models including SVM, k-NN, MLP, OneVsRest, XGB, and GradientBoosting, as well as deep learning (DL) models such as CNN and LSTM, have been explored. These models are often combined with TF-IDF representations of word or character n-grams to effectively address the challenges of code-mixed text processing.

Participants encountered challenges in working with code-mixed text due to the inclusion of non-native script in our corpus. To address this, they acquired pre-trained models from libraries and fine-tuned them for our corpora. However, the availability of resources for Tulu code-mixed text is limited in comparison to Tamil. This scarcity prompted participants to take initiatives in resource generation and training pre-trained models from scratch. Given the data imbalance in the dataset, participants opted to employ resampling techniques like SMOTE to mitigate this imbalance effectively.

Despite efforts, both LSTM and traditional ML algorithms fell short in delivering satisfactory results when contrasted with transformer-based models. Notably, among the various models tested, XLM-RoBERTa and the transformer-based architecture demonstrated the most promising performance. Even though several systems and approaches had F1 scores that were below the average, we accepted those articles in an effort to promote the use of a variety of research techniques to address the issue in Dravidian languages. Most of the submissions in working notes provided comprehensive insights into class-specific precision, recall, and F1 scores. The primary evaluation metric utilized was the weighted F1 score, enabling a comprehensive assessment of model effectiveness.

7 Conclusion

We present the results of the SA shared task on code-mixed Tamil and Tulu text. The dataset utilized in the shared task consisted of code-mixed instances sourced from social media, particularly YouTube comments. To tackle the SA challenge, a majority of the participants employed fine-tuning techniques on pre-trained multilingual language models. This approach allowed them to leverage the existing knowledge captured by the pre-trained models while adapting them to the specific code-mixed Dravidian language context. The top-performing systems in the shared tasks employed additional resources such as multilingual sentiment analysis datasets and fine-tuned pre-trained models. However, despite their success, the results also suggest that there is still potential for improvement in sentiment analysis for all three Dravidian languages: Tamil, Malayalam, and Kannada. The increased number of participants and the improved performance of the systems indicate a growing interest in the field of Dravidian NLP and a positive trend towards advancing research in this domain.

Acknowledgments

The author Bharathi Raja Chakravarthi was supported in part by a research grant from Science Foundation Ireland (SFI) under Grant Number SFI/12/RC/2289_P2 (Insight_2).

References

PJ Antony, Hemant B Raj, BS Sahana, Dimple Sonal Alvares, and Aishwarya Raj. 2012. Morphological Analyzer and Generator for Tulu Language: A Novel Approach. In *Proceedings of the International Conference on Advances in Computing, Communications and Informatics*, pages 828–834.

Kalika Bali, Jatin Sharma, Monojit Choudhury, and Yogarshi Vyas. 2014. "I am Borrowing Ya Mixing?" An Analysis of English-Hindi Code Mixing in Facebook. In *Proceedings of the first workshop on computational approaches to code switching*, pages 116–126.

Fazlourrahman Balouchzahi and HL Shashirekha. 2020. MUCS@ Dravidian-CodeMix-FIRE2020: SACO-SentimentsAnalysis for CodeMix Text. In *FIRE (Working Notes)*, pages 495–502.

Bharathi Raja Chakravarthi, Navya Jose, Shardul Suryawanshi, Elizabeth Sherly, and John P McCrae. 2020a. A Sentiment Analysis Dataset for Code-mixed Malayalam-English. In *arXiv preprint arXiv:2006.00210*.

Bharathi Raja Chakravarthi, Vigneshwaran Muralidaran, Ruba Priyadharshini, and John Philip McCrae. 2020b. Corpus Creation for Sentiment Analysis in Code-Mixed Tamil-English Text. In *Proceedings of the 1st Joint Workshop on Spoken Language Technologies for Under-resourced languages (SLTU) and Collaboration and Computing for Under-Resourced Languages (CCURL)*, pages 202–210, Marseille, France. European Language Resources association.

Bharathi Raja Chakravarthi, Ruba Priyadharshini, Vigneshwaran Muralidaran, Navya Jose, Shardul Suryawanshi, Elizabeth Sherly, and John P McCrae. 2022. Dravidiancodemix: Sentiment Analysis and Offensive Language Identification Dataset for Dravidian Languages in Code-mixed Text. In *Language*

Resources and Evaluation, volume 56, pages 765–806. Springer.

Bharathi Raja Chakravarthi, Ruba Priyadharshini, Vigneshwaran Muralidaran, Shardul Suryawanshi, Navya Jose, Elizabeth Sherly, and John P McCrae. 2020c. Overview of the Track on Sentiment Analysis for Dravidian Languages in Code-mixed Text. In *Forum for information retrieval evaluation*, pages 21–24.

Bharathi Raja Chakravarthi, Ruba Priyadharshini, Sajeetha Thavareesan, Dhivya Chinnappa, Durairaj Thenmozhi, Elizabeth Sherly, John P McCrae, Adeep Hande, Rahul Ponnusamy, Shubhanker Banerjee, et al. 2021. Findings of the Sentiment analysis of Dravidian Languages in Code-mixed Text. In *arXiv preprint arXiv:2111.09811*.

Sharal Coelho, Asha Hegde, Pooja Lamani, Kavya G, and Hosahalli Lakshmaiah Shashirekha. 2023. MUCSD@DravidianLangTech2023: Predicting Sentiment in Social Media Text using Machine Learning Techniques. In *Proceedings of the Third Workshop on Speech and Language Technologies for Dravidian Languages*, Varna, Bulgaria. Recent Advances in Natural Language Processing.

Toqeer Ehsan, Amina Tehseen, Kengatharaiyer Sarveswaran, and Amjad Ali. 2023. AlphaBrains@DravidianLangTech: Sentiment Analysis of Code-Mixed Tamil and Tulu by Training Contextualized ELMo Word Representations. In *Proceedings of the Third Workshop on Speech and Language Technologies for Dravidian Languages*, Varna, Bulgaria. Recent Advances in Natural Language Processing.

Kavya G, Asha Hegde, Sharal Coelho, Pooja Lamani, and Hosahalli Lakshmaiah Shashirekha. 2023. MUNLP@DravidianLangTech2023: Learning Approaches for Sentiment Analysis in Code-mixed Tamil and Tulu Text. In *Proceedings of the Third Workshop on Speech and Language Technologies for Dravidian Languages*, Varna, Bulgaria. Recent Advances in Natural Language Processing.

Asha Hegde, Mudoor Devadas Anusha, Sharal Coelho, Hosahalli Lakshmaiah Shashirekha, and Bharathi Raja Chakravarthi. 2022a. Corpus Creation for Sentiment Analysis in Code-Mixed Tulu Text. In *Proceedings of the 1st Annual Meeting of the ELRA/ISCA Special Interest Group on Under-Resourced Languages*, pages 33–40, Marseille, France. European Language Resources Association.

Asha Hegde, Shubhanker Banerjee, Bharathi Raja Chakravarthi, Ruba Priyadharshini, Hosahalli Shashirekha, John Philip McCrae, et al. 2022b. Overview of the Shared Task on Machine Translation in Dravidian Languages. In *Proceedings of the Second Workshop on Speech and Language Technologies for Dravidian Languages*, pages 271–278.

Asha Hegde and Hosahalli Lakshmaiah Shashirekha. 2022. Leveraging Dynamic Meta Embedding for Sentiment Analysis and Detection of Homophobic/Transphobic Content in Code-mixed Dravidian Languages.

Asha Hegde, Hosahalli Lakshmaiah Shashirekha, Anand Kumar Madasamy, and Bharathi Raja Chakravarthi. 2022c. A Study of Machine Translation Models for Kannada-Tulu. In *Congress on Intelligent Systems*, pages 145–161. Springer.

S Hewavitharana and HC Fernando. 2002. A Two Stage Classification Approach to Tamil Handwriting Recognition. In *Tamil Internet*, volume 2002, pages 118–124.

Braj B Kachru. 1978. Toward Structuring Code-mixing: An Indian Perspective. Walter de Gruyter, Berlin/New York Berlin, New York.

Selam Kanta. 2023. Sentiment Analysis of Code-Mixed Dravidian Texts Using SVM Classification. In *Proceedings of the Third Workshop on Speech and Language Technologies for Dravidian Languages*, Varna, Bulgaria. Recent Advances in Natural Language Processing.

Rachana Kulal, Prajnashree M, Asha Hegde, and Shashirekha H. L. 2023. MUCS@DravidianLangTech2023: Sentiment Analysis in Code-mixed Tamil and Tulu Texts using fastText. In *Proceedings of the Third Workshop on Speech and Language Technologies for Dravidian Languages*, Varna, Bulgaria. Recent Advances in Natural Language Processing.

Kirti Kumari, Shirish Shekhar Jha, Zarikunte Kunal Dayanand, and Praneesh Sharma. 2023. MLAI_IIITRanchi@DravidianLangTech: Fine-Tuning IndicBERT for Exploring Language-specific Features for Sentiment Classification in Code-Mixed Dravadian Language. In *Proceedings of the Third Workshop on Speech and Language Technologies for Dravidian Languages*, Varna, Bulgaria. Recent Advances in Natural Language Processing.

Zhipeng Luo and Jiahui Wang. 2023. Deepblueai@dravidianlangtech. In *Proceedings of the Third Workshop on Speech and Language Technologies for Dravidian Languages*, Varna, Bulgaria. Recent Advances in Natural Language Processing.

Ankit Kumar Mishra, Sunil Saumya, and Abhinav Kumar. 2021. Sentiment Analysis of Dravidian-CodeMix Language. In *Forum for information retrieval evaluation*, pages 1011–1019.

K Padmanabha Kekunnaya. A comparative study of tulu dialects.

Charmathi Ponnusamy, Kishore Kumar andRajkumar, Elizabeth Kumaresan, Prasanna Kumar andSherly, and Ruba Priyadharshini. 2023. VEL@DravidianLangTech: Sentiment Analysis of Tamil and Tulu. In *Proceedings of the Third*

Workshop on Speech and Language Technologies for Dravidian Languages, Varna, Bulgaria. Recent Advances in Natural Language Processing.

Pradeep Kumar Roy and Abhinav Kumar. 2021. Sentiment Analysis on Tamil Code-Mixed Text using Bi-LSTM. In *Forum for information retrieval evaluation*, pages 1044–1050.

K. Shanmugavadivel, V.E. Sathishkumar, and S. Raja. 2022. Deep Learning Based Sentiment Analysis and Offensive Language Identification on Multilingual Code-mixed Data. volume 12, page 21557. nature.

Poorvi Shetty. 2023. Sentiment Analysis on Code-Mixed Tulu and Tamil Corpus. In *Proceedings of the Third Workshop on Speech and Language Technologies for Dravidian Languages*, Varna, Bulgaria. Recent Advances in Natural Language Processing.

R Sivanantham and M Seran. 2019. Keeladi: An Urban Settlement of Sangam Age on the Banks of River Vaigai. In *India: Department of Archaeology, Government of Tamil Nadu, Chennai.*

Mithun Kumar SR, Lov Kumar, and Aruna Malapati. 2022. Sentiment Analysis on Code-Switched Dravidian Languages with Kernel Based Extreme Learning Machines. In *Proceedings of the Second Workshop on Speech and Language Technologies for Dravidian Languages.*, pages 184–190. Association for Computational Linguistics.

R Srinivasan and CN Subalalitha. 2019. Automated Named Entity Recognition from Tamil Documents. In *2019 IEEE 1st international conference on energy, systems and information processing (ICESIP)*, pages 1–5. IEEE.

CN Subalalitha. 2019. Information Extraction Framework for Kurunthogai. In *Sādhanā*, volume 44, page 156. Springer.

Moein Tash, Jesus Armenta-Segura, zahra ahani, Grigori Kolesnikova, Olga andSidorov, and Gelbukh Alexander. 2023. LIDOMA@DravidianLangTech: Convolutional Neural Networks for Studying Correlation Between Lexical Features and Sentiment Polarity in Tamil and Tulu Languages. In *Proceedings of the Third Workshop on Speech and Language Technologies for Dravidian Languages*, Varna, Bulgaria. Recent Advances in Natural Language Processing.

S. Thavareesan and S. Mahesan. 2021. Sentiment Analysis in Tamil Texts using k-means and k-Nearest Neighbour. In *Proceedings of 10th International Conference on Information and Automation for Sustainability (ICIAfS)*, pages 48– 53. IEEE.

S. Yadav and T. Chakraborty. 2021. Unsupervised Sentiment Analysis for Code-mixed Data. In *Proceedings of AAAI Conference on Artificial Intelligence*, pages 15941–15942.

Tadesse Yigezu, Mesay Gemeda andKebede, Olga Kolesnikova, Grigori Sidorov, and Gelbukh Alexander. 2023. Habesha@DravidianLangTech: Utilizing Deep and Transfer Learning Approaches for Sentiment Analysis. In *Proceedings of the Third Workshop on Speech and Language Technologies for Dravidian Languages*, Varna, Bulgaria. Recent Advances in Natural Language Processing.

Findings of the Shared Task on Multimodal Abusive Language Detection and Sentiment Analysis in Tamil and Malayalam

Premjith B[1], Jyothish Lal G[1], Sowmya V[1], Bharathi Raja Chakravarthi[2], Rajeswari Natarajan[3], K Nandhini[4], Abirami Murugappan[5], Bharathi B[6], Kaushik M[1], Prasanth SN[1], R Aswin Raj[1], Vijai Simmon S[1]

[1] Amrita School of Artificial Intelligence, Coimbatore, Amrita Vishwa Vidyapeetham, India
[2]Insight SFI Research Centre for Data Analytics, School of Computer Science, University of Galway, Ireland
[3]SRC Campus, SASTRA Deemed to be University, Kumbakonam, Tamilnadu, India
[4]School of Mathematics and Computer Sciences, Central University of Tamil Nadu
[5]Department of Information Science and Technology, Anna University
[6] SSN college of Engineering, Tamilnadu

Abstract

This paper summarizes the shared task on multimodal abusive language detection and sentiment analysis in Dravidian languages as part of the third Workshop on Speech and Language Technologies for Dravidian Languages at RANLP 2023. This shared task provides a platform for researchers worldwide to submit their models on two crucial social media data analysis problems in Dravidian languages - abusive language detection and sentiment analysis. Abusive language detection identifies social media content with abusive information, whereas sentiment analysis refers to the problem of determining the sentiments expressed in a text. This task aims to build models for detecting abusive content and analyzing fine-grained sentiment from multimodal data in Tamil and Malayalam. The multimodal data consists of three modalities - video, audio and text. The datasets for both tasks were prepared by collecting videos from YouTube. Sixty teams participated in both tasks. However, only two teams submitted their results. The submissions were evaluated using macro F1-score.

1 Introduction

Multimodal social media data analyses the insights from social media data that include multiple modalities such as text, audio, and videos. Conventional social media data involves text data such as tweets, Facebook posts, and YouTube comments, and social media data analysis mainly focuses on processing text data to obtain valuable information. However, multimodal data analysis considers the diverse content shared on various social media platforms (Chakravarthi et al., 2021). Analyzing the data containing multiple modalities can give a more comprehensive understanding of user behavior, opinions, and trends. The features extracted from video and audio data can be considered additional information to enhance the text features of input data. The facial expressions from the video, the pitch, and the tone of the audio signal can help to refine the features for identifying different opinions and expressions more effectively.

Multimodal social media data analysis combines approaches from different domains, including computer vision (CV), speech processing, and natural language processing (NLP), to process and detect different categories of data.

- *Text mining and analysis*: The text data related to the videos posted on different social media platforms can be mined and analysed using NLP techniques to identify the context, sentiment, hate comments, comments with offensive language, and abusive content.

- *Computer vision*: This task involves the analysis of images and videos to understand different categories of data. This analysis can include detecting different objects, scenes, facial expressions, and emotions of people from images and videos.

- *Speech analysis*: Analysis of speech data, specifically spoken words, to extract information, sentiment, or other relevant features.

- *Feature fusion*: Integrating and combining features extracted from different modalities to obtain an extensive understanding of multimodal data.

Third Workshop on Speech and Language Technologies for Dravidian Languages, pages 72–79, Varna, Bulgaria, Sep 7, 2023.
https://doi.org/10.26615/978-954-452-085-4_010

The shared task on multimodal abusive language detection and sentiment analysis in Dravidian languages at DravidianLangTech, organized as part of Recent Advancements in Natural Language Processing 2023, has two subtasks - multimodal abusive language detection in Tamil and multimodal sentiment analysis in Tamil and Malayalam. The main objective of the shared task is to encourage researchers around the globe to participate and submit their approaches and results, with the motivation to support the research in resource-poor languages like Tamil and Malayalam.

Sentiment Analysis (opinion mining) (Medhat et al., 2014), (Chakravarthi et al., 2020b), (Priyadharshini et al., 2021) identifies sentiments or opinions by analyzing the underlying subjective information in the text data. Generally, sentiment analysis involves understanding the emotional tone present in a text to classify it as positive, negative, neutral, or more fine-grained categories. This analysis utilizes NLP embedding algorithms to represent text as a feature vector and classify the text into different categories using machine learning (ML) or deep learning (DL) algorithms. The multimodal sentiment analysis from video data involves the analysis of video or image sequence analysis and speech analysis in addition to the text analysis to identify the sentiments expressed in the data. In this task, the data are in Tamil and Malayalam, two low-resource languages. Both languages are morphologically rich and agglutinative, which makes the analysis more complex. In addition, the code-mixing property, which usually occurs in social media data, increases the complexity as it covers words from multiple languages.

Abusive language detection from social media data is identifying comments with abusive content (Nobata et al., 2016), (Priyadharshini et al., 2022b), (Priyadharshini et al., 2022a), (Chakravarthi et al., 2023), (Prasanth et al., 2022). Generally, in text-based analysis, the algorithms look for the words or phrases (sequence of words) or similar words/phrases that define the abusiveness of the input text. Multimodal abusive language detection includes detecting videos containing abusive information by analyzing video, speech, and text data. This subtask is primarily focused on building models for multimodal data in Tamil.

This paper summarises the shared task on multimodal abusive language detection in Tamil and multimodal sentiment analysis in Tamil and Malayalam. Besides, this paper discusses the findings from the models submitted to the two subtasks mentioned above. The shared task was hosted on CodaLab [1]. We shared the training data and validation data with all the registered participants for building their models. Later, the test data without labels were shared to make predictions using the models built. Sixty teams registered for both subtasks. However, only two teams submitted their results.

The structure of the paper is as follows: Section 2 discusses the research papers published in the domains of multimodal abusive language detection and multimodal sentiment analysis, Section 3 describes the shared tasks, followed by Section 4, which summarizes the systems submitted by participating teams. The paper concludes in Section 5.

2 Related Works

People post messages and comments on various social media platforms in their mother tongue or code-mixed languages. Hence, the machine learning models built with monolingual datasets are unsuitable for identifying abusive language or analyzing sentiments from code-mixed languages. However, researchers are now progressing to develop systems using code-mixed datasets. As stated above, the data collection and annotation process is one key challenge. (Chakravarthi et al., 2020b,a; Hande et al., 2021a; Mandl et al., 2020) released a few Dravidian language datasets for offensive language and hate speech detection. Many models have been proposed using the above-cited datasets (Saumya et al., 2021; Yasaswini et al., 2021; Hande et al., 2021b; Kedia and Nandy, 2021; Renjit and Idicula, 2020; Chakravarthi et al., 2022). The authors (Singh and Bhattacharyya, 2020) have employed an ensemble of multilingual BERT models to detect hate speech and offensive content for Dravidian languages. They have achieved an F-score of 0.95 for hate speech and offensive content detection tasks. in YouTube comments in Malayalam language(code-mixed, script-mixed). For hate speech and offensive content detection tasks for YouTube or Twitter datasets in Malayalam (code-mixed: Tanglish and Manglish), F-scores of 0.86 and 0.72 were achieved, respectively. (Ranasinghe et al., 2020) experimented with multinomial Naive Bayes, support vector machines and random for-

[1] https://codalab.lisn.upsaclay.fr/competitions/11092

est methods to identify the offensive comments in code-mixed Malayalam YouTube comments. They have also used cross-lingual contextual word embeddings and transfer learning models to predict hate and offensive speech in Malayalam data. A weighted average F1-score of 0.89 was achieved.

An ensemble of multilingual transformer networks like XLMRoBERTa has been proposed for offensive speech detection in code-mixed and Romanised variants of three Dravidian languages-Tamil, Malayalam, and Kannada (Sai and Sharma, 2021). Two DL frameworks, namely CNN and Bi-LSTM (Saumya et al., 2021), have been used in parallel to extract the contextual features from the text. These features were concatenated and presented to a fully connected layer for final prediction. They also used conventional machine learning approaches, such as naive Bayes, random forests, support vector machine and transformer-based models to predict content from Dravidian code-mixed scripts. (Yasaswini et al., 2021) explored various transformer models to detect the offensive language in social media posts in Tamil, Malayalam, and Kannada. They achieved F1-scores of 0.9603 and 0.7895 on the Malayalam and Tamil datasets by using the ULMFiT model, respectively. For the Kannada dataset, they obtained an F1-score of 0.7277 by using the distilmBERT model. Two multi-task learning approaches (Hande et al., 2021a) was developed to identify the offensive language for Kannada, Malayalam, and Tamil and analyse the sentiments. The model obtained a weighted F1-score of (59% and 70%), (66.8% and 90.5%), and (62.1% and 75.3%) for Malayalam, Kannada, and Tamil on sentiment analysis and offensive language identification tasks, respectively. An offensive content classification model (Kedia and Nandy, 2021) was built with transformer-based models, namely BERT and RoBERTa, for Dravidian code-mixed languages like Kannada, Malayalam and Tamil. The authors achieved a weighted average F1-scores of 0.72, 0.77, and 0.97 for Kannada-English, Tamil-English, and Malayalam-English datasets.

The authors (Chakravarthi et al., 2022) developed datasets using the YouTube comments of three Dravidian languages, namely Malayalam–English (20,000), Tamil–English (44,000), and Kannada–English (7000) for sentiment analysis and offensive language identification tasks. (Dave et al., 2021) used machine learning and transformer-based models for offensive language identification. The authors represented the sentences using character n-gram and pre-trained word embedding. The F1-scores were 0.95 and 0.71 for Malayalam and Tamil, respectively. (Li, 2021; Dowlagar and Mamidi, 2021; Zhao and Tao, 2021; Chen and Kong, 2021; Dave et al., 2021) have used transformer-based models, such as BERT, RoBERTa and MuRiL for offensive language identification task for Dravidian languages. Besides, research articles (Dowlagar and Mamidi, 2021; Andrew, 2021) have shown the performances of offensive language detection from code-mixed languages using machine learning models such as logistic regression, K-nearest neighbour, support vector machine, decision trees and random forests. (Zhao and Tao, 2021; Chen and Kong, 2021; Sreelakshmi et al., 2021; Sharif et al., 2021) used deep learning techniques for offensive language identification task. All the above-discussed articles cover various methods and evaluations for offensive language identification and hate speech detection. They provide insights into this research's ensemble strategies and deep learning models. Nevertheless, research has to progress deeper and wider to develop a robust model for hate speech and offensive language identification tasks using Dravidian languages. Even though text-based datasets and models are available for abusive language detection and sentiment analysis in Dravidian languages, research on multimodal datasets is yet to kickstart.

3 Task Description

This section discusses the two subtasks - multimodal abusive language detection in Tamil and multimodal sentiment analysis in Tamil and Malayalam, including the dataset used. The subtask, "Multimodal abusive language detection in Tamil", aims to encourage researchers to develop AI/machine learning/deep learning models for classifying video data posted on YouTube into abusive and non-abusive categories. Multimodal sentiment analysis in Tamil and Malayalam" subtask has two tasks - one in Tamil and another in Malayalam. In both tasks, the objective is to develop AI/machine learning/deep learning models for classifying video data into highly positive, positive, neutral, negative, and highly negative categories. In all the tasks mentioned above, video, audio, and text data were provided, and the participants were free to use any combination of modalities to build their models.

The dataset used for conducting both tasks is

insufficient for training a machine learning or deep learning model. However, the availability of pre-trained models can help the participants to resolve this problem by generating meaningful feature representations.

3.1 Multimodal Abusive Language Detection in Tamil

The competition was hosted on the CodaLab platform. We provided training data and test data for this competition. Training data contains 70 videos collected from YouTube with abusive and non-abusive content. We extracted audio signals from the video and prepared the transcripts using the Google automatic speech recognition (ASR) module. The errors in the transcripts were corrected manually in the postprocessing step. After that, 88 videos were labeled with the help of qualified native speakers into two categories - abusive and non-abusive (Ashraf et al., 2021).

- **Abusive**: Abuse content encompasses any communication that
    1. targets an individual, group, or community
    2. is disrespectful, sexist, crude, or obscene
    3. pertains to human shortcomings, aims to provoke offense towards an individual or group, or suggests condescension or victim-blaming.
- **Non-abusive**: Anything that do not belong to the abusive category.

We divided the dataset into training and test data. The training dataset consisted of 70 videos, and the test data contained 18 videos. In addition to videos, both datasets are composed of audio and text data. The training dataset consists of 38 videos in the abusive category and 32 in the non-abusive category. The number of data points in each class shows a slight class imbalance problem. The test data consists of 18 videos, of which nine are abusive, and nine are non-abusive. During the testing phase of the competition, we provided the test data without labels. However, we released the test data with labels after the closure of the competition. Table 1 describes the training and testing data details.

Despite sixty registrations, only two teams submitted their results through the Google form provided.

Table 1: Details of the dataset used for the shared task on multimodal abusive language detection in Tamil

Dataset	Abusive	Non-abusive
Training	38	32
Test	9	9

3.2 Multimodal Sentiment Analysis in Tamil and Malayalam

This subtask is also hosted on the CodaLab platform. This is the second edition of this subtak (Premjith et al., 2022). This subtask has two sections - one for Tamil and another for Malayalam. Like the multimodal abusive language detection task, we collected data for this task from YouTube. The same procedure was followed for collecting the data and annotation. Unlike the abusive language detection task, we provided the participants with training, validation, and test data. Training and validation data were released together, and test data without labels were supplied during the testing phase. The test data without labels were uploaded to the CodaLab after completing the task.

We considered five fine-grained labels for annotating each data point in both languages - Highly Positive, Positive, Neutral, Negative, and Highly Negative.

- **Highly Positive**: A video featuring a reviewer using exaggerated language or expressions.
- **Positive**: A video in which the reviewer delivers positive reviews while maintaining subtle facial expressions
- **Neutral**: There are no direct or indirect indications of the speaker's emotional state. Examples include requests for likes or subscriptions and inquiries about a movie's release date or dialogue.
- **Negative**: Videos featuring the utilization of negative words and sarcastic comments, coupled with understated facial expressions.
- **Highly Negative**: Videos where excessively negative words are employed, accompanied by a gloomy facial expression and a stressed voice.

Training, validation, and test data in both languages contain data from three modalities - video, speech, and text. Tamil data consisted of 64 data

Table 2: Details of the dataset used for the shared task on multimodal Sentiment Analysis in Tamil and Malayalam

Dataset	Tamil	Malayalam
Training	44	50
Validation	10	10
Test	10	10

Table 3: Class-wise distribution of the dataset used for the shared task on multimodal Sentiment Analysis in Tamil and Malayalam

Category	Tamil	Malayalam
Highly Positive	8	9
Positive	38	39
Neutral	8	8
Negative	5	12
Highly Negative	5	2
Total	64	70

samples split into training, validation, and test data in the ratio of 22:5:5. Malayalam corpus had 70 data samples, of which 50 were used as training data, ten each as validation and test data. A detailed description of the split is given in Table 3. Class-wise distribution of the data points in both languages is provided in Table 2. The tables 4 and 5 give the class-wise distribution of the data points used in the training, validation, and test datasets. From the dataset details, it is evident that there is a high-class imbalance problem. The positive category has significantly more data points than other categories.

Similar to the previous task, we had 60 registrations for this task, and only two teams submitted their predictions.

Table 4: Distribution of training, validation, and test datasets used for the shared task on multimodal Sentiment Analysis in Tamil

Category	Train	Validation	Test
Highly Positive	5	3	1
Positive	29	4	5
Neutral	4	2	2
Negative	3	1	1
Highly Negative	3	0	1
Total	44	10	10

Table 5: Distribution of training, validation, and test datasets used for the shared task on multimodal Sentiment Analysis in Malayalam

Category	Train	Validation	Test
Highly Positive	5	2	2
Positive	31	5	3
Neutral	5	1	2
Negative	8	2	2
Highly Negative	1	0	1
Total	50	10	10

4 System Description

We received two submissions for both subtasks. Each team was allowed to submit a maximum of three runs. The run with the highest macro F1 score was considered for preparing the rank list. The descriptions of the systems submitted for the shared tasks are given below.

4.1 Team: hate-alert

Their work involved utilizing three distinct models to extract features from various modalities, such as text, audio, and video (Barman and Das, 2023). Firstly, the authors used the BERT model to extract text-based features from the video. By employing the BERT model, they capture and analyze the textual information and characteristics embedded within the video. Additionally, they incorporated the Mel-frequency cepstral coefficients (MFCC) based feature extraction technique to extract audio-based features from the videos. The advantage of MFCCs is that they will aid in capturing the shape of the vocal tract, giving distinct characteristics to the sound or audio. Moreover, the successful extraction of video-based features was achieved by utilizing the Vision Transformer model. It is a specialized deep learning model designed for processing visual data. This model demonstrated its efficacy in handling visual tasks, enabling us to obtain valuable visual features from the videos. The extracted features included significant visual patterns, objects, and informative content. Furthermore, these features significantly contributed to a comprehensive understanding of the visual aspects of the video data. The proposal entailed applying a fusion-based system or a multimodal model after extracting the specific features from each modality (text, audio, and video). The model utilizes the complementary information or features received from different modalities to make accurate predic-

Table 6: Ranklist for the shared task on multimodal abusive language detection in Tamil

Team	Macro F1	Rank
hate-alert	0.5786	1
AbhiPaw	0.3333	2

Table 7: Ranklist for the shared task on multimodal sentiment analysis in Tamil

Team	Macro F1	Rank
hate-alert	0.1429	1
AbhiPaw	0.1333	2

tions. With this approach, the authors categorized the video based on sub-tasks, considering the amalgamated information from text, audio, and video features. Overall, their approach demonstrates a comprehensive and robust video analysis and classification framework.

4.2 Team: AbhiPaw

In this work (Bala and Krishnamurthy, 2023), the authors created multimodal Transformer-based architecture to make accurate predictions. The proposal drew inspiration from two primary sources: (a) "MISA: Modality-Invariant and -Specific Representations for Multimodal Sentiment Analysis" presented at ACM MM 2020 (Hazarika et al., 2020), and (b) "How you feelin'? Learning Emotions and Mental States in Movie Scenes" presented at CVPR 2023 (Srivastava et al., 2023). They employed different models with varying dimensions to extract features from all three modalities (video, audio, and text). They used the MVIT model for video data, the openl3 library for audio data, and the BERT-based multilingual model for text data. These models were selected based on their respective strengths and capabilities in processing their corresponding modalities. Further, they designed a 2-layer transformer-based architecture for the primary model. Additionally, they incorporated type embeddings for the features, drawing inspiration from the work (b). These types of embeddings were used to signify the modality of each feature, distinguishing between video, audio, and text. The model's raw output consisted of logits corresponding to the predicted classes.

5 Conclusion

This paper reports the findings of the shared task on multimodal abusive language detection in Tamil

Table 8: Ranklist for the shared task on multimodal sentiment analysis in Malayalam

Team	Macro F1	Rank
hate-alert	0.1889	1
AbhiPaw	0.0923	2

and multimodal sentiment analysis in Tamil and Malayalam. The task dataset consisted of videos collected from YouTube and corresponding audio and transcripts. We received sixty registrations for both subtasks. However, only two teams submitted the predictions for the test data provided to the participants. We used macro F1-score to assess the submitted predictions' performance and prepare the rank list.

Acknowledgments

The author Bharathi Raja Chakravarthi was supported in part by a research grant from Science Foundation Ireland (SFI) under Grant Number SFI/12/RC/2289_P2(Insight_2).

References

Judith Jeyafreeda Andrew. 2021. Judithjeyafreedaandrew@ dravidianlangtech-eacl2021: offensive language detection for dravidian code-mixed youtube comments. In *Proceedings of the First Workshop on Speech and Language Technologies for Dravidian Languages*, pages 169–174.

Noman Ashraf, Arkaitz Zubiaga, and Alexander Gelbukh. 2021. Abusive language detection in youtube comments leveraging replies as conversational context. *PeerJ Computer Science*, 7:e742.

Abhinaba Bala and Parameswari Krishnamurthy. 2023. Abhipaw@dravidianlangtech: Multimodal abusive language detection and sentiment analysis. In *Proceedings of the Third Workshop on Speech and Language Technologies for Dravidian Languages*, Varna, Bulgaria. Recent Advances in Natural Language Processing.

Shubhankar Barman and Mithun Das. 2023. hate-alert@dravidianlangtech: Multimodal abusive language detection and sentiment analysis in dravidian languages. In *Proceedings of the Third Workshop on Speech and Language Technologies for Dravidian Languages*, Varna, Bulgaria. Recent Advances in Natural Language Processing.

Bharathi Raja Chakravarthi, Anand Kumar M, John P McCrae, B Premjith, KP Soman, and Thomas Mandl. 2020a. Overview of the track on hasoc-offensive language identification-dravidiancodemix. In *FIRE (Working notes)*, pages 112–120.

Bharathi Raja Chakravarthi, Vigneshwaran Muralidaran, Ruba Priyadharshini, and John P McCrae. 2020b. Corpus creation for sentiment analysis in code-mixed tamil-english text. *arXiv preprint arXiv:2006.00206*.

Bharathi Raja Chakravarthi, Ruba Priyadharshini, Shubanker Banerjee, Manoj Balaji Jagadeeshan, Prasanna Kumar Kumaresan, Rahul Ponnusamy, Sean Benhur, and John Philip McCrae. 2023. Detecting abusive comments at a fine-grained level in a low-resource language. *Natural Language Processing Journal*, 3:100006.

Bharathi Raja Chakravarthi, Ruba Priyadharshini, Vigneshwaran Muralidaran, Navya Jose, Shardul Suryawanshi, Elizabeth Sherly, and John P McCrae. 2022. Dravidiancodemix: Sentiment analysis and offensive language identification dataset for dravidian languages in code-mixed text. *Language Resources and Evaluation*, 56(3):765–806.

Bharathi Raja Chakravarthi, KP Soman, Rahul Ponnusamy, Prasanna Kumar Kumaresan, Kingston Pal Thamburaj, John P McCrae, et al. 2021. Dravidianmultimodality: A dataset for multi-modal sentiment analysis in tamil and malayalam. *arXiv preprint arXiv:2106.04853*.

Shi Chen and Bing Kong. 2021. cs@ dravidianlangtech-eacl2021: Offensive language identification based on multilingual bert model. In *Proceedings of the First Workshop on Speech and Language Technologies for Dravidian Languages*, pages 230–235.

Bhargav Dave, Shripad Bhat, and Prasenjit Majumder. 2021. Irnlp daiict@ dravidianlangtech-eacl2021:+ offensive language identification in dravidian languages using tf-idf char n-grams and muril. In *Proceedings of the First Workshop on Speech and Language Technologies for Dravidian Languages*, pages 266–269.

Suman Dowlagar and Radhika Mamidi. 2021. Offlangone@ dravidianlangtech-eacl2021: Transformers with the class balanced loss for offensive language identification in dravidian code-mixed text. In *Proceedings of the first workshop on speech and language technologies for dravidian languages*, pages 154–159.

Adeep Hande, Siddhanth U Hegde, Ruba Priyadharshini, Rahul Ponnusamy, Prasanna Kumar Kumaresan, Sajeetha Thavareesan, and Bharathi Raja Chakravarthi. 2021a. Benchmarking multi-task learning for sentiment analysis and offensive language identification in under-resourced dravidian languages. *arXiv preprint arXiv:2108.03867*.

Adeep Hande, Karthik Puranik, Konthala Yasaswini, Ruba Priyadharshini, Sajeetha Thavareesan, Anbukkarasi Sampath, Kogilavani Shanmugavadivel, Durairaj Thenmozhi, and Bharathi Raja Chakravarthi. 2021b. Offensive language identification in low-resourced code-mixed dravidian languages using pseudo-labeling. *arXiv preprint arXiv:2108.12177*.

Devamanyu Hazarika, Roger Zimmermann, and Soujanya Poria. 2020. Misa: Modality-invariant and-specific representations for multimodal sentiment analysis. In *Proceedings of the 28th ACM international conference on multimedia*, pages 1122–1131.

Kushal Kedia and Abhilash Nandy. 2021. indicnlp@ kgp at dravidianlangtech-eacl2021: Offensive language identification in dravidian languages. *arXiv preprint arXiv:2102.07150*.

Zichao Li. 2021. Codewithzichao@ dravidianlangtech-eacl2021: Exploring multilingual transformers for offensive language identification on code mixing text. In *Proceedings of the First Workshop on Speech and Language Technologies for Dravidian Languages*, pages 164–168.

Thomas Mandl, Sandip Modha, Anand Kumar M, and Bharathi Raja Chakravarthi. 2020. Overview of the hasoc track at fire 2020: Hate speech and offensive language identification in tamil, malayalam, hindi, english and german. In *Forum for information retrieval evaluation*, pages 29–32.

Walaa Medhat, Ahmed Hassan, and Hoda Korashy. 2014. Sentiment analysis algorithms and applications: A survey. *Ain Shams engineering journal*, 5(4):1093–1113.

Chikashi Nobata, Joel Tetreault, Achint Thomas, Yashar Mehdad, and Yi Chang. 2016. Abusive language detection in online user content. In *Proceedings of the 25th international conference on world wide web*, pages 145–153.

SN Prasanth, R Aswin Raj, P Adhithan, B Premjith, and Soman Kp. 2022. Cen-tamil@ dravidianlangtech-acl2022: Abusive comment detection in tamil using tf-idf and random kitchen sink algorithm. In *Proceedings of the Second Workshop on Speech and Language Technologies for Dravidian Languages*, pages 70–74.

B Premjith, Bharathi Raja Chakravarthi, Malliga Subramanian, B Bharathi, Soman Kp, V Dhanalakshmi, K Sreelakshmi, Arunaggiri Pandian, and Prasanna Kumaresan. 2022. Findings of the shared task on multimodal sentiment analysis and troll meme classification in dravidian languages. In *Proceedings of the Second Workshop on Speech and Language Technologies for Dravidian Languages*, pages 254–260.

Ruba Priyadharshini, Bharathi Raja Chakravarthi, Subalalitha Cn, Thenmozhi Durairaj, Malliga Subramanian, Kogilavani Shanmugavadivel, Siddhanth U Hegde, and Prasanna Kumaresan. 2022a. Overview of abusive comment detection in tamil-acl 2022. In *Proceedings of the Second Workshop on Speech and Language Technologies for Dravidian Languages*, pages 292–298.

Ruba Priyadharshini, Bharathi Raja Chakravarthi, Subalalitha Chinnaudayar Navaneethakrishnan, Thenmozhi Durairaj, Malliga Subramanian, Kogilavani Shanmugavadivel, Siddhanth U Hegde, and

Prasanna Kumar Kumaresan. 2022b. Findings of the shared task on abusive comment detection in tamil. In *Proceedings of the Second Workshop on Speech and Language Technologies for Dravidian Languages. Association for Computational Linguistics.*

Ruba Priyadharshini, Bharathi Raja Chakravarthi, Sajeetha Thavareesan, Dhivya Chinnappa, Durairaj Thenmozhi, and Rahul Ponnusamy. 2021. Overview of the dravidiancodemix 2021 shared task on sentiment detection in tamil, malayalam, and kannada. In *Proceedings of the 13th Annual Meeting of the Forum for Information Retrieval Evaluation*, pages 4–6.

Tharindu Ranasinghe, Sarthak Gupte, Marcos Zampieri, and Ifeoma Nwogu. 2020. Wlv-rit at hasoc-dravidian-codemix-fire2020: Offensive language identification in code-switched youtube comments. *arXiv preprint arXiv:2011.00559.*

Sara Renjit and Sumam Mary Idicula. 2020. Cusatnlp@ hasoc-dravidian-codemix-fire2020: identifying offensive language from manglishtweets. *arXiv preprint arXiv:2010.08756.*

Siva Sai and Yashvardhan Sharma. 2021. Towards offensive language identification for dravidian languages. In *Proceedings of the first workshop on speech and language technologies for Dravidian languages*, pages 18–27.

Sunil Saumya, Abhinav Kumar, and Jyoti Prakash Singh. 2021. Offensive language identification in dravidian code mixed social media text. In *Proceedings of the first workshop on speech and language technologies for Dravidian languages*, pages 36–45.

Omar Sharif, Eftekhar Hossain, and Mohammed Moshiul Hoque. 2021. Nlp-cuet@ dravidianlangtech-eacl2021: Offensive language detection from multilingual code-mixed text using transformers. *arXiv preprint arXiv:2103.00455.*

Pankaj Singh and Pushpak Bhattacharyya. 2020. Cfilt iit bombay@ hasoc-dravidian-codemix fire 2020: Assisting ensemble of transformers with random transliteration. In *FIRE (Working Notes)*, pages 411–416.

K Sreelakshmi, B Premjith, and Soman Kp. 2021. Amrita_cen_nlp@ dravidianlangtech-eacl2021: deep learning-based offensive language identification in malayalam, tamil and kannada. In *Proceedings of the First Workshop on Speech and Language Technologies for Dravidian Languages*, pages 249–254.

Dhruv Srivastava, Aditya Kumar Singh, and Makarand Tapaswi. 2023. How you feelin'? learning emotions and mental states in movie scenes. In *Proceedings of the IEEE/CVF Conference on Computer Vision and Pattern Recognition*, pages 2517–2528.

Konthala Yasaswini, Karthik Puranik, Adeep Hande, Ruba Priyadharshini, Sajeetha Thavareesan, and Bharathi Raja Chakravarthi. 2021. Iiitt@ dravidianlangtech-eacl2021: Transfer learning for offensive language detection in dravidian languages. In *Proceedings of the First Workshop on Speech and Language Technologies for Dravidian Languages*, pages 187–194.

Yingjia Zhao and Xin Tao. 2021. Zyj123@ dravidianlangtech-eacl2021: Offensive language identification based on xlm-roberta with dpcnn. In *Proceedings of the first workshop on speech and language technologies for dravidian languages*, pages 216–221.

Overview of Shared-task on Abusive Comment Detection in Tamil and Telugu

Ruba Priyadharshini[1], Bharathi Raja Chakravarthi[2], Malliga Subramanian[3], Subalalitha Chinnaudayar Navaneethakrishnan[4], Kogilavani Shanmugavadivel[3], Premjith B[5], Abirami Murugappan[6], Prasanna Kumar Kumaresan[2], Karnati Sai Prashanth[5], Mangamuru Sai Rishith Reddy[5], Janakiram Chandu[5]
[1]Gandhigram Rural Institute-Deemed to be University, India
[2]Insight SFI Research Centre for Data Analytics, School of Computer Science, University of Galway, Ireland
[3]Kongu Engineering College, Tamil Nadu, India
[4]SRM Institute of Science and Technology, Kattankulathur, Chennai, India
[5]Amrita School of Artificial Intelligence, Amrita Vishwa Vidyapeetham, India
[6]Department of Information Science and Technology, Anna University

Abstract

This paper discusses the submissions to the shared task on abusive comment detection in Tamil and Telugu codemixed social media text conducted as part of the third Workshop on Speech and Language Technologies for Dravidian Languages at RANLP 2023. The task encourages researchers to develop models to detect the contents containing abusive information in Tamil and Telugu codemixed social media text. The task has three subtasks - abusive comment detection in Tamil, Tamil-English and Telugu-English. The dataset for all the tasks was developed by collecting comments from YouTube. The submitted models were evaluated using macro F1-score, and prepared the rank list accordingly.

1 Introduction

Abusive comment detection from social media has become an essential and challenging task in the current age of technology (Chakravarthi et al., 2023; Priyadharshini et al., 2022b; Prasanth et al., 2022). The proliferation of online platforms helped people to spread information, including harmful and violent comments and posts. Therefore, addressing and mitigating harmful content to keep online platforms clean automatically has become very important (Chakravarthi et al., 2022a,b, 2023; Chakravarthi, 2023). This task is challenging due to the complexities of the languages. However, advanced machine learning algorithms and techniques were proposed to automatically identify and flag abusive comments, ranging from hate speech and cyberbullying to threats and harassment, recently. These systems analyze the content of the posts and the context to determine the presence of abusive language and malicious intent. The complexity of detecting the abusive contents from a code-mixed Dravidian language is even high due to the code-mixed nature of the text and the intricacies of the language, such as morphological richness and agglutinative property (Premjith et al., 2018). In addition, large datasets of labelled abusive content are required to train and fine-tune the Artificial Intelligence (AI)-based models, enabling them to recognize patterns and distinguish between harmful and benign texts.

A considerable amount of research has been conducted to detect abusive and similar harmful content from social media posts and comments (Bharathi and Agnusimmaculate Silvia, 2021; Bharathi and Varsha, 2022b; Swaminathan et al., 2022; Subramanian et al., 2022). In addition, several shared tasks were organized to promote the research for automatically detecting social media comments containing abusive content. This shared task focuses on detecting abusive comments in two Dravidian languages - Tamil and Telugu. Tamil is predominantly spoken in Tamil Nadu, a state in India and nearby countries, whereas Telugu is the official language of two states in India - Andhra Pradesh and Telangana (Vasantharajan et al., 2022; Anita and Subalalitha, 2019; Thavareesan and Mahesan, 2019, 2020a,b; Subalalitha, 2019; Sakuntharaj and Mahesan, 2016, 2017, 2021). This paper summarizes the findings of the research works submitted to the shared task on abusive language detection in Tamil and Telugu. Besides, this paper details the dataset developed and used for conducting the experiments.

Third Workshop on Speech and Language Technologies for Dravidian Languages, pages 80–87, Varna, Bulgaria, Sep 7, 2023.
https://doi.org/10.26615/978-954-452-085-4_011

2 Literature Review

In an attempt by Chakravarthy et. al. (Chakravarthi et al., 2023), a set of four datasets comprising abusive comments in Tamil and code-mixed Tamil-English extracted from YouTube is presented. Each dataset has undergone comment-level annotation, wherein polarities are assigned to the comments. To establish baselines for these datasets, the authors conducted experiments using various machine learning classifiers and presented the results in terms of F1-score, precision, and recall. Prasanth et al. (Prasanth et al., 2022) conducted a study focusing on the detection of abusive comments within given text. The authors employed TF-IDF with char-wb analyzers and utilized the Random Kitchen Sink (RKS) algorithm to generate feature vectors. For classification purposes, they employed the Support Vector Machine (SVM) classifier with a polynomial kernel. The proposed method was applied to both Tamil and Tamil-English datasets, resulting in f1-scores of 0.32 and 0.25, respectively. Priyadharsini et. al. (Priyadharshini et al., 2022a) provides a comprehensive review of a shared task focused on identifying abusive comments encompassing various categories such as Homophobia, Misandry, Counter-speech, Misogyny, Xenophobia, Transphobic, and hope speech. The participants were provided with a dataset extracted from social media, which was labeled with the aforementioned categories in both Tamil and Tamil-English code-mixed languages. The participants employed diverse machine learning and deep learning algorithms for their approaches. The paper presents an overview of this task, including detailed information about the dataset and the results achieved by the participants. The objective of the study by Bharathi and Varsha (Bharathi and Varsha, 2022a) is to automate the identification and categorization of abusive comments into specific categories like Misogynism, Misandry, Homophobia, and Cyberbullying. The datasets utilized in this research were provided by the DravidianLangTech@ACL2022 organizers and consisted of code-mixed Tamil text. The authors trained these datasets using pre-trained transformer models such as BERT, m-BERT, and XLNET. Remarkably, they achieved a weighted average F1 score of 0.96 for Tamil-English code-mixed text and 0.59 for Tamil text. Gupta et al. (Gupta et al., 2022) conducted a study where they introduced a model called AbuseXLMR, designed specifically for detecting abusive content. This model was pre-trained on a vast amount of social media comments in over 15 Indic languages. Notably, AbuseXLMR exhibited superior performance compared to XLM-R and MuRIL when evaluated on multiple Indic datasets. In addition to providing annotations, this study also released mappings between comment, post, and user IDs, enabling the modeling of relationships among them. Furthermore, competitive baselines for monolingual, cross-lingual, and few-shot scenarios were shared, intending to establish the collected dataset as a benchmark for future research. The primary goal of the study by Marreddy et. al. (Marreddy et al., 2022) is to address the challenges posed by limited resources in the Telugu language. The authors make several valuable contributions to enrich resources for Telugu. They have curated a large annotated dataset containing 35,142 sentences for various NLP tasks, including sentiment analysis, emotion identification, hate-speech detection, and sarcasm detection. To enhance model efficiency, the authors have developed separate lexicons for sentiment, emotion, and hate speech and utilized pre-trained word and sentence embeddings. Furthermore, the authors have created different pre-trained language models specifically for Telugu, such as ELMo-Te, BERT-Te, RoBERTa-Te, ALBERT-Te, and DistilBERT-Te, using a sizable Telugu corpus comprising 8,015,588 sentences. Notably, the authors demonstrate that these developed models significantly enhance the performance of the four NLP tasks and provide benchmark results for Telugu.

3 Task Description

We used the CodaLab platform to conduct the task [1]. The task includes three subtasks - abusive language detection in

- **Tamil**: Abusive language detection from Tamil codemixed social media text
- **Tamil-English**: Abusive language detection from Tamil-English codemixed social media text
- **Telugu-English**: Abusive language detection from Telugu-English codemixed social media text

3.1 Tamil

The dataset was compiled utilizing the YouTube comment scraper, capturing comprehensive com-

[1] https://codalab.lisn.upsaclay.fr/competitions/11096

ments in the Tamil script. The comments were sourced from videos addressing subjects related to homophobia, transphobia, misogyny, xenophobia, and misandry. However, procuring Tamil comments from YouTube videos posed challenges due to the extensive array of videos available. An extensive effort was made to exclusively retain comments in the Tamil language, resulting in the exclusion of non-Tamil comments. The comment annotations encompassed seven distinct classes, which are itemized in Table 1. The table provides comment counts for each class within every set.

Table 1: Distribution of training, test, and dev datasets used for the shared task on abusive language detection in Tamil

Categories	Train	Test	Dev
None-of-the-above	1295	416	346
Hope-Speech	86	26	11
Homophobia	35	8	8
Misandry	446	127	104
Counter-speech	149	47	36
Transphobic	9	2	2
Xenophobia	95	25	29
Misogyny	125	48	24
Total	2240	699	560

3.2 Tamil-English

The dataset was acquired from YouTube using the YouTube comment scraper. These comments are specifically in Tamil-English codemixed social media text, where Tamil characters are transliterated into the Latin script. Comments that incorporate both Tamil and English words, written in their respective scripts, were included in the dataset. We adhered to YouTube's guidelines to categorize the comments into 7 labels: Homophobia, Transphobia, Hope-speech, Misandry, Xenophobia, Misogyny, Counter-speech, and None-of-the-above. Table 2 below presents the quantities of comments in each dataset as well as the distribution of comments across each label.

Table 2: Distribution of training, test, and dev datasets used for the shared task on abusive language detection in Tamil-English

Categories	Train	Test	Dev
None-of-the-above	3720	1141	919
Hope-Speech	213	70	53
Homophobia	172	56	43
Misandry	830	292	218
Counter-speech	348	88	95
Transphobic	157	58	40
Xenophobia	297	95	70
Misogyny	211	57	50
Total	5948	1857	1488

3.3 Telugu-English

This task was hosted in CodaLab. This task encourages researchers to build machine learning or deep learning models for detecting hate comments from Telugu-English codemixed social media text. The dataset was prepared by collecting hate comments from YouTube. The initial challenge was identifying the videos where we could find the hate comments. The comments in which Telugu characters are written using Latin scripts and comments containing both Telugu and English words written in respective scripts were considered for preparing the dataset. We followed the regulations of YouTube to annotate the comments into hate and non-hate. The annotators were Telugu native speakers with English proficiency and good academic qualifications. Finally, the dataset consisted of 4500 annotated comments, of which 4000 were used as the training data, and 500 were considered the test data. The training data was released to the participants initially to build the model. The participants were free to choose the validation data. During the testing phase of the competition, we released the test data without labels, and the participants were asked to predict the labels. We published the test data with labels along with the rank list.

The training dataset consisted of 1939 hate and 2061 non-hate comments, whereas the test data had 250 hate and non-hate comments each. The distribution of the data points in each class indicates no considerable class imbalance problem. The train-test split of the dataset and the number of data points in each class is given in Table 3.

Table 3: Distribution of training and test datasets used for the shared task on abusive language detection in Telugu-English

Category	Train	Test
Hate	1939	250
Non-hate	2061	250
Total	4000	250

We received 52 registrations for the competition. However, only eight teams submitted the predictions for the test data. We accepted a maximum of three runs from each team, and the run with the highest performance score was considered for preparing the rank list, which is shown in Table 5. Macro F1-score was used to evaluate the performance of the submitted results and prepare the rank list.

4 System Descriptions

This section summarizes the systems submitted to the Abusive Comment Detection in Tamil and Telugu tasks.

4.1 Team: MUCS

The team MUCS (Hegde et al., 2023) submitted three different models to the competition. In all three approaches, the authors used a resampling approach but used different feature extraction algorithms. The first model was developed by using TF-IDF as the feature extraction algorithm. The second method used the Telugu-bert model to generate the input text's feature representation. In contrast, the authors used the multilingual BERT model in the third model. The third approach achieved the highest macro F1-score of 0.7459, and the team secured first place.

4.2 Team: DeepBlueAI

The team DeepBlueAI (Luo and Wang, 2023) used XLM-RoBERTa to develop their base model for classifying Telugu comments into hate and non-hate categories. They mixed multiple language datasets at different proportions to build the model. In addition, the authors performed cross-validation to develop a generalized model. This team secured the second position in the shared task, and their submission achieved a macro F1-score of 0.7318.

4.3 Team: Habesha

The team followed an LSTM-based approach for modelling the data (Yigezu et al., 2023). They did not use any other algorithms to generate the word embedding. The model consisted of a dropout layer introduced to avoid the overfitting problem, which generally happens when the number of data points is less. In addition, the model was set up to use early stopping based on validation loss, which stops training if the validation loss does not improve for a certain number of epochs. The team was placed third in the competition and scored a macro F1-score of 0.6519.

In the second model, the authors used character-based RNN for training the model.

4.4 Team: AK-NLP

The team submitted two models. In the first model, the authors used Term Frequency-Inverse Document Frequency (TF-IDF) to represent the comments as vectors and further used an LSTM model to learn the text's sequential properties. The second approach used a Word2Vec-based hierarchical attention network for building the model. In this work, the authors used 20,000 external codemixed Telugu data for training the Word2Vec model. The TF-IDF+LSTM model achieved the highest performance among the two submissions, with a macro F1-score of 0.6430. This team achieved the fourth rank in the competition.

4.5 Team: AbhiPaw

The team AbhiPaw (Bala and Krishnamurthy, 2023) achieved the fifth rank in the compeition, and they scored a macro F1-score of 0.6319. The team implemented a Logistic Regression-based classifier for categorizing the Telugu-Englosh comments into hate and non-hate category.

4.6 Team: SuperNova

Team SuperNova (Reddy et al., 2023) used TF-IDF for feature extraction and Support Vector Machine (SVM) for classification. They did not consider any external dataset for feature extraction. The team achieved the sixth position with a macro F1-score of 0.6189.

4.7 Team: Athena

The team Athena (Sivanaiah et al., 2023a) implemented their model using the Logistic Regression classifier. They used the TF-IDF vectorization algorithm to vectorize the text data in the dataset before passing it to the model. They did not utilize any external data for generating the feature. The team was placed in the seventh position with a macro F1-score of 0.6137.

4.8 Team: CSSCUTN

The team used Bag of Words and TF-IDF feature representation algorithms for converting the input text into a feature representation (Pannerselvam et al., 2023). The authors used machine learning algorithms such as Support Vector Machine (SVM), Logistic Regression, and Random Forest for building the model. They did not use any external datasets for training the model. The team obtained the eighth

5 Result Analysis and Discussion

This section discusses the submission by different teams in the shared task.

5.1 Tamil

In the Tamil task, numerous participants took part, contributing a total of 9 submissions. The leading team, MUCS, achieved a macro F1 score of 0.46. This team employed the mBERT pre-trained transformer model using the resample method, along with DistilBERT using the same resample method, both of which delivered the top performance. The second-highest performing team, Harmony, adopted a strategy involving transliteration to Tamil and amalgamation with Tamil data. They balanced class distribution by oversampling minority classes until all classes had an equal count. Additionally, they applied the IndicNLP morphological analyzer for stemming. Subsequently, the data was fed into transformer models: MuRIL and XLM-RoBERTa with fine-tuning. They also employed fast text embedding, which underwent two parallel recurrent layers—two Bi-LSTM and two Bi-GRU and this team got 0.41 macro F1 scores.

5.2 Tamil-English

In the Tamil-English codemixed task, 12 participants submitted their evaluation predictions. A rank list was compiled based on the macro F1 scores. Notably, DeepBlueAI secured the top rank with an F1 score of 0.55, while the team SuperNova achieved the lowest rank with an F1 score of 0.25. The team that claimed the first position employed Fine-tuning with XLM-RoBERTa as the foundational model. They also explored mixing multiple language datasets at various ratios and utilized cross-validation techniques. Conversely, the team that ended up with the last rank adopted a TF-IDF approach in conjunction with basic machine learning models. Interestingly, the teams discovered that the most effective results were achieved when combining Tf-IDF feature extraction with various machine learning and transformer models. Additionally, these teams found success by incorporating resampling techniques into their transformer model implementations.

5.3 Telugu-English

The submissions by different teams include various feature extraction approaches and classification models. Most models were based on TF-IDF feature extraction followed by a machine learning classifier. However, the two teams used BERT-based approaches for developing their models. Another two teams used LSTM and RNN architectures for modelling the Telugu-English codemixed data. It is observed from the macro F1-scores of all the teams that the model based on BERT and its variants achieved the top ranks, followed by LSTM and RNN-based models. The bottom-placed teams used TF-IDF feature extraction algorithms. Therefore, it is evident that the BERT-based embedding algorithms learn better features for classification than conventional approaches such as TF-IDF and Bag of Words.

6 Conclusion

This paper discussed the findings of the shared task conducted as part of the third Workshop on Speech and Language Technologies for Dravidian Languages at RANLP 2023 on abusive comment detection in Tamil, Tamil-English and Telugu-English data. The datasets used for the competition were collected from YouTube comments and annotated with experts' help in compliance with YouTube's regulations. There were nine, eleven and eight submissions in Tamil, Tamil-English and Telugu-English tasks, respectively. Most teams used multilingual BERT-based pre-trained models to transform the input text into the feature vector. The other submissions consisted of models using TF-IDF features and machine learning classifiers. We used macro F1-score for computing the classification performance and prepared the rank list accordingly.

Acknowledgments

The author Bharathi Raja Chakravarthi was supported in part by a research grant from Science Foundation Ireland (SFI) under Grant Number SFI/12/RC/2289_P2(Insight_2).

References

R Anita and CN Subalalitha. 2019. An approach to cluster Tamil literatures using discourse connectives. In *2019 IEEE 1st International Conference on Energy, Systems and Information Processing (ICESIP)*, pages 1–4. IEEE.

Table 4: Rank list for the Tamil subtask

Team Name	macro F1	Rank
MUCS (Hegde et al., 2023)	0.46	1
Harmony (Raaj P et al., 2023)	0.41	2
AK_NLP	0.35	3
KEC_AI_NLP (Shanmugavadivel et al., 2023)	0.35	4
Athena (Sivanaiah et al., 2023a)	0.28	5
AbhiPaw (Bala and Krishnamurthy, 2023)	0.27	6
DeepBlueAI (Luo and Wang, 2023)	0.26	7
Habesha (Yigezu et al., 2023)	0.22	8
Supernova (Reddy et al., 2023)	0.15	9

Table 5: Rank list for the Tamil-English subtask

Team Name	macro F1	Rank
DeepBlueAI (Luo and Wang, 2023)	0.55	1
AK-NLP	0.51	2
Harmony (Raaj P et al., 2023)	0.50	3
MUCS (Hegde et al., 2023)	0.49	4
Avalanche (Sivanaiah et al., 2023b)	0.44	5
KEC_AI_NLP (Shanmugavadivel et al., 2023)	0.42	6
Athena (Sivanaiah et al., 2023a)	0.37	7
Avalanche (Sivanaiah et al., 2023b)	0.35	8
CSSCUTN (Pannerselvam et al., 2023)	0.35	8
AbhiPaw (Bala and Krishnamurthy, 2023)	0.29	9
Habesha (Yigezu et al., 2023)	0.26	10
SuperNova (Reddy et al., 2023)	0.25	11

Table 6: Rank list for the Telugu-English subtask

Team Name	macro F1	Rank
MUCS (Hegde et al., 2023)	0.7459	1
DeepBlueAI (Luo and Wang, 2023)	0.7318	2
Habesha (Yigezu et al., 2023)	0.6519	3
AK-NLP	0.6430	4
AbhiPaw (Bala and Krishnamurthy, 2023)	0.6319	5
Supernova (Reddy et al., 2023)	0.6189	6
Athena (Sivanaiah et al., 2023a)	0.6137	7
CSSCUTN (Pannerselvam et al., 2023)	0.5939	8

Abhinaba Bala and Parameswari Krishnamurthy. 2023. Abhipaw @ abusive comment detection in tamil and telugu-dravidianlangtech. In *Proceedings of the Third Workshop on Speech and Language Technologies for Dravidian Languages*, Varna, Bulgaria. Recent Advances in Natural Language Processing.

B Bharathi and A Agnusimmaculate Silvia. 2021. SSNCSE_NLP@DravidianLangTech-EACL2021: Offensive language identification on multilingual code mixing text. In *Proceedings of the First Workshop on Speech and Language Technologies for Dravidian Languages*, pages 313–318, Kyiv. Association for Computational Linguistics.

B Bharathi and Josephine Varsha. 2022a. Ssncse nlp@ tamilnlp-acl2022: Transformer based approach for detection of abusive comment for tamil language. In *Proceedings of the Second Workshop on Speech and Language Technologies for Dravidian Languages*, pages 158–164.

B Bharathi and Josephine Varsha. 2022b. SSNCSE NLP@TamilNLP-ACL2022: Transformer based approach for detection of abusive comment for Tamil language. In *Proceedings of the Second Workshop on Speech and Language Technologies for Dravidian Languages*, pages 158–164, Dublin, Ireland. Association for Computational Linguistics.

Bharathi Raja Chakravarthi. 2023. Detection of homophobia and transphobia in Youtube comments. *International Journal of Data Science and Analytics*, pages 1–20.

Bharathi Raja Chakravarthi, Adeep Hande, Rahul Ponnusamy, Prasanna Kumar Kumaresan, and Ruba Priyadharshini. 2022a. How can we detect homophobia and transphobia? experiments in a multilingual code-mixed setting for social media governance. *International Journal of Information Management Data Insights*, 2(2):100119.

Bharathi Raja Chakravarthi, Ruba Priyadharshini, Shubanker Banerjee, Manoj Balaji Jagadeeshan, Prasanna Kumar Kumaresan, Rahul Ponnusamy, Sean Benhur, and John Philip McCrae. 2023. Detecting abusive comments at a fine-grained level in a low-resource language. *Natural Language Processing Journal*, 3:100006.

Bharathi Raja Chakravarthi, Ruba Priyadharshini, Thenmozhi Durairaj, John McCrae, Paul Buitelaar, Prasanna Kumaresan, and Rahul Ponnusamy. 2022b. Overview of the shared task on homophobia and transphobia detection in social media comments. In *Proceedings of the Second Workshop on Language Technology for Equality, Diversity and Inclusion*, pages 369–377, Dublin, Ireland. Association for Computational Linguistics.

Vikram Gupta, Sumegh Roychowdhury, Mithun Das, Somnath Banerjee, Punyajoy Saha, Binny Mathew, Animesh Mukherjee, et al. 2022. Multilingual abusive comment detection at scale for indic languages. *Advances in Neural Information Processing Systems*, 35:26176–26191.

Asha Hegde, Sharal G, Kavya andCoelho, and Hosahalli Lakshmaiah Shashirekha. 2023. Mucs@dravidianlangtech2023: Leveraging learning models to identify abusive comments in code-mixed dravidian languages. In *Proceedings of the Third Workshop on Speech and Language Technologies for Dravidian Languages*, Varna, Bulgaria. Recent Advances in Natural Language Processing.

Zhipeng Luo and Jiahui Wang. 2023. Deepblueai@dravidianlangtech. In *Proceedings of the Third Workshop on Speech and Language Technologies for Dravidian Languages*, Varna, Bulgaria. Recent Advances in Natural Language Processing.

Mounika Marreddy, Subba Reddy Oota, Lakshmi Sireesha Vakada, Venkata Charan Chinni, and Radhika Mamidi. 2022. Am i a resource-poor language? data sets, embeddings, models and analysis for four different nlp tasks in telugu language. *ACM Transactions on Asian and Low-Resource Language Information Processing*, 22(1):1–34.

Kathiravan Pannerselvam, Saranya Rajiakodi, Rahul Ponnusamy, and Sajeetha Thavareesan. 2023. Css-cutn@dravidianlangtech:abusive comments detection in tamil and telugu. In *Proceedings of the Third Workshop on Speech and Language Technologies for Dravidian Languages*, Varna, Bulgaria. Recent Advances in Natural Language Processing.

SN Prasanth, R Aswin Raj, P Adhithan, B Premjith, and Soman Kp. 2022. Cen-tamil@ dravidianlangtech-acl2022: Abusive comment detection in tamil using tf-idf and random kitchen sink algorithm. In *Proceedings of the Second Workshop on Speech and Language Technologies for Dravidian Languages*, pages 70–74.

B Premjith, KP Soman, and M Anand Kumar. 2018. A deep learning approach for malayalam morphological analysis at character level. *Procedia computer science*, 132:47–54.

Ruba Priyadharshini, Bharathi Raja Chakravarthi, Subalalitha Cn, Thenmozhi Durairaj, Malliga Subramanian, Kogilavani Shanmugavadivel, Siddhanth U Hegde, and Prasanna Kumaresan. 2022a. Overview of abusive comment detection in tamil-acl 2022. In *Proceedings of the Second Workshop on Speech and Language Technologies for Dravidian Languages*, pages 292–298.

Ruba Priyadharshini, Bharathi Raja Chakravarthi, Subalalitha Chinnaudayar Navaneethakrishnan, Thenmozhi Durairaj, Malliga Subramanian, Kogilavani Shanmugavadivel, Siddhanth U Hegde, and Prasanna Kumar Kumaresan. 2022b. Findings of the shared task on abusive comment detection in tamil. In *Proceedings of the Second Workshop on Speech and Language Technologies for Dravidian Languages. Association for Computational Linguistics*.

Amrish Raaj P, Abirami Murugappan, Lysa Packiam R S, and Deivamani M. 2023. Harmony@dravidianlangtech: Transformer-based ensemble learning for abusive comment detection. In *Proceedings of the Third Workshop on Speech and Language Technologies for Dravidian Languages*, Varna, Bulgaria. Recent Advances in Natural Language Processing.

Ankitha Reddy, Pranav Moorthi, and Ann Maria Thomas. 2023. Supernova@dravidianlangtech 2023@abusive comment detection in tamil and telugu - (tamil, tamil-english, telugu-english). In *Proceedings of the Third Workshop on Speech and Language Technologies for Dravidian Languages*, Varna, Bulgaria. Recent Advances in Natural Language Processing.

Ratnasingam Sakuntharaj and Sinnathamby Mahesan. 2016. A novel hybrid approach to detect and correct spelling in Tamil text. In *2016 IEEE international conference on information and automation for sustainability (ICIAfS)*, pages 1–6. IEEE.

Ratnasingam Sakuntharaj and Sinnathamby Mahesan. 2017. Use of a novel hash-table for speeding-up suggestions for misspelt Tamil words. In *2017 IEEE international conference on industrial and information systems (ICIIS)*, pages 1–5. IEEE.

Ratnasingam Sakuntharaj and Sinnathamby Mahesan. 2021. Missing word detection and correction based on context of Tamil sentences using n-grams. In *2021 10th International Conference on Information and Automation for Sustainability (ICIAfS)*, pages 42–47. IEEE.

Kogilavani Shanmugavadivel, Malliga Subramanian, ShriDurga R, SRIGHA S, Sree Harene J S, and Yasvanth Bala P. 2023. Kec_ai_nlp@dravidianlangtech: Abusive comment detection in tamil language. In *Proceedings of the Third Workshop on Speech and Language Technologies for Dravidian Languages*, Varna, Bulgaria. Recent Advances in Natural Language Processing.

Rajalakshmi Sivanaiah, Angel Deborah S, M Hema, and Anza Prem. 2023a. Athena@dravidianlangtech: Abusive comment detection in code-mixed languages using machine learning techniques. In *Proceedings of the Third Workshop on Speech and Language Technologies for Dravidian Languages*, Varna, Bulgaria. Recent Advances in Natural Language Processing.

Rajalakshmi Sivanaiah, Rajasekar S, Srilakshmisai K, Angel Deborah S, and Mirnalinee ThankaNadar. 2023b. Avalanche@dravidianlangtech:abusive comment detection in code mixed data using machine learning techniques with undersampling. In *Proceedings of the Third Workshop on Speech and Language Technologies for Dravidian Languages*, Varna, Bulgaria. Recent Advances in Natural Language Processing.

CN Subalalitha. 2019. Information extraction framework for Kurunthogai. *Sādhanā*, 44(7):156.

Malliga Subramanian, Rahul Ponnusamy, Sean Benhur, Kogilavani Shanmugavadivel, Adhithiya Ganesan, Deepti Ravi, Gowtham Krishnan Shanmugasundaram, Ruba Priyadharshini, and Bharathi Raja Chakravarthi. 2022. Offensive language detection in Tamil youtube comments by adapters and cross-domain knowledge transfer. *Computer Speech & Language*, 76:101404.

Krithika Swaminathan, Bharathi B, Gayathri G L, and Hrishik Sampath. 2022. SSNCSE_NLP@LT-EDI-ACL2022: Homophobia/transphobia detection in multiple languages using SVM classifiers and BERT-based transformers. In *Proceedings of the Second Workshop on Language Technology for Equality, Diversity and Inclusion*, pages 239–244, Dublin, Ireland. Association for Computational Linguistics.

Sajeetha Thavareesan and Sinnathamby Mahesan. 2019. Sentiment analysis in Tamil texts: A study on machine learning techniques and feature representation. In *2019 14th Conference on industrial and information systems (ICIIS)*, pages 320–325. IEEE.

Sajeetha Thavareesan and Sinnathamby Mahesan. 2020a. Sentiment lexicon expansion using Word2vec and fastText for sentiment prediction in Tamil texts. In *2020 Moratuwa engineering research conference (MERCon)*, pages 272–276. IEEE.

Sajeetha Thavareesan and Sinnathamby Mahesan. 2020b. Word embedding-based part of speech tagging in tamil texts. In *2020 IEEE 15th International conference on industrial and information systems (ICIIS)*, pages 478–482. IEEE.

Charangan Vasantharajan, Ruba Priyadharshini, Prasanna Kumar Kumarasen, Rahul Ponnusamy, Sathiyaraj Thangasamy, Sean Benhur, Thenmozhi Durairaj, Kanchana Sivanraju, Anbukkarasi Sampath, and Bharathi Raja Chakravarthi. 2022. TamilEmo: Fine-grained Emotion Detection Dataset for Tamil. In *International Conference on Speech and Language Technologies for Low-resource Languages*, pages 35–50. Springer.

Mesay Gemeda Yigezu, Selam Kanta, Grigori Kolesnikova, Olga andSidorov, and Gelbukh Alexander. 2023. Habesha@dravidianlangtech: Abusive comment detection using deep learning approach. In *Proceedings of the Third Workshop on Speech and Language Technologies for Dravidian Languages*, Varna, Bulgaria. Recent Advances in Natural Language Processing.

CoPara: The First Dravidian Paragraph-level *n-way* Aligned Corpus

Nikhil E
nikhil.e@research.iiit.ac.in
IIIT Hyderabad

Mukund Choudhary
mukund.choudhary@research.iiit.ac.in
IIIT Hyderabad

Radhika Mamidi
radhika.mamidi@iiit.ac.in
IIIT Hyderabad

Abstract

We present CoPara[1], the first publicly available paragraph-level (n-way aligned) multilingual parallel corpora for Dravidian languages. The collection contains 2856 paragraph/passage pairs between English and four Dravidian languages. We source the parallel paragraphs from the New India Samachar magazine and align them with English as a pivot language. We do human and artificial evaluations to validate the high-quality alignment and richness of the parallel paragraphs of a range of lengths. To show one of the many ways this dataset can be wielded, we finetuned IndicBART, an S2S transformer model on NMT for all XX-En pairs of languages in CoPara which perform better than existing sentence-level models on standard benchmarks (like BLEU) on sentence level translations and longer text too. We show how this dataset can enrich a model trained for a task like this, with more contextual cues and beyond sentence understanding even in low-resource settings like that of Dravidian languages. Finally, the dataset and models are made available publicly at GitHub[2] to help advance research in Dravidian NLP, parallel multilingual, and beyond sentence-level tasks like NMT, etc.

1 Introduction

Public and quality Multilingual data for Indic languages, explorations in NLP for the same, and in general community interest has grown in the last few years which gave us large parallel multilingual sentence level datasets and models (Ramesh et al., 2022; AI4Bharat et al., 2023). More specifically there is also much needed and quality research coming out in Dravidian NLP through community efforts and workshops like DravidianLangTech (Madasamy et al., 2022).

However, while we improve and amass resources & techniques on Dravidian sentence-level NLP, we should also utilize publicly available data to explore if there are structures beyond sentences that can be mined to inform these growing models of longer form texts (Zhang et al., 2019). This information could lead the models one step further into solving straightforward problems like translating a paragraph (and not translating parts of it and stitching it back together) or more subtle ones like coreference resolution or author style feature distinction (Gao and Shih, 2022).

This first paragraph/passage level multilingual n-way aligned (PLA from here on) dataset in Dravidian languages thus is a step towards opening up research for these languages on document level parallel corpus creation/NMT (El-Kishky et al., 2020; Zhang et al., 2022) and be an early part of the rare but growing work in PLA corpus creation & NLP (Thai et al., 2022; Zhang et al., 2019; Devaraj et al., 2021; Gottschalk and Demidova, 2017).

The PLA work cited above and classic sentence-level aligned works (SLA, like Europarl (Koehn, 2005)) show how PLA has directly bettered NMT, has been helpful in obtaining better aligned sentence level texts, linking entities across Wikipedia like databases, better literary & medical text translation, etc. In the context of Dravidian languages, early work like (J et al., 2010) & more recently DravidianLangTech '21 (Chakravarthi et al., 2021) concluded (across 2 works) that sentence length & complexity were crucial barriers to a good translation in this language family as well. With these motivations we present *CoPara* the first public Dravidian languages' PLA corpus (example at Figure 1) which has a fair share of small & long passages, some quality checks, and show how it bettered Dravidian NMT (both sentence and paragraph level) as an example of use.

[1] *CoPara* is a reference to **copra** -meaning *the kernel of a coconut*- that lent its name to English from Dravidian languages (its a cognate - `ko[pp/bb]ar[a/i]`, in all 4 languages we explore) and the fact that the contribution is of an aligned **Para**graph **corpora**.

[2] `https://github.com/ENikhil/CoPara`

Third Workshop on Speech and Language Technologies for Dravidian Languages, pages 88–96, Varna, Bulgaria, Sep 7, 2023.
https://doi.org/10.26615/978-954-452-085-4_012

Figure 1: An example from *CoPara*

2 Literature Review

2.1 The Dravidian Languages

Following is a brief introduction to the 4 Dravidian languages and their morpho-syntactic features of interest to motivate beyond sentence need of context in a corpus, summarised from Gutman and Avanzati (2013)'s compilation (find a more detailed sociolinguistic history at Madasamy et al. (2022)).

Some languages in the Dravidian language family (mainly South India and Asia), lack a written form, but the following 4 prominent ones have developed a large body of written literature. These agglutinative languages are mostly head-final with a flexible Subject-Object-Verb (SOV) word order, requiring the finite verb at the sentence's end. Each sentence permits one finite verb accompanied by one or more non-finite verbs. Subordinate clauses in these languages typically precede the main clause. **Kannada** is a pro-drop language that syntactically depends on case suffixes, postpositions, participles, gerunds, and infinitives. Since this makes the verb rich to express person and number, it allows subject omission. **Tamil** has its subject is usually in the nominative case. Subject-verb agreement exists, and verbs agree in person, number, and gender. It employs postpositions and case inflection to indicate syntactical relations. **Telugu**'s syntactic functions are conveyed through case suffixes and postpositions following the oblique stem. It is a pro-drop language too but lacks coordinating conjunctions, and coordinated phrases lengthen their final vowels. Relative clauses are formed using a relative participle instead of a finite verb. Finally, **Malayalam** closely resembles Tamil, but has diverged since the 8th century. It is agglutinative like Dravidian languages but has lost subject-verb and person-number agreement.

2.2 Related Work

There is some research on PLA pairs in a larger SLA dataset like Europarl but scarce work that focuses exclusively on creating a PLA corpus or NLP tasks on the same. The closest works (Thai et al., 2022; Zhang et al., 2019) respectively contribute the Par3 (multilingual, not n-way) & a Chinese-English translated novels' dataset. Thai et al. (2022) conclude that the current metrics (like BLEU (Papineni et al., 2002)) are insufficient to qualify paragraph alignment or translation etc. (thus we also do human evaluation on our data). They also find that NMT sentence-level translations are too literal as compared to human ones but BLEU prefers Google Translate over Humans. Finally they find paragraphs as a key unit for a literary paraphrase dataset and among Dravidian languages they report BLEU scores around 15-17 only for En-Ta translation quality in the literary domain. Similarly Zhang et al. (2019) innovate a hierarchical model to learn both word level and sentence level features to model a paragraph level unit in the literary domain too. They highlight how paragraph alignment is not a trivial task but make sentence alignment easier while also being a richer context for NMT models. Finally we model our Results and Analysis of the NMT experiment by plotting metric scores across sections of data with increasing average lengths.

Finally, while exploring semi-automatic methods to gauge a translator's style (Gao and Shih, 2022) highlight that sentence level auto textual aligners are more prone to errors than paragraph ones in Chinese-English and that sentence boundaries are not neatly defined by punctuation boundaries making paragraphs preferable, while (Gupta and Pala, 2012) make a Hindi-English aligner & found that it did better with aligned paragraphs, finally (Gottschalk and Demidova, 2017) showed that PLA with overlapping information in partner Wiki articles help make a comprehensive overview over shared entity facets in multilingual editions.

3 The *CoPara* Dataset

The dataset is based on the "New India Samachar" magazine (PIB, 2020), a publication launched by the Information and Broadcasting (I&B) Ministry of India in 2020 and published on a fortnightly basis in English and twelve different Indic languages. The magazine disseminates information on cabinet decisions, features content like 'Mann ki Baat', and discussions on prevailing issues.

We processed (Pipeline at Figure 2) 15 of these issues published in 2022 (subset picked randomly) to create *CoPara*. Thus we had a total of 75 issues as we aimed to align each of the 15 issues in an n-way manner across 5 languages: English and 4 Dravidian languages (Kannada, Tamil, Telugu, and Malayalam). This resulted in 2856 n-way aligned paragraphs with statistics as highlighted by Table 1. These statistics show that *CoPara* is consistent with general relative linguistic features e.g. for each sentence that is a part of an n-way aligned paragraph in English, it will be on an average longer than a Dravidian languages' sentence (more agglutinative) w.r.t. Word Length.

Avg. Len.	kn	ml	ta	te	*en*
Tokens	100.6	105.4	103.2	105.8	*108.6*
Words	49.7	45.8	53.0	52.1	*70.2*
Sentences	3.9	4.1	4.3	4.5	*3.8*

Table 1: Average Lengths of *CoPara* paragraphs on various levels of units across languages

The following sections detail the steps of the data processing and show a detailed analysis of alignment quality too.

3.1 Data Creation

3.1.1 Imaging and Alignment

Given the characteristic presence of image-based text or non-standard encoding in all the Dravidian language magazines (mostly because they were PDFs), direct text extraction was highly erroneous. Thus the first step for an annotator (native speaker of the Dravidian language magazine is in) was to copy an English magazine content and then to capture screenshots of the corresponding Dravidian magazines for more accurate text extraction via standard Optical Character Recognition (OCR) software later.

This process involved 6 annotators who subsequently segmented these magazine contents by indicating breaks throughout the copied/screenshot magazine by using a combination of article breaks (*A*) and paragraph breaks (*#P#*). These breaks were identified by annotators after briefing them on the process of using visual cues like relative positioning, spatial heuristics, and matching design elements.

This was then checked for errors and re-annotated if required until it was satisfactorily aligned. This segmenting was served as the main way to align paragraphs across all language versions of a given magazine.

3.1.2 OCR and cleaning

For the next step of transforming these image documents into the necessary text format, we used *Google Cloud Vision*'s OCR API (Google, 2017) as it is capable of generating outputs with higher confidence than other solutions that we tested (like *Tesseract OCR* and *Amazon Textract*) and supports English & all the Dravidian languages considered.

The generated textual data was then refined by the same team of annotators to maintain quality and de-noise text-image-text conversion by tackling issues such as misinterpreted characters, incorrect order, missing words, inappropriate formatting, and other noisy artifacts.

Following this refinement, the text is subjected to further standard text pre-processing to remove extra punctuations, redundant whitespaces, line breaks, and hyperlink fixes.

3.1.3 Splitting into paragraphs

The text is then aligned using the article breaks, resulting in `1893` n-way aligned articles. To ensure accurate paragraph alignment for the next step, we cross-examine each article in all languages, tallying the number of internal paragraphs. In instances where the count is identical, the corresponding paragraphs are assumed congruent and the tuple is incorporated into the dataset (in line with assumptions of previous work) - this holds even if the count totals to a single paragraph.

Finally, we tokenize each (now aligned) paragraph from all tuples using the **IndicBART-XXEN**[3] (Dabre et al., 2021) tokenizer from the Hugging Face Library, and if the resulting token count surpasses `512`, the corresponding tuple is filtered out to allow for higher compatibility with existing language models. This rigorous procedure

[3]`https://huggingface.co/ai4bharat/IndicBART-XXEN`

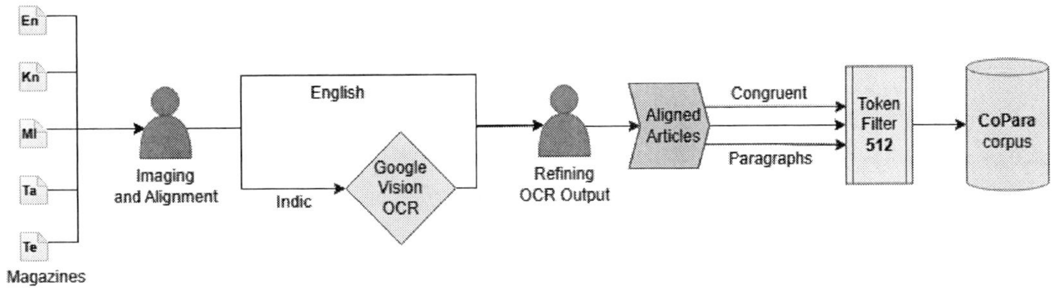

Figure 2: *CoPara* Creation Pipeline

culminates in a parallel paragraph-level corpus containing **2856** n-way aligned passages, where n = 5 (English, Kannada, Tamil, Telugu, Malayalam).

3.2 Data Quality

We adapt previous work in parallel sentences' Indic language multilingual corpus quality estimation (Ramesh et al., 2022) to fit to our paragraph-level corpus quality estimation tasks. We do two experiments to approximate the Semantic Textual Similarity (STS) of our data tuples as a proxy for their alignment quality as a correctly aligned paragraph will be generally highly similar to its other language counterpart too.

The two experiments are conducted on a randomized & length balanced subset (5%) of the data respectively an Artificial estimate (Section 3.2.1) by calculating the cosine similarity of cross-lingual embeddings and a Human estimate (Section 3.2.2) by asking human annotators to rate the same sentences on a 0-5 scale designed for an STS task.

3.2.1 Artificial Alignment Evaluation

To artificially estimate how aligned our data tuples are, we generate cross-lingual embeddings using the **indic-sentence-similarity-sbert**[4] (Deode et al., 2023) (Sentence-BERT) model for all paragraphs from the different languages in our corpus to map them to a shared vector space. These embeddings are reliable as this model is the state-of-the-art for Indic cross-lingual similarity (also we did not need to truncate data as all were bound to be below 512 tokens by design).

We use these to calculate the alignment score for each **XX-En** (Dravidian-English) paragraph pair with the cosine similarity function. Descriptive statistics for the same are shown in Table 2, and the distribution of alignment scores across all tuples for all XX-En pairs are shown in Figure 3.

cos_sim	**kn-en**	**ml-en**	**ta-en**	**te-en**
Mean	0.892	0.819	0.864	0.852
SD	0.047	0.073	0.065	0.064
Min	0.162	0.187	0.137	0.218
Max	0.975	0.948	0.979	0.965

Table 2: Descriptive statistics for xx-en alignment scores

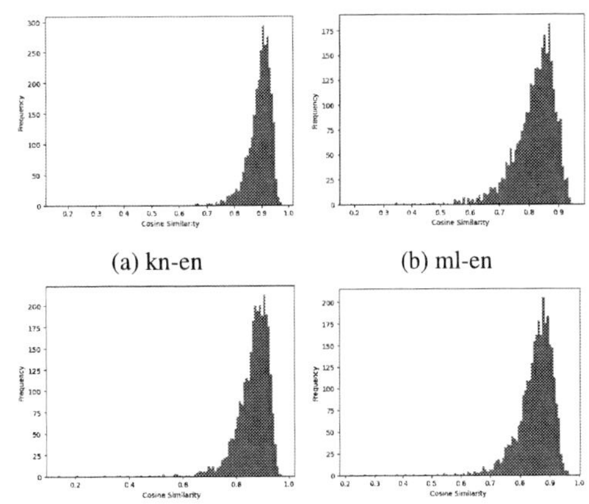

(a) kn-en (b) ml-en

(c) ta-en (d) te-en

Figure 3: The graphs for cosine-similarity (x-axis, goes from 0-1) distribution against number of tuples (y-axis)

We can observe that all XX-En language tuples' averages are above 0.8 making them very similar to each other overall. Kannada comes out to be the best-aligned subset of *CoPara* in terms of the highest means and lowest standard deviations. Meanwhile, Malayalam seems the lowest in the same terms.

A closer look at the lower (<0.5, which are less than 3% data in all of these XX-En tuples) cosine-similar tuples, shows that some of these tuples have a sentence more or less than the other which would have occurred because of how the translation was

[4] https://huggingface.co/l3cube-pune/indic-sentence-similarity-sbert

done and to which paragraph a border sentence fit more. Another set of low-performing tuples shows the existence of a referenced entity in one of the languages of the tuple and just a pronoun referral in the other. In this case, embedding-based cosine-similarity has only limited context outside of paragraphs to understand that the alignment is actually fine (this is a fallback consistent with SLA datasets).

3.2.2 Human evaluation

To assess the semantic textual similarity and gauge alignment quality, we enlisted the assistance of one human annotator for each subset of language pairs. We provided them with guidelines and utilized the scoring system from Agirre (Agirre et al., 2016), ensuring they were adequately briefed on the criteria. Annotators might have differed in their choice of minimum and maximum values when assigning scores. To account for variations in the scoring preferences of annotators, we normalized their marked scores within the range of 0 to 1. Normalizing the scores allows for a more consistent and standardized evaluation across all annotators, which would lead to a fairer assessment of the alignment quality.

score	kn-en	ml-en	ta-en	te-en
Mean	0.850	0.752	0.814	0.850
SD	0.245	0.301	0.278	0.245
Min	0.0	0.0	0.0	0.0
Max	1.0	1.0	1.0	1.0

Table 3: Descriptive statistics for xx-en alignment scores

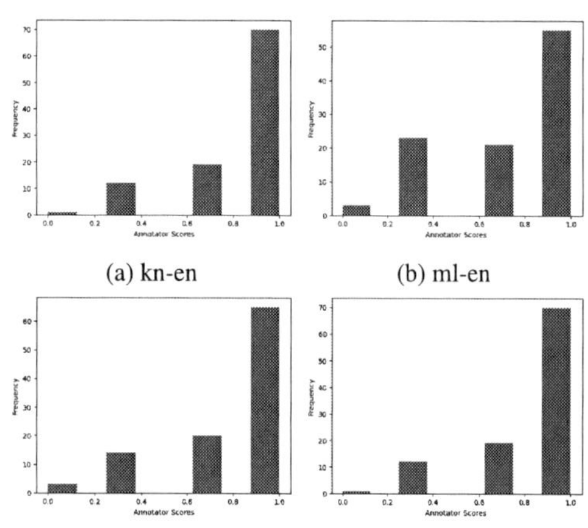

(a) kn-en (b) ml-en (c) ta-en (d) te-en

Figure 4: The graphs for annotator-score (x-axis, goes from 0-1) distribution against the number of tuples (y-axis)

Based on the human evaluation, can observe that all XX-En language tuples' averages are above 0.75, making them quite similar to each other. Kannada and Telugu come out as the best-aligned subsets of *CoPara* with Malayalam being the lowest aligned in terms of the mean and the standard deviation.

We see that both human and artificial STS scores indicate that while Kannada is more highly aligned and Malayalam is the least of the set, *CoPara* as an overall set is aligned well and is a usable dataset for parallel paragraph-level tasks in Dravidian Languages. We show how it actually improves a sentence-level NMT model's performance in Dravidian languages in the next section.

4 Neural Machine Translation by Fine-tuning on *CoPara*

We now show how *CoPara* can be used to improve NMT in Dravidian languages. For the same, we take a multilingual Indic Language Model fine-tuned on the NMT task. We further finetune it on our dataset and check if the performance increases as compared to base model's results.

4.1 Dataset

As this experiment required comparable results to existing models, we sampled 5% data out from the main dataset, for evaluation. This data was a collection of five parts, labeled from 1 to 5, with each section corresponding to a specific number of sentences within a data point.

Section 1 of the evaluation set exclusively contains single sentence-length paragraphs, with an average of 30 token length (other sentence-level Indic datasets have had 25 as an average sentence length) for us to keep it comparable to existing models. In contrast, like (Zhang et al., 2019) our last evaluation section, section 5 comprises paragraphs that exceed five sentences, representing longer texts. While all the sections between 1 and 5 represent the number of sentences each passage has, in that section. Finally we used the embeddings generated from the last section to find out which evaluation paragraphs were very similar (>0.8) to fine-tuning data. We found 28 such data points out of 130 that we sampled, leaving us with 102 aligned passages to run statistics on and infer from them.

Language Pairs →	kn-en		ml-en		ta-en		te-en	
↓ Dataset evaluated	base	*FT*	base	*FT*	base	*FT*	base	*FT*
CoPara section 1	27.99	43.47	18.75	22.20	19.73	23.94	14.85	20.86
FLORES101 devtest	11.87	15.55	12.08	15.38	12.77	15.17	15.19	17.02
CoPara section 2	23.79	40.08	18.92	31.79	21.17	28.34	16.29	23.77
CoPara section 3	22.42	39.33	12.82	27.52	19.19	30.23	12.45	23.68
CoPara section 4	23.12	41.02	8.82	27.57	12.60	25.72	8.95	25.54
CoPara section 5	18.71	35.94	10.95	21.22	8.94	25.58	10.86	21.65
CoPara averaged	24.12	40.63	15.33	26.39	17.92	26.84	13.46	22.93

Table 4: BLEU scores for base vs finetuned on all XX-En pairs across all sections and FLORES101 devtest

4.2 Model

For our experimentation, we employed **IndicBART**, a multilingual sequence-to-sequence Transformer model specifically pretrained on Indic languages. Architecturally, it utilizes 6 encoder and decoder layers with model and filter dimensions of 1024 and 4096 respectively on 16 attention heads (244M parameters). In specific, we utilized the publicly available ***IndicBART-XXEN*** variant, which is already finetuned on the PMI(Haddow and Kirefu, 2020) and PIB(Siripragada et al., 2020) sentence-level datasets for XX-En NMT. This will be our base model from here on.

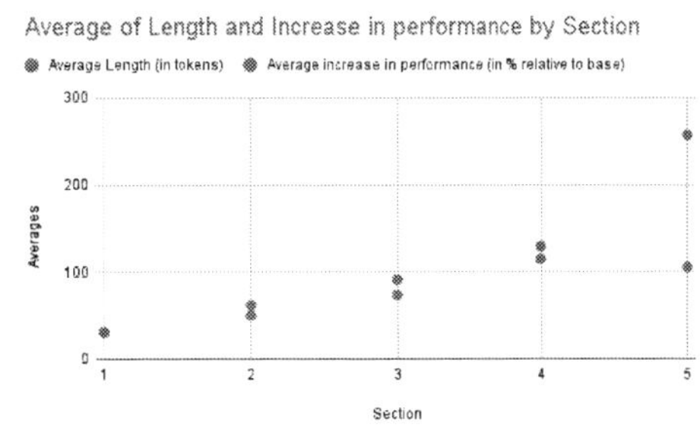

Figure 5: *CoPara* increases performance. Sections are representative of the number of sentences per paragraph and the Increase is in percent increase from baseline scores

4.3 Training

We utilized an 85:10:5 split on our dataset for training, development, and evaluation purposes. The training set was used to fine-tune the model using YANMTT(Dabre and Sumita, 2021), while the development set helped determine early stopping checkpoints. The evaluation set was utilized for qualitative, and quantitative evaluation of translations. Fine-tuning was performed individually for each XX-En language pair, using a batch size of 512 tokens for 10 epochs on an Nvidia V100 GPU. The best-performing checkpoint for each XX-En translation pair was saved as the final model.

4.4 Results

Table 4 presents a comparison of the performance of the IndicBART-XXEN model before and after fine-tuning it with our dataset. The finetuned version performs better than the base model across all language pairs and all sections. For a more generalized result and testing *CoPara* fine-tuned model's increase in performance outside of our corpus, we tested on the similarly sized ***FLORES101 devtest*** (Goyal et al., 2021) as well. Table 5 shows that the fine-tuned model does better on this benchmark as well, across the 4 languages.

Figure 5 summarises the results from *CoPara* evaluation, across different sections/lengths. These results show that the 1-sentence section of the evaluation set showed a 55% increase from the baseline BLEU scores (other metrics were similar) on finetuning. This increase because of finetuning increases as we make the paragraphs contain more sentences until it is composed of 4 sentences, after which there is still an increase from the baseline but not proportionate to the increase in the number of sentences. This implies that *CoPara* does increase a model's paragraph handling capabilities but only up to a certain point, more work needs to be done for article-sized texts.

Across the 4 languages, we independently also calculated the effect of the standard deviation of cosine similarities on the increase in scores from baseline on just 1-sentence paragraphs and found that there was a -0.97 (Pearson's) correlation between the two. This indicates that as a dataset gets less reliable in paragraph alignment, the efficiency of it being able to enrich a sentence-level NMT model decreases. This also helped us explain why

Language Pairs →	kn-en		ml-en		ta-en		te-en	
↓ Dataset evaluated	base	*FT*	base	*FT*	base	*FT*	base	*FT*
CoPara section 1	0.933	0.956	0.916	0.933	0.923	0.930	0.916	0.933
FLORES101 devtest	0.933	0.925	0.925	0.932	0.927	0.925	0.920	0.936

Table 5: BERTScores for base vs finetuned on all XX-En pairs for section 1 and FLORES101 devtest

the Kannada fine-tuned model did consistently better than the Malayalam one.

Finally since BLEU has been shown insufficient as a metric for NMT (especially for longer texts), we tried out BERTScore (Zhang et al., 2020) (Table 5) to confirm results on sentence level performances of out model across languages and on teh FLORES101 devtest set as well. We see that except Kannada & Tamil data in the FLORES101 devtest sets, *CoPara* fine-tuning consistently increases performances and on these two the performance is still comparable.

5 Conclusion

We establish *CoPara* as the first parallel paragraph-level Dravidian n-way corpus by showing how it was formed and its quality by doing various evaluations. We then show that it significantly increases a sentence-level NMT model's performance on not just sentence level but also on paragraph-level data. We show that it does not hamper the base model's performance on sentence-level NMT, while enhancing it for processing paragraphs. These analyses are done on a different benchmark and on two different metrics as well.

We hope that this opens up avenues for long text and document-level NLP in Dravidian languages and that *CoPara* is grown both in quantity and quality by succeeding works.

6 Future Work and Limitations

One big improvement could be to find out better ways to align Malayalam data after finding systematic inaccuracy patterns and make it as good as Kannada data for a better *CoPara*. We can also finetune existing NMT models for the En-XX translation tasks and experiment with multilingual training to see if it can improve performance.

Recent work on Europarl (Amponsah-Kaakyire et al., 2021) showed that using a pivot language could cause deprecation, it would be interesting to see if the same applies to low resource language settings like Dravidian and work more on the same. (Thai et al., 2022) finds that human evaluations are still better than existing sentence-level metrics. One improvement to our work would have been to employ a more paragraph-relevant human evaluation but another improvement that is much needed is for a new set of metrics for this task.

Finally, future work can also try a hierarchical model like (Zhang et al., 2019) on our dataset to see if it can utilize the data better while we can work in parallel to make our models consume bigger paragraphs in innovative ways.

References

Eneko Agirre, Carmen Banea, Daniel Cer, Mona Diab, Aitor Gonzalez-Agirre, Rada Mihalcea, German Rigau, and Janyce Wiebe. 2016. SemEval-2016 task 1: Semantic textual similarity, monolingual and cross-lingual evaluation. In *Proceedings of the 10th International Workshop on Semantic Evaluation (SemEval-2016)*, pages 497–511, San Diego, California. Association for Computational Linguistics.

AI4Bharat, Jay Gala, Pranjal A. Chitale, Raghavan AK, Sumanth Doddapaneni, Varun Gumma, Aswanth Kumar, Janki Nawale, Anupama Sujatha, Ratish Puduppully, Vivek Raghavan, Pratyush Kumar, Mitesh M. Khapra, Raj Dabre, and Anoop Kunchukuttan. 2023. Indictrans2: Towards high-quality and accessible machine translation models for all 22 scheduled indian languages.

Kwabena Amponsah-Kaakyire, Daria Pylypenko, Cristina España-Bonet, and Josef van Genabith. 2021. Do not rely on relay translations: Multilingual parallel direct Europarl. In *Proceedings for the First Workshop on Modelling Translation: Translatology in the Digital Age*, pages 1–7, online. Association for Computational Linguistics.

Bharathi Raja Chakravarthi, Ruba Priyadharshini, Shubhanker Banerjee, Richard Saldanha, John P. McCrae, Anand Kumar M, Parameswari Krishnamurthy, and Melvin Johnson. 2021. Findings of the shared task on machine translation in Dravidian languages. In *Proceedings of the First Workshop on Speech and Language Technologies for Dravidian Languages*, pages 119–125, Kyiv. Association for Computational Linguistics.

Raj Dabre, Himani Shrotriya, Anoop Kunchukuttan, Ratish Puduppully, Mitesh M. Khapra, and Pratyush

Kumar. 2021. Indicbart: A pre-trained model for natural language generation of indic languages. *CoRR*, abs/2109.02903.

Raj Dabre and Eiichiro Sumita. 2021. Yanmtt: Yet another neural machine translation toolkit.

Samruddhi Deode, Janhavi Gadre, Aditi Kajale, Ananya Joshi, and Raviraj Joshi. 2023. L3cube-indicsbert: A simple approach for learning cross-lingual sentence representations using multilingual bert.

A. Devaraj, B. C. Wallace, I. J. Marshall, and J. J. Li. 2021. Paragraph-level Simplification of Medical Texts. *Proc Conf*, 2021:4972–4984. [PubMed Central:PMC5933936] [DOI:10.18653/v1/2021.naacl-main.395] [PubMed:5302480].

Ahmed El-Kishky, Vishrav Chaudhary, Francisco Guzmán, and Philipp Koehn. 2020. CCAligned: A massive collection of cross-lingual web-document pairs. In *Proceedings of the 2020 Conference on Empirical Methods in Natural Language Processing (EMNLP)*, pages 5960–5969, Online. Association for Computational Linguistics.

Zhao-Ming Gao and Jou-An Shih. 2022. A corpus-based computational study on translators' styles based on three chinese translations of the old man and the sea. In *The Routledge Handbook of Asian Linguistics*, pages 583–604. Routledge.

Google. 2017. Google cloud vision ocr api. `https://cloud.google.com/vision/docs/ocr`.

Simon Gottschalk and Elena Demidova. 2017. MultiWiki. *ACM Transactions on the Web*, 11(1):1–30.

Naman Goyal, Cynthia Gao, Vishrav Chaudhary, Peng-Jen Chen, Guillaume Wenzek, Da Ju, Sanjana Krishnan, Marc'Aurelio Ranzato, Francisco Guzman, and Angela Fan. 2021. The flores-101 evaluation benchmark for low-resource and multilingual machine translation.

Ankush Gupta and Kiran Pala. 2012. A generic and robust algorithm for paragraph alignment and its impact on sentence alignment in parallel corpora. In *Proc of the Workshop on Indian Language Data: Resource and Evaluation(WILDRE, Organized under LREC2012)*, pages 18–27.

Alejandro Gutman and Beatriz Avanzati. 2013. [link].

Barry Haddow and Faheem Kirefu. 2020. Pmindia – a collection of parallel corpora of languages of india.

Antony J, Nandini Warrier, and Soman Kp. 2010. Penn treebank-based syntactic parsers for south dravidian languages using a machine learning approach. *International Journal of Computer Applications*, 7.

Philipp Koehn. 2005. Europarl: A parallel corpus for statistical machine translation. In *Proceedings of Machine Translation Summit X: Papers*, pages 79–86, Phuket, Thailand.

Anand Kumar Madasamy, Asha Hegde, Shubhanker Banerjee, Bharathi Raja Chakravarthi, Ruba Priyadharshini, Hosahalli Shashirekha, and John McCrae. 2022. Overview of the shared task on machine translation in Dravidian languages. In *Proceedings of the Second Workshop on Speech and Language Technologies for Dravidian Languages*, pages 271–278, Dublin, Ireland. Association for Computational Linguistics.

Kishore Papineni, Salim Roukos, Todd Ward, and Wei-Jing Zhu. 2002. Bleu: A method for automatic evaluation of machine translation. In *Proceedings of the 40th Annual Meeting on Association for Computational Linguistics*, ACL '02, page 311–318, USA. Association for Computational Linguistics.

Press Information Bureau PIB. 2020. New India Samachar.

Gowtham Ramesh, Sumanth Doddapaneni, Aravinth Bheemaraj, Mayank Jobanputra, Raghavan AK, Ajitesh Sharma, Sujit Sahoo, Harshita Diddee, Mahalakshmi J, Divyanshu Kakwani, Navneet Kumar, Aswin Pradeep, Srihari Nagaraj, Kumar Deepak, Vivek Raghavan, Anoop Kunchukuttan, Pratyush Kumar, and Mitesh Shantadevi Khapra. 2022. Samanantar: The largest publicly available parallel corpora collection for 11 indic languages. *Transactions of the Association for Computational Linguistics*, 10:145–162.

Shashank Siripragada, Jerin Philip, Vinay P. Namboodiri, and C V Jawahar. 2020. A multilingual parallel corpora collection effort for Indian languages. In *Proceedings of the 12th Language Resources and Evaluation Conference*, pages 3743–3751, Marseille, France. European Language Resources Association.

Katherine Thai, Marzena Karpinska, Kalpesh Krishna, Bill Ray, Moira Inghilleri, John Wieting, and Mohit Iyyer. 2022. Exploring document-level literary machine translation with parallel paragraphs from world literature. In *Proceedings of the 2022 Conference on Empirical Methods in Natural Language Processing*, pages 9882–9902, Abu Dhabi, United Arab Emirates. Association for Computational Linguistics.

Biao Zhang, Ankur Bapna, Melvin Johnson, Ali Dabirmoghaddam, Naveen Arivazhagan, and Orhan Firat. 2022. Multilingual document-level translation enables zero-shot transfer from sentences to documents. In *Proceedings of the 60th Annual Meeting of the Association for Computational Linguistics (Volume 1: Long Papers)*, pages 4176–4192, Dublin, Ireland. Association for Computational Linguistics.

Tianyi Zhang, Varsha Kishore, Felix Wu, Kilian Q. Weinberger, and Yoav Artzi. 2020. Bertscore: Evaluating text generation with bert.

Yuqi Zhang, Kui Meng, and Gongshen Liu. 2019. Paragraph-level hierarchical neural machine translation. In *Neural Information Processing: 26th International Conference, ICONIP 2019, Sydney, NSW, Aus-*

tralia, December 12–15, 2019, Proceedings, Part III, page 328–339, Berlin, Heidelberg. Springer-Verlag.

ChatGPT-Powered Tourist Aid Applications: Proficient in Hindi, Yet To Master Telugu and Kannada

Sanjana Kolar
Dublin High School, California, USA
Voice Thesis, California, USA
kolarSanjana@gmail.com

Rohit Kumar
Voice Thesis, Texas, USA
rohit@voicethesis.com

Abstract

This research investigates the effectiveness of ChatGPT, an AI language model by OpenAI, in translating English into Hindi, Telugu, and Kannada languages, aimed at assisting tourists in India's linguistically diverse environment. To measure the translation quality, a test set of 50 questions from diverse fields such as general knowledge, food, and travel was used. These were assessed by five volunteers for accuracy and fluency, and the scores were subsequently converted into a BLEU score. The BLEU score evaluates the closeness of a machine-generated translation to a human translation, with a higher score indicating better translation quality. The Hindi translations outperformed others, showcasing superior accuracy and fluency, whereas Telugu translations lagged behind. Human evaluators rated both the accuracy and fluency of translations, offering a comprehensive perspective on the language model's performance.

1 Introduction

Language barriers often hinder effective communication and can lead to misunderstanding. e.g., a tourist may ask for directions to get to a specific location, but the local person may understand differently. Such communication can lead to getting lost or taking longer. Though English is widely spoken and understood, there could be significant communication issues in understanding the accent and language. For instance, visitors may have a hard time understanding similar-sounding words like "bazaar" (market) and "bizarre" (strange). Accurate and fluent translations play a crucial role in overcoming these challenges and ensuring smooth communication, enhancing visitor satisfaction, and fostering cultural understanding. So, developing efficient communication tools to bridge language barriers has become highly fundamental (Urlana et al., 2023), (Stüker et al., 2006), (Anand et al., 2023).

Generative AI technology learns using supervised and unsupervised algorithms to analyze, synthesize, summarize and transform language data (Radford et al., 2019), (Brown et al., 2020). Such technology provides many solutions, including language translation, to develop tourist-aided applications.

ChatGPT is one of the generative algorithms which can do several tasks, such as summarization, planning, and translation, based on prompts. ChatGPT is a transformer model trained as InstructGPT by openAI (Ouyang et al., 2022). The objective of this study is twofold: 1. To evaluate how well ChatGPT, an AI tool, can translate English into Indian languages like Kannada, Hindi, and Telugu for international visitors looking for information about Indian cuisine and travel. 2. To conduct an error analysis and provide valuable insights to improve these models for the tourist domain, so that such AI language models can be applied to enhance communication and provide better experiences for travelers in foreign countries(Vaswani et al., 2017).

2 Data Collection and Categorization

The initial data for this study was collected using a multi-faceted approach, combining insights from informal interviews with a diverse set of frequent travelers, online searches, and interactions with ChatGPT. Participants were asked questions about their experiences with language barriers, communication difficulties, and their expectations regarding translation services. This ensured a comprehensive understanding of travelers' challenges faced when

Third Workshop on Speech and Language Technologies for Dravidian Languages, pages 97–107, Varna, Bulgaria, Sep 7, 2023.
https://doi.org/10.26615/978-954-452-085-4_013

seeking local information, coupled with online travel websites and blogs. To further help the data collection process, queries were inputted to ChatGPT simulating travelers' interactions. Overall, around Sixty questions were finalized for further analysis.

All these Sixty questions were then analyzed by two independent volunteers to identify the key themes. A third volunteer was asked to resolve any conflicts and discrepancies. From the original set of Sixty questions, Fifty relevant questions were shortlisted and were categorized into 3 themes; General, Food, and Travel. The theme-based categorization allowed for a comprehensive analysis that aligned with research objectives.
You can find the list of 50 questions used for this experiment in the Appendix A.

3 Experiment Methodology

The experiment utilizes the openAI Language Model (LLM) model, specifically the "gpt-3.5-turbo" variant, for translating English text to the target language. The experiment involves a conversation-style interaction between the user and the system, where the system acts as a helpful assistant providing translations(Ouyang et al., 2022).

The prompt used to generate the data consists of two parts: a system role and a user role. The system's role is to introduce the assistant's purpose, which is to assist with English to Target Language translation. The user's role is to instruct the assistant to translate a specific English text to the target language. The provided source text serves as the input for the translation task(Lai et al., 2023).

The prompt used to generate the translation data:

- model="gpt-3.5-turbo"
- You are a helpful assistant that translates English to *Target Language*.
- Translate the following English text to *Target Language*

4 Evaluation Methodology

In this work, we use a subjective and an objective evaluation methodology. Subjective evaluation asks native speakers of a language to rate the accuracy and fluency of the translation (White and O'Connell, 1993).

To assess translation quality, participants were asked specific questions covering several characteristics of translation accuracy and fluency. For example, one question asked participants to assess the translated text on a scale of 1 to 5, indicating how correctly it conveyed the original text's meaning. Another question focused on fluency, asking participants to judge the smoothness and naturalness of the translated text. We aimed to cover multiple aspects of translation quality by incorporating a wide set of questions, ensuring a thorough evaluation procedure.

For accuracy evaluation, "On a scale of 1 to 5, how accurately does the translated text convey the meaning of the original text?"
For fluency evaluation, "On a scale of 1 to 5, how fluent is the translated text?", where 1-Bad, 2 - Poor, 3 - Fair, 4 - Good, 5 - Excellent.

Collecting scores on accuracy and fluency provides a comprehensive evaluation of the translation quality. It helps this study understand how accurately the AI model performs in translating the meaning of the original text while maintaining fluency in the target language.

5 Results and Analysis

Table 1 provides the accuracy and fluency scores. Overall, Hindi translations received the highest average scores, indicating better accuracy and fluency compared to Telugu and Kannada. Kannada translations showed relatively better performance than Telugu, while Telugu had the lowest average scores across all themes.

The average scores for Hindi translations in the General theme indicate high accuracy (4.8) and fluency (4.6) indicating effective translations. Kannada translations received relatively lower average scores for accuracy (3.7) and fluency (3.5) compared to Hindi. However, they moderately demonstrated decent accuracy and fluency. Telugu translations received the lowest average scores for accuracy (2.5) and fluency (2.1), suggesting there is room for development in accurately and fluently interpreting the meaning.

The average scores for Hindi translations in

Table 1: Accuracy and Fluency for Hindi, Kannada and Telugu.

Language	Avg.Accuracy	Avg.Fluency
Hindi	4.2	3.8
Hindi General	4.8	4.6
Hindi Food	3.8	3.3
Hindi Travel	3.7	3.3
Kannada	3.2	3
Kannada General	3.7	3.5
Kannada Food	3	2.9
Kannada Travel	2.6	2.4
Telugu	2.5	2.1
Telugu General	2.6	2.1
Telugu Food	2.5	2.1
Telugu Travel	2.4	1.9

the Food theme suggest moderate accuracy (3.8) and fluency (3.3). While the translations generally convey the meaning satisfactorily, there is some scope for improvement in terms of linguistic fluency. Kannada translations received slightly lower average scores for accuracy (3.0) and fluency (2.9) compared to Hindi. There is room for improvement in both accuracy and fluency in the translations. Telugu translations show a similar trend to the General theme, with relatively lower average scores for accuracy (2.4) and fluency (2.2), indicating the need for improvement.

The average scores for Hindi translations in the Travel theme suggest sufficient accuracy 3.7 for accuracy and 3.2 for fluency. However, there is room for improvement in terms of linguistic fluency to enhance the user experience. Kannada translations in the Travel theme received lower average scores for accuracy (2.6) and fluency (2.4) compared to Hindi. This suggests the need for further improvements to ensure accurate and fluent translations. Telugu translations in the Travel theme received the lowest average scores for accuracy (2.4) and fluency (1.9), indicating the need for significant improvements in both aspects.

6 Objective Evaluation

Table 2 shows an evaluation of the BLEU scores for machine translation of 50 questions into three languages - Telugu, Hindi, and Kannada - has been conducted. The BLEU score is a standard measure of machine translation quality, comparing machine-generated translations to a reference human translation on a scale of 0 to 100(Papineni et al., 2002).

Table 2: BLEU Scores for Hindi, Kannada and Telugu.

Language	BLEU Score
Hindi	72.69
Kannada	46.78
Telugu	13.12

The Hindi translation showed high-quality translation performance, achieving a high BLEU score of 72.69, indicating a high resemblance to reference translations and effective preservation of meaning in phrases. In contrast, the Telugu translation scored low on the BLEU scale (13.12), struggling with maintaining meaning in longer phrases and suggesting substantial room for improvement. There were significant disparities in translation quality across the languages, with Hindi excelling over Telugu and Kannada. These findings suggest a need for refining the translation models or methods, particularly for Telugu and Kannada, to enhance translation quality.

7 Qualitative Evaluation

The evaluators appreciated the comprehensive methodology used for data collection. They commended the use of a multi-faceted approach, combining insights from informal interviews, online searches, and interactions with ChatGPT. Below are some of the comments expressed in the participants' own words:

For Hindi Translation:

"I was amazed with how well Chat GPT has translated some of the questions, few words were translated beautifully. But some did not make much sense and had opposite meaning. But a good start :) "

"I'm pleasantly pleased with some of the translations; they incorporate rich vocabulary and demonstrate good grammar."

"The majority of the translated text shows promising improvements and correctness. With some additional refinement, it will become even more polished and accurate."

For Kannada Translation:

"Quite impressed with some of the translations, using some rich words which do seem grammatically correct. There is room for improvement which I'm sure it'll happen soon. The colloquial and spoken Kannada is quite different from the dramatized version and it does have work to do there."

"Harder questions translations and fluency is really good. Simpler questions are off. Some questions have literary translation gives a different meaning altogether."

"Some of the translations are apt and very good. Majority of them seems to do literal translation instead of intelligent meaningful translation similar to spoken language. Overall work in progress and would need more usage based inputs to correct the responses to make it very close to original intention of the sentence."

"Most of the translated text has half correct translation. It needs lot of refinement."

For Telugu Translation:

"The translation accuracy is not usable. Regional variations or idiomatic expressions are not in the current translation."

"While some parts of the translated text are correct, a significant portion requires further refinement to achieve better accuracy."

"The translation is ambiguous and does not reflect the true meaning in several cases."

8 Limitations

It is important to acknowledge the limitations of this study. Firstly, the sample size, although diverse, may not fully represent the entire population of Indian tourists and visitors.

Secondly, the volunteer ratings used for evaluating the translations introduce a potential source of subjectivity. While efforts were made to ensure consistency and reliability in the ratings, individual preferences and biases may have influenced the results.

Additionally, the study focused on three specific language pairs (English to Hindi, English to Kannada, and English to Telugu), and the findings may not be directly applicable to other language pairs.

Furthermore, a substantial limitation lies in the ambiguity surrounding the employed prompting process. The lack of transparency regarding this critical aspect raises questions about the potential impact of alternative prompts, such as those focused on identifying correct and incorrect translations, or the utilization of different prompts altogether.

Also, this study did not benchmark the performance of ChatGPT against other consumer tools supporting real-time language translation, such as Apple and Google.

Future studies should consider expanding the sample size, involving a wider range of participant demographics, and utilizing objective evaluation measures to complement the volunteer ratings.

9 Conclusion

This research evaluated ChatGPT's efficacy as a digital companion for tourists in India, particularly in translating English to Hindi, Kannada, and Telugu. Hindi outshone the others in accuracy and fluency, whereas Telugu lagged. The study underscores the importance of effective translation tools in facilitating communication amidst India's linguistic diversity and surging foreign tourism. Utilizing 50 diverse questions, participants assessed the translations for accuracy and fluency. The findings showed consistent superior performance by Hindi, moderate results in Kannada, and considerable improvement opportunities in Telugu translations. (Stahlberg, 2020)

The research utilized the BLEU score, a recognized yardstick for machine translation quality, for assessment. Results showed Hindi translations aligning closely with reference translations, while Kannada had a moderate correspondence and Telugu fell behind, needing considerable refinement. Based on this, the study advised enhancing Telugu translations through exploring advanced models, diversifying training data, or employing techniques like transfer learning. The high performance of Hindi should be preserved through ongoing evaluation and training with refreshed datasets. Improvement strategies for Kannada include expanding training data, fine-tuning methods, or leveraging sophisticated translation models.

Continuous evaluation of the translation models and incorporating human review and feedback are recommended practices to ensure ongoing improvements in translation quality. By addressing these recommendations, the virtual tourist companion powered by ChatGPT can provide better experiences for Indian tourists and visitors, enhancing communication and fostering cultural understanding.

10 Future Direction

There are several avenues for future research in this domain. Firstly, exploring additional language pairs, such as translations from English to regional languages of other countries, would provide valuable insights into the effectiveness of language models in diverse linguistic contexts.

Secondly, expanding the study to include more diverse participant groups, such as non-Indian tourists and visitors, would further enhance the generalizability of the findings. Thirdly, investigating different translation models or approaches, beyond the use of ChatGPT, could shed light on the comparative effectiveness of various AI language models for tourism applications.

Moreover, adopting a more rigorous and in-depth analytical strategy would prove indispensable in thoroughly capturing the intricate nuances of translation behavior exhibited by the methods under scrutiny. This strategic enhancement aligns seamlessly with the ambitious objective of facilitating seamless communication across India's multifaceted linguistic landscape, catering to the needs of both its diverse population and the influx of foreign tourists.

Finally, incorporating additional evaluation metrics, such as user satisfaction surveys or qualitative assessments of translation quality, would provide a more comprehensive understanding of the user experience and the impact of translations on effective communication in the tourism context.

References

Sruthy Anand, AM Abhishek Sai, and Moturi Karthikeya. 2023. Chatbot enabled smart tourism service for indian cities: An ai approach. In *2023 11th International Conference on Internet of Everything, Microwave Engineering, Communication and Networks (IEMECON)*, pages 1–7. IEEE.

Tom B Brown, Benjamin Mann, Nick Ryder, Melanie Subbiah, Jared Kaplan, Prafulla Dhariwal, Arvind Neelakantan, Pranav Shyam, Girish Sastry, Amanda Askell, et al. 2020. Language models are few-shot learners. *arXiv preprint arXiv:2005.14165*.

Viet Dac Lai, Nghia Trung Ngo, Amir Pouran Ben Veyseh, Hieu Man, Franck Dernoncourt, Trung Bui, and Thien Huu Nguyen. 2023. ChatGPT beyond english: Towards a comprehensive evaluation of large language models in multilingual learning.

Long Ouyang, Jeff Wu, Xu Jiang, Diogo Almeida, Carroll L. Wainwright, Pamela Mishkin, Chong Zhang, Sandhini Agarwal, Katarina Slama, Alex Ray, John Schulman, Jacob Hilton, Fraser Kelton, Luke Miller, Maddie Simens, Amanda Askell, Peter Welinder, Paul Christiano, Jan Leike, and Ryan Lowe. 2022. Training language models to follow instructions with human feedback.

Kishore Papineni, Salim Roukos, Todd Ward, and Wei-Jing Zhu. 2002. BLEU: a method for automatic evaluation of machine translation. In *Proceedings of the 40th annual meeting of the Association for Computational Linguistics*, pages 311–318.

Alec Radford, Jeffrey Wu, Rewon Child, David Luan, Dario Amodei, and Ilya Sutskever. 2019. Language models are unsupervised multitask learners. *OpenAI Blog*.

Felix Stahlberg. 2020. Neural machine translation: A review. *Journal of Artificial Intelligence Research*, 69:343–418.

Sebastian Stüker, Chengqing Zong, Jürgen Reichert, Wenjie Cao, Muntsin Kolss, Guodong Xie, Kay Peterson, Peng Ding, Victoria Arranz, Jian Yu, et al. 2006. Speech-to-speech translation services for the olympic games 2008. *Lecture notes in computer science*, 4299:297.

Ashok Urlana, Pinzhen Chen, Zheng Zhao, Shay B. Cohen, Manish Shrivastava, and Barry Haddow. 2023. PMIndiaSum: Multilingual and cross-lingual headline summarization for languages in india.

Ashish Vaswani, Noam Shazeer, Niki Parmar, Jakob Uszkoreit, Llion Jones, Aidan N Gomez, Łukasz Kaiser, and Illia Polosukhin. 2017. Attention is all you need. *Advances in neural information processing systems*, 30.

John S White and Theresa A O'Connell. 1993. Evaluation of machine translation. In *Human Language Technology: Proceedings of a Workshop Held at Plainsboro, New Jersey, March 21-24, 1993*.

Appendix

A Questions used in the Survey:

1. How are you?
2. What's your name?
3. Do you know English?
4. What language is spoken here?
5. Can I use your phone?
6. How much does it cost?
7. What is the local currency here?
8. How/Where can I exchange money?
9. Where is the bank?
10. Do you accept debit/credit cards
11. What are some popular places to shop for souvenirs or local products?
12. What time is it?
13. When does this close?
14. Can you help me book a tour or excursion?
15. What is there to see around here?
16. Could you write that down?
17. Could you repeat that?
18. How do I call the police
19. Can you help me with directions?
20. Where is the airport?
21. What time does the bus arrive?
22. What time does the train depart?
23. Is there a hospital nearby?
24. Where is the nearest restroom?
25. Do you have a map of the area?
26. How do I get to restaurant from here?
27. Is it possible to walk to the train from here?
28. Which train do I need to take to go to the park
29. Is there a map or tourist information available in English?
30. How far is it to the hotel
31. Are there any landmarks or notable buildings that can help me navigate?
32. Can you point me to the nearest bank?
33. Can you give me directions to the nearest public transportation stop?
34. Is there a tourist information center nearby where I can ask for directions?
35. Which direction is the museum from here?
36. Can you help me find my way back to my hotel from here?
37. What are the local specialties or traditional dishes that I must try?
38. Are there any vegetarian or vegan options available?
39. Does this food item contain meat?
40. Does this food item contain egg?
41. Can you recommend a good restaurant for local cuisine?
42. Do you have a menu in English?
43. Is tap water safe to drink here?
44. Can you tell me about any food allergies or common ingredients used in local dishes?
45. What time do local restaurants typically serve dinner?
46. Do you offer any dairy-free?
47. Can you recommend a local street food market or food stall?
48. How much does a typical meal cost in this area?
49. Are there any food etiquette or dining customs I should be aware of?
50. Can you recommend a good place to buy local groceries or snacks?

B ChatGPT Translation for Hindi:

1. आप कैसे हैं?
2. तुम्हारा नाम क्या है?
3. क्या आपको अंग्रेज़ी आती है?
4. यहाँ कौनसी भाषा बोली जाती है?
5. क्या मैं आपका फोन उपयोग कर सकता हूँ?
6. यह कितने का है?
7. यहाँ स्थानीय मुद्रा क्या है?
8. मैं पैसे कैसे/कहाँ बदलवा सकता हूँ?
9. बैंक कहाँ है?
10. क्या आप डेबिट/क्रेडिट कार्ड को स्वीकार करते हैं?
11. स्मृतियों या स्थानीय उत्पादों के लिए खरीददारी करने के कुछ लोकप्रिय स्थान क्या हैं?
12. अभी क्या समय हुआ है?
13. यह कब बंद होता है?
14. क्या आप मेरी मदद कर सकते हैं टूर या एक्सकर्शन बुक करने में?
15. यहाँ आस-पास क्या देखने लायक है?
16. क्या आप उसे लिख सकते हैं?
17. क्या आप उसे दोहरा सकते हैं?
18. मैं पुलिस को कैसे बुलाऊं?
19. क्या आप मुझे दिशाओं में मदद कर सकते हैं?
20. एयरपोर्ट कहाँ है?
21. बस कब आती है?
22. ट्रेन किस समय दौड़ेगी?
23. क्या पास में कोई हॉस्पिटल है?
24. सबसे निकट स्नानघर कहाँ है?
25. क्या आपके पास इस इलाके का नक्शा है?
26. यहां से रेस्तोरेंट तक मुझे कैसे पहुंचा जाए?
27. क्या यहाँ से रेलगाड़ी तक पैदल चलकर जाना संभव है?
28. मुझे पार्क जाने के लिए कौन सी ट्रेन लेनी होगी?
29. क्या अंग्रेजी में कोई मानचित्र या पर्यटक सूचना उपलब्ध है?
30. होटल तक कितना दूर है?
31. क्या कोई ऐसे चिह्न या महत्वपूर्ण इमारतें हैं जो मेरी नेवि-गेशन में मदद कर सकती हैं?
32. क्या आप मुझे नज़दीकी बैंक का रास्ता दिखा सकते हैं?
33. क्या आप मुझे सबसे निकट सार्वजनिक परिवहन स्थान के दिशा-निर्देश दे सकते हैं?
34. क्या नज़दीक में कोई पर्यटक सूचना केंद्र है जहाँ मैं दिशा-निर्देश पूछ सकता हूँ?
35. यहाँ से संग्रहालय की दिशा कौन सी है?
36. क्या आप मेरी मदद कर सकते हो कि मैं यहां से अपने होटल तक वापस अपना मार्ग ढूंढूँ?
37. मैं कौन से स्थानिक विशेष पकवान या पारंपरिक भोजन को खाना चाहिए?
38. क्या कोई शाकाहारी या वीगन विकल्प उपलब्ध हैं?
39. क्या ये खाद्य वस्तु मांस शामिल करती है?
40. क्या इस खाद्य वस्तु में अंडा है?
41. क्या आप स्थानिक व्यंजनों के लिए एक अच्छा रेस्टोरेंट सुझाव दे सकते हैं?
42. क्या आपके पास अंग्रेजी में मेनू है?
43. क्या यहाँ का नल का पानी पीने लायक है?
44. क्या आप मुझे कोई भोजन एलर्जी या स्थानीय व्यंजनों में उपयोग किए जाने वाले सामान्य सामग्रियों के बारे में बता सकते हैं?
45. स्थानीय रेस्तरां आम तौर पर नाश्ता/दोपहर का भोजन/रात का खाना किस समय पर सर्विस करते हैं?
46. क्या आप कोई डेयरी-फ्री उपलब्ध कराते हैं?
47. क्या आप कोई स्थानीय स्ट्रीट फूड मार्केट या खाने की ठेली सुझाव दे सकते हैं?
48. इस क्षेत्र में एक सामान्य भोजन की कीमत क्या होती है?
49. क्या कोई खाने की शिष्टाचार या भोजन के रीति-रिवाज हैं, जिनके बारे में मुझे जानकारी होनी चाहिए?
50. क्या आप कोई अच्छी जगह सिफारिश कर सकते हैं जहाँ स्थानीय किराने या स्नैक्स खरीदने के लिए?

C ChatGPT Translation for Telugu:

1. నీవు ఎలా ఉన్నారు?
2. మీ పేరు ఎందుకు అందించారు?
3. మీరు ఆంగ్లము తెలుసుకోవాలా?
4. ఇక్కడ ఏ భాష మాట్లాడబడుతుంది?
5. నీ ఫోన్ ఉపయోగించగలనుకుంటున్నాను?
6. ఇది ఎంత ఖరీదు అవుతుంది?
7. ఇక్కడ స్థానిక కరెన్సీ ఏమిటి?
8. నేను డబ్బును ఎలా/ఎక్కడ మారుస్తాను?
9. బ్యాంకు ఎక్కడ ఉంది?
10. మీరు డెబిట్ / క్రెడిట్ కార్డులను అంగీకరిస్తున్నారా?
11. సావేనీర్ల లేదా స్థానిక ఉత్పత్తులు కొనుగోలు చేయడానికి ప్రసిద్ధిపైన ఎక్కువ ప్రాంధ్యమైన స్థలాలు ఏవివి ఉన్నాయి?
12. ఇటీవల ఎన్నికలు ఉన్నాయి?
13. ఇది ఎప్పటికి ముగిసేది?
14. దయచేసి నేను ఒక టూర్ లేదా ఎక్స్ కర్షన్ బుక్ చేసుకోగలరా?
15. ఇక్కడ చూడాలని ఏమి ఉంది?
16. దయచేసి దానిని నమోదు చేయగలరా?
17. దయచేసి దాంచుకోవచ్చా మీరు మళ్ళీ అందరూమరించారా?
18. నేను పోలీస్ ను ఎలా పిలువుతాను?
19. దయచేసి నాకు దిశలు గుర్తులు కొడించగలరా?
20. విమానాశ్రయం ఎక్కడ ఉంది?
21. బస్ ఎప్పటికి వస్తుంది?
22. రైలు ఎప్పుడు ప్రయాణం చేయడం ప్రారంభమవుతుందా?
23. ఇప్పటి దాకా నెరవేరుగా ఆసుపత్రి ఉందా?
24. అత్యంత అనుకూలంగా ఉన్న శౌచాలయం ఎక్కడ ఉంది?
25. మీకు ప్రాంతం యొక్క మ్యాప్ ఉందా?
26. నేను ఇక్కడ నుండి రెస్టారెంట్ ఎక్కడ రావాలి?
27. ఇక్కడి నుండి రైలు వెళ్ళడం సాధ్యంకా?
28. పార్క్ కోసం నేను ఏ రైలుకు ప్రయాణం చేయాలి?
29. ఇంగ్లీష్లో మ్యాప్ లేదా పర్యటన సమాచారం అందుబాటులో ఉందా?
30. హోటల్ ఎటువంటిది ఎందుకు ఉంది?
31. నావు దిశానిర్దేశాలు కొడదీ మీకు సహాయపడుతున్నాయి కానీ యెమ్మటకు తెలియని భవనాలు లేవా?
32. దయచేసి నాకు తలపండి, అత్యవసరంగా ఉన్న బ్యాంక్ ఎక్కడ ఉంది చెప్పండినా?
33. దయచేసి నేను సమీపంలో ఉన్న ప్రజా రవాణా స్థానం దారిమార్గాలు ఇవ్వగలరా?
34. నిజముగానే నాకు దిక్సూచికలు కోరడానికి నెర్రోట్ టూరిస్ట్ సమాచార కేంద్రం ఉందా?
35. ఇక్కడ నుండి మ్యూజియం ఏ దిశాలో ఉంది?
36. నేను ఇక్కడ నుండి నా హోటల్ తరిమికి ఎలా వెళ్లగలను, మద్దతు చేస్తారా?
37. నేను ప్రయత్నించాల్సిన స్థానిక ప్రత్యేకతలు లేదా పరంపరాగత వంటి వంటకాలు ఏవి ఉన్నాయి?
38. వెజెటేరియన్ లేదా వెగాన్ ఆహార ఎక్కువ ఉందా?
39. ఈ ఆహార ఐటంలో మాంసం ఉందా?
40. ఈ ఆహార అంశం ఎగ్ కనుగొంటుందా?
41. స్థాన వంతులకు ఒక మంచి జాబితాల వెతుకుతారా మీరు?
42. మీకు ఆంగ్లంలో మెనూ ఉందా?
43. ఇక్కడ టాప్ వాటర్ తినేయండి అని ఉందా?
44. మీరు ప్రాంతీయ వంటింటిలో ఉపయోగించనున్న ప్రముఖ శాకాహారాలు లేదా అన్య ఆహార అలెర్జీల గురించి చెప్పగలరా?
45. స్థానిక రెస్టారెంట్‌లు ప్రాతఃకాలం / మధ్యాహ్నం / రాత్రి ఎందుకు సర్వ్ చేస్తాయి?
46. మీరు ఏదో డైరీ ఫ్రీ ఆఫర్ చేస్తున్నారా?
47. మీరు సూచించబడవచ్చున్నారా స్థానిక స్ట్రీట్ ఫుడ్ మార్కెట్ లేదా ఫుడ్ స్టాల్?
48. ఈ ప్రాంతంలో ఒక సామాన్య ఆహారం ఎంత ఖర్చు వస్తుంది?
49. నేను తెలియకపరచాల్సిన ఏదో ఆహార నియమాలు లేక ఉంటాయా?
50. ప్రాంతీయ కిరాణా వస్తువులు లేదా పొట్టిబంగారు కొనుగోలు చేయడానికి ఒక మంచి స్థలాన్ని మీరు సిఫారసు చేయగలరా?

D ChatGPT Translation for Kannada:

1. ನೀವು ಹೇಗಿದ್ದೀರಿ?
2. ನೀವು ಯಾರು?
3. ನೀವು ಆಂಗ್ಲ ಭಾಷೆಯನ್ನು ತಿಳಿದಿರುವುದೇ?
4. ಇಲ್ಲಿ ಯಾವ ಭಾಷೆ ಮಾತಾಡಲಾಗುತ್ತದೆ?
5. ನಾನು ನಿಮ್ಮ ಫೋನ್ ಬಳಸಬಹುದೆ?
6. ಅದರ ವೆಲ್ಲನ್ನು ಎಷ್ಟು ಆಗುತ್ತದೆ?
7. ಇಲ್ಲಿ ಸ್ಥಳೀಯ ಕರೆನ್ಸಿ ಯಾವುದು?
8. ನಾನು ಹೆಚ್ಚಿನ ಹಣವನ್ನು ಹೇಗೆ / ಎಲ್ಲಿ ವಿನಿಮಯ ಮಾಡಬಹುದು?
9. ಬ್ಯಾಂಕ್ ಎಲ್ಲಿದೆ?
10. ದೆಬಿಟ್ / ಕ್ರೆಡಿಟ್ ಕಾರ್ಡ್ಗಳನ್ನು ನೀವು ಸ್ವೀಕರಿಸುತ್ತೀರಾ?
11. ಸ್ಮೃತಿಗಳು ಅಥವಾ ಸ್ಥಳೀಯ ಉತ್ಪನ್ನಗಳನ್ನು ಖರೀದಿಸಲು ಕೆಲವು ಜನಪ್ರಿಯ ಸ್ಥಳಗಳು ಯಾವುವು?
12. ಏನು ಸಮಯವಿದೆ?
13. ಇದು ಯಾವಾಗ ಮುಚ್ಚುವುದು?
14. ನೀವು ನನಗಾಗಿ ಭ್ರಮಣ ಅಥವಾ ಉದ್ಯಾನವನ ಬುಕ್ ಮಾಡುವುದರಲ್ಲಿ ನೆರವು ಮಾಡಬಹುದೇ?
15. ಇಲ್ಲಿ ನೋಡಲು ಏನಿದೆ?
16. ನೀವು ಅದನ್ನು ಬರೆಯಲು ಸಾಧ್ಯವಾದರೆ ಮಾಡುವಿರಾ?
17. ಅದನ್ನು ಮತ್ತೆ ಹೇಳುವಿರಾ?
18. ನಾನು ಪೊಲೀಸನನ್ನು ಹೇಗೆ ಕರೆಯಬಹುದು?
19. ದಾರಿಯನ್ನು ನೀವು ಸಹಾಯಮಾಡಬಹುದೇ?
20. ವಿಮಾನ ನೀಡಿದಾಗ ಎಲ್ಲಿದೆ?
21. ಬಸ್ ಯಾವಾಗ ಬರುತ್ತೇನೆ ಅಥವಾ ಬಸ್ ಬರುವ ಸಮಯವೇನು?
22. ರೈಲು ಯಾವ ಸಮಯದಲ್ಲಿ ಹೊರಟು ಹೋಗುತ್ತದೆ?
23. ಸಮೀಪದಿದೆಯೇ ಆಸ್ಪತ್ರೆ?
24. ಸಮೀಪದಲ್ಲಿರುವ ಶೌಚಾಲಯವು ಎಲ್ಲಿದೆ?
25. ನೀವು ಪ್ರದೇಶದ ನಕ್ಷೆ ಹೊಂದಿದ್ದೀರಾ?
26. ಇಲ್ಲಿಂದ ರೆಸ್ಟೋರೆಂಟ್ಗೆ ಹೇಗೆ ಹೋಗಬೇಕು?
27. ಇಲ್ಲಿಂದ ರೈಲು ಹೋಗುವುದು ನಡೆಯುವುದು ಸಾಧ್ಯವೆ?
28. ಪಾರ್ಕ್ ಹೋಗಲು ನಾನು ಯಾವ ರೈಲುಗೆ ಹೋಗಬೇಕು ಗೊತ್ತೆ?
29. ಆಂಗ್ಲ ಭಾಷೆಯಲ್ಲಿ ನಕ್ಷೆ ಅಥವಾ ಪರ್ಯಟಕ ಮಾಹಿತಿ ಲಭ್ಯವಿದೆಯೇ?
30. ಹೊಟೆಲ್ ಹೇಗೆ ದೂರವಿದೆ ನೀವು?
31. ನಾವು ಹೇಗೆ ಹೋಗಿದ್ದೀರೋ ಗುರುತು ಹಾಕಲು ಯಾವುದೇ ಲ್ಯಾಂಡ್ಮಾರ್ಕ್ ಅಥವಾ ಲೇಖಕಪ್ರಸಿದ್ಧ ಕಟ್ಟಡಗಳಿವೆಯೇ?
32. ನೆರವೇರಿಸಬಹುದಾದ ಬ್ಯಾಂಕ್ ದೂರವೇನುಂಟೋ ಹೇಳಿಕೊಡುವುದು ಸಾಧ್ಯವೇ?
33. ಸಮೀಪದ ಸಾರ್ವಜನಿಕ ಸಾರಿಗೆ ನಿಲ್ದಾಣಕ್ಕೆ ದಾರಿಯನ್ನು ನೀಡಲು ಸಾಧ್ಯವೇ?
34. ನಾನು ದಾರಿಯನ್ನು ಕೇಳಲು ಸಾಧ್ಯವಿರುವ ಹತ್ತಿರದಲ್ಲಿ ಪ್ರಯಾಣಿಕ ಮಾಹಿತಿ ಕೇಂದ್ರ ಇದೆಯೇ?
35. ಇಲ್ಲಿಂದ ಸಂಗ್ರಹಾಲಯಕ್ಕೆ ಯಾವ ದಿಕ್ಕಿಗೆ ಹೋಗಬೇಕು?
36. ನೀವು ನನಗೆ ಇಲ್ಲಿಂದ ನನ್ನ ಹೋಟೆಲ್ಗೆ ಹಿಂತೆಗೆದುಕೊಂಡು ಹೋಗುವ ಮಾರ್ಗವನ್ನು ಹುಡುಕುವುದಕ್ಕೆ ಸಹಾಯ ಮಾಡಬಹುದೇ?
37. ನಾನು ಪ್ರಯತ್ನಿಸಬೇಕಾದ ಸ್ಥಳೀಯ ವಿಶೇಷಗಳು ಅಥವಾ ಸಂಪ್ರದಾಯ ಆಹಾರಗಳು ಯಾವುವು?
38. ಯಾವ ಶಾಕಾಹಾರಿಗಳ ವಿಕಲ್ಪಗಳು ಲಭ್ಯವಿವೆ?
39. ಈ ಆಹಾರದ ವಿಷಯದಲ್ಲಿ ಮಾಂಸ ಇದೆಯೇ? []
40. ಈ ಆಹಾರ ಐಗುವಿನೊಂದಿಗೆ ಹೊಂದಿಕೆಯಾಗಿದೆಯೇ?
41. ಸ್ಥಳೀಯ ಕುಕ್ಕಿನ ಒಳಗಡೆ ಒಳ್ಳೆಯ ರೆಸ್ಟೋರೆಂಟ್ ಯಾವುದನ್ನು ಸಲಹೆ ಮಾಡಬಹುದು?
42. ನೀವು ಆಂಗ್ಲ ಭಾಷೆಯಲ್ಲಿ ಮೆನು ಹೊಂದಿದ್ದೀರಾ?
43. ಇಲ್ಲಿ ಹಾನಿಕರವಾದ ನೀರು ಕುಡಿಯಲು ಸುರಕ್ಷಿತವಾಗಿದೆಯೇ?
44. ಸ್ಥಳೀಯ ಆಹಾರದಲ್ಲಿ ಯಾವುದೇ ಅನ್ನ ವಿಷಯದಲ್ಲಿ ನೀವು ಏನಾದರೂ ಅನಿಸುವುದೆಂದು ಹೇಳಬಹುದೇ ?ಅಥವಾ ಸಾಮಾನ್ಯವಾಗಿ ಬಳಸಲಾಗುವ ಘಟಕಗಳು ಯಾವುವು?
45. ಸ್ಥಳೀಯ ರೆಸ್ತೆರೆಂಟ್ಗಳು ಸಾಮಾನ್ಯವಾಗಿ ಎಂದಿಗೂ ಯಾವ ಸಮಯದಲ್ಲಿ ತಿಂಡಿ/ಊಟ/ಅಡುಗೆ ಸೇವಿಸುತ್ತವೆ?

46. ನೀವು ಯಾವುದೇ ಹಾಲು ಉಳಿದಿಲ್ಲ ಎಂದು ಒಕ್ಕೂರು-ತ್ತೀರಾ?

47. ನೀವು ಸೂಕ್ಷ್ಮ ಸ್ಟ್ರೀಟ್ ಫೂಡ್ ಮಾರ್ಕೆಟ್ ಅಥವಾ ಭೋ-ಜನ ಸ್ಟಾಲ್ ಸೂಚಿಸಬಹುದೇ?

48. ಈ ಪ್ರದೇಶದಲ್ಲಿ ಒಂದು ಸಾಮಾನ್ಯ ಊಟದ ವೆಚ್ಚವೇ-ನು?

49. ಯಾವ ಆಹಾರ ನಿಯಮಗಳು ಅಥವಾ ಊಟದ ರೀತಿ ನಡವಳಿಕೆಗಳು ನನಗೆ ತಿಳಿದಿವೆಯೇ?

50. ಸ್ಥಳದ ಸ್ಥಳಿಕ ಮತ್ತು ಸ್ನ್ಯಾಕ್ಸ್ ಖರೀದಿಸಲು ಒಳ್ಳೆಯ ಸ್ಥಳ-ವನ್ನು ಶಿಫಾರಸು ಮಾಡಬಹುದೇ?

Enhancing Telugu News Understanding: Comparative Study of ML Algorithms for Category Prediction

Manish Rama Gopal Nadella, Venkata Krishna Rayalu Garapati, Eswar Sudhan S.K., Gouthami Jangala, Soman K P, and **Sachin Kumar S**
Amrita School of Artificial Intelligence, Coimbatore,
Amrita Vishwa Vidyapeetham, India.
s_sachinkumar@cb.amrita.edu, manishnadella03@gmail.com

Abstract

Telugu, a widely used language in India, boasts a substantial audience and an extensive repository of news content. Predicting the categories of Telugu news articles not only streamlines organization but also facilitates trend analysis, targeted advertising, and personalized recommendations. This study endeavors to identify the optimal approach for precise Telugu news category prediction, by contrasting diverse machine learning (ML) methods including support vector machines (SVM), random forests, and naive Bayes. Performance metrics like accuracy, precision, recall, and F1-score are employed to gauge algorithm efficacy. This comparative exploration addresses the intricacies of the Telugu language, contributing insights to the field of news category prediction. The study's implications extend to enhancing news organization and recommendation systems for Telugu-speaking consumers, delivering tailored and pertinent news experiences. Our findings underscore that, while other models warrant further investigation, the combination of W2Vec-skip gram and polynomial SVM emerges as the most proficient choice.

1 Introduction

News is the latest information about recent developments and events that are relevant to the general audience (Sundarababu et al. (2020)). It is distributed using a variety of media and covers a broad range of themes. News serves to inform the public, encourage openness, and facilitate informed decision making. The categorization and prediction of news articles have become crucial in the quickly changing environment of information transmission for effective organization and improved user experience. The challenge of predicting news category has significantly advanced with the introduction of machine learning (ML) techniques. We compare many machines learning (ML) techniques for predicting Telugu news category in this research (Sultana et al. (2021)).

One of the most widely used languages in India is Telugu (Sultana et al. (2021)), which has a large audience and an extensive library of news stories. Predicting the categories of Telugu news articles (Boddupalli et al. (2019)) not only allows for effective organization but also makes it possible for trend research, advertising that is specifically targeted, and personalized suggestions. We seek to determine the most efficient strategy for precise Telugu news category prediction by examining and contrasting various ML algorithms.

The comparative study will include numerous kinds of machine learning (ML) techniques, such as support vector machines (SVM), random forests, and naive Bayes (Sheth et al. (2022)). The effectiveness of these algorithms in correctly classifying Telugu news articles will be evaluated based on their performance indicators, such as accuracy, precision, recall, and F1- score.

By performing this comparative analysis, we aim to add to the body of knowledge already available on news category prediction while taking into account the special difficulties and complexities of the Telugu language. The results of this study could improve how Telugu news articles are stored and found, giving users access to more relevant and individualized news consumption experiences (Kumar et al. (2022)).

With the ultimate goal of increasing the effectiveness and efficiency of news organization and recommendation systems for Telugu-speaking users, this study intends to shed light on the comparative analysis of various ML algorithms for Telugu news category prediction.

2 Related Works

In Sheth et al. (2022) a thorough comparative analysis was conducted to assess the effectiveness of various data mining classification techniques. The major goal was to evaluate the performance of the Naive Bayes, Support Vector Machines (SVM), De-

Third Workshop on Speech and Language Technologies for Dravidian Languages, pages 108–115, Varna, Bulgaria, Sep 7, 2023.
https://doi.org/10.26615/978-954-452-085-4_014

cision Trees, and K-Nearest Neighbor classifiers. Accuracy, recall, precision, and F1 score were the evaluation criteria, and several datasets were used for the evaluation. The study's results consistently showed that, in terms of these evaluation measures, the Naive Bayes method performed better than the other classifiers. In comparison to the other algorithms, it regularly shows greater accuracy, recall, precision, and F1 score values. In the comparison, SVM took second place, K-Nearest Neighbor came in third, and Decision Trees came in fourth as the top classifier. These findings emphasize the importance of carefully choosing the right classifier based on the unique properties of the dataset and the surrounding circumstances. It highlights the significance of avoiding a one-size-fits-all strategy and instead taking into account the particular requirements and subtleties of the current challenge. In data mining jobs, selecting the most appropriate classifier based on the particular dataset and context can produce more accurate and dependable results.

In (Sundarababu et al. (2020)), the authors address challenges in mining large electronic data. They focus on accuracy and the Zero Frequency Problem. They propose using Multinomial Naive Bayes Algorithm to forecast online story popularity. Python is highlighted for AI due to adaptability. While Naive Bayes is used in various areas, its assumption of independence is a drawback. Yet, it handles many features, is simple, and offers quick training. Their aim is to enhance news popularity prediction using Multinomial Naive Bayes and discuss its pros and cons in electronic data analysis, noting Python's suitability for AI.

In (Jang et al., 2019) Beakcheol Jang et al., The goal of the study is to assess word2vec Convolutional Neural Networks' (CNNs') performance in classifying news articles and tweets as related or unrelated. In particular, the study looks into how well the word embedding techniques CBOW (Continuous Bag-of-Words) and Skip-gram perform while creating CNN models for classification. The study's experimental analysis shows that the use of word2vec considerably improves the classification models' accuracy. Interesting results are found when the performance of the CBOW and Skip-gram models are compared. When applied to tweets, the Skip-gram model performs better, whereas the CBOW model performs better and more consistently when applied to news items. This performance disparity shows that the word embedding approach selected should be adapted to the unique characteristics of the text under study. Word2vec- enabled CNN models perform better than models without word embedding. These findings help us comprehend how the choice of word embedding models affects CNN-based classification for news articles and tweets. The study emphasizes the potential of utilizing cutting-edge neural network approaches for efficient text categorization in the context of news and social media analysis by highlighting the benefits of word2vec in enhancing classification accuracy.

In Sultana et al. (2021), the authors explore Telugu news sentiment categorization using machine learning. They classify news into categories and sentiment (positive, negative, neutral). Various models are compared based on accuracy, precision, recall, and F1-score. Sentiment analysis's importance for Telugu news, addressing regional languages like Telugu, is highlighted. Techniques like Naive Bayes, Random Forest, SVM, among others, are used. A framework with feature selection, training, testing, and performance evaluation is presented. Passive Aggressive Classifier stands out with 80

In most of the researches, the focus is much tilted towards the various algorithms rather than the multiple features that are associated with natural language processing, this leaves a significant gap for us to make this research a vital part.

3 Feature Extraction and Classification Algorithms

3.1 N_gram

Natural language processing relies heavily on N-grams (Cavnar and Trenkle (2001)). They are groups of (n) items retrieved from text, such as words or characters. N-grams expose word relationships, aid in word prediction, discover common patterns, and make realistic writing. They evaluate the likelihood of word sequences in language modelling to ensure coherent and fluent output.

3.2 Tf_idf

TF-IDF (Sammut and Webb (2010)) is vital in text mining and retrieval. It combines term frequency (TF) and inverse document frequency (IDF) to gauge phrase importance across documents. TF measures word frequency in a doc, IDF gauges term rarity in the collection. TF-IDF shows term relevance compared to full set. It's used for ranking, categorization, keyword extraction, and info retrieval, aiding term identification, text categorization, and info extraction.

3.3 Fasttext

FastText (Bojanowski et al. (2017)) is a notable NLP tool for text tasks and word representation. It creates word vectors using character n-grams, aiding with rare words and semantics. It's efficient in training and inference, supports various loss functions, excelling in tasks like sentiment analysis. FastText offers a Python API and CLI, easy to integrate. Being open source, it's customizable for experimentation by academics and professionals.

3.4 Word2Vec-CBOW

Word2Vec (Jang et al. (2019)) is a popular word embedding technique in NLP. Using dense vectors, it represents words. Continuous Bag of Words (CBOW) predicts a word from its context, adjusting embeddings for semantic links. It's efficient for local context-reliant tasks like sentiment analysis. CBOW is used in sentiment analysis, text categorization, and info retrieval. Compared to Skip-gram (better with rare words but slower), CBOW might struggle with uncommon words.

3.5 Word2Vec-skip gram

Word2Vec (Jang et al. (2019)) is neural network-based for dense word embeddings. Skip-gram, a variant, predicts context words from a target. It learns from large text data, producing embeddings for semantics. Used in tasks like similarity and classification. Skip-gram excels with rare words and links but needs more data due to computational intensity.

3.6 Support Vector Machines

Support Vector Machine (Cortes and Vapnik (2009)) classifies by finding a hyperplane in the feature space for linear separation, maximizing margin between classes. Linear SVM suits linearly separable data but struggles with complex cases. Polynomial and quadratic SVMs tackle this using kernel functions, capturing nonlinear patterns. Polynomial kernel involves raising dot product, quadratic squaring it, enabling complex interactions. Polynomial and quadratic SVMs offer flexible decision boundaries but demand careful kernel choice and regularization to avoid overfitting. Quadratic SVMs handle intricate patterns but are computationally expensive, needing regularization for better generalization.

3.7 KNN

K-Nearest Neighbors (KNN) is for classification and regression. It uses similar data points, based on distance, to predict outcomes. KNN retains the training dataset, finds k closest neighbors for a new point. Majority class among neighbors is used for classification, average/median for regression. Picking k, distance metric (like Euclidean), scaling, handling imbalanced data, and addressing dimensionality through selection/reduction are key KNN considerations.

3.8 Multinomial Naive Bayes

Multinomial Naive Bayes is a text classification method assuming feature independence within a class. It's effective for discrete features like word frequencies. It models class probabilities from features and predicts based on highest probability. It's commonly used in text categorization with representations like bag-of-words or TF-IDF. Despite assuming feature independence and sensitivity to imbalanced data, it's popular due to simplicity and low computational needs, delivering competitive results.

3.9 Random Forest

Random Forest (Louppe (2015)) is an ensemble technique for classification and regression. It uses multiple decision trees that vote or average predictions for better accuracy.The final prediction is determined by majority voting. Trees are trained on different data subsets with random feature selection. It boosts performance using bootstrap sampling. Gini or entropy measures guide node splitting. It's popular for complex data due to robustness.

4 Dataset and Preprocessing

We used an in-house dataset for performing the experiments in this paper. The dataset was prepared by scrapping (Bhardwaj et al. (2021)) an online Telugu news website, gulte.com. This dataset consists of 6 classes with a total of 38637 news articles (Sachin Kumar et al. (2020)). Figure 1 shows the category distribution in the dataset. Figure 2 shows the samples for each category from the dataset.

The data which has been scrapped from the websites consists of several unwanted characters, white

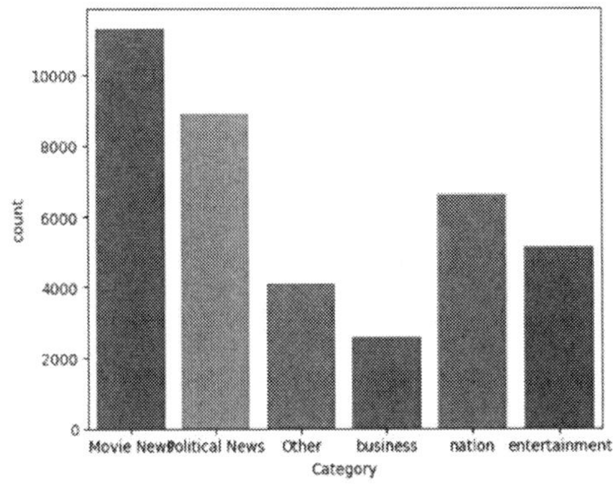

Figure 1: Category Distribution

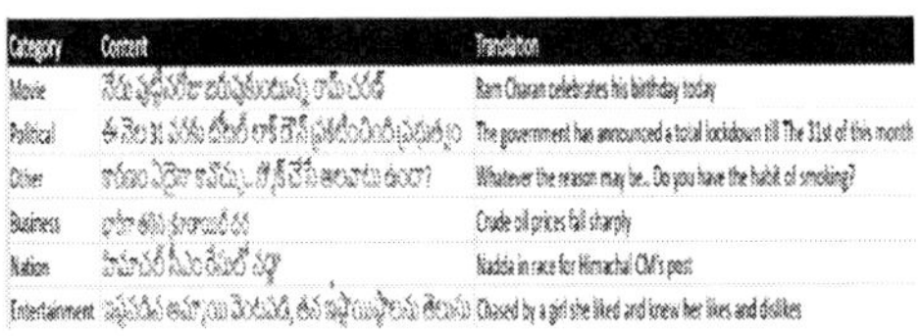

Category	Content	Translation
Movie	[illegible]	Ram Charan celebrates his birthday today
Political	[illegible]	The government has announced a total lockdown till The 31st of this month
Other	[illegible]	Whatever the reason may be.. Do you have the habit of smoking?
Business	[illegible]	Crude oil prices fall sharply
Nation	[illegible]	Nadda in race for Himachal CM's post
Entertainment	[illegible]	Chased by a girl she liked and knew her likes and dislikes

Figure 2: Sample news for each category from dataset

spaces, html tags or some numbers. These kinds of characters have been removed from the entire dataset (Varshini et al. (2023)), furthermore we have also removed stop words, belonging to Telugu language and also perform stemming.

5 Experimental Setup

The pre-processed dataset has been used to perform all the experiments in this paper. We trained Word2vec and fasttext on the pre-processed dataset to get the word embeddings instead of using the pre-trained models. Linear SVM, Quadratic SVM, Polynomial SVM, Random Forest, KNN and Multinomial Naive Bayes models are trained for each of the feature extraction methods.

For feature extraction we have used W2Vec-SG, W2Vec-CBOW, n-gram, Fast Text and TF-IDF. The dimension of feature vectors for n-gram and TF-IDF, is 10,000 whereas for other features W2Vec-SG, W2Vec-CBOW, and Fast Text it is 100.The feature visualization for vectors of such large dimensions can be done through t-SNE. t-SNE is a technique for revealing patterns and correlations in word vectors by visualizing them in a lower-dimensional environment. It entails gathering word vectors, using t-SNE to reduce dimensionality, then presenting the results on a scatter plot. Figure 3 shows t-SNE visualization for TF-IDF word vectors taken for 500 samples where each color represents a category.

Raw Words	35881750
Effective Words	354422
Vocab	477946
Vector size	100
alpha	0.025
window	3
epoch	4

Table 1: Parameters for Word2Vec CBOW-model

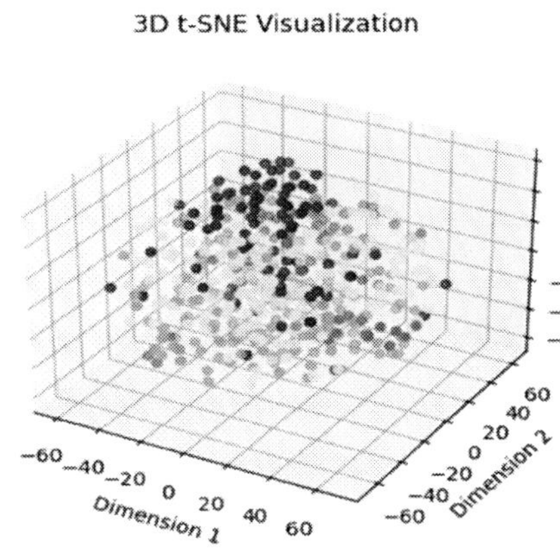

Figure 3: Example t-SNE visualization

To understand the word vectors in a better way, we have also used an online embeddings projector for which the result is shown in Figure 4 where each circle represents a word vector and words which are similar are grouped together.

All the models initially take a set of parameters and train on these set of parameters to find the best fit, then the model is evaluated on the best fit parameters. At N-fold cross validation has also been performed on each of the machine learning algorithms to evaluate the algorithm's performance for unseen data. Table 1 shows the inputs and parameters given to train the Word2Vec model.

6 Results and Discussion

Refer the Tables 2 to 8 for the performance metrics and cross Validation score for various algorithms against popular features. After Studying the performance metrics of all the algorithms, we have observed that quadratic SVM for n-gram is not performing up to the mark. Figure 5 shows the confusion matrix accordingly.

We can observe that there is a huge misclassification for category consisting of news articles that are contained in the 'Nation' class. Furthermore, the number of true classifications or correct

Figure 4: Smoothened Visualization

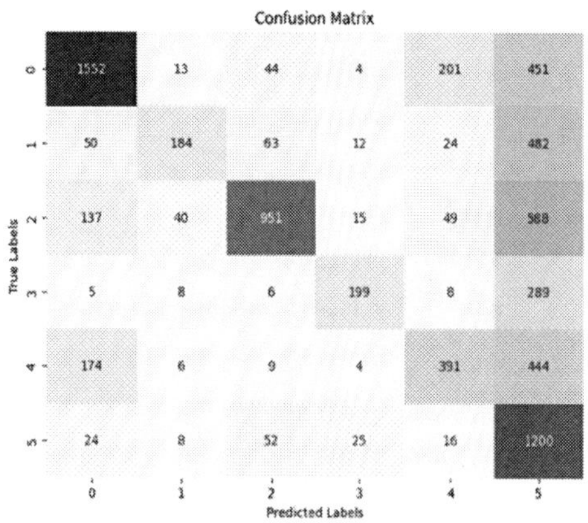

Figure 5: Confusion Matrix for Quadratic SVM using n-gram

classifications for the categories Other, Business, Entertainment are relatively less. This can be because of two factors, one being the huge imbalance in the dataset and the other can be because of use of similar words in the articles, which leads to misclassification.

Figure 6 Confusion Matrix for Word2Vec-CBOW for same method, Quadratic SVM. It is clearly observed that the model performed much better and the number of misclassifications for the category nation are very less compared to that of n-gram, we can also see that the number of true classifications for the categories Others, Business, Entertainment is relatively more compared to n-gram. This can be because Word2Vec model was able to generate better word vectors for the given corpus.

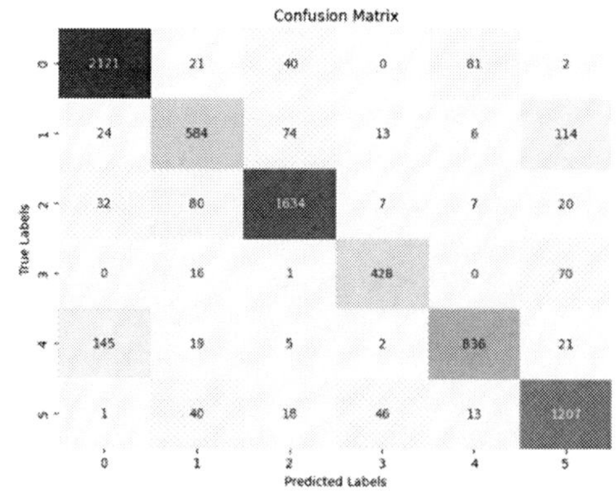

Figure 6: Confusion Matrix for Quadratic SVM using Word2Vec-CBOW

7 Conclusion

Word-2-vec CBOW and Skip gram are the two models which showed constant and reasonable performance for all the algorithms except Multinomial Naive Bayes. The performance of Fast-Text was also consistent except for Multinomial Naive Bayes but it under performed when compared to word-2-vec. N-gram showed the third best performance among the feature extraction methods, its performance was better even for Multinomial Naive Bayes, but it showed poor performance for KNN.

Finally, Tf-IDF showed reasonable performance except for Polynomial SVM and KNN. Further it has been observed that changing the parameter value, 'C' in all three types of SVM, resulted in minute increase of model's accuracy. On setting the 'C' value to 10,000 the models showed up to 5%-10% increase in accuracy. In general, a higher 'C' value in SVM results in higher penalty and smaller margin. It also reduces the regularization strength which may lead to overfitting, these can be some of the reasons for improved performance.

The primary goal of this research has been to choose the best classifier and feature extraction pair from the most popular techniques. We have observed that W2Vec-skip gram and polynomial SVM is the best pair for this task. However, other models may be considered in the future work for comparison and selection.

References

Bhavya Bhardwaj, Syed Ishtiyaq Ahmed, J Jaiharie, R Sorabh Dadhich, and M Ganesan. 2021. Web scraping using summarization and named entity

	Performance metrics				Cross-Validation score			
	Precision	**Recall**	**Accuracy**	**F1-Score**	**Mean-Precision**	**Mean-Recall**	**Mean-Accuracy**	**Mean F1-Score**
W2Vec-SG	0.86	0.85	0.87	0.85	0.85	0.80	0.85	0.81
W2Vec-CBOW	0.81	0.72	0.79	0.77	0.84	0.77	0.83	0.79
n-gram	0.57	0.58	0.62	0.57	0.55	0.55	0.60	0.55
Fast Text	0.68	0.60	0.66	0.61	0.70	0.65	0.71	0.66
TF-IDF	0.57	0.57	0.62	0.57	0.56	0.56	0.61	0.56

Table 2: Performance of Linear SVM

	Performance metrics				Cross-Validation score			
	Precision	**Recall**	**Accuracy**	**F1-Score**	**Mean-Precision**	**Mean-Recall**	**Mean-Accuracy**	**Mean F1-Score**
W2Vec-SG	0.89	0.88	0.90	0.88	0.88	0.87	0.89	0.88
W2Vec-CBOW	0.88	0.87	0.89	0.88	0.87	0.85	0.88	0.86
n-gram	0.70	0.32	0.63	0.30	0.66	0.50	0.56	0.51
Fast Text	0.74	0.71	0.76	0.71	0.74	0.70	0.75	0.71
TF-IDF	0.74	0.62	0.71	0.65	0.67	0.56	0.61	0.57

Table 3: Performance of Quadratic SVM

recognition (ner). In *2021 7th International Conference on Advanced Computing and Communication Systems (ICACCS)*, volume 1, pages 261–265.

Srikiran Boddupalli, Anitha Sai Saranya, Usha Mundra, Pratyusha Dasam, and Padmamala Sriram. 2019. Sentiment analysis of telugu data and comparing advanced ensemble techniques using different text processing methods. In *2019 5th International Conference On Computing, Communication, Control And Automation (ICCUBEA)*, pages 1–6.

Piotr Bojanowski, Edouard Grave, Armand Joulin, and Tomas Mikolov. 2017. Enriching word vectors with subword information.

William Cavnar and John Trenkle. 2001. N-gram-based text categorization. *Proceedings of the Third Annual Symposium on Document Analysis and Information Retrieval.*

Corinna Cortes and Vladimir Vapnik. 2009. Support-vector networks. *Chem. Biol. Drug Des.*, 297:273–297.

Beakcheol Jang, Inhwan Kim, and Jong Kim. 2019. Word2vec convolutional neural networks for classification of news articles and tweets. *PLOS ONE*, 14:e0220976.

Sruthi S. Kumar, S. Sachin Kumar, and K. P. Soman. 2022. Deep learning-based emotion classification of hindi text from social media. In *Advanced Machine Intelligence and Signal Processing*, pages 535–543, Singapore. Springer Nature Singapore.

Gilles Louppe. 2015. Understanding random forests: From theory to practice.

S. Sachin Kumar, M. Anand Kumar, K. P. Soman, and Prabaharan Poornachandran. 2020. Dynamic mode-based feature with random mapping for sentiment analysis. In *Intelligent Systems, Technologies and Applications*, pages 1–15, Singapore. Springer Singapore.

	Performance metrics				Cross-Validation score			
	Precision	**Recall**	**Accuracy**	**F1-Score**	**Mean-Precision**	**Mean-Recall**	**Mean-Accuracy**	**Mean F1-Score**
W2Vec-SG	0.90	0.89	0.91	0.89	0.90	0.89	0.91	0.89
W2Vec-CBOW	0.89	0.88	0.90	0.88	0.88	0.87	0.89	0.88
n-gram	0.70	0.32	0.36	0.30	0.68	0.30	0.33	0.26
Fast Text	0.75	0.72	0.76	0.73	0.75	0.71	0.76	0.72
TF-IDF	0.44	0.21	0.32	0.17	0.60	0.22	0.20	0.15

Table 4: Performance of Polynomial SVM

	Performance metrics				Cross-Validation score			
	Precision	**Recall**	**Accuracy**	**F1-Score**	**Mean-Precision**	**Mean-Recall**	**Mean-Accuracy**	**Mean F1-Score**
W2Vec-SG	0.87	0.86	0.88	0.86	0.87	0.85	0.88	0.86
W2Vec-CBOW	0.86	0.84	0.87	0.85	0.86	0.84	0.87	0.85
n-gram	0.68	0.64	0.70	0.65	0.60	0.59	0.63	0.59
Fast Text	0.71	0.56	0.67	0.58	0.71	0.56	0.67	0.58
TF-IDF	0.83	0.61	0.73	0.64	0.64	0.60	0.66	0.61

Table 5: Performance of Random Forest Classifier

Claude Sammut and Geoffrey I. Webb, editors. 2010. *TF–IDF*, pages 986–987. Springer US, Boston, MA.

Vraj Sheth, Urvashi Tripathi, and Ankit Sharma. 2022. A comparative analysis of machine learning algorithms for classification purpose. *Procedia Computer Science*, 215:422–431. 4th International Conference on Innovative Data Communication Technology and Application.

J. Sultana, Usha Rani Macigi, and G. Priya. 2021. *Telugu News Data Classification using Machine Learning Approach*, pages 181–194.

Mr Sundarababu, Ch Chandramohan, Mahendra Suthar, Ch Harsha, Lubna Juveria, B Blessy, and Sameer Mohammad. 2020. News classification using machine learning. *SSRN Electronic Journal*, 7:657–660.

Surisetty Hima Varshini, Gottimukkala Sarayu Varma, and Supriya M. 2023. A recognizer and parser for basic sentences in telugu using cyk algorithm. In *2023 3rd International Conference on Intelligent Technologies (CONIT)*, pages 1–5.

	Performance metrics				Cross-Validation score			
	Precision	**Recall**	**Accuracy**	**F1-Score**	**Mean-Precision**	**Mean-Recall**	**Mean-Accuracy**	**Mean F1-Score**
W2Vec-SG	0.88	0.87	0.89	0.87	0.87	0.86	0.89	0.87
W2Vec-CBOW	0.86	0.85	0.87	0.85	0.85	0.84	0.87	0.85
n-gram	0.43	0.43	0.41	0.39	0.42	0.41	0.39	0.37
Fast Text	0.66	0.60	0.68	0.62	0.65	0.59	0.66	0.61
TF-IDF	0.46	0.33	0.28	0.30	0.46	0.31	0.27	0.29

Table 6: Performance of KNN

	Performance metrics				Cross-Validation score			
	Precision	**Recall**	**Accuracy**	**F1-Score**	**Mean-Precision**	**Mean-Recall**	**Mean-Accuracy**	**Mean F1-Score**
W2Vec-SG	0.61	0.58	0.67	0.58	0.62	0.58	0.67	0.58
W2Vec-CBOW	0.64	0.62	0.69	0.62	0.64	0.61	0.68	0.62
n-gram	0.67	0.65	0.70	0.66	0.67	0.65	0.69	0.66
Fast Text	0.46	0.46	0.52	0.45	0.46	0.46	0.52	0.45
TF-IDF	0.67	0.65	0.70	0.66	0.67	0.65	0.69	0.66

Table 7: Performance of Multinomial Naive Bayes

	Single Layer		Two Layers	
	Accuracy	**Validation Accuracy**	**Accuracy**	**Validation Accuracy**
W2Vec-SG	0.86	0.855	0.874	0.876
W2Vec-CBOW	0.846	0.842	0.861	0.858
n-gram	0.925	0.666	0.925	0.667
Fast Text	0.736	0.710	0.745	0.73
TF-IDF	0.965	0.734	0.986	0.783

Table 8: Performance of 1D-CNN

Revisiting Automatic Speech Recognition for Tamil and Hindi Connected Number Recognition

Rahul Mishra*, **Senthil Raja Gunaseela Boopathy, Manikandan Ravikiran**
Shreyas Kulkarni, Mayurakshi Mukherjee, Ananth Ganesh, Kingshuk Banerjee
R&D Centre, Hitachi India Pvt Ltd, Bangalore, India
rahul.mishra@hitachi.co.in, senthil.raja@hitachi.co.in

Abstract

Automatic Speech Recognition and its applications are rising in popularity across applications with reasonable inference results. Recent state-of-the-art approaches, often employ significantly large-scale models to show high accuracy for ASR as a whole but often do not consider detailed analysis of performance across low-resource languages applications. In this preliminary work, we propose to revisit ASR in the context of Connected Number Recognition (CNR). More specifically, we (i) present a new dataset HCNR collected to understand various errors of ASR models for CNR, (ii) establish preliminary benchmark and baseline model for CNR, (iii) explore error mitigation strategies and their after-effects on CNR. In the due process, we also compare with end-to-end large scale ASR models for reference, to show its effectiveness.

1 Introduction

Automatic Speech Recognition is a wide variety with a majority of them claiming that these speech-to-text systems are able to deliver high accuracy on some of the well-established benchmarks (Prabhavalkar et al., 2023). Connected Number Recognition (CNR) is a subproblem of ASR that focuses on recognizing spoken numbers that are connected in a continuous sequence. For example, `Toḷḷāyirattu aintu` is a CNR speech sample representing number 905. Extracting such numbers from the speech is helpful in multiple applications (Vajpai and Bora, 2016) ranging from assisting senior citizens to make online purchases to simplification of complex banking functions. Recently there are many works that further augment ASR systems into low-resource languages such as Tamil (Diwan et al., 2021). The motivation for this research work lies in the use of ASR techniques in the sectors (like finance etc.) where the frequency of speaking connected numbers and the importance of each utterance is very high.

However many of these methods largely focus on reporting exclusively the overall Word Error Rate (WER) of the whole without discerning application-specific results and corner cases. These results are not transferable across the subset of ASR applications with different human perceptions (Kim et al., 2022). As such to advance applications of the ASR further there is a need to understand the impact of input in realistic application settings on the final ASR output across specific applications. Moreover, such analysis of errors, will in turn help introduce better post-editing mechanisms that are dynamic and selectable for specific inputs, leading to improved effectiveness of such systems. Specifically, benchmarking of CNR will economic progress by enabling technology for people across the spectrum. Thus, in this work, we analyze ASR systems for the problem of CNR in Tamil and Hindi languages.

Specifically, this work focuses on benchmarking ASR systems for CNR in Tamil, and Hindi and the impact of input data-related errors on the final performance of CNR. For the former case, we study the performance of 4 different models that currently exist for ASR. Accordingly, we find that all the existing models show significant performance degradation for CNR in Tamil and Hindi. In the latter case, we find very few works to focus on input data-related errors of ASR systems, with a majority of them concentrating on the English Language and establishing WER and few of them on other languages (Choudhary et al., 2023; Singh et al., 2020), but not from the point of CNR. Overall the contributions of this paper are as follows.

*Corresponding Author

Third Workshop on Speech and Language Technologies for Dravidian Languages, pages 116–123, Varna, Bulgaria, Sep 7, 2023.
https://doi.org/10.26615/978-954-452-085-4_015

- We create a new CNR dataset (HCNR) for Tamil and Hindi in line with guidelines of Bakhturina et al. (2021) and present comprehensive error analysis.
- We establish preliminary baselines on HCNR with existing state-of-the-art models.
- We identify various errors and associate them with data characterstics.
- Finally, we explore some error mitigation strategies of spectral gating (Sainburg et al., 2020), spectral subtraction (Martin, 1994), speaker diarization (Bredin et al., 2020) and PESQ (Perceptual Evaluation of Speech Quality) (Rix et al., 2001) to reduce impact of few of the common errors to help researchers understand strengths and weaknesses of the developed baseline.

The rest of the paper is organized as follows. In section 2, we present the existing literature, followed by 3 showing HCNR dataset used in this work. Meanwhile in section 4, we discuss various methods, followed by results and key findings in section 5. We conclude with implications on future work in section 6.

2 Related Work

Automatic Speech Recognition systems often aim to learn end to end with output directly conditioned on raw input sample (Schneider et al., 2019). To achieve this, many works add variety of dense architectures (Povey et al., 2011), weak supervision (Radford et al., 2022) and unique components (Kaur et al., 2023). More recently there are a plethora of ASR systems for Indian languages despite low resource constraints (Gupta et al., 2023; Kumar and Mittal, 2021; Sharma et al., 2023; Madhavaraj and Ramakrishnan, 2017; Choudhary et al., 2022).

Number Recognition using speech samples, often limited to recognizing single digits with shallow analysis on few samples. Notable of these include Muhammad et al. (2009) which identifies digits spoken in Bangladesh, Alotaibi (2005) investigated the recognition of Arabic digits from the speech signals using artificial neural network and attempts of Mishra et al. (2011), Krishnamurthy and Prasanna (2017) and Patel and Patel (2017) for languages of Hindi, Malayalam, Gujarati respectively. In this work, we focus on establishing a comprehensive benchmark for connected number recognition using Povey et al. (2011) and Radford et al. (2022).

Datasets often used to train these models are trained on large, clean, and very generic. Few of the notable datasets for Indian languages include Bansal et al. (2023) for Hindi, Rakib et al. (2023) for Bengali, Manjutha et al. (2019) for Tamil, Banga et al. (2019) for emotion-based speech recognition and accented speech data by Rajaa et al. (2022). However to date, there aren't any large datasets specifically developed for connected numbers, accordingly in this work, we create new dataset catering to CNR in Tamil and Hindi.

3 Dataset

Characteristics	Values
Languages Selected	Tamil, Hindi
Number of Train Samples	56000, 35000
Number of Test Samples	8000, 5000
Sampling Rate	16 KHz
Preprocessing at collection	None
Maximum SNR	60%
Dual Talk	Yes
Background Noise	Yes
Inaudible Sound	Yes
Clipping	Yes
Repeated Numbers	Yes
Pitch Variations	Yes
Long Pauses	Yes
SNR	$\geqslant$20

Table 1: Dataset Characteristics of HCNR

The overall HCNR dataset characteristics are as shown in Table 1. Specifically, we collected datasets for two languages namely Tamil and Hindi, with the former used for the main evaluation and the latter to test the scalability of results. For Tamil, we explored various districts of Tamil Nadu, while for Hindi we collected data across Northern states of India. Moreover, each person was randomly shown a number and was asked to repeat the same as per day-to-day usage and these were recorded at the specific sampling frequency. Each of the collected samples was re-sampled at 16KHz inline with Radford et al. (2022).

The dataset was separated into the train, validation, and test splits as shown in Table 1, without any overlap between the speakers themselves. Besides, the speakers used across the sets included both male and female genders. Also, the dataset collected was made sure to include (a) Dual talk (more than one person speaking) (b) Background noise below 300 Hz (c) Inaudible sound, where

Sample Characteristics	Number of Samples	
	Tamil	Hindi
Clean	4721	4432
Dual Talk	11	254
Background Noise	116	78
Inaudible Sound	40	28
Missing Segments	52	18
Repetitions	2	5
Others	58	185

Table 2: Characteristics of `HCNR` from randomly drawn 5000 samples from training set.

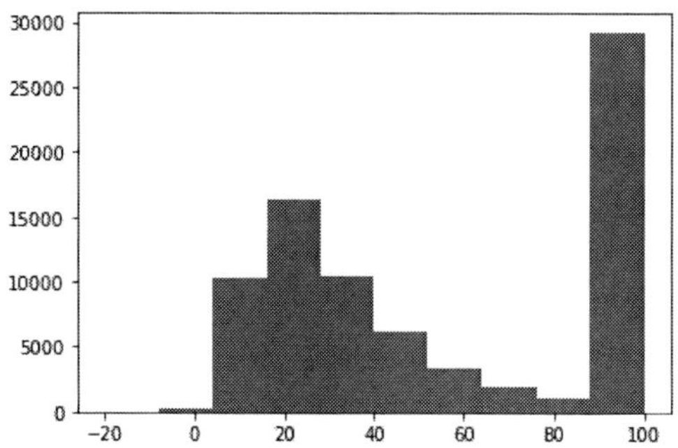

Figure 1: Histogram of SNR of Hindi data.

the quality of spoken number is poor (d) Missing digit Segments where speech doesn't include any digits (e) Clipping in Spoken Number where complete instance of spoken number is not present (f) Repetition of spoken number (g) Long pauses between spoken numbers (h) Pitch variations leading to changes of speech within a sample (See Table 2). Figures 2 and 1, show the signal-to-noise ratio (Kim and Stern, 2008) of the collected dataset. From the histograms, we can see that for the Hindi dataset, around 45% of the total speech samples are having SNR less than 40 db while for the Tamil dataset, around 57% of the total speech samples are having SNR less than 40 dB.

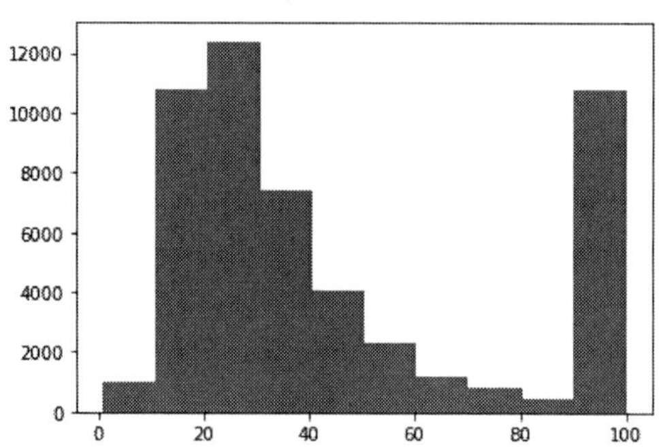

Figure 2: Histogram of SNR of Tamil data.

4 Experimental Setup

Our experimental setup is split into two parts which aim to establish a strong baseline for the problem of connected number recognition. More specifically, we assess WER for the baseline methods that are not end-to-end ASRs, rather widely used hybrid deep learning LSTM-TDNN model. Following this, we understand various errors and relate them to the characteristic of the dataset in turn highlighting the strength and weaknesses of the said baseline methods. Following this, we explore certain mitigation strategies to further ground the method so selected as a strong baseline candidate for connected number recognition. Throughout this work, we employ Word Error Rate (WER) and Sentence Error Rate (SER) inline with Klakow and Peters (2002).

4.1 Methods

Following are the various models used in this work.

- **Baseline Hybrid ASR:** In this work, we use LSTM-TDNN **(LT-Kaldi)** architecture that is part of Kaldi Speech Toolkit (Povey et al., 2011). This baseline model is composed of size convolutional layers and 15 factorized time-delay neural networks with a total of 31M parameters. We follow the standard Kaldi training recipe. The input to this model is high-resolution MFCCs with cepstral mean normalization. The **LT-Kaldi-F** model is trained for a total of 5 epochs on the training samples from Table 1. Additionally, **LT-Kaldi-P** model is trained on 50% of total training samples. This is a standard setup taken from Kaldi Speech Toolkit (Povey et al., 2011).

- **End-to-End ASR:** Though our end goal, is to establish a baseline benchmark for CNR and analyze it thoroughly, we however debate on the merits of end-to-end ASR models specifically, Wav2Vec 2.0 and Whisper. From now on we refer to these models with the following tags (i) **w2v2**: Fine-tuned `wav2vec2-large-xlsr-53` in Tamil and Hindi using the Common Voice (ii) **WH**: This model is a fine-tuned version of openai/whisper-small on the Tamil and Hindi data available from multiple publicly available ASR corpora (For fine tuning Tamil ASR models, Tamil characters are used).

- **Error Mitigation Methods in ASR:** Additionally, we also explore (i) **P1**: Spectral Gating, (ii) **P2:** Spectral Subtraction as two measures to see effect of background noise reduction, that is part of the input, (iii) **P3:** Speaker Diarization to remove samples that consists of more than one speaker and (iv) **P4:** PESQ based score assignment to remove poor quality samples.

5 Results and Discussion

5.1 Evaluation measure

For evaluating the performance of the system, we used **World error rate (WER)**. The motivation for using WER as a performance measure comes from the type of output we are getting. As we are getting the translated text from the process of recognizing speech there is a possibility that some words may be left out or mistranslated. WER can be calculated by taking into account all of these possibilities. Mathematically, WER can be calculated as

$$WER = \frac{S + D + I}{N}, \quad (1)$$

Here, S is the number of substitutions, D is the number of deletions, I is the number of insertions, C is the number of correct words, N is the number of words in the reference ($N = S + D + C$). Sentence error rate (SER) is the number of incorrect sentences divided by the total number of sentences.

We structure the discussion of results by focusing on establishing the suitability of the simple hybrid method of LT-Kaldi as the baseline for the task of CNR. Although ASR-based methods are used for a subset of ASR problems, the overall results for CNR are not well-established with a significantly large dataset as approached by this work. Accordingly, in Table 3, we compare the results of LT-Kaldi across different settings mentioned earlier. From the results we can explicitly see that for both Tamil and Hindi with full data, the individual word error are 15% and 7% respectively, indicating the simple methods indeed show strong performance on the overall dataset with a variety of characteristics. SER depends on the correctness of each word in a complete sentence. If there is a prediction error only in one word of a full sentence, it will make the prediction of the entire sentence wrong. That's why the SER is relatively higher than the WER.

Table 4 shows error statistics of LT-Kaldi in the test set with a breakdown across sample characteristics. Meanwhile, Table 5, shows example predictions and errors in Tamil (Transliterated).

	WER (%)		SER (%)	
Method	**Tamil**	**Hindi**	**Tamil**	**Hindi**
LT-Kaldi	15.11	7.63	25.64	15.40

Table 3: Baseline results on HCNR across different methods.

Sample Characteristics	Erroneous Samples	
	Tamil	**Hindi**
Dual Talk	52	329
Background Noise	514	328
Inaudible Sound	273	138
Missing Segments	160	46
Repetitions	33	8
Others	216	241

Table 4: Error statistics across languages with LT-Kaldi on test set.

From the table 4, we can see that for Tamil, the overall WER is majorly dominated by samples with background noise, repetition of spoken numbers, and Inaudible sound respectively. Meanwhile, in the case of Hindi, the resulting errors are heavily concentrated in background noise, dual talk, and repetition of spoken numbers. For this analysis, we considered all samples of the test set for both Hindi as well as Tamil language. Further contrasting the two languages, one would argue that background noise and dual talk are vital to be handled in the problem of CNR, followed by repetition of spoken number and Inaudible sound respectively. Thus, the languages despite being different the model shows common behavior across its errors, indicating its potential generalization.

Meanwhile, to further verify the effectiveness of LT-Kaldi, we subject the samples of the test set to noise removal using P1 and P2 respectively. For P1, we compare the spectrogram of the input speech and estimate a noise threshold (SNR Threshold) to gate out the unnecessary signals. In this work, we test with three different SNR threshold values namely `None`, `<15`, `<30` respectively. Meanwhile, for P2, we subtract the current speech spectrum with noise to estimate a clean signal. The result with these methods is as shown in Table 6 and 7 respectively. From the tables, we can see that with both spectral gating and spectral subtraction on the overall data, there is indeed a negative impact on the overall results across both languages. This is because of models like LT-Kaldi tempo-spectral properties of any type of speech and noise and adding noise removal method indeed distorts speech samples and in turn effectively removes useful parts. While noise removal using spectral gating had a negative impact, we argue that the method is crude in removing noise and rather verify the same using spectral subtraction to obtain results as shown in Table 7. From the results, we can see that indeed removing noise improves the results of Tamil CNR by 1% with a still negative impact on the Hindi language. The potential reason behind this may be the degradation of signal power with respect to the noise power. In few samples (% of total samples) the SNR is low, which essentially signifies that the signal power is nearly equal to the noise power. In these cases the application of noise cancellation techniques may also result in the degradation of necessary signal information. However, more investigation is required in this regard.

Meanwhile, we also argue that the removal of dual talk would improve the overall results due to inherent distortion created by the voices of multiple people. Accordingly, we employ works of Bredin et al. (2020) where we remove samples that have more than one identified speaker and accordingly obtain results as shown in Table 8. Besides combining all the pre-processing methods shows additional improvement as shown in Table 9.

Apart from the speaker diarization to remove samples, we also employ PESQ based technique to assign score to each speech sample. Its value lies in between -0.5 to 4.5. A higher score indicates a better signal quality. If the score is greater than a threshold, it means that the quality of the speech sample is good and we can consider that sample for further proceedings. This score has been calculated between the raw speech sample and its processed version (speech signal after passing through the spectral subtraction based noise cancellation pipeline). For more details refer to this work. For getting the threshold, we create the histogram of scores of all speech samples of Hindi and Tamil languages (Fig. 3 and Fig. 4). After manually visualizing the histograms, we decided to keep 2.3 and 1.9 as the threshold for the Hindi and Tamil speech samples respectively. However, more experiments can be done to get a more robust threshold value.

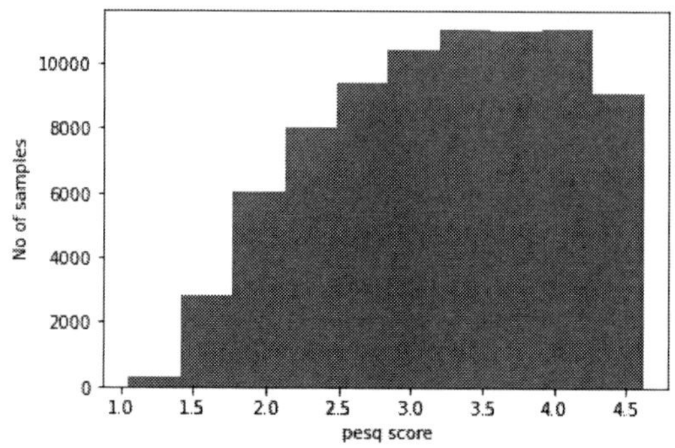

Figure 3: Histogram of PESQ score Hindi data.

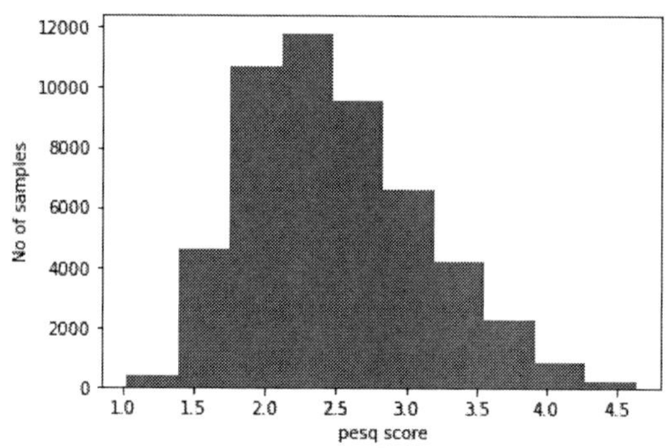

Figure 4: Histogram of PESQ score of Tamil data.

From the result again we can see net effectiveness restricted to only around 1% indicating the effectiveness of preprocessing methods on the problem of CNR is not high, warranting more study in the training process and sample processing. Overall from results across Table 3-9, we can conclude that LT-Kaldi is a descent baseline for CNR with various preprocessing methods having a negligible effect on the results. To further, establish the effectiveness of the results of LT-Kaldi, we compare the results of LT-Kaldi with Wav2vec2 and whisper respectively. To this end, we compare the results of LT-Kaldi trained with HCNR against pre-trained models Wav2vec2 and whisper in Table 10. The poor performance is because the models are trained on general speech data. It also signifies that if we want to use the model for utilizing connected numbers for any specific task, we need to finetune the publicly available SOTA models on

Input Tamil Sample	Prediction	
	LT-Kaldi	WH
Muppattu mūu āyirattu eṇṇūu aupattiraṇṭu	mūu āyirattu muppattu mūu āyirattu eṇṇūu aupattiraṇṭu	nukarppu eṇṇūi aupatti iraṇṭu
Toḷḷāyirattu aintu	eupattaintu	vārttai
Ainūu irupattou	eṭṭu	ea
Muppattu nāku āyirattu eṇpattu mūu	nāku āyirattu eṇpattu mūu	tōṭṭi nāku āyirattu topatti mūu
Ōr āyirattu nūi nāpattu mūu	ōr āyirattu nāpattu mūu āyirattu nāpattu mūu	āyiratti nāppatti mūṇu āyiratti nāppatti mūṇu
Toḷḷāyirattu eṇpattu nāku	toūu eṇpattaintu	coatu

Table 5: Example Errors from Tamil with LT-Kaldi and WH models

Method	SNR Threshold	WER (%)		SER (%)	
		Tamil	Hindi	Tamil	Hindi
LT-Kaldi + P1	None	15.34	8.23	29.23	16.84
LT-Kaldi + P1	<15	15.52	9.40	30.17	16.70
LT-Kaldi + P1	<30	15.81	9.09	30.54	17.09

Table 6: Results on HCNR for LT-Kaldi with spectral gating.

Method	SNR Thresholding	WER (%)		SER (%)	
		Tamil	Hindi	Tamil	Hindi
LT-Kaldi + P2	None	14.37	9.41	26.35	18.09

Table 7: Results on HCNR for LT-Kaldi with spectral subtraction.

	WER (%)		SER (%)	
Method	Tamil	Hindi	Tamil	Hindi
LT-Kaldi + Diarization	14.03	6.35	26.31	12.40

Table 8: Results on HCNR across with LT-Kaldi and Diarization

	WER (%)		SER (%)	
Method	Tamil	Hindi	Tamil	Hindi
LT-Kaldi + P2 + P3	13.57	7.85	26.35	15.62
LT-Kaldi + P2 + P4	13.72	8.49	27.21	16.52

Table 9: Results on HCNR across with LT-Kaldi with P2, P3 and P4

the specific dataset.

From the results it is evident both the models are directly not suitable for CNR with high WER, indeed indicating that simply trained LT-Kaldi is a more suitable baseline method. Table 5, shows various errors obtained using **WH** on Tamil language. From the results it is evident that E2E models indeed being unable to understand the spoken language, indicating the need for domain adaptation. This is in contrast with other applications of ASR where E2E show high results.

	WER (%)		SER (%)	
Method	Tamil	Hindi	Tamil	Hindi
w2v2	98.63	71.08	99.12	87.07
WH	93.37	85.70	97.80	93.70

Table 10: Results on HCNR across Wav2vec2 and Whisper models.

6 Conclusion and Future Work

Overall in this work, we study the problem of CNR by creating a new HCNR dataset and report baseline results with the LT-Kaldi model across Tamil and Hindi languages. In the process, we find that the baseline LT-Kaldi shows WER of around 15% and 7% respectively across the languages. In the due process, we conjectured the sample characteristics might be the key reason leading to higher WER through analysis, for which we studied spectral gating, spectral subtraction, and diarization methods for further improvement. However, we could see that the overall results improved only by 2% for Tamil and 1% for Hindi CNR. Most importantly, we could also see that compared to LT-Kaldi, the pretrained models performed significantly worse, unlike prior works. However, we think this may be attributed to the case of out-of-domain samples, needing further studies. In this regard, a possible question to explore includes evaluating the effect of training the E2E model with HCNR and the effect of in-domain data on CNR performance. Additionally, we plan to explore other methods to remove negative sample characteristics and study their impact on overall CNR results.

Acknowledgements

We thank our anonymous reviewers for their valuable feedback.

References

Yousef Ajami Alotaibi. 2005. Investigating spoken arabic digits in speech recognition setting. *Information Sciences*, 173(1-3):115–139.

Evelina Bakhturina, Vitaly Lavrukhin, and Boris Ginsburg. 2021. A toolbox for construction and analysis of speech datasets. In *Proceedings of the Neural Information Processing Systems Track on Datasets and Benchmarks 1, NeurIPS Datasets and Benchmarks 2021, December 2021, virtual.*

Subham Banga, Ujjwal Upadhyay, Piyush Agarwal, Aniket Sharma, and Prerana Mukherjee. 2019. Indian emospeech command dataset: A dataset for emotion based speech recognition in the wild. *CoRR*, abs/1910.13801.

Vansh Bansal, T. Thishyan Raj, Nagarathna Ravi, Shubham Korde, Jaskaran Kalra, Sudha Murugesan, B. Ramkrishnan, Aboli Gore, and Vipul Arora. 2023. Parturition hindi speech dataset for automatic speech recognition. In *28th National Conference on Communications, NCC 2023, Guwahati, India, February 23-26, 2023*, pages 1–6. IEEE.

Hervé Bredin, Ruiqing Yin, Juan Manuel Coria, Gregory Gelly, Pavel Korshunov, Marvin Lavechin, Diego Fustes, Hadrien Titeux, Wassim Bouaziz, and Marie-Philippe Gill. 2020. Pyannote. audio: neural building blocks for speaker diarization. In *ICASSP 2020-2020 IEEE International Conference on Acoustics, Speech and Signal Processing (ICASSP)*, pages 7124–7128. IEEE.

Tripti Choudhary, Atul Bansal, and Vishal Goyal. 2022. Investigation of cnn-based acoustic modeling for continuous hindi speech recognition. In *IoT and Analytics for Sensor Networks: Proceedings of ICWS-NUCA 2021*, pages 425–431. Springer.

Tripti Choudhary, Vishal Goyal, and Atul Bansal. 2023. WTASR: wavelet transformer for automatic speech recognition of indian languages. *Big Data Min. Anal.*, 6(1):85–91.

Anuj Diwan, Rakesh Vaideeswaran, Sanket Shah, Ankita Singh, Srinivasa Raghavan, Shreya Khare, Vinit Unni, Saurabh Vyas, Akash Rajpuria, Chiranjeevi Yarra, Ashish R. Mittal, Prasanta Kumar Ghosh, Preethi Jyothi, Kalika Bali, Vivek Seshadri, Sunayana Sitaram, Samarth Bharadwaj, Jai Nanavati, Raoul Nanavati, Karthik Sankaranarayanan, Tejaswi Seeram, and Basil Abraham. 2021. Multilingual and code-switching asr challenges for low resource indian languages. *ArXiv*, abs/2104.00235.

Astha Gupta, Rakesh Kumar, and Yogesh Kumar. 2023. An automatic speech recognition system in indian and foreign languages: A state-of-the-art review analysis. *Intell. Decis. Technol.*, 17(2):505–526.

Amrit Preet Kaur, Amitoj Singh, Rohit Sachdeva, and Vinay Kukreja. 2023. Automatic speech recognition systems: A survey of discriminative techniques. *Multim. Tools Appl.*, 82(9):13307–13339.

Chanwoo Kim and Richard M Stern. 2008. Robust signal-to-noise ratio estimation based on waveform amplitude distribution analysis. In *Ninth Annual Conference of the International Speech Communication Association*. Citeseer.

Suyoun Kim, Duc Le, Weiyi Zheng, Tarun Singh, Abhinav Arora, Xiaoyu Zhai, Christian Fuegen, Ozlem Kalinli, and Michael L. Seltzer. 2022. Evaluating user perception of speech recognition system quality with semantic distance metric. In *Interspeech 2022, 23rd Annual Conference of the International Speech Communication Association, Incheon, Korea, 18-22 September 2022*, pages 3978–3982. ISCA.

Dietrich Klakow and Jochen Peters. 2002. Testing the correlation of word error rate and perplexity. *Speech Commun.*, 38(1-2):19–28.

S. Krishnamurthy and S. R. Mahadeva Prasanna. 2017. A hybrid feature extraction technique for continuous number speech recognition in malayalam. In *Proceedings of the 24th International Conference on Machine Learning*, pages 33–40.

Ashok Kumar and Vikas Mittal. 2021. Hindi speech recognition in noisy environment using hybrid technique. *International Journal of Information Technology*, 13:483–492.

A Madhavaraj and AG Ramakrishnan. 2017. Design and development of a large vocabulary, continuous speech recognition system for tamil. In *2017 14th IEEE India Council International Conference (INDICON)*, pages 1–5. IEEE.

Manavalan Manjutha, Parthasarathy Subashini, Marimuthu Krishnaveni, and V. Narmadha. 2019. An optimized cepstral feature selection method for dysfluencies classification using tamil speech dataset. In *2019 IEEE International Smart Cities Conference, ISC2 2019, Casablanca, Morocco, October 14-17, 2019*, pages 671–677. IEEE.

Rainer Martin. 1994. Spectral subtraction based on minimum statistics. *power*, 6(8):1182–1185.

AN Mishra, Mahesh Chandra, Astik Biswas, and SN Sharan. 2011. Robust features for connected hindi digits recognition. *International Journal of Signal Processing, Image Processing and Pattern Recognition*, 4(2):79–90.

Ghulam Muhammad, Yousef A Alotaibi, and Mohammad Nurul Huda. 2009. Automatic speech recognition for bangla digits. In *2009 12th international conference on computers and information technology*, pages 379–383. IEEE.

P. Patel and P. Patel. 2017. A comparative study of continuous digit recognition using mfcc and lpc features for gujarati language. In *Proceedings of the 24th International Conference on Machine Learning*, pages 33–40.

Daniel Povey, Arnab Ghoshal, Gilles Boulianne, Lukas Burget, Ondrej Glembek, Nagendra Kumar Goel, Mirko Hannemann, Petr Motlicek, Yanmin Qian, Petr Schwarz, Jan Silovsky, Georg Stemmer, and Karel Vesely. 2011. The kaldi speech recognition toolkit. IEEE Signal Processing Society.

Rohit Prabhavalkar, Takaaki Hori, Tara N. Sainath, Ralf Schluter, and Shinji Watanabe. 2023. End-to-end speech recognition: A survey. *ArXiv*, abs/2303.03329.

Alec Radford, Jong Wook Kim, Tao Xu, Greg Brockman, Christine McLeavey, and Ilya Sutskever. 2022. Robust speech recognition via large-scale weak supervision. *CoRR*, abs/2212.04356.

Shangeth Rajaa, Swaraj Dalmia, and Kumarmanas Nethil. 2022. Skit-s2i: An indian accented speech to intent dataset. *CoRR*, abs/2212.13015.

Fazle Rabbi Rakib, Souhardya Saha Dip, Samiul Alam, Nazia Tasnim, Md. Istiak Hossain Shihab, Md. Nazmuddoha Ansary, Syed Mobassir Hossen, Marsia Haque Meghla, Mamunur Mamun, Farig Sadeque, Sayma Sultana Chowdhury, Tahsin Reasat, Asif Shahriyar Sushmit, and Ahmed Imtiaz Humayun. 2023. Ood-speech: A large bengali speech recognition dataset for out-of-distribution benchmarking. *CoRR*, abs/2305.09688.

Antony W Rix, John G Beerends, Michael P Hollier, and Andries P Hekstra. 2001. Perceptual evaluation of speech quality (pesq)-a new method for speech quality assessment of telephone networks and codecs. In *2001 IEEE international conference on acoustics, speech, and signal processing. Proceedings (Cat. No. 01CH37221)*, volume 2, pages 749–752. IEEE.

Tim Sainburg, Marvin Thielk, and Timothy Q Gentner. 2020. Finding, visualizing, and quantifying latent structure across diverse animal vocal repertoires. *PLoS computational biology*, 16(10):e1008228.

Steffen Schneider, Alexei Baevski, Ronan Collobert, and Michael Auli. 2019. wav2vec: Unsupervised pre-training for speech recognition. *CoRR*, abs/1904.05862.

Usha Sharma, Hari Om, and AN Mishra. 2023. Hindispeech-net: a deep learning based robust automatic speech recognition system for hindi language. *Multimedia Tools and Applications*, 82(11):16173–16193.

Amitoj Singh, Virender Kadyan, Munish Kumar, and Nancy Bassan. 2020. Asroil: a comprehensive survey for automatic speech recognition of indian languages. *Artif. Intell. Rev.*, 53(5):3673–3704.

Jayashri Vajpai and Avnish Bora. 2016. Industrial applications of automatic speech recognition systems.

Poorvi@DravidianLangTech: Sentiment Analysis on Code-Mixed Tulu and Tamil Corpus

Poorvi Shetty
JSS Science and Technology University
Mysuru, India
poorvishetty1202@gmail.com

Abstract

Sentiment analysis in code-mixed languages poses significant challenges, particularly for highly under-resourced languages such as Tulu and Tamil. Existing corpora, primarily sourced from YouTube comments, suffer from class imbalance across sentiment categories. Moreover, the limited number of samples in these corpus hampers effective sentiment classification.

This study introduces a new corpus tailored for sentiment analysis in Tulu code-mixed texts. The research applies standard pre-processing techniques to ensure data quality and consistency and handle class imbalance. Subsequently, multiple classifiers are employed to analyze the sentiment of the code-mixed texts, yielding promising results. By leveraging the new corpus, the study contributes to advancing sentiment analysis techniques in under-resourced code-mixed languages. This work serves as a stepping stone towards better understanding and addressing the challenges posed by sentiment analysis in highly under-resourced languages.

Keywords sentiment analysis, code-mixed languages, Tulu, Tamil, under-resourced languages, corpus, class imbalance, classification.

1 Introduction

Online social media material is expanding at an exponential rate. Social media platforms allow users to freely express themselves in their native languages thanks to their multilingual user interface. As a result, a linguistic phenomenon known as code-mixing in social media data has become prevalent, attracting the interest of academics in disciplines like sociolinguistics and Natural Language Processing (NLP). The informality of code-mixed text, however, presents a number of difficulties, including those with data extraction and summarization. Sentiment analysis has been a significant research field in the field of code-mixed data analysis in recent years (Ahmad and Singla, 2021) (Patra et al., 2018) (Gambäck and Das, 2014) (Tarihoran and Sumirat, 2022).

India has the greatest population of speakers of English as a Second Language thanks to its rich linguistic past and close relationship with English. Native Indian language speakers don't use Unicode while exchanging information on social media platforms. They employ code-mixing to combine Latin script with English words or phrases in their original language to communicate themselves (Thara and Poornachandran, 2018). Additionally, there has been work done on sentiment analysis on YouTube comments (Alhujaili and Yafooz, 2021).

It is difficult to process these natural languages for diverse language-processing tasks (Srivastava and Singh, 2021). Compared to other languages, the regional languages of India are thought to have few resources (Harish and Rangan, 2020).

This paper introduces a novel methodology for sentiment analysis on code-mixed Tulu and Tamil corpora, considering the challenges associated with class imbalance. An additional corpus is curated by scraping YouTube comments on Tulu videos, enriching the code-mixed Tulu corpus and providing more comprehensive resources for analysis. This paper proposes a new stopwords list, tailored for both English and Tulu languages, and utilizes a synonyms list to address inconsistent spelling variations in the corpus. These contributions advance the field of sentiment analysis on code-mixed languages, offering insights and guidance for effective analysis and improving the overall performance of sentiment classification models.

2 Related Work

There is a lot of research being done right now on code mixing in natural language processing (NLP)

Third Workshop on Speech and Language Technologies for Dravidian Languages, pages 124–132, Varna, Bulgaria, Sep 7, 2023.
https://doi.org/10.26615/978-954-452-085-4_016

jobs. In their thorough investigation of the difficulties code-mixed NLP faces in a multilingual society, Srivastava et al. (Srivastava and Singh, 2021) shed light on the current state of this field's NLP research.

The unique unified approach put out by Choudhary et al. (Choudhary et al., 2018) aims to overcome the drawbacks associated with using code-mixed text in NLP. Their method includes a pre-processing step that groups distinct word variations based on an empirical similarity measure, making analysis and processing more efficient.

Using datasets created expressly to show code-mixing between Bengali, English, and Hindi, Barman et al. (Barman et al., 2014) report an ongoing research project on automatic language recognition on social media platforms. According to their first results, a dictionary-based strategy outperforms supervised classification and sequence labelling techniques in solving this issue.

By creating a new code-switched dataset for Hindi-English language pairings and carrying out a comparative evaluation of conventional machine learning models for word-level language recognition, Mave et al. (Mave et al., 2018) make a contribution to the area. Their research offers insightful information about the performance of these models in contexts with code-mixed linguistics.

The following five language pairs underwent neural machine translation by Vyawahere et al (Vyawahare et al., 2022): Kannada to Tamil, Kannada to Telugu, Kannada to Malayalam, Kannada to Sanskrit, and Kannada to Tulu. The datasets for each of the five language pairings were used to train a variety of translation models, including Seq2Seq models like LSTM, bidirectional LSTM, Conv2Seq, and state-of-the-art transformers from scratch.

Although much research has been done on SA in the English language, data on the web also offers information in various other languages that should be examined. The goal of Shah et al. (Shah and Kaushik, 2019) is to analyse, assess, and debate the methodologies, algorithms, and difficulties encountered by the researchers when conducting the SA on Indigenous languages.

In today's age, Twitter contains a vast array of emotions and viewpoints. It offers a significant volume of sentiment-related information, but extracting data from Twitter necessitates appropriate techniques. The study conducted by Rakshitha et al. (Rakshitha et al., 2021) focuses on analyzing the sentiments expressed in regional languages on Twitter.

Labels	Train Set	Test Set
Positive	3487	344
Negative	736	60
Mixed Feelings	1094	107
Neutral	1921	197

Table 1: Tulu Corpus Details

Labels	Train Set	Test Set
Positive	22327	73
Negative	4751	338
Mixed Feelings	4458	101
Unknown State	6239	137

Table 2: Tamil Corpus Details

3 Corpus Details

In the case of the code-mixed Tulu corpus, a combination of the existing corpus (Hegde et al., 2022) and the newly created dataset proposed in this paper was utilized. For the code-mixed Tamil corpus, the data was obtained from the established dataset (Chakravarthi et al., 2020).

3.1 Existing Corpus

The code-mixed Tulu corpus used in this study was obtained from YouTube comments posted on videos in the Tulu language. These comments exhibited a mixture of languages including English, Kannada, Tulu, and combinations thereof, with varying scripts including Latin and Kannada. The comments in the corpus were manually labelled with sentiment categories, including positive, negative, neutral, and mixed feelings.

The code-mixed Tamil corpus utilized in this research was gathered from YouTube comments posted on videos in the Tamil language. The corpus predominantly consisted of "Tanglish" sentences, which are a combination of Tamil and English. It is noteworthy that the comments did not exclusively comprise fully Tamil or English sentences. To facilitate sentiment analysis, each comment in the corpus was annotated with sentiment labels, including positive, negative, unknown, and mixed feelings.

Labels	Number of Samples
Positive	323
Negative	65
Mixed Feelings	34
Neutral	195
Not Tulu	2932

Table 3: Newly-Created Tulu Corpus Details

Details	Number
Male, Post-graduate	1
Female, Graduate	1
Male, High-school graduate	1

Table 4: Details of Annotators for the Newly-Created Tulu Corpus

3.2 Creation of Additional Resources

3.2.1 New Corpus Creation for Tulu

To overcome the limited availability of samples in the original corpus, a supplementary dataset was curated by extracting comments from Tulu-language videos on YouTube. The YouTube Comment Scraper yielded a total of 3459 samples in this supplementary corpus. These comments were written using a combination of English, Kannada, and Tulu languages.

Notably, Tulu content is commonly articulated in either the Latin or Kannada scripts. I identified any comments not in the Tulu language and labelled them within the dataset manually.

Annotation Process: To ensure consistency, manual annotation was carried out on this new dataset, aligning with the sentiment categories in the corpus mentioned in the previous subsection. The sentiment classifications encompass Positive, Negative, Mixed Feelings, and Neutral tones.

Each sample is presented in a two-column format: 'Text,' which contains the full YouTube comment, and 'Annotations,' denoting the assigned sentiment category for the respective comment.

The annotation process engaged three native Tulu speakers, all proficient in English and Kannada also. The annotation guidelines closely followed the approach outlined by Hegde et al. After a preliminary demonstration featuring two comments from each sentiment class, the annotators independently assigned labels to all comments on their copy of the comment sheet.

For each individual sample, if the majority of annotators provided a consistent label, that label was selected. In instances of discordant labelling, the annotators collaborated in a discussion to reach a consensus.

This supplementary corpus plays a pivotal role in enhancing sentiment analysis tasks for the Tulu language. By augmenting the available dataset, it broadens the potential for more accurate sentiment classification. This corpus will be made available online.

Language	Number of Words
Tulu	193
English	127

Table 5: English-Tulu Stopwords List

3.2.2 Stopwords List Creation for Code-Mixed Tulu

To optimize the sentiment analysis process, a comprehensive list of English and Tulu stop words was meticulously compiled. The stop words in Tulu are presented in the Latin script to align with the character set commonly used in the comments.

The inclusion of stop words removal as a preprocessing step has demonstrated its efficacy in enhancing the performance of classification models in sentiment analysis tasks. (Sarica and Luo, 2021) By eliminating commonly occurring and less informative words, the focus is shifted towards more meaningful and sentiment-rich terms. To address the potential variations in spelling, special attention was given to accommodate different possible spellings of the same word. This consideration ensures a more robust and inclusive stop words list. The compiled list comprises a total of 320 words, encompassing both English and Tulu stop words. This resource facilitates the elimination of irrelevant and redundant terms.

3.2.3 'Synonyms' List Creation for Code-Mixed Tulu

Due to the absence of consistent spelling rules for Tulu in the Latin script, a challenge arises in dealing with the multiple spellings of the same word within the corpus. In response to this concern, with the aim of ensuring consistency in word usage, a meticulously crafted compendium of synonymous terms was developed for the textual corpus. This compilation was particularly attuned to words that have the highest frequencies in this corpus.

Each entry within the synonym list encompassed

Word	Synonyms/Variations in Spelling
super	superb, spr, supper, supr, sooper, sprb, superrrrr
malpule	manpule, malpi, malpere, malpuna, malpode, malpu, malpuni, maldar, malpad, malpun
panda	pand, pandh, pandat, panpar, pather, patherle, pande

Table 6: Sample Entries from 'Synonyms' List

terms sharing akin meanings, yet exhibiting variations in their orthographic representation. This compilation was methodically curated, and tailored exclusively to this specific dataset. It is not exhaustive and sought to collate words that convey identical meanings but had different spellings. Moreover, this compilation aimed to cluster words that share semantic equivalence, yet diverge in their linguistic structure and levels of respect. As an illustrative instance, the juxtaposition of "panper" and "panda" is encompassed within this list.

By incorporating these synonymous terms, the aim was to establish a standardised representation of commonly occurring words and minimize the impact of spelling inconsistencies on model performance.

The utilization of the synonym dictionary played a crucial role in enhancing the overall consistency of word spellings within the corpus. This, in turn, contributed to improved model performance in sentiment analysis tasks. By promoting uniformity in word representations, the dictionary of synonyms mitigated the challenges posed by varied spellings and facilitated more accurate sentiment classification.

4 Data Pre-Processing

The corpus underwent a series of pre-processing steps prior to the application of models. Initially, emojis were replaced with their corresponding names. Following this, a sequence of transformations was performed, which involved the removal of HTML tags, URLs, punctuation marks, special characters, numbers, and excessive whitespace. Additionally, the text was converted to lowercase to ensure uniformity.

Stop words, however, were not removed from the corpus, as their exclusion resulted in a decrease in performance.

To establish consistent spelling, a predefined list of synonyms that I created was utilized to replace words with their appropriate alternatives. Moreover, a label encoder was applied to the annotation labels, facilitating ease of use for the models during training (Shah et al., 2022). The TF-IDF Vectorizer was employed with specific parameters, including a maximum of 5000 features and an n-gram range of (1, 2) (Das and Chakraborty, 2018). In this context, the use of inverse document frequency (IDF) was disabled to optimize vectorisation.

To expand the corpus, the TextAttack EasyDataAugmenter technique was utilized, resulting in a quadrupling of the corpus size. This augmentation process helped to introduce additional variations in the data, thereby enhancing the overall model performance (Morris et al., 2020).

Considering the imbalanced distribution of positive comments within the corpus, the SMOTE (Synthetic Minority Over-sampling Technique) algorithm was employed. This technique ensured an equal representation of samples from each class, ultimately improving the performance of the models.

Class imbalance is a common challenge in many machine learning applications, particularly in sentiment analysis tasks. One effective approach to address this issue is Synthetic Minority Oversampling Technique (SMOTE). SMOTE is a data augmentation technique specifically designed to tackle class imbalance by generating synthetic samples for the minority class (Bowyer et al., 2011). The method works by identifying minority class instances and creating synthetic examples along the line segments connecting them. This process increases the diversity of the minority class and helps to balance the class distribution in the corpus. By introducing synthetic samples, SMOTE not only mitigates the impact of class imbalance but also improves the overall performance of classification models. It allows the classifier to learn from a more balanced representation of the data, leading to enhanced predictive capabilities. Moreover, SMOTE is widely applicable across various machine learning algorithms and has proven to be particularly effective in sentiment analysis tasks, where imbalanced sentiment classes are often encountered.

These pre-processing and data augmentation techniques collectively contributed to the refinement and enrichment of the corpus, thereby facilitating more accurate sentiment analysis results.

5 Classification Models

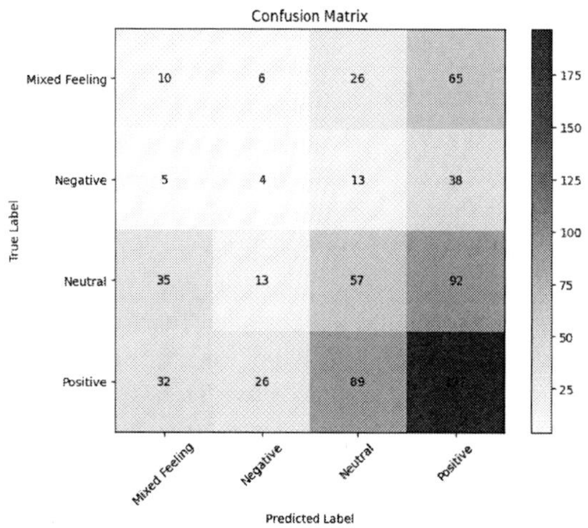

Figure 1: Confusion Matrix: Bagging Model on Tulu Dataset

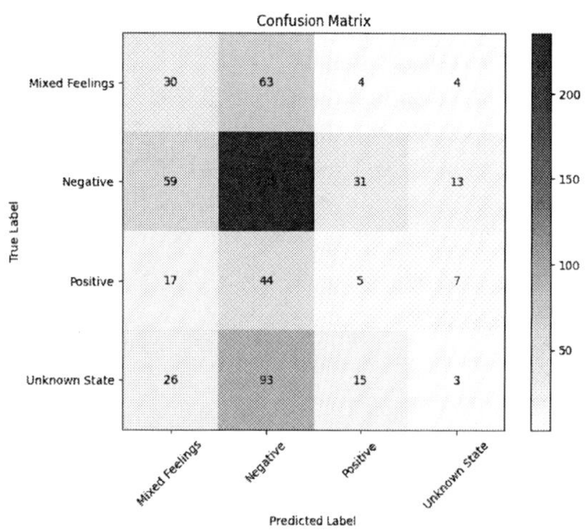

Figure 2: Confusion Matrix: AdaBoost Model on Tamil Dataset

In the study, a range of models (Pedregosa et al., 2018) were employed to analyze the corpus, and their parameters were fine-tuned using 5-fold cross-validation. The application of cross-validation ensures robust evaluation and provides insight into the models' performance. The chosen parameters aim to optimize the models' predictive capabilities while maintaining a balance between bias and variance. The details of the models considered in the analysis are given below.

5.1 Multinomial Naive Bayes

The Multinomial Naive Bayes classifier is a probabilistic model based on Bayes' theorem. It is specifically designed for classification tasks with discrete features, such as text classification. The alpha parameter, set to 0.1, represents the smoothing parameter that helps handle zero probabilities for unseen features.

5.2 Random Forest Classifier

Random Forest is an ensemble learning method that constructs multiple decision trees and combines their predictions to make final decisions. The criterion is set to 'entropy' to measure the quality of a split based on information gain. With a maximum depth of 8, the trees are limited in their growth to prevent overfitting. The max features parameter is set to 'log2' to control the number of features considered at each split. The n estimators parameter is set to 500, indicating the number of trees in the forest. The min samples split parameter is set to 7, determining the minimum number of samples required to split an internal node.

5.3 Logistic Regression

Logistic Regression is a linear classification model that estimates the probabilities of different classes. The C parameter is set to 10.0, controlling the inverse of the regularization strength. A higher C value indicates less regularization and a stronger emphasis on correctly classifying the training data. The max iter is set to 10000, defining the maximum number of iterations for the solver to converge. The penalty is set to 'l1', indicating L1 regularization that encourages sparse feature selection. The solver is set to 'liblinear', which handles L1 penalty efficiently.

5.4 Linear Support Vector Classifier (LinearSVC)

LinearSVC is a linear model for classification tasks based on Support Vector Machines (SVM). The max iter is set to 5000, defining the maximum number of iterations for convergence. The C parameter is set to 0.1, controlling the trade-off between margin maximization and misclassification. The penalty is set to 'l2', indicating L2 regularization that encourages small weights.

5.5 Decision Tree Classifier

The Decision Tree Classifier builds a tree model by recursively partitioning the data based on feature

Classifier	Mixed Feelings	Negative	Neutral	Positive	Macro Avg	Weighted Avg
Mutinomial NB	0.09	0.05	0.29	0.53	0.24	0.36
Random Forest	0.11	0.18	0.41	0.48	0.24	0.36
Logistic Regression	0.16	0.16	0.26	0.42	0.24	0.31
SVM	0.16	0.16	0.34	0.25	0.23	0.29
Decision Tree	0.06	0.03	0.42	0.06	0.14	0.16
KNN	0.25	0.10	0.29	0.02	0.17	0.14
AdaBoost	0.10	0.06	0.38	0.12	0.17	0.18
OneVsRest	0.16	0.07	0.30	0.39	0.23	0.30
XGBoost	0.16	0.10	0.36	0.29	0.23	0.27
GradientBoost	0.19	0.11	0.36	0.31	0.24	0.29
Voting	0.17	0.12	0.32	0.39	0.25	0.31
Stacking	0.06	0.04	0.28	0.49	0.22	0.33
Bagging	0.10	0.07	0.29	0.53	**0.25**	**0.36**

Table 7: F-Score for Tulu

Classifier	Mixed Feelings	Negative	Neutral	Positive	Macro Avg	Weighted Avg
Mutinomial NB	0.11	0.09	0.27	0.48	0.241	0.336
Random Forest	0.22	0.16	0.24	0.28	0.22	0.25
Logistic Regression	0.23	0.11	0.23	0.36	0.23	0.28
SVM	0.23	0.13	0.34	0.22	0.21	0.23
Decision Tree	0.04	0.10	0.88	0.09	0.16	0.18
KNN	0.25	0.13	0.26	0.01	0.16	0.13
AdaBoost	0.08	0.08	0.40	0.10	0.17	0.18
OneVsRest	0.22	0.07	0.26	0.33	0.22	0.27
XGBoost	0.25	0.11	0.37	0.08	0.20	0.19
GradientBoost	0.20	0.14	0.36	0.25	0.24	0.26
Voting	0.21	0.14	0.22	0.23	0.20	0.22
Stacking	0.14	0.11	0.29	0.42	0.24	0.31
Bagging	0.13	0.08	0.27	0.47	**0.243**	**0.336**

Table 8: F-Score for Tulu without 'Synonyms' List

Classifier	Mixed Feelings	Negative	Positive	Unknown	Macro Avg	Weighted Avg
Mutinomial NB	0.10	0.10	0.21	0.06	0.13	0.11
Random Forest	0.21	0.51	0.09	0.08	0.23	0.33
Logistic Regression	0.22	0.22	0.16	0.18	0.20	0.21
SVM	0.17	0.23	0.18	0.10	0.17	0.19
Decision Tree	0.07	0.66	0.02	0.02	0.19	0.36
KNN	0.01	0.02	0.20	0.02	0.06	0.04
AdaBoost	0.25	0.60	0.07	0.03	**0.24**	**0.37**
OneVsRest	0.16	0.22	0.18	0.15	0.17	0.19
XGBoost	0.26	0.46	0.12	0.10	0.23	0.32
GradientBoost	0.26	0.23	0.13	0.10	0.18	0.19
Voting	0.22	0.28	0.15	0.10	0.19	0.22
Stacking	0.13	0.12	0.20	0.04	0.12	0.11
Bagging	0.09	0.10	0.20	0.10	0.12	0.11

Table 9: F-Score for Tamil

values. The ccp alpha is set to 0.0001, representing the complexity parameter used for pruning the tree. The criterion is set to 'gini', which measures the impurity of a split. The max depth is set to 100, limiting the depth of the tree to avoid overfitting. The min samples split is set to 10, specifying the minimum number of samples required to split an internal node.

5.6 K-Nearest Neighbours Classifier (KNN)

K-Nearest Neighbors Classifier is a non-parametric algorithm that classifies samples based on their similarity to the k nearest neighbours. The n neighbours parameter is set to 1, indicating the closest neighbor is used for classification.

5.7 AdaBoost Classifier

AdaBoost is an ensemble method that combines weak classifiers into a strong classifier. The learning rate is set to 0.5, controlling the contribution of each weak classifier. The n estimators is set to 300, indicating the maximum number of estimators at which boosting is terminated.

5.8 One-vs-Rest Logistic Regression Classifier

The One-vs-Rest (OvR) strategy extends binary classifiers to multi-class classification. The logistic regression classifier (with C=10.0 and solver='liblinear') is used as the base classifier, and the OvR classifier combines multiple binary classifiers to handle each class.

5.9 Gradient Boosting Classifier

Gradient Boosting is an ensemble method that combines weak learners in a stage-wise manner, where each model tries to correct the errors made by the previous models. The n estimators is set to 50, indicating the number of boosting stages. The learning rate is set to 0.5, controlling the contribution of each weak learner. The max depth is set to 10, limiting the depth of each weak learner.

5.10 Voting Classifier

The Voting Classifier combines the predictions of multiple individual classifiers by a majority vote (hard voting). It includes three estimators: logistic regression, random forest, and linear support vector machine. The ensemble of these classifiers enables them to make joint decisions (Leon et al., 2017).

5.11 Stacking Classifier

The Stacking Classifier combines multiple classification models (k-nearest neighbours, random forest, and Multinomial Naive Bayes) by training a meta-classifier (Logistic Regression) on their predictions. This allows the meta-classifier to learn patterns from the outputs of the base classifiers and make the final prediction (Alexandropoulos et al., 2019).

5.12 Bagging Classifier

The Bagging Classifier applies the Bagging ensemble method to a base classifier (Multinomial Naive Bayes). It generates multiple subsets of the training data by bootstrapping and trains each subset on the base classifier. The final prediction is obtained through a majority vote of the base classifiers (Kotsiantis et al., 2005). These models and their respective parameters are applied to the corpus to explore their effectiveness in sentiment analysis tasks.

6 Experiments and Results

A series of experiments were conducted to identify the optimal configuration for sentiment analysis on the code-mixed corpus. The evaluation of the classification system's performance was based on the weighted averaged F-Score, which provides a comprehensive measure across all classes. To ensure reliable results, 5-fold cross-validation was employed to determine the best parameters for the models.

The corpus used for analysis exhibited an imbalance among the classes, necessitating the implementation of the Synthetic Minority Over-sampling Technique (SMOTE). This technique effectively addressed the class imbalance issue and led to significant improvements in the performance of most models.

Moreover, data augmentation techniques were employed using the TextAttack library. This approach further enhanced the corpus by generating additional samples, contributing to the overall performance improvement of the models.

After thorough experimentation and analysis, the stacking classifier, specifically the combination K-nearest neighbours, Random Forest, and Multinomial Naive Bayes with Logistic Regression as the meta-classifier, emerged as the best model for sentiment analysis on the code-mixed Tulu language. In contrast, logistic regression alone demonstrated superior performance for sentiment analysis on the code-mixed Tamil language.

These findings highlight the effectiveness of the proposed models and the significance of addressing class imbalance and utilizing data augmentation techniques in code-mixed sentiment analysis tasks.

7 Conclusion

In conclusion, this paper presents a methodology for sentiment analysis on a code-mixed corpus consisting of Tulu and Tamil languages extracted from YouTube comments. The unique characteristics of code-mixed data, such as inconsistent spelling and the absence of stemming and lemmatisation libraries, pose challenges for traditional classifiers. This study looks at various classifiers and their performance of the code-mixed corpora. However, despite achieving notable performance, there remains ample room for further improvement in prediction accuracy. This study highlights the potential for future research endeavours to enhance sentiment analysis techniques specifically tailored for code-mixed languages.

8 Acknowledgements

I thank the organisers of Sentiment Analysis in Tamil and Tulu - DravidianLangTech@RANLP 2023 (Hegde et al., 2023) for giving me a platform to work on this topic.

References

Gazi Imtiyaz Ahmad and Jimmy Singla. 2021. Sentiment analysis of code-mixed social media text (sacmsmt) in indian-languages. In *2021 International Conference on Computing Sciences (ICCS)*, pages 25–33.

Stamatios-Aggelos Alexandropoulos, Christos Aridas, Sotiris Kotsiantis, and Michael Vrahatis. 2019. *Stacking Strong Ensembles of Classifiers*, pages 545–556.

Rawan Fahad Alhujaili and Wael M.S. Yafooz. 2021. Sentiment analysis for youtube videos with user comments: Review. In *2021 International Conference on Artificial Intelligence and Smart Systems (ICAIS)*, pages 814–820.

Utsab Barman, Amitava Das, Joachim Wagner, and Jennifer Foster. 2014. Code mixing: A challenge for language identification in the language of social media. In *Proceedings of the First Workshop on Computational Approaches to Code Switching*, pages 13–23, Doha, Qatar. Association for Computational Linguistics.

Kevin W. Bowyer, Nitesh V. Chawla, Lawrence O. Hall, and W. Philip Kegelmeyer. 2011. SMOTE: synthetic minority over-sampling technique. *CoRR*, abs/1106.1813.

Bharathi Raja Chakravarthi, Vigneshwaran Muralidaran, Ruba Priyadharshini, and John Philip McCrae. 2020. Corpus creation for sentiment analysis in code-mixed Tamil-English text. In *Proceedings of the 1st Joint Workshop on Spoken Language Technologies for Under-resourced languages (SLTU) and Collaboration and Computing for Under-Resourced Languages (CCURL)*, pages 202–210, Marseille, France. European Language Resources association.

Nurendra Choudhary, Rajat Singh, Ishita Bindlish, and Manish Shrivastava. 2018. Sentiment analysis of code-mixed languages leveraging resource rich languages.

Bijoyan Das and Sarit Chakraborty. 2018. An improved text sentiment classification model using TF-IDF and next word negation. *CoRR*, abs/1806.06407.

Björn Gambäck and Amitava Das. 2014. On measuring the complexity of code-mixing. In *Proceedings of the 11th international conference on natural language processing, Goa, India*, pages 1–7.

B. S. Harish and R. Kasturi Rangan. 2020. A comprehensive survey on indian regional language processing. *SN Applied Sciences*, 2(7).

Asha Hegde, Mudoor Devadas Anusha, Sharal Coelho, Hosahalli Lakshmaiah Shashirekha, and Bharathi Raja Chakravarthi. 2022. Corpus creation for sentiment analysis in code-mixed Tulu text. In *Proceedings of the 1st Annual Meeting of the ELRA/ISCA Special Interest Group on Under-Resourced Languages*, pages 33–40, Marseille, France. European Language Resources Association.

Asha Hegde, Bharathi Raja Chakravarthi, Hosahalli Lakshmaiah Shashirekha, Rahul Ponnusamy, SUBALALITHA CN, Lavanya S K, Thenmozhi D, Martha Karunakar, Shreya Shreeram, and Sarah Aymen. 2023. Findings of the shared task on sentiment analysis in tamil and tulu code-mixed text. In *Proceedings of the Third Workshop on Speech and Language Technologies for Dravidian Languages*, Varna, Bulgaria. Recent Advances in Natural Language Processing.

Sotiris Kotsiantis, George Tsekouras, and P. Pintelas. 2005. Bagging model trees for classification problems. pages 328–337.

Florin Leon, Sabina-Adriana Floria, and Costin Badica. 2017. Evaluating the effect of voting methods on ensemble-based classification. pages 1–6.

Deepthi Mave, Suraj Maharjan, and Thamar Solorio. 2018. Language identification and analysis of code-switched social media text. In *Proceedings of the Third Workshop on Computational Approaches to Linguistic Code-Switching*, pages 51–61, Melbourne, Australia. Association for Computational Linguistics.

John X. Morris, Eli Lifland, Jin Yong Yoo, Jake Grigsby, Di Jin, and Yanjun Qi. 2020. Textattack: A framework for adversarial attacks, data augmentation, and adversarial training in nlp.

Braja Gopal Patra, Dipankar Das, and Amitava Das. 2018. Sentiment analysis of code-mixed indian languages: An overview of sail$_{c}ode - mixedsharedtask@icon - 2017$.

Fabian Pedregosa, Gaël Varoquaux, Alexandre Gramfort, Vincent Michel, Bertrand Thirion, Olivier Grisel, Mathieu Blondel, Andreas Müller, Joel Nothman, Gilles Louppe, Peter Prettenhofer, Ron Weiss, Vincent Dubourg, Jake Vanderplas, Alexandre Passos, David Cournapeau, Matthieu Brucher, Matthieu Perrot, and Édouard Duchesnay. 2018. Scikit-learn: Machine learning in python.

Kakuthota Rakshitha, Ramalingam HM, M Pavithra, Advi HD, and Maithri Hegde. 2021. Sentimental analysis of indian regional languages on social media. *Global Transitions Proceedings*, 2(2):414–420. International Conference on Computing System and its Applications (ICCSA- 2021).

Serhad Sarica and Jianxi Luo. 2021. Stopwords in technical language processing. *PLOS ONE*, 16(8):1–13.

Deval Shah, Zi Yu Xue, and Tor M. Aamodt. 2022. Label encoding for regression networks.

Sonali Rajesh Shah and Abhishek Kaushik. 2019. Sentiment analysis on indian indigenous languages: A review on multilingual opinion mining.

Vivek Srivastava and Mayank Singh. 2021. Challenges and limitations with the metrics measuring the complexity of code-mixed text. In *Proceedings of the Fifth Workshop on Computational Approaches to Linguistic Code-Switching*, pages 6–14, Online. Association for Computational Linguistics.

Naf'an Tarihoran and Iin Ratna Sumirat. 2022. The impact of social media on the use of code mixing by generation z. *International Journal of Interactive Mobile Technologies (iJIM)*, 16(7):54–69.

S Thara and Prabaharan Poornachandran. 2018. Code-mixing: A brief survey. In *2018 International Conference on Advances in Computing, Communications and Informatics (ICACCI)*, pages 2382–2388.

Aditya Vyawahare, Rahul Tangsali, Aditya Mandke, Onkar Litake, and Dipali Kadam. 2022. Pict@dravidianlangtech-acl2022: Neural machine translation on dravidian languages.

NLP_SSN_CSE@DravidianLangTech-2023: Fake News Detection in Dravidian Languages using Transformer Models

Varsha Balaji , Shahul Hameed T & B. Bharathi
Department of CSE
Sri Sivasubramaniya Nadar College of Engineering,
Tamil Nadu, India
varsha2010399@ssn.edu.in
shahul2012066@ssn.edu.in
bharathib@ssn.edu.in

Abstract

The objective of the task is to correctly detect and counteract misleading information using machine learning classification algorithms in order to solve the pervasive problem of fake news, eventually protecting the integrity of information distribution and fostering informed decision-making. Detection of fake news is essential in the modern society. Complex models are used in the analysis of data by ML classification algorithms, which accurately detect incorrect information. This safeguards integrity and gives people the confidence to rely on reliable sources. Fake news threatens democracy, diminishes public trust, and intensifies polarisation. Transformer models like M-BERT, ALBERT, BERT, and XLNET were used in this task, and notably, M-BERT surpassed the competition with a strong F1 score of 0.74, while XLNET and ALBERT only managed 0.71 and 0.66 accuracy respectively. Effectively addressing fake news and its negative repercussions requires ML classification, in particular M-BERT.

1 Introduction

Social media has completely changed the way we receive and share information in the digital age. It has become a necessary component of our everyday life(Schmidt and Wiegand, 2017). Instant communication and worldwide connectivity have many advantages, but there is also a negative aspect to this phenomenon: the mass circulation of false information. In order to manipulate public opinion, spark controversy, or forward particular objectives, fake news is defined as information that has been purposefully created to be false or misleading and presented as true news. (Bharathi)The spread of fake news on social media platforms has had a huge impact on society and poses serious problems for the truth, democracy, and social cohesion.

It is impossible to understate the effects of fake news on society. False narratives can easily gain traction and spread to millions of people in a matter of minutes because of the speedy dissemination of information through social media channels. Social media's widespread use increases the power of fake news, blurring the distinction between fact and fiction and serving as a haven for misinformation. This has wide-ranging effects on different facets of society.

The loss of trust in institutions and the media is one of the main issues. Public trust in established news sources declines when fake news stories spread and acquire credence. The underpinnings of democracy are being weakened by this deterioration of confidence, which also threatens the authority of honest media. A healthy democracy depends on knowledgeable citizens, and when incorrect information spreads widely, it limits people's capacity to make informed judgments and actively engage in public dialogue.

Furthermore, fake news has the power to affect political outcomes and change public opinion. Social media platforms can be used by manipulative individuals to spread false information that advances their goals, whether those goals are to alter public opinion, discredit rivals, or even meddle in elections. Fake news can be customized to certain audiences by utilizing social media's extensive reach and targeting algorithms, escalating polarisation and widening socioeconomic gaps.

Fake news has become increasingly prevalent on social media platforms, which has had a significant effect on society. It has eroded confidence, warped public perception, and exacerbated societal polarization. Because of the seriousness of this problem, academics have resorted to ML classification techniques to create tools that can successfully identify and counter bogus news. We can work towards a more informed society where the dissemination of

Third Workshop on Speech and Language Technologies for Dravidian Languages, pages 133–139, Varna, Bulgaria, Sep 7, 2023.
https://doi.org/10.26615/978-954-452-085-4_017

false information is reduced, public trust is restored, and the pillars of democracy are strengthened by utilizing the potential of AI.

The organisation of the paper is as follows: Section 1 describes the task's goals, with a focus on identifying fake news. The associated work analyses of the existing research on this subject are explained in Section 2. The approach details the models employed, such as M-BERT, ALBERT, and BERT, as well as data gathering and preparation are elaborated in Section 3. Section 4, deals with the observations and outcomes that demonstrate how well the classification systems identify bogus news. Section 5 concludes the results and makes recommendations for additional research.

2 Related work

Recent years have seen the development of a number of methods for addressing the issue of spotting fake news. They are largely divided into the following categories: linguistic approaches, topic-agnostic methods, knowledge-based methods, machine learning methods, and hybrid methods. The authors divided the methods into two categories: social context-based learning and news content-based learning(**?**). While the latter is based on latent knowledge that a user learns from a news piece, the former is dependent on the news's publishing practices. Social media users take an active role in identifying fake news. For instance, Facebook prioritizes comments on a post based on how many people have responded to or interacted with it.

(Shu et al., 2017), "Fake News Detection on Social Media: A Data Mining Perspective" The goal of this study is to identify fake news on social media. The researchers employ ML algorithms to extract features from user profiles, network structure, and textual data. They create a classifier that successfully distinguishes between news stories that are real and those that are not. The method achieves excellent accuracy in spotting fake news, which adds to our understanding of the mechanics of fake news propagation on social media.

(Sharma et al., 2019) in "Combating Fake News: A Survey on Identification and Mitigation Techniques": This survey article offers a thorough summary of methods for spotting and avoiding fake news. It covers a variety of machine learning (ML) strategies, such as supervised learning, unsupervised learning, and hybrid techniques. The paper covers the difficulties and possibilities in identifying false news and provides information on the efficacy of ML-based strategies.

(Granskogen, 2018), "Detection of Fake News in Social Media Networks" The authors of this article suggest a framework for identifying bogus news in social media networks. To analyze sentiment, linguistic patterns, and user engagement indicators, they use ML algorithms and NLP approaches. The study offers information on the automatic detection of false information on social media platforms and demonstrates the efficacy of ML-based techniques in precisely recognizing fake news.

(Goldani et al., 2021) "Fake News Detection with Deep Learning Models" (2020): This paper explores the application of deep learning models for fake news detection, including convolutional neural networks and recurrent neural networks. The authors test out various architectures and assess their effectiveness using benchmark datasets. The study emphasizes deep learning's potential for accurately identifying bogus news.

(Ahmad et al., 2020)"Fake News Detection Using Machine Learning Ensemble Methods" examines the use of ensemble approaches in identifying false news. The research focuses on methods that integrate many classifiers to increase prediction accuracy and reliability, including bagging, boosting, and stacking. Ensemble approaches provide strong and reliable solutions for spotting disinformation by utilizing the various viewpoints and advantages of individual classifiers. The paper examines how well ensemble approaches perform in distinguishing between authentic and false news pieces, emphasizing their potential to improve the precision and overall effectiveness of machine learning-based fake news detection systems.

Our proposed methodology included a number of crucial phases for the false news identification task utilizing machine learning. To ensure data quality, the collection of false news stories was first gathered and preprocessed. Next, the preprocessed data was fine-tuned using the contextual language comprehension skills of the transformer models such as BERT, XLNET, ALBERT, and M-BERT. These models were then used to extract significant elements that captured the subtleties of fake news. The retrieved features were then used to train a classification system to discover the patterns and traits of fake news. Finally, the accuracy and efficiency of our approach in identifying bogus news were assessed using the proper criteria of which M-BERT generated the maximum accuracy.

3 Methodology and Data

The fundamental goal of fake news detection using machine learning (ML) classification is to create reliable and accurate models that can distinguish between false news and accurate information with accuracy. In order to make educated assumptions regarding the accuracy of the information presented, ML classification approaches try to analyze numerous textual, visual, and contextual aspects of news articles and social media content.

The main objective is to use labeled datasets with examples of both false and real news articles to train machine learning models. The models can derive patterns, connections, and indications that distinguish between trustworthy and false information by learning from these samples. The goal is to develop algorithms that can reliably and generally categorize as either false or real new occurrences of news articles.

ML classification algorithms seek to lessen the negative effects of disinformation on society by identifying bogus news. Maintaining the credibility of public discourse, fostering media literacy, and reducing the spread of false narratives that might sway public opinion, polarise communities, and threaten democratic processes are some of the things that fall under this category.

The dataset was obtained from the Codalab site. The dataset contains various comments from YouTube in the Malayalam language. The dataset consists of 2 attributes namely the comment itself along with the truthness label. The truth label indicates real or fake news which helps to find whether the data is real or fake. By using these labels classification will be done.

3.1 Data analysis and Preprocessing

Language	Malayalam
Train data	3258
Development data	816
Test data	1020

Table 1: Dataset Description

Machine learning (ML) classification algorithms for detecting fake news rely heavily on data preprocessing(Sivanaiah et al., 2023). To convert unprocessed data into a format appropriate for training

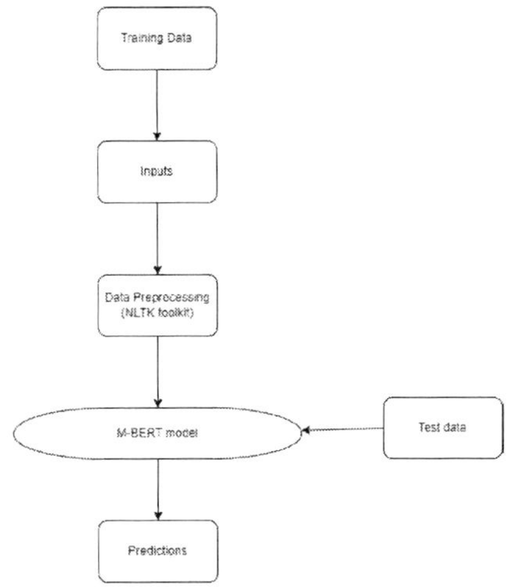

Figure 1: Working Flow of the Proposed model

Text	Label
തൊലിക്കട്ടി മോനേ....	Original
സ്പോൺസർ യുഎസ്	Fake

Figure 2: Dataset sample for Malayalam language

machine learning models, a number of procedures must be taken. Data cleaning is done initially to get rid of extraneous information such as punctuation, special characters, and HTML elements. The dataset's integrity is ensured through the proper handling of missing data. The text is then tokenized, which separates it into distinct words or n-grams to produce a structured representation.The NLTK toolkit was deployed in the preprocessing step.

Stop words are removed in order to get rid of often-appearing words that don't add anything to the meaning. Then, to promote consistency, words are shortened to their base form using stemming and lemmatization processes. Textual data is vectorized using methods like Bag-of-Words or TF-IDF so that ML algorithms may process the resulting numerical representations. To extract additional data, such as sentiment analysis scores or source credibility indicators, feature engineering might be used.

Finally, balancing the dataset reduces the effects of class imbalance by ensuring equal representation of fake and real news samples. ML classification algorithms are better able to learn and recognize patterns that discriminate between authentic and fraudulent news articles thanks to careful data pretreatment, enabling more precise and reliable detection of disinformation.

3.2 Model description

We classified the news dataset with the help of the below transformer models.

3.2.1 BERT Model

A cutting-edge pre-trained model in the area of natural language processing (NLP) is called BERT (Bidirectional Encoder Representations from Transformers). By proposing a cutting-edge method for pre-training language representations, transformed the way researchers approach diverse NLP challenges. Since BERT is built on the transformer architecture, it can recognize contextual dependencies and relationships inside a text.

The fact that BERT is bidirectional is one of its fundamental characteristics. During training, BERT takes into account both left-to-right and right-to-left text processing orientations, in contrast to conventional models(Kaliyar et al., 2021). This enables it to comprehend a word's context and meaning better by taking into account both its left and right surrounding terms.

Massive volumes of unannotated text from books and the internet have been used to pre-train BERT. BERT can learn universal language representations and identify intricate semantic and syntactic links because of this unsupervised training. The two main tasks in the pre-training phase are next-sentence prediction (NSP) and masked language modeling (MLM). While NSP trains BERT to assess whether two phrases in the original text are consecutive, MLM trains BERT to predict words that are randomly masked in the input.

BERT can be fine-tuned for particular downstream tasks such as text classification, named entity identification, and question-answering after pretraining. BERT is trained on task-specific labeled datasets during fine-tuning in order to modify its learned representations to the unique specifications of the target task. With just a small amount of task-specific training data, BERT can nevertheless perform remarkably well by fine-tuning and using its previously learned information.

BERT has excelled in a variety of NLP benchmarks and contests, with impressive results. It is a widely prominent model in the NLP world due to its capacity to capture in-depth contextual understanding and its wide range of applicability. To expand the capabilities of NLP tasks and applications, researchers and practitioners are continuing to investigate and build upon the breakthroughs made by BERT.

Parameters	**Score**
Accuracy	0.63
Macro Avg F1-score	**0.61**
Macro Avg Recall	0.61
Macro Avg Precision	0.63
Weighted Avg F1-score	0.62
Weighted Avg Recall	0.63
Weighted Avg Precision	0.63

Table 2: Performance of the proposed system using BERT

3.2.2 ALBERT Model

The BERT (Bidirectional Encoder Representations from Transformers) model has some drawbacks due to its size and computing demands. ALBERT (A Lite BERT) overcomes these drawbacks. While preserving the performance of BERT, ALBERT introduces model parameter reduction strategies, making it a more scalable and effective choice for diverse natural language processing (NLP) workloads.

Sharing parameters among the layers of the transformer architecture is the central concept of ALBERT. ALBERT uses a "cross-layer parameter sharing" strategy in contrast to BERT, where each layer has its own set of parameters. By drastically reducing the amount of model parameters, this method improves ALBERT's memory efficiency and speeds up its training and inference processes.

ALBERT uses a two-phase training strategy to increase its effectiveness even further. The model is initially pre-trained using a modified version of the BERT pre-training objectives, such as masked language modelling and next-sentence prediction, on a huge corpus of unlabeled text. (Gundapu and Mamidi, 2021)ALBERT fine-tunes on task-specific labelled data in the second phase to update its representations for subsequent challenges.

Despite its parameter reduction strategies, ALBERT performs admirably. On some NLP benchmarks, it shows comparable or even better performance than BERT while using less computational power. Because of this, ALBERT is especially useful in settings with limited resources or when working with huge datasets.

Additionally, ALBERT's lower parameter count permits training with larger batch sizes, which has the effect of hastening convergence and enhancing training effectiveness. Because of this, scaling ALBERT to handle more datasets and speed up the training process is made simpler.

Due to its capacity to balance model performance and efficiency, ALBERT has grown to be a well-known model in the NLP field. To improve its capabilities and use it for a variety of NLP applications, including as text categorization, named entity recognition, and natural language understanding, researchers and practitioners are still researching ALBERT and its variants. Results obtained through ALBERT model are given in Table 3

Parameters	Score
Accuracy	0.67
Macro Avg F1-score	**0.66**
Macro Avg Recall	0.67
Macro Avg Precision	0.70
Weighted Avg F1-score	0.66
Weighted Avg Recall	0.67
Weighted Avg Precision	0.70

Table 3: Performance of the proposed system using ALBERT

3.2.3 XLNET Model

A strong and cutting-edge pre-trained language representation model, XLNet combines the advantages of autoregressive and autoencoding methods. By adding the permutation-based training objective, which enables it to represent dependencies across all points in a sequence, Google AI's XLNet solves the drawbacks of earlier models like BERT.

In contrast to conventional models, which produce text from left to right or right to left, XLNet makes use of the Transformer-XL architecture to simulate the likelihood of a sequence by taking into account all possible input permutations. (Gautam et al., 2021) This makes it possible for XLNet to successfully capture bidirectional dependencies, leading to more accurate and thorough representations of the text.

Pre-training is difficult since XLNet's permutation-based training objective necessitates taking into account every conceivable permutation. In order to solve this problem, XLNet uses a method known as "two-stream self-attention" that factorises the attention function and makes it possible to compute all permutations quickly while training. Because of this, XLNet can recognise word dependencies regardless of where they appear in the input sequence.

The permutation-based objective is used to pre-train the XLNet model using a sizable corpus of unlabeled text. It gains the capacity to forecast a word's likelihood given its context while taking into account all conceivable permutations. With the help of this pre-training, XLNet may learn complex verbal concepts and contextual comprehension.

XLNet can be fine-tuned on particular downstream activities after pre-training. With the use of task-specific labelled data, the model is fine-tuned so that it may adjust its pre-trained representations for jobs like text categorization, named entity identification, or machine translation. Through its competitive performance on benchmark datasets, XLNet has proven its adaptability and efficacy in many NLP tasks. Results obtained through XLNET model is given in Table 4

Parameters	Score
Accuracy	0.71
Macro Avg F1-score	**0.71**
Macro Avg Recall	0.71
Macro Avg Precision	0.72
Weighted Avg F1-score	0.71
Weighted Avg Recall	0.71
Weighted Avg Precision	0.72

Table 4: Performance of the proposed system using XLNET

3.2.4 M-BERT

A version of the BERT (Bidirectional Encoder Representations from Transformers) model called M-BERT (Multilingual BERT) was created specifically to handle multilingual text. It increases BERT's capacity to comprehend and represent languages from various linguistic origins.

M-BERT is trained on a combination of monolingual and multilingual data but shares the same architecture and pre-training technique as BERT. M-BERT gains the ability to produce language representations during pre-training that capture the subtleties and parallels between various languages. As a result, the model can handle cross-lingual, transfer learning, and code-switching tasks with ease.

The ability of M-BERT to handle several languages without the need for distinct models for each language is one of its key advantages.(Nagoudi et al., 2020) M-BERT can process text in many languages by utilising a common lexicon and encoder, making it extremely effective and versatile for multilingual applications.

Training the model on task-specific labelled data in a target language or across many languages is a necessary step in fine-tuning M-BERT. This makes it possible for M-BERT to easily and agnostically adjust its pre-trained representations to certain downstream tasks like sentiment analysis, named entity recognition, or machine translation.

M-BERT has excelled in a number of multilingual NLP tasks and benchmarks. Its adaptability and capacity for managing several languages make it a crucial tool for creating multilingual applications, particularly in environments where the availability of resources and labelled data for specific languages is constrained. It makes it easier to create and use multilingual NLP systems, facilitating cross-lingual comprehension and transfer learning.

By extending its pre-training and fine-tuning methodologies to handle the particular difficulties presented by multilingual text, researchers and practitioners continue to investigate and improve the capabilities of M-BERT. A powerful tool for a variety of multilingual applications and research, M-BERT represents a significant development in the field of multilingual NLP.

4 Result

In terms of accuracy, F1 score, precision, and recall, the M-BERT model surpasses the XLNet, BERT, and ALBERT models in the fake news detection test. When employed to tackle fake news detection tasks, the M-BERT model consistently achieves the highest accuracy, F1 score, precision, and recall when compared to these models. Its proficiency in multiple languages adds versatility to its performance, allowing it to excel across linguistic diversity. While recognizing that each model boasts distinct strengths, the M-BERT model consistently outperforms the XLNet, BERT, and ALBERT models in terms of accuracy and other vital evaluation criteria.

The multilingual capabilities of the M-BERT model are a standout feature. Unlike the other models, it adeptly addresses multiple languages without necessitating separate models. Its reliability and robust performance across all assessment metrics position the M-BERT model as the optimal choice for identifying false news. This capacity instills confidence among academics and professionals, as it serves as a dependable tool for detecting and countering the spread of fake news, thereby upholding information integrity in society. Detailed performance metrics are presented in Table 5.

Parameters	Score
Accuracy	0.75
Macro Avg F1-score	**0.74**
Macro Avg Recall	0.75
Macro Avg Precision	0.75
Weighted Avg F1-score	0.74
Weighted Avg Recall	0.75
Weighted Avg Precision	0.75

Table 5: Performance of the proposed system using M-BERT

5 Error Analysis

Following the implementation of machine learning classification techniques for false news detection, an extensive performance evaluation of the system was conducted. This evaluation aimed to uncover the types and sources of errors made by the system during data classification. By examining instances of misclassification, the objective was to identify patterns, trends, and limitations of the system. This analysis explored common characteristics of misclassified news stories, scrutinized cases of false positives and false negatives, and assessed how various factors affected classification accuracy.

The findings of this comprehensive error analysis provide valuable insights to enhance the system's overall functionality and improve its ability to accurately discern fake news from authentic information.

6 Conclusions

In conclusion, the M-BERT model appears as the most successful method for false news detection using ML classification, in combination with data preparation using the NLTK toolbox. In terms of accuracy, F1 score, precision, and recall, M-BERT clearly outperforms models like XLNet, BERT, and ALBERT. Given the global nature of the spread of fake news, its multilingual capabilities allow it to handle a variety of languages, an essential feature. Additionally, improving the quality of the input data during data preparation with the NLTK toolbox ensures improved performance during model training and evaluation.

Utilising the extensive language representations acquired through pretraining, M-BERT captures the nuanced semantic nuances and complex contextual linkages required for precisely identifying fake news. To further refine the data supplied into the model, the NLTK toolbox assists in preprocessing tasks including tokenization, stemming, and deleting stop words.

In addition to offering effective fake news identification, the M-BERT and NLTK toolkit combination helps to lessen the negative effects of disinformation on society. The promotion of information integrity and assistance in making educated judgements are two benefits of accurate false news identification. This strategy can be used by academics and professionals to stop the spread of false information and maintain the reliability of online information sources.

The M-BERT model combined with NLTK preprocessing is a powerful solution for fake news identification, delivering a useful tool in the battle against misinformation in the current digital era as the fields of ML classification and NLP continue to develop.

References

Iftikhar Ahmad, Muhammad Yousaf, Suhail Yousaf, and Muhammad Ovais Ahmad. 2020. Fake news detection using machine learning ensemble methods. *Complexity*, 2020:1–11.

B Bharathi. Agnusimmaculate silvia a. 2021b. ssncse_nlp@ dravidianlangtech-eacl2021: Offensive language identification on multilingual code mixing text. In *Proceedings of the First Workshop on Speech and Language Technologies for Dravidian Languages*, pages 313–318.

Akansha Gautam, V Venktesh, and Sarah Masud. 2021. Fake news detection system using xlnet model with topic distributions: Constraint@ aaai2021 shared task. In *Combating Online Hostile Posts in Regional Languages during Emergency Situation: First International Workshop, CONSTRAINT 2021, Collocated with AAAI 2021, Virtual Event, February 8, 2021, Revised Selected Papers 1*, pages 189–200. Springer.

Mohammad Hadi Goldani, Reza Safabakhsh, and Saeedeh Momtazi. 2021. Convolutional neural network with margin loss for fake news detection. *Information Processing & Management*, 58(1):102418.

Torstein Granskogen. 2018. Automatic detection of fake news in social media using contextual information. Master's thesis, NTNU.

Sunil Gundapu and Radhika Mamidi. 2021. Transformer based automatic covid-19 fake news detection system. *arXiv preprint arXiv:2101.00180*.

Rohit Kumar Kaliyar, Anurag Goswami, and Pratik Narang. 2021. Fakebert: Fake news detection in social media with a bert-based deep learning approach. *Multimedia tools and applications*, 80(8):11765–11788.

El Moatez Billah Nagoudi, AbdelRahim Elmadany, Muhammad Abdul-Mageed, Tariq Alhindi, and Hasan Cavusoglu. 2020. Machine generation and detection of arabic manipulated and fake news. *arXiv preprint arXiv:2011.03092*.

Anna Schmidt and Michael Wiegand. 2017. A survey on hate speech detection using natural language processing. In *Proceedings of the fifth international workshop on natural language processing for social media*, pages 1–10.

Karishma Sharma, Feng Qian, He Jiang, Natali Ruchansky, Ming Zhang, and Yan Liu. 2019. Combating fake news: A survey on identification and mitigation techniques. *ACM Transactions on Intelligent Systems and Technology (TIST)*, 10(3):1–42.

Kai Shu, Amy Sliva, Suhang Wang, Jiliang Tang, and Huan Liu. 2017. Fake news detection on social media: A data mining perspective. *ACM SIGKDD explorations newsletter*, 19(1):22–36.

Rajalakshmi Sivanaiah, Nishaanth Ramanathan, Shajith Hameed, Rahul Rajagopalan, Angel Deborah Suseelan, and Mirnalinee Thanka Nadar Thanagathai. 2023. Fake news detection in low-resource languages. In *Speech and Language Technologies for Low-Resource Languages: First International Conference, SPELLL 2022, Kalavakkam, India, November 23–25, 2022, Proceedings*, pages 324–331. Springer.

AbhiPaw@ DravidianLangTech: Multimodal Abusive Language Detection and Sentiment Analysis using Transformer based architecture

Abhinaba Bala
IIIT Hyderabad, India
abhinaba.bala@research.iiit.ac.in

Parameswari Krishnamurthy
IIIT Hyderabad, India
param.krishna@iiit.ac.in

Abstract

Detecting abusive language in multimodal videos has become a pressing need in ensuring a safe and inclusive online environment. This paper focuses on addressing this challenge through the development of a novel approach for multimodal abusive language detection in Tamil videos and sentiment analysis for Tamil/Malayalam videos. By leveraging state-of-the-art models such as Multiscale Vision Transformers (MViT) for video analysis, OpenL3 for audio analysis, and the bert-base-multilingual-cased model for textual analysis, our proposed framework integrates visual, auditory, and textual features. Through extensive experiments and evaluations, we demonstrate the effectiveness of our model in accurately detecting abusive content and predicting sentiment categories. The limited availability of effective tools for performing these tasks in Dravidian Languages has prompted a new avenue of research in these domains.

Keywords: abusive language detection, sentiment analysis, multimodal analysis, video analysis, Dravidian languages.

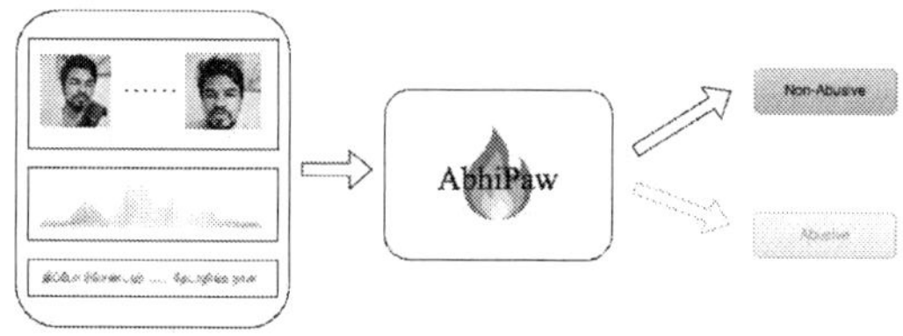

Figure 1: We develop an end-to-end deep network model to learn multimodal representations and perform detection/classification tasks.

1 Introduction

Abusive content, including hate speech, offensive language, and personal attacks, has become prevalent on social media platforms, posing significant challenges to maintaining a safe and inclusive online environment. Detecting and mitigating such abusive language has become an urgent need for social media platforms, content moderators, and society at large. While the detection of abusive language in textual form has received considerable attention, the analysis of multimodal content, specifically videos, incorporating visual, auditory, and textual information, remains a challenging and under explored task (Chakravarthi et al., 2021), (Premjith et al., 2022).

The task of multimodal abusive language detection in videos holds great significance due to several reasons. First, the exponential growth of user-generated video content on social media platforms like YouTube demands efficient mechanisms for content moderation and protection against abuse. As videos can convey rich contextual cues through spoken words, facial expressions, and visual content, analyzing multiple modalities becomes crucial to comprehensively understand the abusive intent and impact within such content. By extending abusive language detection to multimodal videos, we can identify and address abusive behaviors more effectively, ensuring a safer and more inclusive digital space.

Second, focusing on videos expands the scope of abusive language detection beyond textual content alone. Abusive language can be embedded in the audio, visual, and textual components of videos, making it essential to develop models that can holistically analyze and interpret these modalities. By leveraging the combined power of visual information, audio cues, and textual context, we can capture nuanced abusive expressions that might be missed by considering only one modality. This multimodal approach enables us to uncover the full spectrum of abusive content, thereby enhancing our ability to combat online abuse.

In this paper, we address the challenge of mul-

Third Workshop on Speech and Language Technologies for Dravidian Languages, pages 140–146, Varna, Bulgaria, Sep 7, 2023.
https://doi.org/10.26615/978-954-452-085-4_018

timodal abusive language detection and sentiment analysis in videos, specifically focusing on Tamil (one of the major Dravidian languages spoken in South India and Sri Lanka) and Malayalam(spoken in the Indian state of Kerala and the union territories of Lakshadweep and Puducherry). We propose a novel approach that integrates video, audio, and textual features using state-of-the-art models, including Multiscale Vision Transformers (MViT) for video analysis, OpenL3 for audio analysis, and the bert-base-multilingual-cased model for textual analysis. Through our approach, we aim to advance the field of abusive language detection and/or sentiment classification in videos and contribute to the development of robust models capable of understanding and mitigating online abuse in Dravidian Languages and classify sentiments.

2 Related Work

Multimodal analysis, encompassing tasks such as sentiment analysis, hate speech detection, and humor recognition, has garnered significant attention in recent years. Researchers have explored various fusion methods to effectively combine information from different modalities, leading to improved performance in multimodal analysis tasks. In this section, we review relevant studies and highlight their contributions to the field.

(Zadeh et al., 2017) introduced Tensor Fusion Network to pose the problem of multimodal sentiment analysis as *intra-modality* and *inter-modality* dynamics. (Zadeh et al., 2018) introduced a novel interpretable fusion mechanism called Dynamic Fusion Graph (DFG). (Poria et al., 2016b) described a novel temporal deep convolutional neural network for visual and textual feature extraction and used multiple kernel learning to fuse heterogeneous features extracted from different modalities.

(Majumder et al., 2018) introduced an innovative hierarchical feature fusion strategy that sequentially combines modalities in pairs before fusing all three modalities together. (Poria et al., 2016a) employed a combination of feature-level and decision-level fusion techniques to integrate affective information derived from multiple modalities. (Hazarika et al., 2018) introduced a multimodal emotion detection framework that extracts multimodal features from conversational videos and hierarchically models the self- and inter-speaker emotional influences into global memories. (Liu et al., 2023) propose a cascaded multichannel hierarchical fusion method for multimodal emotion recognition.

(Poria et al., 2017) propose a recurrent model that is able to capture contextual information among utterances. They also introduce attention based networks for improving both context learning and dynamic feature fusion. (Chauhan et al., 2019) introduce a recurrent neural network based approach for the multi-modal sentiment and emotion analysis. The proposed model learns the intermodal interaction among the participating modalities through an auto-encoder mechanism. They employ a context-aware attention module to exploit the correspondence among the neighboring utterances. (Ghosal et al., 2018) also proposed a recurrent neural network based multi-modal attention framework that leverages the contextual information for utterance-level sentiment prediction. (Chen and Li, 2020) first applies the cross-modal co-attention mechanism to learn the long range of context information and then use a sentimental words classification auxiliary task to guide and learn the sentimental words aware final multimodal fusion representation.

(Han et al., 2021b) propose a framework named MultiModal InfoMax (MMIM), which hierarchically maximizes the Mutual Information (MI) in unimodal input pairs (inter-modality) and between multimodal fusion result and unimodal input in order to maintain task related information through multimodal fusion. (Han et al., 2021a) propose the Bi-Bimodal Fusion Network (BBFN), a end-to-end network that performs fusion (relevance increment) and separation (difference increment) on pairwise modality representations.

(Zadeh et al., 2018) introduce CMU Multimodal Opinion Sentiment and Emotion Intensity (CMU-MOSEI), then largest dataset of sentiment analysis and emotion recognition. EmotionLines (Hsu et al., 2018) was introduced as the first dataset with emotions labeling on all utterances in each dialogue only based on their textual content. (Poria et al., 2019) was created by enhancing and extending the EmotionLines Dataset.

A comprehensive understanding of the field can be gained through an examination of the historical context and the establishment of baseline methodologies. Notable works such as (Poria et al., 2018), (Cambria et al., 2017), and (Gandhi et al., 2022) provide valuable insights into the broader perspective of the subject.

3 Method

In this section, we present the methodology employed for the multimodal abusive language detection and sentiment analysis tasks. We first provide an overview of the problem statement and task formulation. Then, we discuss the feature extraction process for video, audio, and text modalities. Next, we describe our approach in detail, including the model architecture and the steps involved. Finally, we outline the training and inference procedures.

3.1 Problem Statement

The aim of this study is to determine whether a particular set of video, audio, and text is abusive or non-abusive. Additionally, we seek to predict the sentiment expressed in the given video clip with audio and text information as a seperate problem. Let (V, A, T) denote the input tuple, respectively for video, audio and text.

3.2 Feature Extraction

For the feature extraction process, we utilize specific techniques for each modality:

Video Features To extract video features, we employ Facebook Research's Multiscale Vision Transformers (MViT). MViT connects the concept of multiscale feature hierarchies with transformer models. The architecture consists of multiple stages that hierarchically expand the channel capacity while reducing the spatial resolution. This creates a multiscale pyramid of features, enabling the modeling of both simple low-level visual information and complex, high-dimensional features. MViT has been shown to outperform other vision transformers in terms of computation and parameter efficiency across various video recognition tasks.

$$F_v = \text{MVIT}(V) \tag{1.a.}$$

Audio Features OpenL3 is specifically designed for audio feature extraction using deep learning models. It provides pre-trained models that can generate high-dimensional embeddings for audio signals. OpenL3 supports different audio feature representations, such as raw embeddings and intermediate representations like log-mel spectrograms. It is particularly useful when you want to leverage the power of deep learning for audio analysis tasks.

$$F_a = \text{OpenL3}(A) \tag{1.b.}$$

Text Features To extract text features, we employ the bert-base-multilingual-cased model. This model is pre-trained on a large corpus of text data and is capable of capturing contextual information across multiple languages, including Tamil and Malayalam.

$$F_t = \text{BERT}(T) \tag{1.c.}$$

3.3 Our Approach

In our approach, which we refer to as AbhiPaw, we leverage the given data comprising three modalities, each ranging from 40 to 80 seconds in length. The AbhiPaw model is built upon a transformer-based architecture, enabling the detection of abusive language content in Tamil videos and separate training for multiclass sentiment analysis on video modalities (Tamil and Malayalam videos).

Modality Separation: The input modalities are separately processed, as discussed in Section 3.2.

Neural Layer Fusion: The separated modalities are then passed through a single neural layer to output features with consistent dimensions. This is akin to normalisation. This step is important for fair fusion since different modalities might have different ranges of values.

$$\begin{aligned} F_v' &= \text{Linear}(F_v) \\ F_a' &= \text{Linear}(F_a) \\ F_t' &= \text{Linear}(F_t) \end{aligned} \tag{2}$$

Positional Encoding: We incorporate positional encoding to capture the spatial information of the modalities. This allows the model to understand the relative positions of elements within each modality.

$$F_v'', F_a'', F_t'' = PositionalEncoding(F_v', F_a', F_t') \tag{3}$$

Modality Type Embeddings: Type embeddings corresponding to the three modalities are added. These embeddings do not encode any specific meaning or imposed order but serve to distinguish one modality from another.

$$F_v''', F_a''', F_t''' = TypeEmbedding(F_v'', F_a'', F_t'') \tag{4}$$

Classifier Tokens: Similar to the classic CLS tokens in Transformer models, we employ learnable classifier tokens to detect abuse in videos. A single token is used to generate the output.

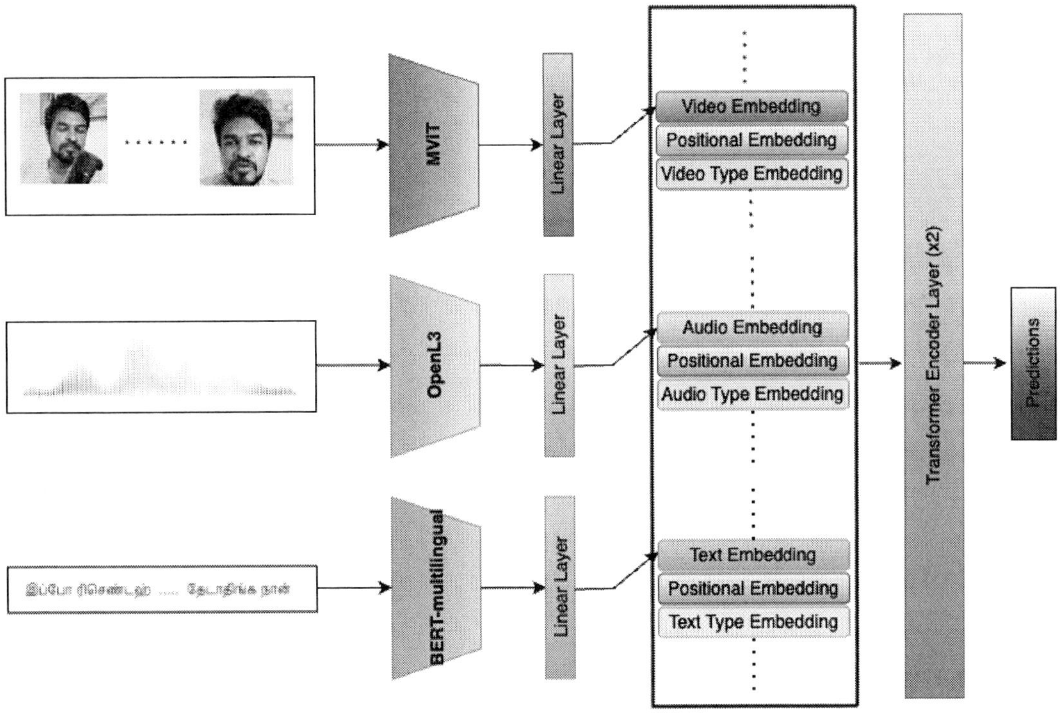

Figure 2: Overview of our work, which is inspired by (Srivastava et al., 2023) and (Hazarika et al., 2020). We utilize separate frozen backbones to get features out of different modalities. We also use linear layers to project them to same dimensionality. To capture positional information between the token we use positional embeddings. For our downstream task of detection, we also add the CLS embeddings before passing to transformer layer followed by linear layer for classification.

Masking: Appropriate masking is applied to prevent self-attention on padded tokens, ensuring accurate attention across the modalities.

Transformer Encoder: The processed features are then passed through a Transformer encoder. Importantly, self-attention across modalities is not applied. For abuse detection, only the outputs corresponding to the classification tokens are considered.

$$z_k = \text{TransformerEncoder}\begin{pmatrix}\text{CLS} + F_v''' \\ + F_a''' + F_t'''\end{pmatrix} \quad (5)$$

Linear Classification: The feature representation from the Transformer encoder is fed into a linear layer for classification. The output logits are compared with the ground truth labels

3.4 Training and Inference

Training Our model is trained end-to-end with *Cross Entropy* Loss and *Adam* optimizer.

Inference We take in un-seen test data and pass to the model to get output.

4 Experiments

4.1 Evaluation Metrics

The evaluation of the model was done based on their F1 score, which is a common metric used in NLP to measure the performance of classification models.

4.2 Datasets

Two different datasets were provided for the shared task at Multimodal Abusive Language Detection and Sentiment Analysis : DravidianLangTech@RANLP 2023.

Task 1 : Multimodal detection of abusive content in Tamil: This sub-task involves developing models that can analyze textual, speech and visual components of videos from social media platforms, such as YouTube, and predict whether they are abusive or non-abusive.

Task 2 : Multimodal sentiment analysis in Dravidian languages: This sub-task involves developing models that can analyze textual, speech and visual components of videos in Tamil and Malayalam from social media platforms, such as YouTube, and identify the sentiments expressed in them. The videos are labelled into five categories: highly positive, positive, neutral, negative and highly negative There are two substasks corresponding to Tamil and Malayalam languages.

4.2.1 Dataset Analysis

Distribution across categories

Figure 3: Pie chart showing the number of instances belonging to each category in abusive comment detection task

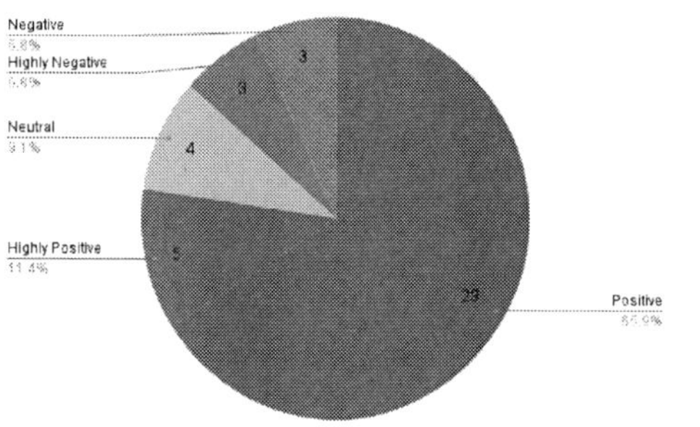

Figure 4: Pie chart showing the number of instances belonging to each category in sentiment analysis task - Tamil

Class Imbalance The training dataset used in our study presents a notable class imbalance issue, with a substantial data points being refered to *Positive*, Figure 4 and 5.

Low sample size The available training data was insufficient in terms of quantity and diversity to fully capture the complexity and variability of the problem domain. We had 70 samples for training for first task, and for second task we had 44 and 50 instances for Tamil and Malayalam sub-tasks respectively.

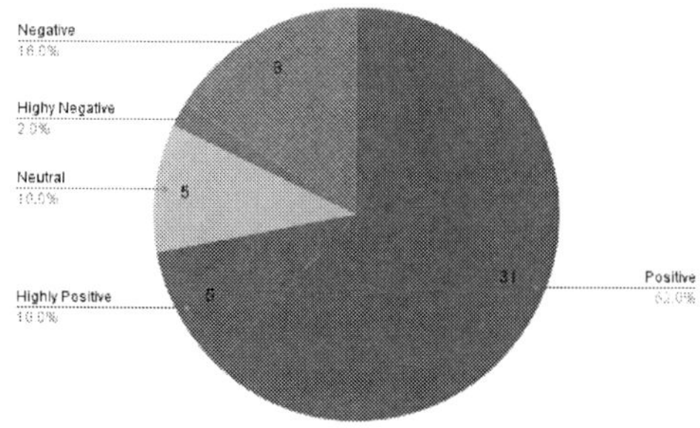

Figure 5: Pie chart showing the number of instances belonging to each category in sentiment analysis task - Malayalam

Table 1: Abusive Language Detection - Tamil

Team	F1-score (macro)	Rank
hate-alert	0.5786	1
AbhiPaw	0.3333	2

4.3 Implementation Details

Our model is trained on a single NVIDIA T4 GPU. We trained our PyTorch model using specific hyperparameters to ensure optimal performance and effective training. The maximum number of epochs was set to 150, allowing the model to undergo multiple iterations through the training dataset. To efficiently process the data, we employed a batch size of 4, which divided the dataset into smaller subsets for parallel computation. Adam optimizer was utilized to optimize the model's weights. Additionally, we set the initial learning rate to 10^{-3}, which determined the step size for adjusting the model's parameters during training. These carefully chosen hyperparameters played a crucial role in achieving the desired results and advancing the effectiveness of our model.

5 Results

We obtain an F1 score of 0.3333 in Abusive Language Detection - Tamil, *Table* 1

For multi-modal sentiment analysis we got an F1 score of 0.1333 for Tamil, *Table* 2 and a score of 0.0923 for Malayalam *Table* 3

Table 2: Sentiment Analysis - Tamil

Team	F1-score (macro)	Rank
hate-alert	0.1429	1
AbhiPaw	0.1333	2

Table 3: Sentiment Analysis - Malayalam

Team	F1-score (macro)	Rank
hate-alert	0.1889	1
AbhiPaw	0.0923	2

6 Conclusion

We present a novel approach for detecting abusive language in low-resource language videos by integrating visual, auditory, and textual features. Our framework demonstrates promising results in accurately identifying abusive content and predicting sentiment categories.

To advance the field, future work should focus on expanding the dataset to address resource scarcity, exploring advanced fusion techniques for multimodal integration, incorporating contextual information and temporal dependencies, and tackling class imbalance challenges. By refining these techniques and considering the linguistic and cultural nuances of Dravidian Languages, we can make significant strides towards ensuring a safer and more inclusive online environment.

7 Acknowledgements

We thank our anonymous reviewers for their invaluable insights and feedback, which have greatly enriched this work. It is important to note that the opinions, conclusions, and findings presented in this material solely represent the views of the authors and do not necessarily reflect the perspectives of their respective graduate institutions or affiliations. We would like to thank Dhruv Srivastava, Aditya Kumar Singh, Prasha Srivastava and Sagar Joshi for their generous assistance and contributions throughout the course of this research. Their support has been instrumental in shaping the development and outcomes of this study. This work was submitted as a part of the DravidianLangTech workshop, 2023 (B et al., 2023).

References

Premjith B, Jyothish Lal G, Sowmya V, Bharathi Raja Chakravarthi, Rajeswari Natarajan, Nandhini K, Abirami Murugappan, Bharathi B, Kaushik M, Prasanth SN, Aswin Raj R, and Vijai Simmon S. 2023. Findings of the shared task on multimodal abusive language detection and sentiment analysis in tamil and malayalam. In *Proceedings of the Third Workshop on Speech and Language Technologies for Dravidian Languages*, Varna, Bulgaria. Recent Advances in Natural Language Processing.

E. Cambria, Devamanyu Hazarika, Soujanya Poria, Amir Hussain, and R. B. V. Subramanyam. 2017. Benchmarking multimodal sentiment analysis. *ArXiv*, abs/1707.09538.

Bharathi Raja Chakravarthi, KP Soman, Rahul Ponnusamy, Prasanna Kumar Kumaresan, Kingston Pal Thamburaj, John P McCrae, et al. 2021. Dravidianmultimodality: A dataset for multi-modal sentiment analysis in tamil and malayalam. *arXiv preprint arXiv:2106.04853*.

Dushyant Singh Chauhan, Md. Shad Akhtar, Asif Ekbal, and Pushpak Bhattacharyya. 2019. Context-aware interactive attention for multi-modal sentiment and emotion analysis. In *Conference on Empirical Methods in Natural Language Processing*.

Minping Chen and Xia Li. 2020. SWAFN: Sentimental words aware fusion network for multimodal sentiment analysis. In *Proceedings of the 28th International Conference on Computational Linguistics*, pages 1067–1077, Barcelona, Spain (Online). International Committee on Computational Linguistics.

Ankita Gandhi, Kinjal Adhvaryu, Soujanya Poria, Erik Cambria, and Amir Hussain. 2022. Multimodal sentiment analysis: A systematic review of history, datasets, multimodal fusion methods, applications, challenges and future directions. *Information Fusion*, 91.

Deepanway Ghosal, Md Shad Akhtar, Dushyant Chauhan, Soujanya Poria, Asif Ekbal, and Pushpak Bhattacharyya. 2018. Contextual inter-modal attention for multi-modal sentiment analysis. In *Proceedings of the 2018 Conference on Empirical Methods in Natural Language Processing*, pages 3454–3466, Brussels, Belgium. Association for Computational Linguistics.

Wei Han, Hui Chen, Alexander F. Gelbukh, Amir Zadeh, Louis-Philippe Morency, and Soujanya Poria. 2021a. Bi-bimodal modality fusion for correlation-controlled multimodal sentiment analysis. *Proceedings of the 2021 International Conference on Multimodal Interaction*.

Wei Han, Hui Chen, and Soujanya Poria. 2021b. Improving multimodal fusion with hierarchical mutual information maximization for multimodal sentiment analysis. *ArXiv*, abs/2109.00412.

Devamanyu Hazarika, Soujanya Poria, Rada Mihalcea, Erik Cambria, and Roger Zimmermann. 2018. ICON: Interactive conversational memory network for multimodal emotion detection. In *Proceedings of the 2018 Conference on Empirical Methods in Natural Language Processing*, pages 2594–2604, Brussels, Belgium. Association for Computational Linguistics.

Devamanyu Hazarika, Roger Zimmermann, and Soujanya Poria. 2020. Misa: Modality-invariant and-specific representations for multimodal sentiment analysis. *arXiv preprint arXiv:2005.03545*.

Chao-Chun Hsu, Sheng-Yeh Chen, Chuan-Chun Kuo, Ting-Hao Huang, and Lun-Wei Ku. 2018. EmotionLines: An emotion corpus of multi-party conversations. In *Proceedings of the Eleventh International Conference on Language Resources and Evaluation (LREC 2018)*, Miyazaki, Japan. European Language Resources Association (ELRA).

Xia Liu, Zhijing Xu, and Huang Kan. 2023. Multimodal emotion recognition based on cascaded multichannel and hierarchical fusion. Florence, Italy. Computational Intelligence and Neuroscience.

N. Majumder, D. Hazarika, A. Gelbukh, E. Cambria, and S. Poria. 2018. Multimodal sentiment analysis using hierarchical fusion with context modeling. *Knowledge-Based Systems*, 161:124–133.

Soujanya Poria, E. Cambria, Devamanyu Hazarika, Navonil Majumder, Amir Zadeh, and Louis-Philippe Morency. 2017. Multi-level multiple attentions for contextual multimodal sentiment analysis. *2017 IEEE International Conference on Data Mining (ICDM)*, pages 1033–1038.

Soujanya Poria, Erik Cambria, Newton Howard, Guang-Bin Huang, and Amir Hussain. 2016a. Fusing audio, visual and textual clues for sentiment analysis from multimodal content. *Neurocomputing*, 174:50–59.

Soujanya Poria, Iti Chaturvedi, Erik Cambria, and Amir Hussain. 2016b. Convolutional mkl based multimodal emotion recognition and sentiment analysis. In *2016 IEEE 16th International Conference on Data Mining (ICDM)*, pages 439–448.

Soujanya Poria, Devamanyu Hazarika, Navonil Majumder, Gautam Naik, Erik Cambria, and Rada Mihalcea. 2019. MELD: A multimodal multi-party dataset for emotion recognition in conversations. In *Proceedings of the 57th Annual Meeting of the Association for Computational Linguistics*, pages 527–536, Florence, Italy. Association for Computational Linguistics.

Soujanya Poria, Navonil Majumder, Devamanyu Hazarika, E. Cambria, Amir Hussain, and Alexander Gelbukh. 2018. Multimodal sentiment analysis: Addressing key issues and setting up the baselines. *IEEE Intelligent Systems*, 33:17–25.

B Premjith, Bharathi Raja Chakravarthi, Malliga Subramanian, B Bharathi, Soman Kp, V Dhanalakshmi, K Sreelakshmi, Arunaggiri Pandian, and Prasanna Kumaresan. 2022. Findings of the shared task on multimodal sentiment analysis and troll meme classification in dravidian languages. In *Proceedings of the Second Workshop on Speech and Language Technologies for Dravidian Languages*, pages 254–260.

Dhruv Srivastava, Aditya Kumar Singh, and Makarand Tapaswi. 2023. How you feelin'? learning emotions and mental states in movie scenes. In *IEEE/CVF Conference on Computer Vision and Pattern Recognition (CVPR)*.

Amir Zadeh, Minghai Chen, Soujanya Poria, E. Cambria, and Louis-Philippe Morency. 2017. Tensor fusion network for multimodal sentiment analysis. In *Conference on Empirical Methods in Natural Language Processing*.

Amir Zadeh, Paul Pu Liang, Soujanya Poria, E. Cambria, and Louis-Philippe Morency. 2018. Multimodal language analysis in the wild: Cmu-mosei dataset and interpretable dynamic fusion graph. In *Annual Meeting of the Association for Computational Linguistics*.

Athena@DravidianLangTech: Abusive Comment Detection in Code-Mixed Languages using Machine Learning Techniques

Hema M, Anza Prem, Rajalakshmi S, Angel Deborah S
Department of Computer Science and Engineering,
Sri Sivasubramaniya Nadar College of Engineering, Chennai - 603110, Tamil Nadu, India
hema19037@cse.ssn.edu.in, anza19020@cse.ssn.edu.in
rajalakshmis@ssn.edu.in, angeldeborahs@ssn.edu.in

Abstract

The amount of digital material that is disseminated through various social media platforms has significantly increased in recent years. Online networks have gained popularity in recent years and have established themselves as go-to resources for news, information, and entertainment. Nevertheless, despite the many advantages of using online networks, mounting evidence indicates that an increasing number of malicious actors are taking advantage of these networks to spread poison and hurt other people. This work aims to detect abusive content in youtube comments written in the languages like Tamil, Tamil-English (code-mixed), Telugu-English (code-mixed). This work was undertaken as part of the "DravidianLangTech@RANLP 2023" shared task. The Macro F1 values for the Tamil, Tamil-English, and Telugu-English datasets were 0.28, 0.37, and 0.6137 and secured 5th, 7th, 8th rank respectively.

1 Introduction

The detection of abusive language has become a major area for research and development in computer linguistics and natural language processing (NLP). The requirement to recognise and filter out harmful or abusive content has multiplied enormously with the rise of Internet platforms and online social media. Detection of abusive or offensive content in English language has been done by many researchers in a wide manner [13, 14, 15]. Recent days, the interest goes on the low resource languages and native languages. In multilingual societies like India, where Tamil and Telugu are widely spoken, this is especially crucial.

Due to the complexity of their linguistic structures and the lack of sufficient labelled data for the training of strong models, the identification of abusive language presents particular difficulties in Tamil and Telugu. A wide range of harmful information is included in abusive language, such as hate speech, cyberbullying, vulgarity, and disparaging remarks. For the sake of upholding a secure and civilised online community, it is essential to accurately identify such offensive language in Tamil and Telugu.

The identification of abusive language in English has advanced significantly in recent years, according to academics. However, adapting these methods to Tamil and Telugu necessitates taking into account these languages' unique traits, cultural quirks, and lack of labelled data. Furthermore, due to variances in syntax, morphology, and the existence of dialectical changes, existing models might not generalise effectively to Tamil and Telugu especially the deep learning techniques as most of them are built for English language.

This work aims to contribute to the development of efficient abusive language detection systems for Tamil and Telugu by tackling the difficulties unique to these languages, promoting a safer and more welcoming online environment for users who communicate in Tamil and Telugu.

In this study, multiple machine learning models were tested in an effort to create an effective system for identifying hate speech and abusive language in Tamil and Telugu comments on YouTube. The paper is organised as follows: Earlier studies on the identification of abusive language in Dravidian languages like Tamil and Telugu are discussed in Section 2. The proposed system along with the architecture diagram and the system modules are explained in Section 3. The datasets and methodologies used in the suggested system are presented in Section 4. The results are discussed in Section 5. The conclusion and future work are presented in Section 6.

Third Workshop on Speech and Language Technologies for Dravidian Languages, pages 147–151, Varna, Bulgaria, Sep 7, 2023.
https://doi.org/10.26615/978-954-452-085-4_019

2 Related Work

F. Balouchzahi et al. [3] centred on the detection of objectionable remarks in texts written in both the native script and Tamil written in code-mixed script. Two models were used to tackle this problem: n-gram-Multilayer Perceptron which makes use of an MLP classifier supplied with character-n-gram features, as well as the (1D ConvLSTM) model, were submitted. The n-gram MLP model performed better than the other two model, corresponding to weighted F1-scores of 0.430 for texts written in the native Tamil script and 0.560 for texts written in code-mixed Tamil, respectively.

Charangan Vasantharajan and Uthayasanker Thayasivam [2] offered a novel and flexible way of selective translation and transliteration operations to improve the results of adjusting and assembling BERT, DistilBERT, and XLM-RoBERTa. The experiment's findings proved that ULMFiT is the best model for the task. ULMFiT and mBERTBiLSTM beat other well-known transfer learning models like DistilBERT and XLM-RoBERTa as well as hybrid deep learning models for this Tamil code-mix dataset.

In the work done by Shantanu Patankar et al. [9] recurrent neural networks, ensemble models, and transformers were used to optimise the results. For the Tamil data, MuRIL and XLM-RoBERTA were utilised. The macro-averaged F1 score generated by the models was 0.43. With a macro-averaged f1 score of 0.45, the top models MuRIL and M-BERT both generated excellent results for the code-mixed data.

Malliga Subramanian et al. [5] worked to identify the offensive utterances, models based on traditional machine learning techniques—such as Bernoulli Naive Bayes, Support Vector Machine, Logistic Regression, and KNearest Neighbor—were constructed. The multilingual transformer-based pre-trained models of natural language processing mBERT, MuRIL (Base and Large), and XLM-RoBERTa (Base and Large) were also used in the experiments.

Pradeep Kumar Roy et al. [6] investigated the use of different machine learning and deep learning approaches. Combining the output of transformer and deep learning-based models, an ensemble model was proposed to detect hate speech and objectionable language on social networking sites. The experimental findings of the suggested weighted ensemble framework outperformed state-of-the-art models for the Malayalam and Tamil code-mixed datasets, achieving weighted F1-scores of 0.802 and 0.933, respectively.

3 Abusive Content Detection System

We have used the deep learning transformer model (BERT), machine learning models (Logistic Regression, Support Vector Machines, Decision Trees, Naive Bayes) and Ensemble model (Random Forest) for abusive content classification. The training dataset is used to build the model by learning the data, development dataset is used to evaluate and fine tune the trained model and test dataset is used for final prediction. The features are extracted from the input text and its matching label are used for learning and training. The texts in the dataset are vectorized using the Term Frequency - Inverse Document Frequency (TF-IDF) vectorization technique for feature extraction. The model that produces the greatest macro F1-Score is selected as the final model to be used for detection after various machine learning models are tested. The model is trained using the training dataset. The performance of the trained model is assessed using the development dataset. By tweaking the parameters, the model is re-trained based on the performance. Finally, predictions are made using the test data and the model. Figure 1 displays the architecture of the system.

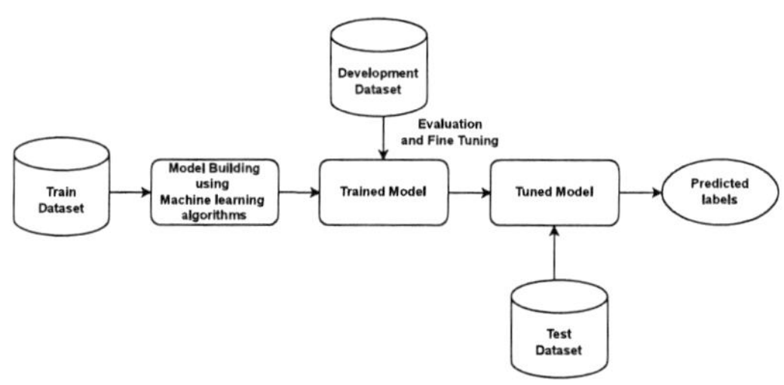

Figure 1: Architecture diagram

4 Implementation Modules

This section elaborates on the datatsets and the methodologies used.

4.1 Datasets Used

The abusive comment detection task consists of 3 datasets: Tamil, Tamil-English and Telugu-English [7, 8].

The **Tamil** dataset consisted of a total of 2240 sentences with their corresponding labels. It was a multi-class classification task which included the following labels: Misandry (446), Counter-speech (149), Misogyny (125), Xenophobia (95), Hope-Speech (86), Homophobia (35), Transphobic (6), Not-Tamil (2), None-of-the-above (1296).

The **Tamil-English** dataset consisted of a total of 5948 sentences with their corresponding labels. The labels present were Misandry (830), Counter-speech (348), Xenophobia (297), Hope-Speech (213), Misogyny (211), Homophobia (172), Transphobic (157), None-of-the-above (3720).

The **Telugu-English** dataset consisted of 4000 sentences along with their labels. This task was a binary classification task and included the labels: non-hate (2061) and hate (1939).

4.2 Methodology

Data Pre-processing: The text presented in the data cannot be passed to the model directly. Hence it is converted into numerical vectors by applying the TF-IDF vectorization on the text data present. After the vectorization the text data in the form of a dense matrix is passed to the model.

Training machine learning models: Logistic Regression (LR), Naive Bayes (NB), Support Vector Machines (SVM), Random Forest (RF), Decision Tree (DT) and BERT techniques are the machine learning models employed. The training dataset is used to train each model.

Evaluating machine learning models: The trained models are evaluated using the development dataset. The parameters of the model are fine-tuned based on the performance. The model that gives the maximum macro F1-Score is chosen as the final detection model.

Running model on test data: Results are obtained once the detection model receives the test data.

5 Results

Several machine learning models are experimented using the given datasets. Evaluation metrics like accuracy (Acc), precision (Prec), Recall and F1-score are used to evaluate the performance of the models. The model that gives the best accuracy and F1-score is chosen to run finally on the test data.

Table 1 displays the models' results on the Tamil dataset. It is evident that SVM provided the highest accuracy and F1-score. The models' results on the Tamil-English dataset are displayed in Table 2. As can be seen, SVM provides the highest level of accuracy and F1-score. Table 3 displays the models' results on the Telugu-English dataset. It is evident that Logistic Regression provides the highest level of accuracy and F1-score.

Model Name	Acc	Prec	Recall	F1-Score
LR	0.66	0.30	0.21	0.22
NB	0.67	0.27	0.16	0.16
SVM	0.68	0.36	0.29	0.26
RF	0.67	0.34	0.30	0.25
DT	0.54	0.23	0.24	0.23
BERT	0.63	0.13	0.16	0.14

Table 1: Comparison results for the Tamil training dataset

Model Name	Acc	Prec	Recall	F1-Score
LR	0.70	0.63	0.27	0.31
NB	0.69	0.42	0.20	0.21
SVM	0.72	0.69	0.33	0.38
RF	0.72	0.55	0.30	0.34
DT	0.65	0.39	0.36	0.37
BERT	0.71	0.35	0.25	0.27

Table 2: Comparison results for the Tamil-English training dataset

Model Name	Acc	Prec	Recall	F1-Score
LR	0.72	0.72	0.72	0.72
NB	0.70	0.70	0.70	0.70
SVM	0.69	0.69	0.69	0.69
RF	0.69	0.69	0.69	0.69
DT	0.65	0.65	0.65	0.65
BERT	0.68	0.71	0.69	0.68

Table 3: Comparison results for the Telugu-English training dataset

The task on the Tamil and the Tamil-English dataset are multi-class classification tasks. SVM has proved to work best on them due to the factors like effective separation of classes and resistance to overfitting.

The task on the Telugu-English dataset is a binary-class classification problem. LR has performed best on this dataset due to its simplicity, interpretability, efficiency with small dataset and robustness to outliers.

6 Performance Analysis

During testing, it was found that simpler machine learning models like SVM and LR performed better than more complex Transformer models like BERT and mBERT. This can be due to the dataset's quantity and quality. Traditional ML models generally require less data than more complex models to perform successfully. ML models might do better than BERT if the dataset isn't too big.BERT excels at a number of NLP tasks, however improved training and classification require a large dataset with a wide variety of texts. The performance of the BERT may suffer if the data are unstable or skewed.

It has been identified that even though the accuracy for all the three datasets (multi class and binary classification) are more or less same, the F1-score of multi-class classification models are very less when compared to the binary classification models. This is due to the imbalance in Tamil and Tamil-English dataset. We belive that this can be rectified using data augmentation in future.

We have also noticed that deep learning transformer model has not performed well as it could not learn the features effectively from the small dataset of low resource language. In order to improve the performance of the deep learning model we have planned to augment the dataset as a future work, so that it can solve the data imbalance as well as increase the number of samples in the dataset.

For the test dataset of Tamil, Tamil-English, Telugu-English languages we have achieved the F1-score of 0.28, 0.37, and 0.6137 respectively.

7 Conclusion and Future Work

This task was taken as a part of "Abusive Comment Detection in Tamil and Telugu at DravidianLangTech@RANLP 2023" shared task. For the Tamil and Tamil-English datasets (multi class classification) Support Vector Machine showed the maximum performance and hence was used to run on the test data and the results were submitted. For the Telugu-English dataset (binary classification) Logistic Regression showed the best performance hence that was used to run on the test data. Our team "Athena" was ranked 5th, 7th, 8th for the Tamil, Tamil-English and Telugu-English datasets respectively.

In the future we would like to improve the results by using larger and more balanced datasets. We would also like to experiment on vectorization feature extraction techniques more suitable for code-mixed and non-English languages.

References

[1] Adaikkan Kalaivani, Durairaj Thenmozhi and Chandrabose Aravindan, TOLD: Tamil Offensive Language Detection in Code-Mixed Social Media Comments using MBERT with Features based Selection, CEUR Workshop Proceedings (2021)

[2] Charangan Vasantharajan, Uthayasanker Thayasivam, Towards Offensive Language Identification for Tamil Code-Mixed YouTube Comments and Posts, arXiv:2108.10939 [cs.CL] (2021)

[3] F. Balouchzahi, M. D. Anusha, H. L. Shashirekha, G. Sidorov, MUCIC@TamilNLP-ACL2022: Abusive Comment Detection in Tamil Language using 1D Conv-LSTM, Proceedings of the Second Workshop on Speech and Language Technologies for Dravidian Languages, ACL (2022)

[4] Gayathri G L, Krithika S, Divyasri K, Durairaj Thenmozhi, B. Bharathi, PANDAS@TamilNLP-ACL2022: Abusive Comment Detection in Tamil Code-Mixed Data Using Custom Embeddings with LaBSE, Proceedings of the Second Workshop on Speech and Language Technologies for Dravidian Languages, ACL (2022)

[5] Malliga Subramanian, Rahul Ponnusamy, Sean Benhur, Kogilavani Shanmugavadivel, Adhithiya Ganesan, Deepti Ravi, Gowtham Krishnan Shanmugasundaram, Ruba Priyadharshini, Bharathi Raja Chakravarthi, Offensive language detection in Tamil YouTube comments by adapters and cross-domain knowledge transfer, Elsevier, Computer Speech & Language (2022)

[6] Pradeep Kumar Roy, Snehaan Bhawal, Chinnaudayar Navaneethakrishnan Subalalitha, Hate speech and offensive language detection in Dravidian languages using deep ensemble framework, Elsevier, Computer Speech & Language (2022)

[7] Priyadharshini, Ruba and Chakravarthi, Bharathi Raja and Chinnaudayar Navaneethakrishnan, Subalalitha and Subramanian, Malliga and Shanmugavadivel, Kogilavani and B, Premjith and Murugappan, Abirami and Karnati, Sai Prashanth and Rishith and Janakiram, Chandu and Kumaresan, Prasanna Kumar, Findings of the Shared Task on Abusive Comment Detection in Tamil and Telugu, Recent Advances in Natural Language Processing (2023)

[8] Priyadharshini, Ruba and Chakravarthi, Bharathi Raja and Cn, Subalalitha and Durairaj, Thenmozhi and Subramanian, Malliga and Shanmugavadivel, Kogilavani and U Hegde, Siddhanth and Kumaresan, Prasanna, Overview of Abusive Comment Detection in Tamil-ACL 2022, Association for Computational Linguistics (2022)

[9] Shantanu Patankar, Omkar Gokhale, Onkar Litake, Aditya Mandke, Dipali Kadam, Optimize-Prime@DravidianLangTech-ACL2022: Abusive Comment Detection in Tamil, arXiv:2204.09675 [cs.CL] (2022)

[10] Snehaan Bhawal, Pradeep Kumar Roy, Abhinav Kumar, Hate Speech and Offensive Language Identification on Multilingual code-mixed Text using BERT, CEUR Workshop Proceedings, FIRE (2021)

[11] Varsha Pathaka, Manish Joshib, Prasad Joshic, Monica Mundadad, Tanmay Joshie, KBCNMUJAL@HASOC-Dravidian-CodeMixFIRE2020: Using Machine Learning for Detection of Hate Speech and Offensive Code-Mixed Social Media text, CEUR Workshop Proceedings, FIRE (2020)

[12] Vikram Gupta, Sumegh Roychowdhury, Mithun Das, Somnath Banerjee, Punyajoy Saha, Binny Mathew, Hastagiri Vanchinathan, Animesh Mukherjee, MACD: Multilingual Abusive Comment Detection at Scale for Indic Languages, 36th Conference on Neural Information Processing Systems, NeurIPS (2022)

[13] Mosquera, Alejandro. "amsqr at SemEval-2020 Task 12: Offensive language detection using neural networks and anti-adversarial features." In Proceedings of the Fourteenth Workshop on Semantic Evaluation, pp. 1898-1905. 2020.

[14] Sivanaiah, Rajalakshmi, Angel Suseelan, S. Milton Rajendram, and Mirnalinee Tt. "TECHSSN at SemEval-2020 Task 12: Offensive language detection using BERT embeddings." In Proceedings of the Fourteenth Workshop on Semantic Evaluation, pp. 2190-2196. 2020.

[15] Sivanaiah, Rajalakshmi, S. Milton Rajendram, Mirnalinee Tt, Abrit Pal Singh, Aviansh Gupta, and Ayush Nanda. "Techssn at semeval-2021 task 7: Humor and offense detection and classification using colbert embeddings." In Proceedings of the 15th International Workshop on Semantic Evaluation (SemEval-2021), pp. 1185-1189. 2021.

Sentiment Analysis of Code-Mixed Tamil and Tulu by Training Contextualized ELMo Representations

Toqeer Ehsan[1], Amina Tehseen[2], Kengatharaiyer Sarveswaran[3], Amjad Ali[4]
[1]Department of Computer Science, University of Gujrat, Pakistan
[2]Department of Information Technology, University of Gujrat, Pakistan
[3]Department of Computer Science, University of Jaffna, Sri Lanka
[4]Information and Computing Technology (ICT) Division, College of Science and Engineering (CSE), Hamad Bin Khalifa University, Doha, Qatar
toqeer.ehsan@uog.edu.pk, amina.tehseen@outlook.com,
sarves@univ.jfn.ac.lk, amsali@hbku.edu.qa

Abstract

Sentiment analysis in natural language processing (NLP), endeavors to computationally identify and extract subjective information from textual data. For low-resourced languages such as Tamil and Tulu, predicting sentiment becomes a challenging task due to the presence of text comprising various scripts and langauges. In this research, we present the sentiment analysis of code-mixed Tamil and Tulu YouTube comments. We have developed Bidirectional Long-Short Term Memory (BiLSTM) networks based models for both languages by deploying contextualized word embeddings at input layers of the models. For that purpose, ELMo embeddings have been trained on larger unannotated code-mixed text like corpora. Our models performed with macro average F_1-scores of 0.2877 and 0.5133 on Tamil and Tulu code-mixed datasets respectively.

1 Introduction

Sentiment analysis, a subfield of Natural Language Processing (NLP), pursuits to computationally identify and extract subjective data, such as opinions, emotions, and attitudes from textual data. It plays a crucial role in understanding human's evaluations expressed in numerous forms of communication, including social media, customer reviews, and online forums (Thavareesan and Mahesan, 2020). The proliferation of social media platforms allows individuals to proportion their perspective public opinions in written form on the internet (Patra et al., 2018). The users having knowledge of multiple languages, often post their thoughts and reaction in multilingualism. It happens due to no restrictions or limitations on the usage of diverse languages or their syntactic rules (Suryawanshi et al., 2020).

The practice of blending multiple languages at various levels, including sentences, words, or subwords within the same text, is known as code-mixing. There are several reasons for code-mixing such as bilingualism, social community, vocabulary, the speaker and their conversation partner, the context or situation, and social prestige (Balahur and Turchi, 2014). These are considered the primary factors influencing code-mixing on social media networks. Code-mixing often occurs due to the unavailability of a particular word or phrase in a particular language, compelling individuals to incorporate words or phrases from their native language in order to enhance comprehension for the receiver (Ahmad et al., 2022).

Although sentiment analysis has gained significant attention in recent years, most of the research has primarily focused on monolingual text, predominantly in English. However, the emergence of code-mixed text brings forth distinctive challenges and opportunities for researchers. The developing presence of code-mixed text presents unique demanding situations and possibilities for sentiment analysis. There is a limited amount of research on sentiment analysis in low-resourced languages particularly for Tamil and Tulu. The datasets for this research, contains various types of languages including Tamil, Tulu, English, Romanized Tamil, and Tulu, as well as mixed text and emoticons. The diverse range of languages in the text presents significant difficulties in achieving higher accuracy of sentiment prediction models.

In this paper, we present the sentiment analysis of code-mixed Tamil and Tulu YouTube comments as a shared task[1]. We propose Bidirectional Long-Short Term Memory (BiLSTM) networks based models for both languages; Tamil and Tulu which further use contextualized word embeddings at input layers of the models. For that purpose, Embeddings from Language Models (ELMo) em-

[1]https://codalab.lisn.upsaclay.fr/competitions/11095

Third Workshop on Speech and Language Technologies for Dravidian Languages, pages 152–159, Varna, Bulgaria, Sep 7, 2023.
https://doi.org/10.26615/978-954-452-085-4_020

beddings have been trained on larger unannotated code-mixed like corpora. For both language, the transfer learning by using trained ELMo models was quite helpful to achieve the improved sentiment prediction results. Our models performed with the macro average F1-scores of 0.2877 and 0.5133 on Tamil and Tulu code-mixed datasets respectively. ELMo Embeddings have shown state of the art performances for low-resourced NLP tasks such as part of speech tagging (Tehseen et al., 2022), phrase chunking (Ehsan et al., 2022), constituency (Ehsan and Hussain, 2020, 2022) and dependency parsing (Ehsan and Butt, 2020). The next sections of the paper present literature review, corpora details, model architecture and results.

2 Literature review

Tamil, being one of the ancient languages with a vibrant literary heritage, is predominantly spoken in the Indian state of Tamil Nadu and certain regions of Sri Lanka (Chakravarthi et al., 2018). There has been a surge in interest regarding sentiment analysis in Tamil, given its extensive usage in diverse domains such as social media, news, and product reviews. Numerous research studies have concentrated on constructing sentiment analysis models specifically for Tamil, employing a range of methodologies, including rule-based techniques, machine learning algorithms, and deep learning architectures.

For code-mixed Tamil-English text's sentiment analysis, Chakravarthi et al. (2020a) developed a corpus, TamilMixSentiment [2], which is a corpus comprising Tanglish (a mix of Tamil and English) comments from YouTube videos. The development of TamilMixSentiment followed guidelines based on the work from Mohammad (2016) and without annotating language tags at the word-level. The inter-annotator agreement was found to be 0.6, indicating a moderate level of agreement among the annotators. They annotated 15,744 comments, making it the largest sentiment corpus for the under-resourced language featuring code-mixing phenomena. They detailed the procedure of developing a code-mixed corpus and attributing polarities. Further, they presented the outcomes of sentiment analysis trained on the corpus, serving as a benchmark.

Chakravarthi et al. (2020b) employed BiLSTM and Recurrent Neural Networks (RNN) with sub-word representation to categorize text based on its polarity. Additionally, for code-mixed Tamil-English corpus, Chakravarthi et al. (2022) introduced three sentiment assessment frameworks: BERT (Bidirectional Encoder Representations from Transformers) and logistic regression classifier, DistilBERT, and rapid Text-mod.

For Tamil code-mixed sentiment analysis, Shanmugavadivel et al. (2022) analyzed machine learning frameworks. The research objective was to develop hybrid deep learning models that combine Convolutional Neural Network (CNN) with LSTM and CNN+BiLSTM. Hybrid models performance was compared with state-of-the-art methods, including traditional machine learning techniques. Among all their developed models, the proposed CNN+BiLSTM framework outperformed with an accuracy of 66%.

Tulu is an Indian language belonging to the Dravidian language family, spoken mainly in the region. It is gaining attention in sentiment analysis research. However, compared to other languages, Tulu has not been extensively studied in this area. The limited focus on sentiment analysis in Tulu can be attributed to the lack of annotated datasets and linguistic resources available for the language.

For sentiment analysis of Tulu-English code-mixed text, Kannadaguli (2021) developed a corpus comprising 5,536 YouTube comments. The dataset construction focused on extracting comments written in the Latin script of Tulu and Tulu-English code-mixed. The annotated Tulu-English dataset was then utilized to implement various machine learning (ML) and deep learning models, and a transformer-based classifier using BERT framework. Keras embeddings and Term-Frequency-Inverse Document-Frequencies (TF-IDF) were used as attributes for deep learning and machine learning models respectively. The BiLSTM framework demonstrated the best performance with notable F_1-scores across all the classes.

Hegde et al. (2022a) worked on corpus creation for code-mixed Tulu Text for sentiment analysis. They scraped 7,171 YouTube comments and subsequently annotated them to predict emotions within the code-mixed Tulu data, establishing a foundational benchmark. They utilized traditional ML algorithms employing TF-IDF features derived from word bigrams and trigrams. In all sentiment classes, the Multi-Layer Perceptron (MLP) and Support Vector Machine (SVM) classifiers performed comparably better and reported an F_1-score of 0.60.

[2] https://github.com/bharathichezhiyan/TamilMixSentiment

3 Code-Mixed Corpora

In this section, we present details of corpora and datasets which have been used to train the sentiment analysis and transfer learning. The train, development and test sets were released by the organizers of the shared task. Moreover, we used additional corpora to train ELMo embeddings to perform transfer learning for both Tamil and Tulu code-mixed text.

3.1 Tamil

Details of the Tamil code-mixed text for training and evaluation sets are given in the Table 1. The number of sentences in the Tamil dataset is greater than that in the Tulu dataset. Tamil train set contains 320,746 tokens in total with 9.4 tokens per sentence on average.

Category	# Sentences	# Tokens
Training set	33,989	320,764
Development set	3,786	35,424
Test set	649	8,019

Table 1: Details of Tamil code-mixed train, development and test sets.

The sentences which are actually YouTube comments, also have emoticons of different types. As the text contains sentences from different scripts and hence has large vocabulary. The Romanized text usually lacks the standard spellings which makes it challenging to train and achieve better predictions. The dataset contains sentences in Tamil script, Romanized Tamil, English, Tamil and Romanized and Tamil with English phrase. Each sentence has been categorized in any of the four sentiment classes; Positive, Negative, Mixed Feelings and Unknown State.

The transfer learning is a suitable method for small to medium sized annotated datasets. We have trained contextualized ELMo embeddings to achieve context-sensitive word vectors and to cater Out-Of-Vocabulary (OOV) words. The ELMo embeddings produce character-based word vectors which are helpful to learn morphology as well as semantics of a language. To perform the transfer learning for code-mixed Tamil, we have used corpora from multiple sources containing text in various scripts. The Table 3 shows statistics of corpora from different sources. The Tamil text corpus has been collected from Kaggle[3], the repository of Tamil - Language Corpus for NLP. We have used a sub-directory containing 357 files of Tamil text with 1,444,046 sentences and 50,743,745 tokens. The Romanized Tamil corpus has been collected from CC100 corpora[4] (Conneau et al., 2019). The corpus contains 6,243,679 sentences and 36,893,050 tokens. The English language text has been collected from Kaggle under the repository IMDB 320.000 Movie Reviews[5]. The repository contains reviews from IMDB[6]. The IMDB dataset contains 320,748 comments and 83,249,225 tokens. As the training dataset has been collected from YouTube comments, therefore, the movie reviews corpus will be useful to perform transfer learning. An additional News and Blogs[7] corpus has been collected from Kaggle to increase the size of the English corpus. The News and Blogs dataset contains 160,036 sentences and 82,627,416 tokens. Overall, the corpus contains 8,168,509 sentences and 253,513,436 tokens from the four sources.

3.2 Tulu

Details of the Tulu code-mixed text provided for training and evaluations are given in the Table 2. Tulu is a low-resourced language with a scarce online corpora. In the shared task, Tulu language has only 6,457 sentences and 36,628 tokens. Similarly, the development and test sets contain 4,729 and 4,077 tokens respectively. The dataset contains sentences in Tulu script, Romanized Tulu, Tulu with Romanized and English text. There are four sentiment classes, which are; Positive, Negative, Neutral and Mixed Feelings.

Category	# Sentences	# Tokens
Training set	6,457	36,628
Development set	781	4,729
Test set	708	4,077

Table 2: Details of Tulu code-mixed train, development and test sets.

To overcome the data scarcity of Tulu text resources, we have performed the transfer learning by using Kannada language corpus. As Tulu is closely related to Kannada with respect to vocabulary and linguistic features (Hegde et al., 2022b; Vyawahare

[3]https://www.kaggle.com/datasets/praveengovi/tamil-language-corpus-for-nlp

[4]https://metatext.io/datasets/cc100-tamil-romanized

[5]https://www.kaggle.com/datasets/nikosfragkis/imdb-320000-movie-reviews-sentiment-analysis

[6]https://www.imdb.com/

[7]https://www.kaggle.com/datasets/patjob/articlescrape

Sr.#	Data source	# Sentences	# Tokens
1	Tamil - Language Corpus for NLP	1,444,046	50,743,745
2	CC100 - Tamil Romanized[8]	6,243,679	36,893,050
3	IMDB 320.000 Movie Reviews	320,748	83,249,225
4	News and Blog	160,036	82,627,416
	Total	8,168,509	253,513,436

Table 3: Details of Tamil code-mixed corpora to perfrom transfer learning by training contextualized ELMo embeddings.

Sr.#	Data source	# Sentences	# Tokens
1	CC100 - Kannada	2,000,000	30,376,315
2	CC100 - Kannada (Romanized)	2,000,000	30,376,315
3	IMDB 320.000 Movie Reviews	320,748	83,249,225
	Total	4,320,748	144,001,855

Table 4: Details of Tulu code-mixed corpora to perform transfer learning by training contextualized ELMo embeddings.

et al., 2022). We further transliterated the Kannada text to Romanized Kannada by using a transliterator called *om-transliterator*[9]. The transliterator is an open source python library which is freely available to use. Table 4 shows statistics of corpora which have been used to train ELMo embeddings. The Kannada corpus has been collected from CC100 corpora[10] (Conneau et al., 2019). We have used two million sentences from this corpus which were further transliterated to the Roman script. Additionally, the IMDB 320.000 Movie Reviews dataset has been included to the code-mixed large corpus for transfer learning.

3.3 Corpus Preparation

A few pre-processing operations have been performed on the labeled datasets as well as unlabeled corpora. In both Tamil and Tulu datasets, Romanized and English text has been converted to lower case. Tokenization is a basic task to perform any NLP task. Initially, the tokenization has been performed on the basis of the space character but there are many non-word tokens like punctuation and symbols which were combined with words. We have separated these types of symbols from words and used them as separate tokens. Both Tamil and Tulu datasets contain emoticons in them which are quite important to represent the sentiments and feelings. In many sentences, there are repeating emoticons without space in them. We have converted all emoticons to the English text in both datasets. For that purpose, we have used a python package *emoji*[11] which has a function to *demojize* the text. This function takes a sentence as input and returns the same sentence by replacing emoticons with equivalent text. The *demojization* was quite helpful to learning contextual word vectors to learn the sentiment labels.

4 Model

We developed the sentiment analysis model by using Bidirectional Long-Short Term Memory (BiLSTM) networks. BiLSTM based neural models are quite capable to learn sequence labels which can also be used to predict sentence level tasks like sentiment analysis. The model has two LSTM layers, first layer scans the word sequences in the forward direction while the other layer scans the word sequences in opposite i.e. backward direction. The LSTM based models learn next and previous words to attain the contextual information within sentences. The input sequence of N words $x_1, x_2, ..., x_n$ is given as input. The BiLSTM($x_{1:n}$,i) function has been shown in the Equation 1 which demonstrates the concatenation of forward and backward layers. $LSTM_f$ represents the forward layer whereas $LSTM_r$ shows the backward layer. The function denotes to a vector *i* by conditioning the past antiquity $x_{1:i}$ and the forthcoming sequence $x_{i:n}$ as well.

$$BiLSTM(x_{1:n}, i) = LSTM_f(x_{1:i}).LSTM_r(x_{n:i}) \quad (1)$$

[9]https://pypi.org/project/om-transliterator

[10]https://metatext.io/datasets/cc100-kannada

[11]https://pypi.org/project/emoji

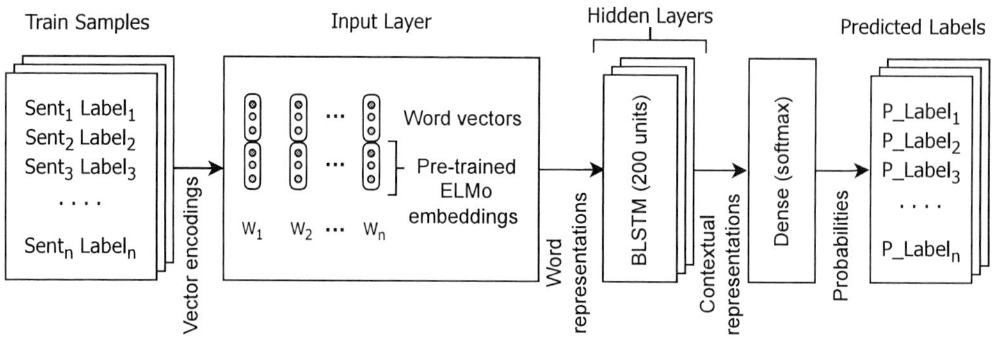

Figure 1: BiLSTM based sentiment analysis model architecture.

The *softmax* non-linearity function is employed at the output layer which performs the multi-class classification returning sentiment label classes l_i for each input sequence of N words $x_1, x_2, ..., x_n$ as shown in Equation 2.

$$o_i = Softmax(Xh_i + b) \tag{2}$$

The Figure 1 shows our BiLSTM based neural model architecture which has been trained for sentiment analysis for the Tamil and Tulu code-mixed datasets. The dataset contains sentences followed by sentiment labels. The training sentences have been transformed to vectors to use them in the neural model at input layer. The word vectors have been concatenated with the contextualized vectors achieved from the EMLMo embeddings. The concatenated vectors are further fed to hidden LSTM layers. We experimented with two hidden LSTM layers. The *Dropout* layers have been added between LSTM layers and before the output layer. The LSTM layers are followed by a *Flatten* layer to perform sentiment labeling. The *Softmax* non-linearity has been used at dense output layer to perform multi-class classification. Finally, the sentiment classes are predicted on the basis of maximum likelihood. The predicted labels have been evaluated against gold labels for development and test sets.

The sentiment analysis model has been developed by using *keras* library with the *Tensorflow* back-end in Python-3. The bidirectional LSTM layers had 200 hidden units. The value for *Dropout* layers was set to 0.2 (20%). Root Mean Squared Propagation (*RMSprop(0.001)*) optimization function has been used in the model. The *categorical cross-entropy* loss function was used in all experiments. The word vectors have been trained to have 128 dimensions, however, ELMo embeddings have been trained with 256 projection dimensions. The LSTM sentence length was set to the longest sentence with padding sequences in the datasets for both Tamil and Tulu. Transfer leaning by training ELMo embeddings were quite useful to achieve better results. The following section describes the details of ELMo embeddings and its parameters.

4.1 Transfer Learning

Deep learning based models are data hungry models as they require a lot of annotated samples to produce the state-of-the-art results. However, the annotation of such huge datasets is quite costly in terms of human resource, expertise and time. Transfer learning is a suitable technique by training word representations on large unannotated corpora. This method helps in the training by learning context and OOV tokens. We have trained ELMo embeddings on code-mixed text for Tamil and Tulu languages.

Context-free word embeddings produce unique vectors for each token in the corpus which represent a single meaning. The well-known context-free word embeddings are GloVe (Pennington et al., 2014), Word2Vec (Mikolov et al., 2013) and fastText (Bojanowski et al., 2017). However, contextualized word representations are able to learn meanings with respect to the contexts of the words because a single word may have multiple meanings in a language. ELMo embeddings (Peters et al., 2018) produce contextualized vectors to learn the meanings with respect to the context. The code-mixed datasets contain Romanized text for both Tamil and Tulu. People usually use the Roman spellings according to their personal practices which results in a lot of variations in the text producing larger

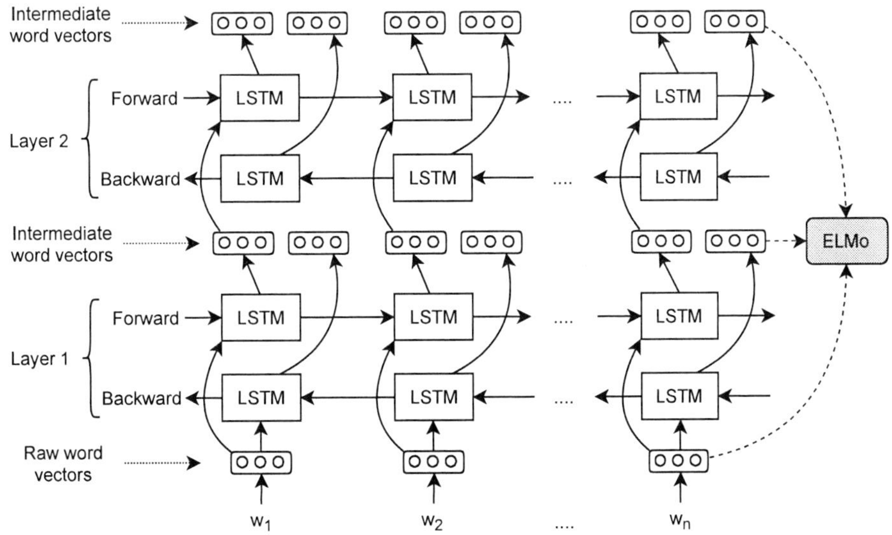

Figure 2: ELMo architecture.

vocabulary. ELMo embeddings are trained on the basis of character sequences creating an ability to learn spelling variations as well as morphology of the languages.

The Figure 2 shows the ELMo architecture which contains three neural network layers. First layer is a convolutional layer which operates on character sequences. The second and third layers are bidirectional layers where each layer contains two concatenated LSTMs. The output of the third layer produces the contextualized word embeddings for the given text. The details of corpora which have been used to train ELMo embeddings for both Tamil and Tulu code-mixed datasets are given in the Table 3 and the Table 4 respectively. The vocabulary for both languages has been used with minimum frequency of 20. The ELMo projection dimension size was set to 256 and the ELMo model was run for five epochs for each language.

5 Results

The macro average metric has been used to evaluate the prediction of the shared task. The findings of the shared task are presented by Hegde et al. (2023). In our submissions, we achieved the macro average F_1-scores of 0.2150 and 0.5220 for Tamil and Tulu code-mixed datasets respectively. However, our initial models lacked English data, proper tokenization and *demojization*. We retrained the models and the updated results for development and test sets which are shown in the Tables 5, 6, 7 and 8.

Category	**Pre.**	**Rec.**	**F_1-score**
Positive	0.7669	0.7944	0.7804
Negative	0.3545	0.6521	0.4593
Mixed feelings	0.3699	0.1461	0.2095
Unknown state	0.5128	0.3290	0.4008
micro avg	0.6263	0.6263	0.6263
macro avg	**0.5010**	**0.4804**	**0.4625**
weighted avg	0.6277	0.6263	0.6124

Table 5: Sentiment analysis results for Tamil code-mixed development set.

Category	**Pre.**	**Rec.**	**F_1-score**
Positive	0.1235	0.4247	0.1914
Negative	0.6340	0.3639	0.4624
Mixed feelings	0.2404	0.2475	0.2439
Unknown state	0.3000	0.2190	0.2532
micro avg	0.3220	0.3220	0.3220
macro avg	**0.3245**	**0.3138**	**0.2877**
weighted avg	0.4448	0.3220	0.3537

Table 6: Sentiment analysis results for Tamil code-mixed test set.

The results for Tamil code-mixed sentiment analysis have been improved by enhancing the size and the quality of the datasets for transfer learning. The macro average F_1-score has been improved with a gain of 0.0727 points. The model performed better on development set with a macro average F_1-score of 0.4625 as compared to the test set. The reason behind the significant difference is the size of evaluation sets for Tamil. The development set contains 3,786 sentence whereas the test set contains only 649 sentences.

On the other hand, the Tulu evaluation sets have almost same number of samples. The Tulu model performed with the macro average F_1-scores of 0.5386 and 0.5133 on development and test set respectively. The Tulu dataset has less variations as compared to Tamil data as it mostly contains Romanized Tulu comments which resulted higher results.

Category	Pre.	Rec.	F_1-score
Positive	0.8506	0.7561	0.8006
Negative	0.5435	0.2778	0.3676
Neutral	0.5096	0.7921	0.6202
Mixed feelings	0.4194	0.3250	0.3662
micro avg	0.6440	0.6440	0.6440
macro avg	**0.5807**	**0.5377**	**0.5386**
weighted avg	0.6607	0.6440	0.6373

Table 7: Sentiment analysis results for Tulu code-mixed development set.

Category	Pre.	Rec.	F_1-score
Positive	0.8615	0.7413	0.7969
Negative	0.5588	0.3167	0.4043
Neutral	0.5034	0.7614	0.6061
Mixed feelings	0.2875	0.2150	0.2460
micro avg	0.6314	0.6314	0.6314
macro avg	**0.5528**	**0.5086**	**0.5133**
weighted avg	0.6494	0.6314	0.6273

Table 8: Sentiment analysis results for Tulu code-mixed test set.

From the results, it is quite evident that transfer learning has the ability to produce competitive results for code-mixed corpora. However, the data preparation is an important task before the training process. There should also be a balance in the corpus having representation of various types of comments. In this way, the sentiment analysis models could perform better. The sentiment analysis of code-mixed text is important research topic which requires more research to analyze online text.

6 Conclusion

This paper presents the sentiment analysis of code-mixed Tamil and Tulu YouTube comments. The code-mixed text contains text from different scripts, such as, Tamil, Tulu, English, Romanized Tamil and Tulu, mixed text and emoticons. The variety of languages makes it quite challenging to predict sentiments with higher accuracy. We proposed a Bidirectional Long-Short Term Memory networks based model for both languages which further uses contextualized word embeddings at the input layers of the model. For that purpose, ELMo embeddings have been trained on larger unannotated code-mixed text corpora. The transfer learning by using trained ELMo models for both language was quite helpful to achieve improved sentiment analysis results. Our models performed with the macro average F_1-scores of 0.2877 and 0.5133 on Tamil and Tulu code-mixed datasets respectively.

References

Gazi Imtiyaz Ahmad, Jimmy Singla, Ali Anis, Aijaz Ahmad Reshi, and Anas A Salameh. 2022. Machine learning techniques for sentiment analysis of code-mixed and switched indian social media text corpus-a comprehensive review. *International Journal of Advanced Computer Science and Applications*, 13(2).

Alexandra Balahur and Marco Turchi. 2014. Comparative experiments using supervised learning and machine translation for multilingual sentiment analysis. *Computer Speech & Language*, 28(1):56–75.

Piotr Bojanowski, Edouard Grave, Armand Joulin, and Tomas Mikolov. 2017. Enriching word vectors with subword information. *Transactions of the association for computational linguistics*, 5:135–146.

Bharathi Raja Chakravarthi, Mihael Arcan, and John Philip McCrae. 2018. Improving wordnets for under-resourced languages using machine translation. In *Proceedings of the 9th Global Wordnet Conference*, pages 77–86.

Bharathi Raja Chakravarthi, Vigneshwaran Muralidaran, Ruba Priyadharshini, and John Philip McCrae. 2020a. Corpus creation for sentiment analysis in code-mixed Tamil-English text. In *Proceedings of the 1st Joint Workshop on Spoken Language Technologies for Under-resourced languages (SLTU) and Collaboration and Computing for Under-Resourced Languages (CCURL)*, pages 202–210, Marseille, France. European Language Resources association.

Bharathi Raja Chakravarthi, Ruba Priyadharshini, Vigneshwaran Muralidaran, Navya Jose, Shardul Suryawanshi, Elizabeth Sherly, and John P McCrae. 2022. Dravidiancodemix: Sentiment analysis and offensive language identification dataset for dravidian languages in code-mixed text. *Language Resources and Evaluation*, 56(3):765–806.

Bharathi Raja Chakravarthi, Ruba Priyadharshini, Vigneshwaran Muralidaran, Shardul Suryawanshi, Navya Jose, Elizabeth Sherly, and John P McCrae. 2020b. Overview of the track on sentiment analysis for dravidian languages in code-mixed text. In *Forum for information retrieval evaluation*, pages 21–24.

Alexis Conneau, Kartikay Khandelwal, Naman Goyal, Vishrav Chaudhary, Guillaume Wenzek, Francisco Guzmán, Edouard Grave, Myle Ott, Luke Zettlemoyer, and Veselin Stoyanov. 2019. Unsupervised Cross-Lingual Representation Learning at Scale. *arXiv preprint arXiv:1911.02116*.

Toqeer Ehsan and Miriam Butt. 2020. Dependency Parsing for Urdu: Resources, Conversions and Learning. In *Proceedings of the 12th Language Resources and Evaluation Conference*, pages 5202–5207.

Toqeer Ehsan and Sarmad Hussain. 2020. Development and Evaluation of an Urdu Treebank (CLE-UTB) and a Statistical Parser. *Language Resources and Evaluation*, pages 1–40.

Toqeer Ehsan and Sarmad Hussain. 2022. *Statistical Parser for Urdu*. Ph.D. dissertation, University of Engineering and Technology, Lahore, Pakistan.

Toqeer Ehsan, Javairia Khalid, Saadia Ambreen, Asad Mustafa, and Sarmad Hussain. 2022. Improving Phrase Chunking by using Contextualized Word Embeddings for a Morphologically Rich Language. *Arabian Journal for Science and Engineering*, pages 1–19.

Asha Hegde, Mudoor Devadas Anusha, Sharal Coelho, Hosahalli Lakshmaiah Shashirekha, and Bharathi Raja Chakravarthi. 2022a. Corpus creation for sentiment analysis in code-mixed Tulu text. In *Proceedings of the 1st Annual Meeting of the ELRA/ISCA Special Interest Group on Under-Resourced Languages*, pages 33–40, Marseille, France. European Language Resources Association.

Asha Hegde, Bharathi Raja Chakravarthi, Hosahalli Lakshmaiah Shashirekha, Rahul Ponnusamy, SUBALALITHA CN, Lavanya S K, Thenmozhi D, Martha Karunakar, Shreya Shreeram, and Sarah Aymen. 2023. Findings of the shared task on sentiment analysis in Tamil and Tulu code-mixed text. In *Proceedings of the Third Workshop on Speech and Language Technologies for Dravidian Languages*, Varna, Bulgaria. Recent Advances in Natural Language Processing.

Asha Hegde, Hosahalli Lakshmaiah Shashirekha, Anand Kumar Madasamy, and Bharathi Raja Chakravarthi. 2022b. A Study of Machine Translation Models for Kannada-Tulu. In *Congress on Intelligent Systems*, pages 145–161. Springer.

Prashanth Kannadaguli. 2021. A code-diverse tulu-english dataset for nlp based sentiment analysis applications. In *2021 Advanced Communication Technologies and Signal Processing (ACTS)*, pages 1–6. IEEE.

Tomas Mikolov, Ilya Sutskever, Kai Chen, Greg S Corrado, and Jeff Dean. 2013. Distributed representations of words and phrases and their compositionality. *Advances in neural information processing systems*, 26.

Saif Mohammad. 2016. A practical guide to sentiment annotation: Challenges and solutions. In *Proceedings of the 7th workshop on computational approaches to subjectivity, sentiment and social media analysis*, pages 174–179.

Braja Gopal Patra, Dipankar Das, and Amitava Das. 2018. Sentiment analysis of code-mixed indian languages: An overview of sail_code-mixed shared task@ icon-2017. *arXiv preprint arXiv:1803.06745*.

Jeffrey Pennington, Richard Socher, and Christopher D Manning. 2014. GloVe: Global Vectors for Word Representation. In *Proceedings of the 2014 conference on empirical methods in natural language processing (EMNLP)*, pages 1532–1543.

Matthew E Peters, Mark Neumann, Mohit Iyyer, Matt Gardner, Christopher Clark, Kenton Lee, and Luke Zettlemoyer. 2018. Deep Contextualized Word Representations. *arXiv preprint arXiv:1802.05365*.

Kogilavani Shanmugavadivel, Sai Haritha Sampath, Pramod Nandhakumar, Prasath Mahalingam, Malliga Subramanian, Prasanna Kumar Kumaresan, and Ruba Priyadharshini. 2022. An analysis of machine learning models for sentiment analysis of tamil code-mixed data. *Computer Speech & Language*, 76:101407.

Shardul Suryawanshi, Bharathi Raja Chakravarthi, Pranav Verma, Mihael Arcan, John Philip McCrae, and Paul Buitelaar. 2020. A dataset for troll classification of tamilmemes. In *Proceedings of the WILDRE5–5th workshop on indian language data: resources and evaluation*, pages 7–13.

Amina Tehseen, Toqeer Ehsan, Hannan Bin Liaqat, Amjad Ali, and Ala Al-Fuqaha. 2022. Neural POS Tagging of Shahmukhi by Using Contextualized Word Representations. *Journal of King Saud University-Computer and Information Sciences*.

Sajeetha Thavareesan and Sinnathamby Mahesan. 2020. Sentiment lexicon expansion using word2vec and fasttext for sentiment prediction in tamil texts. In *2020 Moratuwa engineering research conference (MERCon)*, pages 272–276. IEEE.

Aditya Vyawahare, Rahul Tangsali, Aditya Mandke, Onkar Litake, and Dipali Kadam. 2022. PICT@ DravidianLangTech-ACL2022: Neural Machine Mranslation on Dravidian Languages. *arXiv preprint arXiv:2204.09098*.

HARMONY@DravidianLangTech: Transformer-based Ensemble Learning for Abusive Comment Detection

Amrish Raaj P, Abirami S, Lysa Packiam R S, Deivamani M
Department of Information Science and Technology
College of Engineering Guindy
Anna University, Chennai, India
amrishraaj@gmail.com, abirami@auist.net, mailtolysa@gmail.com
deivamani@auist.net

Abstract

Millions of posts and comments are created every minute as a result of the widespread use of social media and easy access to the internet. It is essential to create an inclusive environment and forbid the use of abusive language against any individual or group of individuals.This paper describes the approach of team HARMONY for the "Abusive Comment Detection" shared task at the Third Workshop on Speech and Language Technologies for Dravidian Languages.A Transformer-based ensemble learning approach is proposed for detecting abusive comments in code-mixed (Tamil-English) language and Tamil language. The proposed architecture achieved rank 2 in Tamil text classification sub task and rank 3 in code mixed text classification sub task with macro-F1 score of 0.41 for Tamil and 0.50 for code-mixed data.

1 Introduction

Online Social Networks (OSNs) have become increasingly significant in recent years and are now considered to be go-to resource for news, knowledge, and entertainment (Halevy et al., 2022; Priyadharshini et al., 2021; Kumaresan et al., 2021) . However, despite the numerous benefits of using OSNs, mounting evidence suggests that an increasing number of illicit actors are taking advantage of these platforms to spread toxicity and harm other people. Numerous risks are brought on by these illicit people, including online abuse, vulgarity, harassment and bullying.

Abusive comments are those that mock or disparage a person or a group based on traits like colour, ethnicity, sexual orientation, nationality, race, or religion (Saumya et al., 2021). Social media abuse can have a negative impact on users' lives in a number of ways. This will have a terrible impact on that person's mental health, leading to depression and insomnia (Chakravarthi et al., 2021; Sean, 2022; Chakravarthi et al., 2022). Some of these remarks have the potential to stir up controversy on social media about a particular person or group of people. This demonstrates the need to prohibit the posting of these kinds of offensive comments on social media. Both the union territory of Puducherry (Pondicherry) and the Indian state of Tamil Nadu speak Tamil as their official language. In addition, it is spoken widely in Malaysia, Mauritius, Fiji, and South Africa. It is also the official language of Singapore and Sri Lanka.(Krishnamurti, 2022)

In the past, text classification was carried out on the text's sentence embedding using linear classifiers. This was followed by Recurrent Neural Networks. Transformers became prominent in the field of natural language processing following the publication (Vaswani et al., 2017). They have an attention layer mechanism that provides context to words in the text. The development of the transformer architecture has resulted in the development of numerous other transformer variations, such as BERT (Devlin et al., 2018), XLMRoBERTa (Conneau et al., 2019), MuRIL (Khanuja et al., 2021), etc.

In this paper, Transformer-based models and Recurrent Neural Network models are used for abusive comment detection in Tamil and code-mixed data(Tamil-English). The results from the performance of individual models and their ensemble are obtained to determine the best-performing model for this task.

2 Related works

Numerous published works have addressed the problem of identifying offensive content in high-resource languages. Umer et al. (2023)analysed the impact of FastText word embedding on text classification. Compared to contextual word embeddings, FastText has limited ability to capture complex se-

Third Workshop on Speech and Language Technologies for Dravidian Languages, pages 160–165, Varna, Bulgaria, Sep 7, 2023.
https://doi.org/10.26615/978-954-452-085-4_021

mantic relationships. Fazil et al. (2023)demonstrated an attentional multi-channel convolutional-BiLSTM network for the classification of hateful content. GloVe embedding used in this paper may struggle with Out-Of-Vocabulary words. The pre-trained BERT model ensembled with Deep Learning (DL) models are the foundation of Mazari et al. (2023)proposed multi-aspect hate speech detection approach.This approach will have difficulty in handling multi-lingual or non-english data. Başarslan and Kayaalp (2023) proposed a deep learning model with multiple Bidirectional Gated Recurrent Units and Convolution layers for social media sentiment analysis.

Compared to English and other high-resource languages, low-resource languages have significantly fewer published studies on the detection of abusive comments. Datasets have been created by Chakravarthi et al. (2020) to promote research in Tamil, one of the Indian Dravidian languages.Rajalakshmi et al. (2023) proposed a method to detect hate speech or offensive content in Tamil. A detailed analysis was made to study the performance of stemming and pre-trained transformer models for word embedding. For the detection of offensive language in Tamil YouTube comments, Subramanian et al. (2022) proposed adapter-based transformer models. It was done using mBERT, MuRIL (Base and Large), and XLM-RoBERTa (Base and Large).Chakravarthi et al. (2023) proposed a novel approach of fusing MPNet with a deep neural network for detecting offensive language content in low-resource Dravidian languages

3 Dataset

The objective of this shared-task (Priyadharshini et al., 2023)is to determine whether a given comment contains abusive language. The annotations in the corpus are done at the comment or post level. Tamil and Tamil-English comments were gathered from the YouTube comment section for the Abusive Comment Detection Dataset (Priyadharshini et al., 2022). The dataset consists of a comment and its corresponding label from one of the nine labels in the dataset: Misandry, Counter-speech, Misogyny, Xenophobia, Hope-Speech, Homophobia, Transphobic, Not-Tamil, and None of-the-above. Only eight classes are classified because the 'Not-Tamil' class has no test or development data instances. A few weeks before the deadline for run submission, the testing dataset, which lacked labels, was made available. The labelled test dataset was made available by the organisers for verification purposes after the results were declared. The number of samples in the training, validation, and testing datasets for each class are listed in Tables 1 and 2.

Table 1: Class Wise Distribution in Training, Validation and Test dataset (Tamil)

Class	Train	Validation	Test
Misogyny	125	24	48
Misandry	446	104	127
Homophobia	35	8	8
Transphobic	6	2	2
Xenophobia	95	29	25
Hope-speech	86	11	26
Counter-speech	149	36	47
None-of-the-above	1296	346	416
Total	2238	560	699

Table 2: Class Wise Distribution of Training, Validation and Test dataset (Tamil-English)

Class	Train	Validation	Test
Misogyny	211	50	57
Misandry	830	218	292
Homophobia	172	43	56
Transphobic	157	40	58
Xenophobia	297	70	95
Hope-speech	213	53	70
Counter-speech	348	95	88
None-of-the-above	3720	919	1141
Total	5948	1488	1857

4 Methodology

The overall architecture for Abusive Comment Detection in Tamil and Tamil-English is given in Figure 1.

4.1 Pre-processing

For Tamil sub-task, Pre-processing is done to remove the noisy elements from the text.Usernames, URLs, Extra spaces and Emojis are removed. Transliteration is the process of changing a word's script while maintaining the sentence's semantic meaning and strictly adhering to the target language's syntactical structure. (Hande et al., 2021). The Tamil-English code-mixed dataset is transliterated to Tamil and combined with the existing Tamil dataset.

Table 1 makes clear that there is severe class

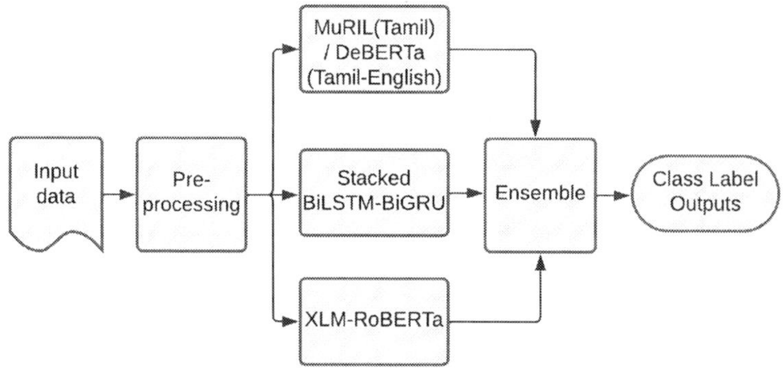

Figure 1: Abusive Comment Detection Architecture

imbalance in the dataset. An issue with class imbalance is when a dataset favours one class over another. By oversampling the minority classes, representation in the dataset is artificially increased, ensuring that the model receives sufficient exposure to learn patterns and make accurate predictions for those classes. Despite the potential benefits, stemming in Tamil NLP tasks is quite rare and hardly used. Tamil has a rich morphology, so the data was stemmed using a stemming algorithm created using the IndicNLP library's morphological analyzer (Kunchukuttan, 2022).

For Tamil-English sub-task, the dataset is preprocessed to remove noisy elements from the text.Usernames, URLs, Extra spaces and Emojis are removed. The pre-processed text is passed into the classification models.

4.2 Classification model

MuRIL (Khanuja et al., 2021) is a transformer based model built explicitly for Indian languages and trained on large amounts of Indic text corpora. XLM-RoBERTa is a multilingual variation of RoBERTa, which in and of itself outperformed BERT in a number of cutting-edge NLP tasks. 100 languages from 2.5 TB of filtered CommonCrawl data served as the basis for XLM-RoBERTa's pretraining (Conneau et al., 2019). DeBERTa improves RoBERTa and outperforms it in most NLP tasks by utilising enhanced mask decoding and disentangled attention (He et al., 2020).

MuRIL and XLM-RoBERTa pre-trained transformers are fine-tuned for Tamil dataset. For Tamil-English code-mixed dataset, DeBERTa and XLM-RoBERTa transformers are fine-tuned respectively. The fastText model is trained for a specified number of epochs(100) using the Skip-gram algorithm separately on Tamil and Tamil-English datasets.The word vectors generated after training are used for creating the embedding layer of the RNN model. The encoded sentences are then fed into two parallel, stacked recurrent layers, consisting of Bi-GRU and Bi-LSTM layers with the same number of units. The hidden states computed over all time steps from these recurrent layers are concatenated. The concatenated hidden states are then passed through global average pooling and global max pooling layers. The outputs of both pooling layers are concatenated again and served as the input for a dense classification layer. 'Adam's optimizer is used with a loss function of sparse_categorical_crossentropy. Table 3 represents the parameters used to finetune the MuRIL, XLM-RoBERTa, DeBERTa base models and the Bi-LSTM-Bi-GRU model.

The output class probabilities obtained from the transformer-based models and the stacked BiLSTM-BiGRU model are ensembled using weighted average method.MuRIL, XLM-RoBERTa and RNN model are ensembled for Tamil text. DeBERTa, XLM-RoBERTa and RNN model are ensembled for Tamil-English text. In the weighted averaging, Each model composing the ensemble model is assigned a weight depending on its individual performance. The values of individual weights range from zero to one , and the total sum of the weights given to the individual models is one.Equation 1 gives the formula for weighted average prediction.W_i: weight assigned to the ith model.Y_i: prediction of the ith model.

$$\hat{y} = \sum_{i=1}^{n} w_i \cdot y_i \tag{1}$$

Table 3: Hyper-parameters used for fine-tuning the models

	Tamil sub-task			Tamil-English sub-task		
Hyper-parameter	**MuRIL**	**XLM-RoBERTa**	**Bi-LSTM-Bi-GRU**	**DeBERTa**	**XLM-RoBERTa**	**Bi-LSTM-Bi-GRU**
Learning Rate	2e-5	2e-5	1e-3	2e-5	2e-5	1e-3
Batch Size	16	16	32	8	8	32
Number of Epochs	3	8	15	10	10	20

Table 4: Results for Abusive Comment Detection in Tamil Language (Validation dataset)

Model	Accuracy	Precision	Recall	F1-Score
MuRIL	0.69	0.44	0.42	0.42
Bi-LSTM-Bi-GRU	0.66	0.31	0.37	0.32
XLM-RoBERTa	0.71	0.44	0.40	0.41
Ensemble	**0.74**	**0.50**	0.41	**0.43**

Table 5: Results for Abusive Comment Detection in Code-Mixed Language (Validation dataset)

Model	Accuracy	Precision	Recall	F1-Score
DeBERTa	0.73	0.57	0.49	0.52
Bi-LSTM-Bi-GRU	0.74	0.45	0.60	0.50
XLM-RoBERTa	0.74	0.52	0.49	0.50
Ensemble	**0.78**	**0.71**	0.49	**0.56**

Table 6: Results for Abusive Comment Detection (Test datasets)

Dataset	Accuracy	Precision	Recall	F1-Score
Tamil	0.69	0.40	0.45	0.41
Tamil-English	0.75	0.46	0.58	0.50

5 Results and Analysis

The training set was used to train all the models, and the development set was used to validate them.The organisers indicated macro F1-score as their primary evaluation metric.Apart from this,a few more performance metrics like accuracy and the macro averages of precision and recall are also used to assess the classification models. In order to determine the classification performance more accurately, all four evaluation metrics are calculated.The performance of the models on the Tamil and Tamil-English validation datasets is shown in Tables 4 and 5, respectively.On analysing the performance of all the models on validation datasets, it is clearly seen that the ensemble model performs better than the individual models. The weighted average ensemble model works better because it combines diverse representations, corrects errors, reduces bias, improves robustness to variability, and leverages the strengths of each model. By integrating multiple perspectives and leveraging their complementary abilities, the ensemble captures a broader range of patterns and linguistic nuances, leading to an improved performance. Due to higher macro-F1 score, the ensemble model is used in both cases for the test dataset. Table 6 contains the result obtained for Tamil and Tamil-English test datasets using ensemble model. The macro-F1 scores obtained using the ensemble model secured rank 2 for Tamil and rank 3 for Tamil-English in the shared task.

According to a comparison between predictions from the ensemble model for Tamil dataset and the original class labels of Tamil test data, the None-of-the-above class has the highest individual F1-score of 0.81 and Transphobic class has the lowest individual F1-score of 0 since it only has two data points in the test data. The None-of-the above class in the Tamil-English dataset has the highest individual F1-score of 0.85, while the Misogyny class has the lowest individual F1-score of 0.27.Table 7 contains the class-wise F1-score for both the datasets.

Table 7: Classwise F1-Score obtained using Ensemble Model on Test datasets

Class Name	Tamil	Tamil-English
Misogyny	0.42	0.27
Misandry	0.66	0.71
Homophobia	0.47	0.45
Transphobic	0.00	0.35
Xenophobia	0.28	0.65
Hope-Speech	0.30	0.33
Counter-speech	0.34	0.40
None-of-the-above	0.81	0.85

6 Conclusion and Future work

In this paper, a new approach has been proposed for abusive comment detection based on ensemble learning. The proposed model combined the pre-trained transformer models(MuRIL, XLM-RoBERTa, DeBERTa) with a deep-learning model built by stacking Bi-LSTMs and Bi-GRUs on Fast-Text embeddings. This ensemble learning has actually reduced the number of misclassified instances and thus improved the precision of the abusive comment detection model. For Tamil dataset, an ensemble of MuRIL, Bi-LSTM-Bi-GRU and XLM-RoBERTa provided the best results with a macro-averaged F1 score of 0.41. For Tamil-English dataset, an ensemble of DeBERTa, Bi-LSTM-Bi-GRU and XLM-RoBERTa provided the best results with a macro-averaged F1 score of 0.50.

Further this work can be extended by exploring the performance of adapter-based transformer models. Ensembling of other transformer models with RNNs can also be explored in future.

References

Muhammet Sinan Başarslan and Fatih Kayaalp. 2023. Mbi-grumconv: A novel multi bi-gru and multi cnn-based deep learning model for social media sentiment analysis. *Journal of Cloud Computing*, 12(1):1–16.

Bharathi Raja Chakravarthi, Manoj Balaji Jagadeeshan, Vasanth Palanikumar, and Ruba Priyadharshini. 2023. Offensive language identification in dravidian languages using mpnet and cnn. *International Journal of Information Management Data Insights*, 3(1):100151.

Bharathi Raja Chakravarthi, Vigneshwaran Muralidaran, Ruba Priyadharshini, and John P McCrae. 2020. Corpus creation for sentiment analysis in code-mixed tamil-english text. *arXiv preprint arXiv:2006.00206*.

Bharathi Raja Chakravarthi, Ruba Priyadharshini, Thenmozhi Durairaj, John Philip McCrae, Paul Buitelaar, Prasanna Kumaresan, and Rahul Ponnusamy. 2022. Overview of the shared task on homophobia and transphobia detection in social media comments. In *Proceedings of the Second Workshop on Language Technology for Equality, Diversity and Inclusion*, pages 369–377.

Bharathi Raja Chakravarthi, Ruba Priyadharshini, Rahul Ponnusamy, Prasanna Kumar Kumaresan, Kayalvizhi Sampath, Durairaj Thenmozhi, Sathiyaraj Thangasamy, Rajendran Nallathambi, and John Phillip McCrae. 2021. Dataset for identification of homophobia and transophobia in multilingual youtube comments. *arXiv preprint arXiv:2109.00227*.

Alexis Conneau, Kartikay Khandelwal, Naman Goyal, Vishrav Chaudhary, Guillaume Wenzek, Francisco Guzmán, Edouard Grave, Myle Ott, Luke Zettlemoyer, and Veselin Stoyanov. 2019. Unsupervised cross-lingual representation learning at scale. *arXiv preprint arXiv:1911.02116*.

Jacob Devlin, Ming-Wei Chang, Kenton Lee, and Kristina Toutanova. 2018. Bert: Pre-training of deep bidirectional transformers for language understanding. *arXiv preprint arXiv:1810.04805*.

Mohd Fazil, Shakir Khan, Bader M Albahlal, Reemiah Muneer Alotaibi, Tamanna Siddiqui, and Mohd Asif Shah. 2023. Attentional multi-channel convolution with bidirectional lstm cell toward hate speech prediction. *IEEE Access*, 11:16801–16811.

Alon Halevy, Cristian Canton-Ferrer, Hao Ma, Umut Ozertem, Patrick Pantel, Marzieh Saeidi, Fabrizio Silvestri, and Ves Stoyanov. 2022. Preserving integrity in online social networks. *Communications of the ACM*, 65(2):92–98.

Adeep Hande, Karthik Puranik, Konthala Yasaswini, Ruba Priyadharshini, Sajeetha Thavareesan, Anbukkarasi Sampath, Kogilavani Shanmugavadivel, Durairaj Thenmozhi, and Bharathi Raja Chakravarthi. 2021. Offensive language identification in low-resourced code-mixed dravidian languages using pseudo-labeling. *arXiv preprint arXiv:2108.12177*.

Pengcheng He, Xiaodong Liu, Jianfeng Gao, and Weizhu Chen. 2020. Deberta: Decoding-enhanced bert with disentangled attention. *arXiv preprint arXiv:2006.03654*.

Simran Khanuja, Diksha Bansal, Sarvesh Mehtani, Savya Khosla, Atreyee Dey, Balaji Gopalan, Dilip Kumar Margam, Pooja Aggarwal, Rajiv Teja Nagipogu, Shachi Dave, et al. 2021. Muril: Multilingual representations for indian languages. *arXiv preprint arXiv:2103.10730*.

B. Krishnamurti. 2022. Tamil language. encyclopedia britannica. `https://www.britannica.com/topic/Tamil-language`.

Prasanna Kumar Kumaresan, Premjith, Ratnasingam Sakuntharaj, Sajeetha Thavareesan, Subalalitha Navaneethakrishnan, Anand Kumar Madasamy, Bharathi Raja Chakravarthi, and John P McCrae. 2021. Findings of shared task on offensive language identification in tamil and malayalam. In *Proceedings of the 13th Annual Meeting of the Forum for Information Retrieval Evaluation*, pages 16–18.

A. Kunchukuttan. 2022. The indicnlp library. https://github.com/anoopkunchukuttan/indic_nlp_library.

Ahmed Cherif Mazari, Nesrine Boudoukhani, and Abdelhamid Djeffal. 2023. Bert-based ensemble learning for multi-aspect hate speech detection. *Cluster Computing*, pages 1–15.

Ruba Priyadharshini, Bharathi Raja Chakravarthi, Subalalitha Cn, Thenmozhi Durairaj, Malliga Subramanian, Kogilavani Shanmugavadivel, Siddhanth U Hegde, and Prasanna Kumaresan. 2022. Overview of abusive comment detection in tamil-acl 2022. In *Proceedings of the Second Workshop on Speech and Language Technologies for Dravidian Languages*, pages 292–298.

Ruba Priyadharshini, Bharathi Raja Chakravarthi, Malliga S, SUBALALITHA CN, Kogilavani S V, Premjith B, Abirami Murugappan, and Prasanna Kumar Kumaresan. 2023. Overview of shared-task on abusive comment detection in tamil and telugu. In *Proceedings of the Third Workshop on Speech and Language Technologies for Dravidian Languages*, Varna, Bulgaria. Recent Advances in Natural Language Processing.

Ruba Priyadharshini, Bharathi Raja Chakravarthi, Sajeetha Thavareesan, Dhivya Chinnappa, Durairaj Thenmozhi, and Rahul Ponnusamy. 2021. Overview of the dravidiancodemix 2021 shared task on sentiment detection in tamil, malayalam, and kannada. In *Forum for Information Retrieval Evaluation*, pages 4–6.

Ratnavel Rajalakshmi, Srivarshan Selvaraj, Pavitra Vasudevan, et al. 2023. Hottest: Hate and offensive content identification in tamil using transformers and enhanced stemming. *Computer Speech & Language*, 78:101464.

Sunil Saumya, Abhinav Kumar, and Jyoti Prakash Singh. 2021. Offensive language identification in dravidian code mixed social media text. In *Proceedings of the first workshop on speech and language technologies for Dravidian languages*, pages 36–45.

Benhur Sean. 2022. Findings of the shared task on emotion analysis in tamil. In *Proceedings of the Second Workshop on Speech and Language Technologies for Dravidian Languages*, pages 279–285.

Malliga Subramanian, Rahul Ponnusamy, Sean Benhur, Kogilavani Shanmugavadivel, Adhithiya Ganesan, Deepti Ravi, Gowtham Krishnan Shanmugasundaram, Ruba Priyadharshini, and Bharathi Raja Chakravarthi. 2022. Offensive language detection in tamil youtube comments by adapters and cross-domain knowledge transfer. *Computer Speech & Language*, 76:101404.

Muhammad Umer, Zainab Imtiaz, Muhammad Ahmad, Michele Nappi, Carlo Medaglia, Gyu Sang Choi, and Arif Mehmood. 2023. Impact of convolutional neural network and fasttext embedding on text classification. *Multimedia Tools and Applications*, 82(4):5569–5585.

Ashish Vaswani, Noam Shazeer, Niki Parmar, Jakob Uszkoreit, Llion Jones, Aidan N Gomez, Łukasz Kaiser, and Illia Polosukhin. 2017. Attention is all you need. *Advances in neural information processing systems*, 30.

Avalanche@DravidianLangTech:Abusive Comment Detection in Code Mixed Data Using Machine Learning Techniques with UnderSampling

Rajalakshmi S, Rajasekar S, Srilakshmisai K, Angel Deborah S, Mirnalinee T T
Department of Computer Science and Engineering,
Sri Sivasubramaniya Nadar College of Engineering, Chennai - 603110, Tamil Nadu, India
rajalakshmis@ssn.edu.in, rajasekar2110857@ssn.edu.in,
srilakshmisai2110452@ssn.edu.in, angeldeborahs@ssn.edu.in,
mirnalineett@ssn.edu.in

Abstract

In recent years, the growth of online platforms and social media has given rise to a concerning increase in the presence of abusive content. This poses significant challenges for maintaining a safe and inclusive digital environment. In order to resolve this issue, this paper experiments an approach for detecting abusive comments. We are using a combination of pipelining and vectorization techniques, along with algorithms such as the stochastic gradient descent (SGD) classifier and support vector machine (SVM) classifier. We conducted experiments on an Tamil-English code mixed dataset to evaluate the performance of this approach. Using the stochastic gradient descent classifier algorithm, we achieved a weighted F1 score of 0.76 and a macro score of 0.45 for development dataset. Furthermore, by using the support vector machine classifier algorithm, we obtained a weighted F1 score of 0.78 and a macro score of 0.42 for development dataset. With the test dataset, SGD approach secured 5th rank with 0.44 macro F1 score, while SVM scored 8th rank with 0.35 macro F1 score in the shared task and to improve the macro F1 score, we used SVC and got a macro F1 score as 0.39.

1 Introduction

In recent times, social media has emerged as a prominent platform for discussions due to its wide reach and accessibility. It has granted individuals the power to express themselves, but unfortunately, it has also become a breeding ground for attacks based on characteristics such as race, gender, sexual orientation, or even threats of violence towards others.

According to the recent survey conducted by Economic Times, India in 2023 [1], 8 out of 10 urban women are using the Internet for various purposes. Nearly 83% of the people surveyed said that the safety measures for the usage of Internet need be enhanced. It states that, "Key concerns of urban Indian women when using the Internet include online sexual harassment, trolling, abuse, extortion and fraud". Hence it is a pressing need to identify the abusive content in Internet and take necessary actions for that.

To address the issue of data imbalance, sampling techniques are employed, and feature extraction is performed using count vectorizer and TF-IDF. Various machine learning classifiers are applied in the process of classifying the text as abusive or not and find the category.

The paper is organized as follows: Section 2 provides an overview of the relevant research conducted in the field. Section 3 examines the provided dataset, and Section 4 outlines the methodology employed for the task. The results obtained are presented in Section 5, and the paper concludes with a summary in the final section.

2 Related work

Nobata et al., published in 2016 [1] specifically addressing the detection of abusive comments. This seminal work introduced a methodology for identifying abusive language in various online platforms and utilized machine learning techniques for classification. It is widely recognized as one of the pioneering contributions in the field of abusive comment detection.

Waseem and Hovy, published in 2016 [7] focused on identifying predictive features for detecting hate speech on the Twitter platform. The objective was to understand the characteristics of hate speech and develop effective detection models.

Davidson et al. (2017) [13] addressed the challenge of automated hate speech detection and offensive language. Their work involved constructing a dataset of Twitter posts annotated for hate speech

[1]https://economictimes.indiatimes.com/news/india

Third Workshop on Speech and Language Technologies for Dravidian Languages, pages 166–170, Varna, Bulgaria, Sep 7, 2023.
https://doi.org/10.26615/978-954-452-085-4_022

and employing machine learning algorithms to classify offensive content. The research aimed to develop robust models capable of identifying hate speech in social media.

In 2018, Founta et al [11] conducted large-scale crowdsourcing to characterize abusive behavior on Twitter. By collecting and analyzing a substantial amount of data, they sought to understand the prevalence and nature of abusive content. This study significantly contributed to the understanding of abusive behavior patterns and provided valuable insights for the development of detection systems.

Badjatiya et al. (2020) [5] explored the application of deep learning techniques for hate speech detection in tweets. Their research employed deep neural network architectures, including convolutional neural networks (CNNs) and long short-term memory (LSTM) networks, to classify tweets into different categories of hate speech. The study aimed to harness the power of deep learning for accurate hate speech detection.

Earlier we have worked on offensive language and misogyny detection for English language. Offensive content is recognized in English tweets using deep learning techniques and machine learning techniques in [15]. Misogyny detection from the multimodal data with English language is done in [16]. Now we are experimenting our work on the low resource languages and code mixed data.

Anusha Gowda [17] Spreading positive vibes or hope content on social media may help many people to get motivated in their life. To address Hope Speech detection in YouTube comments, this paper presents the description of the models submitted by our team-MUCIC, to the Hope Speech Detection for Equality, Diversity, and Inclusion (HopeEDI) shared task at Association for Computational Linguistics (ACL) 2022. This shared task consists of texts in five languages,namely: English, Spanish (in Latin scripts), and Tamil, Malayalam, and Kannada.

3 Dataset analysis and preprocessing

The provided dataset consists of comments extracted from social media platforms, primarily YouTube, and the train data-set contains dimensions of 5948 rows and 2 columns and test dataset contains dimensions of 1856 rows and 1 column, and is available in both Tamil and English languages [16]. These comments are categorized into different classes, namely **Misogyny, Misandry, Xenophobia, Transphobia, Homophobia, Counter-speech, and not abusive**. Initially, the data-set contains unwanted special characters and emojis. Most of the comments in the dataset are short, typically consisting of a single sentence, with an average sentence count close to 1. For reference, the number of classes in training and development dataset with their count have been listed in Table 1.

It is important to note that the dataset exhibits a significant class imbalance, with some categories being more dominant than others. This class imbalance can potentially lead to biased predictions favoring the majority class during model training.

To address the above mentioned issues, it is necessary to preprocess the raw dataset. The preprocessing step involves cleaning the data by removing special characters, punctuation, and irrelevant words that do not contribute significantly to the overall category or meaning of each comment.

4 Methodology

The methodology involves the steps of data preprocessing, class balancing, encoding, feature extracting, model building, evaluating and fine tuning the model. After extracting the necessary features from the cleaned dataset, we used classifier algorithms namely Stochastic Gradient Descent (SGD) and Support Vector Machine (SVM) to train the model and to predict the results i.e type of comment from the comments given in the dataset.

4.1 Encoding

Label Encoding is utilized in this task to handle the categorical features in machine learning. It transforms the categorical data into numerical labels, enabling effective processing by algorithms. In this task, we experimented with the use of label encoder.

4.2 Resampling

Resampling techniques help to balance the class distribution in the dataset which can improve the performance of machine learning models. It involves creating a new dataset by either undersampling or oversampling. Here, for this model, we used undersampling, since the label **none of the above** is significantly over represented compared to other labels.

Undersampling is done to reduce the size of the datasamples of a particular class to match the num-

S.no	Labels	Train dataset	Dev Dataset
1	None-of-the-above	3720	918
2	Misandry	830	218
3	Counter-speech	347	94
4	Xenophobia	297	70
5	Hope-Speech	213	53
6	Misogyny	211	50
7	Homophobia	172	43
8	Transphobic	157	40
9	Counter-speech	1	1

Table 1: Class label distribution of the dataset

ber of samples in other classes. When we are trying to over sample the number of samples of imbalance classes in the range of 1 - 830 to 3720, we are losing the importance features of those particular classes. But when we are under sampling the 3720 samples of non-abusive class to 500, then we are not losing much information. Hence it is planned to use under sampling techniques for balancing the data.

4.3 Feature extraction

Feature extraction involves quantifying or measuring unique properties of a text, reducing the complexity of the dataset used for model training. As part of this process, the text is numerically encoded.

4.3.1 Feature Extraction using Count Vectorizer

Count Vectorizer is employed to tokenize a set of texts by converting them into a vector representation based on token counts. This approach encompasses tokenization, counting, and normalization, collectively known as the n-gram representation.

4.3.2 Feature Extraction using TF-IDF

TF-IDF (Term Frequency - Inverse Document Frequency) is a method for quantifying a sentence based on the words it contains. Each row is vectorized using a scoring technique that evaluates the importance of each word in the text. The scores for commonly used words are decreased, while the scores for rare words are increased.

4.4 Model Building

The machine learning models used for experimenting this task, includes **Stochastic Gradient Descent** (SGD) and **Support Vector Machine** (SVM) classifiers with Pipelining. These experiments are conducted on Tamil-English code-mixed data. The models are built using the training dataset and evaluated and fine tuned using the development dataset. We selected the best-performing models to generate performance scores for the test dataset.

5 Observation Results

For reference, the models under consideration for the Tamil-English dataset have been listed in Table 3 with the evaluation metrics like precision, recall, F1-score and accuracy.

In the study conducted on the Tamil-English dataset, we employed two different classifiers, namely Stochastic Gradient Descent (SGD) and Support Vector Machine (SVM) along with a simple transformer that involved pipelining. To convert categorical data into numerical labels, label encoding was applied. Count vectorizer and TF-IDF vectorizer are used for extracting features from text data. We evaluated the performance of various models and selected the best ones to generate performance scores for the test dataset.

Using the SGD classifier with both count vectorizer and TF-IDF features, our model achieved a F1 score of 0.45 and an accuracy of 0.73 for the development dataset. In the case of the SVM classifier with TF-IDF vectorizer, the model attained a a F1 score of 0.42 and an accuracy of 0.72 for the development dataset. For the test dataset SGD classifier achieved 0.44 F1 score and SVM achieved 0.35 F1 score. Our submission achieved the 5th rank in the test evaluation for SGD and 8th rank for SVM.

6 Inferences

Based on the observation, it can be noted that the datasets used in the study are relatively small, resulting in a limited number of training samples. Since the dataset is small, we identified that deep learning methods are not giving good results when

S.no	Feature extraction	Classifier	Precision	Recall	F1-Score	Accuracy
1	Count vectorizer	SGD	0.75	0.73	0.45	0.73
2	TF-IDF vectorizer	SGD	0.75	0.73	0.45	0.73
3	TF-IDF vectorizer	SVM	0.71	0.71	0.42	0.72
4	TF-IDF vectorizer	SVC	0.68	0.71	0.39	0.73

Table 2: Performance of the selected classifier models on Tamil-English using development data (With Re-sampling)

S.no	Feature extraction	Classifier	Precision	Recall	F1-Score	Accuracy
1	Count vectorizer	SGD	0.73	0.72	0.43	0.71
2	TF-IDF vectorizer	SGD	0.73	0.72	0.46	0.72
3	TF-IDF vectorizer	SVM	0.71	0.71	0.40	0.72
4	TF-IDF vectorizer	SVC	0.72	0.73	0.38	0.73

Table 3: Performance of the selected classifier models on Tamil-English using development data (Without Re-sampling)

compared to ML models. Furthermore, it is evident that both the Count and TF-IDF vectorizers exhibit a comparable accuracy rate. In summary, when comparing the SGD classifier and the SVM classifier, it is observed that the SGD classifier consistently achieves higher scores. Consequently, the SGD classifier can be considered as yielding the best results.

7 Conclusion and Future Work

In this study, we have performed a comprehensive analysis of different models for the DravidianLangTech@RANLP 2023 shared task focused on detecting abusive comments. We investigated the effectiveness of multiple classifiers on the preprocessed data by extracting relevant features. Our findings indicated that the SGD classifier produced comparable results using both vectorizers. Furthermore, we observed that the SVM classifier achieved a similar level of accuracy as the SGD classifier. In future, we have planned to increase the accuracy and F1-score by involving other feature extraction techniques and augmentation techniques. The potential challenges for further research in this field includes Multilingual and Multimodal Settings, Adversarial Attacks and Domain and Cultural Variations. The directions for further research includes User-Adaptive Models, Continuous Learning, Explainable AI and Real-Time Detection.

References

[1] Nobata, C., Tetreault, J., Thomas, A., Mehdad, Y., & Chang, Y. (2016). Abusive language detection in online user content. In Proceedings of the 25th International Conference on World Wide Web (pp. 145-153). ACM.

[2] Fortuna, P., Nunes, M. D., & Cardoso, N. (2018). An analysis of machine learning approaches for abusive language detection on Twitter. In Proceedings of the 9th International Conference on Social Media and Society (pp. 1-5). ACM.

[3] Djuric, N., Zhou, J., Morris, R. R., Grbovic, M., Radosavljevic, V., & Bhamidipati, N. (2015). Hate speech detection with comment embeddings. In Proceedings of the 24th International Conference on World Wide Web (pp. 29-30). ACM.

[4] Wulczyn, E., Thain, N., & Dixon, L. (2017). Ex machina: Personal attacks seen at scale. In Proceedings of the 26th International Conference on World Wide Web (pp. 1391-1399). ACM.

[5] Badjatiya, P., Gupta, S., Gupta, M., & Varma, V. (2017). Deep learning for hate speech detection in tweets. In Proceedings of the 26th International Conference on World Wide Web (pp. 759-760). ACM.

[6] Park, S., & Fung, P. (2017). One-step and two-step classification for abusive language detection on Twitter. In Proceedings of the 11th International Conference on Language Resources and Evaluation (LREC 2018) (pp. 1041-1048).

[7] Waseem, Z., & Hovy, D. (2016). Hateful symbols or hateful people? Predictive features for hate speech detection on Twitter. In Proceedings of the NAACL Student Research Workshop (pp. 88-93).

[8] Dadvar, M., Trieschnigg, D., de Jong, F., & Ordelman, R. (2013). Improving web search by detecting and assigning sentiment to query terms. Information Retrieval Journal, 16(5), 565-586.

[9] Qian, Y., Zhang, H., Li, J., Li, S., & Sun, X. (2018). Offensive tweet detection using convolutional neural networks. Future Generation Computer Systems, 88, 656-663.

[10] Bandyopadhyay, S., Malakar, S., Ganguly, N., & Mitra, P. (2019). Deep learning based abusive language detection in online social media platforms. arXiv preprint arXiv:1904.05772.

[11] Fortuna, P., Nunes, C., Sarmento, L. (2018). Abusive language detection on social media using lexicon-based approaches. In Proceedings of the International Conference Recent Advances in Natural Language Processing (pp. 291-299). INCOMA Ltd.

[12] Mathew, B., & D'Cunha, C. (2020). Hybrid feature-based detection of hate speech on social media using machine learning. IEEE Access, 8, 240354-240366.

[13] Davidson, T., Warmsley, D., Macy, M., Weber, I. (2017). Automated hate speech detection and the problem of offensive language. In Proceedings of the 11th International AAAI Conference on Web and Social Media (pp. 512-515). AAAI.

[14] Sivanaiah, R., Angel, S., Rajendram, S. M., & Mirnalinee, T. T. (2022, July). TechSSN at semeval-2022 task 5: Multimedia automatic misogyny identification using deep learning models. In Proceedings of the 16th International Workshop on Semantic Evaluation (SemEval-2022) (pp. 571-574).

[15] Suseelan, A., Rajalakshmi, S., Logesh, B., Harshini, S., Geetika, B., Dyaneswaran, S.,& Mirnalinee, T. T. (2019, June). TECHSSN at SemEval-2019 task 6: Identifying and categorizing offensive language in tweets using deep neural networks. In Proceedings of the 13th International Workshop on Semantic Evaluation (pp. 753-758).

[16] Priyadharshini, Ruba and Chakravarthi, Bharathi Raja and Cn, Subalalitha and Durairaj, Thenmozhi and Subramanian, Malliga and Shanmugavadivel, Kogilavani and U Hegde, Siddhanth and Kumaresan, Prasanna, Overview of Abusive Comment Detection in Tamil-ACL 2022, Association for Computational Linguistics (2022)

[17] Anusha Gowda, Fazlourrahman Balouchzahi, Hosahalli Shashirekha, and Grigori Sidorov. 2022. MUCIC@LT-EDI-ACL2022: Hope Speech Detection using Data Re-Sampling and 1D Conv-LSTM. In Proceedings of the Second Workshop on Language Technology for Equality, Diversity and Inclusion, pages 161–166, Dublin, Ireland. Association for Computational Linguistics.

DeepBlueAI@DravidianLangTech-RANLP 2023

Zhipeng Luo **Jiahui Wang**
DeepBlue Technology (Shanghai) Co., Ltd, Shanghai, China
{luozp, wangjh}@deepblueai.com

Abstract

This paper presents a study on the language understanding of the Dravidian languages. Three specific tasks related to text classification are focused on in this study, including abusive comment detection, sentiment analysis and fake news detection. The paper provides a detailed description of the tasks, including dataset information and task definitions, as well as the model architectures and training details used to tackle them. Finally, the competition results are presented, demonstrating the effectiveness of the proposed approach for handling these challenging NLP tasks in the context of the Dravidian languages.

1 Introduction

The field of natural language processing (NLP) has made significant progress in recent years, with the development of increasingly powerful models and techniques for understanding and analyzing human language. However, one major challenge that remains is the development of NLP systems that can effectively handle regional and under-resourced languages (Chakravarthi and Raja, 2020), which often lack the resources and support needed for effective NLP research. The Dravidian languages (Kolipakam et al., 2018) are one such family of languages that have received relatively little attention in the NLP community, despite their significant cultural and linguistic importance.

To address this gap, this paper focuses on the language understanding of the Dravidian languages, with a particular emphasis on five specific tasks related to text classification. These tasks include abusive comment detection, sentiment analysis and fake news detection.

As the Transformer model (Vaswani et al., 2017) gained popularity, various pretrained models have been proposed, including BERT (Devlin et al., 2019), RoBERTa (Liu et al., 2019), and the cross lingual pretrained model XLM-RoBERTa (Conneau et al., 2020), etc. Meanwhile, finetuning of pretrained language models has gradually become the standard approach of various natural language understanding tasks, including text classification, as demonstrated in this paper.

In this paper, we provide a detailed description of these tasks, including the dataset information and task definitions, as well as the model architectures and training details used to tackle them. We also present our competition results, demonstrating the effectiveness of our approach for handling these challenging NLP tasks in the context of the Dravidian languages.

2 Task Description

In this section, we describe the task definition and dataset of the 3 tasks we participated in.

2.1 Abusive Comment Detection in Tamil and Telugu

This task requires to indentify whether the given text is an abusive comment. Table 1 describes the dataset (Priyadharshini et al., 2022) information. The dataset contains 7429 samples in total, each sample contains a comment and a label that represents whether it is an abusive comment. The dataset includes 8 label types in total, including misandry, counter-speech, misogyny, xenophobia, hope-speech, homophobia, transphobic, and none-of-the-above.

2.2 Sentiment Analysis in Tamil and Tulu

Given a Youtube comment, this task requires to classify the comment's emotions. Table 2 & 3 describe the provided datasets (Chakravarthi and Raja, 2020) (Hegde et al., 2022) of Tamil and Tulu languages respectively. Both datasets contain Dravidian texts mixed with English collected from social media. The two datasets contains 37775 and

Third Workshop on Speech and Language Technologies for Dravidian Languages, pages 171–175, Varna, Bulgaria, Sep 7, 2023.
https://doi.org/10.26615/978-954-452-085-4_023

Table 1: data distribution of Abusive Comment Detection task.

Label	Count	Percentage (%)
None-of-the-above	4632	62.35
Misandry	1048	14.10
Counter-speech	443	5.96
Xenophobia	367	4.94
Hope-Speech	266	3.58
Misogyny	261	3.51
Homophobia	215	2.89
Transphobic	197	2.65

7238 samples respectively and each contains 4 sentiment labels, including positive, neutral, negative and mixed feelings.

Table 2: data distribution of Sentiment Analysis task of Tamil language.

Label	Count	Percentage (%)
positive	22327	59.11
unknown state	6239	16.52
negative	4751	12.58
mixed feelings	4458	11.80

Table 3: data distribution of Sentiment Analysis task of tulu language.

Label	Count	Percentage (%)
positive	3487	48.18
neutral	1921	26.54
negative	736	10.17
mixed feeling	1094	15.11

2.3 Fake News Detection in Dravidian Languages

Given a comment from Youtube, this task requires to indentify whether it comes from original or fake news. Table 4 describes the dataset information. The dataset contains 4072 samples in total, each sample has an input comment, and a corresponding label. Label 0 means it comes from fake news, and label 1 means original news.

3 Models & Training

3.1 Model architecture

In order to ensure consistency and simplicity across the different tasks we participated in, we used the same model architecture for all five tasks. Specifically, we employed the XLM-RoBERTa (Conneau et al., 2020) as the pretrained language model, which has been shown to achieve state-of-the-art performance on a range of natural language understanding tasks.

Table 4: data distribution of Fake News Detection task.

label	count	percentage (%)
original	2067	50.76
fake	2005	49.24

For each task, we extracted the representation of the [CLS] token, which is a special token added to the input sequence by the BERT family of models, and passed it through an additional linear layer. This final layer was used to generate the task-specific predictions, which were then compared to the ground truth labels using the softmax cross entropy loss function.

Adopting a consistent model architecture across all tasks allowed us to focus on the differences in the data and task-specific nuances, rather than spending time optimizing different model architectures for each task. It also enables us to easily analyze the generalizability of our approach.

3.2 Adversarial Training

Adversarial training (Miyato et al., 2015; Goodfellow et al., 2014; Miyato et al., 2016) is a technique used in machine learning to improve the robustness of models against adversarial attacks. Adversarial attacks are inputs that are specifically crafted to deceive the model and cause it to misclassify or produce incorrect outputs. Adversarial training involves training the model on both normal and adversarial examples, with the goal of making the model more resistant to adversarial attacks.

Word embeddings are an important component of Transformer models, but they can be vulnerable to overfitting and instability. To address these issues, Miyato et al. (2016) have proposed adding perturbations to the embedding layer during training. This technique, known as Fast Gradient Method (FGM), has been shown to improve the stability and generalization of word representations, leading to better performance on unseen data. By introducing small random perturbations to the embeddings, the model learns to be more robust to variations in the input data and can better capture the underlying semantic and syntactic relationships between words.

3.3 Ensembling

Ensembling is a widely-used technique in machine learning competitions, and k-fold cross-validation is a common approach used during training to evaluate and improve model performance.

In k-fold cross-validation, the dataset is randomly split into k parts, with one part used as the validation set and the remaining parts used for training. This process is repeated k times, with each part used once for validation. During testing, the model predictions for the test set are obtained from all k models trained in the cross-validation process, and the predicted label for each sample is determined by selecting the most common label among the k predictions. This ensemble approach has been shown to improve model accuracy and generalization, and is widely used in various deep learning applications.

4 Experiments

This section provides a detailed account of the training settings used in our experiments.

4.1 Abusive Comment Detection in Tamil and Telugu

The task is composed of three subtasks, each with its own unique challenges. To effectively address these challenges, we employed a variety of strategies and techniques throughout our work.

For the Tamil and Tamil-English subtasks, we combined the training data and trained our models based on the F1 score on the validation set. By using this approach, we were able to develop models that performed well on both tasks and effectively leverage the available data. For the Telugu subtask, we solely used the training data provided for the task, as the availability of data for this subtask was more limited.

In addition to our approach to training data, we employed a number of techniques to improve the robustness and generalizability of our models. Specifically, we utilized 10-fold cross-validation for all subtasks, ensuring that our models were validated on unseen data and able to generalize well to new data. Additionally, we employed ensembling techniques to combine the strengths of multiple models and achieve superior performance. These techniques helped to mitigate overfitting and ensure that our models were robust and accurate.

4.2 Sentiment Analysis in Tamil and Tulu

For the sentiment analysis task in Tamil and Tulu, we investigated different training approaches. Initially, we attempted to train 10 models using 10-fold cross validation by merging the two datasets together, resulting in an F1 score of 51.4. Subsequently, we treated the Tamil and Tulu datasets as two seperate tasks, each consisting of training 10 models using 10-fold cross-validation. This approach yielded a slightly higher F1 score of 51.7 and allowed us to better tailor our models to the specific characteristics and nuances of each language. To further improve the performance and robustness of our models, we also utilized ensembling techniques.

4.3 Fake News Detection in Dravidian Languages

Since the dataset for this task only consisted of Malayalam language, we faced the challenge of limited data availability. To address this challenge, we adopted a strategy of training multiple models using 10-fold cross-validation. This approach allowed us to effectively leverage the available data and improve the robustness and generalizability of our models.

Specifically, we divided the dataset into 10 subsets and trained 10 models, each using a different subset for validation, while the remaining subsets were used for training. By doing this, we were able to train our models on the entire dataset while also ensuring that our models were validated on unseen data. This approach helped us to overcome the challenge of limited data availability and ensured that our models were able to generalize well to new data.

Overall, our strategy of training multiple models using 10-fold cross-validation proved to be effective in leveraging the limited data available for this task and improving the generalizability and robustness of our models.

5 Competition Results

Our team participated in this competition and achieved promising results, earning 4 first place rankings as well as 1 second place, as shown in Table 5, 6, 7. These outstanding results demonstrate the effectiveness of our innovative methods. We attribute our success to the utilization of various cutting-edge techniques, such as adversarial training, 10-fold cross-validation, and ensembling. Our use of adversarial training enabled our model to better handle noisy and adversarial inputs, while 10-fold cross-validation helped us to improve the generalizability of our model. Additionally, ensembling multiple models allowed us to combine the strengths of different models and achieve superior performance.These techniques allowed us to develop a robust and accurate model that performed exceptionally well on the competition tasks.

Table 5: F1 Scores and Rankings for Abusive Comment Detection in Tamil and Telugu

Dataset	F1-score (macro)	Rank
Tamil	0.26	7
Tamil-English	0.55	1
Telugu-English	0.7318	2

Table 6: F1 Scores and Rankings for Sentiment Analysis in Tamil and Tulu

Dataset	F1-score (macro)	Rank
Tamil	0.32	1
Tulu	0.542	1

Table 7: F1 Scores and Rankings for Fake News Detection in Dravidian Languages

Dataset	F1-score (macro)	Rank
Malayalam	0.9	1

6 Conclusion

To summarize, this paper focused on five specific text classification tasks related to the Dravidian languages, including abusive comment detection, sentiment analysis and fake news detection.

With the increasing popularity of Transformer-based models such as BERT, RoBERTa, and XLM-RoBERTa, fine-tuning of pre-trained language models has become a standard approach to various natural language understanding tasks.

The paper provided detailed descriptions of the tasks, dataset information and definitions, as well as the model architectures and training details. Our team achieved impressive results in the competition. Our innovative approaches, such as adversarial training, 10-fold cross-validation, and ensembling, played a significant role in our success.

Overall, our findings demonstrate the potential of natural language processing in addressing challenging tasks in the context of the Dravidian languages.

References

Asoka Chakravarthi and Bharathi Raja. 2020. *Leveraging orthographic information to improve machine translation of under-resourced languages.* Ph.D. thesis, NUI Galway.

Alexis Conneau, Kartikay Khandelwal, Naman Goyal, Vishrav Chaudhary, Guillaume Wenzek, Francisco Guzmán, Édouard Grave, Myle Ott, Luke Zettlemoyer, and Veselin Stoyanov. 2020. Unsupervised cross-lingual representation learning at scale. In *Proceedings of the 58th Annual Meeting of the Association for Computational Linguistics*, pages 8440–8451.

Jacob Devlin, Ming-Wei Chang, Kenton Lee, and Kristina Toutanova. 2019. BERT: Pre-training of deep bidirectional transformers for language understanding. In *Proceedings of the 2019 Conference of the North American Chapter of the Association for Computational Linguistics: Human Language Technologies, Volume 1 (Long and Short Papers)*, pages 4171–4186, Minneapolis, Minnesota. Association for Computational Linguistics.

Ian J Goodfellow, Jonathon Shlens, and Christian Szegedy. 2014. Explaining and harnessing adversarial examples. *arXiv preprint arXiv:1412.6572.*

Asha Hegde, Mudoor Devadas Anusha, Sharal Coelho, Hosahalli Lakshmaiah Shashirekha, and Bharathi Raja Chakravarthi. 2022. Corpus creation for sentiment analysis in code-mixed Tulu text. In *Proceedings of the 1st Annual Meeting of the ELRA/ISCA Special Interest Group on Under-Resourced Languages*, pages 33–40, Marseille, France. European Language Resources Association.

Vishnupriya Kolipakam, Fiona M Jordan, Michael Dunn, Simon J Greenhill, Remco Bouckaert, Russell D Gray, and Annemarie Verkerk. 2018. A bayesian phylogenetic study of the dravidian language family. *Royal Society open science*, 5(3):171504.

Yinhan Liu, Myle Ott, Naman Goyal, Jingfei Du, Mandar Joshi, Danqi Chen, Omer Levy, Mike Lewis, Luke Zettlemoyer, and Veselin Stoyanov. 2019. Roberta: A robustly optimized bert pretraining approach. *arXiv preprint arXiv:1907.11692.*

Takeru Miyato, Andrew M Dai, and Ian Goodfellow. 2016. Adversarial training methods for semi-supervised text classification. *arXiv preprint arXiv:1605.07725.*

Takeru Miyato, Shin-ichi Maeda, Masanori Koyama, Ken Nakae, and Shin Ishii. 2015. Distributional smoothing with virtual adversarial training. *arXiv preprint arXiv:1507.00677.*

Ruba Priyadharshini, Bharathi Raja Chakravarthi, Subalalitha Cn, Thenmozhi Durairaj, Malliga Subramanian, Kogilavani Shanmugavadivel, Siddhanth U Hegde, and Prasanna Kumaresan. 2022. Overview of abusive comment detection in Tamil-ACL 2022. In *Proceedings of the Second Workshop on Speech and Language Technologies for Dravidian Languages*, pages 292–298, Dublin, Ireland. Association for Computational Linguistics.

Ashish Vaswani, Noam Shazeer, Niki Parmar, Jakob Uszkoreit, Llion Jones, Aidan N Gomez, Ł ukasz Kaiser, and Illia Polosukhin. 2017. Attention is all you need. In *Advances in Neural Information Processing Systems*, volume 30. Curran Associates, Inc.

Selam@DravidianLangTech:Sentiment Analysis of Code-Mixed Dravidian Texts using SVM Classification

Selam Abitte Kanta
Instituto Politécnico Nacional
Centro de Investigación en Computación
selaminadady300@gmail.com

Grigori Sidorov
Instituto Politécnico Nacional
Centro de Investigación en Computación
sidorov@cic.ipn.mx

Abstract

Sentiment analysis in code-mixed text written in Dravidian languages. Specifically, Tamil-English and Tulu-English. This paper describes the system paper of the RANLP-2023 shared task. The goal of this shared task is to develop systems that accurately classify the sentiment polarity of code-mixed comments and posts. be provided with development, training, and test data sets containing code-mixed text in Tamil-English and Tulu-English. The task involves message-level polarity classification, to classify YouTube comments into positive, negative, neutral, or mixed emotions. This Code-Mix was compiled by RANLP-2023 organizers from posts on social media. We use classification techniques SVM and achieve an F1 score of 0.147 for Tamil-English and 0.518 for Tulu-English.

1 Introduction

Social media platforms have become significant sources of user-generated content, providing a wealth of information about people's opinions, emotions, and attitudes. Sentiment analysis, a subfield of natural language processing, aims to automatically classify the sentiment or emotional tone expressed in textual data. Currently, in the area of NLP, different researchers are developing different NLP applications in code-mixed datasets. Some of the applications are code-mixed sentiments analysis

which involves identifying subjective opinions or emotional responses, has gained significant attention in both academia and industry over the past two decades. One emerging challenge in sentiment analysis is the detection of sentiment in social media texts, particularly in Dravidian languages, where code-mixing is prevalent (Shahiki Tash et al., 2022). Social media platforms have become more integrated into this digital era and have impacted various people's perceptions of networking and socializing (Tonja et al., 2022) machine translation detection, sentiment analysis and language identification (Gemeda Yigezu et al., 2022).

Code-mixing refers to the phenomenon where multiple languages or language varieties are used within a single conversation or text. This linguistic practice is prevalent in multilingual societies, particularly in regions where diverse languages coexist. In the context of Dravidian languages, such as Tamil and English, code-mixing has gained prominence on social media platforms, where users freely express their thoughts using a mixture of both languages. Code-mixing or code-switching is the alternation between two or more languages at the level of the document, paragraph, comments, sentence, phrase, word, or morpheme. It is a distinctive aspect of conversation or dialogue in bilingual and multilingual societies (Barman et al., 2014)

As the classification model for sentiment analysis, we propose using the Support Vector Machine (SVM) algorithm. SVM has proven effective in various natural language processing tasks, including sentiment analysis (Mullen and Collier, 2004).

By utilizing SVM, we aim to leverage its ability to capture complex patterns in text data and its flexibility in handling high-dimensional feature spaces. In social media, low-resourced languages such as Tamil and Malayalam have been increasingly used along with English (Najiha and Romadhony, 2023)

The contribution of this research lies in advancing the understanding of sentiment expression in code-mixed scenarios on social media, within the context of Dravidian languages of Tamil-English and Tulu-English language. Accurate identification of sentiment polarity at the message level provides valuable insights into user emotions and attitudes in code-mixed interactions. also known as opinion mining,(Nandwani and Verma, 2021) is a natural language processing technique that aims to determine the sentiment expressed in a piece of text (Liu et al., 2010).

By applying sentiment analysis to code-mixed

Third Workshop on Speech and Language Technologies for Dravidian Languages, pages 176–179, Varna, Bulgaria, Sep 7, 2023.
https://doi.org/10.26615/978-954-452-085-4_024

interactions, researchers and analysts can gain a deeper understanding of how users feel and their attitudes toward specific topics or situations. accurate identification of sentiment polarity in code-mixed interactions can provide valuable insights into user emotions and attitudes(Saura et al., 2023). Advancements in code-mixed sentiment analysis can contribute to a better understanding of user sentiment in multilingual communities, social media, customer support, and other domains where code-mixing is prevalent(Agüero-Torales et al., 2021).

The findings of this research will facilitate the development of more robust sentiment analysis techniques for analyzing multilingual social media data, enabling improved understanding and interpretation of user sentiments across diverse linguistic contexts(Hegde et al.).

2 Related Work

Along with language-specific preprocessing techniques, the implemented model used sub-word level representations to incorporate features at the morpheme level, the smallest meaningful unit of any language.

It was evaluated by weighted average F1-score, the subword level approach achieved the 5th highest score 47 in the Tamil task, and the 12th rank in the Malayalam task (Shahiki Tash et al., 2022). People use code-mixing because it is much easier and more effective to express their feelings, grab the attention of others, and are not fluent in one of the languages used (Wongso et al., 2022). As a multilingual country, people commonly mix or switch from their regional or native language to Indonesian (Najiha and Romadhony, 2023). It is frequently heard in daily conversations in the neighborhood or on social media. To improve abusive language detection in English social media communications, (Felbo et al., 2017) used the 'deepmoji' technique, which was first announced in 2017(Chakravarthi et al., 2023).

This strategy is primarily based on pretraining a neural network model for offensive language classification using emojis as poorly supervised training labels. A lexical syntactic feature architecture was proposed to strike a balance between identifying offensive content and potentially offensive users in social media (Luo et al., 2015) the challenge of cross-lingual classification due to linguistic differences between languages. mentions that the SVM and KNN algorithms were effective for this task, showcasing the importance of selecting appropriate algorithms for different languages(Ahani et al.)

This data on polarity can help in understanding public opinion. Furthermore, including sentiment analysis can improve the performance of tasks such as recommendation system (Andrew and Gao, 2007) to train some machine learning classifiers with various syntax-based n-gram features.

3 Task A Description and Dataset

The shared task on sentiment analysis in Tamil and Tulu focuses on message-level polarity classification. The dataset provided for this task consists of code-mixed text in Dravidian languages, namely Tamil-English and Tulu-English. Tamil-English code-switched, sentiment-annotated corpus containing 15,744 comment posts from YouTube.(Chakravarthi et al., 2020). and the code-mixed Tulu annotated corpus of 7,171 YouTube comments is created.(Hegde et al., 2022)

The comments and posts in the dataset may contain more than one sentence, but the average sentence length across the corpora is one. Each comment and post is annotated with sentiment polarity at the message level, indicating whether it expresses a positive, negative, neutral, or mixed emotional sentiment.

These datasets reflect the real-world scenarios of social media texts, exhibiting class imbalance issues commonly encountered in sentiment analysis tasks. The datasets provided in this task will facilitate the exploration of innovative approaches and techniques for sentiment analysis in multilingual and multicultural contexts.

4 Methods

For sentiment analysis tasks in code-mixed comments and posts in Tamil-English and Tulu-English, we propose employing the Support Vector Machines (SVM) model as the classification technique. SVM has proven effective in various natural language processing tasks, including sentiment analysis, and has demonstrated robustness in handling high-dimensional feature spaces.

4.1 Feature Engineering

To represent the textual data as numerical features suitable for SVM classification, we will explore various feature extraction techniques. This may include traditional approaches such as bag-of-words (BoW), term frequency-inverse document frequency (TF-IDF), or more advanced methods like word embeddings (e.g., Word2Vec or GloVe) or contextual embeddings (e.g., BERT or Roberta). By representing the text as feature vectors, we can capture the important information relevant to sentiment analysis.

4.2 Model Construction

we trained the SVM model using the labeled training dataset. The SVM algorithm aims to find an optimal hyperplane that separates the different sentiment classes in the feature space. By adjusting the hyperparameters of the SVM model, such as the kernel function and regularization parameters, we can fine-tune the model's performance.

Such as accuracy, precision, recall, and F1 score. Cross-validation techniques like k-fold cross-validation may be employed to ensure the robustness of the results. Additionally, we will analyze the model's performance on the development dataset to identify potential areas for improvement. Parameters that were used in SVM and TF-IDF were as follows. For the SVM classifier, we used C=0.1, kernel='poly', degree=3, and gamma='scale'. For the TF-IDF vectorizer, we used analyzer='char_wb', ngram_range=(2,6), min_df=0, and norm='l1'.

5 Results

In the shared task, a Support Vector Machine (SVM) model was employed for message-level polarity classification of code-mixed text in Tamil-English and Tulu-English. The evaluation metric used was the F1 score, which provides a measure of the model's performance across all sentiment classes. The results obtained for the SVM model on the provided datasets were as follows in Table 1.

Run	language	F1-score
Run1	Tamil	0.147
Run1	Tulu	0.518

Table 1: F1-Score

6 Conclusion

This study shows how different languages may be identified in code-mix data using a classifier that uses two algorithms, SVM and TF-IDF. The first technique produces better results, with the best weighted average F1-score of 0.147 and 0.518.

Acknowledgments

The work was done with partial support from the Mexican Government through grant A1-S-47854 of CONACYT, Mexico, grants 20232138, 20232080, and 20231567 of the Secretaría de Investigación y Posgrado of the Instituto Politécnico Nacional, Mexico. The authors thank the CONACYT for the computing resources brought to them through the Plataforma de Aprendizaje Profundo para Tecnologías del Lenguaje of the Laboratorio de Supercómputo of the INAOE, Mexico, and acknowledge the support of Microsoft through the Microsoft Latin America Masters Award.

References

Marvin M Agüero-Torales, José I Abreu Salas, and Antonio G López-Herrera. 2021. Deep learning and multilingual sentiment analysis on social media data: An overview. *Applied Soft Computing*, 107:107373.

Zahra Ahani, Grigori Sidorov, Olga Kolesnikova, and Alexander Gelbukh. Hope speech detection from text using tf-idf features and machine learning algorithms.

Galen Andrew and Jianfeng Gao. 2007. Scalable training of L1-regularized log-linear models. In *Proceedings of the 24th International Conference on Machine Learning*, pages 33–40.

Utsab Barman, Amitava Das, Joachim Wagner, and Jennifer Foster. 2014. Code mixing: A challenge for language identification in the language of social media. In *Proceedings of the First Workshop on Computational Approaches to Code Switching*, pages 13–23, Doha, Qatar. Association for Computational Linguistics.

Bharathi Raja Chakravarthi, Manoj Balaji Jagadeeshan, Vasanth Palanikumar, and Ruba Priyadharshini. 2023. Offensive language identification in dravidian languages using mpnet and cnn. *International Journal of Information Management Data Insights*, 3(1):100151.

Bharathi Raja Chakravarthi, Vigneshwaran Muralidaran, Ruba Priyadharshini, and John P McCrae. 2020. Corpus creation for sentiment analysis in code-mixed tamil-english text. *arXiv preprint arXiv:2006.00206*.

Bjarke Felbo, Alan Mislove, Anders Søgaard, Iyad Rahwan, and Sune Lehmann. 2017. Using millions of emoji occurrences to learn any-domain representations for detecting sentiment, emotion and sarcasm. *arXiv preprint arXiv:1708.00524*.

Mesay Gemeda Yigezu, Atnafu Lambebo Tonja, Olga Kolesnikova, Moein Shahiki Tash, Grigori Sidorov, and Alexander Gelbukh. 2022. Word level language identification in code-mixed Kannada-English texts using deep learning approach. In *Proceedings of the*

19th International Conference on Natural Language Processing (ICON): Shared Task on Word Level Language Identification in Code-mixed Kannada-English Texts, pages 29–33, IIIT Delhi, New Delhi, India. Association for Computational Linguistics.

Asha Hegde, Mudoor Devadas Anusha, Sharal Coelho, Hosahalli Lakshmaiah Shashirekha, and Bharathi Raja Chakravarthi. 2022. Corpus creation for sentiment analysis in code-mixed tulu text. In *Proceedings of the 1st Annual Meeting of the ELRA/ISCA Special Interest Group on Under-Resourced Languages*, pages 33–40.

Asha Hegde, Bharathi Raja Chakravarthi, Hosahalli Lakshmaiah Shashirekha, Rahul Ponnusamy, SUBALALITHA CN, Lavanya S K, Thenmozhi D, Martha Karunakar, Shreya Shreeram, and Sarah" Aymen. Findings of the shared task on sentiment analysis in tamil and tulu code-mixed text.

Bing Liu et al. 2010. Sentiment analysis and subjectivity. *Handbook of natural language processing*, 2(2010):627–666.

A-Li Luo, Yong-Heng Zhao, Gang Zhao, Li-Cai Deng, Xiao-Wei Liu, Yi-Peng Jing, Gang Wang, Hao-Tong Zhang, Jian-Rong Shi, Xiang-Qun Cui, et al. 2015. The first data release (dr1) of the lamost regular survey. *Research in Astronomy and Astrophysics*, 15(8):1095.

Tony Mullen and Nigel Collier. 2004. Sentiment analysis using support vector machines with diverse information sources. In *Proceedings of the 2004 conference on empirical methods in natural language processing*, pages 412–418.

Hajarot Najiha and Ade Romadhony. 2023. Sentiment analysis on indonesian-sundanese code-mixed data. In *2023 IEEE 8th International Conference for Convergence in Technology (I2CT)*, pages 1–7.

Pansy Nandwani and Rupali Verma. 2021. A review on sentiment analysis and emotion detection from text. *Social Network Analysis and Mining*, 11(1):81.

Jose Ramon Saura, Daniel Palacios-Marqués, and Domingo Ribeiro-Soriano. 2023. Privacy concerns in social media ugc communities: Understanding user behavior sentiments in complex networks. *Information Systems and e-Business Management*, pages 1–21.

M. Shahiki Tash, Z. Ahani, A.l. Tonja, M. Gemeda, N. Hussain, and O. Kolesnikova. 2022. Word level language identification in code-mixed Kannada-English texts using traditional machine learning algorithms. In *Proceedings of the 19th International Conference on Natural Language Processing (ICON): Shared Task on Word Level Language Identification in Code-mixed Kannada-English Texts*, pages 25–28, IIIT Delhi, New Delhi, India. Association for Computational Linguistics.

Atnafu Lambebo Tonja, Mesay Gemeda Yigezu, Olga Kolesnikova, Moein Shahiki Tash, Grigori Sidorov, and Alexander Gelbuk. 2022. Transformer-based model for word level language identification in code-mixed kannada-english texts. *arXiv preprint arXiv:2211.14459*.

Wilson Wongso, Henry Lucky, and Derwin Suhartono. 2022. Pre-trained transformer-based language models for sundanese. *Journal of Big Data*, 9(1):39.

LIDOMA@DravidianLangTech: Convolutional Neural Networks for Studying Correlation Between Lexical Features and Sentiment Polarity in Tamil and Tulu Languages

Moein Shahiki-Tash and **Jesús Armenta-Segura** and **Zahra Ahani** and **Olga Kolesnikova** and **Grigori Sidorov** and **Alexander Gelbukh**
Instituto Politécnico Nacional,
Centro de Investigación en Computación
Mexico City, Mexico.
{mshahikit2022, jarmentas2022, zahani2023, kolesnikova, sidorov, gelbukh} @cic.ipn.mx

Abstract

With the prevalence of code-mixing among speakers of Dravidian languages, DravidianLangTech proposed the shared task on Sentiment Analysis in Tamil and Tulu at RANLP 2023. This paper presents the submission of LIDOMA, which proposes a methodology that combines lexical features and Convolutional Neural Networks (CNNs) to address the challenge. A fine-tuned 6-layered CNN model is employed, achieving macro F1 scores of 0.542 and 0.199 for Tulu and Tamil, respectively.

1 Introduction

In recent years, there has been a significant surge of interest in sentiment analysis on social media platforms for Dravidian languages. The linguistically diverse and multicultural environments in which these languages are spoken have contributed to the prevalence of a linguistic phenomenon known as code-mixing. Code-mixing refers to the occurrence of multiple languages within a single document or utterance (E. Ojo et al., 2022). This phenomenon is particularly prominent in written texts, where non-native scripts and hybrid words combine elements from more than one language.

The Shared Task on Sentiment Analysis in Tamil and Tulu, proposed by DravidianLangTech at RANLP 2023 (B et al., 2023; Hegde et al., 2023), aims to address the challenges associated with sentiment analysis in code-mixed text. This shared task seeks to introduce a new gold standard corpus specifically designed for sentiment analysis in the context of Tamil-English and Tulu-English code-mixing language. Moreover, their dataset (Chakravarthi et al., 2020; Hegde et al., 2022) also has class imbalance problems depicting real-world scenarios.

The main focus of the proposed approach is to identify sentiment polarity in code-mixed comments and posts extracted from social media platforms. These comments and posts often contains more than one sentence, making the sentiment analysis task more complex.

In order to tackle the proposed shared tasks, this paper presents an approach that utilizes lexical features and convolutional neural networks (CNNs) (Fukushima, 1980; LeCun et al., 1989). Lexical features have demonstrated a strong correlation with various pragmatic phenomena, including sentiment analysis tasks such as hope and hate speech detection (Dowlagar and Mamidi, 2021; Balouchzahi et al., 2023). They have also been effective in other pragmatic tasks such as user preferences predictions in entertainment domains (Armenta-Segura and Sidorov, 2023). Additionally, lexical features have shown significant relevance in sentiment analysis when code-mixing is involved, as demonstrated in (E. Ojo et al., 2022) with Kannada and English languages.

On the other hand, CNNs have proven to be effective in detecting relevant features associated with sentiments across different classes (Shahiki-Tash et al., 2023), which is the reason why they were employed on this work. The presented model consists of a 6-layered CNN with the following structure: The first layer generates an embedding from a bag of words vectorization. The second and third layers are convolutional layers designed to learn the lexical features that have the strongest relationship with the labeling of each sample, which in this particular case are *positive*, *negative*, *neutral*, and *mixed feelings*. The fourth and fifth layers help prevent overfitting and reduce the dimensionality of the output by fine-tuning the lexical feature extraction using max pooling (Yamaguchi et al., 1990). Finally, the sixth layer utilizes a sigmoid ac-

Third Workshop on Speech and Language Technologies for Dravidian Languages, pages 180–185, Varna, Bulgaria, Sep 7, 2023.
https://doi.org/10.26615/978-954-452-085-4_025

tivation function to relate the learned features with the binary golden label. The achieved F1 scores were 0.542 for the Tulu-English dataset and 0.199 for the Tamil-English dataset.

The structure of this paper is as follows: in Section 2 it is described some state-of-the-art works on sentiment polarity detection. In Section 3, the methodology is detailed. In Section 4, it is provided a brief description of both datasets, and the experimental workflow is outlined. In Section 5, it is discussed the results of the experiments. Finally, in Section 6, the paper is concluded.

2 Related Work

Sentiment polarity analysis is considered one of the pioneering tasks in computational sentiment analysis. One of the earliest approaches in this field are the General Inquirer (Stone and Hunt, 1963), which is a 1961 IBM system capable to perform content analysis for behavioral sciences, most particular pattern detection in text for categorizing words according to their semantics, related to positive or negative sentiments. In 1997, a most focused approach was proposed with the system Smokey (Spertus, 1997), designed to detect abusive messages by using a rule-based approach to identify offensive language and contexts.

Following on the line of negative sentiment detection, in (Warner and Hirschberg, 2012), the authors proposed a lexicon-based approach for hate speech detection. Their approach focused on analyzing the sense in which selected words were used in sentences to identify hateful or offensive content, making the task close similar to word sense disambiguation. However, they discovered that this hypothesis is vulnerable when faced with incomplete datasets, especially in cases where a word only appears in one type of speech.

On the other hand, in the domain of positive speech, a notable line of research is the peace speech line initiated in (Palakodety et al., 2019b,a), where the authors primarily focused on analyzing peace-oriented discourse, particularly in the context of a conflict between Pakistan and India.

Furthermore, in (Chakravarthi, 2020), the authors focuses more towards the themes of equality, diversity, and inclusion. Notably, Chakravarthi also organized a series of shared tasks (Chakravarthi et al., 2022; Chakravarthi and Muralidaran, 2021), where team LIDOMA utilized a Convolutional Neural Network (CNN) to address the specified task (Shahiki-Tash et al., 2023). This model is a variation to the model presented in this paper.

About code-mixing detection, several computational approaches have been done to address the task in languages from India. For instance, in (Shekhar et al., 2020), the authors worked on code-mixing between Hindi and English, presenting a methodology for language identification in a dataset comprising Facebook, Twitter, and WhatsApp messages. In (Patwa et al., 2020), the authors proposed a shared task at SemEval-2020, in which team LIMSI_UPV (Banerjee et al., 2020) proposed a recurrent convolutional neural network architecture to address the task. In (Ansari et al., 2021), the authors expanded this line by incorporating Urdu into the analysis and utilizing transformer models with attention mechanisms, specifically employing BERT models.

In (Yasir et al., 2021), the authors considered code-mixing involving Saraiki and Bengali. They employed recurrent neural networks and word vectorizations to address the task of language identification in code-mixed texts.

In (Dutta, 2022), the author proposed a setting that aligns closely with the shared tasks mentioned earlier, but with a focus on English-Hindi and English-Bengali code-mixing. Additionally, she introduced an index to measure the level of mixing within the corpora, providing insights into the degree of code-mixing present in the data.

Furthermore, in (E. Ojo et al., 2022), the authors proposed an n-gram-based approach to tackle the task of language identification in Kannada-English code-mixed texts.

3 Methodology

Diving further in the structure outlined in the introduction, the overall followed procedure is explained now, along with the used hiperparameters.

3.1 Preprocessing

All samples written in the latin alphabet were preprocessed by lowercasing and removing special characters. All samples containing kannadian, Tamil and Tulu alphabet characters were letting intact. All URL patterns were removed in all samples. This process helped to enhance the results due to the noise reduction, as in (Shahiki-Tash et al., 2023). After that, word-based tokenization was performed creating a Bag-of-Words representation, ready to be feeded into the first layer of the 6-

layered CNN (see Figure 1 for a summary and an example).

3.2 Layers of the network

The first layer of the CNN embeds the input tokens into a dense vector representation, capturing semantic relationships between them, in a straightforward standard way to convert text into vectors. Concretely, it maps the bag-of-words tokens into 32-dimentional dense vectors. The layer allows a maximum of 2000 features and processes sequences with a maximum length of 40 tokens. Additionally, it applies L_2 regularization with a strength of 0.0005 to the embedding weights. All these hyperparameters were determined through a trial and error fine-tuning process, picking the ones who brought better results. In general, all hyperparameters for every layer in this model were determined in this same fashion.

The second layer is convolutional with small kernels of size 3, allowing it to capture better local parameters. Also, it consists of 128 filters. The kernel regularizer was L_2, with a strength of 0.0005 to the output weights. To prevent overfitting, a bias regularizer is also applied, which is the same as the one applied to the kernels. The chosen activation function for this layer is ReLu (Fukushima, 1969), which maps a value x to $Max\{0, x\}$.

The third layer is similar to the second, but it employs half the number of filters. We included it aiming to refine the output of the second layer.

The fourth layer is a Flatten layer. Its purpose is to reshape the input data to a flat one-dimensional representation, required for the employment of a dense layer.

The fifth layer is a 32-dimensioned dense layer with ReLu as activation function. It also includes a L_2 regularizer for the kernels and a bias reguarizer, both with strenght of 0.001. Its function is to convert the vector into a suitable string able to become a prediction in the last layer.

Finally, the output layer is 4-dimentional and has a sigmoid activation function (Cramer, 2002; Verhulst, 1845). It also includes the same regularizers as the previous dense layer.

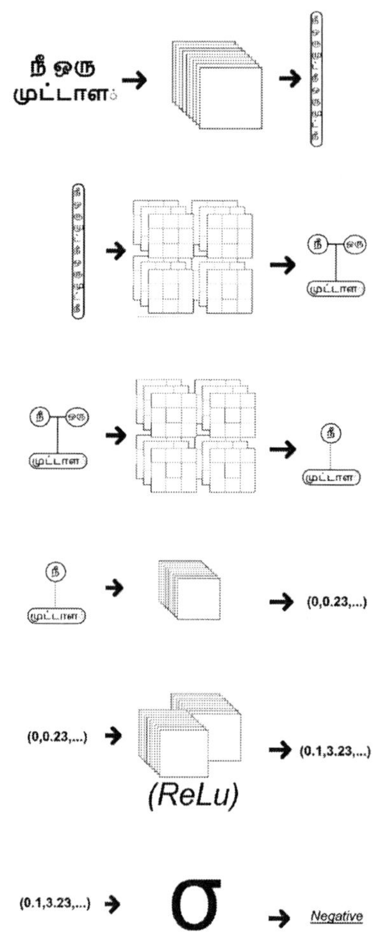

Figure 1: From top to down, ilustrations of the six layers of our CNN model. The example text can be written in latin alphabet as *Nī oru muṭṭāḷ*, which means *you are an idiot* in Tamil. In the first layer, the tokenized text is converted into a dense vector. In the second and third layer, the 3×3 kernels extracts patterns relevant to the golden labels (in this example, represented as a link betweet the tokens *Nī* and *muṭṭāḷ -you* and *idiot-*). The fourth layer convert these patterns into a vector. The fifth layer uses ReLu and, finally, the sixth layer makes a prediction using the sigmoid function. The final output can be *positive*, *negative*, *neutral* and *mixed feelings*.

4 Experimental Setup

4.1 Data

The Tulu training set contains 6,457 samples with labels Positive, Neutral, Negative and Mixed Feelings. The Tamil training set contains 33,989 sam-

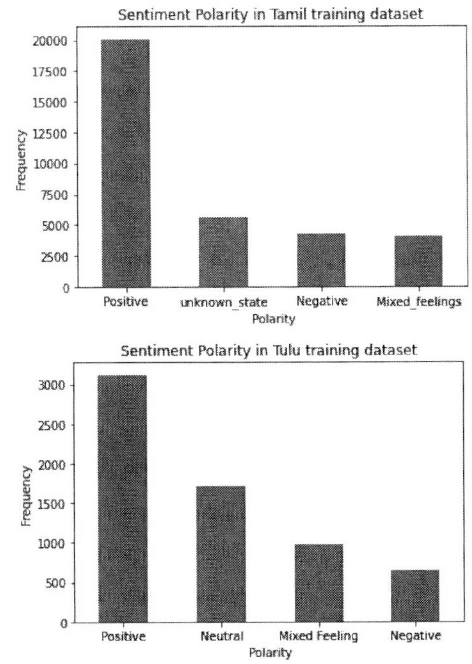

Figure 2: Label distribution among the training sets. Recall that Unknown State corresponds to Neutral in the Tamil training set.

Sample	Polarity
Vani bhojam fans hit like solli 500 like Vangida Vendiyathu than	Neutral
Ithu yethu maathiri illama puthu maathiyaala irukku	Positive
Wow! Back to Baasha mode. thalaivaaaa. petta paraakkkkk	Negative
Kaagam karaindhu koodi unnum, Manidham ennum moodar koodam koodi serdhu pagaimai kollum... Idil yaar uyarthinai yaar agrinai	Mixed Feelings

Table 1: Latin alphabet examples from the Tamil training sets.

ples with labels Positive, Unknown State (Neutral), Negative and Mixed Feelings. In Figure 2 it is shown the distribution of every sample, along with the precise number of samples for each class. In Table 2 it is shown examples per label in the Tulu training set. In Table 1 it is shown for the Tamil training set.

4.2 Experimental Workflow

Every dataset was splitted into a 75 : 25 ratio for training the model. The CNN was trained during 30 epochs.

5 Results

After the 30-epoch training, the model achieved a macro F1 score of 0.516 in the Tulu evaluation set, and 0.199 in the Tamil evaluation set. The most important factors for these results were the notable differences between kannada, Tamil, Tulu and latin alphabets, in which this network was designed, and the nature of the labelling: regardless previous experiences where variations of this CNN was employed, the datasets employed for this task includes the categories of Neutral and Mixed Feelings, while in the other sentiment analysis tasks the labelling was binary in terms of a single polarity,

Sample	Polarity
Bega 2 nd part padle	Neutral
Devdas kapikad no1	Positive
Enchi pankda comedy	Negative
Yan 4 class d uppunaga kallamundkur du thutina cha parka thandada suruta drama	Mixed Feelings

Table 2: Latin alphabet examples from the Tulu training sets

and not mixing it.

Another important factor was the balance of the dataset. As shown in Figure 2, there is a high imbalance in the dataset which led to a general low performance in the proposed methods, being macro F1-score of 0.32 the best for Tamil and 0.542 the best for Tulu, not so far of our results.

6 Conclusions

In this paper, it was presented the LIDOMA submission for the shared task on Sentiment Analysis in Tamil and Tulu, proposed by DravidianLangTech at RANLP2023. They employed CNN's, who have proven being effective in sentiment polarity tasks.

The proposed methodology involved the conversion of labels into categorical values, then basic preprocessing of the samples and finally the training of a 6-layered CNN. The findings highlight the complexities involved in handling non-balanced datasets along with the merge of polarities within the *Mixed Feelings* cathegory.

Future work will focus on adapt the CNN architecture to deal better with mixed cathegories, along with adding more steps of preprocessing adapted to kannada, Tamil and Tulu alphabets. Also, it is possible to add the use of atention mechanisms to enhance results in this and other similar datasets.

Acknowledgments

The work was done with partial support from the Mexican Government through the grant A1-S-47854 of CONACYT, Mexico, grants 20232138, 20232080, 20231567 of the Secretaría de Investigación y Posgrado of the Instituto Politécnico Nacional, Mexico. The authors thank the CONACYT for the computing resources brought to them through the Plataforma de Aprendizaje Profundo para Tecnologías del Lenguaje of the Laboratorio de Supercómputo of the INAOE, Mexico and acknowledge the support of Microsoft through the Microsoft Latin America PhD Award.

References

Mohd Zeeshan Ansari, M M Sufyan Beg, Tanvir Ahmad, Mohd Jazib Khan, and Ghazali Wasim. 2021. Language identification of hindi-english tweets using code-mixed bert. In *2021 IEEE 20th International Conference on Cognitive Informatics Cognitive Computing (ICCI*CC)*, pages 248–252.

Jesús Armenta-Segura and Grigori Sidorov. 2023. Anime Success Prediction Based on Synopsis Using Traditional Classifiers. In *Proceedings of Congreso Mexicano de Inteligencia Artificial, COMIA*.

Premjith B, Jyothish Lal G, Sowmya V, Bharathi Raja Chakravarthi, Rajeswari Natarajan, Nandhini K, Abirami Murugappan, Bharathi B, Kaushik M, Prasanth SN, Aswin Raj R, and Vijai Simmon S. 2023. Findings of the shared task on multimodal abusive language detection and sentiment analysis in tamil and malayalam. In *Proceedings of the Third Workshop on Speech and Language Technologies for Dravidian Languages*, Varna, Bulgaria. Recent Advances in Natural Language Processing.

Fazlourrahman Balouchzahi, Grigori Sidorov, and Alexander Gelbukh. 2023. Polyhope: Two-level hope speech detection from tweets. *Expert Systems with Applications*, 225:120078.

Somnath Banerjee, Sahar Ghannay, Sophie Rosset, Anne Vilnat, and Paolo Rosso. 2020. LIMSI_UPV at SemEval-2020 task 9: Recurrent convolutional neural network for code-mixed sentiment analysis. In *Proceedings of the Fourteenth Workshop on Semantic Evaluation*, pages 1281–1287, Barcelona (online). International Committee for Computational Linguistics.

Bharathi Raja Chakravarthi. 2020. Hopeedi: A multilingual hope speech detection dataset for equality, diversity, and inclusion. In *Workshop on Computational Modeling of People's Opinions, Personality, and Emotions in Social Media*.

Bharathi Raja Chakravarthi and Vigneshwaran Muralidaran. 2021. Findings of the shared task on hope speech detection for equality, diversity, and inclusion. In *Proceedings of the First Workshop on Language Technology for Equality, Diversity and Inclusion*, pages 61–72, Kyiv. Association for Computational Linguistics.

Bharathi Raja Chakravarthi, Vigneshwaran Muralidaran, Ruba Priyadharshini, Subalalitha Cn, John McCrae, Miguel Ángel García, Salud María Jiménez-Zafra, Rafael Valencia-García, Prasanna Kumaresan, Rahul Ponnusamy, Daniel García-Baena, and José García-Díaz. 2022. Overview of the shared task on hope speech detection for equality, diversity, and inclusion. In *Proceedings of the Second Workshop on Language Technology for Equality, Diversity and Inclusion*, pages 378–388, Dublin, Ireland. Association for Computational Linguistics.

Bharathi Raja Chakravarthi, Vigneshwaran Muralidaran, Ruba Priyadharshini, and John Philip McCrae. 2020. Corpus creation for sentiment analysis in code-mixed Tamil-English text. In *Proceedings of the 1st Joint Workshop on Spoken Language Technologies for Under-resourced languages (SLTU) and Collaboration and Computing for Under-Resourced Languages (CCURL)*, pages 202–210, Marseille, France. European Language Resources association.

J. S. Cramer. 2002. The origins of logistic regression. *Econometrics eJournal.*

Suman Dowlagar and Radhika Mamidi. 2021. Edione@lt-edi-eacl2021: Pre-trained transformers with convolutional neural networks for hope speech detection. *Proceedings of the First Workshop on Language Technology for Equality, Diversity and Inclusion*, page 86 – 91. Cited by: 6.

Aparna Dutta. 2022. Word-level language identification using subword embeddings for code-mixed Bangla-English social media data. In *Proceedings of the Workshop on Dataset Creation for Lower-Resourced Languages within the 13th Language Resources and Evaluation Conference*, pages 76–82, Marseille, France. European Language Resources Association.

O. E. Ojo, A. Gelbukh, H. Calvo, A. Feldman, O. O. Adebanji, and J. Armenta-Segura. 2022. Language identification at the word level in code-mixed texts using character sequence and word embedding. In *Proceedings of the 19th International Conference on Natural Language Processing (ICON): Shared Task on Word Level Language Identification in Code-mixed Kannada-English Texts*, pages 1–6, IIIT Delhi, New Delhi, India. Association for Computational Linguistics.

Kunihiko Fukushima. 1969. Visual feature extraction by a multilayered network of analog threshold elements. *IEEE Transactions on Systems Science and Cybernetics*, 5(4):322–333.

Kunihiko Fukushima. 1980. Neocognitron: A self-organizing neural network model for a mechanism of pattern recognition unaffected by shift in position. *Biological Cybernetics*, 36(4):193–202.

Asha Hegde, Mudoor Devadas Anusha, Sharal Coelho, Hosahalli Lakshmaiah Shashirekha, and Bharathi Raja Chakravarthi. 2022. Corpus creation for sentiment analysis in code-mixed Tulu text. In *Proceedings of the 1st Annual Meeting of the ELRA/ISCA Special Interest Group on Under-Resourced Languages*, pages 33–40, Marseille, France. European Language Resources Association.

Chakravarthi Bharathi Raja Hegde, Asha, Hosahalli Lakshmaiah Shashirekha, Rahul Ponnusamy, SUBALALITHA CN, Lavanya S K, Thenmozhi D, Martha Karunakar, Shreya Shreeram, and Sarah Aymen. 2023. Findings of the shared task on sentiment analysis in tamil and tulu code-mixed text. In *Proceedings of the Third Workshop on Speech and Language Technologies for Dravidian Languages*, Varna, Bulgaria. Recent Advances in Natural Language Processing.

Yann LeCun, Bernhard Boser, John S Denker, Donnie Henderson, Richard E Howard, Wayne Hubbard, and Lawrence D Jackel. 1989. Backpropagation applied to handwritten zip code recognition. *Neural computation*, 1(4):541–551.

Shriphani Palakodety, Ashiqur R. KhudaBukhsh, and Jaime G. Carbonell. 2019a. Hope speech detection: A computational analysis of the voice of peace. In *European Conference on Artificial Intelligence.*

Shriphani Palakodety, Ashiqur R. KhudaBukhsh, and Jaime G. Carbonell. 2019b. Voice for the voiceless: Active sampling to detect comments supporting the rohingyas. In *AAAI Conference on Artificial Intelligence.*

Parth Patwa, Gustavo Aguilar, Sudipta Kar, Suraj Pandey, Srinivas PYKL, Björn Gambäck, Tanmoy Chakraborty, Thamar Solorio, and Amitava Das. 2020. SemEval-2020 task 9: Overview of sentiment analysis of code-mixed tweets. In *Proceedings of the Fourteenth Workshop on Semantic Evaluation*, pages 774–790, Barcelona (online). International Committee for Computational Linguistics.

Moein Shahiki-Tash, Jesús Armenta-Segura, Olga Kolesnikova, Grigori Sidorov, and Alexander Gelbukh. 2023. LIDOMA at HOPE2023@IberLEF: Hope Speech Detection Using Lexical Features and Convolutional Neural Networks. In *Proceedings of IberLEF.*

Shashi Shekhar, Dilip Kumar Sharma, and MM Sufyan Beg. 2020. Language identification framework in code-mixed social media text based on quantum lstm—the word belongs to which language? *Modern Physics Letters B*, 34(06):2050086.

Ellen Spertus. 1997. Smokey: Automatic recognition of hostile messages. In *AAAI/IAAI.*

Philip J. Stone and Earl B. Hunt. 1963. A computer approach to content analysis: studies using the general inquirer system. *Proceedings of the May 21-23, 1963, spring joint computer conference.*

P.F. Verhulst. 1845. *Recherches mathématiques sur la loi d'accroissement de la population, par P.F. Verhulst ...* M. Hayez.

William Warner and Julia Hirschberg. 2012. Detecting hate speech on the world wide web. In *Proceedings of the Second Workshop on Language in Social Media*, pages 19–26, Montréal, Canada. Association for Computational Linguistics.

Kouichi Yamaguchi, Kenji Sakamoto, Toshio Akabane, and Yoshiji Fujimoto. 1990. A neural network for speaker-independent isolated word recognition. *First International Conference on Spoken Language Processing (ICSLP 1990).*

Muhammad Yasir, Li Chen, Amna Khatoon, Muhammad Amir Malik, and Fazeel Abid. 2021. Mixed script identification using automated dnn hyperparameter optimization. *Computational Intelligence and Neuroscience.*

nlpt_malayalm@DravidianLangTech-RANLP 2023: Fake News Detection in Malayalam using Optimized XLM-RoBERTa Model

Eduri Raja **Badal Soni** **Samir Kumar Borgohain**
Department of Computer Science & Engineering
National Institute of Technology Silchar
Assam, India, 788010
{eduri_rs, badal, samir}@cse.nits.ac.in

Abstract

The paper demonstrates the submission of the team nlpt_malayalm to the Fake News Detection in Dravidian Languages-DravidianLangTech@LT-EDI-2023. The rapid dissemination of fake news and misinformation in today's digital age poses significant societal challenges. This research paper addresses the issue of fake news detection in the Malayalam language by proposing a novel approach based on the XLM-RoBERTa base model. The objective is to develop an effective classification model that accurately differentiates between genuine and fake news articles in Malayalam. The XLM-RoBERTa base model, known for its multilingual capabilities, is fine-tuned using the prepared dataset to adapt it specifically to the nuances of the Malayalam language. A thorough analysis is also performed to identify any biases or limitations in the model's performance. The results demonstrate that the proposed model achieves a remarkable macro-averaged F-Score of 87% in the Malayalam fake news dataset, ranking 2nd on the respective task. This indicates its high accuracy and reliability in distinguishing between real and fake news in Malayalam.

1 Introduction

Fake news and misinformation proliferation have become pervasive problems in today's digital age. The rapid spread of false information through social media platforms and online news sources has the potential to mislead and deceive individuals, leading to harmful consequences for individuals, communities, and even entire nations.

In recent years, numerous research efforts have focused on developing effective solutions for fake news detection in various languages Hariharan and Anand Kumar (2023). However, even though millions of people worldwide and in the Indian state of Kerala speak Malayalam, a dearth of research is specifically focused on it. As a result, there is a pressing need to address this gap and develop robust models tailored for detecting fake news in Malayalam.

This research paper aims to tackle the challenge of fake news detection in Malayalam by proposing an innovative approach based on the XLM-RoBERTa base model. The XLM-RoBERTa Conneau et al. (2019) model is chosen due to its exceptional performance in multilingual tasks and ability to capture contextual information effectively. By leveraging the power of this model, we aim to develop a classification system capable of accurately identifying fake news articles written in Malayalam.

The contributions of this research paper include the following:

- Fine-tuning the XLM-RoBERTa base model on the Malayalam dataset to enhance its performance for fake news detection.
- Optimize the models' hyperparameters using Bayesian optimization to enhance their detection capabilities.
- Evaluating the proposed model's performance using various metrics, including precision, recall, and F1 score.

2 Related Work

Detecting fake news and misinformation has garnered significant attention from researchers in recent years. Numerous studies have explored various approaches and techniques to address this challenging problem. This section provides an overview of related work in fake news detection, focusing on methods applied to different languages and the specific challenges associated with detecting fake news in Malayalam. Sai and

Third Workshop on Speech and Language Technologies for Dravidian Languages, pages 186–191, Varna, Bulgaria, Sep 7, 2023.
https://doi.org/10.26615/978-954-452-085-4_026

Sharma (2021) used the XLM-R model for offensive language identification in Dravidian languages. Yasaswini et al. (2021) used the transfer learning technique to identify offensive language in Dravidian languages. To obtain optimal results, they used various classifiers like XLMR, mBERT, CNN, and ULMFiT. Ghanghor et al. (2021) used mBERT and XLM-R-based models with sauce loss and class weights for identifying the offensive language in Dravidian languages. Chen and Kong (2021) used mBERT with the TextCNN model to identify offensive language in Dravidian languages. K et al. (2021) used the CNN-BiLSTM hybrid model in shared tasks for identifying offensive language. Saha et al. (2021) proposed transformer-based ensembling strategies for identifying offensive language in Dravidian languages.

García-Díaz et al. (2022) proposed a knowledge integration method using fastText, BERT, and XLM-RoBERETa word embeddings and linguistic features. Palanikumar et al. (2022) used machine learning models and MuRIL for Transliteration as Data Augmentation for Abuse Detection in Tamil. S N et al. (2022) used TF-IDF with a random kitchen algorithm for abusive comment detection in Tamil. LekshmiAmmal et al. (2022) used MuRiL to identify offensive span in Tamil. Biradar and Saumya (2022) used IndicBERT and SVM classifier for identifying abusive comments in Dravidian code mixed data. Raja et al. (2023) used XLM-R and mBERT transformer models with adaptive fine-tuning for fake news detection in Dravidian languages. Transformer-based models have emerged as powerful tools for various NLP tasks, including fake news detection. These models leverage self-attention mechanisms to capture global dependencies in text, enabling them to learn contextual representations effectively. Transformer architectures such as BERT have demonstrated remarkable success in various NLP tasks.

3 Dataset Description

The data sources are diverse social media platforms like Facebook, Twitter, etc. The objective of the shared task is to classify the given social media post as either fake or original news. The competition organizers have released the dataset for fake news detection in Dravidian languages in the Malayalam language S et al. (2022). The dataset's train, validation, and test set distributions are depicted in Table1.

Class	Train	Validation	Test
Original	1658	409	512
Fake	1599	406	507
Total	3257	815	1019

Table 1: Dataset statistics

We see that the given dataset is almost balanced[1]. It consists of transliterated, code-mixed, emojis, and Malayalam-scripted data.

4 System Description

In this section, we present the model architecture for detecting fake news in Malayalam. We experimented with three different transformer-based models to classify the text as fake or real. We used MultilingualBERT (mBERT) Pires et al. (2019) and DistilBERT Sanh et al. (2019) as the base models, and we leveraged the optimized XLM-RoBERTa (XLM-R) as the proposed model, a transformer-based language model known for its effectiveness in various NLP tasks, including text classification.

4.1 mBERT

mBERT is an extension of the original BERT Devlin et al. (2018) model that is designed to handle multiple languages. While the original BERT model was explicitly trained for English, mBERT is trained on a large corpus of text data from various languages, enabling it to understand and process text in different languages. mBERT leverages a masked language modelling (MLM) objective during training, where it learns to predict masked words in a sentence based on the surrounding context. By training in diverse languages, mBERT learns to generate contextualized representations that capture language patterns and relationships across multiple languages.

One of the critical benefits of mBERT is its ability to perform cross-lingual transfer learning. This means that the knowledge learned from one language can be transferred to another, even if the amount of labelled data in the target language is limited. By leveraging the shared representations across languages, mBERT can improve the performance of various NLP tasks for multiple languages, such as text classification, named entity recognition, sentiment analysis, and more. It has become a popular choice for multilingual applications and

[1]https://codalab.lisn.upsaclay.fr/competitions/11176

research in NLP due to its versatility and effectiveness in handling diverse languages.

4.2 DistilBERT

DistilBERT is a variant of the BERT model, a state-of-the-art NLP model developed by Google. DistilBERT is designed to be a smaller and faster version of the original BERT model while maintaining a similar performance level. The "Distil" in DistilBERT stands for "distillation," which refers to training a smaller model to mimic the behaviour and performance of a larger model. It aims to compress the original BERT model using knowledge distillation, parameter sharing, and removing unnecessary components. By distilling the knowledge from BERT, DistilBERT achieves a significantly smaller model size, which leads to faster inference times and reduced memory requirements.

DistilBERT retains most of the critical characteristics of BERT, including its ability to perform a wide range of NLP tasks such as question answering, text classification, named entity recognition, and more. It learns contextual phrases of terms and sentences by training on enormous quantities of unlabeled text data, which allows it to seize intricate language patterns and semantic relationships.

4.3 XLM-RoBERTa

The XLM-RoBERTa model is a multilingual variant of the RoBERTa model based on the transformer architecture. It is pre-trained on a large corpus of multilingual data, allowing it to capture contextual information and semantic representations across multiple languages effectively.

The XLM-RoBERTa model consists of multiple layers of self-attention mechanisms, which enable it to learn contextualized word embeddings. Considering the surrounding context, these embeddings capture the relationships between words in a sentence. By leveraging the transformer's attention mechanism, the model can effectively encode the semantic information of the input text.

4.4 Adaptation for Malayalam

To adapt the XLM-RoBERTa model for detecting fake news in Malayalam, fine-tuning is performed using the annotated Malayalam news dataset. Fine-tuning involves training the model on the labeled data, allowing it to learn the specific patterns and linguistic characteristics of fake news in Malayalam.

During fine-tuning, the XLM-RoBERTa model is augmented with a classification layer on top. This layer maps the contextualized word embeddings generated by the model to a binary classification output, indicating whether the news article is genuine or fake. The parameters of the classification layer and the pre-trained XLM-RoBERTa model are updated simultaneously during the fine-tuning process.

4.5 Training and Optimization

The fine-tuning process involves training the adapted XLM-RoBERTa model on the annotated Malayalam news dataset. The training is performed using a batch-wise approach, where a subset of the dataset is processed at each iteration. The optimizer, Adam, updates the model's parameters based on the computed loss. Tuning hyperparameters is an essential step in developing deep-learning-based models. The implementation of a deep-learning-based model is highly dependent on the choosing of the optimal hyperparameters. Bayesian optimization can help find the best set of hyperparameters that maximize the model's performance, such as precision, recall, and F score. We used a Bayesian optimization Snoek et al. (2015) method to find the optimal hyperparameters for the proposed model and the remaining models. Hyperparameters of the proposed model are depicted in Table 2.

Parameter	Value
Train_batch_size	9
Number of training epochs	10
Max sequence length	128
Learning_rate	1e-5

Table 2: Parameters of the model

To prevent overfitting the model, early stopping was employed. Training would be stopped if the model's performance on the validation set did not improve for a certain number of consecutive epochs.

4.6 Inference and Prediction

Once trained, the model can predict the authenticity of new, unseen Malayalam news articles. The input text undergoes the preprocessing steps, including tokenization and normalization. The preprocessed text is then fed into the trained model, which predicts whether the news article is genuine or fake.

Model	Accuracy	Recall	Precision	F1-score	AUC
DistilBERT	0.8464	0.8753	0.8295	0.8518	0.9068
mBERT	0.8580	0.8845	0.8411	0.8623	0.9127
XLM-RoBERTa	**0.8687**	**0.8973**	**0.8495**	**0.8728**	**0.9384**

Table 3: Performance of the models over the training data

Model	Precision	Recall	F1-score
DistilBERT	0.76	0.82	0.79
mBERT	0.81	0.83	0.82
XLM-RoBERTa	**0.85**	**0.90**	**0.87**

Table 4: Performance of the models over the test data

The prediction can be based on the probability output of the classification layer, where a threshold can be applied to determine the final label.

5 Results and Evaluation

In this section, we present the results and evaluation of the proposed fake news detection model for the Malayalam language. We analyze the model's performance based on the evaluation metrics and provide insights into its effectiveness in distinguishing between real and fake news.

5.1 Performance Metrics

The enactment of the fake news detection model is evaluated using various metrics, including macro-averaged recall, precision, and F1 score. These metrics comprehensively comprehend the model's performance across different aspects.

The precision metric measures the model's ability to accurately identify real and fake news, while recall estimates the model's ability to seize all instances of each class. The F1 score delivers a balanced criterion by assessing both precision and recall.

The performance metrics are calculated for each class (original and fake), and the overall performance is typically reported as macro-averaged or weighted averages of the class-wise metrics.

5.2 Comparative Analysis

To provide a comprehensive evaluation, the performance of the proposed fake news detection model is compared with the existing approaches, such as mBERT and DistilBERT. This comparison helps assess the model's effectiveness and highlights its strengths and weaknesses. Table 3 depicts the performance of the models over the training data. Table 4 represents the performance of the models over the test data.

The proposed optimized XLM-RoBERTa model achieved an impressive macro-averaged F-Score of 87%. It demonstrated superior performance to both the mBERT and DistilBERT models, showcasing its effectiveness in detecting fake news in Malayalam. The mBERT model achieved a macro-averaged F-Score of 82%. While it performed well, it lagged behind the XLM-RoBERTa model in terms of overall performance. The DistilBERT model obtained a macro-averaged F-Score of 79%. It exhibited slightly lower performance compared to both XLM-RoBERTa and mBERT models.

The macro-averaged F-Scores comprehensively evaluate the model's precision and recall performance across all classes. The results highlight the superiority of the XLM-RoBERTa model, which attained the highest macro-averaged F-Score of 87%. This suggests that XLM-RoBERTa is particularly well-suited for fake news detection in Malayalam. The comparative analysis of macro F1 scores indicates that XLM-RoBERTa outperforms both mBERT and DistilBERT models. The XLM-RoBERTa model's ability to capture contextual dependencies and linguistic nuances in the Malayalam language contributes to its superior performance. This finding emphasizes the importance of language-specific modelling approaches for accurate fake news detection in languages with unique characteristics like Malayalam. The results exhibit the potential of transformer-based models for addressing the challenges of fake news detection in Malayalam. By achieving a high macro F1 score, the XLM-RoBERTa model can identify and combat misinformation in the Malayalam news ecosystem.

6 Conclusion

In this research paper, we propose a fake news detection model for the Malayalam language. The model utilizes the XLM-RoBERTa architecture and is finetuned on a dataset of real and fake news articles in Malayalam. We demonstrated through extensive experimentation and evaluation that the proposed model achieves promising results in detecting fake news in Malayalam. The model achieved an impressive macro F1 score of 87%, indicating its ability to balance precision and recall. We compared the proposed model with existing approaches such as mBERT and DistilBERT to fake news detection and discussed its performance, strengths, and limitations. The use of the XLM-RoBERTa model, combined with finetuning, proved advantageous in capturing contextual information and handling the linguistic nuances of the Malayalam language.

References

Shankar Biradar and Sunil Saumya. 2022. IIITDWD@TamilNLP-ACL2022: Transformer-based approach to classify abusive content in Dravidian code-mixed text. In *Proceedings of the Second Workshop on Speech and Language Technologies for Dravidian Languages*, pages 100–104, Dublin, Ireland. Association for Computational Linguistics.

Shi Chen and Bing Kong. 2021. cs@DravidianLangTech-EACL2021: Offensive language identification based on multilingual BERT model. In *Proceedings of the First Workshop on Speech and Language Technologies for Dravidian Languages*, pages 230–235, Kyiv. Association for Computational Linguistics.

Alexis Conneau, Kartikay Khandelwal, Naman Goyal, Vishrav Chaudhary, Guillaume Wenzek, Francisco Guzmán, Edouard Grave, Myle Ott, Luke Zettlemoyer, and Veselin Stoyanov. 2019. Unsupervised cross-lingual representation learning at scale. *CoRR*, abs/1911.02116.

Jacob Devlin, Ming-Wei Chang, Kenton Lee, and Kristina Toutanova. 2018. BERT: pre-training of deep bidirectional transformers for language understanding. *CoRR*, abs/1810.04805.

José García-Díaz, Manuel Valencia-Garcia, and Rafael Valencia-García. 2022. UMUTeam@TamilNLP-ACL2022: Abusive detection in Tamil using linguistic features and transformers. In *Proceedings of the Second Workshop on Speech and Language Technologies for Dravidian Languages*, pages 45–50, Dublin, Ireland. Association for Computational Linguistics.

Nikhil Ghanghor, Parameswari Krishnamurthy, Sajeetha Thavareesan, Ruba Priyadharshini, and Bharathi Raja Chakravarthi. 2021. IIITK@DravidianLangTech-EACL2021: Offensive language identification and meme classification in Tamil, Malayalam and Kannada. In *Proceedings of the First Workshop on Speech and Language Technologies for Dravidian Languages*, pages 222–229, Kyiv. Association for Computational Linguistics.

RamakrishnaIyer LekshmiAmmal Hariharan and Madasamy Anand Kumar. 2023. Impact of transformers on multilingual fake news detection for tamil and malayalam. In *Speech and Language Technologies for Low-Resource Languages*, pages 196–208, Cham. Springer International Publishing.

Sreelakshmi K, Premjith B, and Soman Kp. 2021. Amrita_CEN_NLP@DravidianLangTech-EACL2021: Deep learning-based offensive language identification in Malayalam, Tamil and Kannada. In *Proceedings of the First Workshop on Speech and Language Technologies for Dravidian Languages*, pages 249–254, Kyiv. Association for Computational Linguistics.

Hariharan LekshmiAmmal, Manikandan Ravikiran, and Anand Kumar Madasamy. 2022. NITK-IT_NLP@TamilNLP-ACL2022: Transformer based model for toxic span identification in Tamil. In *Proceedings of the Second Workshop on Speech and Language Technologies for Dravidian Languages*, pages 75–78, Dublin, Ireland. Association for Computational Linguistics.

Vasanth Palanikumar, Sean Benhur, Adeep Hande, and Bharathi Raja Chakravarthi. 2022. DE-ABUSE@TamilNLP-ACL 2022: Transliteration as data augmentation for abuse detection in Tamil. In *Proceedings of the Second Workshop on Speech and Language Technologies for Dravidian Languages*, pages 33–38, Dublin, Ireland. Association for Computational Linguistics.

Telmo Pires, Eva Schlinger, and Dan Garrette. 2019. How multilingual is multilingual BERT? In *Proceedings of the 57th Annual Meeting of the Association for Computational Linguistics*, pages 4996–5001, Florence, Italy. Association for Computational Linguistics.

Eduri Raja, Badal Soni, and Samir Kumar Borgohain. 2023. Fake news detection in dravidian languages using transfer learning with adaptive finetuning. *Engineering Applications of Artificial Intelligence*, 126:106877.

Kayalvizhi S, Thenmozhi Durairaj, Bharathi Raja Chakravarthi, and Jerin Mahibha C. 2022. Findings of the shared task on detecting signs of depression from social media. In *Proceedings of the Second Workshop on Language Technology for Equality, Diversity and Inclusion*, pages 331–338, Dublin, Ireland. Association for Computational Linguistics.

Prasanth S N, R Aswin Raj, Adhithan P, Premjith B, and Soman Kp. 2022. CEN-Tamil@DravidianLangTech-ACL2022: Abusive comment detection in Tamil using TF-IDF and random kitchen sink algorithm. In *Proceedings of the Second Workshop on Speech and Language Technologies for Dravidian Languages*, pages 70–74, Dublin, Ireland. Association for Computational Linguistics.

Debjoy Saha, Naman Paharia, Debajit Chakraborty, Punyajoy Saha, and Animesh Mukherjee. 2021. Hate-alert@DravidianLangTech-EACL2021: Ensembling strategies for transformer-based offensive language detection. In *Proceedings of the First Workshop on Speech and Language Technologies for Dravidian Languages*, pages 270–276, Kyiv. Association for Computational Linguistics.

Siva Sai and Yashvardhan Sharma. 2021. Towards offensive language identification for Dravidian languages. In *Proceedings of the First Workshop on Speech and Language Technologies for Dravidian Languages*, pages 18–27, Kyiv. Association for Computational Linguistics.

Victor Sanh, Lysandre Debut, Julien Chaumond, and Thomas Wolf. 2019. Distilbert, a distilled version of BERT: smaller, faster, cheaper and lighter. *CoRR*, abs/1910.01108.

Jasper Snoek, Oren Rippel, Kevin Swersky, Ryan Kiros, Nadathur Satish, Narayanan Sundaram, Md. Mostofa Ali Patwary, Prabhat, and Ryan P. Adams. 2015. Scalable bayesian optimization using deep neural networks.

Konthala Yasaswini, Karthik Puranik, Adeep Hande, Ruba Priyadharshini, Sajeetha Thavareesan, and Bharathi Raja Chakravarthi. 2021. IIITT@DravidianLangTech-EACL2021: Transfer learning for offensive language detection in Dravidian languages. In *Proceedings of the First Workshop on Speech and Language Technologies for Dravidian Languages*, pages 187–194, Kyiv. Association for Computational Linguistics.

ML&AI_IIITRanchi@DravidianLangTech: Fine-Tuning of Indic-BERT for Exploring Language-Specific Features for Sentiment Classification in Code-Mixed Dravidian Language

Kirti Kumari
IIIT Ranchi, India
kirti@iiitranchi.ac.in

Shirish Shekhar Jha
IISER Bhopal, India
shirish20@iiserb.ac.in

Zarikunte Kunal Dayanand
IISER Bhopal, India
zarikunte20@iiserb.ac.in

Praneesh Sharma
KIIT, Bhubaneswar, India
praneeshsharma30@gmail.com

Abstract

Code-mixing presents challenges to sentiment analysis due to limited availability of annotated data found on low-resource languages such as Tulu. To address this issue, comprehensive work was done in creating a gold-standard labeled corpus that incorporates both languages while facilitating accurate analyses of sentiments involved. Encapsulated within this research was the employed use of varied techniques including data collection, cleaning processes as well as preprocessing leading up to effective annotation along with finding results using fine tuning Indic-BERT and performing experiments over TF-IDF and Bag-of-Words. The outcome is an invaluable resource for developing custom-tailored models meant solely for analyzing sentiments involved with code mixed texts across Tamil and Tulu domain limits; allowing a focused insight into what makes up such expressions. Remarkably, the adoption of hybrid models yielded promising outcomes, culminating in a 10th rank achievement for Tulu, and a 14th rank achievement for Tamil, supported by an macro F1-Score of 0.471 and 0.124, respectively.

1 Introduction

Sentiment analysis is instrumental when it comes to understanding subjective information contained within written language data. Due to extensive language mixing within the realm of electronic communications lately, it's critical that we employ sentiment analysis in practice. This study focuses primarily on conducting a thorough examination of how best sentiments are analyzed when it comes to Tulu and Tamil code-mixed texts since these two languages typically fuse regularly across various social media sites. Code-mixed (Hedge et al., 2023) text becomes uniquely challenging when it blends multiple languages within one sentence or utterance. The addition of Tulu and Tamil to this mix together with English or other regional tongues significantly complicates any attempts at sentiment analysis. One barrier that stands out is the absence of resources as well as annotated datasets for code-mixed Tulu and Tamil scripts' emotion assessment. Consequently, there is an urgent need to compile a corpus that can enable effective interpretation of sentiments revealed through these dialects as well as guidelines on how best to proceed with analyses. In this research paper, we propose an inclusive approach towards developing such a corpus through diverse data collection channels ranging from social media platforms, online discussion forums down other digital sources that exhibit diverse language mixing designs encompassed by these texts; subsequently utilizing human experts' annotation skills to deliver precision sentiment labels required for designing valid models capable of evaluating such analyses. To increase the precision of sentimental analyses applied to mixed-language Tulu-Tamil texts, an interdisciplinary team plans on exploring several critical linguistic and contextual features. They intend on investigating methods like customized lexicons geared towards capturing each language's subtle nuances in expressing emotions - such as part-of-speech-tagging approaches or syntactic parsing methods - amongst others. Leveraging machine-learning-algorithms along with cutting-edge natural-language-processing technologies will enable them to construct reliable models capable of acutely categorizing various emotional states present within mixed-language texts. This research paper has practical implications that could benefit future studies on emotional analysis of code-mixed Tulu and Tamil language texts.

Firstly, the data set developed during this research provides useful information that can be harnessed by researchers exploring this field in greater depth. Secondly, our proposed methodology improves ac-

Third Workshop on Speech and Language Technologies for Dravidian Languages, pages 192–197, Varna, Bulgaria, Sep 7, 2023.
https://doi.org/10.26615/978-954-452-085-4_027

curacy to capture sentiments expressed within hybrid language forms so that results may provide more accurate readings when compared with previous studies or models. Lastly, our insights into developing sentiment-aware applications could have wide-ranging potential benefits for social media monitoring tools, mental health assessment platforms and customer feedback systems. In general, through the utilization of machine-aided analyses to expand upon essential linguistic features, we successfully tackled gaps in current comprehension related to mixed language forms.

Our work is summarised in the following sections. Related Work, it outlines the work that has been done in the related field, Datasets summarises the efforts and intricacies about the dataset on which the task has been performed, Experimental Results and Discussion, discusses about the various methodologies employed and their results obtained, lastly in Section 5, we wrap up our discussion and findings.

2 Related Work

In recent times due to the growth of social media, Sentiment Analysis referred as SA in the text has become significantly important and there is extensive research being carried out on SA of monolingual texts belonging to high-resource languages such as English, German, Russian. However, only few work have been reported on SA in Tulu and Tamil languages and very less number of SA works are found for other Dravidian languages too.

The authors of (Rani et al., 2020) have become imperative to identify hate speech in social media communication in order to avoid confrontations and control bad behaviour. Using techniques created for monolingual datasets to detect hate speech offers a problem because of the presence of multilingual speakers who regularly transition between languages. In this work, the aim was to analyse, identify, and compare hate speech in text from code-mixed social media platforms. Additionally, they collected a dataset of posts and comments from Facebook and Twitter that are code-mixed with text in Hindi and English. Their test findings show that deep learning models that have been trained on this code-mixed corpus perform better.

The research (Agrawal et al., 2018) focuses on finding a solution to the difficulty of handling idioms in Natural Language Processing (NLP) jobs specifically focused at Indian languages. The goal of this study is to close the gap between Indian languages and NLP applications in idiom handling.The authors offer a thorough analysis of idiomatic expressions used in Indian languages and suggest a cutting-edge method for handling and interpreting idioms in the context of NLP tasks. They use linguistic tools like dictionaries and corpora to build a database of idioms in the Indian language. The information in this repository is quite helpful for deciphering and analysing idiomatic idioms.The research also presents a framework for idiom disambiguation that takes into account the syntactic and semantic characteristics of idioms in Indian languages. The suggested framework uses statistical and rule-based methods to separate the meanings of idioms in various circumstances and the authors test their methodology through tests on several NLP tasks, including sentiment analysis and machine translation, utilising datasets in Indian languages. The outcomes show how their method to handling idioms was successful in enhancing these tasks' performance.The accuracy and effectiveness of NLP applications for Indian languages are improved since it offers insights and methods for handling idioms.

The research (Cieliebak et al., 2017) outlines the investigation into the development of a thorough corpus and benchmark resources designed exclusively for sentiment analysis in the German language utilizing Twitter data. Given the distinct linguistic traits and contextual complexities of the German language, the authors recognized the necessity for high-quality datasets and evaluation measures in the field of German sentiment analysis. They compiled a sizable German Twitter corpus by gathering tweets that contain sentiment-related hashtags in order to fill this gap. The corpus includes a wide range of subjects and emotions covered by German tweets.Apart from creating the corpus, the authors of the paper also constructed benchmark resources specifically designed for German sentiment analysis. They performed manual annotation on a portion of the collected tweets, assigning sentiment labels to ensure the availability of labeled data for training and evaluating sentiment analysis models. The labeling process involved categorizing the tweets as positive, negative, or neutral based on their underlying sentiment. To evaluate how well sentiment analysis models perform on the German Twitter corpus, the authors introduced evaluation metrics that are specifically tailored for German sentiment analysis. These metrics take into consideration the intricacies and subtle nuances of sentiment expression in the German language, offering a comprehensive and accurate evaluation framework.

The research (Jiang et al., 2019) centers around tackling aspect-based sentiment analysis (ABSA) through the introduction of a challenge dataset and the proposal of effective models. The authors acknowledged the necessity for high-quality datasets and robust models in ABSA, which involves discerning sentiment polarity towards specific attributes or aspects of a given target entity. To overcome the limitations of current datasets, they meticulously curated a challenge dataset tailored to test the capabilities of ABSA models. This challenge dataset encompasses a diverse array of reviews from various domains such as restaurants, laptops, and hotels. Each review is meticulously annotated with sentiment labels at the aspect-level, indicating the sentiment polarity associated with different aspects mentioned within the review. The dataset provides a comprehensive evaluation framework for assessing the performance of ABSA models. Additionally, the authors put forth effective models for ABSA. They introduce an attention-based neural network model that harnesses the contextual information of words to capture sentiment towards different aspects. This model adeptly addresses the challenges posed by the intricate relationships between aspects and sentiments in ABSA tasks. To assess the proposed model and compare its performance against existing approaches, the authors conducted extensive experiments utilizing the challenge dataset. The results demonstrated that their model surpasses several state-of-the-art models in aspect-based sentiment analysis, underscoring its effectiveness and superiority.

The authors of (Rogers et al., 2018) present research conducted to create a rich sentiment analysis dataset specifically designed for Russian-language social media content. The authors recognized the need for high-quality datasets that meet the unique challenges of sentiment analysis in Russian social media. To overcome the limitations of existing datasets, they developed RuSentiment. This is a large dataset carefully designed to capture the complex nuances and characteristics of emotional expression in Russian social media texts. The RuSentiment dataset contains a diverse collection of Russian social media posts from platforms such as Twitter, VKontakte, and LiveJournal. The dataset covers a wide range of topics and includes various sentiment categories such as positive, negative, neutral, and ambiguous. Additionally, the dataset is enriched with additional annotations such as sentiment strength, sentiment goal, and sentiment frame. Sentiment Strength indicates the strength of the sentiment conveyed in each post, while Sentiment Target identifies the specific entity or aspect that the sentiment targets. Emotion frames provide contextual information about the situations in which emotions are expressed. To ensure the quality and reliability of the dataset, the authors used a careful annotation process involving multiple annotators and checked agreement between the annotators. We have also developed customized guidelines and annotation schemes specifically for sentiment analysis in Russian social media. This paper also describes a baseline experiment using the RuSentiment dataset to evaluate the performance of our sentiment analysis model. The results demonstrate the effectiveness of the dataset in capturing the complex nuances of emotional expression in Russian social media and highlight its potential in developing advanced sentiment analysis models.

The research (Mandalam and Sharma, 2021) presented a method for implementation to classify Dravidian code-shuffled comments according to their polarity. Due to the availability of Tamil and Malayalam datasets with mixed codes, his three methods are proposed: subword-level models, word-embedding-based models, and machine-learning-based architectures. Subword and word embedding-based models use Long Short Term Memory (LSTM) networks with language-specific preprocessing, while machine learning models use Term Frequency-Inverse Document Frequency (TF-IDF) vectors with logistic regression models conversion was used.

In the article (Gupta et al., 2021), the authors explore two popular approaches, namely task-specific pre-training and cross-lingual transfer, for handling code-switched data in the context of sentiment analysis. Specifically, they focus on two Dravidian Code-Switched languages, Tamil-English and Malayalam-English, and evaluate the performance of four different BERT-based models.The goal was to compare the impact of task-specific pre-training and cross-lingual transfer on sentiment analysis tasks. The authors find that task-specific pre-training yields superior results in zero-shot and supervised settings compared to leveraging cross-lingual transfer from multilingual BERT models.

By conducting experiments on our newly created sentiment analysis corpus, we aim to evaluate the performance of fine-tuned Indic-BERT models in comparison to TF-IDF and Bag-of-Words approaches. These experiments will provide insights into the strengths and limitations of each method and their suitability for sentiment analysis in code-mixed Tulu and Tamil text.

3 Datasets

The dataset (Hegde et al., 2022; Chakravarthi et al., 2020, 2022) used for this task aims to address the challenge of identifying sentiment polarity in code-mixed comments and posts in two language pairs: Tamil-English and Tulu-English. These comments and posts were collected from social media platforms, providing a real-world context for sentiment analysis research. The dataset contains annotations of sentiment polarity at the comment or post level, allowing for a comprehensive analysis of the overall sentiment expressed in each instance.

One notable characteristic of the dataset is the sentence structure. While a comment or post may consist of multiple sentences, the average sentence length across the corpora is approximately one sentence. This aspect of the dataset simplifies the task by focusing on individual comments or posts as self-contained units for sentiment analysis.

The dataset captures the intricacies of code-mixing, which refers to the phenomenon of mixing two or more languages within a single communication instance. In this case, the dataset specifically focuses on Tamil-English and Tulu-English code-mixing. Code-mixing is prevalent in multilingual societies, particularly in social media conversations, and understanding sentiment in such mixed-language contexts is crucial for gaining insights into users' opinions and attitudes.

One important consideration when working with this dataset is the presence of class imbalance. Class imbalance refers to an uneven distribution of sentiment polarities in the dataset, where certain sentiments may be over–represented while others are underrepresented. This class imbalance accurately reflects real–world scenarios, as sentiment distribution in social media is often skewed, with certain sentiments being more prevalent than others. Addressing class imbalance is a significant challenge in sentiment analysis, and this dataset has provided an opportunity to explore and develop effective techniques to handle this issue.

Researchers and practitioners can leverage this dataset for various tasks related to sentiment analysis, such as sentiment classification, sentiment intensity estimation, or sentiment trend analysis. The availability of sentiment annotations at the comment or post level enables a fine-grained analysis of sentiment in code-mixed social media content. By utilizing this dataset, one can gain insights into the sentiment patterns and dynamics within the Tamil-English and Tulu-English code-mixed social media landscape.

The dataset for us served as a valuable resource for training and evaluating sentiment analysis models. We were able to develop and fine-tune machine learning or deep learning models using this dataset to improve the accuracy and performance of sentiment analysis algorithms in code-mixed contexts. Additionally, the presence of class imbalance in the dataset provided an opportunity to explore techniques for handling imbalanced data and improving model robustness in real-world scenarios.

In terms of potential challenges, code-mixing introduces linguistic complexities that may pose difficulties for sentiment analysis. Sentiment expression can vary depending on the language used, and the presence of code-mixed phrases, idioms, or cultural references adds an additional layer of complexity to sentiment interpretation. While working with this dataset we considered these linguistic intricacies and explore techniques that effectively capture sentiment in code-mixed contexts.

Furthermore, the dataset's domain, which comprises social media comments and posts, presents its own set of challenges. Social media platforms are characterized by informal language, abbreviations, emoticons, and non-standard grammar, which can impact sentiment analysis accuracy. It was crucial for us to account for these unique characteristics and develop models that can effectively handle the noisy nature of social media data.

4 Experimental Results and Discussion

To evaluate the performance of sentiment analysis models, fine-tuning of Indic-BERT was employed.

Fine-tuning of In-Domain contextualized BERT (Indic-BERT): the fine-tuning of indic BERT

Table 1: Indic-BERT results on the test dataset

Method	Macro F1-Score
Indic-BERT Tamil	0.124
Indic-BERT Tulu	0.471

demonstrated notable improvements in sentiment classification accuracy. By leveraging pre-trained language representations and fine-tuning them on the code-mixed Tulu and Tamil sentiment analysis task, the model achieved enhanced performance in capturing the nuances of sentiment expressed in the code-mixed texts.

Indic-BERT (Kakwani et al., 2020), an ALBERT model, has been exclusively pretrained on 12 major Indian languages. It underwent pre-training using unique monolingual corpus comprising approximately 9 billion tokens, followed by evaluation on diverse tasks. Despite having fewer parameters compared to other multilingual models like mBERT and XLM-R, Indic-BERT achieves comparable or superior performance. It utilizes a vast corpus of text data from Indic languages to acquire contextual representations of words and sentences. Through training on a diverse range of Indic language data, the model captures the specific linguistic patterns, syntactic structures, and semantic relationships inherent in these languages. This empowers the model to comprehend and generate meaningful representations for Indic text.

Notably, Indic-BERT excels in handling code-mixed text, where multiple languages are combined within a single instance of communication. Indic-BERT has been purposefully trained to effectively handle code-mixed text, rendering it suitable for a wide array of applications involving mixed-language data.

The findings in Table 1 highlight the significance of contextualized language models like Indic-BERT in capturing the complex sentiments expressed in code-mixed texts. The fine-tuning process enables the model to adapt specifically to the characteristics of Tulu and Tamil code-mixed data, leading to improved classification performance. Figure 1 shows the utilized architecture of our model.

The utilization of the current corpus and the findings of this research have significant implications for sentiment analysis in code-mixed Tulu and Tamil texts.

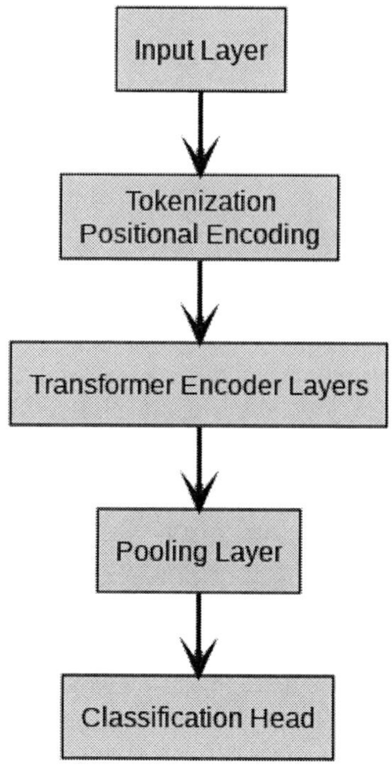

Figure 1: Utilized Indic-BERT Architecture

5 Conclusion

The corpus serves as a valuable resource for future studies and advancements in sentiment analysis techniques for code-mixed languages. Researchers can utilize this corpus to develop and evaluate more accurate sentiment analysis models specific to Tulu and Tamil code-mixed text. Moreover, the incorporation of fine-tuned Indic-BERT and the exploration of traditional approaches contribute to the existing body of knowledge in sentiment analysis. These findings can guide future research in developing effective sentiment analysis models for code-mixed languages.And also the outcomes of this research have practical implications for various applications. The accurate sentiment analysis of code-mixed Tulu and Tamil texts can be leveraged in brand reputation management, political analysis, customer feedback analysis, and mental health monitoring systems. By understanding and interpreting the sentiments expressed in these languages, decision-makers can make informed decisions and provide necessary support.

Now concluding, the research highlights the importance of corpus used for sentiment analysis in code-mixed Tulu and Tamil texts. The incorporation of fine-tuned Indic-BERT and experimentation with traditional approaches contributes to the advancement of sentiment analysis techniques. The developed corpus and the obtained results provide valuable resources for future studies and applications in sentiment analysis, benefiting various domains that rely on accurate sentiment interpretation in code-mixed Tulu and Tamil texts.

Acknowledgements

We are thankful to Indian Institute of Information Technology Ranchi for all the support during our research.

References

Ruchit Agrawal, Vighnesh Chenthil Kumar, Vigneshwaran Muralidharan, and Dipti Misra Sharma. 2018. No more beating about the bush: A step towards idiom handling for indian language nlp. In *Proceedings of the Eleventh International Conference on Language Resources and Evaluation (LREC 2018)*.

Bharathi Raja Chakravarthi, Vigneshwaran Muralidaran, Ruba Priyadharshini, and John Philip McCrae. 2020. Corpus creation for sentiment analysis in code-mixed Tamil-English text. In *Proceedings of the 1st Joint Workshop on Spoken Language Technologies for Under-resourced languages (SLTU) and Collaboration and Computing for Under-Resourced Languages (CCURL)*, pages 202–210, Marseille, France. European Language Resources association.

Bharathi Raja Chakravarthi, Ruba Priyadharshini, Vigneshwaran Muralidaran, Navya Jose, Shardul Suryawanshi, Elizabeth Sherly, and John P McCrae. 2022. Dravidiancodemix: Sentiment analysis and offensive language identification dataset for dravidian languages in code-mixed text. *Language Resources and Evaluation*, 56(3):765–806.

Mark Cieliebak, Jan Milan Deriu, Dominic Egger, and Fatih Uzdilli. 2017. A twitter corpus and benchmark resources for german sentiment analysis. In *5th International Workshop on Natural Language Processing for Social Media, Boston MA, USA, 11 December 2017*, pages 45–51. Association for Computational Linguistics.

Akshat Gupta, Sai Krishna Rallabandi, and Alan Black. 2021. Task-specific pre-training and cross lingual transfer for code-switched data. *arXiv preprint arXiv:2102.12407*.

Asha Hedge, Bharathi Raja Chakravarthi, Hosahalli Lakshmaiah Shashirekha, Rahul Ponnusamy, Subalalitha Chinnaudayar Navaneethakrishnan, Lavanya S.K, Durairaj Thenmozhi, Martha Karunakar, Shreya Sriram, and Sarah Aymen. 2023. Findings of the shared task on sentiment analysis in tamil and tulu code-mixed text. In *Proceedings of the Third Workshop on Speech and Language Technologies for Dravidian Languages*, Varna, Bulgaria. Recent Advances in Natural Language Processing.

Asha Hegde, Mudoor Devadas Anusha, Sharal Coelho, Hosahalli Lakshmaiah Shashirekha, and Bharathi Raja Chakravarthi. 2022. Corpus creation for sentiment analysis in code-mixed Tulu text. In *Proceedings of the 1st Annual Meeting of the ELRA/ISCA Special Interest Group on Under-Resourced Languages*, pages 33–40, Marseille, France. European Language Resources Association.

Qingnan Jiang, Lei Chen, Ruifeng Xu, Xiang Ao, and Min Yang. 2019. A challenge dataset and effective models for aspect-based sentiment analysis. In *Proceedings of the 2019 conference on empirical methods in natural language processing and the 9th international joint conference on natural language processing (EMNLP-IJCNLP)*, pages 6280–6285.

Divyanshu Kakwani, Anoop Kunchukuttan, Satish Golla, Gokul N.C., Avik Bhattacharyya, Mitesh M. Khapra, and Pratyush Kumar. 2020. IndicNLPSuite: Monolingual Corpora, Evaluation Benchmarks and Pre-trained Multilingual Language Models for Indian Languages. In *Findings of EMNLP*.

Asrita Venkata Mandalam and Yashvardhan Sharma. 2021. Sentiment analysis of Dravidian code mixed data. In *Proceedings of the First Workshop on Speech and Language Technologies for Dravidian Languages*, pages 46–54, Kyiv. Association for Computational Linguistics.

Priya Rani, Shardul Suryawanshi, Koustava Goswami, Bharathi Raja Chakravarthi, Theodorus Fransen, and John Philip McCrae. 2020. A comparative study of different state-of-the-art hate speech detection methods in hindi-english code-mixed data. In *Proceedings of the second workshop on trolling, aggression and cyberbullying*, pages 42–48.

Anna Rogers, Alexey Romanov, Anna Rumshisky, Svitlana Volkova, Mikhail Gronas, and Alex Gribov. 2018. Rusentiment: An enriched sentiment analysis dataset for social media in russian. In *Proceedings of the 27th international conference on computational linguistics*, pages 755–763.

ML&AI_IIIT Ranchi@DravidianLangTech: Leveraging Transfer Learning for the Discernment of Fake News within the Linguistic Domain of Dravidian Language

Kirti Kumari
IIIT Ranchi / Ranchi India
kirti@iiitranchi.ac.in

Shirish Shekhar Jha
IISER Bhopal / Bhopal India
shirish20@iiserb.ac.in

Zarikunte Kunal Dayanand
IISER Bhopal / Bhopal India
zarikunte20@iiserb.ac.in

Praneesh Sharma
KIIT / Bhubaneswar India
praneeshsharma30@gmail.com

Abstract

The primary focus of this research endeavor lies in detecting and mitigating misinformation within the intricate framework of the Dravidian language. A notable feat was achieved by employing fine-tuning methodologies on the highly acclaimed Indic-BERT model, securing a commendable 4th rank in a prestigious competition organized by DravidianLangTech 2023 while attaining a noteworthy macro F1-Score of 0.78. To facilitate this undertaking, a diverse and comprehensive dataset was meticulously gathered from prominent social media platforms, including but not limited to Facebook and Twitter. The overarching objective of this collaborative initiative was to proficiently discern and categorize news articles into either the realm of veracity or deceit through the astute application of advanced machine learning techniques, coupled with the astute exploitation of the distinctive linguistic idiosyncrasies inherent to the Dravidian language.

1 Introduction

Text classification has emerged as a critical task that has garnered significant attention and contributions from researchers and practitioners worldwide in recent years. The rapid increase in user enrollment on social media platforms has led to an unprecedented surge in the availability of textual data. This abundance of textual data has played a pivotal role in various domains, including business and research, shaping strategies, and driving advancements in software and applications.

Companies rely on textual data, particularly user reviews and comments, to formulate their business strategies and make informed decisions about their products and services. By analyzing the sentiment and content of textual data, businesses gain valuable insights into customer opinions, preferences, and trends. Furthermore, researchers have recognized the potential of textual data analysis in advancing fields such as natural language processing, sentiment analysis, and information retrieval. The exploration of textual data has paved the way for the development of more intelligent software and applications that can understand and process human language more effectively.

The analysis of textual data assumes even greater significance when considering its multilingual nature. With a diverse range of languages spoken worldwide, understanding and analyzing textual data across different languages is crucial. While most contributions in the field of text classification have focused on the English language domain, it is essential to explore the characteristics and challenges posed by other languages. Low-resource languages, such as the Dravidian languages, often face a scarcity of available methodologies and resources for effective text analysis. This poses a unique challenge that requires innovative approaches and solutions.

The impact of textual data goes beyond business and research, particularly in the era of social media and digital communication. A study conducted by MIT [1] revealed a disconcerting trend: fake news spreads faster than accurate information, particularly on platforms like Twitter, where it can propagate at a rate 10 to 20 times faster. This poses a significant challenge to individuals, organizations, and society as a whole, as the proliferation of misinformation can lead to detrimental consequences. Trust in news sources and the ability to discern reliable information become paramount in such an environment.

Addressing this issue becomes even more challenging when dealing with low-resource languages

[1]https://news.mit.edu/2018/study-twitter-false-news-travels-faster-true-stories-0308

Third Workshop on Speech and Language Technologies for Dravidian Languages, pages 198–206, Varna, Bulgaria, Sep 7, 2023.
https://doi.org/10.26615/978-954-452-085-4_028

like the Dravidian languages. The scarcity of methodologies and resources specifically tailored for these languages poses a barrier to effective fake news detection and mitigation. However, recognizing the urgency and importance of finding solutions, competitions and collaborative initiatives have emerged, bringing together great minds from around the world to tackle this pressing problem. These platforms foster innovation, encourage the development of novel methodologies, and promote advancements in technology that can benefit the human race.

With the aim of contributing to this endeavor, we embarked on an experiment to identify fake news in the Malayalam language, a Dravidian language spoken primarily in the Indian state of Kerala. Leveraging various machine learning and deep learning techniques, we sought to devise a suitable solution that could effectively detect and classify fake news in this language. Our experimentation involved training and fine-tuning models using state-of-the-art approaches, with a particular focus on transfer learning. By fine-tuning Indic-BERT, a language model specifically designed for Indian languages, we aimed to leverage its pre-trained knowledge to improve the accuracy and effectiveness of our classification system.

The results of our experiment were promising, with an achieved macro F1-Score of 0.78. This performance placed us in an admirable 4th position in the competition (Subramanian et al., 2023), reflecting the efficacy of our approach and the efforts invested in tackling the challenges specific to the Malayalam language. By harnessing the power of transfer learning and combining it with domain-specific fine-tuning, we enhanced our system's capabilities and achieved commendable results in detecting and classifying fake news.

Rest of the paper summarised in different sections. Related works are presented in Section 2 followed by Task description and Dataset description in Section 3 and Section 4 respectively. In Section 5, we presented our detailed methodology and validation results followed by Section 6, where we presented the results of test data and analysis of the the results. Finally, we summarise our work in Section 7.

2 Related Work

Due to their potential impact on public discourse and the spread of disinformation, the identification and mitigation of fake news on social media have become key fields of research. This part includes an extensive assessment of the pertinent literature and covers significant contributions to the study of how to spot false news.

In their seminal work, the work (Shu et al., 2017) adopt a data mining perspective to address the challenge of detecting fake news on social media. Their research underscores the significance of employing data mining techniques to extract features and patterns from social media content, enabling accurate identification of fake news. The authors propose a framework incorporating textual, visual, and social features to discern instances of fake news. By highlighting the role of data mining in tackling the issue of fake news on social media platforms, this study contributes valuable insights to the field. The article (Wang, 2017) introduces the benchmark dataset "Liar, liar pants on fire," specifically designed for fake news detection. This dataset consists of statements that have been labeled with varying degrees of truthfulness, enabling researchers to develop and evaluate models for fake news detection. The author emphasizes the significance of high-quality datasets in advancing research in this domain and provides a valuable resource for benchmarking and comparing different approaches. The researches **(Mridha et al., 2021)(Li et al., 2021)(Kim and Jeong, 2019)(Aldwairi and Alwahedi, 2018)** explore deep learning approaches for fake news detection. They extensively review a range of deep learning models and techniques, including Convolutional Neural Networks (CNNs), Recurrent Neural Networks (RNNs), and attention mechanisms, applied in the context of fake news detection. The survey provides valuable insights into the strengths and limitations of different deep learning approaches and highlights their potential for detecting fake news. Conducting a comparative study of computational fake news detection on social media, the research (Manish et al., 2022) evaluate the performance of various machine learning and deep learning algorithms. The authors assess different features, such as linguistic, stylistic, and temporal characteristics, and examine their effectiveness in distinguishing between fake and real news. This comparative analysis offers valuable insights into the strengths and limitations of different computational approaches for fake news detection.

In conclusion, there are many different viewpoints and methods covered in the literature on detecting fake news on social media. The articles discussed in this part highlight how crucial it is to use data mining methods, benchmark datasets, deep learning models, and comparative analyses to progress the field of false news detection. These studies' findings, benchmark datasets, and suggested frameworks are all useful tools for creating computational techniques that can stop fake news from spreading on social media platforms. We attempted to draw inspiration for our work from these references, and after comparing our dataset with theirs, we attempted to develop some useful approaches.

3 Task Description

DravidianLangTech presents an intriguing competition titled "Fake News Detection in Dravidian Languages." The primary objective of this task is to develop a proficient classification system that can effectively distinguish between original and fake news in social media text written in Dravidian languages. The dataset for this task comprises social media posts extracted from diverse platforms like Twitter, Facebook, and others.

Participants have been provided with social media texts in Dravidian languages. They are tasked with building machine learning or deep learning models to accurately classify the given content as either fake or original news. The focus of the competition revolves around the ability to discern authentic information from fabricated or misleading content within the context of Dravidian languages.The outcomes of this task hold significant implications for enhancing the credibility and trustworthiness of information shared on social media platforms in Dravidian linguistic domains. Furthermore, developing effective classification models will contribute to empowering users with reliable information, foster informed decision-making, and combat fake news dissemination.

4 Dataset Description

The dataset (Kayalvizhi et al., 2022) utilized for the Fake News Detection competition in Dravidian Languages comprises a diverse collection of social media posts sourced from prominent platforms, including Twitter and Facebook. It is segmented into three distinct subsets: a training dataset, a development dataset, and a test dataset. The training dataset furnished to us encompasses a substantial volume of social media posts composed in Dravidian languages in code-mixed format. Each post within the training dataset is annotated with labels indicating its categorization as either an original or fake news post. The total texts in the Training dataset were 3257 in number. These labeled annotations served as the ground truth for training classification models, playing a crucial role in facilitating the development and refinement of machine learning or deep learning models.

Table 1: Distribution of the dataset

Class	Training	Development	Test	Total
Original	1658	409	512	2579
Fake	1599	406	507	2512
Total	3257	815	1019	5091

The development dataset, also referred to as the validation dataset, augments the labeled data provided. It allowed us to evaluate models' performance and fine-tune the hyperparameters during the development phase. The labeled information within the development dataset aids in the assessment of the models' efficacy in accurately classifying social media text as either original or fake news.The total text in development dataset were 815. Table 1 summarizes the data distribution in training, development, and test dataset.

5 Methodology and Validation Results

In our study, we employed a range of methodologies on the development dataset with the objective of identifying the most effective approach for making predictions on the test dataset. Different techniques (Chanda et al., 2022) presents a technique where *mBert* has been utilized along with word-level language tag to classify the comments. The article (Varsha et al., 2022) presented an approach where feature extraction has been done in association with transfer learning to perform the classification task. Being inspired by the related work, we have tried to introduce methodologies that could prove effective in this task.

For example, when working with TF-IDF (Term Frequency-Inverse Document Frequency) features and embeddings-based classification, extensive data pre-processing was undertaken to optimize the performance of the models. However, in the case of fine-tuning Indic-BERT, this data pre-processing step was not necessary. Indic-BERT, have been pretrained on a large corpus of social media texts, specifically in Indian languages, incorporates the linguistic nuances and contextual information prevalent in social media language, including the presence of emojis[2]. Consequently, removing emojis in this case could potentially compromise the linguistic semantics captured by IndicBERT.

Data Pre-Processing was conducted specifically for methods such as TF-IDF feature extraction and sentence embedding-based classification. This crucial step encompassed several operations aimed at enhancing the quality and structure of the text data.

The initial phase involved the removal of punctuation marks, Emojis (only for methodologies of section 5.1 to 5.3) and alphanumeric characters to eliminate noise and ensure a cleaner representation of the textual content. Following this, we proceeded with the removal of stop words, which are commonly occurring words that do not contribute significantly to the overall meaning of the text. Additionally, we focused on expanding any contracted words to their full forms, allowing for a more comprehensive analysis of the text.

The final step of the data pre-processing pipeline involved tokenization, which entailed breaking down the text into individual units such as words or sub-words. This process facilitates subsequent analysis and modeling tasks by providing a structured representation of the text data. Furthermore, we applied lemmatization to the tokens, aiming to reduce inflected or variant forms to their base or dictionary form, promoting consistency and coherence within the dataset.

By diligently performing these data preprocessing techniques, we aimed to enhance the quality and reliability of the text data, preparing it for subsequent analysis and classification tasks.

Following the feature extraction stage, we applied several machine learning models and deep learning techniques to perform the classification task. The specific methods utilized are discussed in subsequent subsections of this study, outlining the intricacies and nuances associated with each approach.

By exploring and evaluating multiple methodologies, we aimed to identify the most effective techniques for classifying social media texts as original or fake news in the context of our research.

[2]https://www.frontiersin.org/articles/10.3389/fpsyg.2019.02221/full

5.1 TF-IDF Based Classification

In this research study, we focused on utilizing the TF-IDF technique for classification tasks in machine learning. The primary objective was to explore the effectiveness of TF-IDF-based approaches for text classification.

TF-IDF is a widely used technique in natural language processing that assigns weights to individual terms based on their frequency within a document and their rarity across the entire corpus. By considering both the local and global importance of terms, TF-IDF enables identifying key features that are discriminative for classification.

We employed various machine learning algorithms to implement the TF-IDF-based classification, including the Ridge classifier and Logistic Regression. These algorithms are well-known for their effectiveness in handling text classification tasks. We also explored similar algorithms to assess their performance and compare their results.

The choice of max_df was 0.9, meaning we ignored terms that appeared in more than 90% of documents, and min_df was set to 5, meaning we also ignored words that appeared in less than five documents; it was made to strike a balance between capturing sufficient vocabulary diversity and avoiding computational complexity. By limiting the dictionary to the most frequent and informative terms, we aimed to ensure robust classification performance while managing the dimensionality of the feature space. Table 2 summarizes the results of different machine learning algorithms deployed on training and development datasets.

5.2 Bag-Of-Words Based Classification

Bag-of-Words (BoW) based text classification is a widely adopted approach in natural language processing for representing text documents as numerical feature vectors. In this research study, we also leveraged BoW-based text classification with machine learning algorithms to analyze and classify textual data effectively.

The initial step in BoW-based text classification involved constructing a dictionary or vocabulary of unique words or terms that were utilized to represent the documents. To ensure comprehensive coverage, we created a dictionary consisting of 10,000 terms, encompassing the most frequent and informative terms derived from the training dataset.

Once the dictionary was established, we proceeded to transform each document into a sparse

Table 2: Summary of TF-IDF based Results on Training and Validation Datasets

Classifier	Macro Precision	Macro Recall	Macro F1
Ridge-Classifier	0.76	0.75	0.75
Perceptron-Classifier	0.72	0.71	0.71
SGD-classifier	0.75	0.75	0.74
Passive-AggressiveClassifier	0.74	0.74	0.74
Decision-Tree-Classifier	0.74	0.72	0.72
Random-Forest-Classifier	0.75	0.75	0.75
AdaBoost-Classifier	0.75	0.74	0.73
SVM-Classifier	0.75	0.74	0.75

vector representation. This vector representation captured the presence or absence of dictionary terms within the document, along with their frequency or weighted values using techniques like term frequency-inverse document frequency (TF-IDF).

To train and classify the BoW representations of the documents, we employed a diverse range of machine learning algorithms, including well-known models such as logistic regression, support vector machines, random forests, and decision trees, among others. Each algorithm underwent training using a labeled training dataset comprising documents and their respective class labels.

During the training phase, the machine learning algorithms acquired an understanding of the patterns and relationships between the BoW features and their associated classes. Subsequently, we evaluated the trained models on a development dataset, utilizing metrics such as precision macro, recall macro, and F1-score macro, to assess their performance and generalization capabilities.

We carefully considered the trade-off between capturing sufficient vocabulary diversity and managing computational complexity in selecting the dictionary size. By opting for a dictionary size of 10,000, we aimed to strike an optimal balance.Table 3 summarizes the results of experiments done on training and validation datasets. It was noted that the Bag-Of-Words features were more effective in classifying the text data.

5.3 Sentence Embedding Based Classification

We have employed Sentence-BERT (SBERT) (Reimers and Gurevych, 2019, 2020), a powerful technique for calculating sentence embeddings, to extract meaningful representations from the text data. By leveraging transfer learning, we utilized the pre-trained model xlm-r-100langs-bert-base-nli-stsb-mean-tokens to generate high-quality sentence embeddings.

To perform classification, we fed the sentence embeddings into a Deep Neural Network (DNN) architecture. To enhance the performance of our model, we extracted the features from the last layer of the neural network model. These extracted features were then used as inputs for various machine-learning classifiers. The concept behind approaching such hybrid architecture was to capture the complexity that came with Dravidian languages.

In addition to the DNN-based approach, we also constructed a custom ensemble classifier by combining multiple machine learning algorithms. The ensemble classifier integrated Decision Tree, Gaussian Naive Bayes, Support Vector Machine, Logistic Regression, and Linear Discriminant Analysis (LDA) classifiers. This ensemble classifier leveraged the features extracted from the last layer of the neural network to classify the text data.

To optimize the performance of our models, we carefully tuned the hyperparameters. Details regarding the hyperparameters can be found in Table 6. We aimed to achieve the best possible classification results by fine-tuning these parameters.

The outcomes of our experiments and evaluations are summarized in Table 4. These results provide insights into the effectiveness and performance of the proposed approach.
Overall, this experiment showcased the utilization of SBERT for sentence embedding, combined with DNN-based classification and a custom ensemble classifier. By extracting features from the last layer of the neural network, we were able to leverage the power of transfer learning and machine learning algorithms.

Table 3: Bag-Of-Words bases Results Summary on Training and Validation Datasets

Classifier	**Macro Precision**	**Macro Recall**	**Macro F1**
Ridge-Classifier	0.78	0.76	0.76
Perceptron-Classifier	0.72	0.72	0.72
SGD-classifier	0.79	0.79	0.78
Passive-AggressiveClassifier	0.79	0.78	0.78
Decision-Tree-Classifier	0.76	0.74	0.74
Random-Forest-Classifier	0.80	0.79	0.79
AdaBoost-Classifier	0.76	0.75	0.74
SVM-Classifier	0.78	0.77	0.77

Table 4: Sentence Embedding based Results Summary on Training and Validation Datasets

Classifier	**Macro Precision**	**Macro Recall**	**Macro F1**
SBERT + DNN	0.69	0.69	0.69
SBERT+DNN+Random Forest	0.70	0.69	0.70
SBERT+DNN+AdaBoost	0.68	0.68	0.68
SBERT+DNN+Ensemble	0.67	0.67	0.67

Table 5: Fine Tuned Indic-BERT Results Summary on Training and Validation Datasets

Classifier	**Macro Precision**	**Macro Recall**	**Macro F1**
IndicBERT	0.79	0.78	0.78
IndicBERT+Random Forest	0.75	0.75	0.75
IndicBERTT+AdaBoost	0.78	0.78	0.78
IndicBERT+Extra Trees	0.75	0.75	0.75
IndicBERT+SGD Classifier	0.79	0.78	0.78
IndicBERT+SVM	0.78	0.78	0.78
IndicBERT+Logistic Regression	0.78	0.78	0.78
IndicBERT+Decision Tree	0.75	0.75	0.75

Table 6: Deep Neural Network Architecture and Hyperparameters

Hyperparameters	Values
Number of Layers	4
Activation Function(s)	Tanh and ReLU
Dropout Rate	0.2
Optimizer	Adam
Number of Epochs	50

Table 7: Indic-BERT results on the test dataset

Method	Result
Indic-BERT	**macro F1-Score** 0.78

5.4 Fine Tuning Indic-BERT

In the final stage of our research experimentation, we focused on fine-tuning the pre-trained model Indic-BERT, which AI4BHARAT developed[3]. Indic-BERT represents a multilingual ALBERT model that has been trained on extensive corpora comprising 12 major Indian languages. These languages include Assamese, Bengali, English, Gujarati, Hindi, Kannada, Malayalam, Marathi, Oriya, Punjabi, Tamil, and Telugu. Remarkably, Indic-BERT outperforms other publicly available models such as *mBERT* and XLM-R, despite having a significantly lower parameter count. It has demonstrated state-of-the-art performance across a range of tasks (Dabre et al., 2021; Ganesan et al., 2021; Kunchukuttan et al., 2020; Doddapaneni et al., 2021; Kakwani et al., 2020).

To tailor the Indic-BERT model to our specific classification objectives, we engaged in the process of fine-tuning by adjusting the model weights using the development dataset. This step allowed us to leverage the dataset's unique characteristics and linguistic nuances to enhance the performance and adaptability of Indic-BERT. Through fine-tuning, we aimed to optimize the model's ability to capture the relevant features and patterns necessary for accurate classification. We replaced the last layer for classification with a single neuron to make binary classification. We used the Sigmoid function to make classifications and Adam as our optimizer. With backpropagation, we were able to adjust the weights of the model according to the task. The Indic-BERT architecture can be described in the following flowchart 1.

[3] https://ai4bharat.iitm.ac.in/indic-bert

Figure 1: Utilized Indic-BERT Architecture

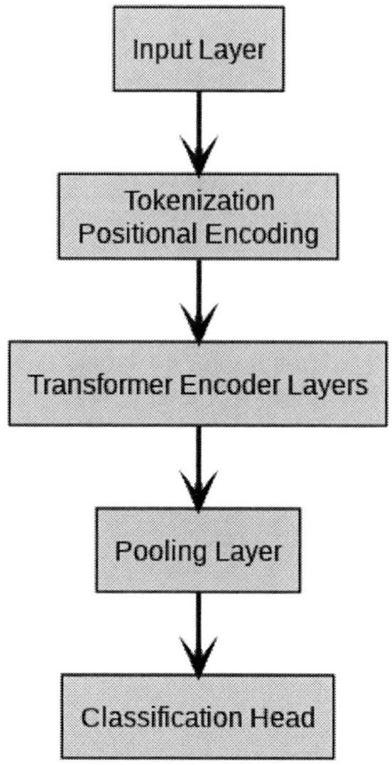

To handle the varying lengths of text sequences within the datasets, we defined maximum sequence lengths for each subset of data. For the training dataset, the maximum sequence length was set to 97, while for the development and test datasets, the respective max sequence lengths were adjusted to 88 and 89. The specification of sequence lengths plays a vital role in optimizing the tokenization process and generating meaningful tokens. Text sequences shorter than the defined length were padded, while longer sequences were truncated, ensuring consistency and compatibility throughout the analysis.

Subsequently, we extracted the features from the last layer of the fine-tuned Indic-BERT model. These features, representing the rich contextual information captured by the model, were utilized as inputs for the machine learning classifiers. By leveraging the combination of the fine-tuned model's representations and the discriminative power of the classifiers, we aimed to harness the benefits of both approaches and construct a hybrid model. This hybrid model would offer a comprehensive and robust solution for text classification tasks.

To evaluate the effectiveness of our approach, we conducted extensive experiments and obtained results for various evaluation metrics. The performance of the hybrid model, including accuracy, precision, recall, and F1 score, was carefully analyzed and documented. These metrics provide valuable insights into the model's capabilities and enable a comprehensive assessment of its performance across different classification tasks.

We present the detailed results of our experiments in Table 5, which serves as a comprehensive summary of the findings. The table provides a holistic view of the model's performance and highlights its effectiveness in accurately classifying text based on the features extracted from the fine-tuned Indic-BERT model. Observing the results, we used the fine-tuned model to make final predictions for our task submission.

6 Results and Analysis

In this section, we present the results of our submitted task. After making predictions using the fine-tuned Indic-BERT, we were evaluated using the macro F1-Score, macro Precision, and macro Recall. We obtained a macro F1 Score of 0.78 on the test dataset.

The confusion matrix has been presented in Figure 2 that tells the classification of various classes along with misclassified classes. It is a critical tool for analyzing the performance and efficiency of our model.

Figure 2: Confusion Matrix of Test Predictions

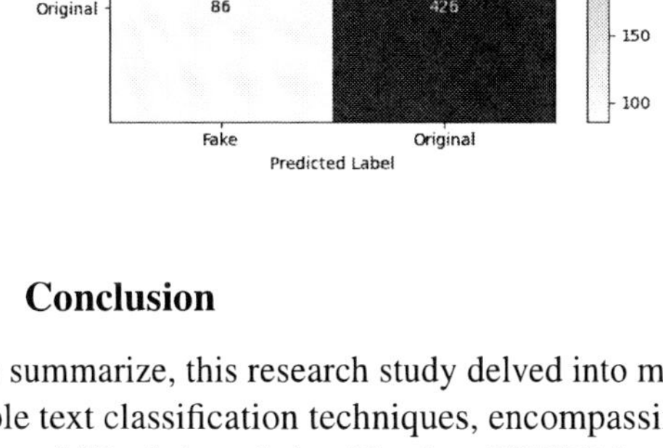

7 Conclusion

To summarize, this research study delved into multiple text classification techniques, encompassing Bag-of-Words based classification, TF-IDF-based classification, Sentence Embedding based classification and the fine-tuning of the pre-trained Indic-BERT model. Each approach exhibited distinct advantages and showcased its effectiveness in accurately categorizing textual data. Our model and experiments performed satisfactorily over task; all the results are summarized in the Tables. We can enhance the performance by fine-tuning the pre-trained model with more data.

Acknowledgements

We are thankful to Indian Institute of Information Technology Ranchi for all the support during our research.

References

Monther Aldwairi and Ali Alwahedi. 2018. Detecting fake news in social media networks. *Procedia Computer Science*, 141:215–222.

Galen Andrew and Jianfeng Gao. 2007. Scalable training of L1-regularized log-linear models. In *Proceedings of the 24th International Conference on Machine Learning*, pages 33–40.

Supriya Chanda, Anshika Mishra, and Sukomal Pal. 2022. Sentiment analysis and homophobia detection of code-mixed dravidian languages leveraging pre-trained model and word-level language tag. In *Working Notes of FIRE 2022-Forum for Information Retrieval Evaluation (Hybrid). CEUR.*

Raj Dabre, Himani Shrotriya, Anoop Kunchukuttan, Ratish Puduppully, Mitesh M Khapra, and Pratyush Kumar. 2021. Indicbart: A pre-trained model for indic natural language generation. *arXiv preprint arXiv:2109.02903.*

Sumanth Doddapaneni, Gowtham Ramesh, Mitesh M Khapra, Anoop Kunchukuttan, and Pratyush Kumar. 2021. A primer on pretrained multilingual language models. *arXiv preprint arXiv:2107.00676.*

Vinod Ganesan, Gowtham Ramesh, and Pratyush Kumar. 2021. Supershaper: Task-agnostic super pre-training of bert models with variable hidden dimensions. *arXiv preprint arXiv:2110.04711.*

Divyanshu Kakwani, Anoop Kunchukuttan, Satish Golla, Gokul N.C., Avik Bhattacharyya, Mitesh M. Khapra, and Pratyush Kumar. 2020. IndicNLPSuite: Monolingual Corpora, Evaluation Benchmarks and Pre-trained Multilingual Language Models for Indian Languages. In *Findings of EMNLP*.

S Kayalvizhi, Thenmozhi Durairaj, Bharathi Raja Chakravarthi, et al. 2022. Findings of the shared task on detecting signs of depression from social media. In *Proceedings of the Second Workshop on Language Technology for Equality, Diversity and Inclusion*, pages 331–338.

Kyeong-Hwan Kim and Chang-Sung Jeong. 2019. Fake news detection system using article abstraction. In *2019 16th International Joint Conference on Computer Science and Software Engineering (JCSSE)*, pages 209–212.

Anoop Kunchukuttan, Divyanshu Kakwani, Satish Golla, Avik Bhattacharyya, Mitesh M Khapra, Pratyush Kumar, et al. 2020. Ai4bharat-indicnlp corpus: Monolingual corpora and word embeddings for indic languages. *arXiv preprint arXiv:2005.00085*.

Xiangyang Li, Yu Xia, Xiang Long, Zheng Li, and Sujian Li. 2021. Exploring text-transformers in aaai 2021 shared task: Covid-19 fake news detection in english. In *Combating Online Hostile Posts in Regional Languages during Emergency Situation: First International Workshop, CONSTRAINT 2021, Collocated with AAAI 2021, Virtual Event, February 8, 2021, Revised Selected Papers 1*, pages 106–115. Springer.

Manish Kumar Singh Manish, Jawed Ahmed Jawed, Mohammad Afshar Alam Alam, Kamlesh Kumar Raghuvanshi Kamlesh, and Sachin Kumar Sachin. 2022. A comparative study of computational fake news detection on social media.

Muhammad F Mridha, Ashfia Jannat Keya, Md Abdul Hamid, Muhammad Mostafa Monowar, and Md Saifur Rahman. 2021. A comprehensive review on fake news detection with deep learning. *IEEE Access*, 9:156151–156170.

Nils Reimers and Iryna Gurevych. 2019. Sentence-bert: Sentence embeddings using siamese bert-networks. In *Proceedings of the 2019 Conference on Empirical Methods in Natural Language Processing*. Association for Computational Linguistics.

Nils Reimers and Iryna Gurevych. 2020. Making monolingual sentence embeddings multilingual using knowledge distillation. In *Proceedings of the 2020 Conference on Empirical Methods in Natural Language Processing*. Association for Computational Linguistics.

Kai Shu, Amy Sliva, Suhang Wang, Jiliang Tang, and Huan Liu. 2017. Fake news detection on social media: A data mining perspective. *ACM SIGKDD explorations newsletter*, 19(1):22–36.

Malliga Subramanian, Bharathi Raja Chakravarthi, Kogilavani Shanmugavadivel, Santhiya Pandiyan, Prasanna Kumar Kumaresan, Balasubramanian Palani, Muskaan Singh, Sandhiya Raja, Vanaja, and Mithunajha S. 2023. Overview of the shared task on fake news detection from social media text. In *Proceedings of the Third Workshop on Speech and Language Technologies for Dravidian Languages*, Varna, Bulgaria. Recent Advances in Natural Language Processing.

Josephine Varsha, B Bharathi, and A Meenakshi. 2022. Sentiment analysis and homophobia detection of youtube comments in code-mixed dravidian languages using machine learning and transformer models. In *Working Notes of FIRE 2022-Forum for Information Retrieval Evaluation (Hybrid). CEUR*.

William Yang Wang. 2017. " liar, liar pants on fire": A new benchmark dataset for fake news detection. *arXiv preprint arXiv:1705.00648*.

NITK-IT-NLP@DravidianLangTech-2023: Impact of Focal Loss on Malayalam Fake News Detection using Transformers

Hariharan R L , Anand Kumar M
hariharanrl.197it003@nitk.edu.in
m_anandkumar@nitk.edu.in
Department of Information Technology
National Institute of Technology Karnataka

Abstract

Fake News Detection in Dravidian Languages is a shared task that identifies YouTube comments in the Malayalam language for fake news detection. In this work, we have proposed a transformer-based model with cross-entropy loss and focal loss, which classifies the comments into fake or authentic news. We have used different transformer-based models for the dataset with modifications in the experimental setup, out of which the fine-tuned model, which is based on MuRIL with focal loss, achieved the best overall macro F1-score of 0.87, and we got second position in the final leaderboard.

1 Introduction

Social media is becoming the most popular media through which people share information happening around them. Online social networks such as Twitter, Facebook, Instagram, Weibo, and many others are major channels for people to obtain an enormous amount of information; meanwhile, there can be unauthentic or fake information among them. The central aspect of fake news is that it fully caters to the audience's curiosity, which is why it spreads faster (Jing et al., 2023). Moreover, research proves that false information or fake news spreads faster than authentic news (Vosoughi et al., 2018). Thus it is very urgent to detect fake news and stop its propagation to prevent potential harm.

Fake news detection in Dravidian Languages is a shared task organized by DravidianLangTech, which focuses on detecting fake news from YouTube comments annotated as fake and original. The dataset was retrieved from YouTube comments which are in Malayalam language. We have proposed a transformer-based model that used cross-entropy and focal loss function.

The rest of the paper is organized as follows. First, in section 2, some related works are explained. Followed by the dataset description in section 3. Then in section 4 we explain the different models and the methodology we have used, followed by data preprocessing and model description in section 5 and 6. The result and discussions are explained in section 7 followed by the conclusions and future scope in section 8

2 Related Works

Fake news detection is one of the popular problems in natural language processing tasks. We can see from the literature that an enormous amount of research has been carried out to tackle the propagation of fake news. In this section, we provide some of the works done on mitigating fake in the Dravidian language, especially in Malayalam. We have also included some recent works developed on fake news detection for other languages.

(Sharma and Arya, 2023) has proposed a Hindi fake news detection model that utilizes linguistic feature-based word embedding. They mainly focus on 24 key features which are extracted and derived for the successful detection of fake news. (Verma et al., 2021) has proposed a method that uses both word embeddings and linguistic features for the identification of textual fake news. (Singhal et al., 2022) has created fact-checked data in 13 different Indian languages covering different news stories from 2013 to 2020. The data were mainly retrieved from social media websites. They have also analyzed the characterization of multilingual, multimedia, and multidomain. (Mirnalinee et al., 2022) has created a dataset for fake news detection in the Tamil language. They have scrapped news snippets from various news media and annotated them into binary, fake, and real labels. The news articles scrapped cover different regions like sports, politics, and science, which they manually annotate. (Hariharan and Anand Kumar, 2022) has studied the impact of different transformer-based models using the data they have created using translation. The dataset covers different domains retrieved from

Third Workshop on Speech and Language Technologies for Dravidian Languages, pages 207–210, Varna, Bulgaria, Sep 7, 2023.
https://doi.org/10.26615/978-954-452-085-4_029

FakeNewsAMT and Celebrity Fake News, which are translated into Tamil and Malayalam languages using Google Translate.

It is evident from the literature the number of works for the Dravidian language, especially Malayalam, is much less than the other languages, the main reason being the lack of proper annotated data resources. Hence, we should develop a system that could address these challenges.

3 Dataset Description

The shared task provided data retrieved from YouTube comments and annotated for fake news detection (Subramanian et al., 2023). The dataset was mainly in Malayalam, and some had code-mixed content. The dataset was labeled into two classes, 'Fake' and 'Original', and the detailed statistics as shown in Table 1. The test data given had 1019 samples for which predictions will be made.

Table 1: Dataset Statistics

Data	Comments		
	Original	Fake	Total
Train	1658	1599	3257
Validation	409	406	815

4 Methodology

The shared task was to classify the YouTube comment into corresponding labels correctly. We were supposed to get a prediction for the test data with the training and validation data provided. Moreover, we were allowed to use external data to train the model. We have employed transformer-based pre-trained models for training the proposed model. Even though the task was for fake news detection in the Dravidian language, and the dataset given was for Malayalam, we had code-mixed samples. Hence we used the multilingual version of the BERT (Devlin et al., 2019) model for training the data. We further experimented with the multilingual version of RoBERTa (Liu et al., 2019) and the MuRIL (Khanuja et al., 2021) model. We used the binary cross entropy loss function as the loss function in all of our models and have experimented with focal loss.

5 Data Preprocessing

As we were using Malayalam and code-mixed to train the model, we applied some basic preprocessing before training the model. The dataset from youtube comments was cleaned using the Python library cleantext, which helps remove the unknown characters and do the ASCII conversions. As mentioned previously, we were using a pre-trained model based on the transformer; hence we had to tokenize the data according to how the model expected. We use the tokenization method from the hugging face library, corresponding to the underlying pre-trained model.

6 Model Description

We mainly used three pre-trained models for training the multilingual BERT (m-BERT) and MuRIL from Google, multilingual RoBERTa (xlmroberta). The m-BERT and xlmroberta were trained on multilingual data, and the MuRIL model was trained specially for the Indian context. The MuRIL model has been pre-trained with multilingual representations from various Indian languages, and they have augmented data that used the translated and transliterated pairs of documents for training. We used recommended hyperparameters for all the models whose particulars are given in Table 2.

6.1 Focal Loss

We can see that most of the classification models used the Cross-Entropy loss (CE) function for their training and learning. The main idea is to have a function that predicts a high probability for a positive class and a low one for a negative class using some threshold. The equation for CE is as follows.

$$CELp_t = -\sum y_i \times log(p_t) \tag{1}$$

The CE loss focussed on penalizing the model based on how far the prediction is from the actual label by giving equal importance to classes. Moreover, CE loss will be the same for any class; given the predicted probability, it will not change based on the class.

Focal Loss (Lin et al., 2020) is a loss function that balances easy and hard examples or positive and negative samples. It is a dynamically scaled CE loss, where the scaling factor decays to zero as the confidence in the correct class increases. The equation for focal loss is as follows.

$$FL_{p_t} = -\alpha \times (1 - p_t)^{\gamma} \times log(p_t) \tag{2}$$

Focal loss is ultimately a weighted CE loss that

Table 2: Hyperparameter Values

Hyperparameters	m-BERT	XLMRoBERTa	MuRIL
Learning rate	2e-5	2e-5	2e-5
Epochs	10	10	10
Batch	32	32	32
Optimizer	AdamW	AdamW	AdamW
Max length	400	400	400

considers the contribution of each sample to the loss based on the classification error.

7 Results and Discussion

This section explains the different experiments we have conducted for the shared task and the results for the same. We used the pre-trained transformer-based models to build our system. We have fine-tuned the transformer-based models using the hyperparameters mentioned in Table, using AdamW as the optimizer. The experiments were conducted on Tesla P100 16 GB GPU on the Kaggle platform.

We initially begin training the data with the m-BERT model after the necessary preprocessing, as explained in the section. We used cross-entropy loss for the experiments. We used the experimental settings for training the model on XLMRoBERTa and MuRIL. The results are shown in Table 3; we can see that the MuRIL model gives the best result, which XLMRoBERTa and m-BERT follow. The result of MuRIL can be because of the better understanding of the Indian language context by the pre-trained model. Among these, the best model was submitted to the shared task.

Table 3: Validation Data Results on different Models using CE Loss

Model	Precision	Recall	F1-score
m-BERT	0.8604	0.8601	0.8601
XLMRoBERTa	0.8761	0.8761	0.8761
MuRIL	0.8853	0.8846	**0.8846**

We started experimenting with focal loss to see how it can perform on complex samples, as we mentioned in the section 6.1 while explaining the focal loss. Moreover, while training the model with CE loss, we could see that the loss did not reduce below 30-35%. Thus we explored the possibility of focal loss whose results are given in Table 4. However, the model did not perform better than the model with cross-entropy loss. We can see that the MuRIL model performed better than the other two models. MuRIL gave 0.8758 for the focal loss model and 0.8846 for the cross-entropy model. Similar is the case for the rest of the models. As we have to give predictions for test data, we included both model results for the final submission.

Table 4: Validation Data Results on different Models using Focal Loss

Model	Precision	Recall	F1-score
m-BERT	0.8587	0.8550	0.8548
XLMRoBERTa	0.8582	0.8577	0.8576
MuRIL	0.8793	0.8759	**0.8758**

Once the test data results and the labels were released, we tested the same with all our models, whose results are given in Tables 5,6. The model performed almost the same for both cross-entropy and focal loss functions; from the tables, it is clear that there is a difference of nearly 0.5% with them. Moreover, XLMRoBERTa and MuRIL performed the same with a small difference in the scores. The final leaderboard result reflected our MuRIL-based model with focal loss function with an F1 score of 0.8692 (which was given as 0.87).

Table 5: Test Data Results on different Models using CE Loss

Model	Precision	Recall	F1-score
m-BERT	0.8450	0.8449	0.8449
XLMRoBERTa	0.8640	0.8637	**0.8636**
MuRIL	0.8640	0.8635	0.8635

Table 6: Test Data Results on different models using Focal Loss

Model	Precision	Recall	F1-score
m-BERT	0.8408	0.8389	0.8388
XLMRoBERTa	0.8728	0.8697	0.8691
MuRIL	0.8728	0.8693	**0.8692**[a]

[a] 2nd Position in the Leaderboard (Score given as 0.87)

8 Conclusions and Future Scope

Currently, social media is the primary influence among people to deliver whatever information is happening around them. Thus it is essential to address the problem of fake information being circulated on online social media platforms. In this work, we have developed a system for fake news identification on Malayalam data retrieved from YouTube comments. We have leveraged the transformer-based model and the focal loss function to address the fake news detection problem. We achieved an F1-score of 0.87 on test data with the proposed model and got second place in the final leaderboard. In the future, we would improve the model's performance by focusing on the code-mixed aspect and language-based fine-tuning.

References

Jacob Devlin, Ming-Wei Chang, Kenton Lee, and Kristina Toutanova. 2019. BERT: Pre-training of deep bidirectional transformers for language understanding. In *Proceedings of the 2019 Conference of the North American Chapter of the Association for Computational Linguistics: Human Language Technologies, Volume 1 (Long and Short Papers)*, pages 4171–4186, Minneapolis, Minnesota. Association for Computational Linguistics.

RamakrishnaIyer LekshmiAmmal Hariharan and Madasamy Anand Kumar. 2022. Impact of transformers on multilingual fake news detection for tamil and malayalam. In *International Conference on Speech and Language Technologies for Low-resource Languages*, pages 196–208. Springer.

Jing Jing, Hongchen Wu, Jie Sun, Xiaochang Fang, and Huaxiang Zhang. 2023. Multimodal fake news detection via progressive fusion networks. *Information Processing and Management*, 60(1):103120.

Simran Khanuja, Diksha Bansal, Sarvesh Mehtani, Savya Khosla, Atreyee Dey, Balaji Gopalan, Dilip Kumar Margam, Pooja Aggarwal, Rajiv Teja Nagipogu, Shachi Dave, et al. 2021. Muril: Multilingual representations for indian languages. *arXiv preprint arXiv:2103.10730*.

Tsung-Yi Lin, Priya Goyal, Ross B. Girshick, Kaiming He, and Piotr Dollár. 2020. Focal loss for dense object detection. *IEEE Trans. Pattern Anal. Mach. Intell.*, 42(2):318–327.

Yinhan Liu, Myle Ott, Naman Goyal, Jingfei Du, Mandar Joshi, Danqi Chen, Omer Levy, Mike Lewis, Luke Zettlemoyer, and Veselin Stoyanov. 2019. Roberta: A robustly optimized BERT pretraining approach. *CoRR*, abs/1907.11692.

TT Mirnalinee, Bhuvana Jayaraman, A Anirudh, R Jagadish, and A Karthik Raja. 2022. A novel dataset for fake news detection in tamil regional language. In *International Conference on Speech and Language Technologies for Low-resource Languages*, pages 311–323. Springer.

Richa Sharma and Arti Arya. 2023. Lfwe: Linguistic feature based word embedding for hindi fake news detection. *ACM Trans. Asian Low-Resour. Lang. Inf. Process.*, 22(6).

Shivangi Singhal, Rajiv Ratn Shah, and Ponnurangam Kumaraguru. 2022. Factdrill: A data repository of fact-checked social media content to study fake news incidents in india. In *Proceedings of the international AAAI conference on web and social media*, volume 16, pages 1322–1331.

Malliga Subramanian, Bharathi Raja Chakravarthi, Kogilavani Shanmugavadivel, Santhiya Pandiyan, Prasanna Kumar Kumaresan, Balasubramanian Palani, Muskaan Singh, Sandhiya Raja, Vanaja, and Mithunajha S. 2023. Overview of the shared task on fake news detection from social media text. In *Proceedings of the Third Workshop on Speech and Language Technologies for Dravidian Languages*, Varna, Bulgaria. Recent Advances in Natural Language Processing.

Pawan Kumar Verma, Prateek Agrawal, Ivone Amorim, and Radu Prodan. 2021. WELFake: Word Embedding over Linguistic Features for Fake News Detection. *IEEE Transactions on Computational Social Systems*, 8(4):881–893.

Soroush Vosoughi, Deb Roy, and Sinan Aral. 2018. The spread of true and false news online. *Science*, 359(6380):1146–1151.

VEL@DravidianLangTech: Sentiment Analysis of Tamil and Tulu

Kishore Kumar Ponnusamy[1], **Charmathi Rajkumar**[2],
Prasanna Kumar Kumaresan[3], **Elizabeth Sherly**[4]
Ruba Priyadharshini[5]
[1] Guru Nanak College, Chennai, Tamil Nadu, India
[2] The American College, Madurai, Tamil Nadu, India
[3] Insight SFI Research Centre for Data Analytics, University of Galway, Ireland
[4]Digital University Kerala, India
[5]The Gandhigram Rural Institute Deemed University, Tamil Nadu, India
{kishorep16002, charmathirajkumar}@gmail.com
prasanna.kumaresan@insight-centre.org
sherly@iiitmk.ac.in, rubapriyadharshini.a@gmail.com

Abstract

We participated in the Sentiment Analysis in Tamil and Tulu - DravidianLangTech 2023-RANLP 2023 task in the team name of VEL. This research focuses on addressing the challenge of detecting sentiment analysis in social media code-mixed comments written in Tamil and Tulu languages. Code-mixed text in social media often deviates from strict grammar rules and incorporates non-native scripts, making sentiment identification a complex task. To tackle this issue, we employ pre-processing techniques to remove unnecessary content and develop a model specifically designed for sentiment analysis detection. Additionally, we explore the effectiveness of traditional machine-learning models combined with feature extraction techniques. Our best model logistic regression configurations achieve impressive macro F1 scores of 0.43 on the Tamil test set and 0.51 on the Tulu test set, indicating promising results in accurately detecting instances of sentiment in code-mixed comments.

1 Introduction

The constant increase in Web and social media usage by the global audience has resulted in a substantial increase in the quantity of textual data expressing opinions (Shanmugavadivel et al., 2022). This publicly available textual data contains valuable insights that can be utilized in numerous disciplines, including marketing, finance, politics, and security (Shaik et al., 2023). These insights provide an excellent opportunity for individuals and businesses to discover the opinions of a user base, allowing them to make informed decisions regarding the enhancement of their brands and services (Chakravarthi et al., 2022).

However, as more opinionated data becomes available on the Internet, it becomes exceedingly difficult to read and trace emotions. This issue can be addressed using techniques of sentiment analysis (Divya et al., 2023). Sentiment analysis is regarded as the computational study of sentiments, opinions, emotions, and evaluations in order to comprehend better a person's reactions and attitudes towards multiple entities (Vasantharajan et al., 2023; Mercha and Benbrahim, 2023).

Due to its prospective applications, the computational treatment of opinion, sentiment, and subjectivity has recently garnered a great deal of attention. Sentiment analysis identifies the perspective(s) underlying a text segment; an example application is classifying a movie review as "thumbs up" or "thumbs down." The situation is more complicated for low-resource languages like Tamil and Tulu due to the poor performance of multilingual or language-specific models and the lack of adequate benchmark datasets (Thenmozhi et al., 2023; Subramanian et al., 2023; Navaneethakrishnan et al., 2023; Chakravarthi, 2023).

Tools and models for sentiment analysis have undergone substantial development over the course of several years, particularly for European languages. On the other hand, comparable tools for Dravidian languages are difficult to come by (Chinnaudayar Navaneethakrishnan et al., 2023; Kumaresan et al., 2022). This is due to the fact that cutting-edge pre-processing tools for Indian languages, such as POS taggers, shallow parsers, and other similar programs, are not easily accessible (Thavareesan and Mahesan, 2019, 2020b; Mahata et al., 2021). It has been observed that people in bilingual and multilingual communities often combine a number of languages when they are speaking or

Third Workshop on Speech and Language Technologies for Dravidian Languages, pages 211–216, Varna, Bulgaria, Sep 7, 2023.
https://doi.org/10.26615/978-954-452-085-4_030

writing informally (B and A, 2021; Karim et al., 2022). Younger generations are increasingly using Dravidian code-mixed languages in a variety of contexts, including but not limited to advertising, entertainment, and social media (Priyadharshini et al., 2022; Subramanian et al., 2022). Examples of these languages include Malayalam and Tamil. Roman script is the most prevalent form used to write the language (Mandalam and Sharma, 2021; Gupta et al., 2021; Chakravarthi, 2022a,b).

We participated in sentiment analysis shared tasks for Tamil and Tulu (Hedge et al., 2023), which focused on detecting sentiment in social media comments. The task was organized by DravidianLangTech 2023. Using the provided dataset, we developed three machine-learning models that utilized TF-IDF feature extraction. Among our models, the logistic regression model yielded the best results, achieving a macro F1 score of 0.43 for Tamil and a macro F1 score of 0.51 for Tulu. These scores indicate the effectiveness of our approach in accurately identifying instances of sentiment in social media comments for the Tamil and Tulu languages. Our participation in this shared task has provided valuable insights into detecting and understanding discriminatory behavior on online platforms.

2 Related Work

Initially, sentiment analysis relies heavily on artificial feature selection and a sentiment dictionary for classification (Thavareesan and Mahesan, 2020a; Jiang et al., 2023). Three levels of sentiment analysis were investigated: document, sentence, and aspect. To categorize the prevailing sentiment of the entire document and sentence, the tasks at the document and sentence levels are virtually identical. On the other hand, the objective at the facet level is to identify opinions expressed about entities and aspects of entities. Earlier research proposed a number of sentiment analysis methods. There are three categories of these approaches: (i) lexicon-based, (ii) machine learning, and (iii) hybrid. The vast majority of research in this area concentrates on a lexicon-based approach that compiles sentiment words. All sentiment analysis tasks require machine learning approaches, the majority of which are either supervised or semi-supervised. A supervised approach is a common solution for sentiment-related tasks. On the basis of labeled datasets, it is frequently employed to ascertain the polarity of sentiments. The advantage of this method is its capacity to adapt and build efficiently trained models for a specific domain. The primary disadvantage of this method, however, is its inefficiency when applied to diverse data across domains. This is due to domain dependence and data scarcity in specific domains. Since 2011, deep learning has been utilized in the field of sentiment analysis research.

3 Task details

Sentiment analysis is the task of identifying subjective opinions or emotional responses about a given topic. It has been an active area of research in the past two decades in academia and industry. There is an increasing demand for sentiment detection on social media texts which are largely code-mixed for Dravidian languages. Code-mixing is a prevalent phenomenon in a multilingual community, and code-mixed texts are sometimes written in non-native scripts. Systems trained on monolingual data fail on code-mixed data due to the complexity of code-switching at different linguistic levels in the text. The shared Task - A presents a new gold standard corpus for sentiment detection of code-mixed text in Dravidian languages (Tamil-English, and Tulu-English)[1].

The goal of this task is to identify the sentiment polarity of the code-mixed dataset of comments/posts in Tamil-English and Tulu-English collected from social media. The dataset description was tabulated in the Table 1. The comment/post may contain more than one sentence, but the average sentence length of the corpora is 1. Each comment/post is annotated with sentiment polarity at the comment/post level. This dataset also has class imbalance problems depicting real-world scenarios. Our proposal aims to encourage research that will reveal how sentiment is expressed in code-mixed techniques on social media.

4 Methodology

Our methodology for the sentiment analysis shared task involved implementing three traditional machine-learning models and performing several data processing steps. We started by importing essential packages such as Pandas, NumPy, and NLTK[2] with sklearn library[3]. These packages

[1] https://codalab.lisn.upsaclay.fr/competitions/11095

[2] https://www.nltk.org/

[3] https://scikit-learn.org/stable/

Table 1: Dataset description for Tamil and Tulu

Classes	Train	Dev	Test
Tamil			
Positive	20,070	2,257	73
Negative	4,271	480	338
unknown_state	5,628	611	137
Mixed_feelings	4,020	438	101
Tulu			
Positive	3,118	369	344
Negative	646	90	60
unknown_state	1,719	202	197
Mixed_feelings	974	120	107

played a crucial role in tasks such as data loading, cleaning, tokenization, vectorization, and modeling.

To begin, we read the train, development, and test files using Pandas, which contained the text data used for training and evaluating the sentiment analysis models. We then proceeded to clean the files by removing unwanted links, '@' symbols, and other characters that could potentially impact the accuracy of our models. Tokenization was performed using the NLTK package, breaking down the text data into individual words or terms. Lowercasing the contents of the files was another important step to ensure consistency, as it helped improve the models' ability to detect sentiment analysis accurately. Once the data was preprocessed, we used the Term Frequency - Inverse Document Frequency (TFIDF) vectorizer method to transform the text data into a numeric representation that could be utilized by our machine-learning models. The models employed for training were logistic regression, multinomial naive Bayes, and linear SVC. We trained these models using the preprocessed train data. To evaluate their performance, we utilized the development data, analyzing metrics such as the confusion matrix[4] and classification report[5]. The macro F1 scores obtained from the development data allowed us to determine the best-performing model.

In the final stage, we assessed the selected best model's performance using the test data. This step provided insights into the model's generalizability and effectiveness in handling new instances of sentiment analysis. Our comprehensive methodology ensured a robust approach to sentiment analysis in social media comments, leveraging traditional machine-learning techniques and effective data processing steps.

[4]https://scikit-learn.org/stable/modules/generated/sklearn.metrics.confusion_matrix.html

[5]https://scikit-learn.org/stable/modules/generated/sklearn.metrics.classification_report.html

5 Results and Discussion

In our evaluation of the machine learning models for sentiment analysis, we employed several performance metrics, including Accuracy (ACC), Macro Precision (M_P), Macro Recall (M_R), Macro F1 (M_F1), Weighted Precision (W_P), Weighted Recall (W_R), and Weighted F1 (W_F1) scores. Our experimentation involved three different models: Logistic Regression (LR), Multinomial Naive Bayes (MNB), and Linear Support Vector Classification (L-SVC), all utilizing TF-IDF feature extraction.

For the Tamil language, the macro F1 scores obtained for the models were as follows: logistic regression achieved a score of 0.43, Multinomial Naive Bayes obtained 0.20, and Linear Support Vector Classification achieved 0.41. Among these models, logistic regression performed particularly well in accurately identifying sentiment in Tamil social media comments when using the TF-IDF vectorizer. The overall classification report is tabulated in Table 2.

Moving on to the Tulu language, we obtained the following macro F1 scores: logistic regression achieved a score of 0.51, Multinomial Naive Bayes obtained 0.25, and Linear Support Vector Classification achieved 0.49. Once again, logistic regression demonstrated superior performance in accurately detecting sentiment in Tulu social media comments when utilizing TF-IDF feature extraction. The overall classification report is tabulated in Table 3.

These results indicate that the logistic regression model outperformed the other models across both Tamil and Tulu languages in terms of macro F1 scores. The TF-IDF vectorizer played a crucial role in capturing important features and enabling accurate sentiment analysis. Overall, our experiments show the effectiveness of logistic regression coupled with TF-IDF feature extraction for sentiment analysis in social media comments for both Tamil and Tulu languages. These findings highlight the potential of machine learning techniques in identifying sentiment and understanding discriminatory

Table 2: Results of the machine learning models with TFIDF in classification report for Tamil

Classifiers	ACC	M_P	M_R	M_F1	W_P	W_R	W_F1
LR	0.64	0.50	0.41	**0.43**	0.59	0.64	0.60
MNB	0.61	0.40	0.26	0.20	0.53	0.61	0.46
L-SVC	0.61	0.46	0.39	0.41	0.56	0.61	0.57

Table 3: Results of the machine learning models with TFIDF in classification report for Tulu

Classifiers	ACC	M_P	M_R	M_F1	W_P	W_R	W_F1
LR	0.66	0.60	0.50	**0.51**	0.64	0.66	0.62
MNB	0.55	0.34	0.30	0.25	0.46	0.55	0.42
L-SVC	0.61	0.53	0.47	0.49	0.58	0.61	0.59

behavior on online platforms in multilingual settings.

6 Conclusion

This study focused on the detection of sentiment analysis in the Tamil and Tulu languages using machine learning models. By employing traditional models with TF-IDF feature extraction, we achieved impressive results, with a macro F1 score of 0.43 on the Tamil test set and 0.51 on the Tulu test set. These findings underscore the effectiveness of our machine learning approach in accurately classifying sentiment analysis instances. We conclude that the TF-IDF with logistic regression (LR) model is a suitable choice for this task, offering potential applications in addressing social issues and promoting inclusivity in online spaces. Future research can further improve the model's performance through fine-tuning techniques and larger datasets. This study contributes to advancing sentiment analysis and highlights the importance of accurate sentiment classification in understanding and addressing social dynamics in multilingual online platforms.

References

Bharathi B and Agnusimmaculate Silvia A. 2021. SSNCSE_NLP@DravidianLangTech-EACL2021: Offensive language identification on multilingual code mixing text. In *Proceedings of the First Workshop on Speech and Language Technologies for Dravidian Languages*, pages 313–318, Kyiv. Association for Computational Linguistics.

Bharathi Raja Chakravarthi. 2022a. Hope speech detection in YouTube comments. *Social Network Analysis and Mining*, 12(1):75.

Bharathi Raja Chakravarthi. 2022b. Multilingual hope speech detection in english and dravidian languages. *International Journal of Data Science and Analytics*, 14(4):389–406.

Bharathi Raja Chakravarthi. 2023. Detection of homophobia and transphobia in youtube comments. *International Journal of Data Science and Analytics*, pages 1–20.

Bharathi Raja Chakravarthi, Adeep Hande, Rahul Ponnusamy, Prasanna Kumar Kumaresan, and Ruba Priyadharshini. 2022. How can we detect homophobia and transphobia? experiments in a multilingual code-mixed setting for social media governance. *International Journal of Information Management Data Insights*, 2(2):100119.

Subalalitha Chinnaudayar Navaneethakrishnan, Bharathi Raja Chakravarthi, Kogilavani Shanmugavadivel, Malliga Subramanian, Prasanna Kumar Kumaresan, Bharathi, Lavanya Sambath Kumar, and Rahul Ponnusamy. 2023. Findings of shared task on sentiment analysis and homophobia detection of youtube comments in code-mixed dravidian languages. In *Proceedings of the 14th Annual Meeting of the Forum for Information Retrieval Evaluation*, FIRE '22, page 18–21, New York, NY, USA. Association for Computing Machinery.

S. Divya, N. Sripriya, Daphne Evangelin, and G. Saai Sindhoora. 2023. Opinion classification on code-mixed Tamil language. In *Speech and Language Technologies for Low-Resource Languages*, pages 155–168, Cham. Springer International Publishing.

Akshat Gupta, Sai Krishna Rallabandi, and Alan W Black. 2021. Task-specific pre-training and cross lingual transfer for sentiment analysis in Dravidian code-switched languages. In *Proceedings of the First Workshop on Speech and Language Technologies for Dravidian Languages*, pages 73–79, Kyiv. Association for Computational Linguistics.

Asha Hedge, Bharathi Raja Chakravarthi, Hosahalli Lakshmaiah Shashirekha, Rahul Ponnusamy, Subalalitha Chinnaudayar Navaneethakrishnan, Lavanya S.K, Durairaj Thenmozhi, Martha Karunakar, Shreya Sriram, and Sarah Aymen. 2023. Findings of the shared task on sentiment analysis in tamil and tulu code-mixed text. In *Proceedings of the Third Workshop on Speech and Language Technologies for Dravidian Languages*, Varna, Bulgaria. Recent Advances in Natural Language Processing.

Lei Jiang, Yuan Li, Jing Liao, Ziwei Zou, and Caoqing Jiang. 2023. Research on non-dependent aspect-level sentiment analysis. *Knowledge-Based Systems*, 266:110419.

Md Rezaul Karim, Sumon Kanti Dey, Tanhim Islam, Md Shajalal, and Bharathi Raja Chakravarthi. 2022. Multimodal hate speech detection from bengali memes and texts. In *International Conference on Speech and Language Technologies for Low-resource Languages*, pages 293–308. Springer.

Prasanna Kumar Kumaresan, Rahul Ponnusamy, Elizabeth Sherly, Sangeetha Sivanesan, and Bharathi Raja Chakravarthi. 2022. Transformer based hope speech comment classification in code-mixed text. In *International Conference on Speech and Language Technologies for Low-resource Languages*, pages 120–137. Springer.

Sainik Mahata, Dipankar Das, and Sivaji Bandyopadhyay. 2021. Sentiment classification of code-mixed tweets using bi-directional RNN and language tags. In *Proceedings of the First Workshop on Speech and Language Technologies for Dravidian Languages*, pages 28–35, Kyiv. Association for Computational Linguistics.

Asrita Venkata Mandalam and Yashvardhan Sharma. 2021. Sentiment analysis of Dravidian code mixed data. In *Proceedings of the First Workshop on Speech and Language Technologies for Dravidian Languages*, pages 46–54, Kyiv. Association for Computational Linguistics.

El Mahdi Mercha and Houda Benbrahim. 2023. Machine learning and deep learning for sentiment analysis across languages: A survey. *Neurocomputing*, 531:195–216.

Subalalitha Chinnaudayar Navaneethakrishnan, Sathiyaraj Thangasamy, Nithya R, Info-farmer, and Neechalkaran. 2023. Exploring the opportunities and challenges in contributing to Tamil Wikimedia. In *Speech and Language Technologies for Low-Resource Languages*, pages 253–262, Cham. Springer International Publishing.

Ruba Priyadharshini, Bharathi raja Chakravarthi, Sajeetha Thavareesan, Dhivya Chinnappa, Durairaj Thenmozhi, and Rahul Ponnusamy. 2022. Overview of the dravidiancodemix 2021 shared task on sentiment detection in tamil, malayalam, and kannada. In *Proceedings of the 13th Annual Meeting of the Forum for Information Retrieval Evaluation*, FIRE '21, page 4–6, New York, NY, USA. Association for Computing Machinery.

Thanveer Shaik, Xiaohui Tao, Christopher Dann, Haoran Xie, Yan Li, and Linda Galligan. 2023. Sentiment analysis and opinion mining on educational data: A survey. *Natural Language Processing Journal*, 2:100003.

Kogilavani Shanmugavadivel, Malliga Subramanian, Prasanna Kumar Kumaresan, Bharathi Raja Chakravarthi, B Bharathi, Subalalitha Chinnaudayar Navaneethakrishnan, Lavanya Sambath Kumar, Thomas Mandl, Rahul Ponnusamy, Vasanth Palanikumar, et al. 2022. Overview of the shared task on sentiment analysis and homophobia detection of youtube comments in code-mixed dravidian languages.

Malliga Subramanian, Ramya Chinnasamy, Prasanna Kumar Kumaresan, Vasanth Palanikumar, Madhoora Mohan, and Kogilavani Shanmugavadivel. 2023. Development of multi-lingual models for detecting hope speech texts from social media comments. In *Speech and Language Technologies for Low-Resource Languages*, pages 209–219, Cham. Springer International Publishing.

Malliga Subramanian, Rahul Ponnusamy, Sean Benhur, Kogilavani Shanmugavadivel, Adhithiya Ganesan, Deepti Ravi, Gowtham Krishnan Shanmugasundaram, Ruba Priyadharshini, and Bharathi Raja Chakravarthi. 2022. Offensive language detection in tamil youtube comments by adapters and cross-domain knowledge transfer. *Computer Speech & Language*, 76:101404.

Sajeetha Thavareesan and Sinnathamby Mahesan. 2019. Sentiment Analysis in Tamil Texts: A Study on Machine Learning Techniques and Feature Representation. In *2019 14th Conference on Industrial and Information Systems (ICIIS)*, pages 320–325.

Sajeetha Thavareesan and Sinnathamby Mahesan. 2020a. Sentiment Lexicon Expansion using Word2vec and fastText for Sentiment Prediction in Tamil texts. In *2020 Moratuwa Engineering Research Conference (MERCon)*, pages 272–276.

Sajeetha Thavareesan and Sinnathamby Mahesan. 2020b. Word embedding-based Part of Speech tagging in Tamil texts. In *2020 IEEE 15th International Conference on Industrial and Information Systems (ICIIS)*, pages 478–482.

Durairaj Thenmozhi, C. Jerin Mahibha, S. Kayalvizhi, M. Rakesh, Y. Vivek, and V. Poojesshwaran. 2023. Paraphrase detection in Indian languages using deep learning. In *Speech and Language Technologies for Low-Resource Languages*, pages 138–154, Cham. Springer International Publishing.

Charangan Vasantharajan, Ruba Priyadharshini, Prasanna Kumar Kumarasen, Rahul Ponnusamy, Sathiyaraj Thangasamy, Sean Benhur, Thenmozhi Durairaj, Kanchana Sivanraju, Anbukkarasi Sampath, and Bharathi Raja Chakravarthi. 2023. Tamilemo: Fine-grained emotion detection dataset for Tamil.

In *Speech and Language Technologies for Low-Resource Languages*, pages 35–50, Cham. Springer International Publishing.

hate-alert@DravidianLangTech-2023: Multimodal Abusive Language Detection and Sentiment Analysis in Dravidian Languages

Shubhankar Barman
BITS Pilani, India
contact.shubhankarbarman@gmail.com

Mithun Das
IIT Kharagpur, India
mithundas@iitkgp.ac.in

Abstract

The use of abusive language on social media platforms is a prevalent issue that requires effective detection. Researchers actively engage in abusive language detection and sentiment analysis on social media platforms. However, most of the studies are in English. Hence, there is a need to develop models for low-resource languages. Further, the multimodal content in social media platforms is expanding rapidly. Our research aims to address this gap by developing a multimodal abusive language detection and performing sentiment analysis for Tamil and Malayalam, two under-resourced languages, based on the shared task "Multimodal Abusive Language Detection and Sentiment Analysis in Dravidian Languages: DravidianLangTech@RANLP 2023". In our study, we conduct extensive experiments utilizing multiple deep-learning models to detect abusive language in Tamil and perform sentiment analysis in Tamil and Malayalam. For feature extraction, we use the mBERT transformer-based model for texts, the ViT model for images and MFCC for audio. In the abusive language detection task, we achieved a weighted average F1 score of **0.5786**, securing the **first** rank in this task. For sentiment analysis, we achieved a weighted average F1 score of **0.357** for Tamil and **0.233** for Malayalam, ranking **first** in this task.

1 Introduction

Social media platforms have been expanding rapidly with a variety of content in different languages. On social media, users express their opinions with a few limitations, the majority of social media platforms allow users to share and express their thoughts and they aim to gather user comments and posts to offer a personalized feed. However, they are also used for negative activities, such as spreading rumors and bullying people with abusive words. Abuse of language has received a lot of attention as social media platforms have grown in popularity (Das et al., 2020; Banerjee et al., 2021; Das et al., 2021b). When someone uses language that is hurtful, disrespectful, or disparaging towards another person or group because of traits like race, ethnicity, gender, religion, sexual orientation, or other personal qualities, that language is considered abusive(Waseem et al., 2017). It has grown to be a major issue in online communities since it not only stifles positive and healthy discourse but also puts those exposed to it at risk for emotional and psychological harm.

Nowadays, people use different kinds of content on the social media platform, including video, audio, memes and text, to share their opinion or interact with other people (Das and Mukherjee, 2023; Das et al., 2023). The complexity of the computational processing of social media is more for multimodal data, which includes video, audio and text modalities because of the ambiguity at various levels as these types of data are more user-oriented and contextual(Schreck and Keim, 2012).

While there has been a study on abusive language identification and sentiment analysis in the English language for multimodal data, there is a significant lack of exploring these subjects specifically in the context of Dravidian languages. The situation for countries like India is more complicated due to the immense language diversity [1]. Tamil, Telugu, Malayalam and Kannada are Dravidian languages(Krishnamurti, 2003) that are largely spoken in southern India and have a rich linguistic heritage. However, the limited examination of abusive language detection and sentiment analysis in these languages presents unique obstacles and potential for research. As part of this shared task, we have explored Tamil and Malayalam languages(Chakravarthi et al., 2021c,a; Premjith et al., 2022). This shared task on multimedia social media analysis in Dravidian languages includes two sub-tasks -

[1] `https://en.wikipedia.org/wiki/Languages_of_India`

Third Workshop on Speech and Language Technologies for Dravidian Languages, pages 217–224, Varna, Bulgaria, Sep 7, 2023.
https://doi.org/10.26615/978-954-452-085-4_031

1. **Multimodal detection of abusive content in Tamil Language**: This sub-task involves developing models that can analyze textual, speech and visual components of videos from social media platforms, such as YouTube and predict whether they are *abusive* or *non-abusive*(Castro et al., 2019).

2. **Multimodal sentiment analysis in Dravidian languages[Tamil and Malayalam]**: This sub-task involves developing models that can analyze textual, speech and visual components of videos in Tamil and Malayalam from social media platforms, such as YouTube and identify the sentiments expressed in them. The videos are labeled into five categories: *highly positive*, *positive*, *neutral*, *negative* and *highly negative*.

The analysis of multi-modalities has gained significant importance, especially in the realm of video data, which encompasses various modalities such as video frames, speech signals and text transcripts. When training a machine learning model for sentiment analysis, it becomes crucial to incorporate features from these three modalities. Our research specifically targets abusive video detection, utilizing multiple modalities. The primary objective is to identify and remove hateful content from social networks. By considering the combined information from video frames, speech signals and text transcripts, our approach aims to effectively detect and mitigate abusive and harmful content circulating within these platforms.

The paper outlines the methodologies we employed to identify abusive content in Tamil, as well as perform sentiment analysis in Tamil and Malayalam languages on the shared task "Multimodal Abusive Language Detection and Sentiment Analysis in Dravidian Languages: DravidianLangTech@RANLP 2023"(Ashraf et al., 2021; Chakravarthi et al., 2021a; B et al., 2023; Chakravarthi et al., 2021c). To extract text features, we employed the transformer-based model mBERT, while for image feature extraction, we utilized the pre-trained ViT Model. Additionally, MFCC was employed for audio feature extraction. These approaches proved successful, leading us to secure the coveted **first** place in the final leaderboard standings for both tasks. Our techniques and models demonstrate the effectiveness of utilizing these feature extraction methods in the context of Dravidian languages.

2 Related Work

It is vital to filter the abusive content and inflammatory material that is constantly being posted on social media platforms. However, manual screening is nearly difficult due to the overwhelming volume of incoming posts. The research community gave this problem a lot of attention. According to numerous studies, posts in various languages on social media platforms are likely to be insulting or hateful. However, the majority of them spoke only English. There hasn't been much work done to address these concerns in Dravidian languages. This section discusses some of the Multimodal abusive language detection and sentiment analysis methods and briefly explains the multi-modal techniques used so far to detect abusive language.

2.1 Multi-modal abusive language detection

Most of the abusive language detection research were carried out considering textual or Image information (Li, 2021; Mandl et al., 2021; Ghanghor et al., 2021; Suryawanshi et al., 2020; Yasaswini et al., 2021; Chakravarthi et al., 2021a; Andrew, 2021) . There is very less work on Tamil language for detecting abusive content due to lack of resources in this language. As per the shared task we have video ,audio and text data for carrying out the research (Chakravarthi et al., 2021c,a). There are almost no work on multi-modal hate speech detection on Tamil language. Though there many researches on multi-modal hate speech detection for different languages other than Tamil (Das et al., 2023; Thapa et al., 2022; Das et al., 2021a) where they have considered video ,audio and text feature. Such multi-modal schemes typically use unimodal methods like CNNs, LSTMs or BERT to encode text and deep learning models such as ResNet, InceptionV3 to encode images and then perform multi-modal fusion using simple concatenation, gated summation, bi-linear trans-formation, or attention-based methods. Multi-modal bi-transformers like ViLBERT and Visual BERT have also been applied(Kiela et al., 2020).

As part of abusive speech detection, an array of techniques with diverse architecture ranging from video-based, text-based model, image-based model and multi-modal models have been employed(Mozafari et al., 2020; Das et al., 2023).

2.2 Multi-modal sentiment analysis in Dravidian languages

Multimodal sentiment analysis has attracted more and more attention recently (Baltrušaitis et al., 2019; Soleymani et al., 2017; Premjith et al., 2022). Most of the sentiment analysis based on audio or Text in English language (Poria et al., 2018, 2019). But in Dravidian Languages there are almost no work on multimodal sentiment analysis due to lack of resources and study in this area still seems to be in its infancy for this language . We have few woks in Dravidian languages but most of them are based on Text or audio (Ou and Li, 2020; Chakravarthi et al., 2021b). A lot of research has concentrated on creating a novel fusion network based on this topology to better capture multimodal representation(Cambria et al., 2018; Williams et al., 2018; Sahay et al., 2020; Blanchard et al., 2018). As per the shared task of sentiment analysis, we have video, audio and text data for carrying out the research (Chakravarthi et al., 2021c,a). Multimodal sentiment analysis mainly focuses on utilizing multiple resources to predict human emotions. Most multimodal models focus on three modalities: acoustic, visual and text; thus, we also experiment with multimodal sentiment analysis in Tamil and Malayalam languages, where we leverage all three modalities – text, audio and video. The videos are labeled into five categories: *highly positive*, *positive*, *neutral*, *negative* and *highly negative*.

3 Dataset Description

The competition organizers have released data sets for two different languages, Tamil and Malayalam (Chakravarthi et al., 2021c).

However, for the abusive language classification shared task, the dataset was only released for the Tamil language. Competition organizers have provided us with Video, Audio and the extracted texts present in them. The train, dev and test set distributions for both of them are as follows in Table 1.

Split	Abusive	Non-Abusive	Total
Train	38	32	70
Test	9	9	18

Table 1: Offensive Language Dataset Distribution (Tamil)

For the sentiment analysis shared task, the datasets were released for both Tamil and Malayalam languages. Sentiments are labeled into five categories for each language: *highly positive*, *positive*, *neutral*, *negative* and *highly negative*. The train, dev and test set distributions for both Tamil and Malayalam languages are showed as follows in the below Table 2.

Category	Tamil			Malayalam		
	Train	Test	Dev	Train	Test	Dev
highly positive	5	1	2	5	2	2
positive	29	5	4	31	3	5
neutral	4	2	2	5	2	1
negative	3	1	1	8	2	2
highly negative	3	1	1	1	1	0
Total	44	10	10	50	10	10

Table 2: Sentiment analysis Dataset Distribution (Tamil & Malayalam)

4 Methodology

In this section, we discuss the different parts of the pipeline that we pursued for the detection of *abusive* or *non-abusive* Language for the Tamil language using the dataset. Initially, we explored the visual aspects of the videos. Subsequently, the textual information is considered and used transformer-based pre-trained model mBERT. Then we considered audio-based MFCC features for the modeling. Finally, the visual, audio and textual features are combined to make more robust abusive content classification and sentiment analysis. Along with this, we will also discuss sentiment analysis in Tamil and Malayalam languages task.

4.1 Problem Formulation:

Task 1: Abusive Language Detection (Binary Classification) for Tamil : We formulate the abusive video detection problem in this paper as follows. Given a video V, the task can be represented as a binary classification problem. Each video is to be classified as abusive (y = 1) or non-abusive (y = 0). A video V can be expressed as a sequence of frames, i.e., F ={f1, f2, .., fn}, the associated audio A and the extracted video transcript T = {w1, w2, ..., wm}, consisting of a sequence of words. We aim to learn such a hate video classifier Z : Z(F; A; T) $\rightarrow$ y, where y belongs to {0, 1} is the ground-truth label of a video.

Task 2: Sentiment Analysis (Multi-class Classification) for Tamil and Malayalam: Given a video V, the objective is to classify its sentiment into one of five categories, denoted by S = {0, 1, 2,

3, 4}, representing *highly positive*, *positive*, *neutral*, *negative* and *highly negative* sentiments, respectively. The video V can be expressed as a sequence of frames, denoted as F = {f1, f2, ..., fn}. It also contains associated audio, denoted as A and an extracted video transcript T = {w1, w2, ..., wm}, consisting of a sequence of words in the specific language. The sentiment classifier is defined as S(F; A; T) $\rightarrow$ y, where y belongs to S represents the ground-truth label of the video, indicating the sentiment category it belongs to.

We have followed the below-mentioned methods for both **Task 1 (Abusive Language Detection)** and **Task 2 (Sentiment Analysis)** . For Task 1, we have done the modeling for the Tamil language; for Task 2, we have done similar modeling for both Tamil and Malayalam Languages separately. Along with it, as the data was very less for sentiment analysis for both languages, hence we have merged the data set for both languages and performed only for Fusion Model.

4.2 Uni-modal Models

As part of our initial experiments, we created the following three uni-model models, utilizing text features, audio features and image-based features.

mBERT:(Devlin et al., 2019) (multilingual BERT) is a transformer-based language model that has been pre-trained on a large corpus of multilingual text data. It is designed to handle multiple languages and exhibits strong cross-lingual transfer learning capabilities. mBERT captures contextualized representations of words and sentences, enabling it to understand the nuances of different languages and perform well on various natural language processing tasks. With its shared architecture and shared vocabulary, mBERT allows for efficient knowledge transfer between languages, making it a versatile and widely used model for multilingual applications. We pass all the texts associated with the video through the mBERT model and extracted 768-dimensional feature vectors.

Vision Transformer: (Dosovitskiy et al., 2020) The Vision Transformer (ViT) model is a transformer-based architecture specifically designed for computer vision tasks. Unlike traditional convolutional neural networks (CNNs), ViT applies self-attention mechanisms to capture global dependencies in images. It divides the input image into patches and treats them as tokens, allowing the model to learn representations for each patch and their interactions. ViT has shown promising results on various vision tasks, such as image classification, object detection and image generation, demonstrating the power of transformer-based models in the field of computer vision. As our focus is to detect abusive videos or sentiments associated with a video, we cannot use Vision Transformer directly. With the help of OpenCV (Open Source Computer Vision Library), we extracted images from the video for each 1 sec. We uniformly take 30 frames for each video and pass it through the pre-trained Vision Transformer(ViT) (Dosovitskiy et al., 2020) model to get a 768-dimensional feature vector for each frame and finally pass it through the LSTM network to obtain the prediction.

MFCC: The Mel Frequency Cepstral Coefficients (MFCC) (Xu et al., 2004) is one of the widely used techniques for describing audio and research has shown that it is efficient for difficult tasks including lung sound classification(Jung et al., 2021) and speaker identification. We use the MFCC features to obtain a representation of the audio in our dataset. Utilizing the free software Librosa[2], we create a 40-dimensional vector to represent the audio in order to build the MFCC characteristics.

4.3 Fusion Model

The models presented in the preceding subsections are unable to take use of the relationship between the features derived from the various modalities (such as video, audio and text transcript). We try to substantially merge the text-based, audio-based and vision-based models in order to harness the benefits of all the modalities effectively. For Task 1 and Task 2, in particular, we build the following models – (**mBERT + ViT + MFCC**), + refers to the combination operation of the three modalities through a trainable neural network (aka fusion layer). We denote this model as **Fusion 1.**

Due to very less dataset for Task 2, along with the above-mentioned Fusion approach **(Fusion 1)** we have merged data set for both languages and build same Fusion Model - (**mBERT + ViT + MFCC**) as mentioned previously. We denote this model as **Fusion 2**.

All the models are trained with cross-entropy loss functions and Adam optimizer for 30 epochs.

In both Binary-class classification and Multi-class classification, data is imbalanced. To balance the data, an extensive study has been conducted in

[2]https://librosa.org/doc/latest/index.html

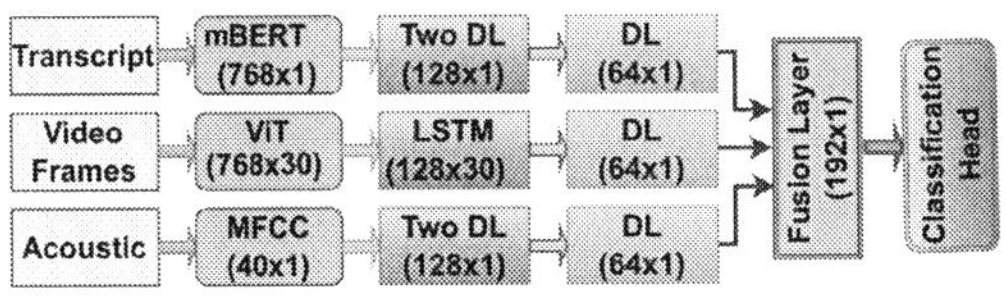

Figure 1: Illustrates the overall modeling pipeline

this area. Both oversampling and under-sampling are widely used techniques for balancing data, although they both have clear drawbacks. Using the class weight procedure, we attempted to reduce the effect of data imbalance.

5 Results

For **Task 1**, we observe among the uni-modal models and fusion-based model, mBERT and MFCC have the highest weighted F1 score of **0.5786** (mBERT: 0.5786, ViT: 0.5555, MFCC: 0.5786, Fusion (mBERT + ViT + MFCC): 0.5555). Table 3 demonstrates the performance of each model.

Abusive Language Detection- Tamil		
Model	**Accuracy**	**F1 Score(w)**
MFCC	**0.611111**	**0.578595**
mBERT	**0.611111**	**0.578595**
ViT	<u>0.555556</u>	<u>0.555556</u>
Fusion	<u>0.555556</u>	<u>0.555556</u>

Table 3: Performance Comparisons of Each Model.w: Weighted-Average. The best performance in each column is marked in **bold** and second best is underlined

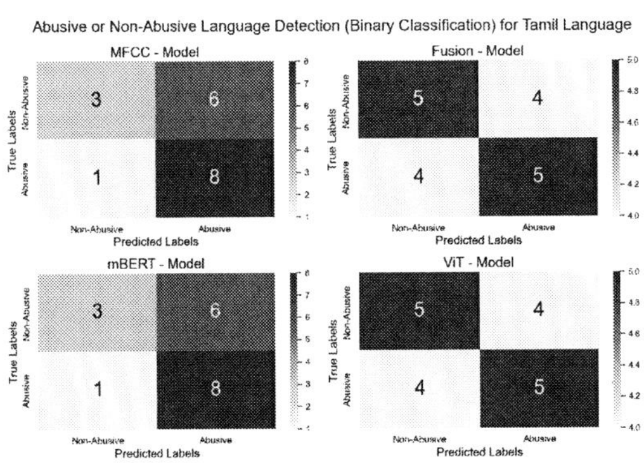

Figure 2: Confusion Matrix on Test Data for Each Model

For **Task 2 -Tamil language**, we observe among the uni-modal models and Fusion Models, ViT has highest weighted F1 score of **0.357** (mBERT: 0.250, ViT: 0.357, MFCC: 0.272, Fusion 1 (BERT

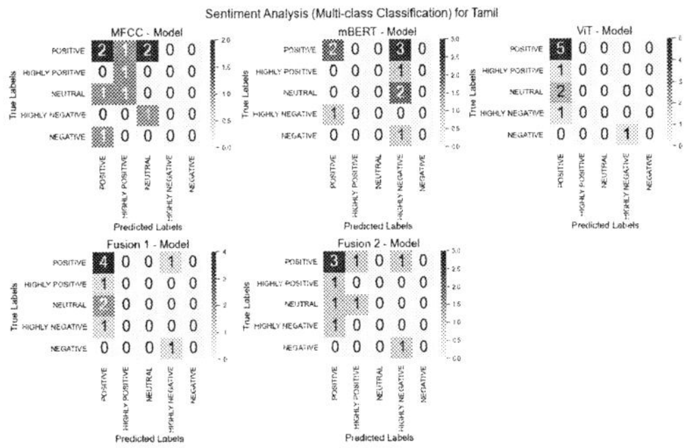

Figure 3: Sentiment Analysis (Multi-class Classification) for Tamil

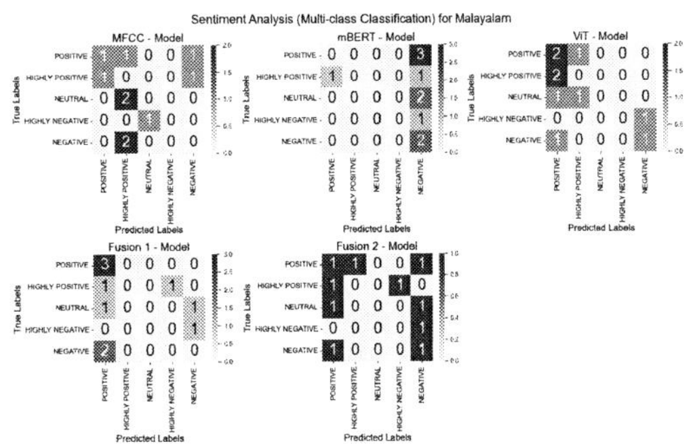

Figure 4: Sentiment Analysis (Multi-class Classification) for Malayalam

+ ViT + MFCC): 0.307 , Fusion 2 (BERT + ViT + MFCC): 0.272).

For **Task 2 -Malayalam language**, we observe among the uni-modal models and Fusion Models, ViT has highest weighted F1 score of **0.233** (mBERT: 0.0727, ViT: 0.233, MFCC: 0.120, Fusion 1 (BERT + ViT + MFCC): 0.180 , Fusion 2 (BERT + ViT + MFCC): 0.152).

To further understand the model's weakness, we show the confusion matrix of each model in Figure 2, 3 and 4 . We observe that both MFCC & BERT model performs better on the abusive language data, ViT performs better on the sentiment analysis data points for Tamil and Malayalam language. Insufficient data is the main reason behind poor performance on sentiment analysis for both languages and data is highly imbalanced for each class.

6 Conclusion

In this shared task, we deal with a novel problem of detecting Tamil abusive language and Sentiment analysis for both Tamil and Malayalam language. We evaluated different uni-modal models and in-

	Sentiment Analysis - Tamil			Sentiment Analysis - Malayalam		
Model	**Accuracy**	**F1 Score(w)**	**F1 Score(m)**	**Accuracy**	**F1 Score(w)**	**F1 Score (m)**
MFCC	0.3	0.272222	0.188889	0.1	0.120000	0.080000
mBERT	0.2	0.250000	0.100000	0.2	0.072727	0.072727
ViT	**0.5**	**0.357143**	**0.142857**	**0.3**	**0.233333**	**0.188889**
Fusion 1	<u>0.4</u>	<u>0.307692</u>	<u>0.123077</u>	<u>0.3</u>	<u>0.180000</u>	<u>0.120000</u>
Fusion 2	0.3	0.272727	0.109091	0.2	0.152381	0.123810

Table 4: Performance Comparisons of Each Model.w: Weighted-Average. m: macro, The best performance in each column is marked in bold and the second best is underlined

troduced a fusion model. We found that text-based model mBERT and Audio based MFCC performs better on the abusive language classification. For the sentiment analysis task, the video-based unimodal model ViT performs better on the sentiment analysis data points for Tamil and Malayalam languages. We plan to explore further other vision-based models to improve performance as an immediate next step.

References

Judith Jeyafreeda Andrew. 2021. JudithJeyafreedaAndrew@DravidianLangTech-EACL2021:offensive language detection for Dravidian code-mixed YouTube comments. In *Proceedings of the First Workshop on Speech and Language Technologies for Dravidian Languages*, pages 169–174, Kyiv. Association for Computational Linguistics.

Noman Ashraf, Arkaitz Zubiaga, and Alexander Gelbukh. 2021. Abusive language detection in youtube comments leveraging replies as conversational context. *PeerJ Computer Science*, 7:e742.

Premjith B, Sowmya V, Jyothish Lal G, Bharathi Raja Chakravarthi, Nandhini K, Rajeswari Natarajan, Abirami Murugappan, Bharathi B, Kaushik M, Prasanth S.N, Aswin Raj R, and Vijai Simmon S. 2023. Findings of the Multimodal Abusive Language Detection and Sentiment Analysis in Dravidian Languages @ dravidianlangtech-ranlp 2023. In *Proceedings of the Third Workshop on Speech and Language Technologies for Dravidian Languages DravidianLangTech 2023*. Recent Advances in Natural Language Processing.

Tadas Baltrušaitis, Chaitanya Ahuja, and Louis-Philippe Morency. 2019. Multimodal machine learning: A survey and taxonomy. *IEEE Transactions on Pattern Analysis and Machine Intelligence*, 41(2):423–443.

Somnath Banerjee, Maulindu Sarkar, Nancy Agrawal, Punyajoy Saha, and Mithun Das. 2021. Exploring transformer based models to identify hate speech and offensive content in english and indo-aryan languages. *arXiv preprint arXiv:2111.13974*.

Nathaniel Blanchard, Daniel Moreira, Aparna Bharati, and Walter J Scheirer. 2018. Getting the subtext without the text: Scalable multimodal sentiment classification from visual and acoustic modalities. *arXiv preprint arXiv:1807.01122*.

Erik Cambria, Devamanyu Hazarika, Soujanya Poria, Amir Hussain, and RBV Subramanyam. 2018. Benchmarking multimodal sentiment analysis. In *Computational Linguistics and Intelligent Text Processing: 18th International Conference, CICLing 2017, Budapest, Hungary, April 17–23, 2017, Revised Selected Papers, Part II 18*, pages 166–179. Springer.

Santiago Castro, Devamanyu Hazarika, Verónica Pérez-Rosas, Roger Zimmermann, Rada Mihalcea, and Soujanya Poria. 2019. Towards multimodal sarcasm detection (an _obviously_ perfect paper). *arXiv preprint arXiv:1906.01815*.

Bharathi Raja Chakravarthi, Ruba Priyadharshini, Navya Jose, Thomas Mandl, Prasanna Kumar Kumaresan, Rahul Ponnusamy, RL Hariharan, John Philip McCrae, Elizabeth Sherly, et al. 2021a. Findings of the shared task on offensive language identification in tamil, malayalam, and kannada. In *Proceedings of the first workshop on speech and language technologies for Dravidian languages*, pages 133–145.

Bharathi Raja Chakravarthi, Ruba Priyadharshini, Sajeetha Thavareesan, Dhivya Chinnappa, Durairaj Thenmozhi, Elizabeth Sherly, John P McCrae, Adeep Hande, Rahul Ponnusamy, Shubhanker Banerjee, et al. 2021b. Findings of the sentiment analysis of dravidian languages in code-mixed text. *arXiv preprint arXiv:2111.09811*.

Bharathi Raja Chakravarthi, KP Soman, Rahul Ponnusamy, Prasanna Kumar Kumaresan, Kingston Pal Thamburaj, John P McCrae, et al. 2021c. Dravidianmultimodality: A dataset for multi-modal sentiment analysis in tamil and malayalam. *arXiv preprint arXiv:2106.04853*.

Mithun Das, Somnath Banerjee, and Punyajoy Saha. 2021a. Abusive and threatening language detection in urdu using boosting based and bert based models: A comparative approach. *arXiv preprint arXiv:2111.14830*.

Mithun Das, Binny Mathew, Punyajoy Saha, Pawan Goyal, and Animesh Mukherjee. 2020. Hate speech in online social media. *ACM SIGWEB Newsletter*, (Autumn):1–8.

Mithun Das and Animesh Mukherjee. 2023. Transfer learning for multilingual abusive meme detection. In *Proceedings of the 15th ACM Web Science Conference 2023*, pages 245–250.

Mithun Das, Rohit Raj, Punyajoy Saha, Binny Mathew, Manish Gupta, and Animesh Mukherjee. 2023. Hatemm: A multi-modal dataset for hate video classification. In *Proceedings of the International AAAI Conference on Web and Social Media*, volume 17, pages 1014–1023.

Mithun Das, Punyajoy Saha, Ritam Dutt, Pawan Goyal, Animesh Mukherjee, and Binny Mathew. 2021b. You too brutus! trapping hateful users in social media: Challenges, solutions & insights. In *Proceedings of the 32nd ACM Conference on Hypertext and Social Media*, pages 79–89.

J. Devlin, Ming-Wei Chang, Kenton Lee, and Kristina Toutanova. 2019. Bert: Pre-training of deep bidirectional transformers for language understanding. In *NAACL*.

Alexey Dosovitskiy, Lucas Beyer, Alexander Kolesnikov, Dirk Weissenborn, Xiaohua Zhai, Thomas Unterthiner, Mostafa Dehghani, Matthias Minderer, Georg Heigold, Sylvain Gelly, et al. 2020. An image is worth 16x16 words: Transformers for image recognition at scale. *arXiv preprint arXiv:2010.11929*.

Nikhil Ghanghor, Parameswari Krishnamurthy, Sajeetha Thavareesan, Ruba Priyadharshini, and Bharathi Raja Chakravarthi. 2021. IIITK@DravidianLangTech-EACL2021: Offensive language identification and meme classification in Tamil, Malayalam and Kannada. In *Proceedings of the First Workshop on Speech and Language Technologies for Dravidian Languages*, pages 222–229, Kyiv. Association for Computational Linguistics.

SY Jung, CH Liao, YS Wu, SM Yuan, and CT Sun. 2021. Efficiently classifying lung sounds through depthwise separable cnn models with fused stft and mfcc features. diagnostics 2021, 11, 732.

Douwe Kiela, Hamed Firooz, Aravind Mohan, Vedanuj Goswami, Amanpreet Singh, Pratik Ringshia, and Davide Testuggine. 2020. The hateful memes challenge: Detecting hate speech in multimodal memes. *Advances in Neural Information Processing Systems*, 33:2611–2624.

Bhadriraju Krishnamurti. 2003. *The dravidian languages*. Cambridge University Press.

Zichao Li. 2021. Codewithzichao@DravidianLangTech-EACL2021: Exploring multimodal transformers for meme classification in Tamil language. In *Proceedings of the First Workshop on Speech and Language Technologies for Dravidian Languages*, pages 352–356, Kyiv. Association for Computational Linguistics.

Thomas Mandl, Sandip Modha, Anand Kumar M, and Bharathi Raja Chakravarthi. 2021. Overview of the hasoc track at fire 2020: Hate speech and offensive language identification in tamil, malayalam, hindi, english and german. In *Proceedings of the 12th Annual Meeting of the Forum for Information Retrieval Evaluation*, FIRE '20, page 29–32, New York, NY, USA. Association for Computing Machinery.

Marzieh Mozafari, Reza Farahbakhsh, and Noel Crespi. 2020. A bert-based transfer learning approach for hate speech detection in online social media. In *Complex Networks and Their Applications VIII: Volume 1 Proceedings of the Eighth International Conference on Complex Networks and Their Applications COMPLEX NETWORKS 2019 8*, pages 928–940. Springer.

Xiaozhi Ou and Hongling Li. 2020. Ynu@ dravidian-codemix-fire2020: Xlm-roberta for multi-language sentiment analysis. In *FIRE (Working Notes)*, pages 560–565.

Soujanya Poria, Devamanyu Hazarika, Navonil Majumder, Gautam Naik, Erik Cambria, and Rada Mihalcea. 2019. MELD: A multimodal multi-party dataset for emotion recognition in conversations. In *Proceedings of the 57th Annual Meeting of the Association for Computational Linguistics*, pages 527–536, Florence, Italy. Association for Computational Linguistics.

Soujanya Poria, Navonil Majumder, Devamanyu Hazarika, Erik Cambria, Alexander Gelbukh, and Amir Hussain. 2018. Multimodal sentiment analysis: Addressing key issues and setting up the baselines. *IEEE Intelligent Systems*, 33(6):17–25.

B Premjith, Bharathi Raja Chakravarthi, Malliga Subramanian, B Bharathi, Soman Kp, V Dhanalakshmi, K Sreelakshmi, Arunaggiri Pandian, and Prasanna Kumaresan. 2022. Findings of the shared task on multimodal sentiment analysis and troll meme classification in dravidian languages. In *Proceedings of the Second Workshop on Speech and Language Technologies for Dravidian Languages*, pages 254–260.

Saurav Sahay, Eda Okur, Shachi H Kumar, and Lama Nachman. 2020. Low rank fusion based transformers for multimodal sequences. *arXiv preprint arXiv:2007.02038*.

Tobias Schreck and Daniel Keim. 2012. Visual analysis of social media data. *Computer*, 46(5):68–75.

Mohammad Soleymani, David Garcia, Brendan Jou, Björn Schuller, Shih-Fu Chang, and Maja Pantic. 2017. A survey of multimodal sentiment analysis. *Image and Vision Computing*, 65:3–14.

Shardul Suryawanshi, Bharathi Raja Chakravarthi, Mihael Arcan, and Paul Buitelaar. 2020. Multimodal meme dataset (MultiOFF) for identifying offensive content in image and text. In *Proceedings of the Second Workshop on Trolling, Aggression and Cyberbullying*, pages 32–41, Marseille, France. European Language Resources Association (ELRA).

Surendrabikram Thapa, Aditya Shah, Farhan Jafri, Usman Naseem, and Imran Razzak. 2022. A multimodal dataset for hate speech detection on social media: Case-study of russia-Ukraine conflict. In *Proceedings of the 5th Workshop on Challenges and Applications of Automated Extraction of Socio-political Events from Text (CASE)*, pages 1–6, Abu Dhabi, United Arab Emirates (Hybrid). Association for Computational Linguistics.

Zeerak Waseem, Thomas Davidson, Dana Warmsley, and Ingmar Weber. 2017. Understanding abuse: A typology of abusive language detection subtasks. *arXiv preprint arXiv:1705.09899*.

Jennifer Williams, Ramona Comanescu, Oana Radu, and Leimin Tian. 2018. Dnn multimodal fusion techniques for predicting video sentiment. In *Proceedings of grand challenge and workshop on human multimodal language (Challenge-HML)*, pages 64–72.

Min Xu, Ling-Yu Duan, Jianfei Cai, Liang-Tien Chia, Changsheng Xu, and Qi Tian. 2004. Hmm-based audio keyword generation. In *Pacific-Rim Conference on Multimedia*, pages 566–574. Springer.

Konthala Yasaswini, Karthik Puranik, Adeep Hande, Ruba Priyadharshini, Sajeetha Thavareesan, and Bharathi Raja Chakravarthi. 2021. IIITT@DravidianLangTech-EACL2021: Transfer learning for offensive language detection in Dravidian languages. In *Proceedings of the First Workshop on Speech and Language Technologies for Dravidian Languages*, pages 187–194, Kyiv. Association for Computational Linguistics.

Supernova@DravidianLangTech2023 @Abusive Comment Detection in Tamil and Telugu - (Tamil, Tamil-English, Telugu-English)

A Ankitha Reddy
SSN College of Engineering
ankithareddy2210178@ssn.edu.in

Ann Maria Thomas
SSN College of Engineering
annthomas2210391@ssn.edu.in

Pranav Moorthi
SSN College of Engineering
pranav2210176@ssn.edu.in

Durairaj Thenmozhi
SSN College of Engineering
theni_d@ssn.edu.in

B. Bharathi
SSN College of Engineering
bharathib@ssn.edu.in

Gayathri G L
SSN College of Engineering
gayathri2010090@ssn.edu.in

Krithika S
SSN College of Engineering
krithika2010039@ssn.edu.in

Abstract

This paper presents our submission for Abusive Comment Detection in Tamil and Telugu - DravidianLangTech 2023 (Tamil, Tamil-English, Telugu-English. The aim is to classify whether a given comment is abusive or not. Support Vector Machines (SVM), Logistic Regression and Linear SVC Classifiers paired with Term Frequency–Inverse Document Frequency feature extraction were used and contrasted to make the classification models. The lack of annotated and balanced datasets for low-resource languages has also been acknowledged.

1 Introduction

Those statements that harbour ill feelings towards a person or a group of people are categorised as abusive comments. These comments consist of either profanity or racist, sexist, xenophobic, homophobic or transphobic connotations targeting members belonging to certain communities (Balouchzahi et al., 2022).

Identification of abuse over online social networks has proven to be a tedious task due to the overwhelming volume of content generated through social media (Ravikiran et al., 2022). These platforms offer a wide reach and the provision of anonymity can empower individuals to partake in hate speech, as they perceive themselves to be protected from facing immediate consequences for their actions.

A large portion of the users on social media platforms engage with other users in their respective native languages and most abusive content detection models are not trained to handle the diversity that exists in these numerous regional languages. The task of identifying abusive comments within the Tamil and Telugu languages (Priyadharshini et al., 2023b) is notably intricate and complex owing to the lack of linguistically tailored resources. This complexity stems from the scarcity of well-annotated datasets (Priyadharshini et al., 2022, 2023a) and proficiently trained models specific to these languages. The distinctive linguistic structures and contextual intricacies inherent in Tamil and Telugu pose obstacles to the creation of precise algorithms for detecting abusive language.

Abusive comments can lead to a hostile online environment, discouraging users from engaging in discussions or expressing themselves freely. Abusive comment detection in these languages allows for targeted content moderation that aligns with the linguistic and cultural context.

Overall, abusive comment detection in social media texts is essential for promoting user safety and enhancing user experience while fostering inclusivity and sustaining a respectful online environment.

2 Related Work

"A Comparison of Classical Versus Deep Learning Techniques for Abusive Content Detection on Social Media Sites" (Chen et al., 2018) addressed the fact that classifiers such as support vector machines (SVM), combined with bag of words or n gram feature representation, have traditionally dominated in text classification for decades. However, in the recent past, concepts under the domain of deep neural networks have begun gaining traction. They explored the impact of numerous levels of training set imbalances on different classifiers. In comparison, it was revealed that deep learning models (CNNs and KNNs) outperformed the traditional SVM classifier when the associated training dataset is seriously imbalanced. However, it was inferred that the performance of the SVM classifier could be dramatically improved through the method of oversampling, surpassing the deep learning models.

Though much work has been done to identify offensive content in major languages such as English (Chakravarthi et al., 2021), it is an arduous

Third Workshop on Speech and Language Technologies for Dravidian Languages, pages 225–230, Varna, Bulgaria, Sep 7, 2023.
https://doi.org/10.26615/978-954-452-085-4_032

task to identify and flag offensive and abusive content in low-resource languages, in the scope of our study, Dravidian languages, due to scarcity and unavailability of annotated datasets (Khan et al., 2021). Due to the predominance of the English script, the datasets involve multiple data points incorporating elements of code-switching or code-mixing (Chakravarthi et al., 2021; Ashraf et al., 2022; Shanmugavadivel et al., 2022). However (Akhter et al., 2021),attempted to detect the same in Urdu and Roman Urdu using, analysing and comparing five diverse ML models (SVM, NB, Logistic, IBK and JRip) and four DL models (BLSTM, CLSTM, LSTM and CNN). It was found that the convolutional neural network outperforms the other models and achieves 96.2 and 91.4 percentage accuracy on Urdu and Roman Urdu. The results also revealed that the one-layer architectures of deep learning models give better results than two-layer architectures.

More relevant to our cause, (Sazzed, 2021) annotated a Bengali corpus of 3000 transliterated Bengali comments and found that support vector machine (SVM) shows the highest efficacy for identifying abusive content. However, it is important to note that the dataset created was unbiased which may potentially be the cause for the outperformance of SVM. The paper delves deeper into the ubiquity of transliterated Bengali comments in social media as it renders monolingual approaches futile. It also addresses the issue of the lack of publicly available data for such low-resource languages. Other notable contributions allied with the scope of our study include (Kannan et al., 2014; Daumé III, 2004) pre-processing, SVM), each providing an extensive analysis of the pre-processing phase and the usage of SVM classifiers respectively, highlighting their merits and efficacy.

3 Dataset Analysis

The task has been furcated into three subdivisions based on the language of choice, namely Tamil-English, Tamil and Telugu-English. The target variables of the given datasets have been described below. The provided labels for the Tamil-English and Tamil tasks include None-of-the-above, Transphobic, Counter-speech, Misandry, Homophobia, Hope-Speech, Xenophobia and Misogyny while the Telugu-English includes hate and non-hate labels. The data distribution of each dataset is provided below.

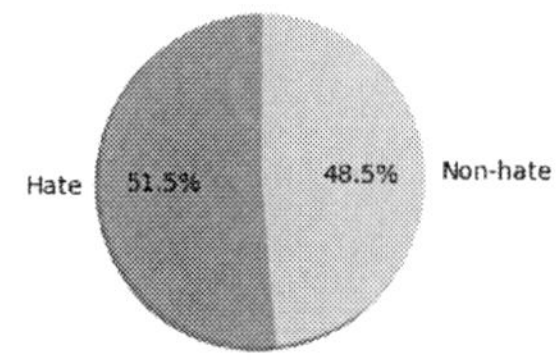

Figure 1: Data distribution of Telugu-English

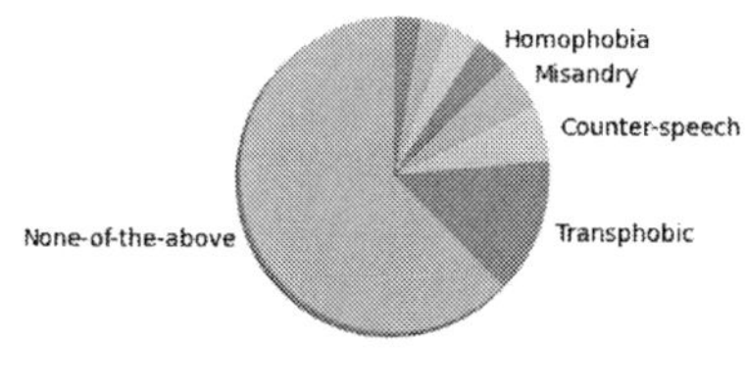

Figure 2: Data distribution of Tamil-English

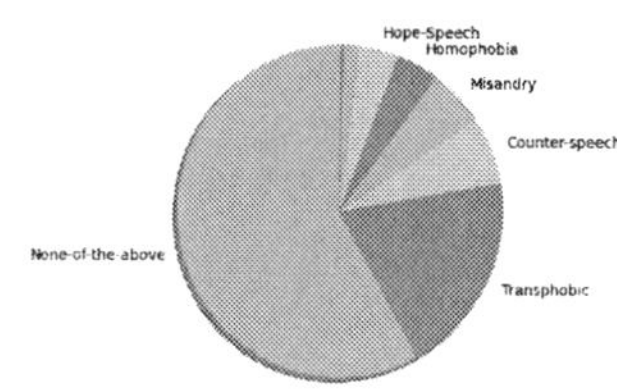

Figure 3: Data distribution of Tamil

Category	Telugu
Hate	1939
Non-Hate	2061

Table 1: Data distribution of Telugu

Category	Tamil	Tamil-English
None of the above	1296	3715
Misandry	446	830
Counter-Speech	149	348
Misogyny	125	211
Xenophobia	95	297
Hopespeech	86	213
Homophobia	35	172
Transphobic	6	157
Not Tamil	2	

Table 2: Data distribution of Tamil and Tamil-English

Analysis of the data distribution provides insights into the class imbalances which could potentially hinder the performance of the models without the appropriate measures in place.

The definition and usage of stop-words is crucial for the effectiveness of such code-mixed and code-switched datasets. While stop-words lists for languages such as English and Spanish have been implemented in the nltk.corpus library, the manual creation of stop-words lists for certain low-resource languages was necessitated. This was executed with the usage of previous domain and linguistic knowledge as well as online resources.

```
Tamil_stopwords = [ஒரு, என்று, மற்றும், இந்த, இது, என்ற, கொண்டு, என்பது, பல, ஆகும், அல்லது, அவர், நான், உள்ள, அந்த, இவர், என, முதல், என்ன, இருந்து, சில, என், போன்ற, வேண்டும், வந்து, இதன், அது, அவன், தான், பலரும், என்னும், மேலும், பின்னர், கொண்ட, இருக்கும், தனது, உள்ளது, போது, என்றும், அதன், தன், பிறகு, அவர்கள், வரை, அவள், நீ, ஆகிய, இருந்தது, உள்ளன, வந்த, இருந்த, மிகவும், இங்கு, மீது, ஓர், இவை, இந்தக், பற்றி, வரும், வேறு, இரு, இதில், போல், இப்போது, அவரது, மட்டும், இந்தப், எனும், மேல், பின், சேர்ந்த, ஆகியோர், எனக்கு, இன்னும், அந்தப், அன்று, ஒரே, மிக, அங்கு, பல்வேறு, விட்டு, பெரும், அதை, பற்றிய, உன், அதிக, அந்தக், பேர், இதனால், அவை, அதே, ஏன், முறை, யார், என்பதை, எல்லாம், மட்டுமே, இங்கே, அங்கே, இடம், இடத்தில், அதில், நாம், அதற்கு, எனவே, பிற, சிறு, மற்ற, விட, எந்த, எனவும், எனப்படும், எனினும், அடுத்த, இதனை, இதை, கொள்ள, இந்தத், இதற்கு, அதனால், தவிர, போல, வரையில், சற்று, எனக்]
```

4 Methodology

4.1 Preprocessing

Preprocessing of data is done to improve the efficiency of the model. The performance metrics of a model could vary drastically with efficient data preprocessing. The different steps involved in preprocessing of data are listed below.

1. Text Normalisation: By expanding contractions, and converting all the characters to lowercase, the text becomes more uniform and easier to analyse.

2. Removal of special characters, symbols and emojis: Special characters such as punctuation marks and emoticons do not donate any meaning to the text. Removal of these characters aids the machine learning model as it reduces the volume of text the model has to sort through.

3. Removal of stop words: Stop words refer to frequently occurring words that lack substantial semantic meaning or contribute minimally to the holistic comprehension of a given text. By eliminating these words, the data payload is reduced, resulting in expedited processing durations and enhanced computational efficacy.

4. Stemming of data: Stemming seeks to minimise words to their morphological base or root form. By stemming words, occurrences of related words are combined, giving a more accurate representation of their true frequency. This process is important for tasks such as sentiment analysis. Through vocabulary size reduction, stemming facilitates expedited model training and diminished memory demands for Natural Language Processing systems.

4.2 TF-IDF feature extraction

TF–IDF or Term Frequency–Inverse Document Frequency is a methodology used to create features from text data. It is a statistical measure of how important a word is in a collection of text or document.

$$TF = \frac{number\ of\ times\ term\ occurs\ in\ document}{total\ number\ of\ terms\ in\ document}$$

$$IDF = log\left(\frac{number\ of\ documents\ in\ corpus}{number\ of\ documents\ in\ corpus\ that\ contain\ the\ term}\right)$$

Words exclusive to a small proportion of documents receive higher importance than words recurring in all documents (e.g., a, the, and). TF-IDF vectorizer matches each feature to a corresponding numerical feature that is calculated from its TF-IDF score. The term frequency and inverse document frequency are multiplied to obtain the score. The term will have a higher TF-IDF score based on its relevance.

For this task, we used the TF-IDF to vectorize the preprocessed data into a classification model as it allows the conversion of unstructured text data into structured numerical representations that natural language processing models can work with. This representation enables the model to identify meaningful patterns and relationships in the text, facilitating sentiment analysis.

4.3 SVM Classifier

Support Vector Machine (SVM) is a supervised learning algorithm used to classify text data into different categories based on the features extracted from the text. SVM uses linear functions in a high dimensional feature space to categorise data using statistical learning theory (Cristianini and Shawe-Taylor, 2000; Daumé III, 2004). By drawing a hyperplane to segregate the classes in an n-dimensional space, it plots the data points as support vectors.

The TF-IDF feature vectors of the training samples are fed into the SVM algorithm. The SVM algorithm learns to find an optimal decision boundary that separates the feature vectors of different classes. Then, the algorithm classifies unlabeled text samples based on the patterns it discovered during the training phase.

4.4 Logistic Regression

Logistic regression establishes a relationship between independent variables and a categorical response or outcome variable by approximating the likelihood that the outcome belongs to a particular class. The regression model serves two objectives: (1) It aids in estimating the outcome variable when faced with new sets of predictive variable values (2) It is instrumental in providing insights into queries related to the subject under investigation. This is achieved through the utilisation of coefficients assigned to each predictive variable, which offer a clear understanding of the extent of each variable's contribution to the final result. (Vimal and Kumar, 2020)

The logistic regression function effectively converts any input values into a numeric range spanning from 0 to 1. The mathematical transformation executed by the logistic function serves to convert the initial linear combination into a reliable probability estimation.

$$P = \frac{e^{a+bX}}{1+e^{a+bX}}$$

4.5 Linear SVC

Linear SVC creates a hyperplane using a linear kernel function to classify the different data points. The data points are grouped into classes with common features. Maximising the margin width between the hyperplanes results in better classification. The support vectors drawn from each point to lines of separation are used to mathematically compute the goal function.

5 Results and Analysis

The evaluation of the task is done based on the following performance metrics: Precision, Recall and F1- score. Recall measures the classifier's ability to identify positive instances correctly while precision is a measure of how accurate the positive predictions are.

$$Recall = \frac{TP}{TP+FN} \quad Precision = \frac{TP}{TP+FP}$$

F1 score provides a harmonised assessment of a model's performance when both precision and recall are important.

$$F1 - score = 2 * \frac{Precision * Recall}{Precision + Recall}$$

	precision	recall	f1-score	support
hate	0.70	0.78	0.74	465
non-hate	0.79	0.71	0.75	535
accuracy			0.74	1000
macro avg	0.75	0.75	0.74	1000
weighted avg	0.75	0.74	0.74	1000

Figure 4: Classification report of SVM on Telugu dataset

	precision	recall	f1-score	support
hate	0.70	0.77	0.73	465
non-hate	0.78	0.71	0.74	535
accuracy			0.74	1000
macro avg	0.74	0.74	0.74	1000
weighted avg	0.74	0.74	0.74	1000

Figure 5: Classification report of Logistic Regression on Telugu dataset

	precision	recall	f1-score	support
hate	0.69	0.77	0.73	465
non-hate	0.78	0.70	0.74	535
accuracy			0.73	1000
macro avg	0.73	0.73	0.73	1000
weighted avg	0.74	0.73	0.73	1000

Figure 6: Classification report of Linear SVC on Telugu dataset

On exploration of the plethora of prospective models, the weighted average and macro average F1 scores of the models implemented for the Telugu dataset were as follows: Logistic Regression (0.74), SVM (0.74) and Linear SVC (0.73) (figures 6, 7 and 8). SVM and Logistic Regression had similar results, which outperformed Linear SVC marginally. Nonetheless, in comparison to Logistic Regression, the precision, recall and class-wise performance metrics of SVM were superior, corroborating the initial hypothesis on the class imbalances in the dataset.

	precision	recall	f1-score	support
0	0.69	0.99	0.81	917
1	0.00	0.00	0.00	40
2	0.00	0.00	0.00	95
3	0.78	0.50	0.61	218
4	1.00	0.02	0.05	43
5	1.00	0.02	0.04	53
6	1.00	0.40	0.57	70
7	1.00	0.02	0.04	50
accuracy			0.70	1486
macro avg	0.68	0.24	0.26	1486
weighted avg	0.69	0.70	0.62	1486

Figure 7: Classification report of SVM on Tanglish dataset

	precision	recall	f1-score	support
0	0.71	0.97	0.82	917
1	0.00	0.00	0.00	40
2	0.58	0.12	0.19	95
3	0.72	0.56	0.63	218
4	1.00	0.07	0.13	43
5	0.17	0.02	0.03	53
6	1.00	0.43	0.60	70
7	1.00	0.04	0.08	50
accuracy			0.71	1486
macro avg	0.65	0.28	0.31	1486
weighted avg	0.70	0.71	0.65	1486

Figure 8: Classification report of Logistic regression on Tanglish dataset

	precision	recall	f1-score	support
0	0.77	0.93	0.84	917
1	0.38	0.07	0.12	40
2	0.51	0.27	0.36	95
3	0.64	0.64	0.64	218
4	0.60	0.21	0.31	43
5	0.31	0.09	0.14	53
6	0.90	0.54	0.68	70
7	0.57	0.24	0.34	50
accuracy			0.73	1486
macro avg	0.59	0.38	0.43	1486
weighted avg	0.70	0.73	0.70	1486

Figure 9: Classification report of Linear SVC on Tanglish dataset

However, a point of interest is the superiority of Linear SVC over Logistic Regression and SVM classifiers on the Tamil and Tamil-English datasets. The classes in Linear SVC are separable by a linear hyperplane as opposed to SVM wherein kernel functions are employed to convert the non linear spaces to linear spaces by transforming data into a higher dimension. Hence, the better performance of the SVC classifier could be attributed to the linear separability of the Tamil and Tamil-English datasets since it minimises the probability of inaccurate classifications.

Furthermore, a deeper analysis of the classification reports substantiated the hypothesis regarding the impact of class imbalances on the model's performance. Evident from the aforementioned performance metrics, though the accuracy of the classifiers are similar for all the datasets utilised, the classifiers proved to perform significantly better with regard to the macro and weighted F1-scores on the Telugu dataset than the Tamil and Tamil-English datasets due to the lack of parity in the latter. Specifically on analysing the label-wise metrics, a predominant inference is the inability of the SVM, Logistic Regression and Linear SVC classifiers to generalise on the test data with a smaller quantity of data points for each label.

6 Conclusion

Our paper describes the models implemented that detect abusive comments in Tamil and Telugu. The objective was to classify comments as abusive or non-abusive. Data preprocessing was undertaken to ensure uniformity and three models were implemented along with Term Frequency–Inverse Document Frequency feature extraction. Support Vector Machines (SVM) Classifiers, Logistic regression and Linear SVC were utilised to build our classification models.

The SVM model performed the best on the Telugu dataset with a macro average and weighted F1-score of 0.74, while the Linear SVC model proved to perform better on the Tamil and Tamil-English datasets due to the relatively linear nature of the datasets utilised. This discrepancy is quite apparent particularly with regard to the macro average F1-score.

From a rudimentary perspective, the issues in dealing with datasets involving low-resource languages were acknowledged and rectified by appropriate measures such as the creation of stop words lists for such languages. Another cardinal drawback of the methods explored is due to the class imbalances. In future works, this could potentially be remedied by implementing clustering methods, bootstrapping or data enrichment techniques.

References

Muhammad Pervez Akhter, Zheng Jiangbin, Irfan Raza Naqvi, Mohammed AbdelMajeed, and Tehseen Zia. 2021. Abusive language detection from social media comments using conventional machine learning and deep learning approaches. *Multimedia Systems*, pages 1–16.

Nsrin Ashraf, Mohamed Taha, Ahmed Abd Elfattah, and Hamada Nayel. 2022. Nayel@ lt-edi-acl2022: Homophobia/transphobia detection for equality, diversity, and inclusion using svm. In *Proceedings of the Second Workshop on Language Technology for Equality, Diversity and Inclusion*, pages 287–290.

Fazlourrahman Balouchzahi, Sabur Butt, Grigori Sidorov, and Alexander Gelbukh. 2022. Cic@ lt-edi-acl2022: Are transformers the only hope? hope speech detection for spanish and english comments. In *Proceedings of the second workshop on language technology for equality, diversity and inclusion*, pages 206–211.

Bharathi Raja Chakravarthi, Ruba Priyadharshini, Sajeetha Thavareesan, Dhivya Chinnappa, Durairaj Thenmozhi, Elizabeth Sherly, John P McCrae, Adeep Hande, Rahul Ponnusamy, Shubhanker Banerjee, et al. 2021. Findings of the sentiment analysis of dravidian languages in code-mixed text. *arXiv preprint arXiv:2111.09811*.

Hao Chen, Susan McKeever, and Sarah Jane Delany. 2018. A comparison of classical versus deep learning techniques for abusive content detection on social media sites. In *Social Informatics: 10th International Conference, SocInfo 2018, St. Petersburg, Russia, September 25-28, 2018, Proceedings, Part I 10*, pages 117–133. Springer.

Nello Cristianini and John Shawe-Taylor. 2000. *An introduction to support vector machines and other kernel-based learning methods*. Cambridge university press.

Hal Daumé III. 2004. Support vector machines for natural language processing. *Lecture Notes*.

Subbu Kannan, Vairaprakash Gurusamy, S Vijayarani, J Ilamathi, Ms Nithya, S Kannan, and V Gurusamy. 2014. Preprocessing techniques for text mining. *International Journal of Computer Science & Communication Networks*, 5(1):7–16.

Lal Khan, Ammar Amjad, Noman Ashraf, Hsien-Tsung Chang, and Alexander Gelbukh. 2021. Urdu sentiment analysis with deep learning methods. *IEEE Access*, 9:97803–97812.

Ruba Priyadharshini, Bharathi Raja Chakravarthi, Subalalitha Chinnaudayar Navaneethakrishnan, Malliga Subramanian, Kogilavani Shanmugavadivel, Premjith B, Abirami Murugappan, Sai Prashanth Karnati, Rishith, Chandu Janakiram, and Prasanna Kumar Kumaresan. 2023a. Findings of the shared task on Abusive Comment Detection in Tamil and Telugu. In *Proceedings of the Third Workshop on Speech and Language Technologies for Dravidian Languages DravidianLangTech 2023*. Recent Advances in Natural Language Processing.

Ruba Priyadharshini, Bharathi Raja Chakravarthi, Subalalitha Cn, Thenmozhi Durairaj, Malliga Subramanian, Kogilavani Shanmugavadivel, Siddhanth U Hegde, and Prasanna Kumaresan. 2022. Overview of abusive comment detection in Tamil-ACL 2022. In *Proceedings of the Second Workshop on Speech and Language Technologies for Dravidian Languages*, pages 292–298, Dublin, Ireland. Association for Computational Linguistics.

Ruba Priyadharshini, Bharathi Raja Chakravarthi, Malliga S, SUBALALITHA CN, Kogilavani S V, Premjith B, Abirami Murugappan, and Prasanna Kumar Kumaresan. 2023b. Overview of shared-task on abusive comment detection in tamil and telugu. In *Proceedings of the Third Workshop on Speech and Language Technologies for Dravidian Languages*, Varna, Bulgaria. Recent Advances in Natural Language Processing.

Manikandan Ravikiran, Bharathi Raja Chakravarthi, Anand Kumar Madasamy, Sangeetha Sivanesan, Ratnavel Rajalakshmi, Sajeetha Thavareesan, Rahul Ponnusamy, and Shankar Mahadevan. 2022. Findings of the shared task on offensive span identification from code-mixed tamil-english comments. *arXiv preprint arXiv:2205.06118*.

Salim Sazzed. 2021. Abusive content detection in transliterated bengali-english social media corpus. In *Proceedings of the Fifth Workshop on Computational Approaches to Linguistic Code-Switching*, pages 125–130.

Kogilavani Shanmugavadivel, Sai Haritha Sampath, Pramod Nandhakumar, Prasath Mahalingam, Malliga Subramanian, Prasanna Kumar Kumaresan, and Ruba Priyadharshini. 2022. An analysis of machine learning models for sentiment analysis of tamil code-mixed data. *Computer Speech & Language*, 76:101407.

Bhartendoo Vimal and S Anupama Kumar. 2020. Application of logistic regression in natural language processing. *Int J Eng Res*, 9.

AbhiPaw@ DravidianLangTech: Abusive Comment Detection in Tamil and Telugu using Logistic Regression

Abhinaba Bala
IIIT Hyderabad, India
abhinaba.bala@research.iiit.ac.in

Parameswari Krishnamurthy
IIIT Hyderabad, India
param.krishna@iiit.ac.in

Abstract

Abusive comments in online platforms have become a significant concern, necessitating the development of effective detection systems. However, limited work has been done in low resource languages, including Dravidian languages. This paper addresses this gap by focusing on abusive comment detection in a dataset containing Tamil, Tamil-English and Telugu-English code-mixed comments. Our methodology involves logistic regression and explores suitablef embeddings to enhance the performance of the detection model. Through rigorous experimentation, we identify the most effective combination of logistic regression and embeddings. The results demonstrate the performance of our proposed model, which contributes to the development of robust abusive comment detection systems in low resource language settings.

Keywords: Abusive comment detection, Dravidian languages, logistic regression, embeddings, low resource languages, code-mixed dataset.

1 Introduction

The widespread prevalence of abusive comments in online social networks (OSNs) has raised serious concerns about the safety and well-being of users. Detecting and mitigating abusive content has become a paramount objective in fostering a respectful and inclusive online environment. While significant progress has been made in abusive comment detection, much of the existing research primarily focuses on high-resource languages, leaving a critical gap in addressing this issue in low resource languages. The lack of resources and research devoted to comprehending and addressing abusive content in these languages poses a hindrance to the development of efficient detection systems.

In recent studies conducted by Abusive Comment Detection in Tamil - ACL 2022 (Priyadharshini et al., 2022), a shared task was introduced to detect categories of abusive comments in social media, focusing on languages such as Tamil and code-mixed language containing Tamil and English scripts. Swaminathan et al. (Swaminathan et al., 2022) proposed a classification model that combines language-agnostic sentence embeddings with TF-IDF vector representation, employing traditional classifiers. Balouchzahi et al. (Balouchzahi et al., 2022) addressed abusive comment detection in native Tamil script texts and code-mixed Tamil texts using n-gram-Multilayer Perceptron (n-gram-MLP) and 1D Convolutional Long Short-Term Memory (1D Conv-LSTM) models. S.N. et al. (S N et al., 2022) employed TF-IDF with char-wb analyzers and the Support Vector Machine (SVM) classifier with a polynomial kernel for classification. These studies demonstrate initial attempts to tackle abusive comment detection in low resource languages, but further research is necessary to address the challenges specific to these languages comprehensively.

The unique linguistic characteristics and nuances of Dravidian languages present significant challenges in detecting abusive comments accurately. Additionally, the limited availability of annotated datasets and language-specific linguistic features further exacerbate these challenges. Therefore, it is crucial to explore novel approaches and methodologies tailored specifically for detecting abusive comments in Dravidian and other low resource languages.

In this paper, we aim to bridge the research gap by comprehensively reviewing the state-of-the-art techniques and methodologies employed in abusive comment detection. Our primary focus will be on addressing the challenges faced in low resource languages, with a specific emphasis on Dravidian languages.

The outcomes of this research have significant

Third Workshop on Speech and Language Technologies for Dravidian Languages, pages 231–234, Varna, Bulgaria, Sep 7, 2023.
https://doi.org/10.26615/978-954-452-085-4_033

implications, as they contribute to building safer online communities in low resource language contexts, empower content moderators, and facilitate the development of automated systems capable of detecting and mitigating abusive comments effectively. By addressing the specific needs of Dravidian languages, we pave the way for further research in other low resource languages, promoting a more inclusive and equitable digital space.

In summary, this paper serves as a significant step towards understanding and combating abusive comment detection in low resource languages, with a particular focus on Dravidian languages. By leveraging innovative techniques and proposing tailored solutions, we aim to make substantial progress in creating a safer and more respectful online environment for users of diverse linguistic backgrounds. This work was submitted as a part of the DravidianLangTech workshop, 2023 (Priyadharshini et al., 2023b).

2 Related Work

Numerous studies have been conducted to identify abusive comments in various languages; however, there has been relatively less work done in low resource languages, highlighting a research gap in this area.

(Priyadharshini et al., 2023a), (Priyadharshini et al., 2022) conducted a shared task (at ACL 2022) that aims at detecting the categories of abusive comments that are posted on social media. They aggregate the comments from social media in two languages, namely, Tamil and in code mixed language containing Tamil and English scripts.

(Swaminathan et al., 2022) approached by building a classification model which includes different methods of feature extraction and the use of traditional classifiers. They propose a novel method of combining language-agnostic sentence embeddings with the TF-IDF vector representation that uses a curated corpus of words as vocabulary, to create a custom embedding, which is then passed to an SVM classifier. (Balouchzahi et al., 2022) addresses the abusive comment detection in native Tamil script texts and code-mixed Tamil texts. To address this challenge, two models: i) n-gram-Multilayer Perceptron (n-gram-MLP) model utilizing MLP classifier fed with char-n gram features and ii) 1D Convolutional Long Short-Term Memory (1D Conv-LSTM) model, were submitted. (S N et al., 2022) used TF-IDF with char-wb analyzers with Random Kitchen Sink (RKS) algorithm to create feature vectors and the Support Vector Machine (SVM) classifier with polynomial kernel for classification.

Transformer is an attention-based technique that effectively captures the contextual connections between words (or subwords) within a text, attracting significant attention in the field. (García-Díaz et al., 2022) sbow a knowledge integration strategy that combines sentence embeddings from BERT, RoBERTa, FastText and a subset of language-independent linguistic features. (Prasad et al., 2022) present XLM-RoBERTa and DeBERTa models for two multi-class text classification tasks in Tamil. (Biradar and Saumya, 2022) used a pre-trained transformer model such as Indic-bert for feature extraction, and on top of that, SVM classifier is used for stance detection. (Pahwa, 2022) presented an exploration of different techniques which can be used to tackle and increase the accuracy of models using data augmentation in NLP. (B and Varsha, 2022) used pre-trained transformer models such as BERT,m-BERT, and XLNET.

Certain works experiment with multiple methods individually to find the best performing model. (Rajalakshmi et al., 2022) approached the task with three methodologies - Machine Learning, Deep Learning and Transformer-based modeling. For Machine Learning, eight algorithms were implemented, among which Random Forest gave the best result with Tamil+English dataset for Deep Learning, Bi-Directional LSTM gave best result with pre-trained word embeddings. In Transformer-based modeling, they used IndicBERT and mBERT with fine-tuning, among which mBERT gave the best result. (Hossain et al., 2022) employed three machine learning (LR, DT, SVM), two deep learning (CNN+BiLSTM, CNN+BiLSTM with FastText) and a transformer-based model (Indic-BERT). The experimental results show that Logistic regression (LR) and CNN+BiLSTM models outperformed the others. (Bhattacharyya, 2022) experimented with logistic regression, SVMs, gradient boost classifier, finetuned MuRIL; with gradient boost classifier emerged to be the best performing method. (Patankar et al., 2022) also used three methods to optimize their results: Ensemble models, Recurrent Neural Networks, and Transformers.

3 Method

The objective of this task is to determine if a given YouTube comment exhibits abusive content.

3.1 Feature Extraction

The TfidfVectorizer is a feature extraction technique commonly used in natural language processing (NLP) and text mining tasks. "TF-IDF" stands for Term Frequency-Inverse Document Frequency, which represents the importance of a word within a document in a corpus [cite :: (Sammut and Webb, 2010)].

The TfidfVectorizer calculates the TF-IDF value for each term (word) in a document by considering its frequency within the document and the inverse document frequency across the entire corpus. The TF-IDF value reflects the significance of a term in a document relative to its frequency in other documents.

The TfidfVectorizer converts a collection of raw text documents into a matrix representation where each row corresponds to a document and each column corresponds to a term. The matrix elements represent the TF-IDF values of the terms in the documents.

This vectorization technique is widely used for tasks such as text classification, information retrieval, and document similarity analysis. It helps capture the discriminative and important terms in a document while downweighting common and less informative terms.

3.2 Classifiers

The Logistic Regression model, trained on the feature vectors, employs a multi-class variant of the algorithm to classify comments into multiple abusive categories. It estimates the probability of each class and assigns the comment to the category with the highest probability. The model's training objective involves optimizing the parameters to minimize the discrepancy between the predicted probabilities and the true class labels across all classes.

4 Experiments and Results

4.1 Evaluation Metrics

The macro average F1-score is the performance metric used to evaluate the overall effectiveness of the detection model. It is derived by calculating the F1-score for each individual class and then taking the average across all classes. Regardless of class size or class imbalance, the macro average F1-score considers the performance of each class independently and then computes the average, giving equal importance to all classes.

4.2 Datasets

The dataset is provided by (Priyadharshini et al., 2023a), (Priyadharshini et al., 2022) as a shared task challenge for Abusive Comment Detection in Tamil and Telugu-DravidianLangTech@RANLP 2023. There are three datasets - Tamil, Tamil-English and Telugu-English

4.3 Results

We achieved a macro F1-score a. 0.27 in Tamil, 0.29 in Tamil-English, 0.6319 in Telugu languages. The current scores are suboptimal, indicating room for enhancement.

5 Conclusion

By transforming textual data into numerical features and employing the logistic function for multi-class classification, Logistic Regression enables accurate identification and categorization of abusive comments into multiple abusive categories, facilitating comprehensive analysis and understanding of the data.

As future work we look forward to use fine tuning on the specific datasets and investigate cross-lingual transfer learning.

References

Bharathi B and Josephine Varsha. 2022. SSNCSE NLP@TamilNLP-ACL2022: Transformer based approach for detection of abusive comment for Tamil language. In *Proceedings of the Second Workshop on Speech and Language Technologies for Dravidian Languages*, pages 158–164, Dublin, Ireland. Association for Computational Linguistics.

Fazlourrahman Balouchzahi, Anusha Gowda, Hosahalli Shashirekha, and Grigori Sidorov. 2022. MUCIC@TamilNLP-ACL2022: Abusive comment detection in Tamil language using 1D conv-LSTM. In *Proceedings of the Second Workshop on Speech and Language Technologies for Dravidian Languages*, pages 64–69, Dublin, Ireland. Association for Computational Linguistics.

Aanisha Bhattacharyya. 2022. Aanisha@TamilNLP-ACL2022:abusive detection in Tamil. In *Proceedings of the Second Workshop on Speech and Language Technologies for Dravidian Languages*, pages 214–220, Dublin, Ireland. Association for Computational Linguistics.

Shankar Biradar and Sunil Saumya. 2022. IIITDWD@TamilNLP-ACL2022: Transformer-based approach to classify abusive content in Dravidian code-mixed text. In *Proceedings of the Second Workshop on Speech and Language Technologies for Dravidian Languages*, pages 100–104, Dublin, Ireland. Association for Computational Linguistics.

José García-Díaz, Manuel Valencia-Garcia, and Rafael Valencia-García. 2022. UMUTeam@TamilNLP-ACL2022: Abusive detection in Tamil using linguistic features and transformers. In *Proceedings of the Second Workshop on Speech and Language Technologies for Dravidian Languages*, pages 45–50, Dublin, Ireland. Association for Computational Linguistics.

Alamgir Hossain, Mahathir Bishal, Eftekhar Hossain, Omar Sharif, and Mohammed Moshiul Hoque. 2022. COMBATANT@TamilNLP-ACL2022: Fine-grained categorization of abusive comments using logistic regression. In *Proceedings of the Second Workshop on Speech and Language Technologies for Dravidian Languages*, pages 221–228, Dublin, Ireland. Association for Computational Linguistics.

Bhavish Pahwa. 2022. BpHigh@TamilNLP-ACL2022: Effects of data augmentation on indic-transformer based classifier for abusive comments detection in Tamil. In *Proceedings of the Second Workshop on Speech and Language Technologies for Dravidian Languages*, pages 138–144, Dublin, Ireland. Association for Computational Linguistics.

Shantanu Patankar, Omkar Gokhale, Onkar Litake, Aditya Mandke, and Dipali Kadam. 2022. Optimize_Prime@DravidianLangTech-ACL2022: Abusive comment detection in Tamil. In *Proceedings of the Second Workshop on Speech and Language Technologies for Dravidian Languages*, pages 235–239, Dublin, Ireland. Association for Computational Linguistics.

Gaurang Prasad, Janvi Prasad, and Gunavathi C. 2022. GJG@TamilNLP-ACL2022: Using transformers for abusive comment classification in Tamil. In *Proceedings of the Second Workshop on Speech and Language Technologies for Dravidian Languages*, pages 93–99, Dublin, Ireland. Association for Computational Linguistics.

Ruba Priyadharshini, Bharathi Raja Chakravarthi, Subalalitha Chinnaudayar Navaneethakrishnan, Malliga Subramanian, Kogilavani Shanmugavadivel, Premjith B, Abirami Murugappan, Sai Prashanth Karnati, Rishith, Chandu Janakiram, and Prasanna Kumar Kumaresan. 2023a. Findings of the shared task on Abusive Comment Detection in Tamil and Telugu. In *Proceedings of the Third Workshop on Speech and Language Technologies for Dravidian Languages DravidianLangTech 2023*. Recent Advances in Natural Language Processing.

Ruba Priyadharshini, Bharathi Raja Chakravarthi, Subalalitha Cn, Thenmozhi Durairaj, Malliga Subramanian, Kogilavani Shanmugavadivel, Siddhanth U Hegde, and Prasanna Kumaresan. 2022. Overview of abusive comment detection in Tamil-ACL 2022. In *Proceedings of the Second Workshop on Speech and Language Technologies for Dravidian Languages*, pages 292–298, Dublin, Ireland. Association for Computational Linguistics.

Ruba Priyadharshini, Bharathi Raja Chakravarthi, Malliga S, SUBALALITHA CN, Kogilavani S V, Premjith B, Abirami Murugappan, and Prasanna Kumar Kumaresan. 2023b. Overview of shared-task on abusive comment detection in tamil and telugu. In *Proceedings of the Third Workshop on Speech and Language Technologies for Dravidian Languages*, Varna, Bulgaria. Recent Advances in Natural Language Processing.

Ratnavel Rajalakshmi, Ankita Duraphe, and Antonette Shibani. 2022. DLRG@DravidianLangTech-ACL2022: Abusive comment detection in Tamil using multilingual transformer models. In *Proceedings of the Second Workshop on Speech and Language Technologies for Dravidian Languages*, pages 207–213, Dublin, Ireland. Association for Computational Linguistics.

Prasanth S N, R Aswin Raj, Adhithan P, Premjith B, and Soman Kp. 2022. CEN-Tamil@DravidianLangTech-ACL2022: Abusive comment detection in Tamil using TF-IDF and random kitchen sink algorithm. In *Proceedings of the Second Workshop on Speech and Language Technologies for Dravidian Languages*, pages 70–74, Dublin, Ireland. Association for Computational Linguistics.

Krithika Swaminathan, Divyasri K, Gayathri G L, Thenmozhi Durairaj, and Bharathi B. 2022. PANDAS@abusive comment detection in Tamil code-mixed data using custom embeddings with LaBSE. In *Proceedings of the Second Workshop on Speech and Language Technologies for Dravidian Languages*, pages 112–119, Dublin, Ireland. Association for Computational Linguistics.

AbhiPaw@ DravidianLangTech: Fake News Detection in Dravidian Languages using Multilingual BERT

Abhinaba Bala
IIIT Hyderabad, India
abhinaba.bala@research.iiit.ac.in

Parameswari Krishnamurthy
IIIT Hyderabad, India
param.krishna@iiit.ac.in

Abstract

This study addresses the challenge of detecting fake news in Dravidian languages by leveraging Google's MuRIL (Multilingual Representations for Indian Languages) model. Drawing upon previous research, we investigate the intricacies involved in identifying fake news and explore the potential of transformer-based models for linguistic analysis and contextual understanding. Through supervised learning, we fine-tune the "muril-base-cased" variant of MuRIL using a carefully curated dataset of labeled comments and posts in Dravidian languages, enabling the model to discern between original and fake news. During the inference phase, the fine-tuned MuRIL model analyzes new textual content, extracting contextual and semantic features to predict the content's classification. We evaluate the model's performance using standard metrics, highlighting the effectiveness of MuRIL in detecting fake news in Dravidian languages and contributing to the establishment of a safer digital ecosystem.

Keywords: fake news detection, Dravidian languages, MuRIL, transformer-based models, linguistic analysis, contextual understanding.x

1 Introduction

The proliferation of fake news has become a pressing concern in the digital age, significantly impacting the accuracy and credibility of information dissemination. Detecting and combating fake news is a critical task to ensure the integrity of news sources and promote informed decision-making. While extensive research has been conducted in various languages and domains, the detection of fake news in the Dravidian language poses unique challenges due to its linguistic characteristics and cultural nuances.

The challenges involved in fake news detection have been widely explored in the literature. Previous studies have examined different task formulations, datasets, and NLP solutions to address this issue (Oshikawa et al., 2020). Understanding the potential and limitations of existing approaches is essential for developing effective strategies in the context of the Dravidian language.

While existing research has made significant contributions to fake news detection, the unique linguistic characteristics and cultural context of the Dravidian language necessitate dedicated efforts and language-specific approaches. This paper aims to address the challenges of fake news detection in the Dravidian language by exploring methodologies, datasets, and potential avenues for future research. By leveraging insights from related work, we aim to contribute to the development of effective and culturally sensitive solutions for detecting fake news in the Dravidian language space.

2 Related Work

To understand the challenges involved in fake news detection (Oshikawa et al., 2020) made a survey, along with describing the related tasks. They systematically review and compare the task formulations, datasets and NLP solutions that have been developed for the task, and also discuss the potentials and limitations of them. (Goldani et al., 2020) propose a new model based on capsule neural networks for detecting fake news, they also propose two architectures for different lengths of news statements.

With increase in popularity of graph networks, following are some works in fake news detection. (Veselý and Veselý, 2021) propose FANG, a novel graphical social context representation and learning framework for fake news detection. Unlike previous contextual models that have targeted performance, their focus is on representation learning. (Ren et al., 2020) present Adversarial Active Learning-based Heterogeneous Graph Neural Net-

Third Workshop on Speech and Language Technologies for Dravidian Languages, pages 235–238, Varna, Bulgaria, Sep 7, 2023.
https://doi.org/10.26615/978-954-452-085-4_034

work (AA-HGNN) which employs a novel hierarchical attention mechanism to perform node representation learning in the heterogeneous information network HIN.

(Liu et al., 2020) show that given a claim and a set of potential evidence sentences that form an evidence graph, Kernel Graph Attention Network (KGAT) introduces node kernels, which better measure the importance of the evidence node, and edge kernels, which conduct fine-grained evidence propagation in the graph, into Graph Attention Networks for more accurate fact verification. For more realisitc scenarios and social media (Lu and Li, 2020) aim at predicting whether a source tweet is fake or not, and generating explanation by highlighting the evidences on suspicious retweeters and the words they concern. They develop a neural network-based model, Graph-aware Co-Attention Networks (GCAN), to achieve the goal.

(Sabarmathi et al., 2021) make two contributions - a. present two new datasets for the undertaking of fake information identification which covers several domains, b. test and train a set of mastering discoveries to create precise fake news detectors.

(Lucas et al., 2022) attempt to detect COVID-19 misinformation (in English, Spanish, and Haitian French) populated in the Caribbean regions. They trained several classification and language models on COVID-19 in the high-resource language regions and transferred the knowledge to the Caribbean claim dataset.

Ensembling machine learning models are quite competant as depicted by - (Akram and Shahzad, 2021), (Kalraa et al., 2021). (Akram and Shahzad, 2021) employ a voting-based approach of the three most effective techniques to decide that the given news article is fake or real. They perform experiments using several classical machine learning techniques, three types of features, unigram, bigram and trigram.

(Kalraa et al., 2021) use ensemble of Various Transformer Based Models for the Fake News Detection Task in the Urdu Language. (Ameer et al., 2021) use transfer learning with BERT algorithm. (Lin et al., 2020) use CharCNN along with Roberta to obtain sentence embeddings with respect to both the word level and character level. They adopt label smoothing to improve the generalization capability of the model.

(Sivanaiah et al., 2023) prepare fake news dataset for low resource languages (Tamil, Kannada, Gujarati, and Malayalam); they experiment with Logistic Regression and BERT models to perform the detection. (De et al., 2021) also offer a multilingual multidomain fake news detection dataset of five languages and seven different domains for resource scarce scenarios. They propose an effective neural model based on the multilingual Bidirectional Encoder Representations from Transformer (BERT) for domain-agnostic multilingual fake news classification.

3 Method

The task is to classifying YouTube comments as either original or fake news.

3.1 Classifier and Feature Extraction

We employed Google's MuRIL (Multilingual Representations for Indian Languages) model, specifically the "muril-base-cased" variant, for our classification task. MuRIL is a state-of-the-art language representation model designed for Indian languages, based on the transformer architecture. It has been pre-trained on a large corpus of text data from various Indian languages, capturing linguistic nuances and semantic relationships specific to these languages.

To adapt MuRIL to our classification task, we fine-tuned the "muril-base-cased" model on our dataset using supervised learning. Labeled examples of YouTube comments were used off the dataset, with labels indicating whether they were original or fake news. This fine-tuning process allowed MuRIL to learn relevant features and patterns for distinguishing between original and fake news in our specific context.

Using the fine-tuned MuRIL model, we performed classification on new, unseen comments or posts. MuRIL computed representations that captured contextual information and semantic meaning, and a classification layer was applied to predict the category of each comment or post (original or fake news. F1 score was used as the evaluation metric to assess MuRIL's performance on our classification task.

3.2 Training and Inference

Through supervised learning, MuRIL adjusts its parameters to minimize the classification loss and optimize its performance on the training data. By fine-tuning on the task-specific dataset, MuRIL learns to capture relevant features and patterns for

Table 1: Data Distribution

Category	Count
Fake	1599
Original	1658

distinguishing between original and fake news.

In the inference phase, the fine-tuned MuRIL model is applied to unseen or new examples to make predictions. Given a comment or post, MuRIL computes representations that capture contextual information and semantic meaning. These representations are then fed into a classification layer, which predicts the category of the input (original or fake news). The predictions are based on the learned patterns and features obtained during the training phase. In this way, MuRIL performs classification on new instances, providing accurate and reliable predictions based on its understanding of the data it has been trained on.

4 Experiments and Results

4.1 Evaluation Metrics

The macro average F1-score is the performance metric used to evaluate the overall effectiveness of the detection model. It is derived by calculating the F1-score for each individual class and then taking the average across all classes. Regardless of class size or class imbalance, the macro average F1-score considers the performance of each class independently and then computes the average, giving equal importance to all classes.

4.2 Datasets

We perform our experiments on "Youtube comments in the Malayalam language" annotated for fake news detection. The dataset is shared as a part of DravidianLangTech@RANLP 2023.

4.2.1 Dataset Analysis

Class Imbalance

As evident from the distribution of labels, there is no class imbalance (Table 1).

4.3 Results

We achieved a macro F1-score of 0.87 which placed us second in the leader-board, Table 2.

Table 2: AbhiPaw @ Fake News Detection in Dravidian Languages

Team	F1-score (macro)	Rank
DeepBlueAI-alert	0.9	1
AbhiPaw	0.87	2
nit-it-nlp	0.87	2
nlpt	0.87	2
MUCS	0.83	3
ML-AL-IIIT-Ranch	0.78	4
DLRG-RR	0.73	5
NLP-SSN-CSE	0.73	6

5 Conclusion

In conclusion, we address the crucial issue of fake news detection in Dravidian languages by harnessing the power of Google's MuRIL (Multilingual Representations for Indian Languages) model. Through fine-tuning and supervised learning, we successfully trained MuRIL to accurately classify comments and posts as original or fake news. The experimental results demonstrate the efficacy of MuRIL in capturing linguistic nuances and contextual information specific to Dravidian languages, enhancing the model's ability to detect fake news. Future research directions include expanding the dataset to improve generalization, addressing code-switching and domain adaptation challenges, exploring ensemble methods, detecting subtle forms of fake news, and extending the research to other low-resource languages for cross-lingual transfer learning.

References

Hammad Akram and Khurram Shahzad. 2021. Ensembling machine learning models for urdu fake news detection. In *Fire*.

Iqra Ameer, Claudia Porto Capetillo, Helena Gómez-Adorno, and Grigori Sidorov. 2021. Automatic fake news detection in urdu language using transformers. In *Fire*.

Arkadipta De, Dibyanayan Bandyopadhyay, Baban Gain, and Asif Ekbal. 2021. A transformer-based approach to multilingual fake news detection in low-resource languages. *ACM Trans. Asian Low-Resour. Lang. Inf. Process.*, 21(1).

Mohammad Hadi Goldani, Saeedeh Momtazi, and Reza Safabakhsh. 2020. Detecting fake news with capsule neural networks. *Appl. Soft Comput.*, 101:106991.

Sakshi Kalraa, Preetika Vermaa, Yashvardhan Sharma, and Gajendra Singh Chauhan. 2021. Ensembling of various transformer based models for the fake news detection task in the urdu language. In *Working Notes of FIRE 2021 - Forum for Information Retrieval Evaluation, Gandhinagar, India, December 13-17, 2021*. CEUR-WS.org.

Nankai Lin, Sihui Fu, and Shengyi Jiang. 2020. Fake news detection in the urdu language using charcnn-roberta. In *Fire*.

Zhenghao Liu, Chenyan Xiong, Maosong Sun, and Zhiyuan Liu. 2020. Fine-grained fact verification with kernel graph attention network. In *Proceedings of the 58th Annual Meeting of the Association for Computational Linguistics*, pages 7342–7351, Online. Association for Computational Linguistics.

Yi-Ju Lu and Cheng-Te Li. 2020. GCAN: Graph-aware co-attention networks for explainable fake news detection on social media. In *Proceedings of the 58th Annual Meeting of the Association for Computational Linguistics*, pages 505–514, Online. Association for Computational Linguistics.

Jason Lucas, Limeng Cui, Thai Le, and Dongwon Lee. 2022. Detecting false claims in low-resource regions: A case study of Caribbean islands. In *Proceedings of the Workshop on Combating Online Hostile Posts in Regional Languages during Emergency Situations*, pages 95–102, Dublin, Ireland. Association for Computational Linguistics.

Ray Oshikawa, Jing Qian, and William Yang Wang. 2020. A survey on natural language processing for fake news detection. In *Proceedings of the Twelfth Language Resources and Evaluation Conference*, pages 6086–6093, Marseille, France. European Language Resources Association.

Yuxiang Ren, Bo Wang, Jiawei Zhang, and Yi Chang. 2020. Adversarial active learning based heterogeneous graph neural network for fake news detection. In *2020 IEEE International Conference on Data Mining (ICDM)*, pages 452–461.

K R Sabarmathi, K Gowthami, and S Sanjay Kumar. 2021. Fake news detection using machine learning and natural language inference (nli). *IOP Conference Series: Materials Science and Engineering*, 1084(1):012018.

Rajalakshmi Sivanaiah, Nishaanth Ramanathan, Shajith Hameed, Rahul Rajagopalan, Angel Deborah Suseelan, and Mirnalinee Thanka Nadar Thanagathai. 2023. Fake news detection in low-resource languages. In *Speech and Language Technologies for Low-Resource Languages*, pages 324–331, Cham. Springer International Publishing.

Dominik Veselý and Marek Veselý. 2021. Reproducibility study - fang: Leveraging social context for fake news detection using graph representation.

Habesha@DravidianLangTech: Utilizing Deep and Transfer Learning Approaches for Sentiment Analysis

Mesay Gemeda Yigezu[1], **Tadesse Kebede**[2], **Olga Kolesnikova** [3], **Grigori Sidorov** [4], **Alexander Gelbukh** [5]

Instituto Politécnico Nacional (IPN), Centro de Investigación en Computación (CIC), Mexico [1], [3], [4], [5]

Haramaya University, Ethiopia [2]

Correspondence: mgemedak2022@cic.ipn.mx

Abstract

This research paper focuses on sentiment analysis of Tamil and Tulu texts using a BERT model and an RNN model. The BERT model, which was pretrained, achieved satisfactory performance for the Tulu language, with a Macro F1-score of 0.352. On the other hand, the RNN model showed good performance for Tamil language sentiment analysis, obtaining a Macro F1-score of 0.208. As future work, the researchers aim to fine-tune the models to further improve their results after the training process.

1 Introduction

The recent rise of the internet as websites, blogs, social networks, online portals, and content-sharing services contribute to the huge amount of user-generated sentiment texts Kebede (2019). These sentiment texts are very important to get feedback from people. Thus, the sentiment analysis fields that help to automatically examine sentiment from texts are required in various areas. Sentiment analysis is a task of subjectivity analysis with some linkage to effective computing principles (Pang et al., 2008). Sentiment analysis is an interdisciplinary theme that exploits natural language processing (NLP) methods, text mining, and computational linguistics to recognize and extract subjective information from source materials (Khan et al., 2009). It involves classifying the sentiment data into different polarity levels such as positive, negative, and neutral. Sentiment analysis is used by the sectors such as advertisers, movie creators, booksellers, political parties, supermarkets, industries, restaurants, etc. that demand their customers' feedback on a particular issue to improve themselves afterward. For example, (1), sentiment analysis is used in government elections to examine the people's sentiments, appraisals, attitudes, and emotions on the candidates of the election. (2), business companies introduce new products to the market and then usefully extract the sentiment of the people on the internet about the product, and settle the future feasibility of this new product. It is possible to gather the sentiment from customers using surveys, blogs, and suggestion committees but this may result in a waste of resources and not provide us the comment in a short period. Automatically gathering and classifying the sentiment that is expressed by natural language on social networks eradicates those problems with minimum time and resources. The objective of this work is to develop a sentiment analysis for Tamil and Tulu languages adopting the pre-trained model and Deep Learning algorithm and to evaluate the model's performance. Getting the sentiment of people in the business sector organizations engaged leads to success in the field or business(Kebede, 2019). The rest of the study is organized as follows. Currently, opinions of the people towards any organization in the world are collected by holding different conferences/meetings by using oral and manual collection methods. Such ways of gathering people's feedback consume much time and resources. In order to solve this, knowing what people are interacting with in their day-to-day life helps us to collect sentiments regarding some issues in a little time. Nowadays, the internet technology that is invented in the world like Facebook, Twitter, Blogs, Websites, etc. is usable in using Tulu and Tamil language. So, the Tamil and Tulu language usage on internet technology provides us with massive sentiment data. Even though the Tamil and Tulu language sentiment data is generated by different organizers, there is no sufficient sentiment analysis task that classifies the sentiment text into their polarity level. Thus, collecting this sentiment and classifying it into their polarity level is the intention of this work. This may optimize oral and survey-based sentiment collection by adopting pre-trained and deep-learning algorithms. Thus, the aim of this research is:

- To find the best data processing techniques for Tulu and Tamil sentiment data.

Third Workshop on Speech and Language Technologies for Dravidian Languages, pages 239–243, Varna, Bulgaria, Sep 7, 2023.
https://doi.org/10.26615/978-954-452-085-4_035

- To investigate techniques that should be applied to perform Tamil and Tulu language sentiment classification into their polarity level.
- To evaluate the Tamil and Tulu sentiment analyzer model using Macro F1-score.

2 Related Work

In this part, related sentiment analysis research investigating Tamil or Tulu languages using different approaches is presented. Besides, the recent sentiment analysis task which is developed by state of art methods is reviewed. (Thavareesan and Mahesan, 2018) performed a review to analyze the recent literature in the area of sentiment analysis in Tamil texts. This study considered the preprocessing, corpus and techniques, and success rate for review. The paper finds that the performance of the model relies on the preprocessing steps such as negation handling and stop word removal. The review concluded that SVM and RNN classifiers taking Word level feature representation using TF-IDF and Word2vec provide better performance than grammar rules-based classifications and other classifiers with usage of words, TF, and BoW features. The review revealed that resources such as Tamil SentiWordNet, adjective rules, and n-grams also can be used in SA on Tamil text as it proves a significant performance.

To analyze the sentiment content of Tamil Movie reviews sentiment analysis task is investigated by (Ramanathan et al., 2021). The aim of this work was to categorize the sentiment of Tamil movies based on Tamil tweets using Tamil SentiWordNet (TSWN). Term Frequency - Inverse Document Frequency (TF-IDF) feature extraction methods are applied to identify the sentiment polarity of the Tamil movie data set. In this work, Tamil SentiWordNet is used with adjectives to classify the sentiment. Since the adjectives are not sufficient to detect the sentiment in the Tamil texts as future work, the paper intended to use adverbs in the Tamil language to identify the sentiment. Finally, the paper recommended the adjective wordnet for any language is appropriate for the sentiment analysis.

This research (Roy and Kumar, 2021) developed the sentiment analysis on Tamil code-mixed text using Bi-LSTM. The code-mixed data like Hindi-English, Malayalam-English, and similar ones; are used to detect the sentiment from Tamil review data. The proposed Bi-LSTM framework automatically extracts the features from input sentences and predicts their sentiment with a 0.552 F1 score for the best case using. (Divyasri et al., 2022) studied emotion analysis of Tamil texts using Language Agnostic Embeddings. The paper invented a multilingual transformer model for the emotion analysis of Tamil text as required by the DravidianTechLang ACL 2022 shared task. In this paper, LaBSE, a pre-trained language agnostic BERT model, was found to perform comparatively well on the Tamil dataset. The paper claimed the result of Tamil Sentiment Analysis can be optimized by utilizing custom embeddings, based on a statistical analysis of the language, to process the data before training the model. A code-diverse Tulu-English data for NLP-based sentiment analysis applications are developed by this paper (Kannadaguli, 2021). The research concentrated on NLP for emotion and sentiment detection of Tulu, a vibrant South Indian language, to start with. Development of the standard corpus for NLP applications of code-diverse text in Tulu-English is contributed by this work. The performance analysis of the dataset is performed through Krippendorff's Alpha value of 0.9 indicates that it is a benchmark in the development of the Automatic Sentiment Analysis system for Tulu. Though research (Kurniasari and Setyanto, 2020), (Topbaş et al., 2021) are conducted for different languages using deep learning and transformer learning the Tulu and Tamil sentiment analysis is very limited using these methods.

3 Task description

To identify the sentiment polarity of the code-mixed dataset of comments and posts in Tamil-English and Tulu-English collected from social media by DravidianLangTech2023 (Chakravarthi et al., 2020) is used. The comment/post may contain more than one sentence but the average sentence length of the corpora is 1. Each comment or post is annotated with sentiment polarity at the comment or post level. This dataset also has class imbalance problems depicting real-world scenarios. Our proposal aims to encourage research that will reveal how sentiment is expressed in code-mixed scenarios on social media. The purpose of this task is to perform sentiment analysis for Tulu and Tamil languages. The given Tulu sentiment text is classified into mixed feelings, negative, neutral, and positive. On the other hand, the Tamil sentiment data is classified into classes such as negative, mixed feelings, positive and unknown (Hedge et al., 2023).

The given data is full of noise and to upgrade the performance of the model the data cleaning task is performed at the pre-processing stage for both languages. The participants were provided with the Tamil and Tulu development, training, and test dataset. This is a message-level polarity classification task. Given a Youtube comment, systems have to classify it into positive, negative, neutral, or mixed emotions. The participants will be provided development, training, and test dataset code-mixed text in Dravidian languages (Tamil-English and Tulu-English).

4 Methodology

(Roy and Kumar, 2021) (Divyasri et al., 2022) (Kurniasari and Setyanto, 2020) (Topbaş et al., 2021) (Talaat, 2023) (Zhang et al., 2023) researchers suggested the pre-trained model like BERT and deep learning algorithms perform great for the sentiment analysis. The review paper (Cui et al., 2023) recommends the deep learning technology, with its hybrid methods combining sentiment dictionary and semantic analysis, fine-grained sentiment analysis methods, and non-English language analysis methods, and cross-domain sentiment analysis techniques have gradually become the research trends. The overall proposed framework of Tamil and Tulu sentiment analysis is depicted in Figure 1.

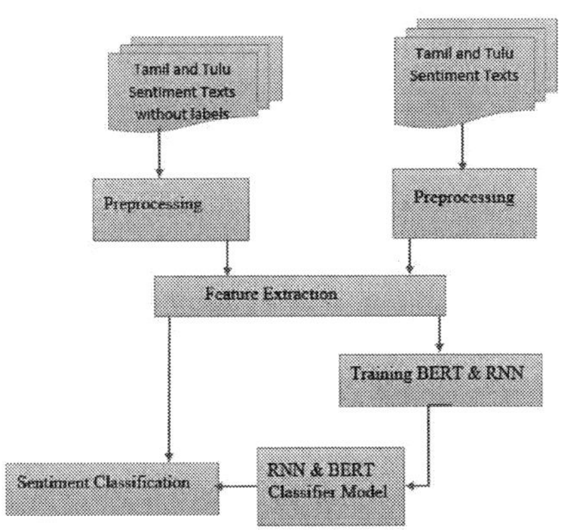

Figure 1: Proposed architecture for sentiment analysis

The proposed framework incorporates data preprocessing, feature extraction, training a model, and sentiment classification evaluation. The dataset used in this study is found on DravidianLangTech2023. Majorly the dataset of the Tamil language belongs to the positive sentiment class. The rest of the Tamil data set is distributed to Negative, mixed feelings, and unknown state sentiment classes. Likewise, the Tulu sentiment is majorly included as a positive sentiment class and the others are distributed as Negative, Neutral, and Mixed feeling sentiment categories. Figure 2 shows the distribution of the Tamil and Tulu sentiment analysis data.

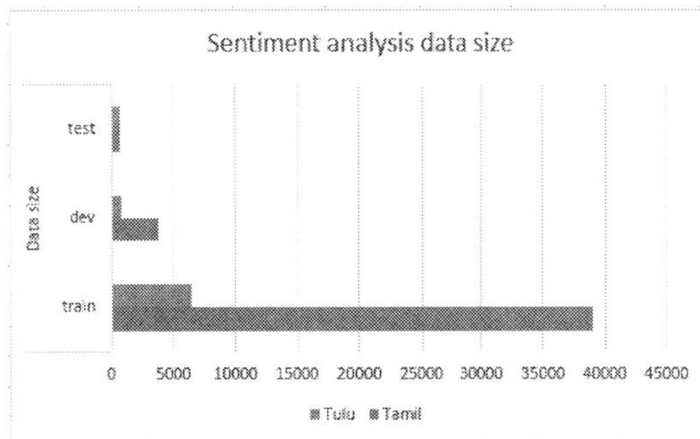

Figure 2: distribution of data size for sentiment analysis

Based on the provided figure, it is evident that there is a limited quantity of both development and training data. The only exception is the training data for the Tamil language, although even these datasets are unbalanced. As a result, this situation causes the model to exhibit reduced or inaccurate performance.

4.1 Data pre-processing

In the data preprocessing stage the unnecessary noises are removed from the original Tamil and Tulu sentiment data. The pre-processing stage removes HTML tags, URLs, digits, and punctuation marks, and lowercasing is performed. In addition to this, the emoji is replaced by the text in both Tamil and Tulu sentiment data.

4.2 Feature extraction

The feature is extracted from the processed data before it can be used in a model. First, for the RNN model, TextVectorization and embedding are used to extract the feature. During embedding the one vector per word is stored. Secondly, before training the BERT to convert our Tulu and Tamil sentiment data into numerical values methods such as Bag of words, TFIDF, and Word Embedding are used to extract the features. In this task, the Tokenizer class from pre-trained DistilBert is used in order to tokenize the Tamil and Tulu sentiment data.

4.3 Model Training

In this work to generate the Tulu and Tamil sentiment analysis model a pre-trained BERT model and deep learning algorithm: RNN is used. BERT is a machine learning technique developed by Google based on the Transformers mechanism. Sometimes, BERT models are used in place of conventional RNN based because the BERT model suffered from information loss in large sequential text. While the BERT can easily understand the context of a word in a sentence based on previous words in the sentences due to its bi-directional approach. RNNs are a form of Artificial Neural networks that can memorize arbitrary-length sequences of input patterns by capturing connections between sequential data types. A neural network that is intentionally run multiple times, where parts of each run feed into the next run. Specifically, hidden layers from the previous run provide part of the input to the same hidden layer in the next run. Recurrent neural networks are particularly useful for evaluating sequences so that the hidden layers can learn from previous runs of the neural network on earlier parts of the sequence.

4.4 Performance metrics

To evaluate the model performance, the classification metrics called F1-score are used. The classification system's performance will be measured in terms of macro-averaged Precision, macro-averaged Recall, and macro-averaged F-Score across all the classes. The macro average F1-score is the harmonic mean of the precision and recall (Pang et al., 2008). Precision is defined as the number of correctly predicted sentiment categories among the retrieved instances of the particular sentiment category. The recall is defined as the number of correctly predicted sentiment categories among the total number of instances of that particular sentiment category.

5 Experiments and Results

5.1 Experimental

The experimentation is done on the Python Tensorflow which is a popular and widely used machine learning framework for developing deep learning applications. Installing Libraries and dependencies make ready all the necessary libraries and packages. To ensure that the GPU is enabled, the TensorFlow API: 'tf. config' is used. In this article, the BERT and RNN are used for developing a sentiment analysis for Tamil and Tulu Sentiment Analysis. BERT is trained on 3 epochs, 16 batch sizes, and using a 5e-5 Learning rate (Adam). The RNN is trained using parameters: buffer size: 10000, batch size: 8, and vocab size:10000. Finally, Both BERT and RNN model is developed for both Tulu and Tamil sentiment classification.

5.2 Results

In this task, we assess the effectiveness of development models for sentiment analysis in two different languages, Tamil and Tulu. The evaluation of these models is based on the Macro F1-Score metric, which provides an overall measure of performance across multiple classes.

Upon analyzing the test dataset, the results reveal that the BERT model outperformed other models in the Tulu language, achieving a Macro F1-Score of 0.35. On the other hand, for sentiment analysis in the Tamil language, the developed RNN model exhibited superior performance, attaining a Macro F1-Score of 0.20.

These findings highlight the suitability of the BERT model for sentiment analysis in the Tulu language, indicating its capability to capture and understand the nuances of sentiment expressed in Tulu text. Conversely, the RNN model demonstrates its proficiency in capturing the sentiment complexities of the Tamil language, making it the preferred choice for sentiment analysis in Tamil. Table 1 depicts a summary of the result.

Tasks	Macro-score			
	P	R	F1	Acc
Tamil	0.25	0.21	0.20	0.40
Tulu	0.36	0.35	0.35	0.57

Table 1: Experimental result

6 Conclusion

In this research paper, we have trained a BERT and RNN model for the sentiment analysis of Tamil and Tulu texts as the need of DravidianLangTech 2023-RANLP 2023. A pre-trained BERT language BERT model performed well for the Tulu language comparing it with the Tulu language yielding a Macro F1 score of 0.352. In another way, the RNN model performance is good for Tamil language sentiment analysis with a Macro F1 score of 0.208. The researchers take as future work fine-tuning the models to improve the results of the models after training.

Acknowledgments

The work was done with partial support from the Mexican Government through the grant A1S-47854 of CONACYT, Mexico, grants 20220852, 20220859, and 20221627 of the Secretaría de Investigación y Posgrado of the Instituto Politécnico Nacional, Mexico. The authors thank the CONACYT for the computing resources brought to them through the Plataforma de Aprendizaje Profundo para Tecnologías del Lenguaje of the Laboratorio de Supercómputo of the INAOE, Mexico and acknowledge the support of Microsoft through the Microsoft Latin America Ph.D. Award.

References

Bharathi Raja Chakravarthi, Vigneshwaran Muralidaran, Ruba Priyadharshini, and John Philip McCrae. 2020. Corpus creation for sentiment analysis in code-mixed Tamil-English text. In *Proceedings of the 1st Joint Workshop on Spoken Language Technologies for Under-resourced languages (SLTU) and Collaboration and Computing for Under-Resourced Languages (CCURL)*, pages 202–210, Marseille, France. European Language Resources association.

Jingfeng Cui, Zhaoxia Wang, Seng-Beng Ho, and Erik Cambria. 2023. Survey on sentiment analysis: evolution of research methods and topics. *Artificial Intelligence Review*, pages 1–42.

K Divyasri, GL Gayathri, Krithika Swaminathan, Thenmozhi Durairaj, B Bharathi, et al. 2022. Pandas@ tamilnlp-acl2022: Emotion analysis in tamil text using language agnostic embeddings. In *Proceedings of the Second Workshop on Speech and Language Technologies for Dravidian Languages*, pages 105–111.

Asha Hedge, Bharathi Raja Chakravarthi, Hosahalli Lakshmaiah Shashirekha, Rahul Ponnusamy, Subalalitha Chinnaudayar Navaneethakrishnan, Lavanya S.K, Durairaj Thenmozhi, Martha Karunakar, Shreya Sriram, and Sarah Aymen. 2023. Findings of the shared task on sentiment analysis in tamil and tulu code-mixed text. In *Proceedings of the Third Workshop on Speech and Language Technologies for Dravidian Languages*, Varna, Bulgaria. Recent Advances in Natural Language Processing.

Prashanth Kannadaguli. 2021. A code-diverse tulu-english dataset for nlp based sentiment analysis applications. In *2021 Advanced Communication Technologies and Signal Processing (ACTS)*, pages 1–6. IEEE.

Tadesse Kebede. 2019. *MACHINE LEARNING BASED MULTI-SCALE SENTIMENT ANALYSIS FOR AFAAN OROMO POSTS*. Ph.D. thesis, Haramaya university.

Khairullah Khan, Baharum B Baharudin, Aurangzeb Khan, et al. 2009. Mining opinion from text documents: A survey. In *2009 3rd IEEE International Conference on Digital Ecosystems and Technologies*, pages 217–222. IEEE.

Lilis Kurniasari and Arif Setyanto. 2020. Sentiment analysis using recurrent neural network. In *Journal of Physics: Conference Series*, volume 1471, page 012018. IOP Publishing.

Bo Pang, Lillian Lee, et al. 2008. Opinion mining and sentiment analysis. *Foundations and Trends® in information retrieval*, 2(1–2):1–135.

Vallikannu Ramanathan, T Meyyappan, and SM Thamarai. 2021. Sentiment analysis: An approach for analysing tamil movie reviews using tamil tweets. *Recent Advances in Mathematical Research and Computer Science*, 3:28–39.

Pradeep Kumar Roy and Abhinav Kumar. 2021. Sentiment analysis on tamil code-mixed text using bi-lstm. In *Working Notes of FIRE 2021-Forum for Information Retrieval Evaluation (Online). CEUR*.

Amira Samy Talaat. 2023. Sentiment analysis classification system using hybrid bert models. *Journal of Big Data*, 10(1):1–18.

Sajeetha Thavareesan and Sinnathamby Mahesan. 2018. Review on sentiment analysis in tamil texts.

Ayşenur Topbaş, Akhtar Jamil, Alaa Ali Hameed, Syed Muzafar Ali, Sibghatullah Bazai, and Syed Attique Shah. 2021. Sentiment analysis for covid-19 tweets using recurrent neural network (rnn) and bidirectional encoder representations (bert) models. In *2021 International Conference on Computing, Electronic and Electrical Engineering (ICE Cube)*, pages 1–6. IEEE.

Xiangsen Zhang, Zhongqiang Wu, Ke Liu, Zengshun Zhao, Jinhao Wang, and Chengqin Wu. 2023. Text sentiment classification based on bert embedding and sliced multi-head self-attention bi-gru. *Sensors*, 23(3):1481.

Habesha@DravidianLangTech: Abusive Comment Detection using Deep Learning Approach

Mesay Gemeda Yigezu, Selam Abitte , Olga Kolesnikova, Grigori Sidorov, Alexander Gelbukh
∀ Instituto Politécnico Nacional (IPN), Centro de Investigación en Computación (CIC), Mexico
Correspondence: mgemedak2022@cic.ipn.mx

Abstract

This research focuses on identifying abusive language in comments. The study utilizes deep learning models, including Long Short-Term Memory (LSTM) and Recurrent Neural Networks (RNNs), to analyze linguistic patterns. Specifically, the LSTM model, a type of RNN, is used to understand the context by capturing long-term dependencies and intricate patterns in the input sequences. The LSTM model achieves better accuracy and is enhanced through the addition of a dropout layer and early stopping. For detecting abusive language in Telugu and Tamil-English, an LSTM model is employed, while in Tamil abusive language detection, a word-level RNN is developed to identify abusive words. These models process text sequentially, considering overall content and capturing contextual dependencies.

1 Introduction

In recent years, online social networks (OSNs) have gained significant significance and have become a popular platform for obtaining news, information, and entertainment. However, despite the various advantages of utilizing OSNs, there is a mounting body of evidence indicating the presence of an escalating number of malicious individuals who exploit these networks to disseminate harmful content and cause damage to others. The negative consequences of these malicious activities are increasingly evident. The spread of poisonous content, such as hate speech, misinformation, and cyberbullying, can have severe psychological, emotional, and even physical effects on targeted individuals. Moreover, the virality and reach of OSNs amplify the potential harm caused by malevolent actors, as harmful content can quickly spread across networks, reaching a vast audience and causing widespread damage. In order to mitigate this activity the organizer provide this shared task.

Natural language processing (NLP) focuses on the practical manipulation of textual components, converting them into a format suitable for machines. Additionally, NLP plays a crucial role in Artificial Intelligence (AI) by providing vital insights to determine the positivity or negativity of information based on numerous comparisons. Hence we combat to fix the above-mentioned problems by applying the NLP concept.

2 Related Work

The objective of this study Chen et al. (2017) was to explore the use of core text mining techniques in automatically detecting abusive content in various social media platforms such as blogs, forums, media-sharing sites, Q and A platforms, and chat services. The research utilized datasets from popular platforms like Twitter, YouTube, MySpace, Kongregate, Formspring, and Slashdot. By employing supervised machine learning, the study compared different text representations and dimension reduction methods, including feature selection and feature enhancement. The results demonstrated the significant influence of these techniques on the accuracy of abusive content detection. Ultimately, the researcher concluded that employing a balanced dataset positively impacts the accuracy of detecting abusive content on social media platforms. They conducted to use minority class and majority class and obtain the best result on the minority class. In addition to that using feature reduction will improve efficiency whilst maintaining detection accuracies.

(Eshan and Hasan, 2017) investigates different machine learning algorithms to detect Bengali abusive text. After experiments, they analyzed that the SVM Linear kernel performs the best with trigram TfidfVectorizer features.

Awal et al. (2018) designed to detect abusive comments in social media by using Naïve Bayes. The researcher collected the corpus from YouTube. To calculate the occurrence of particular words in a particular comment used a bag of words (BOW)

Third Workshop on Speech and Language Technologies for Dravidian Languages, pages 244–249, Varna, Bulgaria, Sep 7, 2023.
https://doi.org/10.26615/978-954-452-085-4_036

vector. In order to evaluate the performance of the model they applied 10-fold cross-validation.

The researcher (Akhter et al., 2021) undertook a comprehensive study focusing on the detection of abusive language in both Urdu and Roman Urdu comments. This investigation encompassed the utilization of a diverse set of machine learning and deep learning models. Specifically, the author employed five ML models, namely Naive Bayes, Support Vector Machine, Instance-Based Learning , Logistic Regression, and JRip. Additionally, four DL models, including CNN, LSTM, BLSTM, and Convolutional LSTM, were also harnessed in the analysis. The research methodology consisted of applying these models to two distinct datasets: a sizable collection comprising tens of thousands of Roman Urdu comments, and a comparatively smaller dataset containing over two thousand comments in Urdu. The primary objective was to assess the performance of these models in both linguistic variations. The outcomes of the experiments conducted revealed noteworthy insights. Notably, the CNN exhibited superior performance compared to the other models. Impressively, it achieved accuracy rates of 96.2% for Urdu comments and 91.4% for Roman Urdu comments. This marked the CNN as the most adept model in accurately identifying abusive language within these linguistic contexts.

This study (Emon et al., 2019) delves into the crucial task of identifying various forms of abusive content within the realm of online platforms. The research extensively explores the utilization of diverse machine learning and deep learning methodologies to address this challenge. The algorithms under scrutiny encompass a range of models, including the Linear Support Vector Classifier (LinearSVC), Logistic Regression (Logit), Multinomial Naïve Bayes (MNB), Random Forest (RF), Artificial Neural Network (ANN), and a RNN featuring aLSTM cell. This author introduces a pioneering dimension by devising novel stemming rules tailored specifically for the Bengali language. These rules substantially contribute to enhancing the efficacy and overall performance of the algorithms employed in the study. Notably, the deep learning-powered RNN model emerges as the frontrunner among the examined algorithms, boasting an impressive peak accuracy rate of 82.20%.

This scholarly investigation involves a comprehensive evaluation of the efficacy of Deep Learning (DL) models in contrast to Machine Learning (ML) models for the purpose of detecting instances of abusive language. The researcher, a notable contributor in this domain, undertook an empirical study wherein a comparative analysis was conducted between Logit and BLSTM models. The primary objective was to discern their effectiveness in identifying abusive language within the context of the Danish language. The study's findings showcase a distinct trend: the BLSTM model, a sophisticated variant of recurrent neural networks, emerged as the standout performer. It outshone the competing models in terms of accurately categorizing comments sourced from prominent social media platforms such as Reddit, Facebook, and Twitter.(Sigurbergsson and Derczynski, 2019) comprehensive experimentation and analysis revealed that the BLSTM model exhibited remarkable capabilities in dealing with the intricacies and nuances of abusive language present in user-generated content.

The studies discussed earlier have provided us with a valuable insight, demonstrating that the utilization of deep learning methodologies offers a straightforward means of detecting the intended content. What's even more advantageous about employing deep learning is that it eliminates the necessity for employing supplementary feature extraction techniques. This implies that the inherent capability of deep learning models allows them to discern patterns and features directly from the data, obviating the need for manual feature engineering. The integration of deep learning into content detection thus emerges as a pivotal advancement in the field, heralding a new era of intelligent and efficient detection mechanisms. This transformative approach holds promise for a wide array of applications where accuracy and automation are paramount.

3 Task description

The objective of the task is to determine whether a comment includes any form of abusive content. The data sets consist of YouTube comments written in the Tamil and Telugu-English languages. The comments or posts in the corpus can consist of multiple sentences, but the average sentence length of the corpus is one. The annotations in the corpus are made at the comment or post level, rather than at the sentence level. This means that the task involves analyzing comments or posts as a whole to determine if they contain abusive content, rather than focusing on individual sentences within the comment. The annotations or labels indicating whether a comment is abusive or not are assigned based on the overall content of the comment or post (Priyadharshini et al., 2023).

4 Methodology

4.1 Data pre-processing

After receiving the data from shared task organizer (Priyadharshini et al.), it was split into three distinct parts: the training set, the development set, and the testing set. However, prior to utilizing this data for training purposes, it is crucial to perform pre-processing on it. The data is currently in an unsuitable format for training a model effectively. Therefore, it requires transformation into a readable and structured format that aligns with the requirements of the training process.

One of the primary tasks during pre-processing is the removal of various unwanted elements present in the data. These elements include links, HTML tags, numbers, and symbols that may hinder the training process or introduce noise into the dataset. By eliminating these unwanted components, the data becomes cleaner and more focused, enabling the model to better discern patterns and relationships within the text.

Once these unwanted elements have been removed, the data will be better suited for training the model. Pre-processing allows the model to focus on the relevant linguistic features and patterns within the text, improving its ability to generalize and make accurate predictions or classifications.

By performing the necessary pre-processing steps, such as transforming the data into a readable format and removing unwanted elements, the dataset will be optimized for training the model, facilitating more accurate and meaningful results in subsequent analysis or applications. The data size provided by the organizers of the shared task is visually represented in Figure 1.

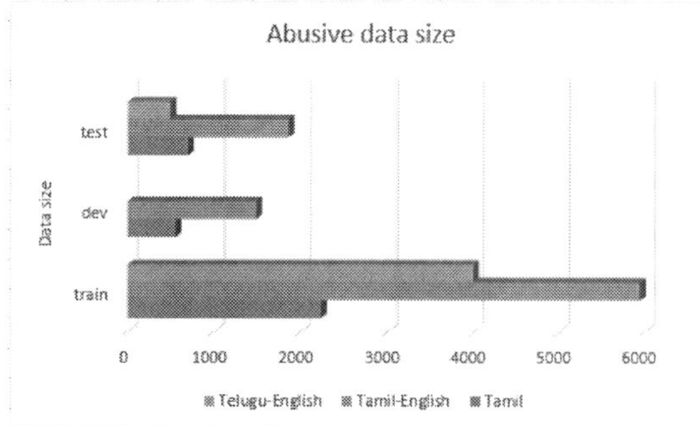

Figure 1: data set size for abusive comment detection

4.2 Algorithms

Within this section, we delve into the algorithms employed within this research paper. The realm of linguistic modeling predominantly relies on the utilization of deep learning models (Yigezu et al., 2021; Arif et al., 2022). These models, such as Convolutional Neural Networks (CNN) and RNN, are commonly employed due to their ability to identify intricate patterns within textual data. More specifically, the LSTM model, which exhibits a tree-like structure, is employed as a recurrent neural network to effectively analyze sequential data of varying lengths (Yigezu et al., 2022).

To detect Telugu and Tamil-English abusive language, an LSTM model was employed. In the implementation, a dropout layer was added after the RNN layer. This dropout layer aids in mitigating the risk of overfitting, which can occur when the model excessively learns from the training data, leading to reduced generalization performance. Additionally, the model was configured to utilize early stopping based on validation loss. This mechanism halts the training process if the validation loss fails to exhibit improvement for a specified number of epochs. This approach helps prevent unnecessary computational effort and ensures that the model is not trained beyond a point where it ceases to benefit from further iterations. The LSTM model employed in our experiment exhibits better accuracy and significantly improves the contextual understanding of the data. By leveraging the capabilities of the LSTM, our model is able to effectively capture long-term dependencies and intricate patterns within the input sequences, enabling a deeper comprehension of the data.

Table 1 shows a comprehensive overview of the parameters utilized in our LSTM model. These parameters, carefully selected and fine-tuned, play a crucial role in shaping the model's architecture and optimizing its performance. By configuring the LSTM model with the appropriate parameters, we were able to enhance its ability to process sequential data and achieve notable accuracy in identifying abusive language.

In the context of Tamil abusive language detection, we developed and trained a rudimentary RNN at the word level to effectively identify abusive

Parameters	Values
embed_units	100
hidden_units	128
dropout	0.5
optimizer	adam
batch_size	64
loss	categorical_crossentropy
epoch	25
activation	softmax
restore best weights	True

Table 1: parameters used in LSTM

Parameters	Values
embedding_size	100
hidden_size	128
optimizer	adam
batch_size	32
crossentropy loss	reduction = sum
num_iteration	30

Table 2: parameters used in RNN

words. Word-level RNNs process text by considering words as a sequential input, generating predictions and hidden states at each step, and forwarding the most recent hidden state to the subsequent step. This iterative process allows the model to capture contextual dependencies and patterns within the sequence of words. RNNs have been widely employed as fundamental components in contemporary neural networks designed for language identification tasks.

To facilitate the mapping of tokens (i.e., words) to numerical representations, we utilized the Dictionary class. This class serves as a tool to assign unique and consecutive integer indexes to each token in the vocabulary. By mapping tokens to indexes, the model can efficiently handle text data and perform computations based on these numerical representations. This enables the RNN model to process and analyze the textual information effectively, aiding in the identification of abusive language.

To ensure fair and unbiased predictions, we employed a balanced dataset during our experimentation. By using a balanced dataset, we aimed to mitigate any potential bias that may arise from an imbalanced distribution of abusive and non-abusive instances. A balanced dataset consists of an equal number of instances from each class, which helps to prevent the model from favoring one class over the other during training and prediction.

By utilizing a balanced dataset, we strived to create a more equitable and reliable predictive model. This approach allows the model to learn from an unbiased representation of both abusive and non-abusive language, enhancing its ability to generalize and make accurate predictions on unseen data. Ultimately, the use of a balanced dataset contributes to the fairness and integrity of the abusive language detection system we developed. Table 2 depicts the parameters which we used in this experiment.

We used PyTorch, a popular deep learning framework. It creates an instance of the CrossEntropyLoss class from the torch.nn module and sets the reduction parameter to 'sum'. Torch.nn.CrossEntropyLoss is a loss function commonly used for multi-class classification problems. It combines the softmax function and the negative log-likelihood loss. It expects the input logits (unnormalized scores) and the target labels. The reduction parameter determines how the loss is aggregated over the batch. In this case, 'sum' means that the loss values for each element in the batch will be summed together to produce a single scalar loss value.

5 Result and Discussion

According to the findings presented in Table 3, we employed an RNN model to detect Tamil abusive languages. The evaluation results indicated that the RNN model achieved a precision of 0.26, a recall of 0.23, and an F1 score of 0.22. These metrics provide insights into the model's performance, with precision representing the accuracy of positive predictions, recall indicating the model's ability to correctly identify positive instances, and the F1 score representing the harmonic mean of precision and recall.

In the second experiment, our primary objective was to detect Tamil-English and Telugu-English languages using an LSTM model. The results demonstrated that the LSTM model performed better in the Telugu-English detection task, achieving a precision of 0.65, a recall of 0.65, and an F1 score of 0.65. On the other hand, for the Tamil-English detection, the LSTM model achieved a precision of 0.27, a recall of 0.25, and an F1 score of 0.26.

The performance metrics offer valuable insights into how effectively the models can identify instances of abusive language in Tamil-English and Telugu-English texts. The higher precision, recall, and F1-score in the Telugu-English detection task indicate that the LSTM model exhibited superior performance in accurately identifying abusive language in that language pair. However, it is important to note that the model's performance was relatively lower in the Telugu-English detection task, suggesting the need for further refinements and improvements in the model's ability to identify abusive language in that specific language pair.

Task	Macro-score			
	P	R	F1	Acc
Tamil	0.26	0.23	0.22	0.46
Telugu-English	0.65	0.65	0.65	0.65
Tamil-English	0.27	0.25	0.26	0.51

Table 3: Experimental results

6 Conclusion

The research paper utilizes deep learning models, specifically LSTM and RNNs, to analyze language patterns. The LSTM model is employed to enhance contextual understanding by capturing long-term dependencies and intricate patterns in the input sequences. When detecting abusive language in Telugu and Tamil-English, an LSTM model is utilized, resulting in improved accuracy and a deeper understanding of the context. In the context of Tamil abusive language detection, a word-level RNN is created and trained to identify abusive words. This type of RNN processes text sequentially, capturing contextual dependencies and patterns within the sequence of words.

To attain enhanced and superior performance levels, our focus will center on the utilization of a transformer-based approach (Aurpa et al., 2022; Gupta et al., 2022). Our strategy involves intricately configuring the parameters of this approach, meticulously fine-tuning them to yield outcomes that hold great promise. This deliberate effort aims to extract the utmost potential from the transformer model, thereby optimizing its performance for optimal results. Through this approach, we intend to unlock new dimensions of efficiency and effectiveness, pushing the boundaries of achievement in our pursuit of excellence.

Acknowledgments

The work was done with partial support from the Mexican Government through the grant A1S-47854 of CONACYT, Mexico, grants 20220852, 20220859, and 20221627 of the Secretaría de Investigación y Posgrado of the Instituto Politécnico Nacional, Mexico. The authors thank the CONACYT for the computing resources brought to them through the Plataforma de Aprendizaje Profundo para Tecnologías del Lenguaje of the Laboratorio de Supercómputo of the INAOE, Mexico and acknowledge the support of Microsoft through the Microsoft Latin America Ph.D. Award.

References

Muhammad Pervez Akhter, Zheng Jiangbin, Irfan Raza Naqvi, Mohammed AbdelMajeed, and Tehseen Zia. 2021. Abusive language detection from social media comments using conventional machine learning and deep learning approaches. *Multimedia Systems*, pages 1–16.

Muhammad Arif, Atnafu Lambebo Tonja, Iqra Ameer, Olga Kolesnikova, Alexander Gelbukh, Grigori Sidorov, and Abdul Gafar Manuel Meque. 2022. Cic at checkthat! 2022: multi-class and cross-lingual fake news detection. *Working Notes of CLEF*.

Tanjim Taharat Aurpa, Rifat Sadik, and Md Shoaib Ahmed. 2022. Abusive bangla comments detection on facebook using transformer-based deep learning models. *Social Network Analysis and Mining*, 12(1):24.

Md Abdul Awal, Md Shamimur Rahman, and Jakaria Rabbi. 2018. Detecting abusive comments in discussion threads using naïve bayes. In *2018 International Conference on Innovations in Science, Engineering and Technology (ICISET)*, pages 163–167. IEEE.

Hao Chen, Susan Mckeever, and Sarah Jane Delany. 2017. Harnessing the power of text mining for the detection of abusive content in social media. In *Advances in Computational Intelligence Systems: Contributions Presented at the 16th UK Workshop on Computational Intelligence, September 7–9, 2016, Lancaster, UK*, pages 187–205. Springer.

Estiak Ahmed Emon, Shihab Rahman, Joti Banarjee, Amit Kumar Das, and Tanni Mittra. 2019. A deep learning approach to detect abusive bengali text. In *2019 7th International Conference on Smart Computing & Communications (ICSCC)*, pages 1–5. IEEE.

Shahnoor C Eshan and Mohammad S Hasan. 2017. An application of machine learning to detect abusive bengali text. In *2017 20th International conference of computer and information technology (ICCIT)*, pages 1–6. IEEE.

Vikram Gupta, Sumegh Roychowdhury, Mithun Das, Somnath Banerjee, Punyajoy Saha, Binny Mathew, Animesh Mukherjee, et al. 2022. Multilingual abusive comment detection at scale for indic languages. *Advances in Neural Information Processing Systems*, 35:26176–26191.

Ruba Priyadharshini, Bharathi Raja Chakravarthi, Subalalitha Chinnaudayar Navaneethakrishnan, Malliga Subramanian, Kogilavani Shanmugavadivel, Premjith B, Abirami Murugappan, Sai Prashanth Karnati, Rishith, Chandu Janakiram, and booktitle = Kumaresan, Prasanna Kumar". Findings of the shared task on Abusive Comment Detection in Tamil and Telugu.

Ruba Priyadharshini, Bharathi Raja Chakravarthi, Malliga Subramanian, Subalalitha Chinnaudayar Navaneethakrishnan, Kogilavani Shanmugavadivel, Premjith B, Abirami Murugappan, Prasanna Kumar Kumaresan, Karnati Sai Prashanth, Mangamuru Sai Rishith Reddy, and Janakiram Chandu. 2023. Overview of shared-task on abusive comment detection in tamil and telugu. In *Proceedings of the Third Workshop on Speech and Language Technologies for Dravidian Languages*, Varna, Bulgaria. Recent Advances in Natural Language Processing.

Gudbjartur Ingi Sigurbergsson and Leon Derczynski. 2019. Offensive language and hate speech detection for danish. *arXiv preprint arXiv:1908.04531*.

Mesay Gemeda Yigezu, Atnafu Lambebo Tonja, Olga Kolesnikova, Moein Shahiki Tash, Grigori Sidorov, and Alexander Gelbukh. 2022. Word level language identification in code-mixed kannada-english texts using deep learning approach. In *Proceedings of the 19th International Conference on Natural Language Processing (ICON): Shared Task on Word Level Language Identification in Code-mixed Kannada-English Texts*, pages 29–33.

Mesay Gemeda Yigezu, Michael Melese Woldeyohannis, and Atnafu Lambebo Tonja. 2021. Multilingual neural machine translation for low resourced languages: Ometo-english. In *2021 International Conference on Information and Communication Technology for Development for Africa (ICT4DA)*, pages 89–94. IEEE.

Multimodal Sentiment Analysis of Tamil and Malayalam

Abhinav Patil, Sam Briggs, Tara Wueger, D. D. O'Connell
Department of Linguistics, University of Washington
Seattle, WA
{abhinavp, briggs3, taraw28, danieloc}@uw.edu

Abstract

We present several models for sentiment analysis of multimodal movie reviews in Tamil and Malayalam into 5 separate classes: highly negative, negative, neutral, positive, and highly positive, based on the shared task, "Multimodal Abusive Language Detection and Sentiment Analysis" at RANLP-2023. We use transformer language models to build text and audio embeddings and then compare the performance of multiple classifier models trained on these embeddings: a Multinomial Naive Bayes baseline, a Logistic Regression, a Random Forest, and an SVM. To account for class imbalance, we use both naive resampling and SMOTE. We found that without resampling, the baseline models have the same performance as a naive Majority Class Classifier. However, with resampling, logistic regression and random forest both demonstrate gains over the baseline. In the shared task, our best-performing model outperformed all ranked models with a macro-F_1 of 0.29 for Tamil and of 0.28 for Malayalam. Nevertheless, we found that this result was not stable across experimental random seeds.

1 Introduction

Sentiment analysis is the application of natural language processing techniques to identify, quantify, and examine the subjective attitudes and affective content of language. It has a rich history and many methods have been used in the past (Cui et al., 2023). While sentiment analysis tasks most frequently occur in the text domain, analysis of multimodal content has become an increasingly important task in recent decades as such content has become much more common. Users of popular social media websites, for instance, have long grown accustomed to creating and interacting with content which has either a textual, auditory, or visual form, or some combination of these three modalities, e.g., a YouTube video with subtitles features all three at once. Sentiment analysis models trained for such contexts must reflect features of all modalities concerned. Practically speaking, this task can be constructed in many ways: as a binary classification task (i.e. categorizing language into either Positive or Negative sentiment), an ordinal regression problem, or a multi-class classification problem. In our case, the task was the latter. We are classifying multimodal (text, audio, and video) data in Tamil and Malayalam into 5 separate sentiment classes: highly negative, negative, neutral, positive, and highly positive (B et al., 2023).

1.1 Motivation

Although Dravidian languages, such as Telugu, Tamil, Kannada, or Malayalam, are spoken by more than 250 million people, very few natural language processing resources exist for them. This paper considers data in two Dravidian languages, Tamil and Malayalam. The agglutination and high degree of morphological complexity exhibited by both languages present significant challenges in the development of useful NLP resources. This makes them ideal candidates for a sentiment analysis task, firstly because approaches which can more effectively extract useful information from limited data are especially useful in this kind of low-resource context, and secondly because progress in the development of such approaches may prove useful to those working with Dravidian languages, morphologically-complex languages, or low-resource languages more generally.

2 Related Work

Previous work on sentiment analysis on Dravidian languages was done in last year's shared task where only one team submitted their sentiment analysis project (Premjith et al., 2022). Also, previous work on sentiment analysis on Dravidian languages has used code-switched data (English

Third Workshop on Speech and Language Technologies for Dravidian Languages, pages 250–257, Varna, Bulgaria, Sep 7, 2023.
https://doi.org/10.26615/978-954-452-085-4_037

and either Tamil or Malayalam) (Chakravarthi et al., 2021a). Our data is not code-switched, and contains only one language. Like many tasks in Natural Language Processing, different Neural Network architectures have been used to perform sentiment analysis (Habimana et al., 2019).

Text Vectorization Synthesizing text documents into feature vectors for text classification is a difficult problem; common methods (Rani et al., 2022; Anita and Shashi, 2019) for doing so include Bag-of-Words, N-Gram, TF-IDF, Word2Vec (Mikolov et al., 2013), GloVE (Pennington et al., 2014), and Sentence2Vec/Doc2Vec (Le and Mikolov, 2014). Previous work has used features present in the orthography of low resource languages, especially Dravidan languages (Chakravarthi et al., 2021b). Using pre-trained ELMo (Peters et al., 2018) or BERT (Devlin et al., 2019) word embeddings has become increasingly popular, since they better encode semantic information (Anita and Shashi, 2019). Sun and Zhou (2020) uses the last three hidden layers of the pretrained multilingual model XLM-RoBERTa (Conneau et al., 2019) in conjunction with a convolutional neural network (CNN) to encode Tamil-English, as well as Malayalam-English code-mixed data into feature vectors.

Audio Vectorization Speech technologies have progressed a lot in the recent years, especially in multilingual and low-resource areas. The introduction of pseudo-labeling has improved the efficiency of semi-supervised deep neural network learning (Lee et al., 2013). Multitask learning approaches in conjunction with deep neural networks has enabled improvements in speech recognition for low-resource languages (Chen and Mak, 2015). Wav2Vec2 utilizes transformer-based unsupervised pre-training (Jiang et al., 2019) which works well with little training data. It also does this pre-training via masked reconstruction loss which has benefits similar to data augmentation methods (Wang et al., 2020). M-CTC-T, XLS-R (Cross-lingual Speech Representations), and UniSpeech, on the other hand, make use of supervised/self-supervised pre-training methods which often allow for better accuracy (Baevski et al., 2019).

3 Dataset Description

The shared task organizers have provided 54 training samples for Tamil and 60 training samples for Malayalam, as well as 10 test samples for both (Chakravarthi et al., 2021c). Each sample consists of an audio file of speech and a (sometimes partial) transcript of it. (They have also provided video files which we do not use.) Every sample is a movie review collected from YouTube and labeled by human annotators.

They have also provided a train and dev split over the data set, which is further subdivided by language (Tamil and Malayalam). The 54 Tamil samples are split 44/10 train/dev while the Malayalam samples are split 50/10. However, instead of using the official split, we combine train and dev data and use k-fold validation.

4 Methodology

4.1 System Overview

Our system pipeline has four main stages (see Figure 1): preprocessing/tokenization, vectorization, resampling, and k-fold cross-validation.

First, we preprocess and tokenize the data. To preprocess the data, we use two different tokenization methods. For the baseline models, we use whitespace tokenization after removing stopwords, punctuation, and numbers. For more sophisticated models, we use the SentencePiece algorithm used in XLM-RoBERTa (Conneau et al., 2019).

Second, we vectorize each input sample to produce document feature vectors. We have three main vectorization methods. The baseline models use TF-IDF vectorization. We also try two different vectorization methods using XLM-RoBERTa, namely using TF-IDF weighted average token embeddings from the first layer of XLM-RoBERTa base model, as well as using CLS token representations from hidden layers n through m of the XLM-RoBERTa base model.

For the audio data, we first pass raw audio into the built-in feature extractors from two models, Wav2Vec2 (Baevski et al., 2020) and M-CTC-T (Lugosch et al., 2022) using HuggingFace (Wolf et al., 2020). We then pass the output of the feature extractors into the three different pretrained models: XLS-R (Conneau et al., 2019), UniSpeech (Wang et al., 2021), and SpeechBrain (Lugosch et al., 2022). To extract document feature vectors, we then perform an element-wise average of the second to last hidden layer of the chosen pretrained model.

Third, we do resampling, using two methods, namely random resampling with replacement as

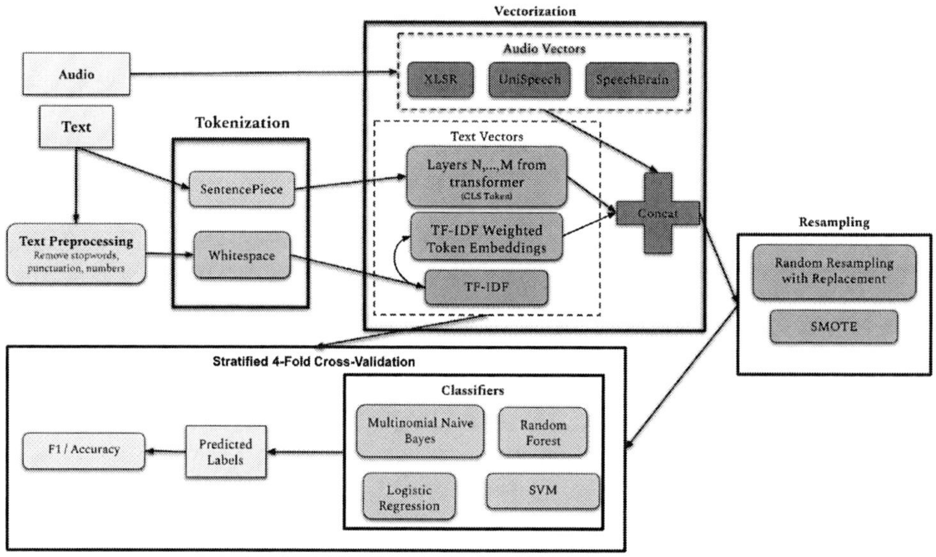

Figure 1: End-to-End System Architecture

well as Synthetic Minority Over-sampling Technique (SMOTE) (Chawla et al., 2002).

Finally, we run stratified k-fold cross-validation with $k = 4$. K-fold cross-validation consists of two main components: classification and evaluation. For classification, we first train various models using the training data, then use these models to predict the sentiment of the development documents specified by the current fold. For evaluation, we evaluate the performance of each model using accuracy and F_1 score.

4.2 Language Pooling

To create more training data, we pooled the data for Tamil and Malayalam together to create a new larger training data set and with which we trained a single model. Doing so produced better results than for language-specific models.

4.3 Preprocessing/Tokenization

WhiteSpace During preprocessing for the baseline, we first tokenized the data by whitespace. We then removed any tokens containing punctuation or numbers, as well as stop words. We used the list of stop words provided by `spaCy`[1] for both Tamil and Malayalam.

SentencePiece For the more sophisticated models, we use the XLM-RoBERTa (Conneau et al., 2019) tokenizer, which was trained using the SentencePiece algorithm (Kudo and Richardson, 2018), as well as IndicBert (Kakwani et al., 2020; Doddapaneni et al., 2022). Text longer than the model maximum input length (512, or 510 after accounting for special tokens) is truncated, while text shorter than it is padded.

4.4 Text Vectorization

TF-IDF Vectors We then create one TF-IDF vector per document in the data set. To create the TF-IDF vectors, we run each document through the TF-IDF vectorizer provided by `sklearn`.[2]

To calculate TF-IDF, we used the unsmoothed TF-IDF provided by `sklearn`. Given a document set D with n documents, a document $d \in D$, and a term t with document frequency $df(t)$, we calculate TF-IDF for term t as follows:

$$\text{TFIDF}(t, d, D) = \text{tf}(t, d) \cdot \text{idf}(t) \quad (1)$$

$$\text{tf}(t, d) = \text{count}(t) \in d \quad (2)$$

$$\text{idf}(t, D) = \log\left(\frac{n}{\text{df}(t)}\right) + 1 \quad (3)$$

Pretrained Multilingual Model Concatenated Hidden State Embeddings In this approach, we pass each document through a pretrained transformer language model and extract the hidden state

[1]We used spaCy v3.*. The Tamil and Malayalam language models can be found here.

[2]We used sklearn v1.*. `Sklearn`'s TF-IDF vectorizer documentation can be found here

representation for a specific set of layers, e.g. the last four, final, the second-to-last, third-to-last, etc. Then, we extract the vector corresponding to the CLS token from each layer and concatenate them together. We tried a variety of model and layer number combinations. For models, we looked at XLM-RoBERTA (base and large) and Indic Bert. For the layers, we looked at the last four concatenated, and each of the last four separately. We found the second-to-last layer of XLM-RoBERTA (base) performed the best, and we present these results below.

TF-IDF Weighted XLM-RoBERTa Token Embeddings We implemented a tokenization strategy using TF-IDF weighted average token embeddings from the embedding (first) layer of the XLM-RoBERTa base model. To obtain document feature vectors, we tokenize a document d using SentencePiece as outlined in section 4.3.

We thus have a sequence of n tokens, $\{t_n\} = d$. For each token $t_i \in d$, we obtain the embedding, $\vec{e_i}$, corresponding to token t_i. To obtain $\vec{e_i}$, we pull $\vec{e_i}$ from the embedding (first) layer of XLM-RoBERTa. We also obtain the TF-IDF score[3], $\mathrm{tf\_idf}(t_i, d)$, corresponding to each token t_i in document d. Then the document feature vector $\vec{f_d}$ for document d is exactly:

$$\vec{f_d} = \sum_{i=1}^{n} \mathrm{tf\_idf(t_i, d)} \cdot \vec{e_i} \tag{4}$$

In other words, each document feature vector is the weighted average of token embeddings, using TF-IDF weights.

4.5 Audio Vectorization

XLS-R For XLS-R we used Facebook's XLSR-Wav2Vec2 pretrained model `facebook/wav2vec2-large-xlsr-53`[4]. This model builds on and shares the same architecture as Wav2Vec2. This model was trained on CommonVoice, Babel, and Multilingual LibriSpeech (MLS) (53 total languages), including Tamil but not Malayalam.

UniSpeech For UniSpeech, we used Microsoft's pretrained model `microsoft/unispeech-large-multi-lingual-1500h-cv`[5]. This model builds on and shares the same architecture as Wav2Vec2. This model was trained on languages from CommonVoice, not including Tamil and Malayalam. This model was trained on the phoneme level rather than the character level, and thus we believe that this model is good for transfer learning.

SpeechBrain For SpeechBrain, we used Meta's pretrained model `speechbrain/m-ctc-t-large`[6]. This model builds on and shares the same architecture as M-CTC-T. This model was trained on all languages from CommonVoice 6.1 (Ardila et al., 2020) and VoxPopuli (79 total languages), including Tamil but not Malayalam.

4.6 Data Augmentation

SMOTE For Tamil, we also resampled the data using SMOTE with $k = 2$. In cross-validation, we could not use SMOTE for Malayalam due to the fact that there was only a single HIGHLY NEGATIVE sample, meaning three folds lacked it altogether. We were constrained to a small k for a similar reason.

Random Resampling with Replacement For both languages, we also tried random resampling with replacement, where we augmented each minority label with duplicates randomly drawn with replacement from the same label, until all classes had an equal number of samples.

4.7 Ridge Regression Feature Selection

We used a ridge regression model (linear regression with L2 regularization) for feature selection. All coefficients of the ridge regression model whose absolute values were smaller than the mean absolute value of all coefficients were dropped from consideration in the final classifier. We used a regularization strength hyperparameter (α) of 0.30. In all experimental settings, this reduced the number of features by between 35-75%, thereby decreasing the immense feature sparsity that we were faced with in this task.

4.8 Classifiers

Multinomial Naive Bayes For our baseline, we trained a multinomial Naive Bayes classifier on the TF-IDF feature vectors from section 4.4. To run Naive Bayes, we used the `sklearn` library (Pedregosa et al., 2011).

[3]As calculated in section 4.3

[4]HF: wav2vec2-large-xlsr-53

[5]HF: UniSpeech

[6]HF: m-ctc-t-large

	Tamil				Malayalam				Tamil+Malayalam			
	Dev		Test		Dev		Test		Dev		Test	
	Acc	F_1	Acc	F_1	Acc	F_1	Acc	F_1	Acc	F_1	Acc	F_1
Baseline (Majority classifier)	0.61	0.15	0.30	0.09	0.60	0.15	0.50	0.13	0.61	0.15	0.40	0.11
Text Only (5-seed average)	0.28	0.26	0.35	**0.19**	0.53	0.40	0.30	**0.14**	–	–	–	–
Text Only (seed=573)	0.26	0.26	0.50	**0.29**	0.40	0.31	0.40	**0.28**	–	–	–	–
Text+Audio (5-seed average)	–	–	0.50	**0.13**	–	–	0.61	**0.15**	0.60	0.35	0.56	0.14

Table 1: Results on the test set comparing our baselines (equivalent performance to a majority vote classifier), and our best systems using text as well as text and audio data. The "Dev" columns refer are the averages of four-fold cross-validation in the train set, while the test columns are calculated based on inference over the test set. See Appendix A.1 for hyperparameters.

Logistic Regression, Random Forest, and SVM We trained a linear Logistic Regression classifier, a Random Forest Classifier, and an SVM using `sklearn` (Pedregosa et al., 2011). We tested different combinations of hyperparameters, such as the solver, penalty, regularization strength, C, loss, alpha, learning rate, and the maximum number of iterations. Although these classifiers, under certain (relatively rare) conditions, could replicate the results of the Naive Bayes classifier on default settings, they never outperformed it.

5 Results

To evaluate our classifiers, we pooled the official train and dev splits into one large training set, and then ran k-fold cross-validation. This allowed us to train our models on more training data, as there was not a lot of training data provided. For k-fold cross-validation, we used 4 folds. To be able to compare the different models that we created, we used a deterministic algorithm to shuffle the data. This ensures that the same four train and dev splits were used for all the models, making the performance of our different models comparable.

First, for reference, in table 1 we provide the results of a majority-class classifier (one that assigns all classes the majority class, `POSITIVE`) as a baseline. This is identical to the performance of all of our Multinomial Naive Bayes as presented in section 4.8.

We have selected the best-performing model in terms of the pooled dev macro-F_1 score, training just on text data, as well as training on text in conjunction with audio data. For this model, we report the validation pooled F_1 scores and accuracy averaged across five seeds.[7] For the test data, we report the same metrics averaged across the same seeds in table 1.

We also report the dev and test results of the best model for any specific seed in terms of F_1 score on the test data. This "best model" was trained with only the text modality (across the board, the text audio models did worse due to greater feature sparsity). Note that this single seed happened to perform especially well, but is not representative of overall model performance.

6 Discussion

6.1 Data Set Imbalance

As we see in figure 2, the data set was both very small and highly imbalanced. Out of 70 Malayalam training samples, only one was of the 'Highly Negative' class, while thirty-six of them were 'Positive'. The fifty-four Tamil samples were likewise highly imbalanced, with 'Highly Negative' and 'Negative' both appearing only four times each and 'Positive' appearing thirty-three times. This imbalance could have negatively impacted the accuracy of our model to a great extent.

6.2 Discussion of Results

Without resampling, our baseline classifiers did not perform better than a majority class classifier, due to the fact that the amount of data available to train on is fairly small and most of the instances are POSITIVE.

Because our models were trained on so few samples, the use of too many features resulted in over-

[7]0, 42, 100, 573, 2023.

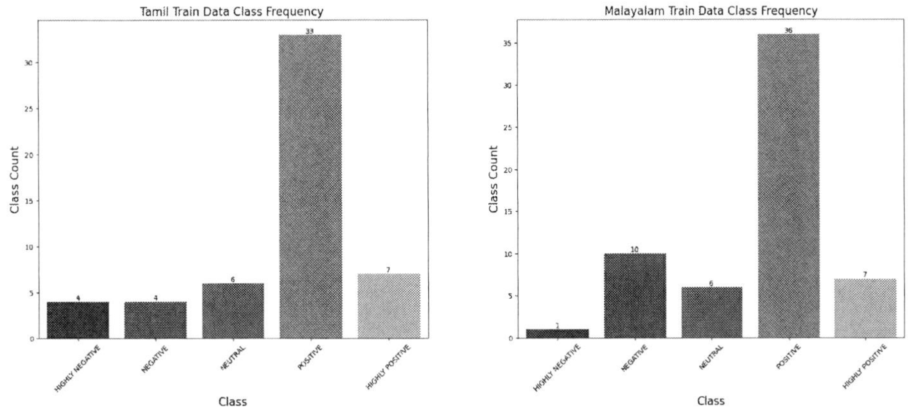

(a) Tamil (total: 54)

(b) Malayalam (total: 60)

Figure 2: Training Data Class Distribution

fitting; for this reason, models with fewer features generally performed better. Because there are only ten test instances per language, across seeds we saw a great amount of variance in scores. We chose to submit the best results among all random seeds, achieved in the text-only setting, but we do not feel that these are necessarily indicative of our model performance in general.

As we see in Table 1, when including text and audio data, we found that pooling the language data into one large training data set featuring both Malayalam and Tamil improved the performance of our models. We believe that this occurred for two reasons. Firstly, pooling enabled us to train our models on a substantially larger amount of data. Secondly, Tamil and Malayalam are very closely related languages, and the model may have been able to leverage salient linguistic features present in both languages to better classify sentiment. However, Tamil and Malayalam use different orthographies, so pooling their data only increased performance when using text and audio, and made no impact when using only text data.

Because there was only one HIGHLY NEGATIVE Malayalam instance, it cannot be in the train and dev data simultaneously. This means that the maximum F_1 score for Malayalam dev data is 0.8, and the evaluation of the models on Malayalam dev data might not be indicative of the actual performance of our models.

6.3 Future Work

One clear route for future work is to focus on mitigating the limitations of such a small and imbalanced data set. For example, one may conduct a more thorough exploration of data augmentation strategies. The sole augmentation procedure we used (besides simple random resampling) operated at the vector level (SMOTE). However, other data augmentation strategies that operate at the text and/or audio level may improve results.

In pooling our language data, we did not convert the text data for Tamil and Malayalam into a script compatible with both, e.g., via Romanization. Doing so may have improved results when pooling, not just for audio data, but for text data as well.

Another route one could take would be to translate all the data into a high-resource language (e.g. English) and then use existing and proven NLP tools on the translations.

7 Conclusion

We performed multimodal sentiment analysis on text and audio data from the Dravidian languages Tamil and Malayalam. To perform sentiment analysis, we built an end-to-end system, trying different vectorization methods, resampling techniques, and classifiers. We evaluated the system's performance using only text data, as well as jointly using text and audio data.

We created baseline systems using TF-IDF vectors and a Multinomial Naive Bayes classifier with no resampling and found that these baseline models performed no better than a majority class classifier.

As discussed elsewhere in this paper, we found that significant challenges stemming from the small size of our data set and its highly imbalanced distribution of classes proved largely insurmountable in improving the success of our models. We were not able to be formally ranked however our model did outperform the other ranked models.

References

Kumari S. Anita and Mogalla Shashi. 2019. Vectorization of text documents for identifying unifiable news articles. *International Journal of Advanced Computer Science and Applications*, 10(7). Copyright - © 2019. This work is licensed under https://creativecommons.org/licenses/by/4.0/ (the "License"). Notwithstanding the ProQuest Terms and Conditions, you may use this content in accordance with the terms of the License; Last updated - 2023-05-01.

Rosana Ardila, Megan Branson, Kelly Davis, Michael Kohler, Josh Meyer, Michael Henretty, Reuben Morais, Lindsay Saunders, Francis Tyers, and Gregor Weber. 2020. Common voice: A massively-multilingual speech corpus. In *Proceedings of the Twelfth Language Resources and Evaluation Conference*, pages 4218–4222, Marseille, France. European Language Resources Association.

Premjith B, Sowmya V, Jyothish Lal G, Bharathi Raja Chakravarthi, Nandhini K, Rajeswari Natarajan, Abirami Murugappan, Bharathi B, Kaushik M, Prasanth S.N, Aswin Raj R, and Vijai Simmon S. 2023. Findings of the Multimodal Abusive Language Detection and Sentiment Analysis in Dravidian Languages @ dravidianlangtech-ranlp 2023. In *Proceedings of the Third Workshop on Speech and Language Technologies for Dravidian Languages DravidianLangTech 2023*. Recent Advances in Natural Language Processing.

Alexei Baevski, Michael Auli, and Abdelrahman Mohamed. 2019. Effectiveness of self-supervised pre-training for speech recognition. *arXiv preprint arXiv:1911.03912*.

Alexei Baevski, Henry Zhou, Abdelrahman Mohamed, and Michael Auli. 2020. wav2vec 2.0: A framework for self-supervised learning of speech representations.

Bharathi Raja Chakravarthi, Ruba Priyadharshini, Vigneshwaran Muralidaran, Shardul Suryawanshi, Navya Jose, Elizabeth Sherly, and John P. McCrae. 2021a. Overview of the track on sentiment analysis for dravidian languages in code-mixed text. In *Proceedings of the 12th Annual Meeting of the Forum for Information Retrieval Evaluation*, FIRE '20, page 21–24, New York, NY, USA. Association for Computing Machinery.

Bharathi Raja Chakravarthi, Priya Rani, Mihael Arcan, and John P. McCrae. 2021b. A survey of orthographic information in machine translation. *SN Computer Science*, 2(4):330.

Bharathi Raja Chakravarthi, KP Soman, Rahul Ponnusamy, Prasanna Kumar Kumaresan, Kingston Pal Thamburaj, John P McCrae, et al. 2021c. Dravidianmultimodality: A dataset for multi-modal sentiment analysis in tamil and malayalam. *arXiv preprint arXiv:2106.04853*.

Nitesh V. Chawla, Kevin W. Bowyer, Lawrence O. Hall, and W. Philip Kegelmeyer. 2002. Smote: Synthetic minority over-sampling technique. *J. Artif. Int. Res.*, 16(1):321–357.

Dongpeng Chen and Brian Kan-Wing Mak. 2015. Multitask learning of deep neural networks for low-resource speech recognition. *IEEE/ACM Transactions on Audio, Speech, and Language Processing*, 23(7):1172–1183.

Alexis Conneau, Kartikay Khandelwal, Naman Goyal, Vishrav Chaudhary, Guillaume Wenzek, Francisco Guzmán, Edouard Grave, Myle Ott, Luke Zettlemoyer, and Veselin Stoyanov. 2019. Unsupervised cross-lingual representation learning at scale. *CoRR*, abs/1911.02116.

Jingfeng Cui, Zhaoxia Wang, Seng-Beng Ho, and Erik Cambria. 2023. Survey on sentiment analysis: evolution of research methods and topics. *Artificial Intelligence Review*.

Jacob Devlin, Ming-Wei Chang, Kenton Lee, and Kristina Toutanova. 2019. Bert: Pre-training of deep bidirectional transformers for language understanding.

Sumanth Doddapaneni, Rahul Aralikatte, Gowtham Ramesh, Shreyansh Goyal, Mitesh M. Khapra, Anoop Kunchukuttan, and Pratyush Kumar. 2022. Indicxtreme: A multi-task benchmark for evaluating indic languages. *ArXiv*, abs/2212.05409.

Olivier Habimana, Yuhua Li, Ruixuan Li, Xiwu Gu, and Ge Yu. 2019. Sentiment analysis using deep learning approaches: an overview. *Science China Information Sciences*, 63(1):111102.

Dongwei Jiang, Xiaoning Lei, Wubo Li, Ne Luo, Yuxuan Hu, Wei Zou, and Xiangang Li. 2019. Improving transformer-based speech recognition using unsupervised pre-training. *arXiv preprint arXiv:1910.09932*.

Divyanshu Kakwani, Anoop Kunchukuttan, Satish Golla, Gokul N.C., Avik Bhattacharyya, Mitesh M. Khapra, and Pratyush Kumar. 2020. IndicNLPSuite: Monolingual Corpora, Evaluation Benchmarks and Pre-trained Multilingual Language Models for Indian Languages. In *Findings of EMNLP*.

Taku Kudo and John Richardson. 2018. SentencePiece: A simple and language independent subword tokenizer and detokenizer for Neural Text Processing. *CoRR*, abs/1808.06226.

Quoc V. Le and Tomas Mikolov. 2014. Distributed representations of sentences and documents.

Dong-Hyun Lee et al. 2013. Pseudo-label: The simple and efficient semi-supervised learning method for deep neural networks. In *Workshop on challenges in representation learning, ICML*, volume 3, page 896. Atlanta.

Loren Lugosch, Tatiana Likhomanenko, Gabriel Synnaeve, and Ronan Collobert. 2022. Pseudo-labeling for massively multilingual speech recognition.

Tomas Mikolov, Kai Chen, Greg Corrado, and Jeffrey Dean. 2013. Efficient estimation of word representations in vector space.

F. Pedregosa, G. Varoquaux, A. Gramfort, V. Michel, B. Thirion, O. Grisel, M. Blondel, P. Prettenhofer, R. Weiss, V. Dubourg, J. Vanderplas, A. Passos, D. Cournapeau, M. Brucher, M. Perrot, and E. Duchesnay. 2011. Scikit-learn: Machine learning in Python. *Journal of Machine Learning Research*, 12:2825–2830.

Jeffrey Pennington, Richard Socher, and Christopher Manning. 2014. GloVe: Global vectors for word representation. In *Proceedings of the 2014 Conference on Empirical Methods in Natural Language Processing (EMNLP)*, pages 1532–1543, Doha, Qatar. Association for Computational Linguistics.

Matthew E. Peters, Mark Neumann, Mohit Iyyer, Matt Gardner, Christopher Clark, Kenton Lee, and Luke Zettlemoyer. 2018. Deep contextualized word representations.

B Premjith, Bharathi Raja Chakravarthi, Malliga Subramanian, B Bharathi, Soman Kp, V Dhanalakshmi, K Sreelakshmi, Arunaggiri Pandian, and Prasanna Kumaresan. 2022. Findings of the shared task on multimodal sentiment analysis and troll meme classification in dravidian languages. In *Proceedings of the Second Workshop on Speech and Language Technologies for Dravidian Languages*, pages 254–260.

Deepa Rani, Rajeev Kumar, and Naveen Chauhan. 2022. Study and comparision of vectorization techniques used in text classification. In *2022 13th International Conference on Computing Communication and Networking Technologies (ICCCNT)*, pages 1–6.

Ruijie Sun and Xiaobing Zhou. 2020. Srj @ dravidian-codemix-fire2020: Automatic classification and identification sentiment in code-mixed text. In *Fire*.

Chengyi Wang, Yu Wu, Yao Qian, Kenichi Kumatani, Shujie Liu, Furu Wei, Michael Zeng, and Xuedong Huang. 2021. Unispeech: Unified speech representation learning with labeled and unlabeled data.

Weiran Wang, Qingming Tang, and Karen Livescu. 2020. Unsupervised pre-training of bidirectional speech encoders via masked reconstruction. In *ICASSP 2020-2020 IEEE International Conference on Acoustics, Speech and Signal Processing (ICASSP)*, pages 6889–6893. IEEE.

Thomas Wolf, Lysandre Debut, Victor Sanh, Julien Chaumond, Clement Delangue, Anthony Moi, Pierric Cistac, Tim Rault, Rémi Louf, Morgan Funtowicz, Joe Davison, Sam Shleifer, Patrick von Platen, Clara Ma, Yacine Jernite, Julien Plu, Canwen Xu, Teven Le Scao, Sylvain Gugger, Mariama Drame, Quentin Lhoest, and Alexander M. Rush. 2020. Transformers: State-of-the-art natural language processing. In *Proceedings of the 2020 Conference on Empirical Methods in Natural Language Processing: System Demonstrations*, pages 38–45, Online. Association for Computational Linguistics.

A Appendix

A.1 Model Hyperparameters

Text Only: Logistic Regression ($C = 5.0$), Ridge Regression feature selection, random resampling with replacement; text vectorization: second-to-last layer.

Text+Audio: Pooled language training, Logistic Regression ($C = 5.0$), Ridge Regression feature selection, random resampling with replacement; text vectorization: second-to-last layer; audio vectorization: XLSR, third-to-last layer.

MUCS@DravidianLangTech2023: Sentiment Analysis in Code-mixed Tamil and Tulu Texts using fastText

Rachana K[a], Prajnashree M[b], Asha Hegde[c], H L Shashirekha[d]
Department of Computer Science, Mangalore University, Mangalore, Karnataka, India
{[a]rachanak749,[b]prajnapushparaj27,[c]hegdekasha}@gmail.com
[d]hlsrekha@mangaloreuniversity.ac.in

Abstract

Sentiment Analysis (SA) is a field of computational study that focus on analyzing and understanding people's opinions, attitudes, and emotions, towards any entity. An entity could be an individual, an event, a topic, a product etc., which is most likely to be covered by reviews and such reviews can be found in abundance on social media platforms. The increase in the number of social media users and the growing amount of user-generated code-mixed content such as reviews, comments, posts etc., on social media, have resulted in a rising demand for efficient tools capable of effectively analyzing such content to detect the sentiments. However, SA of social media text is challenging due to the complex nature of the code-mixed text. To tackle this issue, in this paper, we - team MUCS, describe the learning models submitted to the shared task "Sentiment Analysis in Tamil and Tulu" - DravidianLangTech@Recent Advances in Natural Language Processing (RANLP) 2023. Using fastText embeddings to train the Machine Learning (ML) models to perform SA in code-mixed Tamil and Tulu texts, the proposed methodology exhibited F1 scores of 0.14 and 0.204 respectively.

1 INTRODUCTION

In this digital era, social media platforms have become an integral part of the life of many people, especially the younger generation and have impacted people's perception of networking and socialising to a greater extent (Bharathi and Agnusimmaculate Silvia, 2021; Bharathi and Varsha, 2022; Swaminathan et al., 2022). This concept has influenced people to communicate efficiently and quickly using various social media platforms and has resulted in the increase in large amount of user-generated text data in the form of posts, comments, opinions, emotions, attitudes and reviews, making them a best source for user sentiments (Chakravarthi et al., 2022a,b; Chakravarthi, 2023). Identifying the sentiments of these text as positive, negative, neutral, etc., is the objective of SA as it is useful for various applications (Anita and Subalalitha, 2019; Thavareesan and Mahesan, 2019, 2020a,b). For example, SA can be used to determine which videos are liked by people on YouTube, based on the words/phrases in the comments for the video. SA can also help to determine whether a user is happy, sad, or angry, with the video.

As there is no barrier of language and content on social media, users feel convenient to post comments very informally by mixing words and sentences of more than one language (usually with one language being English) in more than one script, usually the native script and roman script. Further, due to the limitations of keyboard/keypad in computers/smart phones, users find it easy to key in the posts/comments in roman script (Chakravarthi, 2022b; Kumaresan et al., 2022; Chakravarthi, 2022a). This phenomena of mixing the linguistic units of more than language in one utterance or text is called as Code-mixing and it has almost become the official language of social media due to the increased number of users using this language (Chakravarthi et al., 2023a,b). Analyzing the user sentiments in code-mixed language is challenging due to inadequate resources and tools to address the text in code-mixed language. The complexity of the task increases if the code-mixed text is in low-resource languages such as Kannada, Tulu, Tamil, Malayalam, etc. As the code-mixed language is free from the grammar of any languages, users create words/sentences according to their whims and fancies which makes it interesting and challenging to analyze such texts.

To address the challenges of processing code-mixed Dravidian Languages for SA, in this pa-

Third Workshop on Speech and Language Technologies for Dravidian Languages, pages 258–265, Varna, Bulgaria, Sep 7, 2023.
https://doi.org/10.26615/978-954-452-085-4_038

Language	Comments	English Translation
Tamil	Today trailer paaka yaarellam wait panreenga	who is waiting to watch today's trailer
	indha gilli padam yaara yematha pakre	This is gilli movie whom you are thinking to cheat
	Nalla concept ana nalla eruintha nalla erukkum	Good concept but if it was good it will be good
Tulu	Supar bro irna comedy masth ista apudu	Super bro I like your comedy so much
	Title d spoiler alert pad doli	Could have include a spoiler alert in the title
	Ithe Encha ullariye?!	How are you now?

Table 1: Examples of Tamil and Tulu comments in romanized script

per, we - team MUCS, describe the models submitted to "Sentiment Analysis in Tamil and Tulu" shared task at DravidianLangTech@RANLP 2023[1] (Hegde et al., 2023). The shared task consists of a message-level polarity classification task for SA in code-mixed Tamil (Chakravarthi et al., 2020) and Tulu (Hegde et al., 2022). Given a Youtube comment in Tamil/Tulu, the aim of the shared task is to develop models to classify the given comment into positive, negative, neutral, or mixed emotions. Few Tulu and Tamil comments in romanized script and their English translations are shown in a Table 1. This shared task is modeled as a multi-class text classification problem with two distinct models: i) Support Vector Machine (SVM) classifier and ii) ensemble of ML classifiers, both trained with fastText embeddings. As the given datasets are imbalanced, Text Augmentation approaches are explored to increase the size of the minority classes in the training set.

Tulu language, a member of the Dravidian language family, is spoken by a community of more than three million people known as Tuluvas. The Tulu-speaking region is primarily located in the coastal districts of Dakshina Kannada and Udupi in the state of Karnataka, India. Tuluvas can also be found in Mumbai, Maharashtra, and various Gulf countries. Tamil is a Dravidian language spoken in the Tamil Nadu and Puducherry states of India and also some parts of Sri Lanka. Tamil has a long literary history, and is spoken by almost 225 million people. Tamil is a Multilingualism language which means that there is a large variation between the written form of the language and the spoken form. Both Tulu and Tamil languages, belong to the category of low-resourced languages. While some Natural Language Processing (NLP) activity is being explored in Tamil language for various applications, NLP in Tulu is yet to takeoff as there is no availability of digital data in Tulu. The only resources available for Tulu are: a small Wikipedia[2], Byte Pair embeddings (BPEmb)[3] and fastText[4] embeddings.

The rest of the paper is organized as follows: Section 2 contains related work and Section 3 describes the methodology. Section 4 describes the experiments and results followed by conclusion and future work in Section 5.

2 RELATED WORK

Many of the techniques explored by researchers for SA focus on high-resource languages like English, Spanish etc. Off late, SA is also being explored in code-mixed low-resource languages. Description of some of the relevant SA works in code-mixed low-resource languages are given below:

CoSaD - a code-mixed SA model for Dravidian Languages proposed by Balouchzahi et al. (2021) makes use of char n-grams, char sequences, and syllables, to train an ensemble (Linear Support Vector Machine (LSVM), Logistic Regression (LR) and Multi-Layer Perceptron (MLP) classifers) model with majority voting to identify sentiments in code-mixed Kannada, Malayalam, and Tamil languages. Their models obtained average weighted F1-scores of 0.628, 0.726,and 0.619 for code-mixed Kannada, Malayalam, and Tamil languages respectively. Ensemble of Random Forest (RF), Multi-Layer Perceptron (MLP) and gradient boosting is proposed by Hegde et al. (2021) to identify hate speech and offensive content in monolingual English, Hindi, and Marathi languages and code-mixed English-Hindi language pairs. These ensemble models trained using a combination of the Term Frequency - Inverse Document Frequency (TF-IDF) of word uni-grams, character n-grams in the range (2, 3),

[1]https://codalab.lisn.upsaclay.fr/competitions/11095

[2]https://en.wikipedia.org/wiki/Tulu_language

[3]https://bpemb.h-its.org/tcy/

[4]https://fasttext.cc/docs/en/pretrained-vectors.html

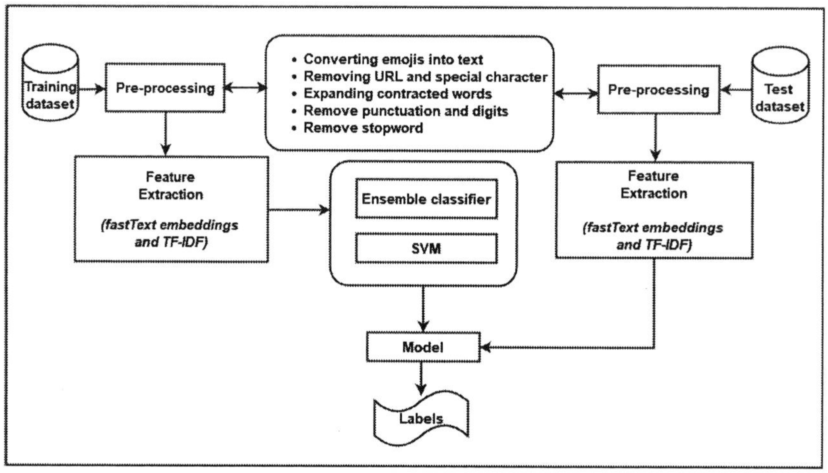

Figure 1: Framework of the proposed methodology

pre-trained word embeddings (Word2Vec), Hashtag embeddings (HastagVec), and Emo2Vec embeddings, obtained F1 scores 0.8251, 0.6323, 0.7830 and 0.6721 for English, Hindi, Marati and code-mixed English-Hindi language pair respectively.

SA of YouTube comments in code-mixed Tamil, Malayalam and Kannada language explored by Babu and Eswari (2021) using Paraphrase Cross-lingual Language Model-Robustly Optimized Bidirectional Encoder Representations from Transformers (XLM-RoBERTa) trained with hyperparameters (epochs = 12, learning rate = 3e-5, batchsize = 16, and dropout = 0.5.) obtained F1-scores of 0.71, 0.75 and 0.62 on Tamil, Malayalam and Kannada languages respectively. Chanda and Pal (2020) experimented feature extraction using Bidirectional Encoder Representations from Transformers (BERT), DistilBERT and fastText to train the LR classifiers to perform SA in code-mixed Tamil and Malayalam languages. Among these models, LR model trained with fastText embeddings outperformed other models with F1 scores of 0.58 and 0.63 for code-mixed Tamil and Malayalam languages respectively.

XLM-Roberta fine-tuned on code-mixed Malayalam and Tamil texts by Bai et al. (2021), to automatically detect sentiments, achieved F1 scores of 0.804 and 0.676 for Malayalam and Tamil languages respectively. Convolutional Neural Networks and Bi-directional Long Short-Term Memory (CNN+Bi-LSTM) model trained with fastText and GloVe pre-trained models by Mengistie and Kumar (2021) for SA of COVID-19 Public Reviews achieved 99.33 and 97.55 accuracy. Zhu and Dong (2020) proposed SA of Dravidian code-mixed text using multilingual Bidirectional Encoder Representations from Transformer (mBERT) model and used self-attention to assign a weight to the output of the BiLSTM. Their models achieved F1-scores of 0.73 and 0.64 for Malayalam and Tamil languages respectively.

From the literature review, it is evident that even though there are many models for SA of code-mixed low-resource languages, very few works have been reported for SA of code-mixed Tamil language and no work has been reported for the SA of code-mixed Tulu language. Hence, there is lot of scope to develop SA models for code-mixed low-resource Tulu and Tamil languages.

3 METHODOLOGY

The proposed methodology for SA in code-mixed Tulu and Tamil includes: Text Augmentation, Pre-processing, Feature extraction, and Model Construction. The framework of the proposed methodology is shown in Figure 1 and the steps are explained below:

3.1 Text Augmentation

Text augmentation is an important aspect of NLP to generate an artificial corpus. This helps in improving the NLP models to generalize better over a lot of different sub-tasks like intent classification, machine translation, chatbot training, image summarization, etc. The training sets for the task shared by the organizers are highly imbalanced and this may affect the performance of the learning models. Hence, several text augmentation methods are

Before Text Augmentation		
Labels	Training set	Development set
Positive	20,070	2,257
Unknown_state	5,628	611
Negative	4,271	480
Mixed_feelings	4,020	438
Total	33,989	3786
After Text Augmentation		
Labels	Training set	Development set
Positive	20,070	2,257
Unknown_state	6,239	611
Negative	4,751	480
Mixed_feelings	4,458	438
Total	35,518	3786

Table 2: Distribution of classes in Tamil dataset

Before Text Augmentation		
Labels	Training set	Development set
Positive	3,118	369
Neutral	1,719	202
Mixed feeling	974	120
Negative	646	90
Total	6,457	781
After Text Augmentation		
Labels	Training set	Development set
Positive	3,118	369
Neutral	1,719	202
Mixed feeling	1,297	120
Negative	1,016	90
Total	7,150	781

Table 3: Distribution of classes in Tulu dataset

explored to overcome the data imbalance to some extent in the training set.

In Tamil training set, the samples belonging to 'Unknown-state', 'Negative' and 'Mixed feelings' classes are less compared to that of 'Positive' class. Hence, the samples belonging to these classes from the Development set are added to the Training set, to balance the dataset to some extent.

In Tulu training set, 'Mixed feeling' and 'Negative' are the two minority classes which are highly imbalanced as compared to 'Positive' class. Hence, to balance the data to some extent, 'Mixed feeling' and 'Negative' classes are upsampled as follows: i) the samples belonging to the above two classes from the Development set are added to the Training set and ii) samples similar to those belonging to the above mentioned classes are collected from various sources (YouTube and Facebook post/comments and WhatsApp chat) and added to the corresponding classes in the training set. The distribution of classes in Tamil and Tulu datasets before and after augmentation are shown in Tables 2 and 3 respectively.

3.2 Pre-processing

Text pre-processing involves removing noise, normalizing and converting the normalized text to a format suitable for feature extraction.

- As emojis mainly depict user's intention, it would be imperative to replace them with their meanings to pick up their cues. Hence, emojis are converted to text using demoji[5] library.

- A contraction is a shortened form of a group of words. For example: hasn't, I'm, I'll etc. Contractions are often used in both written and oral communication. Expanding contractions into their natural form (hasn't – has not, I'm – I am, I'll – I will) will be more useful for processing particularly to extract embeddings from pre-trained models. The contracted words are expanded using the Contractions[6] library.

- URLs (Uniform Resource Locators) in a text are references to a location on the web. URLs, user mentions, hash tags, special characters, punctuation, and numeric information, present in the text data do not contribute to the classification task and hence are removed.

- Stop words are a set of commonly used words in any language. As they are not the distinguishing words, they do not contribute significantly to the classification task and hence are removed. English stopwords available at the Natural Language Tool Kit (NLTK)[7] and Tamil[8] stopwords available at GitHub repository are used as references to remove the English and Tamil stopwords respectively.

[5]https://pypi.org/project/demoji/
[6]https://pypi.org/project/pycontractions/
[7]https://pythonspot.com/nltk-stop-words/
[8]Tamil stopwords

The remaining words are the content bearing words which goes as input to feature extraction.

3.3 Feature Extraction

The process of extracting distinguishing features from the given data is called as Feature Extraction. fastText[9] is an open-source library of pre-trained models providing word embeddings for a total of 157 languages including Tamil and Tulu, developed by Facebook AI Research laboratory. These models trained on character n-grams represent word as the average of character embeddings of the characters a word is made up of. The advantage of using fastText is that it provides word representation even for Out of Vocabulary (OOV) words using their character n-grams. The feature extraction process using fastText pre-trained models for the datasets in both the languages are given below:

- **Tulu** - As the dataset is code-mixed, it consists of English words and Tulu words in native and romanized script. fastText Tulu pre-trained embeddings are used to represent Tulu words in native script and fastText English pre-trained embeddings are used to represent English words. However, Tulu words in romanized script cannot be represented by Tulu or English pre-trained models and hence they result in OOV words. These OOV words are represented as TF-IDF vectors. The vocabulary size of Tulu/English pre-trained models are 7,000 and 20,00,000 respectively and the vector dimension is 300. Concatenation of Tulu and English embeddings and TF-IDF of OOV words is used to train and evaluate the learning models.

- **Tamil** - As the datset is code-mixed, it consist of English words and Tamil words in native and romanized script. fastText Tamil pre-trained embeddings are used to represent Tamil words in native script and fastText English pre-trained embeddings are used to represent English words. The vocabulary size of both Tamil/English pre-trained models is 20,00,000 and the vector dimension is 300. Concatenation of Tamil and English embeddings are used to train and evaluate the learning model.

[9]https://fasttext.cc/docs/en/crawl-vectors.html

3.4 Model Construction

SVM and Ensemble Voting Classifier are used to detect the sentiments in the given unlabeled Tamil and Tulu comments.

- **Support Vector Machine** - maps data to a high-dimensional feature space so that data points can be categorised, even when the data are not otherwise linearly separable. The objective of the SVM Ahmad et al. (2017) algorithm is to find a hyperplane in an n-dimensional space that distinctly classifies the data points. The dimension of the hyperplane depends upon the number of features.

- **Ensemble model** - is a method of generating a new classifier from multiple base classifiers taking advantage of the strength of one classifier to overcome the weakness of another classifier with the intention of getting better performance for the classification task. This arrangement of more than one classifier will outperform when compared to the performance of any constituent classifier in the ensemble. It may be noted that any number of classifiers can be ensembled with compatible parameters Hegde and Shashirekha (2021). As more than one classifier is used in the ensemble model, majority voting of the classifiers is used to predict the class labels for the given unlabeled sample and hence, ensemble of classifiers is also called as Voting classifier.

  An ensemble of three ML classifiers, namely: Logistic Regression (LR), Bernoulli Naive Bayes (BNB) and Support Vector Classifer (SVC) classifiers with hard voting is used to identify the sentiment of the given unlabeled comment.

  LR is a ML classifier utilized for predicting categorical variables, employing dependent variables and regularization to mitigate overfitting. In LR, features from the input data are linearly combined and then transformed using the logistic function, allowing the algorithm to make predictions and classify instances into one of the two classes (Hassan et al., 2022).

  BNB classifier is a probabilistic ML algorithm based on the Naive Bayes principle, specifically designed for binary classification tasks. This algorithm computes the probability of a specific class label based on a set of binary

Model Name		Hyper-parameter and values
SVM		kernal='linear'
Ensemble	LR	random_state=1
	BNB	-
	SVC	penalty='l2', c=1.0

Table 4: Hyperparameters and their values used in ensemble model

Before Text Augmentation			
Language	Model	Development set	Test set
Tamil	SVM	0.20	0.05
	Ensemble	0.29	**0.13**
Tulu	SVM	0.33	0.35
	Ensemble	0.39	**0.35**
After Text Augmentation			
Language	Model	Development set	**Test set**
Tamil	SVM	-	0.05
	Ensemble	-	**0.14**
Tulu	SVM	0.16	**0.20**
	Ensemble	0.15	0.15

Table 5: Results of the proposed models

features using Bayes' theorem by incorporating the assumption of feature independence, making it efficient for text classification tasks (Singh et al., 2019).

SVC is an ML algorithm commonly used for text classification tasks. It aims to find the optimal hyperplane that best separates different classes of text data in a high-dimensional feature space. SVC seeks to find the most discriminative features that can separate different classes of documents/text effectively (Kalcheva et al., 2020). The hyperparameters and their values used in the classifiers of the ensemble model is shown in Table 4.

4 EXPERIMENTS AND RESULTS

Several experiments were conducted by combining various features and classifiers. The combination of features and classifiers which gave good performance on the Development sets are used to train the proposed models. The proposed models are evaluated on the Test set and the predictions are assessed by the organizers based on macro F1-score for the final evaluation and ranking. The performance of the proposed models for both Tamil and Tulu datasets are shown in Table 5.

The results illustrate that, ensemble model exhibited better performance over the other model with macro F1 score of 0.13 for Tamil text. Even though text augmentation is used to increase the samples of the minority classes (3 classes in Tamil and 2 classes in Tulu) to some extent, the datasets still remains imbalanced. Tamil dataset has a very large difference between the number of samples in 'Positive' class and other classes where as the difference between the number of samples in 'Positive' class and other classes in Tulu dataset is comparatively less. This clearly indicates the effect of data imbalance on the performance of the classifiers.

5 CONCLUSION

This paper describes the models submitted to "Sentiment Analysis in Tamil and Tulu" - DravidianLangTech@RANLP 2023 shared task. The proposed methodology consists of balancing the imbalance data using text augmentation, using fastText embeddings and TF-IDF as features to train SVM and ensemble model (LR, BNB and SVC models) with hard voting to perform SA. The proposed models exhibited F1 scores of 0.14 and 0.20 securing 13th and 15th rank for Tamil and Tulu datasets respectively.

References

Munir Ahmad, Shabib Aftab, and Iftikhar Ali. 2017. Sentiment Analysis of Tweets Using SVM. In *Int. J. Comput. Appl*, pages 25–29.

R Anita and CN Subalalitha. 2019. An approach to cluster Tamil literatures using discourse connectives. In *2019 IEEE 1st International Conference on Energy, Systems and Information Processing (ICESIP)*, pages 1–4. IEEE.

Yandrapati Prakash Babu and Rajagopal Eswari. 2021. Sentiment Analysis on Dravidian Code-Mixed YouTube Comments using Paraphrase XLM-RoBERTa Model. In *Working Notes of FIRE*.

Yang Bai, Bangyuan Zhang, Y Gu, T Guan, and Q Shi. 2021. Automatic Detecting the Sentiment of Code-Mixed Text by Pre-training Model. In *Working Notes of FIRE*.

Fazlourrahman Balouchzahi, Hosahalli Lakshmaiah Shashirekha, and Grigori Sidorov. 2021. CoSaD-Code-Mixed Sentiments Analysis for Dravidian Languages. In *CEUR Workshop Proceedings*, pages 887–898. CEUR-WS.

B Bharathi and A Agnusimmaculate Silvia. 2021. SSNCSE_NLP@DravidianLangTech-EACL2021: Offensive language identification on multilingual code mixing text. In *Proceedings of the First Workshop on Speech and Language Technologies for Dravidian Languages*, pages 313–318, Kyiv. Association for Computational Linguistics.

B Bharathi and Josephine Varsha. 2022. SSNCSE NLP@TamilNLP-ACL2022: Transformer based approach for detection of abusive comment for Tamil language. In *Proceedings of the Second Workshop on Speech and Language Technologies for Dravidian Languages*, pages 158–164, Dublin, Ireland. Association for Computational Linguistics.

Bharathi Raja Chakravarthi. 2022a. Hope speech detection in Youtube comments. *Social Network Analysis and Mining*, 12(1):75.

Bharathi Raja Chakravarthi. 2022b. Multilingual hope speech detection in English and Dravidian languages. *International Journal of Data Science and Analytics*, 14(4):389–406.

Bharathi Raja Chakravarthi. 2023. Detection of homophobia and transphobia in Youtube comments. *International Journal of Data Science and Analytics*, pages 1–20.

Bharathi Raja Chakravarthi, Adeep Hande, Rahul Ponnusamy, Prasanna Kumar Kumaresan, and Ruba Priyadharshini. 2022a. How can we detect homophobia and transphobia? experiments in a multilingual code-mixed setting for social media governance. *International Journal of Information Management Data Insights*, 2(2):100119.

Bharathi Raja Chakravarthi, Manoj Balaji Jagadeeshan, Vasanth Palanikumar, and Ruba Priyadharshini. 2023a. Offensive language identification in Dravidian languages using MPNet and CNN. *International Journal of Information Management Data Insights*, 3(1):100151.

Bharathi Raja Chakravarthi, Vigneshwaran Muralidaran, Ruba Priyadharshini, and John Philip McCrae. 2020. Corpus Creation for Sentiment Analysis in Code-Mixed Tamil-English Text. In *Proceedings of the 1st Joint Workshop on Spoken Language Technologies for Under-resourced languages (SLTU) and Collaboration and Computing for Under-Resourced Languages (CCURL)*, pages 202–210, Marseille, France. European Language Resources association.

Bharathi Raja Chakravarthi, Ruba Priyadharshini, Shubanker Banerjee, Manoj Balaji Jagadeeshan, Prasanna Kumar Kumaresan, Rahul Ponnusamy, Sean Benhur, and John Philip McCrae. 2023b. Detecting abusive comments at a fine-grained level in a low-resource language. *Natural Language Processing Journal*, 3:100006.

Bharathi Raja Chakravarthi, Ruba Priyadharshini, Thenmozhi Durairaj, John McCrae, Paul Buitelaar, Prasanna Kumaresan, and Rahul Ponnusamy. 2022b. Overview of the shared task on homophobia and transphobia detection in social media comments. In *Proceedings of the Second Workshop on Language Technology for Equality, Diversity and Inclusion*, pages 369–377, Dublin, Ireland. Association for Computational Linguistics.

Supriya Chanda and Sukomal Pal. 2020. IRLab@ IITBHU@ Dravidian-CodeMix-FIRE2020: Sentiment Analysis for Dravidian Languages in Code-Mixed Text. In *FIRE (Working Notes)*, pages 535–540.

Sayar Ul Hassan, Jameel Ahamed, and Khaleel Ahmad. 2022. Analytics of Machine Learning-Based Algorithms for Text Classification. In *Sustainable Operations and Computers*, pages 238–248. Elsevier.

Asha Hegde, Mudoor Devadas Anusha, Sharal Coelho, Hosahalli Lakshmaiah Shashirekha, and Bharathi Raja Chakravarthi. 2022. Corpus Creation for Sentiment Analysis in Code-Mixed Tulu Text. In *Proceedings of the 1st Annual Meeting of the ELRA/ISCA Special Interest Group on Under-Resourced Languages*, pages 33–40, Marseille, France. European Language Resources Association.

Asha Hegde, Mudoor Devadas Anusha, and Hosahalli Lakshmaiah Shashirekha. 2021. Ensemble Based Machine Learning Models for Hate Speech and Offensive Content Identification. In *Forum for Information Retrieval Evaluation (Working Notes)(FIRE), CEUR-WS. org*.

Asha Hegde and Hosahalli Lakshmaiah Shashirekha. 2021. Urdu Fake News Detection Using Ensemble of Machine Learning Models.

Chakravarthi Bharathi Raja Hegde, Asha, Hosahalli Lakshmaiah Shashirekha, Rahul Ponnusamy, Lavanya CN, SUBALALITHA andS K, Thenmozhi D, Martha Karunakar, Shreya Shreeram, and Sarah Aymen. 2023. "Findings of the Shared Task on Sentiment Analysis in Tamil and Tulu Code-Mixed Text". In *Proceedings of the Third Workshop on Speech and Language Technologies for Dravidian Languages*, Varna, Bulgaria. Recent Advances in Natural Language Processing.

Neli Kalcheva, Milena Karova, and Ivaylo Penev. 2020. Comparison of the Accuracy of SVM Kemel Functions in Text Classification. In *2020 International Conference on Biomedical Innovations and Applications (BIA)*, pages 141–145. IEEE.

Prasanna Kumar Kumaresan, Rahul Ponnusamy, Elizabeth Sherly, Sangeetha Sivanesan, and Bharathi Raja Chakravarthi. 2022. Transformer based hope speech comment classification in code-mixed text. In *International Conference on Speech and Language Technologies for Low-resource Languages*, pages 120–137. Springer.

Tajebe Tsega Mengistie and Deepak Kumar. 2021. Deep Learning Based Sentiment Analysis On COVID-19 Public Reviews. In *2021 International*

Conference on Artificial Intelligence in Information and Communication (ICAIIC), pages 444–449.

Gurinder Singh, Bhawna Kumar, Loveleen Gaur, and Akriti Tyagi. 2019. Comparison between Multinomial and Bernoulli Naïve Bayes for Text Classification. In *2019 International Conference on Automation, Computational and Technology Management (ICACTM)*, pages 593–596. IEEE.

Krithika Swaminathan, Bharathi B, Gayathri G L, and Hrishik Sampath. 2022. SSNCSE_NLP@LT-EDI-ACL2022: Homophobia/transphobia detection in multiple languages using SVM classifiers and BERT-based transformers. In *Proceedings of the Second Workshop on Language Technology for Equality, Diversity and Inclusion*, pages 239–244, Dublin, Ireland. Association for Computational Linguistics.

Sajeetha Thavareesan and Sinnathamby Mahesan. 2019. Sentiment analysis in Tamil texts: A study on machine learning techniques and feature representation. In *2019 14th Conference on industrial and information systems (ICIIS)*, pages 320–325. IEEE.

Sajeetha Thavareesan and Sinnathamby Mahesan. 2020a. Sentiment lexicon expansion using Word2vec and fastText for sentiment prediction in Tamil texts. In *2020 Moratuwa engineering research conference (MERCon)*, pages 272–276. IEEE.

Sajeetha Thavareesan and Sinnathamby Mahesan. 2020b. Word embedding-based part of speech tagging in tamil texts. In *2020 IEEE 15th International conference on industrial and information systems (ICIIS)*, pages 478–482. IEEE.

Yueying Zhu and Kunjie Dong. 2020. YUN111@ Dravidian-CodeMix-FIRE2020: Sentiment Analysis of Dravidian Code Mixed Text. In *FIRE (Working Notes)*, pages 628–634.

MUCS@DravidianLangTech2023: Leveraging Learning Models to Identify Abusive Comments in Code-mixed Dravidian Languages

Asha Hegde[a], **Kavya G**[b], **Sharal Coelho**[c],
Hosahalli Lakshmaiah Shashirekha[d]
Department of Computer Science, Mangalore University, Mangalore, India
{[a]hegdekasha, [b]kavyamujk, [c]sharalmucs}@gmail.com
[e]hlsrekha@mangaloreuniversity.ac.in

Abstract

Abusive language detection in user-generated online content has become a pressing concern due to its negative impact on users and challenges for policy makers. Online platforms are faced with the task of moderating abusive content to mitigate societal harm and foster inclusivity. Despite numerous methods developed for automated detection of abusive language, the problem continues to persist. This ongoing challenge necessitates further research and development to enhance the effectiveness of abusive content detection systems and implement proactive measures to create safer and more respectful online space. To address the automatic detection of abusive languages in social media platforms, this paper describes the models submitted by our team - MUCS, to the shared task "Abusive Comment Detection in Tamil and Telugu" at DravidianLangTech - in Recent Advances in Natural Language Processing (RANLP) 2023. This shared task addresses the abusive comment detection in code-mixed Tamil and Telugu texts, that includes the comments in both native script and romanized script, and romanized Tamil (RTamil) text. Two distinct models: i) AbusiveML - a model implemented utilizing Linear Support Vector Classifier (LinearSVC) algorithm fed with Term Frequency - Inverse Document Frequency (TF-IDF) of n-grams of words and character sequences within word boundary (char_wb) both in the range (1, 3) and ii) AbusiveTL - a Transfer Learning (TL) approach with three different Bidirectional Encoder Representations from Transformers (BERT) models, for three datasets along with random oversampling to deal with data imbalance, are submitted to the shared task for detecting abusive language in the given code-mixed texts. The AbusiveTL model fared well among these two models, with macro F1 scores of 0.46, 0.74, and 0.49 securing 1st, 1st, and 4th rank for code-mixed Tamil, Telugu, and RTamil texts respectively.

1 Introduction

Abusive language encompasses the use of words to insult, demean, or harm others, often through vulgar or profane language, and can include sexism, misogyny, and other forms of discrimination (Mandl et al., 2020; Subramanian et al., 2022; Chinnaudayar Navaneethakrishnan et al., 2023; Chakravarthi et al., 2023a,b). It may include words that provokes or aggravates an individual or a group of people. The phrase "abusive language" is also used synonymously with phrases like "offensive language" and "hate speech" (Hegde et al., 2021b). Over the past few years, the prevalence of offensive behavior targeting individuals, groups, or entire communities on social media platforms has significantly increased (Balouchzahi et al., 2021b; Hande et al., 2020; Chakravarthi et al., 2022a,b; Chakravarthi, 2023). This rise is creating negative impact such as, cyber-bullying, usage of offensive language, hate speech, and triggering content etc., on the well-being of online users. Hence, such negative content should be removed from the social media to keep online platforms healthy (Chakravarthi, 2022b; Kumaresan et al., 2022; Chakravarthi, 2022a).

Despite the efforts of social media companies to combat offensive/abusive language, the problem continues to escalate due to the limitations of existing algorithms used for detecting such content (Balouchzahi and Shashirekha, 2020; Bharathi and Agnusimmaculate Silvia, 2021; Bharathi and Varsha, 2022; Swaminathan et al., 2022a). These algorithms often fail to grasp the nuances of subjectivity and context that are crucial in accurately identifying abusive language. For instance, a single message might seem innocuous when taken out of context, but within a thread of previous conversations, it can reveal a pattern of abusive behavior. Similarly, certain phrases or words may have dif-

Third Workshop on Speech and Language Technologies for Dravidian Languages, pages 266–274, Varna, Bulgaria, Sep 7, 2023.
https://doi.org/10.26615/978-954-452-085-4_039

ferent meanings depending on the context, making it challenging for algorithms to accurately assess their intent. This complexity poses difficulties for human reviewers who have to navigate through vast amounts of content. Hence, achieving an effective and comprehensive solution to detect abusive language on online platforms require advancements in Natural Language Processing (NLP), Machine Learning (ML) techniques and the ability to capture context in a more nuanced manner (Balouchzahi et al., 2021a). It is a complex problem that necessitates ongoing research, collaboration between experts,
mechanisms to create safer online environments.

One of the challenges in addressing abusive language on social media is the prevalence of code -mixed data where regional languages like Tamil, Kannada, Malayalam, etc., are combined with English at various levels such as sub-word, word, or sentence (Hegde and Shashirekha, 2022a). This linguistic diversity makes it difficult for abusive comment detection algorithms to accurately identify and categorize the offensive content. Further, the use of internet slangs, abbreviations, words in short forms, words from other languages, and emojis complicates the issue. Lack of annotated datasets specifically in low-resource languages like Tamil and Telugu pose an additional hurdle in developing effective abusive content detection algorithms for these languages (Ravikiran et al., 2022). Bridging this gap requires efforts to gather and annotate data in these languages to train models that can better understand and detect abusive content in diverse linguistic settings.

"Abusive Comment Detection in Tamil and Telugu-DravidianLangTech@RANLP - 2023[1]" shared task encourages researchers to develop models to identify whether the given code-mixed Tamil and Telugu texts and RTamil texts is abusive or not (Priyadharshini et al., 2023). Code-mixed Tamil comments are distributed into nine classes (None-of-the-above, Misandry, Counter-speech, Misogyny, Xenophobia, Hope-Speech, Homophobia, Transphobic, Not-Tamil), Telugu comments into two classes (Non-Hate, Hate), and RTamil comments into eight classes (None-of-the-above, Misandry, Counter-speech, Xenophobia, Hope-Speech, Misogyny, Homophobia, Transphobic), in the dataset provided by the shared task organizers.

To address the challenges of this shared task, in this paper, we - team MUCS, describe the two classification models: i) AbusiveML model utilizing LinearSVC fed with TF-IDF of n-grams of words and char_wb both in the range (1, 3) and ii) AbusiveTL - a TL model trained using three different versions of BERT (Tamil BERT, Telugu BERT, and Distilled Multilingual BERT (DistilmBERT)).

The rest of the paper is arranged as follows: a review of related work is included in Section 2 and the methodology is discussed in Section 3. Experiments and results are described in Section 4 followed by concluding the paper with future work in Section 5.

2 Related work

Abusive comments are statements that offend a person or a group of people. These comments are directed at people who belong to certain nationality, gender, caste, race, sexuality, etc. The objective of abusive content detection is to find abusive speech on social media platforms, such as hate speech, derogatory language, misogyny, and racism. The description of some works that are carried out to perform a similar task is given below:

S N et al. (2022) presented Support Vector Machine (SVM) classifier for abusive comment detection in code-mixed Tamil and RTamil texts. They used TF-IDF with char_wb features in the range (1, 5) along with Random Kitchen Sink (RKS) algorithm to create feature vectors to train SVM classifier. Their proposed model obtained macro F1 scores of 0.32 and 0.25 for code-mixed Tamil and RTamil texts respectively. Palanikumar et al. (2022) proposed ML models (Light Gradient-boosting Machine (LGBM), Categorical Boosting (Catboost), Random Forest (RF), SVM and Multinomial Naive Bayes (MNB)) on fine-grained abusive detection in Tamil. To increase the size of the minority class in the dataset, they transliterated the given code-mixed dataset and combined it with the dataset. ML models are trained with TF-IDF of char_wb n-grams and MURIL - a pretrained BERT model. The proposed ML model trained with MURIL outperformed other models with macro average F1 score of 0.290 and weighted F1 score of 0.590.

Swaminathan et al. (2022b) proposed the ML models (SVM, MultiLayer Perceptron (MLP), and k-Nearest Neighbours Classifier (k-NN)) to classify abusive content in RTamil code-mixed text. In their study, they combined language-agnostic sentence embeddings with the TF-IDF of word

[1]https://codalab.lisn.upsaclay.fr/competitions/11096

vectors to train SVM classifier and obtained an accuracy of 0.520 and macro F1 score 0.54. Nayel and Shashirekha (2019) described the ML models (SVM, Linear Classifier, MLP) for binary classification and, multi-class classification to detect the type of offensive content in three languages (English, German, and Hindi). For both binary and multi-class classification, SVM classifier trained with TF-IDF of word n-grams in the range (1, 2) exhibited macro F1 scores of 0.66, 0.75, 0.46 and 0.42, 0.47, 0.23 for English, Hindi and German languages respectively. Balouchzahi et al. (2021c) submitted two distinct models: COOLIEnsemble - an ensemble model of MLP, eXtreme Gradient Boosting (XGboost) and Logistic Regression (LR) trained using term frequencies and COOLI-Keras - a Deep Learning (DL) classifier, to identify offensive language in code-mixed Kannada-English, Malayalam-English, and RTamil texts. Out of the two models, COOLI-Ensemble model outperformed the other model with weighted F1 scores of 0.97, 0.75, and 0.69 for Malayalam-English, RTamil, and Kannada-English respectively.

Hegde and Shashirekha (2022b) proposed Dynamic Meta Embedding (DME) based Long Short Term Memory (LSTM) classifier to perform sentiment analysis and homophobia detection as Task A (Malayalam and Kannada) and Task B (Tamil, English, RTamil) respectively. Their proposed methodology exhibited macro F1 scores of 0.61, and 0.44 for Malayalam, and Kannada respectively in Task A and for Task B their models obtained macro F1 scores of 0.74 and 0.58 for English and RTamil languages respectively. Das et al. (2021) explored three learning models (XGboost, LGBM, mBERT) for abusive and threatening content detection in Urdu. They trained XGboost and LGBM classifiers using pre-trained Urdu laser embeddings. Further, they fine-tuned mBERT and dehatebert-mono-arabic pretrained models for abusive and threatening content detection in Urdu. Their fine-tuned mBert models outperformed the other models with macro F1 scores of 0.88 and 0.54 for abusive and threatening content detection respectively. Balouchzahi and Shashirekha (2020) proposed three distinct models to identify hate speech in English, German, and Hindi languages. They implemented i) ensemble of ML classifiers (RFC, LR, and SVM) trained with TF-IDF of word n-gram in the range (1, 2) and character n-grams in the range (1, 5), ii) TL based classifier using Universal Language Model Fine-tuning (ULMFiT) model, and iii) a hybrid model which is an ensemble of ML (i)) and TL (ii)) models. The ensembled ML classifier obtained macro F1 score of 0.5044 for German and hybrid model obtained macro F1 score of 0.5182 for Hindi.

From the above related work, it is found that among ML, DL, and TL models, TL models outperformed the other models indicating the efficiency of the TL models in detecting abusive content on social media. Though there are several models to identify abusive content in social media text, there is still scope for developing models for low-resource languages like Tamil and Telugu as these languages are not much explored in the realm of code-mixed content.

3 Methodology

The objective of this work is to identify abusive comments in code-mixed Tamil, Telugu, and RTamil texts. This is achieved by proposing two distinct models, AbusiveML and AbusiveTL. Detailed description of the models are given below:

3.1 Preprocessing

Preprocessing the raw text is an important initial step in text processing to enhance the performance of the learning models. During preprocessing, punctuation, numerical data, hashtags, user mention and stopwords are removed. English stopwords list available in Natural Language Tool Kit (NLTK) [2] and Tamil[3] and Telugu[4] stopwords lists available in github repository are used as reference to remove the stopwords.

3.2 Models Construction

The framework of AbusiveML and AbusiveTL are visualized in Figures 1 and 2. AbusiveML uses LinearSVC classifer and AbusiveTL uses transformer based classifier - ClassificationModel. Model descriptions are as follows:

3.2.1 AbusiveML

n-grams are widely used in text processing projects due to their ease of implementation and scalability. By increasing the 'n' value up to a certain level, a model can capture larger contexts and store more

[2]https://pythonspot.com/nltk-stop-words/

[3]https://gist.github.com/arulrajnet/e82a5a331f78a5cc9b6d372df13a919c

[4]https://github.com/Xangis/extra/_stopwords/blob/master/telugu

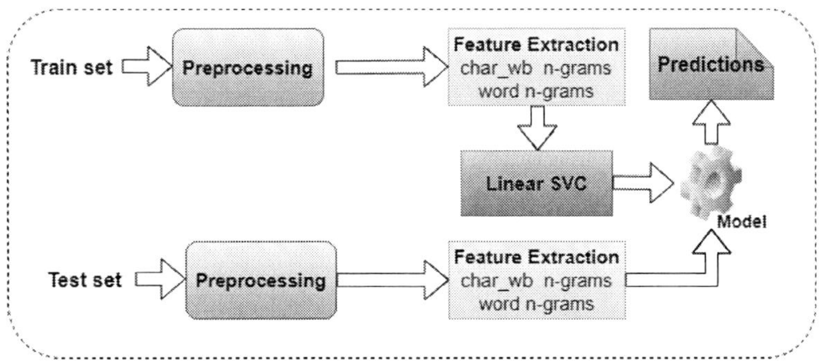

Figure 1: The framework of the AbusiveML model

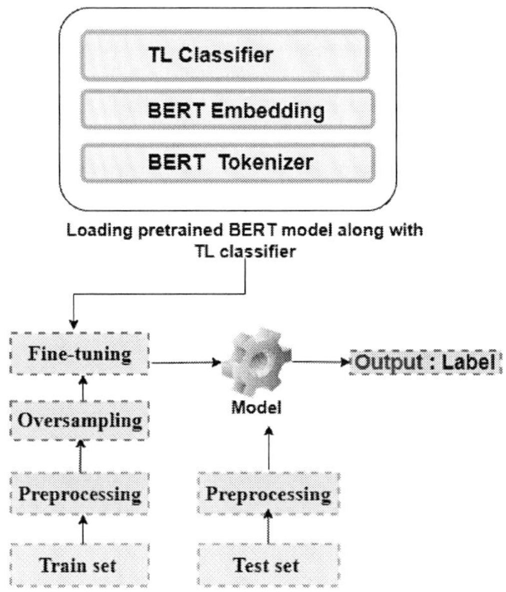

Figure 2: The framework of the AbusiveTL model

information about word/character sequences, enabling a better understanding of the relationships between words. This space-time trade-off is well-understood, allowing text processing experiments to scale up efficiently by adjusting the 'n' value based on the requirements of the task at hand viz. for simpler language tasks (e.g. autocomplete suggestions) smaller values of n (1, 2) is used, whereas, for complex tasks (e.g. text generation) larger values of n (3, 6) is used (Hegde and Shashirekha, 2021). However, larger value of 'n' introduces sparsity and increases the complexity of the learning algorithms.

n-grams of words and char_wb, both in the range (1, 3) extracted from the texts are vectorized using TfidfVectorizer[5] to train LinearSVC model. The

Hyperparameters	Values
penalty	l2
C	1.0
class_weight	balanced
max_iter	max_iter
random_state	100
loss	squared_hinge

Table 1: Hyperparameters and their values used in LinearSVC algorithm

hypermeters and their values used in LinearSVC model are shown in Table 1. The hyperparameters which are not mentioned in Table 1 are used with their default values.

In LinearSVC, setting the hyperparameter 'class_weight' to 'balanced' enables automatic adjustment of class weights based on their frequencies, effectively addressing data imbalance without the need for manual intervention.

3.2.2 AbusiveTL

TL is an ML technique that leverages knowledge gained from one task to improve the performance of a related but different task (Hegde et al., 2021a). It involves using pretrained models as a starting point and fine-tuning them for a specific task or domain (Hegde et al., 2022). In the proposed AbusiveTL model, random oversampling[6] - an oversampling technique which increases the instances in the minority class by replicating the synthetic samples, is used before fine-tuning the pretrained models. DistilmBERT[7], Tamil BERT[8], and Telugu

[5]https://scikit-learn.org/stable/modules/generated/sklearn.feature_extraction.text.TfidfVectorizer.html

[6]https://imbalanced-learn.org/stable/over_sampling.html

[7]https://huggingface.co/distilbert-base-multilingual-cased

[8]https://huggingface.co/l3cube-pune/tamil-bert

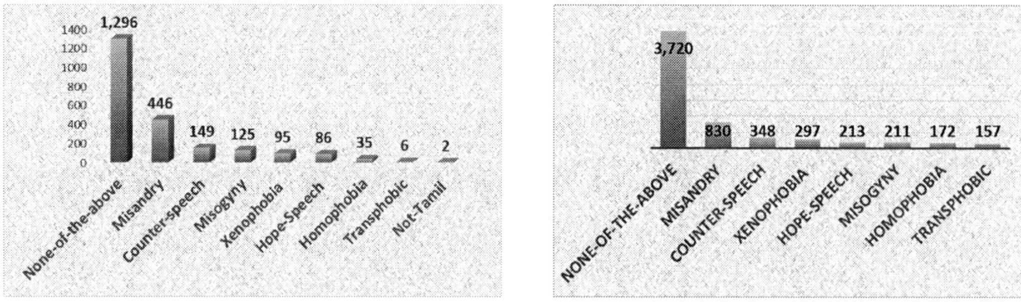

(a) Tamil (b) RTamil

Figure 3: Classwise distribution of code-mixed Tamil and RTamil datasets

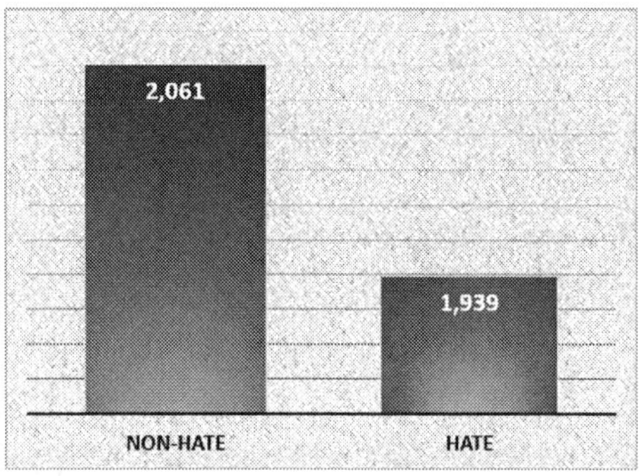

Figure 4: Classwise distribution of Telugu dataset

Hyperparameters	Values
Layers	6
Dimension	768
Attention heads	12
Learning Rate	2e-5
Batch Size	32
Maximum Sequence Length	128
Dropout	0.3

Table 2: Hyperparameters and their values used in AbusiveTL model

BERT[9] from huggingface library[10] are used to load the corresponding pretrained BERT versions which includes pretrained BERT tokenizer, embeddings and a TL classifier. Eventually this model is used to fine-tune the labeled Train set. Hyperparameters and their values used to implement AbusiveTL model are shown in Table 2. The hyperparameters which are not mentioned in Table 2 are used with their default values. The steps involved in fine-tuning the pretrained BERT models are given below:

- Tokenization - input text is passed through BERT's positional encoding-based tokenizer, which segments the text into individual tokens and adds positional information
- BERT encoder - tokens are transformed into contextualized embeddings using BERT encoder that helps to capture the contextual information and semantic representations
- Training - contextualized embeddings are fed into the model's classifiers viz. transformers based classifier for training

[9]https://huggingface.co/l3cube-pune/telugu-bert
[10]https://huggingface.co/docs/hub/models-libraries

Prediction is carried out by the transformers based classifier (ClassificationModel).

4 Experiments and Results

Train, Development, and Test sets are provided by the shared task organizers (Priyadharshini et al., 2022) for abusive language detection in code-mixed Tamil and Telugu along with RTamil texts. Multiple experiments are carried out, incorporating different resampling techniques (Synthetic Minority Over-sampling TEchnique (SMOTE), random oversampling, and downsampling), feature combinations (pretrained word vectors, character count, and word count), and classifiers (LR, LinearSVC, NB, and MLP). The models that exhibited considerably good performances on the Development set were subsequently evaluated on the Test set. Figures 3 (a), 3 (b), and 4 show the label distribution in code-mixed Tamil, RTamil, and Telugu datasets respectively.

The predictions of the proposed models are evaluated by the organizers of the shared task based on macro F1 score and performance of the proposed models on Test and Development sets are shown in Table 3. As illustrated in Table 3 AbusiveTL model outperformed the other model with macro F1 scores of 0.74, 0.46, and 0.49 securing 1st, 1st, and 4th rank in the shared task for Telugu, Tamil, and RTamil, Test sets respectively.

In spite of using data imbalance handling mechanisms, for Tamil and RTamil texts the macro F1 scores are still less. This may be due to the overlapping feature distributions in the Train set. Further, adding class_weight='balanced' as a hyperparameter to a LinearSVC model can help to address the class imbalance by assigning higher weights to the minority class during training. While it generally helps to improve the performance, the macro F1 scores might decrease even after using this technique in certain scenarios, such as, data complexity, loss information, and features used. Further, as random oversampling technique increase the instances in minority classes by duplicating samples, this can lead the model to become overly focused on the minority class, potentially causing overfitting. This means the model might perform exceptionally well on the Train set but fail to generalize to new, unseen data. Table 4 shows the misclassifications for Telugu and Tamil comments along with their English translations, actual labels, predicted labels (obtained from AbusiveTL models for Tamil, Telugu, and RTamil Test sets) and remarks. From Table 4, it is clear that removing stopwords and digits may also lead to misclassification in addition to rare words and wrong annotation. This underscores the importance of a balanced preprocessing approach that carefully considers the impact of each step on the overall classification performance, as eliminating stopwords and digits might inadvertently remove context and information necessary for classification. Figures 5 (a), 5 (b), and 6 illustrate the comparison of macro F1 scores of all the participating teams for code-mixed Tamil and RTamil and Telugu texts respectively.

5 Conclusion

This paper describes the models submitted by our team - MUCS, to "Abusive Comment Detection in Tamil and Telugu" shared task at DravidianLangTech@RANLP 2023, to identify abusive content in code-mixed Tamil, Telugu, and RTamil texts. Two models: i) AbusiveML model that utilizes LinearSVC algorithm fed with TF-IDF of n-grams of words and char_wb both in the range (1, 3) and ii) AbusiveTL model fine-tuned on oversampled Train set with three different BERT models (for three different languages), are proposed to detect abusive comments in the input text. AbusiveTL models outperformed the other models with macro F1 scores of 0.74, 0.46, and 0.49 securing 1st, 1st, and 4th rank in the shared task for Telugu, Tamil, and RTamil texts respectively. Efficient resampling techniques for handling imbalanced data with effective feature extraction will be explored further.

References

F Balouchzahi, S Bashang, G Sidorov, and HL Shashirekha. 2021a. CoMaTa OLI-Code-mixed Malayalam and Tamil Offensive Language Identification. In *Working Notes of FIRE 2021-Forum for Information Retrieval Evaluation (Online). CEUR.*

Fazlourrahman Balouchzahi, BK Aparna, and HL Shashirekha. 2021b. MUCS@ DravidianLangTech-EACL2021: COOLI-Code-Mixing Offensive Language Identification. In *Proceedings of the First Workshop on Speech and Language Technologies for Dravidian Languages*, pages 323–329.

Fazlourrahman Balouchzahi, Aparna B K, and H L Shashirekha. 2021c. MUCS@DravidianLangTech-EACL2021:COOLI-Code-Mixing Offensive Language Identification. In *Proceedings of the First Workshop on Speech and Language Technologies for Dravidian Languages*, pages 323–329, Kyiv. Association for Computational Linguistics.

Fazlourrahman Balouchzahi and HL Shashirekha. 2020. LAs for HASOC-Learning Approaches for Hate Speech and Offensive Content Identification. In *FIRE (Working Notes)*, pages 145–151.

B Bharathi and A Agnusimmaculate Silvia. 2021. SSNCSE_NLP@DravidianLangTech-EACL2021: Offensive language identification on multilingual code mixing text. In *Proceedings of the First Workshop on Speech and Language Technologies for Dravidian Languages*, pages 313–318, Kyiv. Association for Computational Linguistics.

B Bharathi and Josephine Varsha. 2022. SSNCSE NLP@TamilNLP-ACL2022: Transformer based approach for detection of abusive comment for Tamil language. In *Proceedings of the Second Workshop on Speech and Language Technologies for Dravidian Languages*, pages 158–164, Dublin, Ireland. Association for Computational Linguistics.

Bharathi Raja Chakravarthi. 2022a. Hope speech detection in Youtube comments. *Social Network Analysis and Mining*, 12(1):75.

Bharathi Raja Chakravarthi. 2022b. Multilingual hope speech detection in English and Dravidian languages. *International Journal of Data Science and Analytics*, 14(4):389–406.

Model	Language	Development set		Test set	
		With imbalanced data	With balanced data	With imbalanced data	With balanced data
AbusiveML	**Telugu**	0.61	0.65	0.66	**0.70**
	Tamil	0.31	0.39	0.30	0.32
	RTamil	0.41	0.46	0.38	0.43
AbusiveTL	**Telugu**	0.73	0.77	0.65	**0.74**
	Tamil	0.08	0.39	0.07	0.46
	RTamil	0.15	0.51	0.16	0.49

Table 3: Performance of the proposed models with imbalanced and balanced datasets

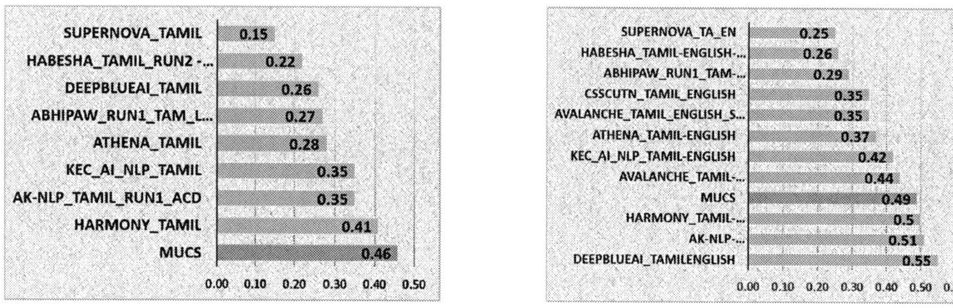

(a) Tamil

(b) RTamil

Figure 5: Comparison of macro F1 scores of the participating teams in the shared task for code-mixed Tamil and RTamil datasets

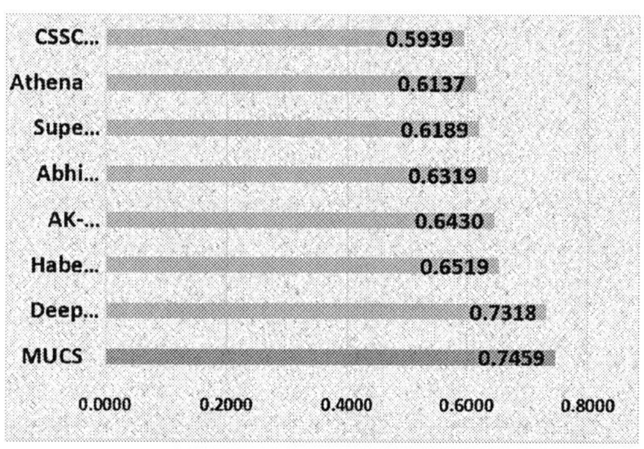

Figure 6: Comparison of macro F1 scores of the participating teams in the shared task for code-mixed Telugu dataset

Bharathi Raja Chakravarthi. 2023. Detection of homophobia and transphobia in Youtube comments. *International Journal of Data Science and Analytics*, pages 1–20.

Bharathi Raja Chakravarthi, Adeep Hande, Rahul Ponnusamy, Prasanna Kumar Kumaresan, and Ruba Priyadharshini. 2022a. How can we detect homophobia and transphobia? experiments in a multilingual code-mixed setting for social media governance. *International Journal of Information Management Data Insights*, 2(2):100119.

Bharathi Raja Chakravarthi, Manoj Balaji Jagadeeshan, Vasanth Palanikumar, and Ruba Priyadharshini. 2023a. Offensive language identification in Dravidian languages using MPNet and CNN. *International Journal of Information Management Data Insights*, 3(1):100151.

Bharathi Raja Chakravarthi, Ruba Priyadharshini, Shubanker Banerjee, Manoj Balaji Jagadeeshan, Prasanna Kumar Kumaresan, Rahul Ponnusamy, Sean Benhur, and John Philip McCrae. 2023b. Detecting abusive comments at a fine-grained level in a low-resource language. *Natural Language Processing Journal*, 3:100006.

Bharathi Raja Chakravarthi, Ruba Priyadharshini, Thenmozhi Durairaj, John McCrae, Paul Buitelaar, Prasanna Kumaresan, and Rahul Ponnusamy. 2022b. Overview of the shared task on homophobia and transphobia detection in social media comments. In *Proceedings of the Second Workshop on Language Technology for Equality, Diversity and Inclusion*, pages 369–377, Dublin, Ireland. Association for Computational Linguistics.

Subalalitha Chinnaudayar Navaneethakrishnan, Bharathi Raja Chakravarthi, Kogilavani Shanmugavadivel, Malliga Subramanian, Prasanna Kumar Kumaresan, Bharathi, Lavanya Sambath Kumar, and Rahul Ponnusamy. 2023. Findings of shared task on sentiment analysis and homophobia detection

Language	Comment	English Translations	Actual Label	Predicted Label	Remarks
Telugu	ఓటమి ఎంతో నేర్చుకోవచ్చు దానికిక్కే వేరు ఉంటుంది	Defeat can learn a lot, but it's different	non-hate	hate	The word "defeat" carries a negative connotation and may be due to this the comment is classified as 'hate'.
	అదే 420 పరిపాలన	Same 420 administration	hate	non-hate	'420' is a slang term that is often used in the negative tone and it is removed during preprocessing (usually numeric information will be removed). The remaining words has nothing to do with 'hate' class and hence the comment is classified as 'non-hate'.
Tamil	அந்த தமிழன் ஒரு சாதிவெறி	That Tamil is a caste fanatic	None	Xenophobia	The comment is incorrectly annotated as 'None' because the terms 'caste' and 'fanatic' indicates the class 'Xenophobia'.
	வாழ்த்துக்கள் h ராஜா ஜி	Congratulations h Raja G	None	Hope-Speech	In this comment, the characters 'h' and 'G' will be removed during preprocessing and because the word 'Raja' is a noun, it may not have a representation. Further, the term 'congratulations' is associated with 'Hope-speech' class in the train set and hence it is classified as hope.

Table 4: Samples of misclassification for code-mixed Telugu and Tamil texts

of Youtube comments in code-mixed Dravidian languages. In *Proceedings of the 14th Annual Meeting of the Forum for Information Retrieval Evaluation*, FIRE '22, page 18–21, New York, NY, USA. Association for Computing Machinery.

Mithun Das, Somnath Banerjee, and Punyajoy Saha. 2021. Abusive and Threatening Language Detection in Urdu using Boosting based and Bert based Models: A Comparative Approach. In *arXiv preprint arXiv:2111.14830*.

Adeep Hande, Ruba Priyadharshini, and Bharathi Raja Chakravarthi. 2020. KanCMD: Kannada CodeMixed Dataset for Sentiment Analysis and Offensive Language Detection. In *Proceedings of the Third Workshop on Computational Modeling of People's Opinions, Personality, and Emotion's in Social Media*, pages 54–63.

Asha Hegde, Mudoor Devadas Anusha, Sharal Coelho, and Hosahalli Lakshmaiah Shashirekha. 2021a. MUM at ComMA@ICON: Multilingual Gender Biased and Communal Language Identification using Supervised Learning Approaches. In *Proceedings of the 18th International Conference on Natural Language Processing: Shared Task on Multilingual Gender Biased and Communal Language Identification*, pages 64–69, NIT Silchar. NLP Association of India (NLPAI).

Asha Hegde, Mudoor Devadas Anusha, and Hosahalli Lakshmaiah Shashirekha. 2021b. Ensemble Based Machine Learning Models for Hate Speech and Offensive Content Identification. In *Forum for Information Retrieval Evaluation (Working Notes)(FIRE), CEUR-WS. org*.

Asha Hegde, Sharal Coelho, Ahmad Elyas Dashti, and Hosahalli Shashirekha. 2022. MUCS@ Text-LT-EDI@ ACL 2022: Detecting Sign of Depression from Social Media Text using Supervised Learning Approach. In *Proceedings of the Second Workshop on Language Technology for Equality, Diversity and Inclusion*, pages 312–316.

Asha Hegde and Hosahalli Lakshmaiah Shashirekha. 2021. Urdu Fake News Detection Using Ensemble of Machine Learning Models.

Asha Hegde and Hosahalli Lakshmaiah Shashirekha. 2022a. Learning Models for Emotion Analysis and Threatening Language Detection in Urdu Tweets.

Asha Hegde and Hosahalli Lakshmaiah Shashirekha. 2022b. Leveraging Dynamic Meta Embedding for Sentiment Analysis and Detection of Homophobic/Transphobic Content in Code-mixed Dravidian Languages.

Prasanna Kumar Kumaresan, Rahul Ponnusamy, Elizabeth Sherly, Sangeetha Sivanesan, and Bharathi Raja Chakravarthi. 2022. Transformer based hope speech comment classification in code-mixed text. In *International Conference on Speech and Language Technologies for Low-resource Languages*, pages 120–137. Springer.

Thomas Mandl, Sandip Modha, Anand Kumar M, and Bharathi Raja Chakravarthi. 2020. Overview of the

Hasoc Track at Fire 2020: Hate speech and Offensive Language Identification in Tamil, Malayalam, Hindi, English and German. In *Forum for information retrieval evaluation*, pages 29–32.

Hamada Nayel and H. Shashirekha. 2019. DEEP at HASOC2019 : A Machine Learning Framework for Hate Speech and Offensive Language Detection. pages 336–343.

Vasanth Palanikumar, Sean Benhur, Adeep Hande, and Bharathi Raja Chakravarthi. 2022. DE-ABUSE@TamilNLP-ACL 2022: Transliteration as Data Augmentation for Abuse Detection in Tamil. In *Proceedings of the Second Workshop on Speech and Language Technologies for Dravidian Languages*, pages 33–38, Dublin, Ireland. Association for Computational Linguistics.

Ruba Priyadharshini, Bharathi Raja Chakravarthi, Subalalitha Cn, Thenmozhi Durairaj, Malliga Subramanian, Kogilavani Shanmugavadivel, Siddhanth U Hegde, and Prasanna Kumaresan. 2022. Overview of Abusive Comment Detection in Tamil-ACL 2022. In *Proceedings of the Second Workshop on Speech and Language Technologies for Dravidian Languages*, pages 292–298, Dublin, Ireland. Association for Computational Linguistics.

Ruba Priyadharshini, Bharathi Raja Chakravarthi, Malliga S, SUBALALITHA CN, Kogilavani S V, Premjith B, Abirami Murugappan, and Prasanna Kumar Kumaresan. 2023. Overview of Shared-task on Abusive Comment Detection in Tamil and Telugu. In *Proceedings of the Third Workshop on Speech and Language Technologies for Dravidian Languages*, Varna, Bulgaria. Recent Advances in Natural Language Processing.

Manikandan Ravikiran, Bharathi Raja Chakravarthi, Anand Kumar Madasamy, Sangeetha Sivanesan, Ratnavel Rajalakshmi, Sajeetha Thavareesan, Rahul Ponnusamy, and Shankar Mahadevan. 2022. Findings of the Shared Task on Offensive Span Identification from Code-Mixed Tamil-English Comments. In *arXiv preprint arXiv:2205.06118*.

Prasanth S N, R Aswin Raj, Adhithan P, Premjith B, and Soman Kp. 2022. CEN-Tamil@DravidianLangTech-ACL2022: Abusive Comment Detection in Tamil using TF-IDF and Random Kitchen Sink Algorithm. In *Proceedings of the Second Workshop on Speech and Language Technologies for Dravidian Languages*, pages 70–74, Dublin, Ireland. Association for Computational Linguistics.

Malliga Subramanian, Rahul Ponnusamy, Sean Benhur, Kogilavani Shanmugavadivel, Adhithiya Ganesan, Deepti Ravi, Gowtham Krishnan Shanmugasundaram, Ruba Priyadharshini, and Bharathi Raja Chakravarthi. 2022. Offensive language detection in Tamil youtube comments by adapters and cross-domain knowledge transfer. *Computer Speech & Language*, 76:101404.

Krithika Swaminathan, Bharathi B, Gayathri G L, and Hrishik Sampath. 2022a. SSNCSE_NLP@LT-EDI-ACL2022: Homophobia/transphobia detection in multiple languages using SVM classifiers and BERT-based transformers. In *Proceedings of the Second Workshop on Language Technology for Equality, Diversity and Inclusion*, pages 239–244, Dublin, Ireland. Association for Computational Linguistics.

Krithika Swaminathan, Divyasri K, Gayathri G L, Thenmozhi Durairaj, and Bharathi B. 2022b. PANDAS@Abusive Comment Detection in Tamil Code-Mixed Data Using Custom Embeddings with LaBSE. In *Proceedings of the Second Workshop on Speech and Language Technologies for Dravidian Languages*, pages 112–119, Dublin, Ireland. Association for Computational Linguistics.

MUNLP@DravidianLangTech2023: Learning Approaches for Sentiment Analysis in Code-mixed Tamil and Tulu Text

Kavya G[a], **Asha Hegde**[b], **Sharal Coelho**[c],
Pooja Lamani[d], **Hosahalli Lakshmaiah Shashirekha**[e]
Department of Computer Science, Mangalore University, Mangalore, India
{[a]kavyamujk,[b]hegdekasha,[c]sharalmucs,[d]poojamucs}@gmail.com
[e]hlsrekha@mangaloreuniversity.ac.in

Abstract

Sentiment Analysis (SA) examines the subjective content of a statement, such as opinions, assessments, feelings, or attitudes towards a person, product or anything. The increase in the online users has also increased the SA content demanding the automated tools to analyze such content. Though several models are developed for SA in high-resource languages like English, Spanish, German, etc., under-resourced languages like Dravidian languages are less explored. Added to this is the complexity of code-mixed texts on social media. To address the challenges of SA in code-mixed under-resourced Dravidian language texts, in this paper, we team - MUNLP, describe the models submitted to "Sentiment Analysis in Tamil and Tulu - DravidianLangTech" shared task at Recent Advances in Natural Language Processing (RANLP)-2023. Three models: i) n-gramsSA - an n-grams based model in which Term Frequency-Inverse Document Frequency (TF-IDF) of word n-grams and characters sequences within the word boundary (char_wb) both in the range (1, 3), is used to train Linear Support Vector Classifier (LinearSVC), ii) EmbeddingsSA - a Linear SVC model trained with a concatenation of fastText and Byte Pair word embeddings, and iii) BERTSA - a Transfer Learning (TL) model with Tamil sentiment Bidirectional Encoder Representations from Transformers (BERT) are proposed for SA. Among the three models, BERTSA exhibited a macro F1 score of 0.26 for code-mixed Tamil texts securing 2nd place in the shared task and EmbeddingsSA exhibited a macro F1 score of 0.53 securing 2nd place for Tulu code-mixed texts.

1 Introduction

The dynamic nature of social media platforms like Twitter, Facebook, and YouTube, characterized by rapidly evolving user-generated content, underscores the importance of automated SA, opinion mining, hate speech detection and offensive language detection (Hegde et al., 2022b; Chinnaudayar Navaneethakrishnan et al., 2023). Analyzing the sentiments of opinions, reviews, comments, etc., about the photos, videos, songs, movies or anything, on social media platforms such as YouTube and Facebook, can offer valuable insights to the organizations and individuals to make informed decisions about the content (Bharathi and Agnusimmaculate Silvia, 2021; Bharathi and Varsha, 2022; Swaminathan et al., 2022; Subramanian et al., 2022; Chakravarthi et al., 2023a,b). By analyzing the opinions of the users', content providers can also tailor their strategies to better align the content with the preferences and expectations of users, fostering a stronger connection with the users with the intention of potentially enhancing their reputation. Such sentiment-driven insights enable effective engagement, enabling them to address concerns, capitalize on positive feedback, and adapt their approaches for the improved outcomes (Balouchzahi and Shashirekha, 2021; Chakravarthi et al., 2022a,b; Chakravarthi, 2023).

SA is the process of computationally identifying and categorizing opinions, emotions, and attitudes expressed in written or spoken language. It has emerged as a crucial field of study due to the significant marks it leaves on the online users. SA is witnessing the growing adoption on social media platforms like YouTube, where it is leveraged as a recommender system due to its significant impact on viewers. (Balouchzahi et al., 2021; Hegde and Shashirekha, 2022a)..

Technological limitations often lead users to express their sentiments and opinions in their native languages using the roman script, along with the inclusion of English words. This practice arises from the convenience of keying in roman letters compared to the more complex key combinations

Third Workshop on Speech and Language Technologies for Dravidian Languages, pages 275–281, Varna, Bulgaria, Sep 7, 2023.
https://doi.org/10.26615/978-954-452-085-4_040

required for native language scripts, particularly in the case of Indian languages (Balouchzahi et al., 2022a; Hegde and Lakshmaiah, 2022). This results in code-mixed text, where more than one languages are combined at sentence, word, or sub-word level within the same text. With the rise of social media platforms and user generated content like sentiments and emotions, code-mixing texts have become increasingly prevalent as users find it easier to communicate their thoughts mixing the words of different languages they are very much familiar.

The complexity of SA is significantly increased in code-mixed texts as they combine words from different languages at various linguistic-levels (Varsha et al., 2022; Balouchzahi et al., 2022b). Analyzing sentiments in such texts require the language models and algorithms that are capable of effectively handling code-mixed content, accurately identifying sentiment-bearing units, and deciphering the sentiments expressed in different languages. Overcoming these challenges is crucial for obtaining accurate and meaningful insights for code-mixed SA.

Indian languages in general and Dravidian languages in particular, are under-resourced languages and code-mixing adds further dimension, mainly due to the problems with collecting and annotating code-mixed data for various applications. "Sentiment Analysis in Tamil and Tulu" is a shared task in DravidianLangTech at RANLP 2023 with the aim of promoting SA of code-mixed texts in Tamil and Tulu (Hegde et al., 2023). We, team MUCS, submitted three distinct models: i) n-gramsSA - an n-grams based model in which Term Frequency-Inverse Document Frequency (TF-IDF) of word n-grams and char_wb in the range (1, 3) are used to train LinearSVC, ii) EmbeddingsSA - a Linear SVC model trained using concatenation of fastText and Byte Pair word embeddings, and iii) BERTSA - a model constructed by fine-tuning Tamil sentiment BERT (only for Tamil language), to address the challenges provided by the shared task.

The rest of paper is organized as follows: while Section 2 describes the recent literature on code-mixed text processing and SA, Section 3 focuses on the description of the models submitted to the shared task followed by the experiments and results in Section 4. Conclusion and future works are included in Section 5.

2 Related Work

SA aims to identify and classify sentiments expressed in text data into one of the predefined set of sentiments such as positive, negative, neutral, and mixed feelings. Machine Learning (ML), Deep Learning (DL), and Transfer Learning (TL), are the commonly used approaches for SA and few of the relevant works are described below:

Kumar et al. (2021) presented an ensemble of ML classifiers (Support Vector Machine (SVM), Logistic Regression (LR), and Random Forest (RF)) trained with TF-IDF of character n-grams in the range (1, 3). to classify code-mixed Kannada, Malayalam, and Tamil texts for SA. Their models exhibited weighted F1 scores of 0.63, 0.73, and 0.62 for Kannada, Malayalam, and Tamil code-mixed texts respectively. Babu et al. (2020) proposed two distinct Sentence BERT (SBERT) models, one which uses Manglish features as additional features during fine-tuning cross entropy loss and another that utilizes Class Balanced Loss (CBL) to handle data imbalance for SA in code-mixed Malayalam-English text. Out of these models SBERT with CBL outperformed the other model with macro F1 score of 0.71. Puranik et al. (2021) fine-tuned two pretrained models: Universal Language Model FIne-Tuning (ULMFiT) and multilingual BERT (mBERT) models for SA in code-mixed Dravidian languages (Kannada, Tamil, and Malayalam) and obtained macro F1 scores of 0.63, 0.65 and 0.70 for code-mixed Kannada, Tamil and Malayalam texts respectively.

Hegde and Shashirekha (2022b) describe Long Short Term Memory (LSTM) models trained using Dynamic Meta Embedding (DME) features to perform SA and homophobia detection as Task A (code-mixed Kannada and Malayalam texts) and Task B (code-mixed Tamil-English and English texts) respectively. Their proposed models exhibited macro F1 scores of 0.61, and 0.44 for code-mixed Malayalam and Kannada texts respectively in Task A and macro F1 scores of 0.58 and 0.74 for code-mixed Tamil-English and English texts respectively in Task B. Balouchzahi et al. (2021) proposed ensemble model (LR, SVM, and Multilayer Perceptron (MLP)) with majority voting for SA in code-mixed Kannada, Malayalam, and Tamil texts. Using TF-IDF of character n-grams in the range (1, 5) and syllables in the range (1, 6), to train the ensemble model, they obtained weighted average F1 scores of 0.628, 0.726, and 0.619 for Kannada,

Hyperparameters	Values
penalty	l2
C	1.0
class_weight	balanced
max_iter	max_iter
random_state	100
loss	squared_hinge

Table 1: Hyperparameters and their values used in LinearSVC algorithm

Malayalam, and Tamil code-mixed texts respectively. Three models: SACo-Ensemble, SACo-Keras, and SACo-ULMFiT, using ML, DL, and TL respectively are proposed by Balouchzahi and Shashirekha (2021) for SA in Tamil and Malayalam code-mixed texts. SACo-Ensemble is an ensemble model (MLP, eXtreme Gradient Boosting (XGB) and LR) trained with the count vectors of character sequences in range (2, 6), sub-words extracted from Byte Pair embeddings, syntactic bi-grams, and tri-grams, vectorized using CountVectorizer[1]. These features are also used to train SACo-Keras models. To build SACo-ULMFiT model, the authors pre-trained it with raw text (Dakshina dataset along with code-mixed Tamil and Malayalam texts) and they fine-tuned with their Train sets for SA. Among the three models, SACo-Ensemble models obtained weighted average F1 scores of 0.62 and 0.72 for code-mixed Tamil and Malayalam texts respectively.

From the above literature, it is clear that the researchers explored several models to perform SA in both high-resource and low-resource languages. However, for most of the low-resource languages, performances of the models are still less indicating the scope for developing models for SA in low-resource languages. Further, the code-mixed nature of the social media comments in low-resource languages intensifies the SA task.

3 Methodology

Three distinct models: n-gramsSA, EmbeddingsSA, and BERTSA, are proposed for SA of code-mixed Tamil and Tulu texts. The steps involved in building the proposed models are given below:

3.1 Preprocessing

Preprocessing step includes removing punctuation, numerical data, user mentions, hashtags as well as stopwords. English stopwords available at the Natural Language Tool Kit (NLTK)[2] library and Tamil[3] stopwords available at GitHub repository are used as references to remove the English and Tamil stopwords respectively. Emojis are transformed into English text using demoji[4] library.

Hyper Parameters	Values
Learning Rate	2e-5
Batch Size	16
Number of Epochs	2
Dropout Rate	0.1
Optimizer	Adam
Weight Decay	0.01
Warmup Steps	500
Maximum Sequence Length	128
Embedding size	768

Table 2: Hyperparameters and their values used in BERTSA

3.2 Model Description

The framework of n-gramsSA and EmbeddingsSA models is visualized in Figure 1. Both the models use LinearSVC classifer and the hyperparameters and their corresponding values used in LinearSVC classifier are shown in Table 1. The hyperparameters which are not mentioned in table are used with their default values. The description of the models follows:

n-gramsSA model - n-grams are sequential collections of lexical units viz, words/characters which capture the context by the sequential patterns present in the text/words facilitating a deeper comprehension of relationships between word/characters. Selecting the appropriate value for 'n' in n-grams involves the desired level of context. Larger 'n' values, such as 3 or more, capture longer sequences and dependencies between words, which is beneficial for text classification tasks like, SA, hate speech detection, and emotion analysis but also increases the complexity of the learning models (Balouchzahi and Shashirekha, 2021). Word and character n-grams in the range of (1, 3) are extracted and vectorized using TfidfVectorizer[5] to train the LinearSVC model for SA.

[1]https://scikit-learn.org/stable/modules/generated /sklearn.feature_extraction.text.CountVectorizer.html

[2]https://pythonspot.com/nltk-stop-words/

[3]https://gist.github.com/arulrajnet/ e82a5a331f78a5cc9b6d372df13a919c

[4]https://pypi.org/project/demoji/

[5]https://scikit-learn.org/stable/modules/generated/ sklearn.feature_extraction.text.TfidfVectorizer.html

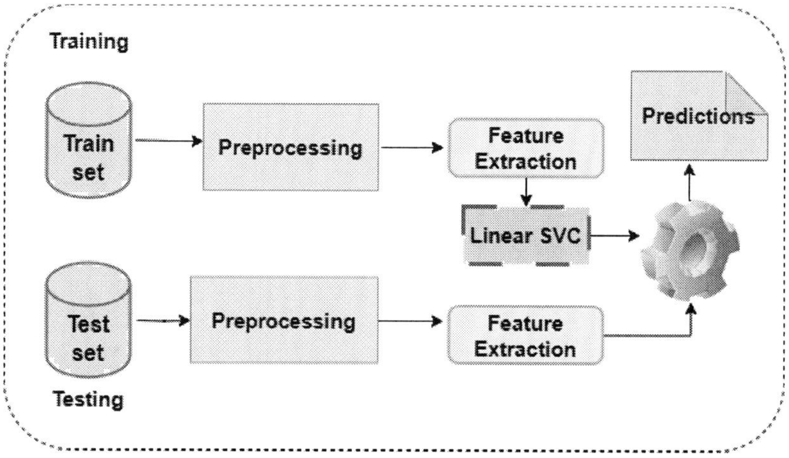

Figure 1: Framework of n-gramsSA and EmbeddigsSA models

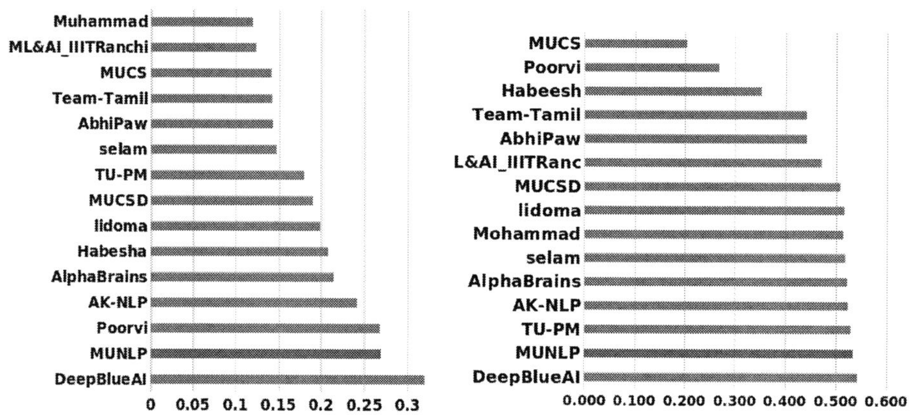

(a) Tamil (b) Tulu

Figure 2: Comparison of macro F1 scores of the participating teams in the shared task

EmbeddingsSA model - distributed representation of words, also known as word embeddings, is a popular word representation technique, where each word is represented by a low-dimensional dense vector such that words having the same meaning will have a similar representation. Sub-word embeddings are dense vector representations of sub-word units - linguistic units that are smaller than complete words but larger than individual characters, that capture their semantic and syntactic properties. The advantage of sub-word embeddings is that it helps to capture the morphological structure even for rare or unseen words. Word embeddings extracted from fastText[6] and Byte Pair embeddings[7] are concatenated to train the LinearSVC model for SA.

[6]https://fasttext.cc/docs/en/crawl-vectors.html
[7]https://bpemb.h-its.org/

Label	Train Set		Development Set	
	Tulu	Tamil	Tulu	Tamil
Positive	3,118	20,070	369	2,257
Neutral	1,719	5,628	202	611
Mixed Feeling	974	4,020	120	480
Negative	646	4,271	90	438

Table 3: Classwise distribution of code-mixed Tamil and Tulu texts

BERTSA - BERT pretrained models have shown remarkable performance in capturing subtle information in text, making them one of the most trending approaches for text classification tasks (Sun et al., 2019). By leveraging large-scale pretraining on diverse text data, BERT models excel in understanding contextual relationships, handling syntactic and semantic information and capturing

Language	Model	Development set		Test set	
		With imbalanced data	With balanced data	With imbalanced Data	With balanced Data
Tamil	n-gramsSA	0.40	0.45	0.16	0.18
	EmbeddingsSA	0.40	0.46	0.15	0.18
	BERTSA	0.45	0.48	0.23	0.26
Tulu	n-gramsSA	0.30	0.33	0.40	0.45
	EmbeddingsSA	0.54	0.56	0.48	**0.53**

Table 4: Performance of the proposed models with imbalanced and balanced dataset

the fine-grained details present in the text.

Tamil sentiment BERT[8] is a variant of the BERT model specifically trained for SA in Tamil text catering to the specific linguistic and cultural intricacies of the language. This variant is fine-tuned to capture the subtle information of sentiments in Tamil text which helps to identify the emotions and opinions effectively. This model leverages the power of pretraining on a large amount of text data and fine-tuning on SA tasks to classify the sentiments in Tamil language. Hyperparameters and their values of Tamil sentiment BERT are shown in Table 2. The hyperparameters which are not mentioned in Table 2 are used with their default values.

4 Experimental results

The dataset provided by the shared task organizers includes code-mixed Tamil (Chakravarthi et al., 2020) and Tulu (Hegde et al., 2022a) texts and the distribution of the labels across the Train and Development sets for these two languages are shown in Table 3. The imbalance nature in both the datasets motivated to use LinearSVC with the hyperparameter - class weight = 'balanced'. The proposed models are evaluated on the unlabeled Test set provided by the organizers and the predictions are evaluated based on macro F1 score. The performance of the proposed models on the Development and Test sets with imbalanced and balanced data are shown in Table 4.

The results illustrate that, both n-gramsSA and EmbeddingsSA models exhibited similar performance with the same macro F1 score of 0.18. Further, BERTSA model outperformed the other models with a macro F1 score of 0.26 securing 2nd rank for code-mixed Tamil text. For Tulu, among n-gramsSA and EmbeddingsSA models, EmbeddingsSA model outperformed the other with macro F1 score of 0.53 on Test set securing 2nd rank in the shared task. However, the macro F1 score obtained by the proposed models are below average. The macro F1 scores are very low due to the imbalance in the Train set. Though the hyperparameter 'class_weight' set to 'balanced' resolves the data imbalance issue to some extent, the extreme data imbalance in the Train set leads to overfitting.

The misclassified comments in Tamil and Tulu Test sets along with the English translations, actual labels, model predictions (obtained from BERTSA and EmbeddingsSA models evaluated for Tamil and Tulu Test sets respectively), and probable reasons for misclassification are shown in Table 5. It can be observed that the wrong classifications may also be due to the incorrect annotations.

The comparison of macro F1 scores of all the participating teams for SA in both code-mixed Tamil and Tulu text is shown in Figure 2.

5 Conclusion

This paper describes the models submitted by our team - MUNLP, to the shared task "Sentiment Analysis in Tamil and Tulu" in DravidianLangTech at RANLP 2023, for SA in code-mixed Tamil and Tulu texts. Three distinct models: i) n-gramsSA - an n-grams based model trained with n-grams of words and char_wb both in the range (1, 3) are used to train LinearSVC, ii) EmbeddingsSA - a model built using combination of fastText and Byte Pair embeddings to train LinearSVC, and iii) BERTSA - a model constructed by fine-tuning Tamil sentiment BERT (only for Tamil language), to address the challenges of the shared task. Among the proposed models, BERTSA and EmbeddingsSA models obtained macro F1 scores of 0.26 and 0.53 for code-mixed Tamil and Tulu datasets respectively both securing 2nd rank.

The results indicate that the macro F1 scores are low. Suitable oversampling or text augmentation techniques will be explored to improve macro F1

[8]https://huggingface.co/vishnun/bert-base-cased-tamil-mix-sentiment

Language	Comments	English Translations	Actual Label	Predicted Label	Remarks
Tamil	முதலில் இவர்கள் மீது பாவம் வரும் இப்போ வெறுப்பு வருகிறது	First there is sin against them, now there is hatred	Mixed Feeling	unknown_state	The content words 'முதலில்' and 'வருகிறது' are associated with the class 'unknown_state' rather than with the class 'Mixed Feeling' in the Train set. Further, as the other content words (இவர்கள், இப்போ, and வெறுப்பு) will not give any hint about 'Mixed Feeling' class, the comment is classified as 'unknown_state'.
	இதுபோன்ற சம்பவம் எங்கள் புதுமனை புகுவிழாவில் நடந்தது	A similar incident happened at our New Year's Eve party	Negative	Positive	This comment is annotated as 'negative' because of the emoji. However, the content words (இதுபோன்ற, எங்கள், புதுமனை, புகுவிழாவில், and நடந்தது) speaks about positive sentiment because of which the comment is classified as 'positive'.
Tulu	Embe onji mage karmda	A scolding Tulu comment	Negative	Neutral	The wrong classification may be because of only four words in the comment. Moreover, only one word (karmda) belongs to negative polarity and the rest speaks about positive polarity.
	Kandani ...gode gode panpuna part...sakath	The part in which the husband is repeatedly telling is good	Positive	Mixed Feeling	The word 'sakath', which makes the entire comment as positive, has rarely appeared in the Train set. This has lead to the wrong classification of the comment.

Table 5: Samples of misclassification for code-mixed Tamil and Tulu text

scores of the proposed models. Efficient resampling techniques will be explored further to handle imbalanced classes with effective feature extraction.

References

Yandrapati Prakash Babu, Rajagopal Eswari, and K Nimmi. 2020. CIA_NITT@ Dravidian-CodeMix-FIRE2020: Malayalam-English Code mixed Sentiment Analysis Using Sentence BERT And Sentiment Features. In *FIRE (Working Notes)*, pages 566–573.

Fazlourrahman Balouchzahi, Sabur Butt, A Hegde, Noman Ashraf, HL Shashirekha, Grigori Sidorov, and Alexander Gelbukh. 2022a. Overview of CoLI-Kanglish: Word Level Language Identification in Code-mixed Kannada-English Texts at ICON 2022. In *Proceedings of the 19th International Conference on Natural Language Processing (ICON): Shared Task on Word Level Language Identification in Code-mixed Kannada-English Texts*, pages 38–45.

Fazlourrahman Balouchzahi and HL Shashirekha. 2021. LA-SACo: A Study of Learning Approaches for Sentiments Analysis in Code-mixing Texts. In *Proceedings of the First Workshop on Speech and Language Technologies for Dravidian Languages*, pages 109–118.

Fazlourrahman Balouchzahi, Hosahalli Lakshmaiah Shashirekha, and Grigori Sidorov. 2021. CoSaD-Code-Mixed Sentiments Analysis for Dravidian Languages. In *CEUR Workshop Proceedings*, volume 3159, pages 887–898. CEUR-WS.

Fazlourrahman Balouchzahi, Hosahalli Lakshmaiah Shashirekha, Grigori Sidorov, and Alexander Gelbukh. 2022b. A Comparative Study of Syllables and Character Level N-grams for Dravidian Multi-Script and Code-mixed Offensive Language Identification. In *Journal of Intelligent & Fuzzy Systems*, Preprint, pages 1–11. IOS Press.

B Bharathi and A Agnusimmaculate Silvia. 2021. SSNCSE_NLP@DravidianLangTech-EACL2021: Offensive language identification on multilingual code mixing text. In *Proceedings of the First Workshop on Speech and Language Technologies for Dravidian Languages*, pages 313–318, Kyiv. Association for Computational Linguistics.

B Bharathi and Josephine Varsha. 2022. SSNCSE NLP@TamilNLP-ACL2022: Transformer based approach for detection of abusive comment for Tamil language. In *Proceedings of the Second Workshop on Speech and Language Technologies for Dravidian Languages*, pages 158–164, Dublin, Ireland. Association for Computational Linguistics.

Bharathi Raja Chakravarthi. 2023. Detection of homophobia and transphobia in Youtube comments. *International Journal of Data Science and Analytics*, pages 1–20.

Bharathi Raja Chakravarthi, Adeep Hande, Rahul Ponnusamy, Prasanna Kumar Kumaresan, and Ruba Priyadharshini. 2022a. How can we detect homophobia and transphobia? experiments in a multilingual code-mixed setting for social media governance. *International Journal of Information Management Data Insights*, 2(2):100119.

Bharathi Raja Chakravarthi, Manoj Balaji Jagadeeshan, Vasanth Palanikumar, and Ruba Priyadharshini. 2023a. Offensive language identification in Dravidian languages using MPNet and CNN. *International Journal of Information Management Data Insights*, 3(1):100151.

Bharathi Raja Chakravarthi, Vigneshwaran Muralidaran, Ruba Priyadharshini, and John Philip McCrae. 2020. Corpus Creation for Sentiment Analysis in Code-Mixed Tamil-English text. In *Proceedings of the 1st Joint Workshop on Spoken Language Technologies for Under-resourced languages (SLTU) and Collaboration and Computing for Under-Resourced Languages (CCURL)*, pages 202–210, Marseille, France. European Language Resources association.

Bharathi Raja Chakravarthi, Ruba Priyadharshini, Shubanker Banerjee, Manoj Balaji Jagadeeshan, Prasanna Kumar Kumaresan, Rahul Ponnusamy, Sean Benhur, and John Philip McCrae. 2023b. Detecting abusive comments at a fine-grained level in a low-resource language. *Natural Language Processing Journal*, 3:100006.

Bharathi Raja Chakravarthi, Ruba Priyadharshini, Thenmozhi Durairaj, John McCrae, Paul Buitelaar, Prasanna Kumaresan, and Rahul Ponnusamy. 2022b. Overview of the shared task on homophobia and transphobia detection in social media comments. In *Proceedings of the Second Workshop on Language Technology for Equality, Diversity and Inclusion*, pages 369–377, Dublin, Ireland. Association for Computational Linguistics.

Subalalitha Chinnaudayar Navaneethakrishnan, Bharathi Raja Chakravarthi, Kogilavani Shanmugavadivel, Malliga Subramanian, Prasanna Kumar Kumaresan, Bharathi, Lavanya Sambath Kumar, and Rahul Ponnusamy. 2023. Findings of shared task on sentiment analysis and homophobia detection of Youtube comments in code-mixed Dravidian languages. In *Proceedings of the 14th Annual Meeting of the Forum for Information Retrieval Evaluation*, FIRE '22, page 18–21, New York, NY, USA. Association for Computing Machinery.

Asha Hegde, Mudoor Devadas Anusha, Sharal Coelho, Hosahalli Lakshmaiah Shashirekha, and Bharathi Raja Chakravarthi. 2022a. Corpus Creation for Sentiment Analysis in Code-Mixed Tulu Text. In *Proceedings of the 1st Annual Meeting of the ELRA/ISCA Special Interest Group on Under-Resourced Languages*, pages 33–40.

Asha Hegde, Bharathi Raja Chakravarthi, Hosahalli Lakshmaiah Shashirekha, Rahul Ponnusamy, SUBALALITHA CN, Lavanya S K, Thenmozhi D, Martha Karunakar, Shreya Shreeram, and Sarah" Aymen. 2023. Findings of the Shared Task on Sentiment Analysis in Tamil and Tulu Code-mixed Text. In *Proceedings of the Third Workshop on Speech and Language Technologies for Dravidian Languages*, Varna, Bulgaria. Recent Advances in Natural Language Processing.

Asha Hegde, Sharal Coelho, Ahmad Elyas Dashti, and Hosahalli Shashirekha. 2022b. MUCS@ Text-LT-EDI@ ACL 2022: Detecting Sign of Depression from Social Media Text using Supervised Learning Approach. In *Proceedings of the Second Workshop on Language Technology for Equality, Diversity and Inclusion*, pages 312–316.

Asha Hegde and Shashirekha Lakshmaiah. 2022. Mucs@ mixmt: Indictrans-Based Machine Translation for Hinglish Text. In *Proceedings of the Seventh Conference on Machine Translation (WMT)*, pages 1131–1135.

Asha Hegde and Hosahalli Lakshmaiah Shashirekha. 2022a. Learning Models for Emotion Analysis and Threatening Language Detection in Urdu Tweets.

Asha Hegde and Hosahalli Lakshmaiah Shashirekha. 2022b. Leveraging Dynamic Meta Embedding for Sentiment Analysis and Detection of Homophobic/Transphobic Content in Code-mixed Dravidian Languages.

Abhinav Kumar, Sunil Saumya, and Jyoti Prakash Singh. 2021. An Ensemble-based Model for Sentiment Analysis of Dravidian Code-mixed Social Media Posts. In *Working Notes of FIRE 2021-Forum for Information Retrieval Evaluation (Online). CEUR.*

Karthik Puranik et al. 2021. IIITT@ Dravidian-CodeMix-FIRE2021: Transliterate or Translate? Sentiment Analysis of Code-mixed Text in Dravidian Languages. In *arXiv preprint arXiv:2111.07906.*

Malliga Subramanian, Rahul Ponnusamy, Sean Benhur, Kogilavani Shanmugavadivel, Adhithiya Ganesan, Deepti Ravi, Gowtham Krishnan Shanmugasundaram, Ruba Priyadharshini, and Bharathi Raja Chakravarthi. 2022. Offensive language detection in Tamil youtube comments by adapters and cross-domain knowledge transfer. *Computer Speech & Language*, 76:101404.

Chi Sun, Luyao Huang, and Xipeng Qiu. 2019. Utilizing BERT for Aspect-based Sentiment Analysis via Constructing Auxiliary Sentence. In *arXiv preprint arXiv:1903.09588.*

Krithika Swaminathan, Bharathi B, Gayathri G L, and Hrishik Sampath. 2022. SSNCSE_NLP@LT-EDI-ACL2022: Homophobia/transphobia detection in multiple languages using SVM classifiers and BERT-based transformers. In *Proceedings of the Second Workshop on Language Technology for Equality, Diversity and Inclusion*, pages 239–244, Dublin, Ireland. Association for Computational Linguistics.

Josephine Varsha, B Bharathi, and A Meenakshi. 2022. Sentiment Analysis and Homophobia Detection of YouTube Comments in Code-Mixed Dravidian Languages using Machine Learning and Transformer Models. In *Working Notes of FIRE 2022-Forum for Information Retrieval Evaluation (Hybrid). CEUR.*

MUCSD@DravidianLangTech2023: Predicting Sentiment in Social Media Text using Machine Learning Techniques

Sharal Coelho[a], **Asha Hegde**[b], **Pooja Lamani**[c], **Kavya G**[d], **Hosahalli Lakshmaiah Shashirekha**[e]
Department of Computer Science, Mangalore University, Mangalore, India
{[a]sharalmucs,[b]hegdekasha,[c]poojalmucs,[d]kavyamujk}@gmail.com
[e]hlsrekha@mangaloreuniversity.ac.in

Abstract

Social media users utilize online platforms to express their thoughts, sentiments, and views through posts/comments. Identifying such sentiments expressed in reviews or comments on a given concept/topic is known as Sentiment Analysis (SA). SA has considerable applications including customer service, social media monitoring, product reviews analysis, and so on. Content creators, bloggers, and researchers can evaluate public opinions, obtain feedback, and make informed choices by analyzing reviews and comments on social media platforms. Online users often express their sentiments using mixing words/scripts of more than one language leading to code-mixed texts. Analysing the code-mixed text to predict sentiments is challenging and lack of resources for code-mixed low-resource languages enhances the complexity further due to complexities of code-mixed texts.

To address the challenges of predicting sentiments in code-mixed low-resource languages, in this paper, we - team MUCSD, describe Machine Learning (ML) models submitted to "Sentiment Analysis in Tamil and Tulu" shared task at DravidianLangTech@RANLP 2023. The proposed methodology makes use of ML models: i) Linear Support Vector Classifier (LinearSVC), ii) Logistic Regression (LR), and iii) Ensemble model (LR, Decision Tree (DT), and Support Vector Machine (SVM)) with hard voting, trained with Term Frequency-Inverse Document Frequency (TF-IDF) of word unigrams, to perform SA in Tamil and Tulu languages. Among these models, LinearSVC model performed better with macro F1-scores of 0.189 and 0.508 and obtained 8th and 9th rank for Tamil and Tulu code-mixed texts respectively.

1 Introduction

Social media usage is increasing continuously due to the ease of use to share reviews even for those who are not familiar about the technologies (Asghar et al., 2015; Bharathi and Agnusimmaculate Silvia, 2021; Bharathi and Varsha, 2022; Swaminathan et al., 2022; Anita and Subalalitha, 2019; Subalalitha, 2019; Sakuntharaj and Mahesan, 2016, 2017, 2021). This has led to the increased user-generated text of opinions or reviews, comments, and posts on social media like Twitter, Facebook, YouTube, etc (Yue et al., 2019). Understanding the users' comments on topics/events in social media allows for more informed decision-making. It helps the content creators like YouTubers to evaluate the emotional impact of their videos on viewers (Chakravarthi et al., 2022a,b; Chakravarthi, 2023). For example, while positive comments about a video indicate satisfaction, negative comments indicate the need for improvement (Asghar et al., 2015).

SA is the task of analysing the reviews, opinions or comments to identify their polarity. This analysis provides insights into public opinions, ideas, and statements, which can be valuable for bloggers, researchers, and even individuals (Hussein, 2018; Thavareesan and Mahesan, 2019, 2020a,b). Social media posts/comments such as YouTube comments, Facebook posts, and tweets, often contain slang, misspellings, contractions, etc. which may impair the ability of the learning models to recognize patterns in the social media content and produce precise predictions. As there is no restriction on the use of language in social media, users often use more than one language to write comments on social media platforms. They may even use more than one script to key in the comments leading to code-mixed data.

Majority of the SA works focus on high-resource languages like English and Spanish giving less importance for low-resource languages and code-mixed low-resource languages (Hegde and Shashirekha, 2021). To promote the SA research

Third Workshop on Speech and Language Technologies for Dravidian Languages, pages 282–287, Varna, Bulgaria, Sep 7, 2023.
https://doi.org/10.26615/978-954-452-085-4_041

work on low-resource languages, in this paper, we - team MUCSD, describe the ML models submitted to the shared task on "Sentiment Analysis in Tamil and Tulu" at DravidianLangTech@RANLP 2023[1] (Hegde et al., 2023). The aim of the shared task is to classify the comments in code-mixed Tamil and Tulu languages, into one of the four categories: Positive, Neutral/Unknown state, Mixed Feelings, and Negative. The proposed methodology makes use of LinearSVC, LR, and Ensemble of classifiers (LR, DT, and SVM) with hard voting, trained with TF-IDF of word unigrams to predict the sentiment of the given text.

The rest of the paper is structured as follows: The related work is briefly described in Section 2. Section 3 describes the methodology, while Section 4 discusses experiments with the results. The study concludes with future work in Section 5.

2 Related Work

Researchers have developed several ML approaches to handle monolingual and code-mixed texts for SA. A brief description of few of the relevant works are given below:

Das and Chakraborty (2018) proposed LinearSVM using TF-IDF along with Next Word Negation (NWN) for sentiment classification of three different datasets (Movie Review Dataset, Product Review Dataset, and SMS Spam Dataset). They obtained accuracies of 89.91%, 88.86%, and 96.83% on IMDB review datasets, Amazon product review, and SMS spam datasets respectively. To perform SA in Code-Mixed Dravidian languages (Tamil and Malayalam) and English language, Hegde and Shashirekha (2022) used Long Short Term Memory (LSTM) model trained with Dynamic Meta Embedding (DME) and obtained F1-scores of 0.36, 0.74, and 0.37 for Tamil, English, and Malayalam languages respectively. Balouchzahi and Shashirekha (2020) proposed Hybrid Voting Classifier (HVC) using char and word n-grams in the range (1, 5) and (1, 3) respectively and word embeddings, as features to train Multi-Layer Perceptron (MLP) and Multinomial Naive Bayes (MNB) classifiers and sub-words embeddings to train Bidirectional Long Short Term (BiLSTM) classifier. With majority voting, their HVC model obtained a weighted F1-score of 0.62 and 0.68 on Tamil-English and Malayalam-English language pairs respectively.

To solve the Arabic sentiment classification problem, Elgeldawi et al. (2021) used various hyperparameter tuning techniques on six ML algorithms (LR, SVM, DT, Ridge Classifier, Random Forest (RF), and Naive Bayes (NB)) trained using TF-IDF of word unigrams. All algorithms were experimented with and without the hyperparameter tuning process and among all the algorithms, they obtained highest accuracy for SVM with an accuracy of 95.62% using Bayesian Optimization. Hande et al. (2020) proposed multitask learning for Offensive Language Detection (OLD) and SA and experimented on the dataset Kannada Code-Mixed Dataset (KanCMD) created by scraping the YouTube comments. ML algorithms (DT, LR, SVM, MNB, k-Nearest Neighbors (k-NN), and RF) are trained with TF-IDF of n-grams in the range (1, 3) for both OLD and SA tasks. The RF model outperformed other models with macro F1-scores of 0.59 and 0.66 for SA and OLD respectively. Poornima and Priya (2020) proposed ML classifiers (MNB, SVM, and LR) trained with word bigrams for SA of Malayalam Tweets and obtained an accuracy of 86.23% for LR classifier.

In spite of several approaches explored for SA, the performance of many of the approaches are still low for low-resource languages, indicating the need to explore models for SA in to improve the performance.

3 Methodology

The proposed methodology for SA in code-mixed Tamil and Tulu (Dravidian languages) includes three major steps: Pre-processing, Feature Extraction, and Classifier Construction. The framework of the proposed methodology is shown in Figure 1 and the steps are briefly explained below:

3.1 Pre-processing

The procedure of cleaning text data with the goal of enhancing the classifier's performance is known as Pre-processing. In this procedure, punctuation marks, digits, stopwords, and extra spaces are removed and English text is converted to lowercase. English stopwords[2] list available in Natural Language Toolkit (NLTK) library and Tamil stopwords[3] list available in github are used as references to remove the stopwords. Sentiments are

[1]https://codalab.lisn.upsaclay.fr/competitions/11095

[2]https://www.nltk.org/nltk_data/

[3]https://gist.github.com/arulrajnet/e82a5a331f78a5cc9b6d372df13a919c

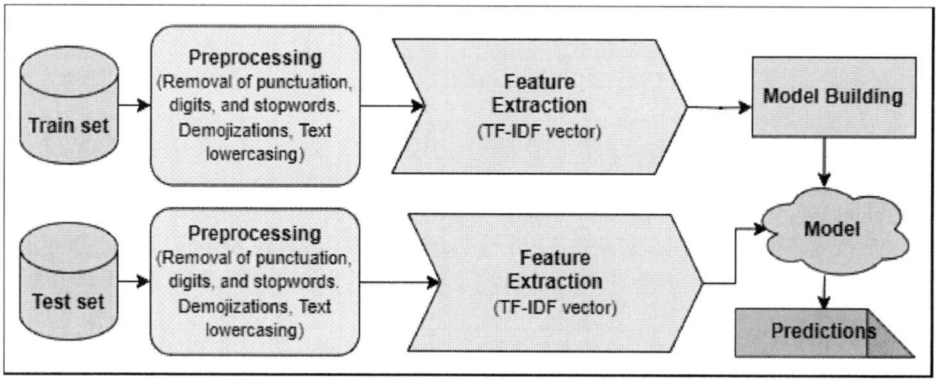

Figure 1: The proposed framework of ML classifiers

Dataset:	Tamil-English			Tulu-English		
Classes	**Train set**	**Dev set**	**Test set**	**Train set**	**Dev set**	**Test set**
Positive	20070	2257	338	3118	369	344
Negative	4271	480	101	646	90	60
Neutral / Unknown state	5628	611	137	1719	202	197
Mixed feelings	4020	438	73	974	120	107
Total	33989	3786	649	6457	781	781

Table 1: Class-wise distribution of Tamil-English and Tulu-English dataset

	Tamil-English		Tulu-English	
Classifier	**Dev set**	**Test set**	**Dev set**	**Test set**
LR	0.444	0.117	0.516	0.442
LinearSVC	**0.464**	**0.189**	**0.555**	**0.508**
Ensemble model	0.437	0.103	0.509	0.461

Table 2: Macro F1-scores of the proposed models

sometimes expressed through emojis. So instead of removing the emojis, they are converted into text to capture the useful information for SA.

3.2 Feature Extraction

The process of extracting the features from the dataset is known as Feature Extraction. In the proposed work, TF-IDF of word unigrams are obtained using TfidfVectorizer[4] from the scikit-learn library to train the model. 12,515 and 62,516 word unigrams are extracted for Tulu and Tamil datasets respectively.

3.3 Classifier Construction

The three learning models, namely: LinearSVC, LR, and Ensemble (LR, DT, and SVM) classifier with hard voting, are trained using TF-IDF of word unigrams to perform SA. LinearSVC learns the decision boundary by separating different classes and it is suitable for linearly separable problems. The LR model provide a simple approach that predicts the probability that an input belongs to a certain class. LinearSVC is used to find a hyperplane that separates data points of different classes in a way that maximizes the margin between them. To improve the accuracy and robustness of predictions, specifically if the individual classifiers have various weaknesses or strengths, the ensemble techniques can be applied. In the proposed methodology, an Ensemble of ML classifiers (LR, DT, and SVM) with hard voting is used.

4 Experiments and Result

The statistics of code-mixed Tamil (Chakravarthi et al., 2020) and Tulu (Hegde et al., 2022) datasets shared by the organisers of the shared task in shown in Table 1. It can be observed that the both datasets are imbalanced.

The performance of the proposed model for Development (Dev) set and Test sets for both the languages are shown in Table 2. The results illustrate that LinearSVC model outperformed the other two models by achieving F1-scores of 0.189 and 0.508

[4]https://scikit-learn.org/stable/modules/generated/sklearn.feature_extraction.text.TfidfVectorizer.html

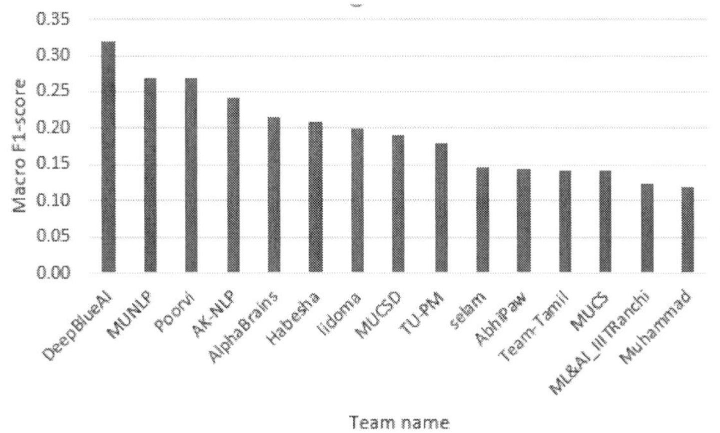

Figure 2: Comparison of macro F1-scores of the LinearSVC model with other teams (participants') for Tamil-English Dataset

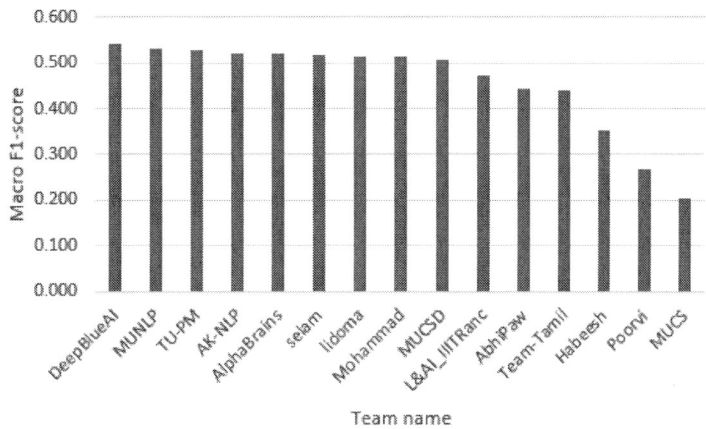

Figure 3: Comparison of macro F1-scores of the LinearSVC model with other teams (participants') for Tulu-English Dataset

Tulu Text	English Translation	Actual Label	Predicted Label	Remarks
ajji baari joruller....jagrthe d patherodu	Grandmother is very strict. Should be careful while talking	Mixed Feeling	Positive	The words like "baari", and "ajji" are associated with sentences of 'Positive' class in the Train set. Hence, this sample is classified as 'Positive'.
Ipl,gangnam style,,pili ,,avu matha common adu ippundu,,,	Ipl, Gangam style, tiger, all those things are very common	Neutral	Positive	The model has associated "Ipl" and "Pili" words with 'Positive' class and hence has classified the comment as 'Positive'.
ಕುಸಾಲ್ ಇತ್ತುಂಡು. ಪ್ರಾಕ್ಟಿಸ್ ಕಮ್ಮಿ. ಒಟ್ಟುಗ್ ಓಕೆ.	It was funny, they have less practice, totally okay	Mixed Feeling	Neutral	The words "ಕಮ್ಮಿ", is associated with 'Neutral' sentiment and hence, the model has the comment as "Neutral" class.

Table 3: Samples of misclassified Tulu Test set with their English translation, actual and predicted (using LinearSVC model) labels and remarks

for code-mixed Tamil and Tulu datasets respectively. The comparison of the macro F1-scores of other participants' models with our proposed model for Tamil and Tulu Datasets are shown in Figure 2 and 3 respectively. The misclassified samples of the Tulu Test test along with actual and predicted labels and remarks, for LinearSVC model are shown in Table 3.

5 Conclusion

In this paper, our team MUCSD describes the three proposed models, namely: LR, LinearSVC, and an Ensemble (LR, DT, and SVM) classifier with hard voting, trained with TF-IDF of word unigrams, to perform SA of Tulu and Tamil code-mixed texts. These models are submitted to the "Sentiment Analysis in Tamil and Tulu" shared task at DravidianLangTech@RANLP 2023. Among the proposed models, LinearSVC achieved F1-scores of 0.189 and 0.508 and secured 8th and 9th rank for Tamil and Tulu texts respectively. Different feature sets and different classifications will be investigated to improve the performance of the proposed models in the future.

References

R Anita and CN Subalalitha. 2019. An approach to cluster Tamil literatures using discourse connectives. In *2019 IEEE 1st International Conference on Energy, Systems and Information Processing (ICESIP)*, pages 1–4. IEEE.

Muhammad Zubair Asghar, Shakeel Ahmad, Afsana Marwat, and Fazal Masud Kundi. 2015. Sentiment Analysis on YouTube: A Brief Survey. *arXiv preprint arXiv:1511.09142*.

Fazlourrahman Balouchzahi and HL Shashirekha. 2020. MUCS@ Dravidian-CodeMix-FIRE2020: SACO-Sentiments Analysis for CodeMix Text. In *FIRE (Working Notes)*, pages 495–502.

B Bharathi and A Agnusimmaculate Silvia. 2021. SSNCSE_NLP@DravidianLangTech-EACL2021: Offensive language identification on multilingual code mixing text. In *Proceedings of the First Workshop on Speech and Language Technologies for Dravidian Languages*, pages 313–318, Kyiv. Association for Computational Linguistics.

B Bharathi and Josephine Varsha. 2022. SSNCSE NLP@TamilNLP-ACL2022: Transformer based approach for detection of abusive comment for Tamil language. In *Proceedings of the Second Workshop on Speech and Language Technologies for Dravidian Languages*, pages 158–164, Dublin, Ireland. Association for Computational Linguistics.

Bharathi Raja Chakravarthi. 2023. Detection of homophobia and transphobia in Youtube comments. *International Journal of Data Science and Analytics*, pages 1–20.

Bharathi Raja Chakravarthi, Adeep Hande, Rahul Ponnusamy, Prasanna Kumar Kumaresan, and Ruba Priyadharshini. 2022a. How can we detect homophobia and transphobia? experiments in a multilingual code-mixed setting for social media governance. *International Journal of Information Management Data Insights*, 2(2):100119.

Bharathi Raja Chakravarthi, Vigneshwaran Muralidaran, Ruba Priyadharshini, and John Philip McCrae. 2020. Corpus Creation for Sentiment Analysis in code-Mixed Tamil-English Text. In *Proceedings of the 1st Joint Workshop on Spoken Language Technologies for Under-resourced languages (SLTU) and Collaboration and Computing for Under-Resourced Languages (CCURL)*, pages 202–210, Marseille, France. European Language Resources association.

Bharathi Raja Chakravarthi, Ruba Priyadharshini, Thenmozhi Durairaj, John McCrae, Paul Buitelaar, Prasanna Kumaresan, and Rahul Ponnusamy. 2022b. Overview of the shared task on homophobia and transphobia detection in social media comments. In *Proceedings of the Second Workshop on Language Technology for Equality, Diversity and Inclusion*, pages 369–377, Dublin, Ireland. Association for Computational Linguistics.

Bijoyan Das and Sarit Chakraborty. 2018. An Improved Text Sentiment Classification Model using TF-IDF and Next Word Negation. *arXiv preprint arXiv:1806.06407*.

Enas Elgeldawi, Awny Sayed, Ahmed R Galal, and Alaa M Zaki. 2021. Hyperparameter Tuning for Machine Learning Algorithms Used for Arabic Sentiment Analysis. In *Informatics*, volume 8, page 79. Multidisciplinary Digital Publishing Institute.

Adeep Hande, Ruba Priyadharshini, and Bharathi Raja Chakravarthi. 2020. KanCMD: Kannada CodeMixed Dataset for Sentiment Analysis and Offensive Language Detection. In *Proceedings of the Third Workshop on Computational Modeling of People's Opinions, Personality, and Emotion's in Social Media*, pages 54–63.

Asha Hegde, Mudoor Devadas Anusha, Sharal Coelho, Hosahalli Lakshmaiah Shashirekha, and Bharathi Raja Chakravarthi. 2022. Corpus Creation for Sentiment Analysis in Code-mixed Tulu Text. In *Proceedings of the 1st Annual Meeting of the ELRA/ISCA Special Interest Group on Under-Resourced Languages*, pages 33–40, Marseille, France. European Language Resources Association.

Asha Hegde, Bharathi Raja Chakravarthi, Hosahalli Lakshmaiah Shashirekha, Rahul Ponnusamy, SUBALALITHA CN, Lavanya S K, Thenmozhi D, Martha

Karunakar, Shreya Shreeram, and Sarah" Aymen. 2023. Findings of the Shared Task on Sentiment Analysis in Tamil and Tulu Code-Mixed Text. In *Proceedings of the Third Workshop on Speech and Language Technologies for Dravidian Languages*, Varna, Bulgaria. Recent Advances in Natural Language Processing.

Asha Hegde and Hosahalli Lakshmaiah Shashirekha. 2021. Urdu Fake News Detection Using Ensemble of Machine Learning Models.

Asha Hegde and Hosahalli Lakshmaiah Shashirekha. 2022. Leveraging Dynamic Meta Embedding for Sentiment Analysis and Detection of Homophobic/Transphobic Content in Code-mixed Dravidian Languages.

Doaa Mohey El-Din Mohamed Hussein. 2018. A Survey on Sentiment Analysis Challenges. *Journal of King Saud University-Engineering Sciences*, 30(4):330–338.

A Poornima and K Sathiya Priya. 2020. A Comparative Sentiment Analysis Of Sentence Embedding Using Machine Learning Techniques. In *2020 6th international conference on advanced computing and communication systems (ICACCS)*, pages 493–496. IEEE.

Ratnasingam Sakuntharaj and Sinnathamby Mahesan. 2016. A novel hybrid approach to detect and correct spelling in Tamil text. In *2016 IEEE international conference on information and automation for sustainability (ICIAfS)*, pages 1–6. IEEE.

Ratnasingam Sakuntharaj and Sinnathamby Mahesan. 2017. Use of a novel hash-table for speeding-up suggestions for misspelt Tamil words. In *2017 IEEE international conference on industrial and information systems (ICIIS)*, pages 1–5. IEEE.

Ratnasingam Sakuntharaj and Sinnathamby Mahesan. 2021. Missing word detection and correction based on context of Tamil sentences using n-grams. In *2021 10th International Conference on Information and Automation for Sustainability (ICIAfS)*, pages 42–47. IEEE.

CN Subalalitha. 2019. Information extraction framework for Kurunthogai. *Sādhanā*, 44(7):156.

Krithika Swaminathan, Bharathi B, Gayathri G L, and Hrishik Sampath. 2022. SSNCSE_NLP@LT-EDI-ACL2022: Homophobia/transphobia detection in multiple languages using SVM classifiers and BERT-based transformers. In *Proceedings of the Second Workshop on Language Technology for Equality, Diversity and Inclusion*, pages 239–244, Dublin, Ireland. Association for Computational Linguistics.

Sajeetha Thavareesan and Sinnathamby Mahesan. 2019. Sentiment analysis in Tamil texts: A study on machine learning techniques and feature representation. In *2019 14th Conference on industrial and information systems (ICIIS)*, pages 320–325. IEEE.

Sajeetha Thavareesan and Sinnathamby Mahesan. 2020a. Sentiment lexicon expansion using Word2vec and fastText for sentiment prediction in Tamil texts. In *2020 Moratuwa engineering research conference (MERCon)*, pages 272–276. IEEE.

Sajeetha Thavareesan and Sinnathamby Mahesan. 2020b. Word embedding-based part of speech tagging in tamil texts. In *2020 IEEE 15th International conference on industrial and information systems (ICIIS)*, pages 478–482. IEEE.

Lin Yue, Weitong Chen, Xue Li, Wanli Zuo, and Minghao Yin. 2019. A Survey of Sentiment Analysis from Social Media Data. *Knowledge and Information Systems*, 60:617–663.

MUCS@DravidianLangTech2023: Malayalam Fake News Detection Using Machine Learning Approach

Sharal Coelho[a], **Asha Hegde**[b],
Kavya G[c], **Hosahalli Lakshmaiah Shashirekha**[d]
Department of Computer Science, Mangalore University, Mangalore, India
{[a]sharalmucs,[b]hegdekasha,[c]kavyamujk}@gmail.com
[d]hlsrekha@mangaloreuniversity.ac.in

Abstract

Social media is widely used to spread fake news which can lead to individuals or group making wrong judgments based on fake news. The fake news can even create confusion, panic, anxiety, etc., leading to taking inappropriate actions by the individuals. Fake news creators with their tactics may use legitimate sources and mimic the style of reputed publications to create fake news, making it difficult and challenging to identify such content. To address the challenges of detecting fake news in this paper, we - team MUCS, describe the Machine Learning (ML) models submitted to "Fake News Detection in Dravidian Languages" at DravidianLangTech@RANLP 2023 shared task. Three different models, namely: Multinomial Naive Bayes (MNB), Logistic Regression (LR), and an Ensemble model (MNB, LR, and Support Vector Machine (SVM)) with hard voting, are trained using Term Frequency - Inverse Document Frequency (TF-IDF) of word unigrams, to detect fake news in code-mixed Malayalam text. Among the three models ensemble model performed better with a macro F1-score of 0.831 and placed 3rd rank in the shared task.

1 Introduction

With the overwhelming growth of social media like Twitter, Facebook, YouTube, etc., and the ease with which the information can be shared widely and quickly on these social media platforms (Ahmed et al., 2017; Chakravarthi et al., 2022a,b; Chakravarthi, 2023), creation and sharing of fake news has seen the unprecedented growth. The anonymity of users on social media has given a chance to fake news spreaders to divert people's beliefs, trust, and opinions by intentionally spreading fake information. Usually rumors and fake news spread fast and damage personal relationships and social connections (Kaliyar et al., 2021). Further, they may also cause anxiety and emotional distress through unfavorable perceptions, scrutiny from the public, and social isolation (Sadeghi et al., 2022). In order to prevent harm and discomfort from fake news, to the users, organizations, and communities, identifying and filtering out such fake news automatically has become the need for the day (Khanam et al., 2021).

The majority of the fake news detection systems have focused on high-resource languages like Spanish and English (Hegde et al., 2022c) giving no or less importance for low-resource Dravidian languages, such as Tulu, Malayalam, Tamil, Telugu, and Kannada, due to lack of resources (Hegde et al., 2022a). Among the low-resource languages, Malayalam is relatively spoken by a smaller population in Indian states of Kerala and the Lakshadweep Islands (Thara and Poornachandran, 2022). Unlike other Dravidian languages, Malayalam has its own linguistic complexities, including dialect variations, word semantics, idiomatic expressions, and so on. These complexities can make it harder to process and analyze the Malayalam text.

As there are no guidelines to create any post/comment on social media, users usually combine words and sub-words belonging to more than one language they know, leading to code-mixed text. Further, they may use more than one script to create the post/comment. These factors make it difficult to process the code-mixed texts. Learning approaches that work well for monolingual text may not give good results for code-mixed texts. Further, there are no pretrained models/specific techniques for code-mixed texts in low-resource languages.

The "Fake News Detection in Dravidian Languages" shared task organised at DravidianLangTech@RANLP 2023[1] (Subramanian et al., 2023) promotes fake news detection in code-mixed Malayalam text. To address the challenges of de-

[1]https://codalab.lisn.upsaclay.fr/competitions/11176

Third Workshop on Speech and Language Technologies for Dravidian Languages, pages 288–292, Varna, Bulgaria, Sep 7, 2023.
https://doi.org/10.26615/978-954-452-085-4_042

tecting fake news in Malayalam, in this shared task, we - team MUCS, implemented three distinct models: i) MNB, ii) LR, and iii) Ensemble models (LR, MNB, and SVM) with hard voting, trained with TF-IDF of word unigrams.

The rest of the paper is organised as follows: Section 2 gives a brief description of the related work. While Section 3 explains the methodology, Section 4 is about experiments and outcomes. Finally, the paper concludes in Section 5 with future work.

2 Related Work

Fake news detection in low-resource languages and code-mixed low-resource languages are getting prominence gradually. Researchers have tried to explore several techniques to identify fake news using available benchmarked corpora in low-resource languages. A brief description of few of the relevant works are given below:

A novel Kurdish fake news corpus created by Azad et al. (2021) to detect fake news in Kurdish language consists of two datasets (i) Crawled fake news and (ii) Texts that are altered from real news. TF-IDF of words is used to train ML models (Naïve Bayes (NB), SVM, LR, Decision Tree (DT), and Random Forest (RF)) to detect fake news. The SVM classifier outperformed all other classifiers with an accuracy of 88.71% for 'Crawled fake news' and LR classifier outperformed all the other algorithms on 'Texts that are altered from real news' with an accuracy of 83.26%. Hegde and Shashirekha (2021) explored ensemble (RF, MLP, Gradient Boosting (GB), and Adaptive Boosting) model with soft voting for Urdu fake news detection. Using a combination of TF-IDF of word unigrams, character n-grams in the range (2, 3), and fastText vectors, to train the ensemble model, they obtained a macro F1-score of 0.552 and an accuracy of 0.713%. To detect fake news in Malayalam language, Bijimol and Santhosh (2022) proposed a model using Passive Aggressive classifier - an online learning algorithm, trained with TF-IDF of words and achieved an accuracy of 98.4%.

Balouchzahi et al. (2021) developed an ensemble model (LinearSVM, LR, Multilayer Perceptron (MLP), XGB, and RF) with soft voting, trained with TF-IDF of char and word n-grams in the range (1, 3) and (2, 5) respectively. They applied feature selection techniques (Chi-square, Mutual Information Gain (MIG), and f_classif) to select the relevant

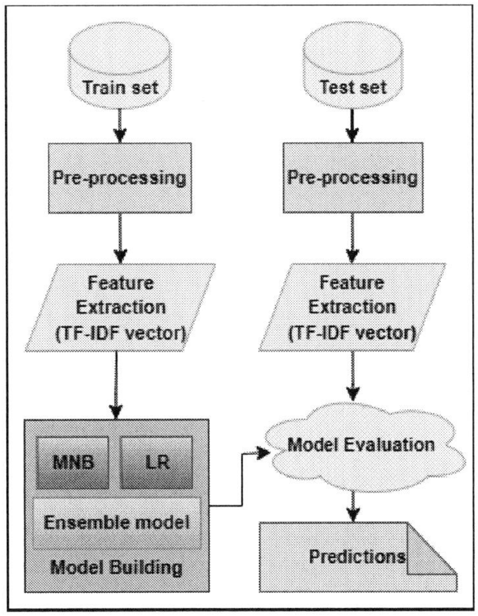

Figure 1: The proposed framework of ML classifiers

features and obtained a macro F1-score of 0.592. In another work, Balouchzahi and Shashirekha (2020) developed an ensemble model (MNB, LR, and MLP) with hard voting for the binary classification of fake news in Urdu. Using term frequency of word and character n-grams in the range (1, 2) and (1, 5) respectively to train the ensemble model, they obtained a macro F1-score of 0.770. The approach to detect fake news in the political domain on the "Liar" dataset is proposed by Khanam et al. (2021). They trained ML models (XGB, RF, NB, k-Nearest Neighbors (k-NN), DT, and SVM) using TF-IDF of word n-gram features and obtained an accuracy of 75% using XGB and 73% accuracy using both SVM and RF models.

The related work reveals that several ML algorithms trained with TF-IDF of word and char n-grams are explored to detect the fake news in low-resource Dravidian languages. However, as the performance of many of the existing works are low, there is scope to develop models to detect fake news in code-mixed low-resource Dravidian languages.

3 Methodology

The framework of the proposed ML models to identify fake news detection in code-mixed Malayalam text is shown in Figure 1 and the steps involved in the proposed methodology are described below:

Classes	Train set	Development set	Test set
Original	1658	409	512
Fake	1599	406	507
Total	3257	815	1019

Table 1: Class-wise distribution of the dataset

Malayalam Text	English Translation	Label
ഇത് പിന്നീട് ട്രോൾ ആകുവെന്നുള്ള ബോധം പോലും പാർട്ടിക്കില്ലേ.. കഷ്ടം	Doesn't the party even realize that this will become a troll later.. Too bad	Original
Sammelanam kazhinjhal eallavarum covid manadhandam paalikkanam ok	After the conference, everyone can follow the Covid criteria	Original
ചില മാധ്യമങ്ങൾ മാധ്യമ ധർമ്മം മറക്കുന്നു	Some media forget media principle	Fake
Vijayane Naattil Ninnum Thalli Odikanam	Vijayan can be pushed out of the country	Fake

Table 2: Samples of code-mixed Malayalam text from the given dataset

3.1 Pre-processing

Malayalam code-mixed data consists of noise such as punctuation, alphanumeric, and special characters (slash, brackets, ampersands, etc.) which are removed during pre-processing. Text written in Roman script is lowercased and emojis are converted to their corresponding English text as they convey emotions which will be useful for classification. The pre-processed data is used for feature extraction.

3.2 Feature Extraction

TF-IDF is used to preserve the relative importance of a word within a document (Hegde et al., 2022b). A higher TF-IDF score indicates that a term is important within a specific document while being relatively less common in the entire corpus. In the proposed work, TF-IDF vectors of word unigrams is obtained from the pre-processed data using TfidfVectorizer[2]. 15,280 word unigrams are obtained from Train set to train the classifiers.

3.3 Model Building

The three ML models: i) MNB, ii) LR, and iii) Ensemble of ML classifiers (MNB, LR, and SVM) with hard voting, are proposed to identify fake news in code-mixed Malayalam text. The strength of MNB model is its capacity to effortlessly handle word occurrences and distribution, capturing distinctive patterns in the text (Abbas et al., 2019). From the training set, the classifier learns the frequency of each class and each word within a class and applies this to the test sample to determine the most likely class from the words it contains. LR model works by transforming the linear combination of extracted features from the given samples through the logistic function, yielding a probability score representing the given data point belonging to a certain class. Ensemble models are a group of diversified classifiers designed with the aim of overcoming the weakness of one classifier with the strength of the others. An Ensemble of ML classifiers (MNB, LR, and SVM) with hard voting is applied to obtain the benefits of SVM classifier to handle complex decision boundaries and high-dimensional data, LR classifier for its simplicity and probabilistic interpretation, and MNB classifier for its efficiency in text-based categorization. This improves the performance of the ensemble models as compared to individual classifiers.

[2]https://scikit-learn.org/stable/modules/generated/sklearn.feature_extraction.text.TfidfVectorizer.html

Classifier	Precision	Recall	Accuracy	Macro F1-score
MNB	0.831	0.831	0.831	0.830
LR	0.820	0.819	0.819	0.819
Ensemble model	**0.831**	**0.831**	**0.831**	**0.830**

Table 3: Performance of the proposed models

4 Experiments and Results

The goal of the shared task is to classify the given Malayalam code-mixed text into "Original" or "Fake" news. The statistics of the Malayalam code-mixed dataset for fake news detection provided by the shared task organisers is shown in Table 1. This dataset contains user-generated text extracted from various social media platforms such as Twitter, Facebook, etc. These texts in Malayalam and/or English will be written in Malayalam and/or Roman scripts. The sample texts from the dataset along with the English translation are shown in Table 2. Predictions on the Test set are evaluated by the organizers of the shared task based on macro F1-scores. The performance of the proposed models for the Development set and Test sets in terms of precision, recall, accuracy, and macro F1-score are shown in Table 3. Among the proposed models, MNB and Ensemble model obtained better results, both with a F1-score of 0.831 securing 3rd rank in the shared task. The comparison of the macro F1-scores of all the participating teams of the shared

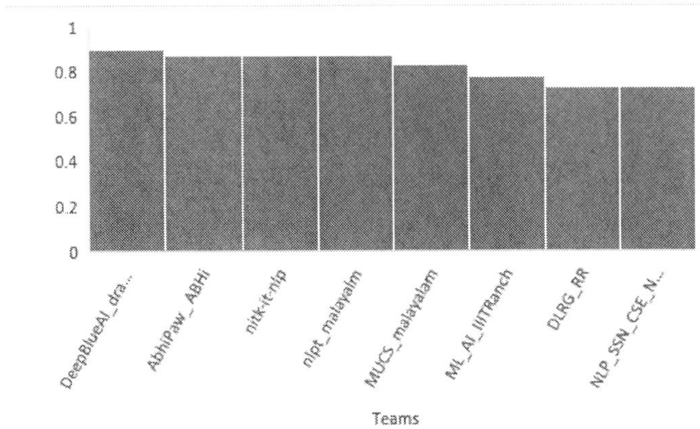

Figure 2: Comparison of macro F1-scores of the proposed ensemble model with other participants' models

Malayalam Text	English Translation	Actual Label	Predicted Label	Remarks
എല്ലാവരും കേക്കുന്നുണ്ടല്ലോ അല്ലേ.........	Everyone is listening right.....	Fake	Original	The words "അല്ലേ" and "എല്ലാവരും" are associated with the class 'original' in Train set. Hence, this sample is classified as original.
Party paruvadikk Corona marinilkumm	When there is a party program then corona concept will take aside	Original	Fake	The words "corona" and "party" are associated with the class 'Fake' in the Train set. Hence, this sample is classified as Fake.

Table 4: Sample misclassified texts from the Test set with predictions generated by ensemble model

task are shown in Figure 2. The misclassified samples along with their English translation, remarks, true and predicted labels for ensemble model are shown in Table 4.

5 Conclusion and Future work

In this paper, we describe the three models: MNB, LR, and Ensemble (LR, RF, and SVM) classifiers with hard voting, submitted to the "Fake News Detection in Dravidian Languages" at DravidianLangTech@RANLP 2023 shared task. The proposed models are trained with TF-IDF of word unigrams, for detecting fake news in code-mixed Malayalam texts. Among the three models, ensemble model obtained 3rd rank with a macro F1-score of 0.831. As a future work, fake news detection in low-resource languages like Tulu, Kannada, and other Dravidian languages will be explored.

References

Muhammad Abbas, K Ali Memon, A Aleem Jamali, Saleemullah Memon, and Anees Ahmed. 2019. Multinomial Naive Bayes Classification model for Sentiment Analysis. *IJCSNS Int. J. Comput. Sci. Netw. Secur*, 19(3):62.

Hadeer Ahmed, Issa Traore, and Sherif Saad. 2017. Detection of Online Fake News Using N-Gram Analysis and Machine Learning Techniques. In *Intelligent, Secure, and Dependable Systems in Distributed and Cloud Environments: First International Conference, ISDDC 2017, Vancouver, BC, Canada, October 26-28, 2017, Proceedings 1*, pages 127–138. Springer.

Rania Azad, Bilal Mohammed, Rawaz Mahmud, Lanya Zrar, and Shajwan Sdiqa. 2021. Fake News Detection in Low-resourced Languages "Kurdish language" using Machine Learning Algorithms. *Turkish Journal of Computer and Mathematics Education (TURCOMAT)*, 12(6):4219–4225.

Fazlourrahman Balouchzahi and HL Shashirekha. 2020. Learning Models for Urdu Fake News Detection. In *FIRE (Working Notes)*, pages 474–479.

Fazlourrahman Balouchzahi, Hosahalli Lakshmaiah Shashirekha, and Grigori Sidorov. 2021. Ensembled Feature Selection for Urdu Fake News Detection. In *CEUR Workshop Proceedings*, volume 3159, pages 1117–1126. CEUR-WS.

TK Bijimol and Anit Sara Santhosh. 2022. Malayalam Fake News Detection using Machine Learning. In

National Conference on Emerging Computer Applications, volume 4.

Bharathi Raja Chakravarthi. 2023. Detection of homophobia and transphobia in Youtube comments. *International Journal of Data Science and Analytics*, pages 1–20.

Bharathi Raja Chakravarthi, Adeep Hande, Rahul Ponnusamy, Prasanna Kumar Kumaresan, and Ruba Priyadharshini. 2022a. How can we detect homophobia and transphobia? experiments in a multilingual code-mixed setting for social media governance. *International Journal of Information Management Data Insights*, 2(2):100119.

Bharathi Raja Chakravarthi, Ruba Priyadharshini, Thenmozhi Durairaj, John McCrae, Paul Buitelaar, Prasanna Kumaresan, and Rahul Ponnusamy. 2022b. Overview of the shared task on homophobia and transphobia detection in social media comments. In *Proceedings of the Second Workshop on Language Technology for Equality, Diversity and Inclusion*, pages 369–377, Dublin, Ireland. Association for Computational Linguistics.

Asha Hegde, Shubhanker Banerjee, Bharathi Raja Chakravarthi, Ruba Priyadharshini, Hosahalli Shashirekha, John Philip McCrae, et al. 2022a. Overview of the Shared Task on Machine Translation in Dravidian Languages. In *Proceedings of the Second Workshop on Speech and Language Technologies for Dravidian Languages*, pages 271–278.

Asha Hegde, Sharal Coelho, Ahmad Elyas Dashti, and Hosahalli Shashirekha. 2022b. MUCS@ Text-LT-EDI@ ACL 2022: Detecting Sign of Depression from Social Media Text using Supervised Learning Approach. In *Proceedings of the Second Workshop on Language Technology for Equality, Diversity and Inclusion*, pages 312–316.

Asha Hegde, Sharal Coelho, and Hosahalli Shashirekha. 2022c. MUCS@DravidianLangTech@ACL2022: Ensemble of Logistic Regression Penalties to Identify Emotions in Tamil Text. In *Proceedings of the Second Workshop on Speech and Language Technologies for Dravidian Languages*, pages 145–150.

Asha Hegde and Hosahalli Lakshmaiah Shashirekha. 2021. Urdu Fake News Detection Using Ensemble of Machine Learning Models.

Rohit Kumar Kaliyar, Anurag Goswami, and Pratik Narang. 2021. FakeBERT: Fake news Detection in Social Media with a BERT-based Deep Learning Approach. *Multimedia tools and applications*, 80(8):11765–11788.

Z Khanam, BN Alwasel, H Sirafi, and Mamoon Rashid. 2021. Fake News Detection Using Machine Learning Approaches. In *IOP conference series: materials science and engineering*, volume 1099, page 012040. IOP Publishing.

Fariba Sadeghi, Amir Jalaly Bidgoly, and Hossein Amirkhani. 2022. Fake News Detection on Social Media Using A Natural Language Inference Approach. *Multimedia Tools and Applications*, 81(23):33801–33821.

Malliga Subramanian, Bharathi Raja Chakravarthi, Kogilavani Shanmugavadivel, Santhiya Pandiyan, Prasanna Kumar Kumaresan, Balasubramanian Palani, Muskaan Singh, Sandhiya Raja, Vanaja, and Mithunajha S. 2023. Overview of the Shared Task on Fake News Detection from Social Media Text. In *Proceedings of the Third Workshop on Speech and Language Technologies for Dravidian Languages*, Varna, Bulgaria. Recent Advances in Natural Language Processing.

S Thara and Prabaharan Poornachandran. 2022. Social Media Text Analytics of Malayalam–English Code-Mixed using Deep Learning. *Journal of big Data*, 9(1):45.

KEC_AI_NLP@DravidianLangTech:Abusive Comment Detection in Tamil Language using Machine Learning Techniques

Kogilavani Shanmugavadivel[1], Malliga Subramanian[1], Shri Durga R[1], Srigha S[1], Sree Harene J S[1], Yasvanth Bala P[1]
[1]Department of AI, Kongu Engineering College, Perundurai, Erode.
{kogilavani.sv, mallinishanth72}@gmail.com
{shridurgar.21aim, srighas.21aim}@kongu.edu
{sreeharenijs.21aim, yasvanthbalap.21aim}@kongu.edu

Abstract

Social media, online news reporting sites, and many other public forums on the Internet are becoming increasingly aware of abusive comments. This also leads to harassment and abusive messages that can cause anxiety and harm others. This research work aims to identify the negative comments that are associated with Counter-speech, Xenophobia, Homophobia, Transphobia, Misandry, Misogyny, and None-of-the-above categories, In order to identify these categories from the given data set, we propose three different models such as machine learning techniques, deep learning model and transfer learning model called BERT is also used to analyze the texts. In the Tamil data set, we are training the models with a train data set and testing the models with validation data. Our team participated in the shared task organized by DravidianLangTech[1] (Priyadharshini et al., 2023a)and secured fourth rank in the task of abusive comment detection in Tamil with a macro- f1 score of 0.35. Also, our run was submitted for abusive comment detection in code-mixed languages (Tamil-English) and secured sixth rank with a macro-f1 score of 0.42 using the Random Forest model.

1 Introduction

Social media platforms that provide communications, education, and information exchange in the digital age have become an essential part of our lives. But this increased online communication has also raised concerns about the spread of slander, hate speech, and online bullying (Park et al., 2018). Slander is a statement made against a person or group of people. In recent years there has been a growing awareness of the harm that negative comments (Narang and Brew, 2020) can do to individuals and society as a whole. Insults not only cause psychological harm to the victim, but also cause the spread of humor, division, and dissatisfaction online. Given the detrimental impact hate speech has on the general public, major platforms such as YouTube, Facebook, Instagram, and Twitter have implemented policies (Caselli et al., 2021) and protocols to address hateful content and combat negative behaviors. It is crucial to prioritize the identification and management of such comments to minimize their adverse effects on individuals.

Over the past few years, a growing body of research has been addressing the issue of tackling abusive comments (Mubarak et al., 2017) in the fields such as natural language processing (NLP), network science, and Artificial Intelligence (AI). Early studies relied on machine learning (ML) classes such as Support Vector Machine (SVM) with word and attribute n-gram features and Logistic Regression (LR) (Ibrohim and Budi, 2019). Analyzing the illegal language in Tamil requires a good understanding of the features of the language, its cultural context, and certain language patterns associated with abusive content. This has required the development of Tamil-adapted artificial intelligence algorithms and machine learning models that can identify and neutralize illegal words with higher accuracy (Davidson et al., 2019).

Machine learning models that possess specific options share similarities and present a simpler alternative to Transformer models (Koufakou et al., 2020). Recent studies on advancements in offensive language detection indicate a growing trend in utilizing deep learning-based transformer models (Mishra et al., 2019). Transfer learning is a concept where models are initially trained on extensive sets of unlabeled text using self-supervised learning, and subsequently employed on labeled text corpora. For our project, we employ the Bidirectional Encoder Representation from Transformers (BERT) model (Corazza et al., 2020).

Our task is to analyze and detect abusive com-

[1]https://codalab.lisn.upsaclay.fr/competitions/11096

Third Workshop on Speech and Language Technologies for Dravidian Languages, pages 293–299, Varna, Bulgaria, Sep 7, 2023.
https://doi.org/10.26615/978-954-452-085-4_043

ments in Tamil (Priyadharshini et al., 2022; Shanmugavadivel et al., 2022). Tamil has an agglutinative grammar, that is, the last word is used to denote class, number case, verb tenses, and other grammatical forms. Abusive Comment Detection is a text classification problem (Priyadharshini et al., 2023b). Text classification is a technique for extracting features from the text, giving it a preset category. It is always done by the linear classifier of sentence embeddings of text. In this paper, we trained various machine learning models, deep learning, and transfer learning models for detecting abusive comments in the Tamil language. We compared the results of all the methods to determine the best model.

2 Literature Review

The paper by Mubarak et al. (ALW 2017) highlight the challenges associated with Arabic abusive language detection, such as the presence of dialects and informal language usage. The review in (Mubarak et al., 2017) provides valuable insights into the state-of-the-art methods, data sets, and evaluation metrics used in this domain. The paper by Mishra et al. (NAACL 2019) presents a novel approach for abusive language detection using Graph Convolutional Networks (GCNs). The authors propose a graph-based model that captures both syntactic and semantic dependencies between words in a sentence to effectively identify abusive content. (Mishra et al., 2019)leverage graph convolutional layers to learn contextual representations from the sentence's dependency graph, enabling the model to capture the structural information crucial for identifying abusive language. The paper by Park et al. (EMNLP 2018) addresses the issue of gender bias in abusive language detection systems. The authors propose a method to reduce gender bias by incorporating gender information into the training process. (Park et al., 2018) introduce a gender-balanced data set and develop a fine-tuning strategy that takes into account the gender of both the author and target of abusive language. The experimental results show that their approach effectively reduces gender bias in the detection system while maintaining good overall performance. The paper by Ibrohim and Budi (ALW 2019) focuses on the task of multi-label hate speech and abusive language detection in Indonesian Twitter. The authors present a comprehensive analysis of various approaches for addressing this challenge, including feature-based, deep learning, and ensemble methods.

(Ibrohim and Budi, 2019) discuss the importance of handling multiple labels, as hate speech and abusive language can exhibit different characteristics and require distinct detection techniques. The paper by Narang and Brew (ALW 2020) presents an approach for abusive language detection that utilizes syntactic dependency graphs. The authors propose a method that incorporates information from these graphs, including node representations and graph-based features, to identify abusive content.(Narang and Brew, 2020) demonstrate the effectiveness of this approach by comparing it with baseline models on multiple data sets and achieving superior performance. The paper by Caselli et al. (WOAH 2021) introduces HateBERT, a retraining approach for BERT (Bidirectional Encoder Representations from Transformers) specifically tailored for abusive language detection in English. The authors fine-tune BERT using a large-scale data set of annotated abusive language to enhance its ability to identify and classify abusive content accurately.

(Caselli et al., 2021) compare HateBERT's performance with other existing models and demonstrate its superiority in terms of precision, recall, and F1-score. The paper by Davidson et al. (ALW 2019) investigates the presence of racial bias in hate speech and abusive language detection data sets. The authors analyze several widely-used data sets and identify potential biases in the annotation process, particularly regarding racial and ethnic slurs. (Davidson et al., 2019) highlight the importance of addressing such biases to ensure fair and unbiased evaluation of detection models. The paper by Koufakou et al. (ALW 2020) introduces HurtBERT, a model that combines BERT with lexical features for the detection of abusive language. The authors incorporate various lexical features, such as n-grams, sentiment scores, and part-of-speech tags, alongside BERT embeddings to enhance the model's understanding of abusive content.

(Koufakou et al., 2020) evaluate HurtBERT on multiple data sets and demonstrate its improved performance compared to BERT alone and other baseline models. The paper by Corazza et al. (Findings 2020) introduces a novel approach for zero-shot abusive language detection using hybrid emoji-based masked language models. The authors propose incorporating emojis as a form of contextual information to enhance the model's ability to identify and classify abusive content. They leverage pre-trained language models and mask out abusive terms, replacing them with emoji representations during inference. The experimental results in (Corazza et al., 2020) demonstrate the effectiveness of their approach in zero-shot detection, achieving competitive performance compared to existing methods. (Chakravarthi, 2020) introduces HopeEDI, a multilingual data set for hope speech detection (Subramanian et al., 2022) in the context of equality, diversity, and inclusion. The data set aims to facilitate research on understanding and promoting positive discourse in social media. The study in (Chakravarthi, 2020) describes the data collection process, and annotation guidelines, and provides an analysis of the data set's characteristics.

3 Dataset Description

The goal of this shared task on abusive comment detection is to detect and reduce abusive comments on social media. The dataset used here is shared by the shared task (Priyadharshini et al., 2022). The primary goal of this project is to develop methods for detecting and classifying instances of hate speech in Tamil. The Abusive Comment Detection data set is made up of Tamil comments retrieved from the YouTube comments area (Priyadharshini et al., 2023b). The data set consists of a comment and its related label from one of the nine labels: Misandry, Counter-speech, Misogyny, Xenophobia, Hope-Speech, Homophobic, Transphobic, Not-Tamil, and None-of-the-above.SMOTE, which stands for Synthetic Minority Over-sampling data augmentation Technique, is a widely used technique in the field of machine learning specifically in the context of handling imbalanced datasets.Imbalanced datasets occur when the classes have significantly different numbers of instances, leading to a bias in the model's performance towards the majority class.

SMOTE is designed to solve this issue by generating synthetic samples for the minority class, thereby balancing the class distribution.Synthetic samples are artificially created data points that are generated based on existing data points in a dataset.In our dataset,'Misandry' belongs to the minority class,thereby we use SMOTE technique to balance the class distribution.

3.1 Tamil Data

The Train, Test, and Development data sets each comprise 2239, 559, 900 comments. The text in Tamil is followed by the appropriate label for each comment in the training data. In the data set, there is a significant class imbalance. Because there is no test or development data of examples for the 'Not-Tamil' label, classification is limited to the other seven labels.

Dataset	No. of Comments
Train	2,239
Validation	559
Test	698

Table 1: Dataset Description

Class	Train	Dev	Test
None Of The Above	1296	345	416
Misandry	446	104	127
Counter Speech	149	36	47
Misogyny	125	29	48
Xenophobia	95	24	25
Hope Speech	85	11	26
Trans-phobic	35	8	2

Table 2: Class Description

4 Methodology

Machine learning and deep learning models cannot access raw texts. Feature extraction is required to train classification models. The TF-IDF representation is utilized in ML techniques to extract features. We use three ways to analyze the results and create the best model possible: Machine Learning, Deep Learning, and Transformer-based Learning.

4.1 Machine Learning Models

Machine learning has come a long way in recent years, changing the way people understand important applications such as image recognition, data mining, and natural language processing(NLP). This section outlines the machine learning models utilized in the present study for text classification. We used several different kinds of machine learning algorithms such as Decision tree, Random Forest, GaussianNB, XGBoost, AdaBoost, KNN, Linear Regression, Multinomial NB, Support Vector Machine, MLP Classifier, Gradient Boost, and Ensemble models.

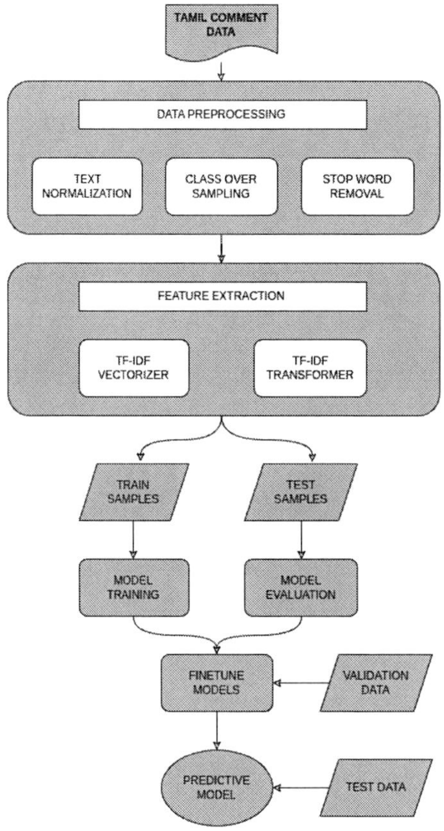

Figure 1: Proposed System Workflow

4.2 Deep Learning Model

Text classification tasks have witnessed the efficacy of deep learning models like Convolutional Neural Networks (CNN) and Long Short-Term Memory (LSTM) networks. CNN models excel in capturing localized patterns and features within text data by utilizing convolutional filters. On the other hand, LSTM models are specifically designed to capture long-term dependencies and sequential information.

LSTM, which belongs to the family of recurrent neural networks (RNNs), is renowned for its capability to capture long-term dependencies in sequential data. This quality makes it highly suitable for analyzing sequences of comments. The comments are pre-processed to remove noise and irrelevant information and then fed into an LSTM model for training and evaluation.

The LSTM model is designed to learn the patterns and relationships within the comment sequences. By considering the temporal information of the comments, the model can effectively capture the context and dependencies that exist between words and phrases. The model is trained using the processed training data set, and the validation data set is used to tune the hyper-parameters and evaluate the performance of each model. Various evaluation metrics such as accuracy, precision, recall, and F1 score are used to evaluate the efficacy of the LSTM model in identifying abusive comments in Tamil.

However, it is important to note that these deep learning models can be computationally intensive and require substantial training time. This is primarily due to the high input dimensionality of text features and the large number of parameters that need to be trained. As a result, training deep learning models can often be time-consuming and resource-intensive.In conclusion, this research demonstrates the effectiveness of LSTM for abusive comment detection in YouTube content. It provides insights into the application of deep learning techniques, specifically LSTM in addressing the challenges associated with analyzing sequential comment data.

4.3 Transfer Learning Model

Transfer learning is a powerful technique that leverages pre-trained models to enhance the performance of models on new tasks. BERT(Bidirectional Encoder Representations from Transformers) is a powerful language model that has achieved remarkable results in various natural language processing tasks. To leverage the capabilities of BERT, it is possible to utilize pre-trained BERT models that have been trained on extensive amounts of text data from diverse sources.

The pre-trained BERT model is tuned-up on the particular task of abusive comment detection using the YouTube comments data set. Fine-tuning involves adapting the previously trained model to the target task by training it on the labeled data. This process allows BERT to learn the specific patterns and features relevant to identifying abusive comments in YouTube content.

During the fine-tuning process, appropriate classification techniques, such as adding a classification layer on top of BERT or employing additional neural network layers for improved performance can be done. The fine-tuned BERT model is evaluated on a separate test set to measure its accuracy score, precision, recall, and F1 score metrics. Additionally,the advantages of transfer learning with BERT include the ability to capture semantic meaning, context, and nuanced language patterns. It also addresses potential limitations, such as the need for large amounts of labeled data and computational resources for fine-tuning BERT.

5 Performance Evaluation

From the comprehensive results presented in Table 3 and Table 4, it becomes apparent that out of the 13 models tested, comprising 11 machine learning models, deep learning model, and transfer learning model, SVC, a machine learning model, emerged as the top performer in term of precision and recall. It outperformed both the deep learning and transfer learning models in terms of precision, recall, and F1 score, signifying its superiority in predictive capabilities. Figure 2 displayed the confusion matrix of the Random Forest Model.

With its ability to leverage an ensemble of decision trees and feature importance estimation, the random forest model demonstrated its prowess in capturing complex patterns within the data set and making accurate predictions. The performance advantage of the random forest model can be attributed to its ability to handle high-dimensional data, effectively deal with noisy and missing values, and mitigate overfitting concerns. By leveraging a combination of feature subsampling and bootstrap aggregating, the model achieved robust generalization and reduced the risk of overfitting.

The deep learning model, which often requires significant computational resources and extensive parameter tuning, fell short in this evaluation. It might have struggled to extract meaningful representations from the given data set or faced challenges in optimizing its numerous parameters, thereby resulting in comparatively lower accuracy and F1 score. Similarly, the transfer learning model, which typically leverages pre-trained neural networks and fine-tunes them for specific tasks, failed to outperform the random forest model. Although transfer learning has proven to be effective in various domains, it appears that the unique characteristics of the data set did not lend themselves well to this particular transfer learning approach.

Overall, the exceptional performance of the support vector classifier model highlights the strength of traditional machine learning algorithms, particularly in scenarios where the data-set is not excessively large or lacks the complexity that deep learning models excel at handling. This outcome underscores the importance of carefully selecting the appropriate modeling technique based on the specific characteristics and requirements of the problem at hand, ultimately leading to improved predictive performance.

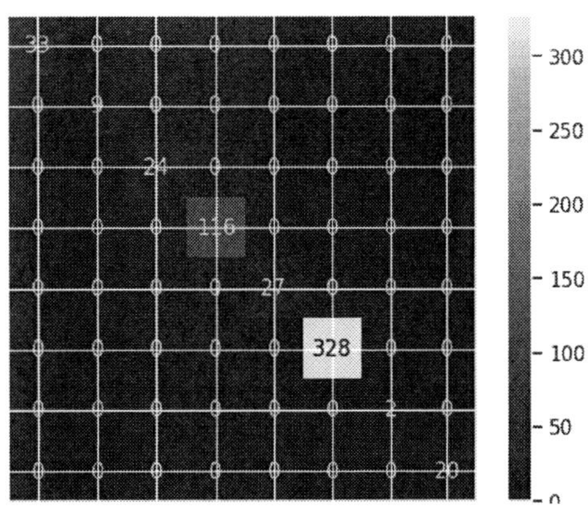

Figure 2: Confusion Matrix Of Support Vector Classifier Model- Train Data

Model	Precision	Recall	F1-score
Multilayer perceptron	0.80	0.66	0.70
K-Nearest Neighbour	0.66	0.35	0.34
Xtreme Gradient Boost	0.81	0.69	0.70
Decision Tree	0.80	0.79	0.79
Random Forest	0.85	0.81	0.81
Logistic Regression	0.81	0.83	0.85
Support Vector Classifier	0.99	0.99	0.99
Multinomial Naive Bayes	0.60	0.53	0.64
Gradient Boost Classifier	0.94	0.94	0.94
Ensemble	0.98	0.98	0.98
Adaboost Classifier	0.52	0.55	0.64
BERT	0.76	0.76	0.79
CNN	0.65	0.52	0.62

Table 3: Tamil-Validation-Train Data Evaluation Metrics

Model	Precision	Recall	F1-score
Multilayer perceptron	0.45	0.45	0.54
K-Nearest Neighbour	0.51	0.51	0.44
Xtreme Gradient Boost	0.55	0.52	0.46
Decision Tree	0.46	0.52	0.54
Random Forest	0.49	0.52	0.44
Logistic Regression	0.66	0.68	0.62
Support Vector Classifier	0.64	0.67	0.64
Multinomial Naive Bayes	0.53	0.60	0.47
Gradient Boost Classifier	0.65	0.68	0.65
Ensemble	0.66	0.69	0.64
Adaboost Classifier	0.64	0.64	0.55
BERT	0.59	0.66	0.60
CNN	0.41	0.50	0.45

Table 4: Tamil-Train Data Evaluation Metrics

6 Conclusion

The study focuses on the detection of abusive comments in the Tamil language. We compare the performance of different models in this task. Deep Learning and Transformer models did not achieve superior results when trained and evaluated on Tamil data. Instead, Machine Learning models outperformed the Deep Learning and Transformer-based models. It is important to note that contextualized embeddings such as ELMO or FLAIR, which have shown potential in enhancing the performance of language models has not been utilized. The absence of these embeddings might have limited the effectiveness of the models used in our study.

We acknowledge this limitation and suggest that future work should explore the implementation of contextualized embeddings using deep learning techniques. We believe that incorporating these advanced embeddings could potentially improve the detection of abusive comments in Tamil. Additionally, other models like Indic BERT and Muril BERT were not utilized at this stage. However, we highlight the possibility of implementing these models in the future as our project advances. This indicates the potential for further exploration and improvement in the detection of abusive comments in Tamil using more advanced language models.

References

Tommaso Caselli, Arjan Schelhaas, Marieke Weultjes, Folkert Leistra, Hylke van der Veen, Gerben Timmerman, and Malvina Nissim. 2021. Dalc: the dutch abusive language corpus. In *Proceedings of the 5th*

Workshop on Online Abuse and Harms (WOAH 2021), pages 54–66.

Bharathi Raja Chakravarthi. 2020. Hopeedi: A multilingual hope speech detection dataset for equality, diversity, and inclusion. In *Proceedings of the Third Workshop on Computational Modeling of People's Opinions, Personality, and Emotion's in Social Media*, pages 41–53.

Michele Corazza, Stefano Menini, Elena Cabrio, Sara Tonelli, and Serena Villata. 2020. A multilingual evaluation for online hate speech detection. *ACM Transactions on Internet Technology (TOIT)*, 20(2):1–22.

Thomas Davidson, Debasmita Bhattacharya, and Ingmar Weber. 2019. Racial bias in hate speech and abusive language detection datasets. *arXiv preprint arXiv:1905.12516*.

Muhammad Okky Ibrohim and Indra Budi. 2019. Multi-label hate speech and abusive language detection in indonesian twitter. In *Proceedings of the third workshop on abusive language online*, pages 46–57.

Anna Koufakou, Endang Wahyu Pamungkas, Valerio Basile, Viviana Patti, et al. 2020. Hurtbert: Incorporating lexical features with bert for the detection of abusive language. In *Proceedings of the fourth workshop on online abuse and harms*, pages 34–43. Association for Computational Linguistics.

Pushkar Mishra, Marco Del Tredici, Helen Yannakoudakis, and Ekaterina Shutova. 2019. Abusive language detection with graph convolutional networks. *arXiv preprint arXiv:1904.04073*.

Hamdy Mubarak, Kareem Darwish, and Walid Magdy. 2017. Abusive language detection on arabic social media. In *Proceedings of the first workshop on abusive language online*, pages 52–56.

Kanika Narang and Chris Brew. 2020. Abusive language detection using syntactic dependency graphs. In *Proceedings of the Fourth Workshop on Online Abuse and Harms*, pages 44–53.

Ji Ho Park, Jamin Shin, and Pascale Fung. 2018. Reducing gender bias in abusive language detection. *arXiv preprint arXiv:1808.07231*.

Ruba Priyadharshini, Bharathi Raja Chakravarthi, Subalalitha Cn, Thenmozhi Durairaj, Malliga Subramanian, Kogilavani Shanmugavadivel, Siddhanth U Hegde, and Prasanna Kumaresan. 2022. Overview of abusive comment detection in Tamil-ACL 2022. In *Proceedings of the Second Workshop on Speech and Language Technologies for Dravidian Languages*, pages 292–298, Dublin, Ireland. Association for Computational Linguistics.

Ruba Priyadharshini, Bharathi Raja Chakravarthi, Malliga S, SUBALALITHA CN, Kogilavani S V, Premjith B, Abirami Murugappan, and Prasanna Kumar Kumaresan. 2023a. Overview of shared-task on abusive comment detection in tamil and telugu. In *Proceedings of the Third Workshop on Speech and Language Technologies for Dravidian Languages*, Varna, Bulgaria. Recent Advances in Natural Language Processing.

Ruba Priyadharshini, Bharathi Raja Chakravarthi, Malliga Subramanian, Subalalitha Chinnaudayar Navaneethakrishnan, Kogilavani Shanmugavadivel, Premjith B, Abirami Murugappan, Prasanna Kumar Kumaresan, Karnati Sai Prashanth, Mangamuru Sai Rishith Reddy, and Janakiram Chandu. 2023b. Overview of shared-task on abusive comment detection in tamil and telugu. In *Proceedings of the Third Workshop on Speech and Language Technologies for Dravidian Languages*, Varna, Bulgaria. Recent Advances in Natural Language Processing.

Kogilavani Shanmugavadivel, Siddhanth U Hegde, and Prasanna Kumar Kumaresan. 2022. Overview of abusive comment detection in tamil-acl 2022. *DravidianLangTech*, 2022:292.

Malliga Subramanian, Ramya Chinnasamy, Prasanna Kumar Kumaresan, Vasanth Palanikumar, Madhoora Mohan, and Kogilavani Shanmugavadivel. 2022. Development of multi-lingual models for detecting hope speech texts from social media comments. In *International Conference on Speech and Language Technologies for Low-resource Languages*, pages 209–219. Springer.

KEC_AI_NLP@DravidianLangTech:Sentiment Analysis using Hybrid Model

Kogilavani Shanmugavadivel[1], Malliga Subramanian[1], VetriVendhan S[1], Pramoth Kumar M[1], Karthickeyan S[1], Kavin Vishnu N[1]

[1]Department of AI, Kongu Engineering College, Perundurai, Erode.

{kogilavani.sv, mallinishanth72}@gmail.com

{vetrivendhans.21aim, pramothkumarm.21aim}@kongu.edu

{karthickeyans.21aim, kavinvishnun.21aim}@kongu.edu

Abstract

Sentiment Analysis is a process that involves analyzing digital text to determine the emotional tone, such as positive, negative, neutral, or unknown. In this study, we obtained the dataset from the CodaLab website by participating in a competition and accessing code-mixed format train and development data. Later, on May 10th, the test data was provided, including an unlabeled class. Sentiment Analysis of code-mixed languages presents challenges in natural language processing due to the complexity of code-mixed data, which combines vocabulary and grammar from multiple languages and creates unique structures. The scarcity of annotated data and the unstructured nature of code-mixed data are major challenges. To address these challenges, we explored various techniques, including Machine Learning (ML), Deep Learning, and Transfer Learning. ML models such as Decision Trees, Random Forests, Logistic Regression, and Gaussian Naïve Bayes were employed. Deep Learning models, such as Long Short-Term Memory (LSTM), and Transfer Learning models like BERT, were also utilized. The results demonstrated promising performance in sentiment analysis of code-mixed text. Overall, this study contributes to the field of sentiment analysis by addressing the challenges posed by code-mixed language and employing diverse ML and Deep Learning techniques for accurate sentiment classification.This dataset was taken in the competition in Codalab with dataset description of (Chakravarthi et al., 2020)and (Hegde et al., 2022). Our team participated in the shared task organized by (Hegde et al., 2023)

Key Words Sentiment Analysis, Emotional tone, Natural language processing, Tokenizer, padded sequence, Machine Learning, BERT, LSTM

1 Introduction

Sentiment Analysis, also referred to as opinion mining, is a computational process that utilizes natural language processing (NLP), text analysis, and computational linguistics to uncover the emotional sentiment expressed in each text. It aims to categorize and determine opinions regarding a product, service, or idea, by extracting polarity (positivity or negativity), subject matter, and the opinion holder within the text. Sentiment Analysis can be performed on various levels, including full documents, paragraphs, sentences, or even smaller units. It finds applications in diverse domains such as product reviews, social media analysis, and market research. Different types of Sentiment Analysis exist, such as aspect-based Sentiment Analysis, grading Sentiment Analysis, multilingual Sentiment Analysis, and emotion detection. Approaches for Sentiment Analysis include knowledge-based techniques, statistical methods, and Machine Learning algorithms. Social media platforms serve as significant sources of data for Sentiment Analysis, as they generate vast and interconnected information in the form of user-generated content.

2 Literature Survey

(Pang et al., 2008) Pang, Bo, and Lillian Lee. "Opinion mining and sentiment analysis." Foundations and Trends in Information Retrieval. This seminal work provides an overview of sentiment analysis techniques, including both traditional machine learning approaches and early deep learning methods.(Kim, 2014) Kim, Yoon. "Convolutional Neural Networks for Sentence Classification." Proceedings of the 2014 Conference on Empirical Methods in Natural Language Processing (EMNLP). The author introduces a simple yet effective model architecture that utilizes multiple parallel convolutional filters with different kernel sizes

Third Workshop on Speech and Language Technologies for Dravidian Languages, pages 300–305, Varna, Bulgaria, Sep 7, 2023.
https://doi.org/10.26615/978-954-452-085-4_044

to capture various n-gram features for sentence classification.(Socher et al., 2013) Socher, Richard, et al. "Recursive deep models for semantic compositionality over a sentiment treebank." Proceedings of the 2013 conference on empirical methods in natural language processing (EMNLP). The authors propose a recursive deep model that captures the hierarchical nature of sentiment in sentences, achieving improved accuracy by leveraging fine-grained sentiment information.[3] Tang, Duyu, et al. "Learning sentiment-specific word embedding for Twitter sentiment classification." Proceedings of the 52nd Annual Meeting of the Association for Computational Linguistics. This study focuses on learning sentiment-specific word embeddings for Twitter sentiment classification, demonstrating the effectiveness of incorporating sentiment information into word representations.(Zhang et al., 2015) Zhang, Lei, et al. "Character-level convolutional networks for text classification." Advances in neural information processing systems. The authors propose character-level convolutional networks for text classification tasks, showcasing their effectiveness in sentiment analysis by capturing local and compositional features at the character level.[6] Devlin, Jacob, et al. "BERT: Pre-training of deep bidirectional transformers for language understanding." arXiv preprint arXiv:1810.04805. This paper introduces BERT, a pre-training approach based on bidirectional transformers, which has shown remarkable performance in various natural language processing tasks, including sentiment analysis.[7] Tang, Duyu, et al. "Attention-over-attention neural networks for reading comprehension." Proceedings of the 2018 Conference of the North American Chapter of the Association for Computational Linguistics: Human Language Technologies, Volume 1 (Long Papers). The authors propose attention-over-attention neural networks for reading comprehension tasks, demonstrating their effectiveness in capturing intricate relationships within sentences for sentiment analysis.(Zhang et al., 2015) Zhang, Xu, et al. "Character-level attentive recurrent neural networks for sentiment analysis." Proceedings of the AAAI Conference on Artificial Intelligence. Vol.This work introduces character-level attentive recurrent neural networks for sentiment analysis, showcasing the significance of character level attention mechanisms in capturing fine-grained sentiment information.(Young et al., 2018) Yang, Zichao, et al. "Hierarchical attention networks for document classification." Proceedings of the 2016 conference of the North American chapter of the association for computational linguistics: human language technologies. The authors propose hierarchical attention networks that capture contextual dependencies at different levels of granularity, achieving state-of-the-art results in document classification, which is applicable to sentiment analysis.[10] Xing, Wei, et al. "Recurrent convolutional neural networks for text classification." Proceedings of the 2015 conference on empirical methods in natural language processing. This study presents recurrent convolutional neural networks and machine learning techniques for text classification tasks, combining the strengths of both recurrent and convolutional neural networks to capture long-term dependencies.

3 Methodology

Machine learning models have revolutionized the field of artificial intelligence by enabling computers to learn and make predictions or decisions without being explicitly programmed. In this introduction, we will explore several popular machine-learning models and their applications in sentiment analysis. The proposed system workflow is presented in Figure 1.

Decision trees are a powerful supervised learning technique that can be used for both classification and regression tasks. They create a tree-like model where each internal node represents a feature, each branch represents a decision rule, and each leaf node represents an outcome or prediction. Decision trees are intuitive, easy to interpret, and can handle both numerical and categorical data. They are often used in sentiment analysis to classify text into positive, negative, or neutral sentiments. Random forests are an ensemble learning method that combines multiple decision trees to make more accurate predictions. It works by constructing a multitude of decision trees, each trained on a different subset of the training data and using random feature subsets. The final prediction is made by aggregating the predictions of individual trees. Random forests are known for their robustness, ability to handle high-dimensional data, and resistance to overfitting. They are commonly used in sentiment analysis to improve classification accuracy. Logistic regression is a popular classification algorithm used to predict the probability of a binary outcome based on input variables. Despite its

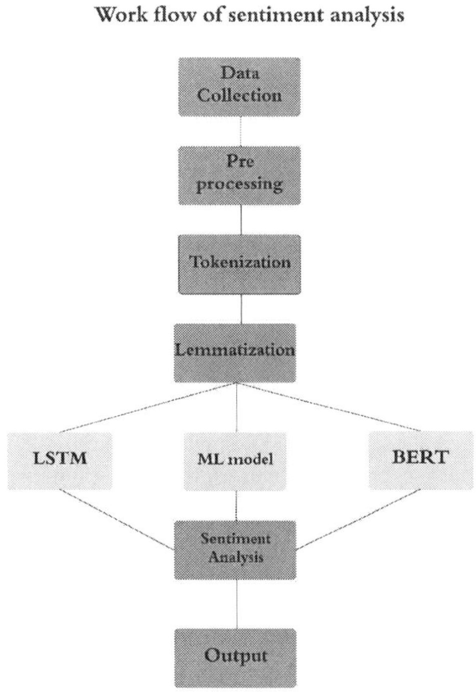

Figure 1: proposed system workflow

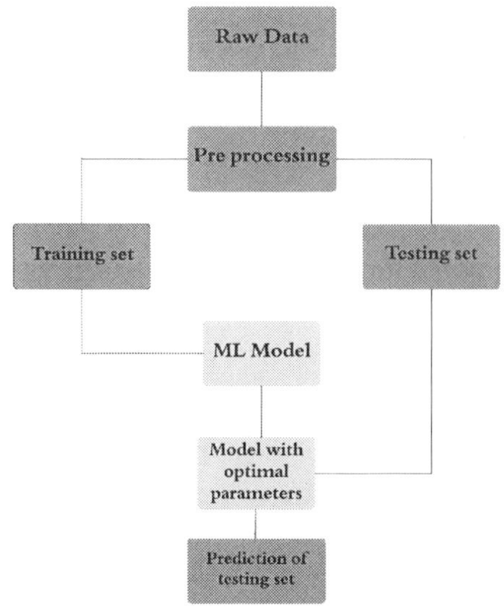

Figure 2: Sentiment Analysis by Machine Learning Models

name, logistic regression is a linear model, but it applies a logistic function to the linear output to transform it into a probability. It is widely used in sentiment analysis to determine the likelihood of a given text belonging to a specific sentiment class. Logistic regression is computationally efficient and can provide interpretable results. Gaussian Naïve Bayes is a probabilistic classifier based on Baye's theorem and assumes independence between features. Gaussian Naïve Bayes specifically assumes that the features follow a Gaussian distribution. It is a simple yet effective algorithm that works well with high-dimensional data and requires a small amount of training data. Gaussian Naïve Bayes is often used in sentiment analysis to classify text based on the likelihood of belonging to a particular sentiment class. Performing sentiment analysis using machine learning models are depicted in Figure 2.

Deep learning models, such as LSTM, are a type of artificial neural network [7-11] with multiple layers that can learn complex patterns and dependencies in data. LSTM networks are specifically designed to capture long-term dependencies by using memory cells and gates that regulate the flow of information. LSTMs have been highly successful in natural language processing tasks, including sentiment analysis. They can learn contextual information, understand sequential patterns, and effectively model text sentiment over longer sequences. Performing Sentiment Analysis by LSTM is represented in Figure 3.

Transfer Learning - BERT (Bidirectional Encoder Representations from Transformers) is a state-of-the-art deep learning model for natural language processing tasks. It is based on the Transformer architecture and is pre-trained on a large corpus of text data. BERT has achieved remarkable results in various NLP tasks, including sentiment analysis, by leveraging its ability to understand contextualized word representations. Transfer learning with BERT involves fine-tuning the pre-trained model on a specific sentiment analysis task, which can significantly improve performance even with limited training data. Sentiment analysis by BERT is presented in Figure 4.

4 Performance Evaluation

Whether utilising machine learning or deep learning techniques, performance evaluation for sentiment analysis models often incorporates multiple indicators to gauge the model's efficacy. Following are a few typical evaluation measures for sentiment analysis: Accuracy: The ratio of examples that

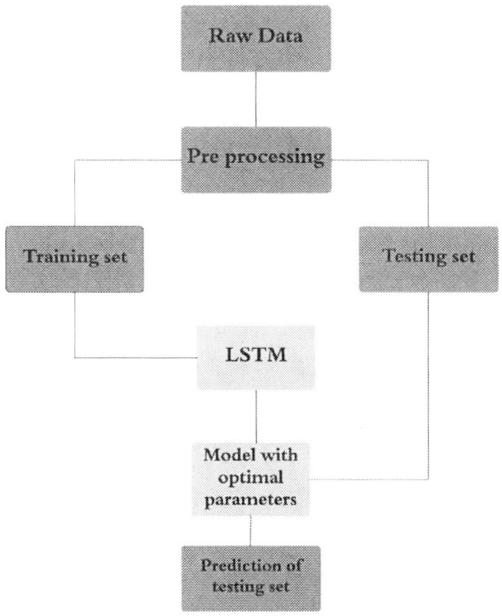

Figure 3: Sentiment Analysis by LSTM

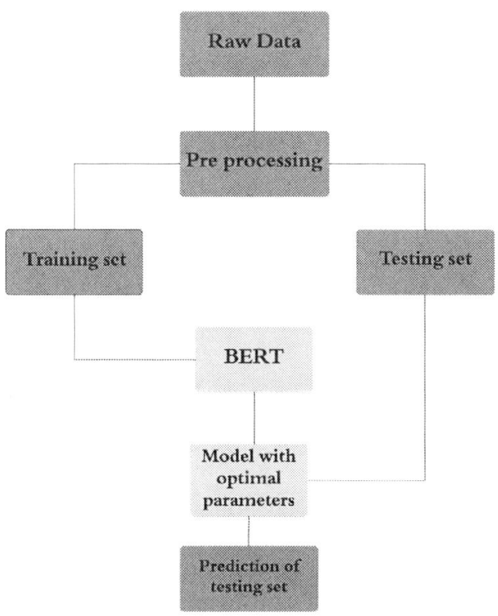

Figure 4: Sentiment Analysis by BERT

were successfully classified to all instances is used to determine the overall accuracy of the model's predictions. However, accuracy by itself could not give a full picture, particularly when dealing with datasets that are unbalanced. Precision: Out of all instances anticipated as positive (or negative), precision represents the percentage of accurately predicted positive (or negative) cases. The accuracy of positive (or negative) predictions is the main focus, and it aids in determining the model's capacity to prevent false positives. Confusion Matrix: A confusion matrix displays the predictions of the model in comparison to the actual classes in a tabular format. Insights into true positives, true negatives, false positives, and false negatives are provided, assisting in the identification of certain areas that require improvement. Table 1 lists the accuracy of each proposed model, and it is evident from the findings that the LSTM model offers superior accuracy with a score of 0.61.Tables 2, 3, and 4 show the Precision, Recall, and f1-Score for each suggested model, respectively. The proportion of accurately predicted positive (or negative) cases out of all actual positive (or negative) instances is determined by recall (also known as sensitivity or true positive rate). It demonstrates how the model can recognise positive (or negative) cases and prevent false negatives. F1-Score: The F1-score is a balanced indicator of a model's performance because it is the harmonic mean of precision and recall. It is helpful when the dataset is unbalanced since it takes precision and recall into account.

Model	Accuracy
Random Forest	0.54
Decision Tree	0.42
Logistic Regression	0.60
GaussianNb	0.14
LSTM	0.61
BERT	0.59

Table 1: Accuracy of proposed models

Model	Precision	Recall	F1-score
GNB	0.62	0.07	0.12
LR	0.36	0.10	0.15
DT	0.14	0.15	0.14
RF	0.22	0.15	0.18

Table 2:
Classification Report of Mixed Feeling Class Label

Model	Precision	Recall	F1-score
GNB	0.13	1.00	0.23
LR	0.14	0.0	0.0
DT	0.15	0.16	0.15
RF	0.22	0.12	0.16

Table 3: Classification Report of Negative Class Label

Model	Precision	Recall	F1-score
GNB	0.35	0.02	0.03
LR	0.42	0.01	0.03
DT	0.18	0.19	0.18
RF	0.23	0.10	0.81

Table 4: Classification Report of Unknown State Class Label

Model	Precision	Recall	F1-score
GNB	0.0	0.0	0.0
LR	0.61	0.98	0.75
DT	0.64	0.59	0.62
RF	0.63	0.82	0.71

Table 5:
Classification Report of Positive Class Label

5 Conclusion

In this research work, sentiment analysis is performed using machine learning, deep learning and transfer learning techniques, specifically Gaussian Naive Bayes, Decision Trees,Random Forests,BERT, and LSTM. For the machine learning approach, we employed logistic regression, decision tree, and random forest algorithms, while for the deep learning approach, we utilized LSTM models and for transfer learning approach, we utilized BERT. After evaluating the models, we obtained an accuracy of 42 percent for the decision tree and 61 percent for the LSTM. In summary, the LSTM model outperformed the decision tree algorithm's precision, achieving a higher accuracy of 61 percent for sentiment analysis. However, the performance can be further improved by fine-tuning hyperparameters, exploring different architectures, or incorporating ensemble methods.

References

Erik Cambria and Bebo White. 2014. Jumping nlp curves: A review of natural language processing research. *IEEE Computational intelligence magazine*, 9(2):48–57.

Bharathi Raja Chakravarthi, Vigneshwaran Muralidaran, Ruba Priyadharshini, and John Philip McCrae. 2020. Corpus creation for sentiment analysis in code-mixed Tamil-English text. In *Proceedings of the 1st Joint Workshop on Spoken Language Technologies for Under-resourced languages (SLTU) and Collaboration and Computing for Under-Resourced Languages (CCURL)*, pages 202–210, Marseille, France. European Language Resources association.

Cicero Dos Santos and Maira Gatti. 2014. Deep convolutional neural networks for sentiment analysis of short texts. In *Proceedings of COLING 2014, the 25th international conference on computational linguistics: technical papers*, pages 69–78.

Asha Hegde, Mudoor Devadas Anusha, Sharal Coelho, Hosahalli Lakshmaiah Shashirekha, and Bharathi Raja Chakravarthi. 2022. Corpus creation for sentiment analysis in code-mixed Tulu text. In *Proceedings of the 1st Annual Meeting of the ELRA/ISCA Special Interest Group on Under-Resourced Languages*, pages 33–40, Marseille, France. European Language Resources Association.

Asha Hegde, Bharathi Raja Chakravarthi, Hosahalli Lakshmaiah Shashirekha, Rahul Ponnusamy, SUBALALITHA CN, Lavanya S K, Thenmozhi D, Martha Karunakar, Shreya Shreeram, and Sarah" Aymen. 2023. Findings of the shared task on sentiment analysis in tamil and tulu code-mixed text. In *Proceedings of the Third Workshop on Speech and Language Technologies for Dravidian Languages*, Varna, Bulgaria. Recent Advances in Natural Language Processing.

Yoon Kim. 2014. Convolutional neural networks for sentence classification. *arXiv preprint arXiv:1408.5882*.

Andrew Maas, Raymond E Daly, Peter T Pham, Dan Huang, Andrew Y Ng, and Christopher Potts. 2011. Learning word vectors for sentiment analysis. In *Proceedings of the 49th annual meeting of the association for computational linguistics: Human language technologies*, pages 142–150.

Bo Pang, Lillian Lee, et al. 2008. Opinion mining and sentiment analysis. *Foundations and Trends® in information retrieval*, 2(1–2):1–135.

Adrien Pavao, Isabelle Guyon, Anne-Catherine Letournel, Dinh-Tuan Tran, Xavier Baro, Hugo Jair Escalante, Sergio Escalera, Tyler Thomas, and Zhen Xu. 2023. Codalab competitions: An open source platform to organize scientific challenges. *Journal of Machine Learning Research*, 24(198):1–6.

Richard Socher, Alex Perelygin, Jean Wu, Jason Chuang, Christopher D Manning, Andrew Y Ng, and Christopher Potts. 2013. Recursive deep models for semantic compositionality over a sentiment treebank. In *Proceedings of the 2013 conference on empirical methods in natural language processing*, pages 1631–1642.

Sida I Wang and Christopher D Manning. 2012. Baselines and bigrams: Simple, good sentiment and topic classification. In *Proceedings of the 50th Annual Meeting of the Association for Computational Linguistics (Volume 2: Short Papers)*, pages 90–94.

Tom Young, Devamanyu Hazarika, Soujanya Poria, and Erik Cambria. 2018. Recent trends in deep learning based natural language processing. *ieee Computational intelligenCe magazine*, 13(3):55–75.

Xiang Zhang, Junbo Zhao, and Yann LeCun. 2015. Character-level convolutional networks for text classification. *Advances in neural information processing systems*, 28.

CSSCUTN@DravidianLangTech: Abusive comments Detection in Tamil and Telugu

Kathiravan Pannerselvam[1], **Saranya Rajiakodi**[1], **Rahul Ponnusamy**[2], **Sajeetha Thavareesan**[3]
[1]Department of Computer Science, Central University of Tamil Nadu,
Thiruvarur, Tamil Nadu, India
[2]Insight SFI Research Centre for Data Analytics, University of Galway, Ireland,
[3]Eastern University, Sri Lanka.
saranya@cutn.ac.in

Abstract

Code-mixing is a word or phrase-level act of interchanging two or more languages during a conversation or in written text within a sentence. This phenomenon is widespread on social media platforms, and understanding the underlying abusive comments in a code-mixed sentence is a complex challenge. We present our system in our submission for the DravidianLangTech Shared Task on Abusive Comment Detection in Tamil and Telugu. Our approach involves building a multiclass abusive detection model that recognizes 8 different labels. The provided samples are code-mixed Tamil-English text, where Tamil is represented in romanised form. We focused on the Multiclass classification subtask, and we leveraged Support Vector Machine (SVM), Random Forest (RF), and Logistic Regression (LR). Our method exhibited its effectiveness in the shared task by earning the ninth rank out of all competing systems for the classification of abusive comments in the code-mixed text. Our proposed classifier achieves an impressive accuracy of 0.99 and an F1-score of 0.99 for a balanced dataset using TF-IDF with SVM. It can be used effectively to detect abusive comments in Tamil, English code-mixed text.

1 Introduction

In the age of rapidly advancing technology and increased social media usage, online platforms have become integral to our daily lives, facilitating global communication and connection (Anita and Subalalitha, 2019; Thavareesan and Mahesan, 2019, 2020a,b; Subalalitha, 2019; Sakuntharaj and Mahesan, 2016, 2017, 2021). However, this interconnectedness has also led to the proliferation of abusive content and hate speech, posing severe challenges to maintaining a safe and respectful online environment (Bharathi and Agnusimmaculate Silvia, 2021; Bharathi and Varsha, 2022b; Swaminathan et al., 2022; Subramanian et al., 2022; Chinnaudayar Navaneethakrishnan et al., 2023). Automated classification of abusive comments is paramount to curb the spread of harmful content and protect users from online harassment (Priyadharshini et al., 2022). Moreover, abusive comments often emerge as a complex interplay of code-mixed text in multilingual communities, such as those in regions where Tamil and English speakers coexist and interact. Code-mixing is word or phrase level interchanging two or more languages within a single sentence or conversation (Chakravarthi et al., 2023a,b). The prevalence of code-mixed text in social media interactions further intensifies the difficulty of abusive comment classification, as traditional natural language processing techniques may not be directly applicable (Thara and Poornachandran, 2018; Chakravarthi et al., 2022a,b; **?**). This research article addresses the challenges of abusive comment classification in Tamil and English code-mixed text using machine learning techniques and the Synthetic Minority Over-sampling Technique (SMOTE) to handle imbalanced data (Chawla et al., 2002; Kathiravan et al., 2023). We explore the effectiveness of employing SMOTE to create a balanced dataset, thereby mitigating the skewed distribution of abusive and non-abusive comments.

To achieve accurate and robust classification results, we explore two popular data representation techniques: Bag-of-Words (BoW) and Term Frequency-Inverse Document Frequency (TF-IDF). BoW represents text data by counting the occurrence of words in documents, while TF-IDF considers the importance of words based on their frequency and rarity in the corpus (Akuma et al., 2022). We apply these representations to our balanced dataset and utilize three different machine learning algorithms: Support Vector Machines (SVM), Logistic Regression (LR), and Random Forest (RF).

Third Workshop on Speech and Language Technologies for Dravidian Languages, pages 306–312, Varna, Bulgaria, Sep 7, 2023.
https://doi.org/10.26615/978-954-452-085-4_045

One of the pivotal contributions of our research lies in showcasing the significance of SMOTE in enhancing the performance of the classifiers. By addressing the class imbalance issue, SMOTE enables the classifiers to better capture patterns and nuances related to abusive comments, improving classification accuracy and reducing the risk of misclassifying harmful content (Satriaji and Kusumaningrum, 2018). Our findings indicate that TF-IDF representation consistently outperforms BoW in SVM, LR, and RF models. The ability of TF-IDF to capture the semantic relevance and rareness of words provides a more substantial discriminatory power, leading to better classification results. Leveraging TF-IDF representation with SMOTE-balanced data yields an accuracy demonstrating the potential for more effective content moderation in code-mixed text environments.

However, despite the success achieved in our research, we recognize that addressing abusive comment classification in code-mixed text is an ongoing challenge. The dynamic nature of online content and the continuous evolution of abusive language demand continuous efforts in refining and updating our classification models.

2 Related works

The growing presence of Tamil and English, code-mixed data on social media platforms has sparked increased research interest in addressing abusive comments. As the multilingual nature of code-mixed content poses unique challenges, several studies have been conducted to develop effective methods for detecting and classifying abusive language in these contexts.

The research by Rajalakshmi et al. (2022) focuses on abusive comment detection in Tamil using multilingual transformer models. They explored the effectiveness of multilingual transformer models in handling the complexities of Tamil code-mixed text for abusive comment detection. The results demonstrated the potential of transformer-based approaches in achieving accurate and robust classification, significantly promoting a safer online environment. The research contributes valuable insights to the field of natural language processing for Dravidian languages, particularly in the context of abusive content moderation.

The research conducted by Prasanth et al. (2022) focuses on abusive comment detection in Tamil language text using the TF-IDF representation and the random kitchen sink algorithm. The authors addressed the challenge of identifying abusive content in the context of the Tamil language, which is particularly relevant for content moderation and user safety on social media platforms. The TF-IDF representation, known for capturing word importance and rarity, was combined with the random kitchen sink algorithm, a randomized feature mapping technique, to classify abusive comments.

Biradar and Saumya (2022) conducted research that focuses on the classification of abusive content in Dravidian code-mixed text using a Transformer-based approach. Their methodology leverages advanced natural language processing techniques to address the challenges of code-mixing in Tamil and other Dravidian languages. The study aims to improve content moderation systems and create a safer online environment by accurately detecting and handling abusive comments in multilingual communities. The paper provides valuable insights into using Transformers for abusive content classification in code-mixed text, contributing to the ongoing research efforts in Natural Language Processing (NLP) and content moderation.

Bharathi and Varsha (2022a) conducted the study on detecting abusive comments in the Tamil language using a Transformer-based approach. Transformers have proven to be highly effective in natural language processing tasks, and the authors explored their application for abusive comment classification in Tamil. Their work contributes to the growing body of research in content moderation and speech technologies for Dravidian languages, addressing the crucial issue of abusive language online. The detailed methodology, experimental setup, and results presented in the paper offer valuable insights into the effectiveness of the proposed approach, providing a significant contribution to the field of NLP for Tamil language processing.

The research conducted by Balouchzahi et al. (2022) focuses on abusive comment detection in the Tamil language. They employed a 1D Conv-LSTM model for classification. The study addressed the crucial issue of identifying abusive content in online Tamil text, considering the challenges posed by multilingual code-mixing. The proposed model demonstrated promising results in detecting abusive comments, and its effectiveness was showcased during the shared task. It also provides insights into the approach, methodology, and results achieved, contributing to developing content moderation systems in multilingual environments.

3 System Description

In this section, we provide comprehensive information about the dataset and elaborate on the experiments conducted in our study. Figure 1 illustrates the system architecture designed for multiclass abusive comments classification using machine learning (ML) techniques, including SMOTE. The diagram depicts the overall flow of the classification process.

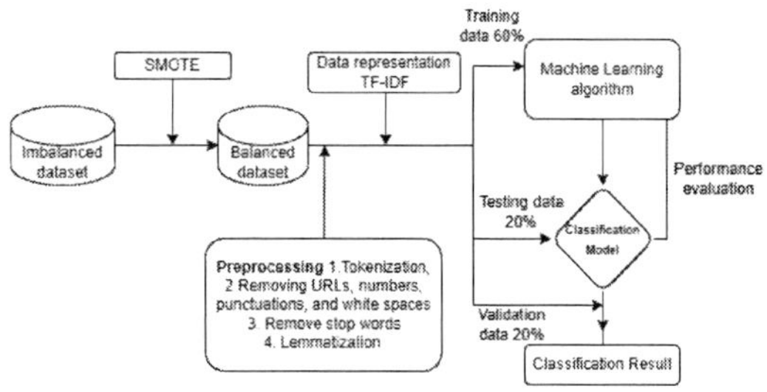

Figure 1: ML based Architecture.

3.1 Dataset

The dataset for the Abusive Comment Detection shared task, provided by the organizers, consists of code-mixed Tamil-English comments ("Priyadharshini et al., "2023") (Priyadharshini et al., 2022). It is important to note that the dataset is imbalanced, as depicted in Figure 2, showing the class-wise distribution of the data in percentages. The categories and their corresponding values are as follows: None-of-the-above (4633 comments), Misandry (1048 comments), Counter-speech (443 comments), Xenophobia (367 comments), Hope-Speech (266 comments), Misogyny (261 comments), Homophobia (215 comments), and Transphobic (197 comments). The imbalanced nature of the dataset poses challenges for effective classification and warrants careful consideration during model training and evaluation.

3.2 SMOTE

SMOTE (Synthetic Minority Over-sampling Technique) addresses the class imbalance in imbalanced datasets by generating synthetic samples for the minority class (Chawla et al., 2002). First, it identifies the minority class and selects k nearest neighbors for each instance within that class. Then, synthetic samples are created by interpolating between the

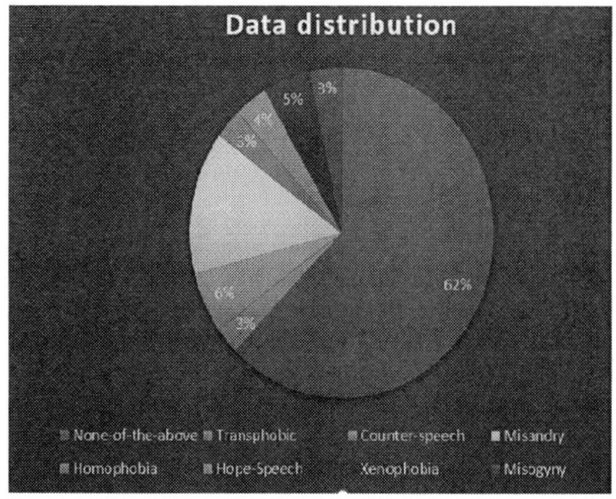

Figure 2: Data distribution

instance and one of its neighbors based on random proportions. This process is repeated for all instances in the minority class, resulting in a balanced dataset. The synthetic samples improve the representation of the minority class, allowing machine learning models to learn from a more diverse dataset and make more accurate predictions, particularly in abusive comment classification in code-mixed textual data (Shanmugavadivel et al., 2022). (Roy and Kumar, 2021) After applying the SMOTE to the initial imbalanced dataset, a significant transformation occurred, resulting in a balanced class distribution. Before SMOTE, the dataset had varying sample counts for each class, with the majority class "None-of-the-above" having 4633 comments. However, after SMOTE was applied, the number of samples in each class was equalized, with all classes containing 4633 comments. This process involved generating synthetic samples for the minority classes, effectively increasing their instances to match the majority class. The balanced dataset achieved through SMOTE addresses the class imbalance challenge, enabling machine learning models to train on a more representative and equitable dataset. Consequently, the classification models are better equipped to detect abusive comments in code-mixed Tamil-English data with enhanced accuracy and performance.

3.3 Preprocessing

We performed several preprocessing activities to clean and prepare the text data for further analysis. Firstly, we remove white spaces and punctuation to standardize the text and eliminate unnecessary things. Next, we eliminate stop words, which are commonly occurring words with little semantic value, to reduce noise in the data. We then tokenize the text, breaking it into individual words or tokens, enabling more granular analysis (Kathiravan and Haridoss, 2018). Additionally, we apply lemmatization to reduce words to their base or root form, aiding in normalization and reducing word variations. These preprocessing activities collectively improve the quality of the text data, making it more suitable for subsequent steps in the abusive comment classification process using machine learning techniques.

3.4 Data representation

Bag-of-Words (BoW) and Term Frequency-Inverse Document Frequency (TF-IDF) are standard text representation techniques used in natural language processing tasks. BoW converts a text document into a numerical vector by counting the frequency of each word present in the document (Qader et al., 2019). It disregards the word order and context, treating each word as an independent entity. The resulting vector represents the occurrence of words in the document, enabling the comparison and analysis of text data based on word frequencies. On the other hand, TF-IDF aims to capture the importance of words in a document relative to the entire corpus. It calculates the product of Term Frequency (TF), which is the frequency of a word in a document, and Inverse Document Frequency (IDF), which measures the rarity of the word across the entire corpus. TF-IDF assigns higher weights to words that are frequent in a document but rare in the corpus, indicating their significance in differentiating documents. As a result, TF-IDF representation allows for the emphasis of relevant terms while downplaying commonly occurring words, offering a more informative vector representation of the text data (Akuma et al., 2022). Both BoW and TF-IDF play crucial roles in text classification tasks, aiding in feature extraction and representing textual information in a format suitable for machine learning algorithms.

3.5 ML models

Support Vector Machine (SVM) is a robust and widely used supervised learning algorithm for classification and regression tasks. In classification, SVM aims to find the optimal hyperplane that best separates the data points of different classes in a high-dimensional space (Valero-Carreras et al., 2023) . The "support vectors" are the data points closest to the hyperplane and play a crucial role in defining the decision boundary. SVM effectively handles both linearly separable and non-linearly separable data through kernel functions, such as polynomial or radial basis function (RBF) kernels, which map the data into a higher-dimensional space. SVM is known for handling high-dimensional data and generalizing to new, unseen data.

Logistic Regressionis a popular statistical method used for binary classification tasks, where the goal is to predict the probability that a given data point belongs to a particular class (Xu et al., 2023). Despite its name, logistic Regression is primarily used for classification, not Regression. The algorithm models the relationship between the input features and the probability of the binary outcome using the logistic function (sigmoid function). The logistic function maps any real-valued number to the range [0, 1], which is then used to make the final classification decision. The model is trained by optimizing the parameters through maximum likelihood estimation. Logistic Regression is relatively simple, interpretable, and computationally efficient, making it a popular choice for binary classification tasks.

Random Forest is an ensemble learning method that combines multiple decision trees to achieve more accurate and robust predictions. Each decision tree is trained in a random forest on a random subset of the data (bootstrap samples) and a random subset of the features. This randomness helps reduce overfitting and increases the diversity among the individual trees (Das et al., 2023) . During prediction, the final output is determined by aggregating the predictions of all the trees, either through majority voting (for classification) or averaging (for Regression). Random forests are known for their ability to handle complex datasets, high-dimensional data, and non-linear relationships. They are also less prone to overfitting than a single decision tree and are widely used in machine learning tasks.

4 Result

In this research, we investigated the application of three machine learning algorithms, namely Support Vector Machine (SVM), Logistic Regression, and Random Forest, in conjunction with two data representation techniques: Bag-of-Words (BoW) and Term Frequency-Inverse Document Frequency

Model	Feature set	Precision	recall	F1-score	Accuracy
Support Vector Machine	BoW	0.98	0.97	0.97	0.97
Random Forest	BoW	0.98	0.98	0.98	0.98
Logistic Regression	BoW	0.98	0.97	0.97	0.97
Support Vector Machine	TF-IDF	0.99	0.99	0.99	0.99
Random Forest	TF-IDF	0.98	0.98	0.98	0.98
Logistic Regression	TF-IDF	0.97	0.97	0.97	0.97

Table 1: Evaluation metrics of various ML models.

(TF-IDF). After employing SMOTE to address the class imbalance, the models were evaluated for abusive comment classification in code-mixed Tamil-English text. This experimental research with TF-IDF representation and SMOTE-balanced data, SVM achieved an outstanding F1 score of 0.99, showcasing its ability to identify abusive comments in the dataset accurately. Logistic Regression, combined with TF-IDF, delivered an F1 score of 0.97, displaying competitive performance in abusive comment classification. Random Forest, with both BoW and TF-IDF representations on SMOTE-balanced data, attained F1 scores of 0.98 and 0.98, respectively. This highlights the algorithm's robustness in handling code-mixed text and class imbalance Table 1 illustrates it briefly.

5 Conclusion

In conclusion, this research delves into the critical issue of abusive comment classification in code-mixed text, particularly in Tamil and English code-mixed data. The escalating growth of social media and online platforms has amplified the need for compelling content moderation to ensure a safe and respectful digital environment. We have achieved promising results in accurately identifying abusive comments by harnessing the power of machine learning techniques and SMOTE for handling class imbalance. The utilization of SVM, Logistic Regression, and Random Forest in combination with TF-IDF representation has proven to be highly effective in capturing the nuances of abusive language, leading to improved classification accuracy. Notably, the application of SMOTE has significantly contributed to overcoming the challenges of class imbalance, enabling our models to make more reliable predictions.

Limitation is encountering out-of-vocabulary words or linguistic phenomena not accounted for during preprocessing. Code-mixing can introduce linguistic variations that may not be adequately handled by the existing language processing techniques, leading to potential misclassifications. Addressing these linguistic complexities in future research could enhance the model's performance and generalization capabilities. Notably, in the shared task, our approach secured the 9th rank out of all participating systems. Despite the competition's challenges and intense competition from other participants, our model's performance demonstrates its effectiveness in abusive comment classification in code-mixed text.

Future work investigating more advanced and context-aware feature extraction techniques will contribute to a more comprehensive analysis of code-mixed content. We continuously refine and update our models to develop robust and adaptive content moderation systems, creating a safer online environment for diverse, multilingual communities. we are optimistic that future work will address these limitations and elevate the performance of abusive comment classification in code-mixed text, contributing to a more inclusive and respectful online space for all users.

References

Stephen Akuma, Tyosar Lubem, and Isaac Terngu Adom. 2022. Comparing Bag of Words and TF-IDF with different models for hate speech detection from live tweets. *International Journal of Information Technology*, 14(7):3629–3635.

R Anita and CN Subalalitha. 2019. An approach to cluster Tamil literatures using discourse connectives. In *2019 IEEE 1st International Conference on Energy, Systems and Information Processing (ICESIP)*, pages 1–4. IEEE.

Fazlourrahman Balouchzahi, Anusha Gowda, Hosahalli Shashirekha, and Grigori Sidorov. 2022. MUCIC@TamilNLP-ACL2022: Abusive Comment Detection in Tamil Language using 1D Conv-LSTM. In *Proceedings of the Second Workshop on Speech and Language Technologies for Dravidian Languages*, pages 64–69.

B Bharathi and A Agnusimmaculate Silvia. 2021. SSNCSE_NLP@DravidianLangTech-EACL2021: Offensive language identification on multilingual code mixing text. In *Proceedings of the First Workshop on Speech and Language Technologies for Dravidian Languages*, pages 313–318, Kyiv. Association for Computational Linguistics.

B Bharathi and Josephine Varsha. 2022a. SSNCSE NLP@ TamilNLP-ACL2022: Transformer based approach for detection of abusive comment for Tamil language. In *Proceedings of the Second Workshop on Speech and Language Technologies for Dravidian Languages*, pages 158–164.

B Bharathi and Josephine Varsha. 2022b. SSNCSE NLP@TamilNLP-ACL2022: Transformer based approach for detection of abusive comment for Tamil language. In *Proceedings of the Second Workshop on Speech and Language Technologies for Dravidian Languages*, pages 158–164, Dublin, Ireland. Association for Computational Linguistics.

Shankar Biradar and Sunil Saumya. 2022. IIITDWD@TamilNLP-ACL2022: Transformer-based approach to classify abusive content in Dravidian code-mixed text. In *Proceedings of the Second Workshop on Speech and Language Technologies for Dravidian Languages*, pages 100–104, Dublin, Ireland. Association for Computational Linguistics.

Bharathi Raja Chakravarthi, Adeep Hande, Rahul Ponnusamy, Prasanna Kumar Kumaresan, and Ruba Priyadharshini. 2022a. How can we detect homophobia and transphobia? experiments in a multilingual code-mixed setting for social media governance. *International Journal of Information Management Data Insights*, 2(2):100119.

Bharathi Raja Chakravarthi, Manoj Balaji Jagadeeshan, Vasanth Palanikumar, and Ruba Priyadharshini. 2023a. Offensive language identification in Dravidian languages using MPNet and CNN. *International Journal of Information Management Data Insights*, 3(1):100151.

Bharathi Raja Chakravarthi, Ruba Priyadharshini, Shubanker Banerjee, Manoj Balaji Jagadeeshan, Prasanna Kumar Kumaresan, Rahul Ponnusamy, Sean Benhur, and John Philip McCrae. 2023b. Detecting abusive comments at a fine-grained level in a low-resource language. *Natural Language Processing Journal*, 3:100006.

Bharathi Raja Chakravarthi, Ruba Priyadharshini, Thenmozhi Durairaj, John McCrae, Paul Buitelaar, Prasanna Kumaresan, and Rahul Ponnusamy. 2022b. Overview of the shared task on homophobia and transphobia detection in social media comments. In *Proceedings of the Second Workshop on Language Technology for Equality, Diversity and Inclusion*, pages 369–377, Dublin, Ireland. Association for Computational Linguistics.

Nitesh V Chawla, Kevin W Bowyer, Lawrence O Hall, and W Philip Kegelmeyer. 2002. Smote: synthetic minority over-sampling technique. *Journal of artificial intelligence research*, 16:321–357.

Subalalitha Chinnaudayar Navaneethakrishnan, Bharathi Raja Chakravarthi, Kogilavani Shanmugavadivel, Malliga Subramanian, Prasanna Kumar Kumaresan, Bharathi, Lavanya Sambath Kumar, and Rahul Ponnusamy. 2023. Findings of shared task on sentiment analysis and homophobia detection of Youtube comments in code-mixed Dravidian languages. In *Proceedings of the 14th Annual Meeting of the Forum for Information Retrieval Evaluation*, FIRE '22, page 18–21, New York, NY, USA. Association for Computing Machinery.

Sunanda Das, Md Samir Imtiaz, Nieb Hasan Neom, Nazmul Siddique, and Hui Wang. 2023. A hybrid approach for bangla sign language recognition using deep transfer learning model with random forest classifier. *Expert Systems with Applications*, 213:118914.

P Kathiravan and N Haridoss. 2018. Preprocessing for mining the textual data-a review. *International Journal of Scientific Research in Computer Science Applications and Management Studies IJSRCSAMS*, 7(5).

P Kathiravan, P Shanmugavadivu, and R Saranya. 2023. Mitigating imbalanced data in online social networks using stratified k-means sampling. In *2023 8th International Conference on Business and Industrial Research (ICBIR)*, pages 883–888. IEEE.

SN Prasanth, R Aswin Raj, P Adhithan, B Premjith, and Soman Kp. 2022. CEN-Tamil@ DravidianLangTech-ACL2022: Abusive comment detection in Tamil using TF-IDF and random kitchen sink algorithm. In *Proceedings of the Second Workshop on Speech and Language Technologies for Dravidian Languages*, pages 70–74.

Ruba "Priyadharshini, Bharathi Raja Chakravarthi, Subalalitha Chinnaudayar Navaneethakrishnan, Malliga Subramanian, Kogilavani Shanmugavadivel, Premjith B, Abirami Murugappan, Sai Prashanth Karnati, Rishith, Chandu Janakiram, and Prasanna Kumar" Kumaresan. "2023". Findings of the shared task on Abusive Comment Detection in Tamil and Telugu. In *"Proceedings of the Third Workshop on Speech and Language Technologies for Dravidian Languages DravidianLangTech 2023"*. "Recent Advances in Natural Language Processing".

Ruba Priyadharshini, Bharathi Raja Chakravarthi, Subalalitha Cn, Thenmozhi Durairaj, Malliga Subramanian, Kogilavani Shanmugavadivel, Siddhanth U Hegde, and Prasanna Kumaresan. 2022. Overview of abusive comment detection in Tamil-ACL 2022. In *Proceedings of the Second Workshop on Speech and Language Technologies for Dravidian Languages*, pages 292–298, Dublin, Ireland. Association for Computational Linguistics.

Wisam A Qader, Musa M Ameen, and Bilal I Ahmed. 2019. An overview of bag of words; importance, implementation, applications, and challenges. In *2019 international engineering conference (IEC)*, pages 200–204. IEEE.

Ratnavel Rajalakshmi, Ankita Duraphe, and Antonette Shibani. 2022. DLRG@ DravidianLangTech-ACL2022: Abusive comment detection in Tamil using multilingual transformer models. In *Proceedings of the Second Workshop on Speech and Language Technologies for Dravidian Languages*, pages 207–213.

Pradeep Kumar Roy and Abhinav Kumar. 2021. Sentiment Analysis on Tamil Code-Mixed Text using Bi-LSTM. In *Working Notes of FIRE 2021-Forum for Information Retrieval Evaluation (Online). CEUR*.

Ratnasingam Sakuntharaj and Sinnathamby Mahesan. 2016. A novel hybrid approach to detect and correct spelling in Tamil text. In *2016 IEEE international conference on information and automation for sustainability (ICIAfS)*, pages 1–6. IEEE.

Ratnasingam Sakuntharaj and Sinnathamby Mahesan. 2017. Use of a novel hash-table for speeding-up suggestions for misspelt Tamil words. In *2017 IEEE international conference on industrial and information systems (ICIIS)*, pages 1–5. IEEE.

Ratnasingam Sakuntharaj and Sinnathamby Mahesan. 2021. Missing word detection and correction based on context of Tamil sentences using n-grams. In *2021 10th International Conference on Information and Automation for Sustainability (ICIAfS)*, pages 42–47. IEEE.

Widi Satriaji and Retno Kusumaningrum. 2018. Effect of synthetic minority oversampling technique (smote), feature representation, and classification algorithm on imbalanced sentiment analysis. In *2018 2nd International Conference on Informatics and Computational Sciences (ICICoS)*, pages 1–5. IEEE.

Kogilavani Shanmugavadivel, Sai Haritha Sampath, Pramod Nandhakumar, Prasath Mahalingam, Malliga Subramanian, Prasanna Kumar Kumaresan, and Ruba Priyadharshini. 2022. An analysis of machine learning models for sentiment analysis of Tamil code-mixed data. *Computer Speech & Language*, 76:101407.

CN Subalalitha. 2019. Information extraction framework for Kurunthogai. *Sādhanā*, 44(7):156.

Malliga Subramanian, Rahul Ponnusamy, Sean Benhur, Kogilavani Shanmugavadivel, Adhithiya Ganesan, Deepti Ravi, Gowtham Krishnan Shanmugasundaram, Ruba Priyadharshini, and Bharathi Raja Chakravarthi. 2022. Offensive language detection in Tamil youtube comments by adapters and cross-domain knowledge transfer. *Computer Speech & Language*, 76:101404.

Krithika Swaminathan, Bharathi B, Gayathri G L, and Hrishik Sampath. 2022. SSNCSE_NLP@LT-EDI-ACL2022: Homophobia/transphobia detection in multiple languages using SVM classifiers and BERT-based transformers. In *Proceedings of the Second Workshop on Language Technology for Equality, Diversity and Inclusion*, pages 239–244, Dublin, Ireland. Association for Computational Linguistics.

S Thara and Prabaharan Poornachandran. 2018. Code-mixing: A brief survey. In *2018 International conference on advances in computing, communications and informatics (ICACCI)*, pages 2382–2388. IEEE.

Sajeetha Thavareesan and Sinnathamby Mahesan. 2019. Sentiment analysis in Tamil texts: A study on machine learning techniques and feature representation. In *2019 14th Conference on industrial and information systems (ICIIS)*, pages 320–325. IEEE.

Sajeetha Thavareesan and Sinnathamby Mahesan. 2020a. Sentiment lexicon expansion using Word2vec and fastText for sentiment prediction in Tamil texts. In *2020 Moratuwa engineering research conference (MERCon)*, pages 272–276. IEEE.

Sajeetha Thavareesan and Sinnathamby Mahesan. 2020b. Word embedding-based part of speech tagging in tamil texts. In *2020 IEEE 15th International conference on industrial and information systems (ICIIS)*, pages 478–482. IEEE.

Daniel Valero-Carreras, Javier Alcaraz, and Mercedes Landete. 2023. Comparing two svm models through different metrics based on the confusion matrix. *Computers & Operations Research*, 152:106131.

Yang Xu, Bern Klein, Genzhuang Li, and Bhushan Gopaluni. 2023. Evaluation of logistic regression and support vector machine approaches for xrf based particle sorting for a copper ore. *Minerals Engineering*, 192:108003.

Author Index

Association for Computational Linguistics
209 N. Eighth Street
Stroudsburg, Pennsylvania 18360

ISBN 978-1-7138-9043-0

CURRAN ASSOCIATES INC.
proceedings.com